T0212380

Lecture Notes in Computer Science   12774

More information about this subseries at http://www.springer.com/series/7409

Gabriele Meiselwitz (Ed.)

Social Computing and Social Media

Experience Design and Social Network Analysis

13th International Conference, SCSM 2021
Held as Part of the 23rd HCI International Conference, HCII 2021
Virtual Event, July 24–29, 2021
Proceedings, Part I

 Springer

Editor
Gabriele Meiselwitz
Department of Computer Science
Towson University
Towson, MD, USA

ISSN 0302-9743   ISSN 1611-3349   (electronic)
Lecture Notes in Computer Science
ISBN 978-3-030-77625-1   ISBN 978-3-030-77626-8   (eBook)
https://doi.org/10.1007/978-3-030-77626-8

LNCS Sublibrary: SL3 – Information Systems and Applications, incl. Internet/Web, and HCI

This Springer imprint is published by the registered company Springer Nature Switzerland AG
The registered company address is: Gewerbestrasse 11, 6330 Cham, Switzerland

Foreword

Human-Computer Interaction (HCI) is acquiring an ever-increasing scientific and industrial importance, and having more impact on people's everyday life, as an ever-growing number of human activities are progressively moving from the physical to the digital world. This process, which has been ongoing for some time now, has been dramatically accelerated by the COVID-19 pandemic. The HCI International (HCII) conference series, held yearly, aims to respond to the compelling need to advance the exchange of knowledge and research and development efforts on the human aspects of design and use of computing systems.

The 23rd International Conference on Human-Computer Interaction, HCI International 2021 (HCII 2021), was planned to be held at the Washington Hilton Hotel, Washington DC, USA, during July 24–29, 2021. Due to the COVID-19 pandemic and with everyone's health and safety in mind, HCII 2021 was organized and run as a virtual conference. It incorporated the 21 thematic areas and affiliated conferences listed on the following page.

A total of 5222 individuals from academia, research institutes, industry, and governmental agencies from 81 countries submitted contributions, and 1276 papers and 241 posters were included in the proceedings to appear just before the start of the conference. The contributions thoroughly cover the entire field of HCI, addressing major advances in knowledge and effective use of computers in a variety of application areas. These papers provide academics, researchers, engineers, scientists, practitioners, and students with state-of-the-art information on the most recent advances in HCI. The volumes constituting the set of proceedings to appear before the start of the conference are listed in the following pages.

The HCI International (HCII) conference also offers the option of 'Late Breaking Work' which applies both for papers and posters, and the corresponding volume(s) of the proceedings will appear after the conference. Full papers will be included in the 'HCII 2021 - Late Breaking Papers' volumes of the proceedings to be published in the Springer LNCS series, while 'Poster Extended Abstracts' will be included as short research papers in the 'HCII 2021 - Late Breaking Posters' volumes to be published in the Springer CCIS series.

The present volume contains papers submitted and presented in the context of the 13th International Conference on Social Computing and Social Media (SCSM 2021), an affiliated conference to HCII 2021. I would like to thank the Chair, Gabriele Meiselwitz, for her invaluable contribution to its organization and the preparation of the proceedings, as well as the members of the Program Board for their contributions and support. This year, the SCSM affiliated conference has focused on topics related to computer-mediated communication, experience design in social computing, and social network analysis, as well as social media applications in marketing and customer behavior, learning and education, and health and wellbeing.

I would also like to thank the Program Board Chairs and the members of the Program Boards of all thematic areas and affiliated conferences for their contribution towards the highest scientific quality and overall success of the HCI International 2021 conference.

This conference would not have been possible without the continuous and unwavering support and advice of Gavriel Salvendy, founder, General Chair Emeritus, and Scientific Advisor. For his outstanding efforts, I would like to express my appreciation to Abbas Moallem, Communications Chair and Editor of HCI International News.

July 2021   Constantine Stephanidis

HCI International 2021 Thematic Areas and Affiliated Conferences

Thematic Areas

- HCI: Human-Computer Interaction
- HIMI: Human Interface and the Management of Information

Affiliated Conferences

- EPCE: 18th International Conference on Engineering Psychology and Cognitive Ergonomics
- UAHCI: 15th International Conference on Universal Access in Human-Computer Interaction
- VAMR: 13th International Conference on Virtual, Augmented and Mixed Reality
- CCD: 13th International Conference on Cross-Cultural Design
- SCSM: 13th International Conference on Social Computing and Social Media
- AC: 15th International Conference on Augmented Cognition
- DHM: 12th International Conference on Digital Human Modeling and Applications in Health, Safety, Ergonomics and Risk Management
- DUXU: 10th International Conference on Design, User Experience, and Usability
- DAPI: 9th International Conference on Distributed, Ambient and Pervasive Interactions
- HCIBGO: 8th International Conference on HCI in Business, Government and Organizations
- LCT: 8th International Conference on Learning and Collaboration Technologies
- ITAP: 7th International Conference on Human Aspects of IT for the Aged Population
- HCI-CPT: 3rd International Conference on HCI for Cybersecurity, Privacy and Trust
- HCI-Games: 3rd International Conference on HCI in Games
- MobiTAS: 3rd International Conference on HCI in Mobility, Transport and Automotive Systems
- AIS: 3rd International Conference on Adaptive Instructional Systems
- C&C: 9th International Conference on Culture and Computing
- MOBILE: 2nd International Conference on Design, Operation and Evaluation of Mobile Communications
- AI-HCI: 2nd International Conference on Artificial Intelligence in HCI

List of Conference Proceedings Volumes Appearing Before the Conference

1. LNCS 12762, Human-Computer Interaction: Theory, Methods and Tools (Part I), edited by Masaaki Kurosu
2. LNCS 12763, Human-Computer Interaction: Interaction Techniques and Novel Applications (Part II), edited by Masaaki Kurosu
3. LNCS 12764, Human-Computer Interaction: Design and User Experience Case Studies (Part III), edited by Masaaki Kurosu
4. LNCS 12765, Human Interface and the Management of Information: Information Presentation and Visualization (Part I), edited by Sakae Yamamoto and Hirohiko Mori
5. LNCS 12766, Human Interface and the Management of Information: Information-rich and Intelligent Environments (Part II), edited by Sakae Yamamoto and Hirohiko Mori
6. LNAI 12767, Engineering Psychology and Cognitive Ergonomics, edited by Don Harris and Wen-Chin Li
7. LNCS 12768, Universal Access in Human-Computer Interaction: Design Methods and User Experience (Part I), edited by Margherita Antona and Constantine Stephanidis
8. LNCS 12769, Universal Access in Human-Computer Interaction: Access to Media, Learning and Assistive Environments (Part II), edited by Margherita Antona and Constantine Stephanidis
9. LNCS 12770, Virtual, Augmented and Mixed Reality, edited by Jessie Y. C. Chen and Gino Fragomeni
10. LNCS 12771, Cross-Cultural Design: Experience and Product Design Across Cultures (Part I), edited by P. L. Patrick Rau
11. LNCS 12772, Cross-Cultural Design: Applications in Arts, Learning, Well-being, and Social Development (Part II), edited by P. L. Patrick Rau
12. LNCS 12773, Cross-Cultural Design: Applications in Cultural Heritage, Tourism, Autonomous Vehicles, and Intelligent Agents (Part III), edited by P. L. Patrick Rau
13. LNCS 12774, Social Computing and Social Media: Experience Design and Social Network Analysis (Part I), edited by Gabriele Meiselwitz
14. LNCS 12775, Social Computing and Social Media: Applications in Marketing, Learning, and Health (Part II), edited by Gabriele Meiselwitz
15. LNAI 12776, Augmented Cognition, edited by Dylan D. Schmorrow and Cali M. Fidopiastis
16. LNCS 12777, Digital Human Modeling and Applications in Health, Safety, Ergonomics and Risk Management: Human Body, Motion and Behavior (Part I), edited by Vincent G. Duffy
17. LNCS 12778, Digital Human Modeling and Applications in Health, Safety, Ergonomics and Risk Management: AI, Product and Service (Part II), edited by Vincent G. Duffy

18. LNCS 12779, Design, User Experience, and Usability: UX Research and Design (Part I), edited by Marcelo Soares, Elizabeth Rosenzweig, and Aaron Marcus

19. LNCS 12780, Design, User Experience, and Usability: Design for Diversity, Well-being, and Social Development (Part II), edited by Marcelo M. Soares, Elizabeth Rosenzweig, and Aaron Marcus

20. LNCS 12781, Design, User Experience, and Usability: Design for Contemporary Technological Environments (Part III), edited by Marcelo M. Soares, Elizabeth Rosenzweig, and Aaron Marcus

21. LNCS 12782, Distributed, Ambient and Pervasive Interactions, edited by Norbert Streitz and Shin'ichi Konomi

22. LNCS 12783, HCI in Business, Government and Organizations, edited by Fiona Fui-Hoon Nah and Keng Siau

23. LNCS 12784, Learning and Collaboration Technologies: New Challenges and Learning Experiences (Part I), edited by Panayiotis Zaphiris and Andri Ioannou

24. LNCS 12785, Learning and Collaboration Technologies: Games and Virtual Environments for Learning (Part II), edited by Panayiotis Zaphiris and Andri Ioannou

25. LNCS 12786, Human Aspects of IT for the Aged Population: Technology Design and Acceptance (Part I), edited by Qin Gao and Jia Zhou

26. LNCS 12787, Human Aspects of IT for the Aged Population: Supporting Everyday Life Activities (Part II), edited by Qin Gao and Jia Zhou

27. LNCS 12788, HCI for Cybersecurity, Privacy and Trust, edited by Abbas Moallem

28. LNCS 12789, HCI in Games: Experience Design and Game Mechanics (Part I), edited by Xiaowen Fang

29. LNCS 12790, HCI in Games: Serious and Immersive Games (Part II), edited by Xiaowen Fang

30. LNCS 12791, HCI in Mobility, Transport and Automotive Systems, edited by Heidi Krömker

31. LNCS 12792, Adaptive Instructional Systems: Design and Evaluation (Part I), edited by Robert A. Sottilare and Jessica Schwarz

32. LNCS 12793, Adaptive Instructional Systems: Adaptation Strategies and Methods (Part II), edited by Robert A. Sottilare and Jessica Schwarz

33. LNCS 12794, Culture and Computing: Interactive Cultural Heritage and Arts (Part I), edited by Matthias Rauterberg

34. LNCS 12795, Culture and Computing: Design Thinking and Cultural Computing (Part II), edited by Matthias Rauterberg

35. LNCS 12796, Design, Operation and Evaluation of Mobile Communications, edited by Gavriel Salvendy and June Wei

36. LNAI 12797, Artificial Intelligence in HCI, edited by Helmut Degen and Stavroula Ntoa

37. CCIS 1419, HCI International 2021 Posters - Part I, edited by Constantine Stephanidis, Margherita Antona, and Stavroula Ntoa

38. CCIS 1420, HCI International 2021 Posters - Part II, edited by Constantine Stephanidis, Margherita Antona, and Stavroula Ntoa
39. CCIS 1421, HCI International 2021 Posters - Part III, edited by Constantine Stephanidis, Margherita Antona, and Stavroula Ntoa

http://2021.hci.international/proceedings

13th International Conference on Social Computing and Social Media (SCSM 2021)

Program Board Chair: **Gabriele Meiselwitz,** *Towson University, USA*

- Francisco Alvarez, Mexico
- Andria Andriuzzi, France
- Karine Berthelot-Guiet, France
- James Braman, USA
- Adheesh Budree, South Africa
- Adela Coman, Romania
- Panagiotis Germanakos, Germany
- Hung-Hsuan Huang, Japan
- Aylin Ilhan, Germany
- Ayaka Ito, Japan
- Carsten Kleiner, Germany
- Takashi Namatame, Japan
- Hoang D. Nguyen, Singapore
- Kohei Otake, Japan
- Daniela Quiñones, Chile
- Cristian Rusu, Chile
- Christian W. Scheiner, Germany
- Pavel Strach, Czech Republic
- Jacqui Taylor-Jackson, Australia
- Simona Vasilache, Japan
- Giovanni Vincenti, USA
- Yuanqiong Wang, USA
- Brian Wentz, USA

The full list with the Program Board Chairs and the members of the Program Boards of all thematic areas and affiliated conferences is available online at:

http://www.hci.international/board-members-2021.php

HCI International 2022

The 24th International Conference on Human-Computer Interaction, HCI International 2022, will be held jointly with the affiliated conferences at the Gothia Towers Hotel and Swedish Exhibition & Congress Centre, Gothenburg, Sweden, June 26 – July 1, 2022. It will cover a broad spectrum of themes related to Human-Computer Interaction, including theoretical issues, methods, tools, processes, and case studies in HCI design, as well as novel interaction techniques, interfaces, and applications. The proceedings will be published by Springer. More information will be available on the conference website: http://2022.hci.international/:

General Chair
Prof. Constantine Stephanidis
University of Crete and ICS-FORTH
Heraklion, Crete, Greece
Email: general_chair@hcii2022.org

http://2022.hci.international/

Contents – Part I

Social Network Analysis

Experience Design in Social Computing

Contents – Part II

Computer Mediated Communication

Social Media, Leadership and Organizational Culture: The Case of Romanian Leaders

Adela Coman[(⊠)], Ana-Maria Grigore, and Andreea Ardelean

The University of Bucharest, Bucharest, Romania
{adela.coman,andreea.ardelean}@faa.unibuc.ro

Abstract. Starting with the late 2010s, the importance of social media in leadership was acknowledged and researched. While a promising beginning was first made by Kotter (1990) who discovered that effective managers spend more than 80% of their time interacting with others, later on researchers argued that social media is important when people need to accomplish work, gain upward mobility and develop personally and professionally (Ibarra 2007). Therefore, leaders and managers must understand how to use social media in order to influence team performance, strengthen the existing relationships and establish new connections between individuals, groups and other entities.

Social media are also an important tool for building the organizational culture of companies: it facilitates different types of relationships between leaders, managers, employees and other stakeholders, expressed in various forms; are good at conveying information and tasks to people working in time zones, locations and communities all around the world (Birkinshaw 2011); and are particularly fit for the younger generation of leaders (Millennials) known as being "digitally native".

The purpose of this paper is to examine the use of social media by Romanian leaders and managers and to identify possible connections between social media, leadership styles and the organizational culture of companies. We based our research on Blake and Mouton's managerial grid (Blake and Mouton 1964) and Goffee and Jones' work on organizational culture (1996). Data analysis and correlation analysis were used in order to establish hypothesis; identify leadership styles; assess the organizational culture correctly. The participants in this study are managers and leaders working in 45 small and medium sized companies (SMEs) in Romania.

The paper is organized in 3 sections; the first is dedicated to the literature review (social media, Blake and Mouton's grid and the matrix of social architecture, namely the concepts of sociability and solidarity); in Sect. 2 we discuss data, methodology and results. In the final section, based on our findings (team leadership style and communal organizational culture prevailing in Romanian companies) we conclude on the challenges all organizations face when leaders and managers need to decide what type of organizational culture works best for their companies looking for success in times of crisis.

Keywords: Social media · Blake and mouton's managerial grid · The matrix of social architecture · Sociability · Solidarity

© Springer Nature Switzerland AG 2021
G. Meiselwitz (Ed.): HCII 2021, LNCS 12774, pp. 3–17, 2021.
https://doi.org/10.1007/978-3-030-77626-8_1

1 Introduction

The phenomenon of social media pervades now every aspect of our personal and business lives, and this revolution continues. In its most basic sense, social media has created a shift in how people communicate with each other, how we read and share information. This has implications for leaders and leadership in that leaders need to optimize their influence by understanding and acknowledging the changing nature of the leader-follower relationships. As Kotter (1990) suggested, effective leaders and managers spend most of their time interacting with others, so it is quite obvious that a greater number of activities on a social media platform to interact with others is a key driver of the network's usefulness. Through interactions and activities, managers are able to foster relationship building and general team building (Kayworth and Leidner 2001).

There are several studies that are worth to be mentioned regarding leadership and organizational culture in Romanian SMEs. For example, Craciun et al. (2015) in their survey on 930 subjects identified characteristics of a leader that influence the organization's results (as seen by employees): adaptability; cooperation; authority; charisma; confidence; motivation. In another research done by Romanian specialists (Nastase and Radu 2013) more entrepreneurs and their staff have been asked to choose the most important values for their companies. Regarding the hierarchy of the values taken into account the most important seemed to be the high focus on customers, performance orientation and professionalism. MKOR (2017) conducted a qualitative survey of nearly 650 Romanian business and NGO leaders and discovered that 19.5% of respondents think they have a rather more collegiate leadership style; 19.1% of respondents think they have a rather democratic leadership style; 18.6% of respondents believe that they have a rather visionary leadership style and, interestingly, only 7.2% of respondents think they have a rather more authoritarian style of leadership.

The purpose of this paper is to identify possible connections between leadership styles and the organizational culture of Romanian companies and to analyze what is the role of social media in mediating these connections.

The paper is organized in 3 sections; the first is dedicated to the literature review; in Sect. 2 we discuss data, methodology and results. In the final section, we discuss the style of leadership and type of organizational culture identified as prevailing in the Romanian companies as well as the challenges these organizations face when leaders and managers need to decide what should be their primary focus (tasks/people) in the context of profound transformations induced by the present pandemic.

2 Literature Review

There is a plethora of leadership definitions in the specialized literature. For example, Northouse (2012) defines leadership as a "process whereby an individual influences a group of individuals to achieve a common goal" (p. 5) while Russell (2005) suggests that leadership is the 'interpersonal influence exercised by a person or persons through the process of communication, toward the attainment of an organization's goals" (p. 16). Furthermore, Rue and Bryars (2009) define leadership as "the ability to influence people to willingly follow one's guidance or adhere to one's decisions" (p. 465). Finally, according to Kane (2009), "Leadership is an influence relationship aimed at moving organizations or groups of people toward an imagined future that depends upon alignment of values and establishment of mutual purposes".

This last definition builds on the following ideas: first, leadership is more than just a role assigned to a person: leadership is about the behaviors one exhibits in this role. Leadership is also interactive and dynamic, calling upon actions in order to influence followers or subordinates, or put it differently, "The true measure of leadership is influence. Nothing more, nothing less" (Maxwell 2007, p. 25). Second, power is an essential component of leadership in that it will constantly alter the type of influence one has with one's followers. Finally, alignment between leaders and followers on values and mutual purposes or outcomes that benefit both the organization and the people involved – is necessary for leadership in order to be successful. Followers need to understand why a certain action is required.

According to Maxwell (2007), leadership ability determines one's success and effectiveness as a leader. A fundamental ability for leaders is to effectively connect with people, and in the era of technological progress and speed, social media has become a modern and challenging tool for nowadays leaders who want to maintain an open communication with their followers/subordinates.

Social media is also important for leadership as it changes the way relationships develop: information flows from one department to another, tasks are accomplished by teams that work in different time-zones and locations while private online conversations between employees and leaders make virtual meetings by far more productive than in the usual face-to-face settings.

Social media has, however, altered what it means to be a follower. 'To follow' used to refer to behavior that meant to go behind someone else and so a follower would tread in the footsteps of a leader. The traditional organizational hierarchy between leaders and their followers has eroded over time, partly due to social movements and the growing empowerment of followers through their ability to access information more easily. To be a follower nowadays implies a choice made by the follower regarding information or communications while leaders are no longer the sole source of information about their companies. The workplace choices made by followers are now much more selective, voluntary, multi-channeled and arguably better informed as new business models arise and blur the distinction between leaders and followers.

In addition to the leader/follower relationship dynamics there is evidence that people are more likely to trust a company whose leadership team engages with social media, and that they would prefer to work for a company where leaders are active on social media. Most people also believe that use of social media improves CEO engagement with employees and that this is mission-critical for a business (according to a BRANDfog 2016 survey).

A more recent Brandfog survey (2020) also shows that CEOs who actively participate in social media can build better connections with customers, employees and investors (92% of respondents agreed to that) and 9 in 10 respondents (88%) agreed that "CEOs on social media who take a stand in the key social issues of our time can act as role models for the next generation of leaders". Furthermore, 82% of survey respondents stated they were more likely to purchase from a company whose leadership communicates openly on social media channels regarding their efforts during the Covid-19 crisis while two thirds (66%) say that social media engagement makes CEOs more effective leaders (Brandfog Survey 2020).

Blake and Mouton's managerial grid was first developed in the 1960s and ever since has been through many transformations (1964, 1978, 1985, 1994). It is widely accepted as a critical and important analysis of leadership behavior. The Grid is similar in some respect to the Ohio State Studies which combines a leader/manager's focus on tasks and a focus on the relationship with the subordinates. However, the managerial grid develops these concepts further by quantifying the degree to which the focus is on tasks or "concern for results" and the focus is on the relationship with the subordinates or "concern for people". The 1 to 9 scale allows differentiation among the variable responses regarding concern for production or people, where 1 represents a low concern and 9 represents a high concern.

Blake and Mouton (1964) postulated there were 5 leadership types:

1.1. Impoverished management – describes a situation in which there is both low concern for results and low concern about people. The apathetic nature of this leader results in behavior that is indifferent to both-success and human relationships.

1.9. Country Club Management – leaders/managers manifest a low concern for results combined with high concern for people. This translates in a leader who is more interested in pleasing people than in the performance of tasks while attempting to create an environment that is both friendly and welcoming.

9.1. Authority-Compliance Management – is a combination of high concern for results and a low concern for people. This controlling leadership style is characterized by a focus on results (delivering instructions and tasks) while manifesting no compassion or concern for subordinates.

5.5. Middle-of –the Road Management – is a style of compromise as leaders try to balance concern for results with satisfying relationships.

9.9. Team management – where emphasis is placed both on results and people. This optimal balance of developing human relationships and effective results attainment provides for the most comfortable and satisfying work environment.

Leadership styles (how leaders deal with tasks and people) together with social media make their mark on the organizational culture of companies.

The specialized literature contains many definitions of the concept of "organizational culture." However, two perspectives dominate the relevant literature, which are not necessarily mutually exclusive: the managerial and social sciences approach. According to the first, a leader or a management team creates and affects the culture, while the social sciences approach supports that culture is shaped by the shared experiences between individuals, often developed on an ad hoc basis.

Based on the second approach, the intersection of the various definitions refers to the common characteristics, perceptions, values, beliefs, and fundamental principles that a group of employees follow, in order to adjust to new external environmental conditions and contribute to inter-organizational integration and operation, and all these guide and constrain employees' behavior (Schein 2004; Bourantas 2006; Kondalkar 2007). Konteh, et al. (2008) observed that culture constitutes a lens through which an organization can be understood and interpreted while Chapman (2002, p. 14) stressed that organizational culture is dynamic and "emerges in the complex interactions of human behavior" and is also structural, because of "such interactions produce particular patterns (or structures) which, in turn, influence the interactions themselves". Simply put, culture depicts the character or identity of an organization, on how things are done and is reflected by artifacts that someone sees when visiting a company, such as office spaces, the dressing code of employees, etc. (Ribière 2001).

Goffee and Jones (2009) pointed out that culture is simply a "community," which is built on shared interests and mutual obligations and thrives on cooperation and friendships.

Organizational culture guides employees' behavior toward operational effectiveness (Schein 2004) and particularly to an organization's performance (Denison 1990; Kotter and Heskett 1992; Alvesson 2002). But businesses rely on patterns of social interactions that sustain them over time. From this perspective, Goffee and Jones attribute to business organizations two characteristics that are present in any organizational culture: sociability and solidarity (1996). Sociability is about human relations. Employees perceive each other as friends while working in such an environment is enjoyable. Sociability has many benefits: it fosters team work, sharing of information, creativity and openness to new ideas. Solidarity, on the other hand, is more about the mind. Relationships within organizations are based on mutual interests and common tasks, shared goals and focus on profit that will benefit both the employees and the organization (Goffee, Jones 1996). While sociability and solidarity come as natural in all types of organizations, assessing where one stands in both dimensions may be particularly useful for leaders and managers. According to Goffee and Jones (1996), the intersection of sociability and responsibility results in four types of organizational culture: networked, mercenary, fragmented and communal.

Networked organizations are high in sociability and low on solidarity: people collaborate more as friends and act as a family; decisions are often made before the business meetings (lack of hierarchy). Their low level of solidarity means that managers and leaders have often trouble when trying to make employees commit to rules, procedures and shared objectives.

Mercenary organizations (low sociability and high solidarity) are focused on business issues: deadlines, common tasks, shared objectives. Work takes priority on private life and individual interests coincide with the company's goals. Poor performance is not tolerated while employees are driven more by competition and a strong will to win. In this case, low sociability drives people towards less cooperation and sharing of ideas.

Fragmented organizations (low sociability and low solidarity) are the ones in which members rarely agree on performance standards and organizational objectives. Employees perceive themselves as experts and because they have a high sense of self- worth, many of them prefer to work alone. This makes a leader's job very difficult: it is hard to align people to the company's goals when they do not identify themselves with the organization and act solely on a "what's in it for me" basis. Teamwork in this type of organizations is difficult to achieve because there is little interdependence in the work itself.

Communal organizations (high sociability and high solidarity) seem to be the ideal type of organization: employees identify with the organization; share equitably risks and rewards; value fairness and justice while being committed to the company's goals. Teamwork and creativity thrive because commitment and focus are high (Goffee, Jones 1996).

As unstable as these four types of organizational culture may be, knowing where the organizations stand in terms of sociability and solidarity is important for managers and leaders: They need to know where and how to act on these dimensions in order to gain a competitive advantage and drive their companies to success. Measuring these two dimensions is a challenge particularly in times of crisis such as the present pandemic. Businesses need to become more dynamic and flexible because technological progress puts its mark both on human relations and performance. Therefore deciding what type of organizational culture you want to build up is essential for leaders and managers who know where they are heading in the long run.

Some authors, however, including Scott, et al. (2003), have pointed out that there is little evidence in the research literature on the relationship between organizational culture and performance. However, leaders should develop a clear understanding of organizational culture (Reigle 2001), as this is important for guiding the operations of the whole organization, in order to know its strengths and weaknesses and to use them appropriately. In addition, they should uncover the probable causal relationships between the different kinds of cultures and organizational performance and then implement this most suited to their needs (Alvesson 2002).

The role of leadership is important in shaping the appropriate culture, affecting its main characteristics, such as attitudes to risk, rituals, and autonomy that respond to their organizations' needs (Konteh et al. 2008). Thus, top management needs to understand the culture of their organization or enterprise and must then decide how this can be changed in order to improve both their employees' experience of the workplace and their organization's profitability, despite this being a complicated task (Sadri and Lees 2001). Many challenges must be overcome in order to implement and sustain beneficial cultural change (Konteh, et al. 2008). The relevant literature shows that there are a number of standard steps and appropriate values that managers can follow in order to achieve an efficient organizational cultural change (Kotter 1996; Momen 2015).

Leaders and managers can manipulate the levels of sociability and responsibility in their organizations through the decisions they make. Therefore, their leadership styles generate patterns of organizational cultures that affect the organizational climate and the way work is done while social networking platforms are being used to provide much more support and input for employees. If the chosen leadership style is directly related to the organizational performance of the company, this implies that leaders and managers should invest in their leadership abilities as a leader's effectiveness is always determined by his/her leadership skills (Maxwell 2007).

3 Data and Results

Our study was conducted among 45 Romanian managers/entrepreneurs, the data being collected in January 2021 and processed in SPSS and Excel. The applied questionnaire that consists of 24 questions was build based on fundamental principles related to organizational culture and leadership (Goffee & Jones 1996; Blake and Mouton 1964).

Table 1. Results

Questions	Very important/important	Neutral	Less important/unimportant
1) I encourage my team to participate when it comes to decision-making time and I try to implement their ideas and suggestions	91%	7%	2%
2) Nothing is more important than accomplishing a goal or a task	69%	27%	4%
3) I enjoy coaching people in new tasks and procedures	84%	13%	3%
4) The more challenging a task is, the more I enjoy it	82%	13%	5%
5) I encourage my employees to be creative about their job	89%	11%	–
6) I enjoy reading articles, books and journals about training, leadership and psychology and then putting what I have read into action	78%	18%	4%
7) I manage my time very efficiently	80%	15%	5%
8) When seeing a complex task through completion, I ensure that every detail is accounted for	89%	9%	2%
9) Counseling my employees to improve their performance or behavior is second nature to me	64%	31%	5%

(*continued*)

Table 1. (*continued*)

Questions	Very important/important	Neutral	Less important/unimportant
10) I enjoy reading articles, books and trade journals about my profession and then implementing the new procedures I have learned	78%	18%	4%
11) People in my company try to make friends and to keep their relationships strong	80%	16%	4%
12) People in my company often socialize outside the office	58%	35%	7%
13) When people leave the company, we stay in touch	62%	22%	16%
14) People in this company do favors for others because they like one another	51%	29%	20%
15) People in this company often confide in one another about personal matters	55%	33%	12%
16) Our group/team understands and shares the same business objectives	82%	13%	5%
17) Work gets done effectively and productively	89%	7%	4%
18) Our group/team/company takes strong action to address poor performance	71%	27%	2%
19) Our collective will to win is high	80%	18%	2%

(*continued*)

Table 1. (*continued*)

Questions	Very important/important	Neutral	Less important/unimportant
20) when opportunities for competitive advantage arise, we move quickly to capitalize them	76%	20%	4%

Source: Authors' calculations based on questionnaires filled in by respondents.

The demographic structure of the respondents is presented, as follows: 37.8% women, 62.2% men, from which most of them work in IT (13%) or retail (15%), but also in fields like banking, education, professional services or transportation. The respondents who were between 26 and 39 years old were the majority – 37.8%, followed by those that are between the ages 40 and 49–26.7%. The respondents who under 25 years old represent 20% whereas people between the ages 50–59 represent 11.1%. Only 4.4% from the total number registered by the statistics were people over 60 years old.

The formulated hypotheses are the following:

1. Over 60% of Romanian managers/entrepreneurs practice a team management style, supporting both sociability and solidarity in their organizations.
2. The most important social media platform for entrepreneurs to connect with their employees are Facebook and LinkedIn.
3. Sociability is predominantly encouraged by managers and CEOs under 25 years of age while solidarity is supported mainly by leaders who belong to the 26–39 years of age segment.
4. Most managers/entrepreneurs develop their leadership abilities by constantly reading professional books and articles.

The following table provides information regarding aspects that define the managers/entrepreneurs in organizational culture and leadership:

As we can see from the table above:

– At most of the questions we have a percentage that is higher than 60% regarding that Romanian managers/entrepreneurs practice a team management style, supporting both sociability and solidarity in their organizations.
– Most managers/entrepreneurs develop their leadership abilities by constantly reading professional books and articles, having a high percentage in each question regarding this aspect (approx. 80%). The Somers' D and Kendall tests (Garson 2012) were applied to see if there were significant statistical differences among groups regarding age or gender. The p-value for the tests were not smaller than 0.05 meaning that no differences were identified.

The most important social media platform for entrepreneurs to connect with their employees are Facebook (82%) and WhatsApp (69%), as we can see in the graph below (Fig. 1). Younger entrepreneurs, besides Facebook and WhatsApp, are closer to Instagram, while the more experienced ones are more familiar with Linkedin.

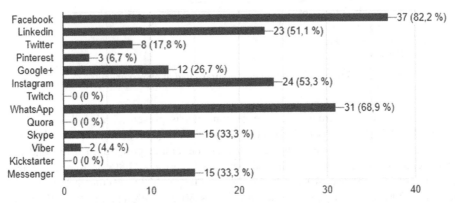

Fig. 1. Distribution of entrepreneurs regarding social media

Even though the difference is insignificant, the Romanian managers/entrepreneurs are slightly more oriented on tasks rather than people and – based on the Blake and Mouton Managerial Grid – their leadership style is team leadership, meaning that they are strong on both tasks and people skills. While meaningful differences between segments of age do not exist, it appears that younger entrepreneurs are barely a bit more targeting tasks rather than people.

To see if there were differences based on age whether sociability or solidarity is predominantly encouraged by managers and CEOs, the Somers' D and Kendall tests were again applied. For each question, p-value was not less or equal to 0.05 which means that there is not sufficient evidence to conclude that there are age differences regarding the way entrepreneurs deal with sociability and solidarity. But as an observation, the sample was rather small, so further investigation may be required to look into this matter.

Nevertheless, using the Somers' D, Kendall and Pearson Chi Square tests, we found that there are some differences regarding age in the following statements:

1. Nothing is more important than accomplishing a goal or a task
2. I enjoy reading articles, books and trade journals about my profession and then implementing the new procedures I have learned.
3. People in my company try to make friends and to keep their relationships strong.
4. Our group/team understands and shares the same business objectives.

Most of the statements where we found differences are oriented more towards solidarity rather than sociability. However, our results indicate a communal organizational culture that prevails in the Romanian entrepreneurial companies. Only the second statement out of the fourth is not sensitive to order (only chi-square p-value being relevant with a value smaller than 0.05). In all other three statements the order of ages is important, in this case Somers' D and Kendall p-values being smaller than 0.05.

Yet, an interesting fact is that there are no statistical significant differences regarding gender when we refer to leadership and organizational culture.

4 Discussion

In the analysis of the results obtained we must take into account both the specificity of the SME sector and the current pandemic context.

Willingly or unwillingly, the societal crisis generated by the pandemic, through its surprising appearance and its all-encompassing and virulent manifestation, forced management at all levels of society and economy to make decisions, to take actions and have reactive behaviors. At the forefront have been and still are, in many areas, especially at company level, the survival and/or ensuring a "reasonable" level of functionality, given that economic challenges and difficulties are closely interconnected with those of medical and social nature (Nicolescu 2020a). Organizational resilience and agility have become coordinates of management in many companies. Among the new managerial elements, crystallized in 2020 under the impact of the Covid-19 pandemic are:

- the ascendancy of pivoting in the forefront of management, i.e. the ability of the management and entrepreneurs to quickly change decision and action directions, when the context changes rapidly and with unique and often atypical manifestations;
- promoting a new type of distributed leadership and a collaborative culture, able to facilitate organizational changes and transformations at an alert and efficient pace.
- highlighting humanistic management, focused on people in its complexity and based on taking into account changes in perception, expectations, aspirations, motivations, feedback, behaviors and emotional intelligence, at the individual and community level;
- intensifying the virtualization of management, aimed at using online applications, digital transformations, increasing use of new concepts, approaches and tools on artificial intelligence "internet of things (IOT) and connected devices", "big data analysis", "metrics and clouds", "custom manufacturing and 3D printing" (Nicolescu 2020b).

The surprising homogeneity in the survey results is obviously explained by the particular context that organizations live in the midst of the pandemic, a context that requires similar reactions: communication methods, leadership in the sense of strengthening the team, real-time collective reactions, reactive and opportunistic strategies, solidarity, agility and organizational resilience. In crisis situations, the differences in the approach of leaders depending on age, gender, field of activity are blurred.

For small companies, the perspective is often dominated and therefore restricted by the personal perspective of the entrepreneur. The company reproduces the personal imprint of the entrepreneur, in many respects: the main purpose of the company (profit, growth, stability, job satisfaction); orientation (technical, commercial, social); working conditions, internal and external communication style, etc. (Nooteboom 1993).

Organizational culture is shaped not only by the values and norms of the entrepreneur, but also by the way these values and norms are communicated to the employees (Grigore 2019).

The know-how in SMEs flows very fast due especially to the informal networks and high interactions between the entrepreneur-leader and his subordinates. We could see this informality in the results of our research regarding the most used platforms: Facebook, 82% and WhatsApp, 69%.

Usually the climate within SMEs is very much associated with that of a family, with a lot of informality, with a parental figure, with clear support for professional and personal development.

The use of SMEs' capabilities is possible only to the extent that the entrepreneurs are able to develop leadership competencies. That means to be able to attract high quality human resources, to unleash their potential, to build up and implement together a realistic vision.

The entrepreneur's success is highly dependent to the extent that his/her decisions and actions come to meet his/her employees' aspirations and needs. Nothing is more important than the solidarity of human resources to their leaders' values and vision. (Nastase and Grigore 2014).

Collaborative business culture is another major pillar of the collaboration. The lack of a business culture that encourages collaboration both within organizations and developing collaborative relationships in the outside will be a real barrier to conducting collaborative strategies.

Another important factor for a strong organizational culture is represented by the leaders' capacity to build up and work in teams. It is often said that entrepreneurship is mainly characterized by individualism. However, entrepreneurs need to develop professional networks inside and outside the company. Moreover, It is important to build up a strong, supportive culture within a SME, especially in times of crisis: the way that the entrepreneur is treating the people around him, starting with his/her employees, customers, suppliers, etc. is about to undergo profound changes.

In this regard, leaders-entrepreneurs try to become role models for their employees; show empathy and support and a significant involvement in the problems they face; they inspire not so much through the vision they have about the future of the company, but through their personal example. Productivity and resilience seem to be two of the manifestations that characterize leaders in times of crisis.

Direct, open and fast communication with employees tends to become the number 1 feature on the list of leadership skills. From this perspective, browsing social media platforms has become a "must": entrepreneurial leaders use Facebook and WhatsApp groups to transmit information and be in constant contact with employees. Most Romanian leaders-entrepreneurs have accounts on at least 3 social media platforms, and this finding is in line with specialized studies that show that leaders who know how to use social media are more appreciated by their employees compared to those who cannot or do not want to use them. Moreover, social media is also a very good tool to strengthen sociability between team members: people rarely gather for coffee face-to-face, and more on WhatsApp for the exchange of information and ideas, but also for socializing (Mocanu 2020). If, prior to the crisis, the main tool used by leaders was email, today it has given way to social media platforms.

The organizational culture of Romanian companies in the period before the pandemic was a mercenary one, characterized by competitive individualism and personal achievements, a culture that did not exclude cooperative activities in situations where benefits can be obtained for both individuals and the organization (Nastase and Grigore 2014). Pragmatism in labor relations is what dominated, and still dominates in many companies. However, the pandemic brought with it a more pronounced orientation towards sociability: the need to strengthen relations between team members is greater because the risks are high, and sincere friendship and collegiality help employees face challenges more easily. Solidarity, in this context, tends to acquire a double meaning: solidarity, in the sense of focusing on tasks and performance, but also solidarity – as mutual support in times of crisis.

Specialized literature (Goffee and Jones 1996) has shown that communal organizational cultures are unstable by definition, the balance between solidarity and sociability constantly oscillating between the 4 types of known cultures, depending on the context. In the Romanian communal cultures, according to our study and, in accordance with Blake and Mouton's Grid, team leadership prevails. The question we can ask ourselves is this: is this leadership style, together with the communal cultures present in SMEs, only a temporary effect of the pandemic or is it rather a long-term shift?

5 Conclusions

We are living in times of great transformations with many and numerous challenges ahead for states, companies and leaders. In this dynamic environment, the leaders' role is becoming vital for the functionality and performance of all systems, at macro or micro levels.

Intensifying VUCA (volatility, uncertainty, complexity and ambiguity) implies both creative, pragmatic and intense efforts of management experts and the need to capitalize on "forced progress" in digitization, online work, communication and blended teams, adaptive leadership – made in the present crisis (Nicolescu 2020a).

Limits of the study and future research directions:

1) The small number of respondents who wanted to participate in our research prevents us from generalizing our observations to all Romanian companies and leaders;
2) The homogeneity of participants – entrepreneurs of small and medium enterprises.

In this regard, we believe that future research in the field should include a significant number of large Romanian companies, private and state, as well as the non-governmental sector.

Changes in the social architecture of Romanian companies are already visible in the Romanian business environment. The teams of many companies are now operating online, and online businesses have exploded. Leaders need to redefine the concept of "performance" in order to put it back in an acceptable balance, according to Blake and Mouton, with human resource (human-oriented) tasks. We believe this should be one of the important directions of research in the coming years.

Acknowledgement. We would like to thank the entrepreneurs who chose to answer our questions. The book (coordinated by Vlad Mocanu) where we found their success stories inspired us.

References

Alvesson, M.: Understanding Organizational Culture. Sage, London (2002)

Blake, R., Mouton, J.: The Managerial Grid: The Key to Leadership Excellence. Gulf Publishing Co, Houston (1964)

Birkinshaw, J.M.: Reinventing Management: Smarter Choices for Getting Work Done. Jossey-Bass (2011)

Brandfog Survey. CEOs, Social Media and Brand reputation (2016). https://www.slideshare.net/BRANDfog/brandfog-2016-survey-ceos-social-media-brand-reputation

Brandfog Survey. CEO Social Media Communications in the Age of COVId-19 (2020). https://brandfog.com/brandfog/wp-content/uploads/2020/07/Brandfog_survey_CEO_social_media_com_in_the_age_of_covid.pdf

Bourantas, D., Papalexandris, N.: Differences in leadership behavior and influence between public and private organizations in greece. Int. J. Hum. Res. Manage. **4**(4), 859–871 (2006)

Chapman, J.A.: A framework for transformational change in organizations. Leaders. Organ. Dev. J. **23**(1), 16–25 (2002)

Crăciun, L., Năstase, M., Stamule, T., Vizitiu, C.: Leadership in romanian small to medium enterprises. Sustainability **7**, 4183–4198 (2015). https://doi.org/10.3390/su7044183

Denison, D.R., Haaland, S., Goelzer, P.: Corporate culture and organizational effectiveness: is there a similar pattern? Advances in Global Leadership, pp. 205–227. Emerald Group Publishing, Bingley (1991)

Garson, G.: Correlation (Statistical Associates "Blue Book" Series Book 3). Statistical Associates (2012)

Goffee, R., Jones, G.: What holds the modern company together? Harv. Bus. Rev. **74**, 133–148 (1996)

Goffee, R., Jones, G.: What holds the modern company together?. Harvard Business School Press, Boston (2009)

Grigore, A-M.: Antreprenoriat si management pentru afaceri mici si mijlocii, Editura Beck (2019)

Ibarra, H., Hunter, M.: How leaders create and use networks. Harv. Bus. Rev. **85**(1), 40–47 (2007)

Kane, G.: Leadership theories (2009). https://pdfs.semanticscholar.org/00d2/81b028786a4ef53c140a0fc870d90fc84c0c.pdf?_ga=2.116158214.1880154633.1614074356-1971896466.1614074356

Kayworth, T., Leidner, D.: Leadership effectiveness in global virtual teams. J. Manage. Inf. Syst. **18**(3), 7–40 (2001)

Kondalkar, V.G.: Organisational Behaviour. New Age International Ltd (2007)

Konteh, F.H., Mannion, R., Davies, H.T.O.: Clinical governance views on culture and quality improvement. Clin. Gov. Int. J. **13**(3), 200–207 (2008)

Kotter, J.: What leaders really do. Harv. Bus. Rev. **68**(3) (1990)

Kotter, J., Heskett, J.L.: Corporate Culture and Performance. Free Press, New York (1992)

Kotter, J.P.: Leading Change. Harvard Business School Press, Boston (1996)

Maxwell, J.: The 21 Irrefutable Laws of Leadership, 2nd Revised Edition. Thomas Nelson Publishers (2007)

Mocanu, V(.: Esecuri de success ale antreprenorilor romani. Evrika, Bucuresti (2020)

Momen, N.: The role of leadership in shaping organizational culture (2015). https://www.linkedin.com/pulse/role-leadership-shaping-organizational-culture-momen

Nastase, M., Grigore, A-M.: Leadership impact over the organizational culture within the SME's sector. In: CSOL-UB Conference, 9 May 2014

Nastase, M., Radu, C.: Leadership's characteristics within the Romanian SME's. In: The Best Romanian Management Studies 2011–2012, Lambert Academic Publishing (2013)

Nooteboom, B.: Firm size effects on transaction costs. Small Bus. Econ. **5**, 285–297 (1993)

Nicolescu, O.: Refocalizarea de la managementul reactiv la managementul anticipativ, SAMRO, Newsletter #139 (2020). https://sites.google.com/site/samronewsletter/2018/nl139#TOC-Refocalizarea-de-la-managementul-reactiv-la-managementul-anticipativ

Nicolescu, O.: "Virtualizarea" și "umanizarea managementului" - cele două tendințe impulsionate de noua pandemie, SAMRO, Newsletter #137 (2020). https://sites.google.com/site/samronewsletter/2018/nl137#TOC-Virtualizarea-i-umanizarea-managementului—celedou-tendin-e-impulsionate-de-noua-pandemie

MKOR. Romanian leaders profile research report (2017). https://mkor.eu/research/romanian-leaders-profile-report/

Northouse, P.G.: Leadership: Theory and Practice. Sage, Thousand Oaks (2012)

Reigle, R.F.: Measuring organic and mechanistic cultures. Eng. Manage. J. **13**, 3–8 (2001)

Ribiere, V.: Assessing knowledge management initiative successes as a function of organizational culture. Ph.D. thesis (2001). https://www.researchgate.net/publication/269574017_Assessing_Knowledge_Management_Initiative_Successes_as_a_Function_of_Organizational_Culture

Rue, L.W., Byars, L.L.: Management: Skills and Application. McGraw-Hill, New York (2009)

Russell, R.V.: Leadership in Recreation, 3rd edn. McGraw-Hill, New York (2005)

Sadri, G., Lees, B.: Developing corporate culture as a competitive advantage. J. Manage. Dev. **20**, 853–859 (2001)

Schein, E.H.: Organizational Culture and Leadership, 3rd edn. Jossey-Bass, San Francisco (2004)

Scott, et al.: The quantitative measurement of organizational culture in health care: a review of the available instruments. Health Serv. Res. **38**(3), 923–945 (2003)

Adolescent Sexting and Its Associations with Parenting Styles and Sense of Parental Social Control

Michal Dolev-Cohen[✉] 🆔 and Tsameret Ricon 🆔

Oranim Academic College of Education, Tivon, Israel
michal@netvision.net.il

Abstract. In this study, online questionnaires were used to examine the sexting (sexual correspondence) habits of 547 students (113 boys and 434 girls) attending grades seven through 12, in an attempt to identify the correlation between parenting styles and the sense of social control experienced by the participants regarding their sexting habits. Findings of the study indicate that sexting was more prevalent among boys, of high-school age, attending mainstream secular schools in Israel (compared to girls, in middle school, attending national-religious schools, respectively). However, eliminating the religious students from the sample resulted in no gender difference in terms of sexting habits. Furthermore, it was also found that the weaker the degree of social control perceived by the adolescent, the greater was the likelihood that the adolescent was engaging in sexting activities. These findings shed light on sexting, a phenomenon which–despite its prevalence among youths in Israel and throughout the world–is insufficiently addressed by the significant adults in their lives. The implications of these findings for educators and school counselors are considered and discussed.

Keywords: Sexting · Adolescence · Internet · Parenting style · Social control

1 Introduction

Nowadays, as technology constitutes an integral part of adolescents' lives (Lenhart et al. 2010), it seems natural that they choose to express themselves online and to exploit the abundance of Internet apps for their needs. Given the sense of privacy afforded by the smartphone, the disinhibition effect as identified by Suler (2004), the increasing importance of the peer group, and the changes that take place during adolescence (Steinberg 2008), it seems inevitable that adolescents now explore their sexuality in the virtual world of cyberspace and through sexting activities (Gordon-Messer et al. 2013). Consequently, parents should address their children's sexting activities when educating them about sex, emphasizing that sexting can have a negative effect on both the sender (if the sender's image is distributed) and on the recipient (who might find the sexual content offensive). The style of parenting and parents' efforts to exert social control over their adolescent children may influence their offspring's behavior overall, including their risk

© Springer Nature Switzerland AG 2021
G. Meiselwitz (Ed.): HCII 2021, LNCS 12774, pp. 18–35, 2021.
https://doi.org/10.1007/978-3-030-77626-8_2

behaviors. Hence, given parents' role as socialization agents, they can play a significant part by educating their children about the potentially negative outcomes of sexting (Vanwesenbeeck et al. 2018).

1.1 Sexting

The term "sexting" refers to the sending of sexual text messages and pictures, as well as engaging (as requestor or responder) in the exchange of nude or semi-nude photographs. Despite the moral alarm to which this phenomenon gives rise, in the research literature it is described as an expression of sexuality in cyberspace; indeed, researchers agree that sexting is used by adolescents to explore their sexuality (Dir et al. 2013; Döring 2014; Henderson and Morgan 2011). It appears that adolescents engage in sexting at the request of their sexual/romantic partners, or to maintain a sense of intimacy when they are physically away from each other (Drouin et al. 2013; Englander 2012; Gil-Llario et al. 2012). Other reasons for engaging in sexting described in the literature include flirting, attracting attention, or proving one's love to one's partner (Van Ouytsel et al. 2017).

A Spanish study of the factors that motivate sexting found that among girls, cyber-gossip and the need for popularity were the most prevalent driving factors, whereas, among boys, these were the desire to demonstrate acceptance of the adolescent culture's norms and a straightforward interest in sexting (Gaston et al. 1996). For adolescents, sexting often appears to be a means of flirtation and harmless entertainment when feeling good about themselves and their sexuality (Dir et al. 2013; Lenhart 2009).

Sexting between romantic partners was not found to be a marker of risk behaviors (Van Ouytsel et al. 2018); by contrast, sexting among adolescents in general has been associated with sexual offenses, such as the trading or possession of pornographic images (Arcabascio 2010). In a recent study, non-partnered adolescents who engaged in sexting outside a romantic relationship were also more likely to report substance use (compared to their non-sexting peers) (Van Ouytsel et al. 2018). Although–as noted—sexting can be considered merely an expression of sexuality, the fact that it is an online activity has certain negative implications, namely, exposing users to risks, such as privacy violation due to distribution, harassment, cyberbullying, sextortion, revenge porn after a breakup, etc. (Madigan et al. 2018; Van Ouytsel et al. 2017).

As to its prevalence, sexting is a frequent phenomenon among adolescents. A study involving students in grades six-12 found that on average, 17% of the participants engaged in sexting; while only 3% of the 12-year-olds engaged in such activities, the rate among 18-year-olds was 32% (Dake et al. 2012). A study of 1,839 seventh-12th graders in the US found that 15% of smartphone owners engaged in sexting (Rice et al. 2012), whereas a study of 3,503 Swedish students found that 20.9% of the adolescents had posted nude photos of themselves online (Jonsson et al. 2014).

A meta-analysis of articles published between 2011 and 2015 on the subject of sexting found that the prevalence of sexting ranged from 2.5% to 24%, with an estimated mean of 10.2% (Kosenko et al. 2017). A more recent study revealed that the rate of adolescents that send sexting messages was one in seven, while the rate of involvement as recipients was one in four. It appears that over the years, sexting has become more common among adolescents (Madigan et al. 2018).

1.2 Sexting and Gender

The use of media differs by gender and, as to sexting, it appears that the research literature is inconclusive regarding the effects of the gender variable. Some studies report finding no gender differences (Hudson and Fetro 2015; Lenhart 2009; Madigan et al. 2018), whereas others report that girls engage in sexting more than do boys (Mitchell et al. 2012; Reyns et al. 2014), and still others suggest that boys are more likely to sext than girls (Delevi and Weisskirch 2013; Garcia et al. 2016; Klettke et al. 2018). A systematic review showed that although findings relating to gender are somewhat mixed, there is some evidence that female texters may be more likely than their male counterparts to send sexts and, accordingly, male texters may be more likely to receive them (Klettke et al. 2014). These gender differences may be explained, in part, by the finding that being pressured by others was a causal factor in female sexting behavior (Englander 2012; Reed et al. 2020).

A different study found that in traditional countries, boys typically engage in sexting behaviors more than do girls, whereas, in non-traditional countries, gender differences were scarce (Baumgartner et al. 2014). Given that Israeli society exhibits a high degree of traditionalism (Lavee and Katz 2003), it is characterized by unequal gender roles (Boehnke 2011). Accordingly, girls tend to be more protected by their parents and hence are subjected to more rules, intended to restrict their sexual activity (Gaston et al. 1996) and promote sexual passivity (Kiefer and Sanchez 2007).

1.3 Parenting and Parenting Styles

Parents play a pivotal role in adolescents' socialization. According to a qualitative study, it was found that boys often ask girls to engage in sexting to demonstrate their mutual love and that the girls feel emotionally pressured to acquiesce (Van Ouytsel et al. 2017; Van Ouytsel et al. 2017). However, when boys' parents set down rules about sending and receiving sexual messages, the boys were less likely to engage in sexting (West et al. 2014). This raises the possibility that sexting may be linked either to the absence of parental social control or to permissive education; hence, it is worth examining whether parenting styles and practices have an impact on the extent and manner of sexting among adolescents.

As sexting behavior becomes a more common form of intimate communication among adolescents, the question of the effects of parenting styles and parental mediation becomes ever more crucial. Parents need to address the risks inherent in this type of communication in the context of their children's sexual education (Vanwesenbeeck et al. 2018).

The term parenting style refers to the way in which parents operate vis-à-vis their children. The most common and accepted conceptualization in the field is based on the work of Baumrind (1977), who defined three basic constructs that differ in terms of the extent to which the parent sets boundaries, explains and justifies expectations and demands, uses force and control, and offers acceptance and emotional support (Smetana 2017; Moreno-Ruiz et al. 2019).

The authoritative parent combines discipline, boundary setting, along with the expression of warmth and emotional support. The authoritarian parent is characterized by a high degree of control over the children and a low degree of emotional availability in support. The authoritarian parent nurtures the child's respect for authority him and him and advocates obedience and rule-following. Finally, the permissive parent is characterized by a moderate degree of control over the child, accompanied by emotional support and expressions of warmth (Baumrind 1991).

Studies have found that the relationship between the authoritative parenting style and children's behaviors and attitudes was associated to a much greater extent with children's normative functioning compared to the relationship in the case of either of the other two parenting styles (McKinney et al. 2008; Rossman and Rea 2005). Indeed, an examination of the relationship between parenting styles and adolescents' emotional state revealed that adolescents who reported an authoritative parenting style, characterized by a warm parent–child relationship exhibited much fewer symptoms of distress, depression, and behavioral problems than did adolescents who experienced parental intrusiveness and strict supervision (Jacobson and Crockett 2000).

As mentioned, parenting styles differ in terms of the extent of parental demands and the degree of parents' responsiveness to their children (Baumrind 1991); not surprisingly, the variable of parenting style has been associated with the mediating role that parents play in their children's online behaviors (Vanwesenbeeck et al. 2018). As such, it is reasonable to assume that the factor of parenting style would affect also adolescents' sexting activities. The authoritative style is associated with healthier child behaviors than either the authoritarian or the permissive styles, which are linked to higher risk behavior, such as sexting (de Graaf et al. 2011).

1.4 Control Theory and Parental Social Control

According to control theory, social bonds may prevent individuals from engaging in socially deviant behaviors (Fagan and Pabon 1990; Hirschi 1969). Four components of social bonds were identified by Hirschi (1969): attachment, commitment, involvement, and belief. Hirschi (1969) claimed that strong bonds not only help individuals to avoid acting on a deviant disposition but also discourage them from associating with delinquent companions. Given that socialization occurs in the context of close relationships (Pugliese and Okun 2014), parenting has been identified as one of the most important factors influencing the degree of social control manifested by adolescents (Gottfredson and Hirschi 1990; Unnever et al. 2003). Hence, the establishment of a healthy bond between parents and children, which entails parental attachment and involvement in shared activities, is viewed as an essential component of parental social control influence over their adolescent children. Parental social control, which refers to parents' efforts to influence and regulate their children's behavior (Pugliese and Okun 2014), appears to be associated with parents' rule regulation and adolescents' rule compliance (Lewis et al. 2004).

1.5 The Current Study

The aim of the current study was to assess the frequency of Israeli adolescents' involvement in sexting and examine the relationship between parenting styles, adolescents' reported sense of parental social control, and their reported use of sexting.

2 Methods

2.1 Participants

The current study included 547 participants: 434 female students (79.3%) and 113 male students (20.7%) from various regions in Israel. Participants' ages ranged from 12 to 18 (mean/M = 15.7 years, standard deviation/SD = 1.51); 206 of them (37.7%) were attending middle school and 341 (62.3) were attending high school; finally, 440 (80.4%) were enrolled in schools affiliated with the secular Jewish sector and 89 (16.3%) were enrolled in schools affiliated with the religious Jewish sector. All of the participants reported owning a smartphone.

Participation in the study was on a voluntary basis. The participants were recruited via an online ad placed on social networks (Facebook and Instagram), which invited them to complete an anonymous online questionnaire for an academic research project. Before they were given access to the questionnaire, they had to indicate that their parents did not object to their participation. Participants were not identified and results are presented in the form of group data rather than individual data.

2.2 Instruments

Demographics and Sexting Questionnaire. The questionnaire was composed of general questions regarding the participant's age, grade in school, gender, and use of chat apps. Participants were asked four yes/no questions about their sexting behavior: (1) sending sexual messages, (2) sending messages containing either nude or semi-nude images, (3) asking someone else to send nude or semi-nude images, and (4) asking someone else to receive nude or semi-nude images from the participant. Additional questions were related to reporting and telling others about sexting messages that were sent and received. The questionnaire was compiled for the purpose of this study and therefore, was written in Hebrew.

Parental Authority Questionnaire (Buri 1991). This questionnaire includes 30 items, through which adolescents indicate how they perceive the parenting style by which they are raised and educated. Three types of parenting styles are examined: permissive, authoritarian, and authoritative. Each type is represented by 10 items on the questionnaire. Participants responded on a 5-point Likert scale, ranging from 1 = strongly disagree to 5 = strongly agree. Parenting style was measured for both parents together. In the present study, internal consistency was $\alpha = 0.72$ for permissive parenting style, $\alpha = 0.86$ for authoritarian style, and $\alpha = 0.87$ for authoritative style.

Social Control Theory Questionnaire (Hirschi 1969). The questionnaire was used to examine participants' perceptions of parental social control. For the purpose of the current study, a briefer Hebrew version (Wilchek-Aviad 2005) was used, namely, only the bonds of attachment and involvement were examined, as they are directly related to and considered evidence of parental social control. Thus, a total of 27 items were used. Participants rated the items on a 5-point Likert scale ranging from "strongly disagree" to "strongly agree" and "don't know." Internal consistency was $\alpha = 0.92$.

2.3 Data Analysis

Data were analyzed using SPSS version 25. Descriptive statistics were used to measure participants' sexting behaviors, and χ^2 was used to analyze group relationships with respect to gender and age groups. Sexting variables were formulated as dichotomous or categorical variables. Principal component factor analysis was applied to the Parental Authority Questionnaire and to the Control Theory Questionnaire to validate their factors. Note that the adolescents responded to the questionnaires anonymously and online, so that data related to their schools, cities, and neighborhoods were not available. For this reason, multilevel modeling was not used. The means, standard deviations, and Pearson correlations between parenting styles and parental social control were calculated. Logistic regressions were calculated to assess how sexting was related to gender, age group, parenting styles, and parental social control.

3 Results

Results of the study indicate that all of the adolescents were using instant messaging: 100% were chatting on WhatsApp, 65 6.5% were using Snapchat, and 61.4% were using Facebook chat.

3.1 Sexting

As shown in Table 1 regarding sending and receiving sexts, 22% of the adolescents reported that they had sent text messages and 18% that they had sent nude or seminude photos; that is, approximately one-quarter (n = 145, 26.5%) reported sending text messages with or without photos (with photos n = 97, 66.9%; without photos n = 48, 33.1%). Approximately one-half of the participants sent these messages to their partners, others sent them either to grade-level peers, someone with whom they wanted to have a relationship, or to strangers. Of these, 71% did not share with or inform anyone about this action and 27% shared this information with a friend. Approximately 11% of the adolescents admitted that they had requested (full or semi-) nude photographs from others; the majority asked this of their partners (45%) while others asked this from either a grade-level peer, someone with whom they wished to have a relationship, or strangers. Approximately one-third of the adolescents (31%) reported that they were asked by others to send nude photos of themselves; approximately half of these requests (49%) came from strangers, whereas the rest were sent by either partners, friends, or acquaintances. Fifty-three percent of the adolescents did not tell anyone about this incident; those who did share this information, reported it to a friend (44%), a sibling, a school counselor, a teacher, neighbor, or parent.

3.2 Sexting—By Gender, Age Group, and School Sector

Sexting (transmitting sexual messages with or without photographs) was found to be more prevalent among boys (than girls), high school-age students (compared to middle-school students), and those attending secular (versus religious) schools (Table 2). The age group and school sector -related differences were due mainly to a difference in sending photographs rather than in sending texts. Similarly, requesting a photograph of sexual content from others was more prevalent among boys, high-school-age students,

Table 1. Sexting frequency ($N = 547$)

	Affirmative response N (%)	To who/By whom		Told someone else about sexting/ being asked to	
Sent sext messages	**121 (22.1)**	Girlfriend/Boyfriend	64 (52.9)	No one	103 (71.0)
		Friends in the peer group	15 (12.4)	Friend	39 (26.9)
		Potential girlfriend/boyfriend	19 (15.7)	Sibling	4 (2.7)
		Stranger	20 (16.5)	Counselor teacher, parent, other adult	3 (2.1)
		Other	3 (2.5)	Told someone*	4 (2.8)
Sent semi/nude self-photos	97 (17.7)	Girlfriend/Boyfriend	48 (49.5)		
		Friends in the peer group	13 (13.4)		
		Potential girlfriend/boyfriend	11 (11.3)		
		Stranger	17 (17.5)		
		Close friend	5 (5.2)		
		Other	3 (3.1)		
	Affirmative response N (%)	To who/By whom	Sharing/Informing		Affirmative response N (%)
Asked someone else to send semi/nude self-photo	60 (11.0)	Girlfriend/Boyfriend	27 (45.0)	No one	
		Friends in the peer group	11 (18.4)	Friend	

(continued)

Table 1. (*continued*)

	Affirmative response N (%)	To who/By whom		Told someone else about sexting/ being asked to	
		Potential girlfriend/boyfriend	8 (13.3)	Sibling	
		Stranger	12 (20.0)	School counselor, teacher, parent, other adult	
		Other	2 (3.3)	Other	
Was asked by someone else to send a semi/nude self-photo	171 (31.3)	Girlfriend/Boyfriend	26 (15.2)	No one	90 (52.6)
		Friends in the peer group	39 (22.8)	Friend	76 (44.4)
		Potential girlfriend/boyfriend	17 (10.0)	Sibling	8 (4.7)
		Stranger	84 (49.1)	School counselor, teacher, parent, other adult	10 (5.8)
		Other	5 (2.9)	Other	12 (7.0)

* Note that "Told someone" is not the sum of the numbers/percentages above, because often, those who shared the information told more than one person.

and students in secular schools. No gender, age group, or school sector-related difference was found for either receiving a request to send a photograph with sexual content or for sharing with others information about one's sexting activities.

Given that the participants attending religious schools constituted only 16.3% of all participants, results were analyzed also without the participants attending religious schools (N = 458).

The results depicted in Table 3 show no gender differences in sexting (sending messages with or without photos), but indicate that sexting is more common among high-school students (age range 15–18, $M = 16.52$, $SD = 0.92$) than among middle-school students (age range 12–15, $M = 14.02$, $SD = 0.85$). Asking others to send nude or semi-nude photos was more common among boys than among girls, and more common among high-school students than among middle-school students.

Table 2. Distribution of sexting by gender, age group, and the school's sectorial affiliation ($N = 547$)s

Variable	Boys N (%)	Girls N (%)	χ^2	Middle School N (%)	High School N (%)	χ^2	Jewish sector–secular affiliation	Jewish sector–religious affiliation	χ^2
	39 (34.5)	106 (24.4)	$\chi^2(1) = 4.69^*$	33 (16.0)	112 (32.8)	$\chi^2(1) = 18.66^{***}$	129 (29.3)	13 (14.6)	$\chi^2(1) = 8.16^{**}$
	13 (11.5)	35 (8.1)	$\chi^2(2) = 4.69$	15 (7.3)	33 (9.7)	$\chi^2(2) = 20.86^{***}$	40 (9.1)	7 (7.9)	$\chi^2(2) = 9.81^{**}$
	26 (23.0)	71 (16.4)		18 (8.7)	79 (23.2)		89 (20.2)	6 (6.7)	
	26 (23.0)	34 (7.8)	$\chi^2(1) = 21.14^{***}$	13 (6.3)	47 (13.8)	$\chi^2(1) = 7.34^{**}$	53 (12.0)	4 (4.5)	$\chi^2(1) = 4.39^*$
	29 (25.7)	142 (32.7)	$\chi^2(1) = 2.08$	55 (26.7)	116 (34.0)	$\chi^2(1) = 3.20$	141 (32.0)	25 (28.1)	$\chi^2(1) = 0.54$
	9 (23.1)	33 (31.1)	$\chi^2(1) = 0.90$	10 (30.3)	32 (28.6)	$\chi^2(1) = 0.04$	36 (27.9)	5 (38.5)	$\chi^2(1) = 0.64$
	11 (37.9)	70 (49.3)	$\chi^2(1) = 1.25$	31 (56.4)	50 (43.1)	$\chi^2(1) = 2.63$	69 (48.9)	9 (36.0)	$\chi^2(1) = 1.43$

$^*p < 0.05$, $^{**}p < 0.01$, $^{***}p < 0.001$

Table 3. Distribution of sexting by gender and age group excluding religious participants ($N = 458$)

Variable	Total N (%)	Boys N (%)	Girls N (%)	$\chi^2(1)$	OR (95% CI)	Middle School N (%)	High School N (%)	$\chi^2(1)$	OR (95% CI)
Sent sexual messages with or without photos	132 (28.8)	35 (34.7)	97 (27.2)	2.15	0.70 (0.44, 1.13)	32 (18.3)	100 (35.3)	15.32***	2.44 (1.55, 3.85)
Sent sexual message(s) including photo(s)	91 (19.9)	24 (23.8)	67 (18.8)	1.58	0.71 (0.41, 1.21)	17 (9.7)	74 (26.1)	19.08***	3.40 (1.92, 6.02)
Asked another person to send nude or semi-nude photos of themselves	56 (12.2)	23 (22.8)	33 (9.2)	13.43***	2.89 (1.61, 5.21)	12 (6.9)	44 (15.5)	7.61**	0.40 (0.20, 0.78)
Was asked by another person to send nude or semi-nude self-photo(s)	146 (31.9)	25 (24.8)	121 (33.9)	3.03	0.64 (0.39, 1.06)	49 (28.0)	97 (34.3)	1.96	0.75 (0.49, 1.12)
Told others about sending sexual messages ($n = 132$)	37 (28.0)	7 (20.0)	30 (30.9)	1.52	1.79 (0.70, 4.55)	10 (31.3)	27 (27.0)	0.22	0.81 (0.34, 1.94)
Told others that someone asked them to send nude or semi-nude photos ($n = 146$)	72 (49.3)	11 (44.0)	61 (50.4)	0.34	1.29 (0.54, 3.08)	28 (57.1)	44 (45.4)	1.81	0.62 (0.31, 1.24)

Note. Middle school (age range 12–15, $M = 14.02$, $SD = 0.85$), high school (age range 15–18, $M = 16.52$, $SD = 0.92$).
*$p < 0.05$, **$p < 0.01$, ***$p < 0.001$.

3.3 Parenting Style and Social Control

Logistic regressions were calculated to predict sexting by gender, age group, type of school, parenting style, and social control (Table 4). The sexting variables were defined dichotomously (1 – exists, 0 – does not exist) and the dichotomous predictors were gender (1 – boys, 0 – girls), age group (1 – high school, 0 – middle school), and type of school affiliation (1 – secular, 0 – religious).

Table 4. Logistic regressions to predict sexting by gender, age group, school affiliation, parenting style, and social control

	Sexting with or without photos		Asking someone else for nudity photos		Asked (by someone) to send self-nudity photos	
	B (SE)	OR (CI95%)	B (SE)	OR (CI95%)	B (SE)	OR (CI95%)
Gender	0.45 (0.24)	1.56 (0.97–2.52)	1.17*** (0.31)	3.21 (1.76–5.85)	−0.36 (0.25)	0.70 (0.42–1.15)
Age group	0.92*** 0.23)	2.51 (1.59–3.95)	0.85* (0.35)	2.33 (1.17–4.67)	0.32 (0.20)	1.38 (0.92–2.06)
School affiliation	1.00** (0.33)	2.71 (1.42–5.16)	0.94 (0.55)	2.55 (0.87–7.46)	0.33 (0.27)	1.39 (0.82–2.35)
Authoritative parenting	0.12 (0.17)	1.12 (0.80–1.58)	−0.23 (0.24)	0.79 (0.49–1.28)	0.15 (0.16)	1.17 (0.85–1.60)
Permissive parenting	−0.08 (0.19)	0.92 (0.63–1.34)	0.59* (0.28)	1.81 (1.05–3.13)	−0.07 (0.18)	0.93 (0.66–1.33)
Authoritarian parenting	−0.09 (0.14)	0.91 (0.69–1.20)	−0.10 (0.20)	0.90 (0.61–1.33)	0.08 (0.13)	1.08 (0.84–1.39)
Social control	−0.53* (0.22)	0.59 (0.38–0.90)	−0.51 (0.31)	0.60 (0.33–1.10)	−0.54** (0.20)	0.58 (0.39–0.87)
χ^2 (9)	40.56***		40.51***		24.53**	

*$p < 0.05$, **$p < 0.01$, ***$p < 0.001$

Sexting with or without accompanying photographs was positively and significantly predicted by the age group and type of school affiliation and negatively and significantly predicted by social control. It was found that the more the degree of social control was perceived to below, the greater the risk/likelihood of engaging in texting with or without photographs, above and beyond the background variables. As noted, sexting with or without photographs was defined as a variable with three different levels: no sexting, sexting via text alone, and sexting with photographs. This variable was analyzed using multinomial logistic regression. Significant results were found for age group χ^2 (2) = 19.18, $p < 0.001$, type of school χ^2 (2) = 13.30, $p < 0.001$, and social control χ^2 (2) = 6.60, $p = 0.037$, while in each the differences were between no sexting and sexting with photographs. No difference was found between no sexting and sexting the text only or between sexting with text only and sexting was photographs. In other words, the main difference according to the findings described in Table 3 is between text messages without sexting and messages with photographs. Beyond the background variables, low social control was found to be associated with a higher risk for sexting with photographs.

Requesting a photograph with social content from someone else was positively and significantly predicted by gender and age group, as shown in Table 3, as well as by permissive parenting. Thus, the perception of permissive parenting was found to be related to a higher risk of requesting sexual photographs from someone else.

Receiving a request from someone else for a sexual photograph of oneself was negatively and significantly predicted by social control. The lower the degree of social control perceived, the greater was the risk of being asked by someone else to send a self-photo with sexual content, this–beyond the effects of the background variables.

The two models for sharing information about sexting activities were found to be insignificant: sharing information about sexting (χ^2 (9) = 5.95, $p = 0.745$, $n = 145$, and sharing about being asked to send one's nude or seminude photo to someone else (χ^2 (9) = 8.63, $p = 0.472$, $n = 171$).

4 Discussion

The present study examined sexting among adolescents and its relationship to gender, perceived parenting style, and parental social control, as evidenced through adolescents' self-reported questionnaires. The findings of the study indicate that the phenomenon is widespread in the age group examined, and it is evident among both boys and girls, affiliated with the secular as well as in the religious sector, with 26.5% of the participants reporting that they had sent sexted or had sent messages containing self-nude or semi-nude photographs. These findings are similar to those of other studies conducted in recent years, which found that the frequency of this phenomenon reached 32%, manifesting more prominently among the older adolescents (compared to the younger ones (Cooper et al. 2016; Dake et al. 2012; Mitchell et al. 2012; Rice et al. 2012).

As regards the issue of gender, the current study found that when examining the secular and religious sectors together, sexting was more frequent among boys than among girls; however, when examining only the secular participants, no gender difference was found. This finding is extremely important because girls have testified that they are afraid that participating in sexting might have a negative effect on their reputation (Spencer et al. 2015), which in turn could explain why they were found to engage less than did boys in sending nude photographs of themselves (Jonsson et al. 2014). This is especially true for young women in traditional countries, where they are expected to maintain a high degree of modesty and morality (Ciclitira 2004; Efrati 2018).

In a study of 480 adolescents, one-fifth of the participants reported being involved in sexting against their will (Drouin et al. 2015), whereas in the present study, almost one-third of the participants reported that others asked them to send nude photos of themselves, with half of these requests coming from strangers. These prevalence rates suggest that sexting is becoming another sign of adolescents' sexual development in the modern age. At the same time, this finding of prevalence is very important in view of the correlation found between more time spent online and sexual harassment, sexual exploitation, and receiving inappropriate requests in the online space (Baumgartner et al. 2010; Jonsson et al. 2014). In Israel, daily screen time among adolescents is relatively higher than that reported in other European countries (Boniel-Nissim et al. 2015).

More than half of the participants refrained from telling anyone of having received requests for sexting content, and of those who did only a few chose to share this with an adult. Indeed, it appears that parents are not aware of the extent or the severity of their children's exposure in the sense. A large study conducted in Europe found that only 21% of parents whose children had been exposed to sexting were aware of this situation, 52% of the parents thought that their children would never be exposed to sexting, and 27% responded that they did not know (Livingstone et al. 2012). It is evident that the percentage of adolescents who report to their parents about sexting involvement is low, which is characteristic of the period of adolescence when children begin to distance themselves from their parents and favor the peer group (Steinberg 2008). A low percent of reporting is characteristic also of victims of online harassment (Heirman and Walrave 2008). This suggests that adolescents feel a need for more assistance, support, and parental guidance regarding their online activities (D'Antona et al. 2010). This state of affairs is problematic given the importance of parents' communication with and support of their adolescent children, which have been shown to act as a factor that moderates the negative effects of online Internet use (Boniel-Nissim et al. 2015). It might be that for many parents, a conversation about sexting might be too embarrassing for them to manage.

Although the focus of the current study was on the frequency of the sexting phenomenon in Israel and its description from the perspective of the adolescents involved, it is impossible to ignore its implications in terms of the findings regarding parental supervision, which indicate that the absence of supervision is related to an increased level of risk for sending nude self-photos. Furthermore, the adolescents' perception of a permissive parenting style being exercised by their parents was found to correlate with requesting others for nude or semi-nude photos. These two findings confirm those of other studies. Thus, for example, the study of, Temple et al. (2014) found a relationship between sexting and the absence of parental supervision, and the study of Lenhart (2009) found that parents who limited the number of messages sent by their children per day substantially reduced chances that their adolescent children would send messages containing nude or semi-nude photographs. Nevertheless, even when parents posed several limitations on their adolescents, a study by Cox Communications (2009) found that one-quarter of the adolescents found a way around these limitations. Hence, it appears that in order to play a significant and educational role, parents must prefer a strategy implementing the discourse of acceptance, containment, and explanations over the strategy of limitations and surveillance (Shin and Li 2017). Such parental presence can enable the adolescent to learn to behave responsibly in the online environment and to seek help if needed.

This study examined the perspective of male and female adolescents through the lands of sexting. The importance of this approach is in revealing the sexting phenomenon as an expression of sexual development among adolescents in the online environment, which is perceived to be private and devoid of parental presence. The results of this study indicate that sexting is prevalent among adolescents but is not always recognized or supervised in either the family or the educational framework; hence the need for active parental involvement and direct communication, mediated through the work of the school counselors.

Furthermore, treating the phenomenon as an expression of a normative developmental stage rather than as pornographic activity can help educate adolescents to consider appropriate means of communication, ways to modulate their actions and reactions, so as to consider excitement and pleasure alongside the potential risks of communicating in the online environment which is devoid of prominent privacy.

We should consider changing the terminology from 'risky' to 'healthy' (Döring 2014). School counselors who partake in the sex education programs in their schools must understand that the adolescents learning environment now includes media and a variety of Internet actions involving their friends, parents, educators, and teachers, as well as more distant and remote circles of acquaintances and even strangers. All of these are components in the adolescents' experience of learning about sexuality and relationships (Davidson 2015). Consequently, all of these components and spaces should be targeted in the educational process. Moreover, the adolescents need to recognize the needs of the sexting message recipients and to determine whether there is a potential sexting partner is interested in receiving such content, rather than assuming that it will be well received or accepted in the manner intended.

Understanding the phenomenon and its driving factors will enable the establishment of counseling educational programs and interventions that are age-appropriate and which can address these online experiences as a normative part of adolescents' sexual development, and thus from an approach that respects the privacy of the adolescents and of their messaging partners.

4.1 Limitations and Further Research

This study had several limitations, which must be addressed. The participants in this study represent a fairly circumscribed cultural population; hence, to ascertain the replicability and generalizability of the findings, future studies are behest to examine this phenomenon among additional age groups as well as among adolescents of diverse religious and cultural populations. The participants of this study were recruited using a convenience sample, gathered online. As such, its findings represent only those who were already online and willing to respond to questions about sexting behaviors. Given that this was not a representative sample, the gender ratio could not be controlled. It would be interesting to compare the results of the current study with those of a study using a more representative sample.

The research in this field must contend with several questions that arise when participants are recruited via the Internet. On the one hand, this recruitment method inherently indicates responders' willingness to participate in the study, enables quick and direct data collection, preserves participants' anonymity (which is particularly important In the context of sexting research), and potentially encourages open and honest responses. On the other hand, this recruitment method may entail a certain degree of bias, given that the participants are already drawn to the topic of investigation. However, it should be noted that to a certain extent, this recruitment method nevertheless, is contextually appropriate, seeing as sexting is an activity that relies on the use of digital communication.

In the current study, the exploration of the social control theory was focused solely on the aspect of parental social control, as a manifestation of the social bonds that enable parental influence. However, given the results of the study, it is important to address the other bonds (friends, and teachers) that may affect adolescents' social control. Despite these lacunae, we view the current study as taking an important step in understanding sexting and its correlation with parental presence.

The original paper was published in *Cyberpsychology: Journal of Psychosocial Research on Cyberspace.*

References

Arcabascio, C.: Sexting and teenagers OMG Ru going 2 jail??? Richmond. J. Law Technol. **16**(3), 1–444 (2010)

Baumgartner, S.E., Sumter, S.R., Peter, J., Valkenburg, P.M., Livingstone, S.: Does country context matter? Investigating the predictors of teen sexting across Europe. Comput. Hum. Behav. **34**, 157–164 (2014). https://doi.org/10.1016/j.chb.2014.01.041

Baumgartner, S.E., Valkenburg, P.M., Peter, J.: Unwanted online sexual solicitation and risky sexual online behaviour across the lifespan. J. Appl. Dev. Psychol. **31**(6), 439–447 (2010). https://doi.org/10.1016/j.appdev.2010.07.005

Baumrind, D.: What research is teaching us about the differences between authoritative and authoritarian child-rearing styles. In: Hamachek, D.E. (ed.) Human Dynamics in Psychology and Education: Selected Readings, 3rd edn., pp. 213–220. Allyn & Bacon, Boston (1977)

Baumrind, D.: The influence of parenting style on adolescent competence and substance use. J. Early Adolesc. **11**(1), 56–95 (1991). https://doi.org/10.1177/0272431691111004

Boehnke, M.: Gender role attitudes around the globe: Egalitarian vs. traditional views. Asian J. Soc. Sci. **39**(1), 57-74 (2011).https://www.jstor.org/stable/43500538

Boniel-Nissim, M., Lenzi, M., Zsizos, E., Gaspar de Matos, M., Gommans, R., Harel-Fisch, Y., Djalovski, A., van der Sluijs, W.: International trends in electronic media communication (EMC) among 11- to 15-year-olds in 30 countries from 2002 to 2010: association with ease of communication with friends of the opposite sex. Eur. J. Publ. Heal. **25**(Suppl. 2), 41–45 (2015). https://doi.org/10.1093/eurpub/ckv025

Buri, J.R.: Parental Authority Questionnaire. J. Pers. Assess. **57**(1), 110–119 (1991). https://doi.org/10.1207/s15327752jpa5701_13

Ciclitira, K.: Pornography, women and feminism: Between pleasure and politics. Sexualities **7**(3), 281–301 (2004). https://doi.org/10.1177/1363460704040143

Cooper, K., Quayle, E., Jonsson, L., Vedin, C.G.: Adolescents and self-taken sexual images: a review of the literature. Comput. Hum. Behav. **55**(Part B), 706–716 (2016). https://doi.org/10.1016/j.chb.2015.10.003

Cox Communications. Teen Online & Wireless Safety Survey: Cyberbullying, sexting, and parental controls (2009). http://www.scribd.com/doc/20023365/2009-Cox-Teen-Online-Wireless-Safety-Survey-Cyberbullying-Sexting-and-Parental-Controls

Dake, J.A., Price, J.H., Maziarz, L., Ward, B.: Prevalence and correlates of sexting behavior in adolescents. Am. J. Sex. Educ. **7**(1), 1–15 (2012). https://doi.org/10.1080/15546128.2012.650959

D'Antona, R., Kevorkian, M., Russom, A.: Sexting, texting, cyberbullying and keeping youth safe online. J. Soc. Sci. **6**(4), 523–528 (2010). https://doi.org/10.3844/jssp.2010.523.528

Davidson, J. (2015). *Sexting: Gender and teens.* Springer.

De Gaston, J.F., Weed, S., Jensen, L.: Understanding gender differences in adolescent sexuality. Adolescence **31**(121), 217–231 (1996)

de Graaf, H., Vanwesenbeeck, I., Woertman, L., Meeus, W.: Parenting and adolescents' sexual development in western societies. Eur. Psychol. **16**(1), 21–31 (2011). https://doi.org/10.1027/1016-9040/a000031

Delevi, R., Weisskirch, R.S.: Personality factors as predictors of sexting. Comput. Hum. Behav. **29**(6), 2589–2594 (2013). https://doi.org/10.1016/j.chb.2013.06.003

Dir, A.L., Coskunpinar, A., Steiner, J.L., Cyders, M.A.: Understanding differences in sexting behaviors across gender, relationship status, and sexual identity, and the role of expectancies in sexting. Cyberpsychol. Behav. Soc. Netw. **16**(8), 568–574 (2013). https://doi.org/10.1089/cyber.2012.0545

Döring, N.: Consensual sexting among adolescents: risk prevention through abstinence education or safer sexting? Cyberpsychol. J. Psychosoc. Res. Cyberspace. **8**(1), 1–15 (2014). https://doi.org/10.5817/CP2014-1-9. Article 9

Drouin, M., Ross, J., Tobin, E.: Sexting: a new, digital vehicle for intimate partner aggression? Comput. Hum. Behav. **50**, 197–204 (2015). https://doi.org/10.1016/j.chb.2015.04.001

Drouin, M., Vogel, K.N., Surbey, A., Stills, J.R.: Let's talk about sexting, baby: computer-mediated sexual behaviors among young adults. Comput. Hum. Behav. **29**(5), A25–A30 (2013). https://doi.org/10.1016/j.chb.2012.12.030

Efrati, Y.: Adolescent compulsive sexual behavior: is it a unique psychological phenomenon? J. Sex Marital Ther. **44**, 687–700 (2018). https://doi.org/10.1080/0092623X.2018.1452088

Englander, E.: Low risk associated with most teenage sexting: a study of 617 18-year-olds. MARC Research Reports (2012). https://vc.bridgew.edu/marc_reports/6

Fagan, J., Pabon, E.: Contributions of delinquency and substance use to school dropout among inner-city youths. Youth Soc. **21**(3), 306–354 (1990). https://doi.org/10.1177/0044118X9002 1003003

Garcia, J.R., Gesselman, A.N., Siliman, S.A., Perry, B.L., Coe, K., Fisher, H.E.: Sexting among singles in the USA: prevalence of sending, receiving, and sharing sexual messages and images. Sex. Heal. **13**(5), 428–435 (2016). https://doi.org/10.1071/SH15240

Gil-Llario, M. D., Morell-Mengual, V., Giménez García, C., Ballester-Arnal, R.: The phenomenon of sexting among Spanish teenagers: Prevalence, attitudes, motivations and explanatory variables (2020). https://www.sciencedirect.com/science/article/pii/S0147176720301760

Gordon-Messer, D., Bauermeister, J.A., Grodzinski, A., Zimmerman, M.: Sexting among young adults. J. Adolesc. Heal. **52**(3), 301–306 (2013). https://doi.org/10.1016/j.jadohealth.2012.05.013

Gottfredson, M.R., Hirschi, T.: A general theory of crime. Stanford University Press, Redwood City (1990)

Heirman, W., Walrave, M.: Assessing concerns and issues about the mediation of technology in cyberbullying. Cyberpsychol. J. Psychosoc. Res. Cyberspace. **2**(2), 1–12 (2008). https://cyberpsychology.eu/article/view/4214/3256

Henderson, L., Morgan, E.: Sexting and sexual relationships among teens and young adults. McNair Scholars Res. J. **7**(1), 1–9 (2011). https://scholarworks.boisestate.edu/mcnair_journal/vol7/iss1/9

Hirschi, T.: Causes of delinquency. University of California Press, Berkeley (1969)

Hudson, H.K., Fetro, J.V.: Sexual activity: predictors of sexting behaviors and intentions to sext among selected undergraduate students. Comput. Hum. Behav. **49**, 615–622 (2015). https://doi.org/10.1016/j.chb.2015.03.048

Jacobson, K.C., Crockett, L.J.: Parental monitoring and adolescent adjustment: An ecological perspective. J. Res. Adolesc. **10**(1), 65–97 (2000). https://psycnet.apa.org/record/2000-133 51-004

Jonsson, L.S., Priebe, G., Bladh, M., Svedin, C.G.: Voluntary sexual exposure online among Swedish youth – social background, internet behavior and psychosocial health. Comput. Hum. Behav. **30**, 181–190 (2014). https://doi.org/10.1016/j.chb.2013.08.005

Kiefer, A.K., Sanchez, D.T.: Scripting sexual passivity: a gender role perspective. Pers. Relat. **14**(2), 269–290 (2007). https://doi.org/10.1111/j.1475-6811.2007.00154.x

Klettke, B., Hallford, D.J., Mellor, D.J.: Sexting prevalence and correlates: a systematic literature review. Clin. Psychol. Rev. **34**(1), 44–53 (2014)

Klettke, B., Mellor, D., Silva-Myles, L., Clancy, E., Sharma, M.: Sexting and mental health: a study of Indian and Australian young adults. Cyberpsychol. J. Psychosoc. Res. Cyberspace. **12**(2), 1–15 (2018). https://doi.org/10.5817/CP2018-2-2

Kosenko, K., Luurs, G., Binder, A.R.: Sexting and sexual behavior, 2011–2015: a critical review and meta-analysis of a growing literature. J. Comput.-Mediat. Commun. **22**(3), 141–160 (2017)

Lavee, Y., Katz, R.: The family in Israel: Between tradition and modernity. Marriage Fam. Rev. **35**(1–2), 193–217 (2003). https://doi.org/10.1300/J002v35n01_11

Lenhart, A.: Teens and sexting: how and why minor teens are sending sexually suggestive nude or nearly nude images via text messaging. Pew Research Center: Internet & Technology (2009). https://www.pewresearch.org/internet/2009/12/15/teens-and-sexting/

Lenhart, A., Ling, R., Campbell, S., Purcell, K.: Teens and mobile phones: text messaging explodes as teens embrace it as the centerpiece of their communication strategies with friends. Pew Research Center: Internet & Technology (2010). https://www.pewresearch.org/internet/2010/04/20/teens-and-mobile-phones/

Lewis, M.A., Butterfield, R.M., Darbes, L.A., Johnston-Brooks, C.: The conceptualization and assessment of health-related social control. J. Soc. Pers. Relat. **21**(5), 669–687 (2004). https://doi.org/10.1177/0265407504045893

Livingstone, S. M., Haddon, L., Görzig, A.: Children, Risk and Safety on the Internet: Research and Policy Challenges in Comparative Perspective. Policy Press (2012)

Madigan, S., Ly, A., Rash, C.L., Van Ouytsel, J., Temple, J.R.: Prevalence of multiple forms of sexting behavior among youth: a systematic review and meta-analysis. JAMA Pediatr. **172**(4), 327–335 (2018). https://doi.org/10.1001/jamapediatrics.2017.5314

McKinney, C., Donnelly, R., Renk, K.: Perceived parenting, positive and negative perceptions of parents, and late adolescent emotional adjustment. Child Adolesc. Mental Heal. **13**(2), 66–73 (2008)

Mitchell, K.J., Finkelhor, D., Jones, L.M., Wolak, J.: Prevalence and characteristics of youth sexting: a national study. Pediatrics **129**(1), 13–20 (2012). https://doi.org/10.1542/peds.2011-1730

Moreno-Ruiz, D., Martínez-Ferrer, B., García-Bacete, F.: Parenting styles, cyberaggression, and cybervictimization among adolescents. Comput. Hum. Behav. **93**, 252–259 (2019)

Pugliese, J.A., Okun, M.A.: Social control and strenuous exercise among late adolescent college students: parents versus peers as influence agents. J. Adolesc. **37**(5), 543–554 (2014). https://doi.org/10.1016/j.adolescence.2014.04.008

Reed, L.A., Boyer, M.P., Meskunas, H., Tolman, R.M., Ward, L.M.: How do adolescents experience sexting in dating relationships? Motivations to sext and responses to sexting requests from dating partners. Child Youth Serv. Rev. **109**, 104696 (2020)

Reyns, B.W., Henson, B., Fisher, B.S.: Digital deviance: low self-control and opportunity as explanations of sexting among college students. Sociol. Spectr. **34**(3), 273–292 (2014). https://doi.org/10.1080/02732173.2014.895642

Rice, E., et al.: Sexually explicit cell phone messaging associated with sexual risk among adolescents. Pediatrics **130**(4), 667–673 (2012). https://doi.org/10.1542/peds.2012-0021

Rossman, B.B.R., Rea, J.G.: The relation of parenting styles and inconsistencies to adaptive functioning for children in conflictual and violent families. Journal of Family Violence **20**(5), 261–277 (2005). https://doi.org/10.1007/s10896-005-6603-8

Shin, W., Li, B.: Parental mediation of children's digital technology use in Singapore. J. Child. Media **11**(1), 1–19 (2017)

Smetana, J.G.: Current research on parenting styles, dimensions, and beliefs. Curr. Opin. Psychol. **15**, 19–25 (2017)

Spencer, J., Olson, J., Schrager, S., Tanaka, D., Belzer, M.: 40. Sexting and adolescents: a descriptive study of sexting and youth in an urban population. J. Adolesc. Heal. **56**(2), S22 (2015). https://doi.org/10.1016/j.jadohealth.2014.10.044

Steinberg, L.: Adolescence. McGraw-Hill, New York (2008)

Suler, J.: The online disinhibition effect. Cyberpsychol. Behav. **7**(3), 321–326 (2004). https://doi.org/10.1089/1094931041291295

Temple, J.R., Le Donna, V., van den Berg, P., Ling, Y., Paul, J.A., Temple, B.W.: Brief report: teen sexting and psychosocial health. J. Adolesc. **37**(1), 33–36 (2014). https://doi.org/10.1016/j.adolescence.2013.10.008

Unnever, J.D., Cullen, F.T., Pratt, T.C.: Parental management, ADHD, and delinquent involvement: reassessing Gottfredson and Hirschi's general theory. Justice Q. **20**(3), 471–500 (2003). https://doi.org/10.1080/07418820300095591

Van Ouytsel, J., Torres, E., Jeong Choi, H., Ponnet, K., Walrave, M., Temple, J.R.: The associations between substance use, sexual behaviors, bullying, deviant behaviors, health, and cyber dating abuse perpetration. J. Sch. Nurs. **33**(2), 116–122 (2017). https://doi.org/10.1177/1059840516683229

Van Ouytsel, J., Van Gool, E., Walrave, M., Ponnet, K., Peeters, E.: Sexting: Adolescents' perceptions of the applications used for, motives for, and consequences of sexting. J. Youth Stud. **20**(4), 446–470 (2017)

Van Ouytsel, J., Walrave, M., Lu, Y., Temple, J.R., Ponnet, K.: The Associations between substance use, sexual behavior, deviant behaviors and adolescents' engagement in sexting: does relationship context matter? J. Youth Adolesc. **47**(11), 2353–2370 (2018). https://doi.org/10.1007/s10964-018-0903-9

Vanwesenbeeck, I., Ponnet, K., Walrave, M., Van Ouytsel, J.: Parents' role in adolescents' sexting behaviour. In: Walrave, M.J., Van Ouytsel, K.P., Temple, J. (eds.) Sexting, pp. 63–80. Palgrave Macmillan, London (2018)

West, J.H., Lister, C.E., Hall, P.C., Crookston, B.T., Snow, P.R., Zvietcovich, M.E., West, R.P.: Sexting among Peruvian adolescents. BMC Public Health **14**(1), 1–7 (2014). https://doi.org/10.1186/1471-2458-14-811

Wilchek-Aviad, Y.: Model for predicting learning perseverance among boarding school students in Israel. Int. J. Disabil. Hum. Develop. **4**(2), 121–130 (2005). https://doi.org/10.1515/IJDHD.2005.4.2.121

Up for Debate: Effects of Formal Structure on Argumentation Quality in a Crowdsourcing Platform

Stephen L. Dorton$^{(\boxtimes)}$ ⓘ, Samantha B. Harper, Glory A. Creed,
and H. George Banta ⓘ

Sonalysts, Inc., Waterford, CT 06385, USA
`hail@sonalysts.com`

Abstract. We examined the use of formal structure (more specifically, the Toulmin model and the use of abstraction laddering) in argument assertion templates in a crowdsourcing platform, to determine its effects on argument quality, as rated by other peer contributors. Contrary to our hypotheses, the attempt to add rigor to asserted arguments resulted in a significant decrease in quality across several measures, including the pathos, kairos, and overall level of agreement with the assertion. We found that the way participants voted (a binary outcome of supporting or dissenting) aligned more strongly with whether they agreed with the assertion (regardless of quality) rather than with the quality of the assertion. We provide multiple potential explanations for why the use of the Toulmin model was not a reliable predictor of argument quality in a crowdsourcing application.

Keywords: Crowdsourcing · Argumentation · Toulmin model · Collective intelligence · Rhetorical analysis

1 Introduction

The overarching objective of this research was to assess whether or not adding formal structure to an argumentation assertion template would increase the quality of the resultant argument in a web-based crowdsourcing environment for identifying and resolving organizational inefficiencies. First, we discuss the various core concepts pertaining to this study before describing the methods and results.

1.1 Crowdsourcing and Collective Intelligence

The use of crowdsourcing has become more widespread since Howe [1] coined the term as a play on "outsourcing." Crowdsourcing is a combination of a bottom-up creative process with top-down organizational goals, where the interplay of the crowd (hereinafter referred to as contributors) and the overall organization is critical to achieving outcomes that are mutually beneficial to both parties (i.e., the crowd of contributors and the organization itself) [2]. Crowdsourcing has also been defined more simply as

© Springer Nature Switzerland AG 2021
G. Meiselwitz (Ed.): HCII 2021, LNCS 12774, pp. 36–53, 2021.
https://doi.org/10.1007/978-3-030-77626-8_3

the act of taking a job done by a single person or team, and outsourcing it to a larger, often undefined group, usually via the internet [3]. Crowdsourcing has been successfully applied to a variety of applications, including simple contests to name products, as well as more complex tasks such as creative writing or taxonomy development [4, 5]. Generally speaking, all of these applications involve iterative content creation followed by voting or consensus-forming: An alternating divergent and convergent activity. More recently, research shows that argumentation can significantly increase the quality or accuracy of crowdsourced products, which is a primary focus of this study [6].

Crowdsourcing is often conflated with other related ideas such as collective intelligence, the higher-level concept that large groups of people can accomplish more together than they can individually [3]. Another positive aspect of collective intelligence is that it leverages intellectual diversity, where the coordination of contributors with diverse knowledge, skills, and abilities can be used to solve exceptionally challenging problems that a more homogeneous team may not have overcome [7]. These concepts of increased quantity and diversity of contributors have been leveraged to great effect for decades in the field of computer-supported cooperative work, of which crowdsourcing is a specific application thereof [8]. Given the various successful uses of crowdsourcing and the positive impact of argumentation on crowdsourcing quality, we seek to understand how best to structure argumentation in order to consistently generate assertions that are perceived by others as high quality in a crowdsourcing system.

1.2 The Toulmin Model

The Toulmin model is an argumentation model that is widely cited as a means to analyze the soundness or quality of an argument [9, 10]. The Toulmin model suggests that a comprehensive or quality argument must have three components [11, 12]: A claim, evidence to support the claim, and a warrant to tie the evidence to the claim. Toulmin's inclusion of a connective (i.e., warrant) between the claim and evidence distinguishes his model from a simpler premise and conclusion approach to argumentation [10]. In practice, the Toulmin model is often used as a dependent measure of argument quality, where arguments are coded based on the presence or absence of the different components; however, some studies have adapted the model and have coded arguments based on the presence of additional argumentation components, including backing, qualifiers, and reservations [13]. As far as we are aware, Kim and Benbasat [14] have run the only study that used the Toulmin model as an Independent Variable (IV), where they manipulated the number of Toulmin model elements present in an eCommerce trust assuring argument. Outside of this effort, we found no other study in the literature that used the Toulmin model as an IV or mechanic for data entry in a computer-mediated communication system; rather, it is more frequently used as a dependent measure of argument quality. We have used the less typical approach of using the Toulmin model as an IV, and have investigated the use of the Toulmin model as a template for writing arguments that other contributors find to be of high quality and agreeableness.

The strength of the Toulmin model is that it forms structurally-sound arguments (resonating with the logical tradition). Using the structural integrity of an argument (offered by the Toulmin model) as a quality measure is advantageous in that it avoids the haphazard means of rating believable arguments as strong, or treating valence as quality

[15]. A chief weakness of the Toulmin model is its relative esotericism, where a high barrier of entry exists for those who have not previously engaged in formal argumentation [16]. Further, the Toulmin model may become unwieldy or even struggle to hold up to complex scenarios where argumentation is not as cut-and-dry, and assertions cannot be simply scored as valid or invalid, or where the interpretation of rules or values is required [17].

1.3 Abstraction Laddering

Abstraction laddering is a metacognitive design thinking process/tool used to refine a problem statement or initial solution by asking the asserter a series of questions in order to create refined problem statements at a greater or lesser level of detail. By taking an example initial statement such as "Access to scholarly literature is too difficult," one would move up the abstraction ladder by asking "Why is that a problem?" and down the ladder by asking "How?" Abstraction laddering has been used as a qualitative research method in conjunction with the Means-End Chain (MEC) model, where asking how and why result in new perspectives that are more abstract or concrete, respectively [18]. MEC is based on the premise that if such a chain is established via laddering interviews with participants, one may identify core values underpinning their beliefs [19]. Aside from creating a greater understanding of an individual's beliefs, research has shown that the reflective or metacognitive aspect of abstraction laddering can lead to more effective communications for a variety of underlying reasons [20].

Although abstraction laddering is rooted in more formal qualitative research methods, it is currently a tool that design thinking practitioners use to rapidly expound upon an initial problem or solution statement to better frame subsequent ideation activities. Abstraction laddering is used in a design context (more analogous to this use case) by helping an asserter to better frame their assertion through the process of creating a variety of different problem statements at different levels of abstraction so that the asserter can then pick the best possible assertion to share with the crowd [21]. In this particular study, we used a version of abstraction laddering that required participants to reframe their problem statement a minimum of three times after answering the question, "why is that a problem?" This method forced participants to undergo a degree of metacognition before choosing the most meaningful and actionable problem statement to submit for review, hoping to harness the advantages described by Senge et al. [20].

1.4 Assessing the Quality of Argumentation

There are multiple methods and measures to assess the quality of argumentation. These various methods generally fall under one of three different traditions: Logical, rhetorical, or dialectical [22]. The logical tradition is primarily concerned with the soundness and acceptability of premises and conclusions (arguments are valid or invalid, and valid arguments are of higher quality), and is concerned less with how the audience perceives the argument [23]. More rigid argumentation models that rely on deductive logic such as syllogisms and the Toulmin model are part of the logical tradition, which are well-fitted for rational persuasion. Conversely, the rhetorical tradition places quality on arguments that persuade or otherwise affect the audience through a variety of appeals [23, 24]. The

Scriven model is one such rhetorical model, which includes seven components by which one may assess argument quality [25]. Rhetorical analysis is more appropriate argumentation conducted in a domain where arguments or assertions are not simply valid or invalid, but instead may have varying levels of quality or appeal. Finally, the dialectical tradition places quality on arguments based on the degree to which they have satisfactorily answered questions and objections that have been raised against them [23]. The Walton model is one example of a dialectical method for evaluating arguments, which relies more on an analytical framework than the structure of the argument, as in the Toulmin model [26]. Dialectical methods are most appropriate for ongoing argumentation where two or more people engage in multiple rounds of making assertions and raising objections/asking questions.

Engendering quality argumentation is an important endeavor, as argumentation is present in several domains. More classically, quality logical argumentation is a cornerstone of law, where lawyers argue cases to convince a jury or judge. These arguments are relatively structured and formal, aiming to be both logically cogent and dialectically satisfactory [23]. Rhetorical argumentation is also crucial in marketing, where the quality of argumentation has been shown to affect consumer trust, attitude, and whether or not a customer purchases something [14]. Dialectical argumentation (along with other styles) is used in education for both conversational and evaluative settings, where teachers can evaluate students' reasoning and understanding as evidenced by their dialogue or essays of written work [9, 27]. Argumentation is also a component of news media, as many articles and reports reflect personal biases, and attempt to persuade others to adopt a certain viewpoint [28]. The specific quality measures chosen for assessing crowdsourced argumentation in this study are discussed later in greater detail.

1.5 Use Case and Research Goals

This study was conducted in the context of developing Visual Argumentation for Resolving Inefficiencies (VARI), a web-based crowdsourcing platform to enable the identification and characterization of organizational inefficiencies, then ideation and consensus-building of different solutions. An overarching goal of the program is to elicit and exploit knowledge that is typically spread across organizational silos (e.g., business units, technical fields, or geographic locations) to provide organizational decision makers with prioritized inefficiencies and the best solutions for resolving them. Another goal is to yield the highest quality crowdsourced products with the least amount of collective time from contributors (the system should not be an inefficiency itself). In concept, VARI blends asynchronous argumentation and iterative voting with a visualization-based collective intelligence approach [6, 29]. This study focused on the first step of the overall VARI process, which is to assert and clearly articulate the problem, a necessary step to resolving organizational issues [30].

To encourage efficiency, VARI provides contributors with an argumentation template that they fill out by entering concise snippets of text (140 characters or less) into a web form (Fig. 1) to describe their asserted inefficiency, which is then compiled into a formatted "problem card" for others to review and vote on. This use of structured argumentation was inspired by Structured Analytic Techniques (SATs) commonly used in intelligence analysis, where analysts of various backgrounds and expertise can use

SATs to compile information into concise and structured formats in order to glean insights that are then shared with decision makers [31].

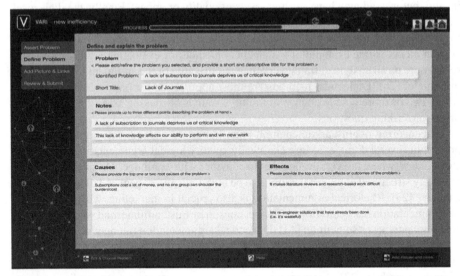

Fig. 1. An example of the argument assertion interface shown with an example inefficiency. For those in the abstraction laddering condition, the statement they chose was automatically populated in the "Identified Problem" field.

Thus, the research questions we aimed to answer in this study (and their associated hypotheses) include:

i.   Will use of the Toulmin model generate higher quality arguments? H_1: Arguments generated in the Toulmin model condition will be of higher quality.
ii. Will use of abstraction laddering generate higher quality arguments? H_2: Arguments generated in the abstraction laddering condition will be of higher quality.
iii. What are the underlying relationships among different measures of argument quality, agreeability, and overall support? H_3: All measures will be positively correlated to overall support.

2   Methods

2.1   Experimental Design

The study was a $2 \times 2 \times 3$, fully factorial, mixed-subjects design which included three IVs, two of which were examined during the argument assertion phase (Toulmin Structure and Abstraction Laddering) and one which was examined during the argument review phase (Level of Information). The Toulmin Structure IV had two conditions, the presence of Toulmin structured text fields to describe their asserted inefficiency (i.e., claim, evidence, and warrant), and no structure (i.e., participants used three text fields simply defined as "notes" to describe their problem). The Abstraction Laddering IV had two conditions, the presence of an abstraction laddering technique as a tool for the participant to identify their problem statement, and the absence of the abstraction laddering technique, where the participant moved straight onto the problem card to identify their problem statement.

The Level of Information IV during the argument review phase had three conditions, which specified the amount of content from a problem card that would be shown. These conditions were All Information (included problem title and description, causes and effects, and external content like pictures, tags, and links), No Causes and Effects (the asserted causes and effects were removed for review), and No External Content (pictures, hyperlinks to websites with supporting evidence, and metadata tags were removed for review). This IV aimed to investigate the tradeoff in the collective time to write arguments and the time to review the arguments to provide quality ratings. This assesses the overarching goal of having the highest quality with the least collective time for the crowd to write and read content before voting). We focus on the effects of formality (i.e., abstraction laddering and the use of the Toulmin model) on argumentation quality in this manuscript. Acknowledging that, the information level IV predominantly served to add variability to the different quality ratings, and the associated analysis for this IV is not discussed in detail in this manuscript.

2.2 Procedure

The study involved three interactions with participants, which took place over roughly 30 days from start to finish. In the first interaction, we obtained informed consent, informed participants of the purpose of the study, told participants to start thinking of an inefficiency at their organization, and scheduled a time to come back and enter data. Approximately five to 10 days later (depending on schedule), participants used the VARI argumentation interface to assert their inefficiency on a desktop computer in a private lab setting (to protect anonymity and confidentiality). After all 40 participants had completed this step, they were recalled to review and provide ratings for other assertions in a round-robin manner where each participant reviewed nine other asserted arguments. That is, participant 10 reviewed arguments from participants 1–9, participant 11 reviewed arguments from participants 2–10, and so on. The procedure resulted in the generation of a total sample of 360 peer reviews of argument quality.

Of the nine arguments each participant rated, the first three were left unaltered, the second three had the "causes" and "effects" fields removed, and the final three arguments had the external information (i.e., pictures, hyperlinks to sites with supporting information, and metadata tags) removed. We systematically masked information to provide insights as to which information in the VARI template was most important to argument quality. As previously discussed, this also offered the benefit of adding diversity to the quality ratings and avoiding a potential ceiling effect.

2.3 Participants

We recruited 40 participants from a mid-size technology company (between 300 and 500 employees) to participate in this study. The majority of the sample was male ($n = 35, 87.5\%$), with few females participating ($n = 5, 12.5\%$). The mean age of participants was 42.6 years ($SD = 12.3$), filling a range from 23 to 60 years of age. Participants had spent a mean of 11.2 years ($SD = 9.7$) at the company, and a mean of 20.8 years ($SD = 12.8$) of overall professional experience following their education. It should be noted that all participant demographics except for sex were bi-modally distributed, showing two somewhat distinct "generations" of contributors.

2.4 Dependent Measures

There is a somewhat unique challenge to measuring quality in the context of VARI as there is no single "right answer." Crowdsourcing studies typically use a "gold standard" question to gauge performance of an algorithm [6], or they might use expert judgements to compare human-created products and crowd-created products [4, 5]. These methods are incompatible with this application since there is not one correct way to assert an inefficiency or solution. Further, being logically cogent alone is not a guarantee of quality or effectiveness of an argument [23]. Therefore, the most viable means of assessing argument quality was to conduct peer reviews based on specific criteria, which also has the greatest external validity since the crowd will ultimately review and curate their own content in the implemented system.

Quality ratings were based largely upon Aristotle's rhetorical appeals for persuasion. Although some object to the term "appeals" as an indication of pleading [32], the logos (the quality and relevancy of evidence), ethos (the credibility of the asserter), pathos (the emotional appeal or relevance to the audience), and kairos (the timeliness or urgency) of an argument are well recognized as building blocks for successful communications, including online and computer-mediated communications [24, 33–35].

We chose rhetorical analysis since it was already acknowledged that logic alone is not a measure of quality in this context (making strictly logical measures inappropriate), and there was only an assertion and review phase rather than an ongoing conversation (making dialectical measures inappropriate). We expanded on these rhetorical appeals with additional low-level measures and high-level measures to enable a holistic analysis. Table 1 provides an overview of the dependent measures of argument quality used in this study. The first five measures were collected together, followed by individual questions for the overall quality, agreement, and support. This was done to prevent reviewers from "gaming the system" and making aggregate judgments. Each measure (with exception of overall support), was rated by contributors on a scale of $1 - 10$, where 1 indicated the lowest value, and 10 indicated the highest value. The overall support vote was a binary yes/no vote that represented how an argument would be received by the crowd in VARI, which uses a simple agree/disagree binary voting system for arguments.

Table 1. Measures of argument quality

Measure	Rhetorical appeal	Description
Clarity	NA	The degree to which information is presented in a logical structure and in readily understandable terms
Quality & Relevance of evidence	Logos	How meaningful the evidence is towards supporting the asserted argument
Asserter credibility	Ethos	The perceived intelligence, character, and goodwill of the person asserting the argument
Personal relevance	Pathos	The degree to which the asserted inefficiency personally affects the rater*
Urgency	Kairos	The perceived urgency of the asserted inefficiency (i.e., how quickly does the inefficiency need to be mitigated, as reflected in the argument)**
Overall quality	NA	The overall quality of the argument, regardless of whether or not you agree with it
Overall agreement	NA	The overall level of agreement or concurrence with the argument, regardless of the quality
Overall support	NA	Whether or not the argument presents a legitimate inefficiency that needs to be resolved by the organization

* The more personally relevant the argument is to somebody, the more persuasive it should be [36, 37].
** Kotter [38] asserts that a sense of urgency is the first step in organizational change (mitigating/removing inefficiencies), therefore, urgency should correlate to quality.

3   Results

3.1   Toulmin Model and Argument Quality

The primary aim of this study was to assess the impact of the Toulmin model on argument quality. The total sample ($N = 360$) was split evenly across each condition (Toulmin model and no structure), resulting in a sample of 180 ratings for each. As shown in Table 2, the use of the Toulmin model for framing assertions had no effect on any measure of argument quality. There were no significant differences between mean ratings for the 'no structure' condition and the 'Toulmin model' condition for any of the argument quality criteria; therefore, we accept the null hypothesis and reject H_1 (that Toulmin arguments will be of higher quality). This result was surprising as the Toulmin model is commonly cited as the measure of argument quality throughout a wide variety of applications and domains. This lack of significant difference led to the examination of several follow-on questions discussed in the following sections.

Table 2. Effects of Toulmin model on argumentation quality.

Quality measure	Mean rating (SD)		ANOVA (one-tailed)		
	No structure	Toulmin	$F(1,358)$	p	η^2
Clarity	6.79 (2.07)	6.68 (2.22)	.24	.62	.00
Quality of evidence	5.93 (2.41)	5.93 (2.51)	.00	.99	.00
Asserter credibility	6.90 (2.05)	6.98 (2.11)	.13	.72	.00
Personal relevance	6.35 (2.70)	6.44 (2.76)	.11	.74	.00
Urgency	6.05 (2.33)	5.84 (2.24)	.73	.39	.00
Overall quality	6.35 (2.29)	6.29 (2.29)	.06	.80	.00
Overall agreement	7.33 (2.38)	7.27 (2.43)	.06	.81	.00

Compliance with the Toulmin Model. Given the lack of significant difference across conditions, we then asked the question "did those in the Toulmin model experimental condition actually create arguments that were compliant with the Toulmin model?" Although the use of the Toulmin model was an explicit condition, we cannot safely assume that all arguments from that condition were actually compliant with the Toulmin model. We also cannot assume that those in the 'no structure' condition did not make Toulmin model arguments. A team of three coders reviewed all 40 asserted arguments and coded for the presence (1) or absence (0) of the three core elements of the Toulmin model [11]: Claim, evidence, and warrant. The initial coding, using Cohen's Kappa to measure inter-rater reliability, proved unreliable ($K_{TOULMIN} = .22$, $K_{CLAIM} = .30$, $K_{EVIDENCE} = .15$, $K_{WARRANT} = .21$). Therefore, all three coders met and adjudicated each argument to determine if it was a proper Toulmin argument. As shown in Table 3, only 7 of the 20 participants (35%) in the Toulmin model condition actually created a complete Toulmin argument. Only 10 of the 40 (25%) total participants (from either condition) asserted arguments that were compliant with the Toulmin model.

Table 3. Presence of Toulmin assertions across structure conditions

Outcome count (% of Total)			
Condition	Toulmin argument	Non-Toulmin argument	Total
No structure	3 (7.5%)	17 (42.5%)	20 (50.0%)
Toulmin structure	7 (17.5%)	13 (32.5%)	20 (50.0%)
Total	10 (25.0%)	30 (75.0%)	40 (100.0%)

The Quality of Actual Toulmin Arguments. We performed a one-way ANOVA on the manually-coded arguments to again evaluate the effect of the Toulmin model on argument quality (regardless of which experimental condition they were from). Surprisingly, the arguments which were coded as Toulmin compliant resulted in significantly lower ratings of quality for measures of clarity, $F(1,358) = 5.56, p < .05, \eta^2 = .02$; personal relevance (pathos), $F(1,358) = 6.94, p < .01, \eta^2 = .02$; urgency (kairos), $F(1, 358) = 7.00, p < .01, \eta^2 = .02$; and overall agreement, $F(1, 358) = 12.76, p < .01, \eta^2 = .03$ (Table 4 shows a summary of the results). Thus, we were still required to reject H_1, as the use of the Toulmin model created lower quality arguments, as rated by other contributors. Not only did the Toulmin model create arguments with decreased clarity, but it also decreased the personal relevance, sense of urgency, and drastically decreased the overall level of agreeability.

Table 4. Effects of actual Toulmin structure on argumentation quality

Quality measure	Mean rating (*SD*)		ANOVA (one-tailed)		
	No structure	Toulmin	$F(1,358)$	p	η^2
Clarity	6.90 (2.07)	6.30 (2.28)	**5.56**	**.02**	**.02**
Quality of evidence	6.02 (2.41)	5.69 (2.58)	1.34	.25	.00
Asserter credibility	7.03 (2.05)	6.69 (2.13)	2.02	.16	.01
Personal relevance	6.63 (2.70)	5.79 (2.73)	**6.94**	**.01**	**.02**
Urgency	6.14 (2.16)	5.43 (2.53)	**7.00**	**.01**	**.02**
Overall quality	6.45 (2.23)	5.97 (2.42)	3.21	.07	.01
Overall agreement	7.57 (2.21)	6.58 (2.72)	**12.76**	**.00**	**.03**

Note. Significant results are shown in bold

Abstraction Laddering and Argument Quality. Another method to add formality and/or rigor into crowdsourced argumentation was to use abstraction laddering as a metacognitive aid to refine assertions. The total sample ($N = 360$) was split evenly across each conditions (abstraction laddering and no laddering) such that each condition had a sample of 180 cases. As shown in Table 5, a one-way ANOVA showed that there were multiple significant differences in argument quality based on the use of abstraction laddering. Counter to H_2 (the use of this critical thinking method would increase argumentation quality), all significant results showed lower quality associated with using abstraction laddering.

The personal relevance (pathos) of arguments built without abstraction laddering ($M = 6.81, SD = 2.61$) was significantly higher than those made with abstraction laddering ($M = 5.98, SD = 2.79$), $F(1,178) = 8.47, p < .01, \eta^2 = .02$. Similarly, the urgency (kairos) of arguments built without abstraction laddering ($M = 6.35, SD = 2.15$) was significantly higher than those built with abstraction laddering ($M = 5.54, SD = 2.35$), $F(1,178) = 11.53, p < .01, \eta^2 = .03$. Finally, the overall level of agreement was significantly higher for arguments made without abstraction laddering ($M = 7.73, SD$

Table 5. Effects of abstraction laddering on argumentation quality

Quality measure	Mean rating (SD)		ANOVA (one-tailed)		
	No laddering	Laddering	$F(1,358)$	p	η^2
Clarity	6.84 (2.00)	6.63 (2.28)	.87	.35	.00
Quality of evidence	5.96 (2.35)	5.90 (2.57)	.06	.81	.00
Asserter credibility	6.87 (2.09)	7.01 (2.07)	.37	.54	.00
Personal relevance	6.81 (2.61)	5.98 (2.79)	**8.47**	**.00**	**.02**
Urgency	6.35 (2.15)	5.54 (2.35)	**11.53**	**.00**	**.03**
Overall quality	6.42 (2.20)	6.22 (2.37)	.73	.40	.00
Overall agreement	7.73 (2.16)	6.87 (2.55)	**11.96**	**.00**	**.03**

Note. Significant results are shown in bold

$= 2.16$) than those made with abstraction laddering ($M = 6.87, SD = 2.55$), $F(1,178) = 11.96, p < .01, \eta^2 = .03$. Thus, we were required to reject H_2, as abstraction laddering negatively affected argument quality.

Factors Affecting Support of Crowdsourced Argumentation. We looked at the correlations in the dependent measures to better understand any underlying relationships between specific measures of argument quality, overall quality (the perceived quality of the argument, regardless of whether one agrees with it), overall agreeability (how much one agrees with the argument, regardless of its quality), and overall support (whether or not they ultimately voted to support a given argument). Spearman's Rho was used to assess correlations for the entire sample of reviews ($N = 360$). Table 6 and Fig. 2 provide an overview of these results, where all specific measures of argument quality were significantly correlated ($p < .01$, one-tailed) to all high-level or overall measures, as well as the level of support (a point-biserial correlation).

Table 6. Correlations of quality measures and overall ratings

Quality factor	Overall quality	Overall agreeability	Overall support
Clarity	.83	.56	.36
quality of evidence	.79	.51	.34
Asserter credibility	.76	.52	.33
Personal relevance	.33	.61	.36
Urgency	.40	.62	.49

Note. All results are using a one-tailed Spearman's Rho (R_S), and are significant to the $p < .01$ level

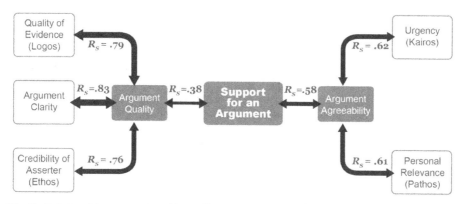

Fig. 2. Relationships among specific quality measures, overall measures, and overall support. Line thickness corresponds to the relative strength of each correlation

One should note that while all quality factors are significantly correlated to all three of the overall ratings (quality, agreeability, and support), different factors have greater correlations to different overall ratings. Arguments with high ratings of clarity and logical organization of the argument ($R_S = .83, p < .01$), quality of evidence ($R_S = .79, p < .01$), and perceived credibility of the asserter ($R_S = .76, p < .01$) were more highly positively correlated with the measure of overall quality. Conversely, the most highly correlated factors to overall agreeability were the sense of urgency ($R_S = .62, p < .01$) and the personal relevance of the argument ($R_S = .61, p < .01$). Additionally, the level of overall support for an argument was most highly correlated to the sense of urgency conveyed by the argument ($R_S = .49, p < .01$).

These correlations nominally explain why critical thinking (via abstraction laddering) and structured argumentation (via the Toulmin model) have negative effects on argument quality as rated by peer contributors. In other wsupportords, if a contributor wishes to assert an inefficiency that is perceived as being high quality, they should focus on logical organization of their argument, presenting quality evidence, and conveying a sense of credibility. However, if contributors want people to agree with them (and to ultimately their assertions with votes), they must convince other contributors that the inefficiency is personally relevant to them, and craft their argument to convey a sense of urgency. In the context of crowdsourcing organizational inefficiencies, this notion supports the work of Kotter [38], who claims that the first step to creating organizational change is to create a sense of urgency (i.e., nothing will be accomplished if people do not believe there is an urgent need to do something).

We also examined the correlations between overall quality, overall agreeability, and overall support to determine if they were entangled. That is, do the identified differences in what makes a quality argument from an agreeable argument matter, or are they equally important in driving contributor support for an argument? Overall argument quality was positively correlated to overall agreeability ($R_S = .58, p < .01$), although not to a high enough degree to use them interchangeably when estimating whether contributors will vote for an argument. This is further supported by the disparity in voting support for agreeable arguments ($R_S = .57, p < .01$) over quality arguments ($R_S = .38, p < .01$).

In other words, contributors are more likely to vote for arguments that they agree with (which are based on personal relevance and sense of urgency) than arguments that they perceive as high quality (which are based on clarity, quality evidence, and presenting oneself as credible). These relationships, and the more prominent correlations identified in Table 6, are illustrated in Fig. 2. Although there are relative differences in correlation strength, we can reject the null hypothesis, and accept H_3, since both overall quality and overall agreeability are positively correlated to overall support.

4 Discussion

Despite entering assumptions about critical thinking and structured argumentation (namely, that they would increase the quality of asserted arguments), the use of both abstraction laddering and the Toulmin model did not result in higher quality argumentation (as rated by a group of peers). Instead, they resulted in significantly lower quality across a variety of measures. Further, we found that argument quality was not the strongest predictor of whether an argument would garner support from the crowd. Instead, the degree to which they agree with the argument (regardless of quality) was the strongest predictor of crowd support. This section discusses possible explanations for these findings, as well as limitations of the study, and practical implications for developing argumentation-based computer-mediated communication systems.

4.1 Prevailing Explanations for Findings

The counterintuitive results of critical thinking and formal argumentation causing lower quality assertions merits discussion. Because of the considerable user feedback regarding usability issues with the abstraction laddering interface, and the fact that it can be considered another form of structure or formalism, we focus the majority of the following discussion more specifically on explanations regarding the use of the Toulmin model. The following are the prevailing explanations for the results obtained, ordered roughly from the most grounded to the most philosophical in nature.

The Toulmin Model is Not Appropriate for Crowdsourcing. One possible explanation is that the Toulmin model is simply not an appropriate quality measure for crowdsourcing applications. In the context of VARI, each contributor is asserting an argument to convince other contributors to support their assertion. As such, a source of discordance may be that we measured the effects of a *logical* manipulation such as the Toulmin model with *rhetorical* measures [23]. The largely rhetorical (i.e., appeals-based) nature of crowdsourced argumentation without a strict right/wrong outcome may explain why logical-based templates were ineffective. Further, the Toulmin model may be too esoteric or complex for a crowdsourcing environment where contributors will receive relatively little training. Bizup [16] acknowledges that many components of the Toulmin model are theoretical and difficult to comprehend, let alone act upon. We attempted to overcome this challenge by including training in the form of text-based definitions, with concrete examples of each component of the model; however, this explanation is plausible as even the research team, with multiple textbooks at their fingertips and no time pressure, still failed to reliably agree on whether each argument complied with the Toulmin model. Therefore, it is likely that there is some degree of mismatch between the quality measure and the application.

The Toulmin Model is Not an Appropriate Measure of Argument Quality. A similar explanation is that compliance with the Toulmin model, however prevalent the practice may be, is not an appropriate means to measure argument quality. Ironically, there may be no warrant to support the argument that compliance with the Toulmin model is a fair measure of argument quality. Many articles that use the Toulmin model as a dependent measure of quality define the Toulmin model and then cite the seminal work, stating that it was created to make quality arguments, and therefore, arguments that use it are quality [12, 14, 15]. This tautology appeals to the credibility of Stephen Toulmin (whom we do not argue against), but does not provide a connective or warrant as to *why* the use of the model makes an argument high quality. It may be that the Toulmin model argument is commonly used as a quality measure because it has face validity, and is simple to encode (at least in theory).

This is supported in various ways throughout the literature. Some have pointed out that structural integrity (what the Toulmin model really measures) is accepted as analogous to quality so that manipulations can be performed with the argument [15]. Nussbaum [27] stated that there are multiple misconceptions surrounding the Toulmin model. First, Toulmin himself stated that some elements may be implied, and in fact, are often left out unless explicitly required. Therefore, coding argument quality based on the explicit presence or absence of components may be misleading. Similarly, Nussbaum [27] discusses how the Toulmin model is normative, and not an accurate representation of how people actually communicate with each other. The Toulmin model is a basic framework for an argument and not a measure of quality, as two arguments could each have all required components, but be viewed differently based on rhetorical and dialectical qualities [27, 39]. This serves as at least a notional explanation of why increased structural integrity (from the Toulmin model and the abstraction laddering) was associated with lower quality arguments.

People Cannot Disentangle Argument Quality from Agreeability in Contemporary Online Communications. Another prevailing explanation is that relatively untrained contributors in a crowdsourcing environment cannot disentangle quality from agreeability. Worded differently, people in the age of ubiquitous social media and connectivity have short attention spans, and vote with quick and visceral reactions rather than deliberate and logical thought. It is therefore possible that a logical structure from the 1950s (when printed media was more commonplace) has not adapted to the fluidity of human language and communication (where the internet is a more prominent communication channel).

Aside from the results of this study, there are empirical, theoretical, and philosophical contributions to support this explanation. Coincidentally, Bizup [16] comments on the fluidity of Toulmin's terms and the relationships among them, where students and teachers blended or adopted the model components and their meanings to fit their ends, rather than taking the time to study and apply them as intended by Toulmin. Kahneman [40] demonstrated that humans are not rational decision makers, and further, that humans would prefer to use a fast, automatic, and error-prone thinking process (referred to as System 1) over a slow, conscious, effortful, and reliable thinking process (referred to as System 2). Carenini [41] supported this notion by showing that the use of Toulmin statements in the context of advertising were received poorly by the audience, and that they preferred concise and tailored (i.e., personally relevant) statements instead.

Far earlier than Kahneman, sociologists noted that Western culture in the 1900s shifted from an ideational or idealistic culture, where people are more prone to use System 2 thinking, towards that of a sensate culture, where sensory inputs drive the majority of reasoning and decision making, greatly predisposing people towards System 1 thinking [42]. In the last few decades, this drive towards sensory-based decision making has been observed and exploited to commercial and political ends. Approaches such as fear appeals are commonplace in contemporary online communications, especially from more ideologically-oriented groups [43]. The significant positive correlation between overall agreeability and overall quality ($R_S = .58, p < .01$) combined with these findings suggest that it is possible that contributors may be conflating the quality of an argument with how much they agree with the argument, regardless of the clarity, evidence, or credibility of the asserter.

4.2 Limitations

Every attempt was made to conduct a study that balanced internal and external validity; however, this study was not without its limitations. The following are the primary limitations of this study, which we will address in future work:

i. The abstraction laddering interface was not instrumented to capture which level of statement was ultimately selected (the initial statement, or a statement abstracted to a higher level). This knowledge would have been beneficial in examining whether or not abstracting arguments to a higher level affected various quality measures. We plan to collect this data with asserted solutions to inefficiencies in another study.

ii. Only one set of rhetorical-based measures were used to code the data. Ideally, we would have coded the data with multiple methods and examined whether the IVs had any positive (or negative) effects on argument quality when using other measures. We have begun a subsequent recoding and analysis of assertions from this study, and will publish the results separately.

4.3 Implications for Design

In addition to reporting these findings, we desire to make practical recommendations towards designing effective computer-mediated communications systems such as crowdsourcing platforms. The following should be considered as guidelines for those developing similar systems:

i. Training: Ensuring contributors reliably conduct formal argumentation is, in fact, quite difficult. Even with ordered and labeled text fields, explanations of each component, and textbook examples, we still only had 17.5% of participants successfully complete a Toulmin-model argument. To be effective, other efforts must consider training beyond simple text-based explanations when attempting to train complex argumentation concepts (e.g., in future efforts we are exploring the use of dynamic content such as videos to explain more esoteric topics).

ii. Holistic Quality: Simply adding structure and form does not ensure quality argumentation. There are dozens of considerations with regards to quality assurance in crowdsourcing systems that must be holistically considered [44].

iii. External Content: We must carefully choose whether to include or exclude external content (pictures, links, tags, other media, etc.) depending on whether the aim of the system is for quality (not persuasion). Pictures can affect peripheral persuasion, which may be unduly powerful when people generally avoid central processing that is associated with using text-based argumentation to consider an argument's quality [45].

Acknowledgements. This material is based upon work supported by the Office of Naval Research under Contract No. N00014-19-C-1012. Any opinions, findings, and conclusions or recommendations expressed in this material are those of the authors, and do not necessarily reflect the views of the Office of Naval Research.

References

1. Howe, J.: The rise of crowdsourcing. wired, June 2006. https://www.wired.com/2006/06/cro wds/
2. Brabham, D.C.: Crowdsourcing. The MIT Press, Cambridge, MA (2013)
3. Quinn, A.J., Bederson, B.B.: Human computation: a survey and taxonomy of a growing field. CHI **2011**, 1403–1412 (2011)
4. Kim, J., Sterman, S., Cohen, A.A.B., Bernstein, M.: Mechanical novel: crowdsourcing complex work through reflection and revision. In: ACM Conference on Computer-Supported Cooperative Work and Social Computing (2017)
5. Chilton, L., Little, G., Edge, D., Weld, D.S., Landay, J.A.: Cascade: crowdsourcing taxonomy creation (Report No. UW-CSE-12–11–02) (2012)
6. Drapeau, R., Chilton, L.B., Bragg, J., Weld, D.S.: MicroTalk: using argumentation to improve crowdsourcing accuracy. In: Fourth AAAI Conference on Human Computation and Crowdsourcing, AAAI Press (2016)
7. Hackman, J.R.: Collaborative Intelligence: Using Teams to Solve Hard Problems. Berrett-Koehler Publishers, San Francisco, CA (2011)
8. Smith, J.B.: Collective Intelligence in Computer-Based Collaboration. Lawrence Erlbaum, Hillsdale, NJ (1994)
9. Erduran, S., Simon, S., Osborne, J.: TAPping into argumentation: developments in the application of Toulmin's argument pattern for studying science discourse. Sci. Educ. **88**(6), 015–933 (2004). https://doi.org/10.1002/sce.20012
10. Verheij, B.: Evaluating arguments based on Toulmin's scheme. In: OSSA Conference Archive, vol. 115, pp. 1–17 (2001). https://scholar.uwindsor.ca/cgi/viewcontent.cgi?article=1700&context=ossaarchive
11. Herrick, J.A.: Argumentation Understanding and Shaping Arguments. Pearson, New York (1995)

12. Toulmin, S.: The Uses of Argument. Cambridge University Press, Cambridge (1958)
13. Spatariu, A., Hartley, K., Bendixen, L.D.: Defining and measuring quality in online discussions. J. Interact. Online Learn. **2**(4), 1–15 (2004)
14. Kim, D., Benbasat, I.: The effects of trust-assuring arguments on consumer trust in Internet stores: application of Toulmin's model of argumentation. Inf. Syst. Res. **17**(3), 286–300 (2006). https://doi.org/10.1287/isre.1060.0093
15. Boller, G.W., Swasy, J.L., Munch, J.M.: Conceptualizing argument quality via argument structure. Adv. Consum. Res. **17**, 321–328 (1990)
16. Bizup, J.: The uses of Toulmin in composition studies. CCC **61**(1), 1–23 (2009)
17. Tans, O.: The fluidity of warrants: Using the Toulmin model to analyse practical discourse. In: Hitchcock, D., Verheij, B. (eds.) Arguing on the Toulmin Model, pp. 219–230. Springer, Dordrecht (2006)
18. Schultze, U., Avital, M.: Designing interviews to generate rich data for information systems research. Inf. Organ. **21**, 1–16 (2011)
19. Veludo-de-Oliveira, T.M., Ikeda, A.A., Campomar, M.C.: Laddering in the practice of marketing research: barriers and solutions. Qual. Mark. Res. **9**(3), 297–306 (2006). https://doi.org/10.1108/13522750610671707
20. Senge, P.M., Kleiner, A., Roberts, C., Ross, R.B., Smith, B.J.: The Fifth Discipline Fieldbook: Strategies and Tools for Building a Learning Organization. Doubleday, New York, NY (1994)
21. Barry, C.: How/why Laddering (2010). https://dschool-old.stanford.edu/groups/k12/wiki/afdc3/HowWhy_Laddering.html
22. Wenzel, J.W.: Three perspectives on argument: Rhetoric, dialectic, logic. In: Trapp, R., Schuetz, J. (eds.) Perspectives on Argumentation: Essays in Honor of Wayne Brockriede, pp. 9–26. Waveland Press, Prospect Heights, IL (1990)
23. Cohen, D.H.: Evaluating arguments and making meta-arguments. Inf. Logic **21**(2), 73–84 (2001). https://doi.org/10.22329/il.v21i2.2238
24. Rife, M.C.: Ethos, pathos, logos, kairos: using a rhetorical heuristic to mediate digital-survey recruitment strategies. IEEE. Prof. Commun. **53**(3), 260–277 (2010). https://doi.org/10.1109/TPC.2010.2052856
25. Scriven, M.: Reasoning. McGraw-Hill Book Co, New York (1976)
26. Walton, D.: The new dialectic: Conversational contexts of argument. University of Toronto Press, Toronto (1998)
27. Nussbaum, E.M.: Argumentation, dialogue theory, and probability modeling: alternative frameworks for argumentation research in education. Educ. Psychol. **46**(2), 84–106 (2011). https://doi.org/10.1080/00461520.2011.558816
28. Winter, S., Krämer, N.C.: Selecting science information in Web 2.0: how source cues, message sidedness, and need for cognition influence users' exposure to blog posts. J. Comput. Mediat. Commun. **18**(1), 80–96 (2012)
29. Dorton, S.L., Smith, C.M., Upham J.B.: Applying visualization and collective intelligence for rapid group decision making. In: Proceedings of the 2018 International Annual Meeting of the Human Factors and Ergonomics Society, pp. 167–171 (2018). doi: https://doi.org/10.1177/1541931218621039
30. Repenning, N.P., Kieffer, D., Astor, T.: The most underrated skill in management. MIT Sloan Manag. Rev. **58**(3), 39–48 (2017)
31. Heuer, R.J.: Psychology of Intelligence Analysis. Echo Point Books & Media, Brattleboro, VT (2017)
32. Killingsworth, M.J.: Rhetorical appeals: a revision. Rhetor. Rev. **24**(3), 249–263 (2005)
33. Hunt, K.: Establishing a presence on the world wide web: a rhetorical approach. Techn. Commun. **43**(4), 376–387 (1996)
34. Higgins, C., Walker, R.: Ethos, logs, pathos: Strategies of persuasion in social/environmental reports. Acc. Forum **36**, 194–208 (2012). https://doi.org/10.1016/j.accfor.2012.02.003

35. Wachsmuth, H., Stede, M., El Baff, R., Al-Khatib, K., Skeppstedt, M., Stein, B.: Argumentation synthesis following rhetorical strategies. In: Proceedings of the 27th Annual Conference on Computational Linguistics, pp. 3753–3765 (2018). https://www.aclweb.org/anthology/C18-1318

36. Petty, R.E., Cacioppo, J.T.: Source factors and the elaboration likelihood model of persuasion. Adv. Consum. Res. **11**, 668–672 (1984)

37. Areni, C.S., Lutz, R.J.: The role of argument quality in the elaboration likelihood model. Adv. Consum. Res. **15**, 197–203 (1988)

38. Kotter, J.: Leading Change. Harvard Business Review Press, Boston, MA (2012)

39. Corner, A., Hahn, U.: Evaluating science arguments: evidence, uncertainty, and argument strength. J. Exp. Psychol. Appl. **15**(3), 199–212 (2009). https://doi.org/10.1037/a0016533

40. Kahneman, D.: Thinking. Fast and Slow. Farrar Straus and Giroux, New York (2011)

41. Carenini, G.: A task-based framework to evaluate evaluative arguments. Proc. First Int. Conf. Nat. Lang. Gener. **14**, 9–16 (2000). https://doi.org/10.3115/1118253.1118256

42. Sorokin, P.A.: The Crisis of Our Age. Dutton, New York (1941)

43. Dunbar, N.E., et al.: Fear appeals, message processing cues, and credibility in the websites of violent, ideological, and nonideological groups. J. Comput.-Mediat. Commun. **19**, 871–889 (2014). https://doi.org/10.1111/jcc4.12083

44. Daniel, F., Kucherbaev, P., Cappiello, C., Benatallah, B., Allahbakhsh, M.: Quality control in crowdsourcing: a survey of quality attributes, assessment techniques, and assurance actions. ACM Comput. Surv. **51**(1), 1–39 (2018). https://doi.org/10.1145/0000000.0000000

45. Rains, S.A., Karmikel, C.D.: Health information-seeking and perceptions of website credibility: Examining web-use orientation, message characteristics, and structural features of websites. Comput. Hum. Behav. **25**(2), 544–553 (2009)

The Faceless Vicinity: Who Uses Location-Based Anonymous Social Networks Like Jodel and Why?

Karoline Jüttner[✉], Philipp Nowak, Katrin Scheibe, Franziska Zimmer,
and Kaja J. Fietkiewicz

Department of Information Science, Heinrich Heine University, Universitätsstr. 1,
40225 Düsseldorf, Germany
{Karoline.Juettner,Philipp.Nowak,Katrin.Scheibe,
Franziska.Zimmer,Kaja.Fietkiewicz}@hhu.de

Abstract. Anonymous social networks, such as Jodel, are enjoying increasing popularity. But what are the reasons? At first, the connection of social networks, usually associated with exchanging and making contacts, and anonymity seems to be somehow contradictory. But as the user statistics of Jodel show, it works. This study explores the question of what exactly motivates people to use anonymous social networks like Jodel. For this purpose, different user roles, usage motivations, and gamification elements were examined by means of correlation and cluster analyses. To generate results for the evaluation a user survey with 874 participants was conducted, which was based among others on the Uses and Gratifications Theory by Blumler and Katz [1]. Following the classification by Shao [2], the participating users were divided into the user roles producer, commenter, rater, and consumer. The study shows that boredom and entertainment are among the most common usage reasons, while additional motivations are rather specific for each user role.

Keywords: Jodel · Anonymous social networks · Usage motivations · Uses and Gratifications · User roles · Gamification

1 Introduction

Anonymity on the internet became more and more of a rarity over the years. Numerous websites, forums, and especially social networks require a registration for the use (some networks even initiated a real-name policy in contrast to common practice of pseudonymization of online profiles), which includes the specification of personal data. This fact makes it comprehendible that anonymous social networks, such as Jodel or formerly Yik Yak, enjoy great popularity, as they allow full use without the disclosure of any personal information. They enable the anonymous exchange between platform users in the vicinity, which people look for in vain on other social networks. But what makes it so desirable to be anonymous in social networks, especially since the establishment of an actual "network" is rather impossible for users in this way? There are

G. Meiselwitz (Ed.): HCII 2021, LNCS 12774, pp. 54–73, 2021.
https://doi.org/10.1007/978-3-030-77626-8_4

already several studies concerning anonymity on the Internet [3–6]. However, there is barely any scientific literature about the anonymous location-based social media app Jodel, although the app is becoming more and more popular in many countries worldwide. For example, Kasakowskij, Friedrich, Fietkiewicz, and Stock [7] investigated the influence of anonymity (and non-anonymity) on user behavior using the example of Jodel and Instagram. Nowak, Jüttner, and Baran [8] examined the quality of Jodel as an information service in an earlier study. This investigation differs from previous studies by addressing the question of what motivates people to use a completely anonymous social network such as Jodel and how can its users be characterized based on their user behavior. In order to answer these questions, a representative user survey about usage motivations, gamification, and user roles was conducted. The object of this study is the German mobile application Jodel, since the comparable American service Yik Yak has been shut down in May 2017 [9] and Jodel shows the potential to occupy its former monopoly position.

1.1 Jodel

The location-based social network Jodel was released in October 2014 in Germany [10]. Meanwhile, the app has gained awareness in numerous other countries [11], especially in all the Nordic (European) countries [8]. An expansion into the US has also been planned for a while [12], but has not yet been accomplished. Jodel allows its users to anonymously send postings, so-called "jodels", in the form of short texts, photos, or video clips into a feed, which is visible for other users within an area of ten kilometers [13]. Postings can be commented, pinned, shared, or reported by others and every content, including comments, can be either up- or down-voted. If a posting receives five down-votes, it automatically gets deleted from the feed. Three different categories determine the postings order: "newest," "most commented," and "loudest." The "loudest" category orders the postings descending by the number of up-votes. For own postings getting up-voted and for active contribution to the community (e.g., for voting other postings), users collect so-called "karma points." In "channels," users have the opportunity to discuss specific topics such as politics, pets, or fitness. Furthermore, the moderator system is the main aspect in which Jodel distinguishes itself from Yik Yak. Every user can become a moderator, since an algorithm, which regards aspects like positive contribution and the number of karma points, automatically chooses suitable users. These users receive access to an additional area, where they have the permission to allow or block reported postings. A decision is always made collectively by many moderators.

The scientific literature published so far about Jodel can be briefly summarized as follows. Johann, Wiedel, Tonndorf, and Windscheid [14] investigated social behavior in anonymous environments using Jodel with regard to aspects of (toxic) disinhibition, self-disclosure, and prosocial behavior. In an extract from their study, Johann et al. [15] showed that social identification with the group promotes prosocial behavior, communication on obscene topics, and self-disclosure, whereas there is no connection to antisocial behavior. Böhm, Taubmann, and Reiser [16] examined the localization of the location from which a post was published. Nowak et al. [8] carried out an evaluation of Jodel based on the Information Service Evaluation (ISE) model by Schumann and Stock [17], which includes aspects such as the quality of the information service, the user characteristics, and acceptance of the information system. Lately, Kasakowskij et al. [7] investigated user behavior in the anonymous social network Jodel compared to the popular non-anonymous social network Instagram.

On the other hand, there are more scientific publications about Yik Yak, especially about related topics like user behavior and motivation, partly with psychological background. O'Leary and Murphy [18], for example, investigated consumer behavior on Yik Yak. Wombacher, Reno, Williams, and Johnson [19] analyzed how healthy and risky behavior is discussed on Yik Yak's anonymous feed and whether these behaviors are encouraged or discouraged. Seigfried-Spellar and Lankford [20] found that distinct posting behaviors are associated with different personality and online environmental factors. Lane, Das, and Hiaeshutter-Rice [21] examined the political expression of young people on Yik Yak in the course of the US election in 2016.

In this study the focus is set on the different motivations of Jodel's users as well as detection of different user types or roles based on their usage behavior.

1.2 User Roles

On every social media platform, we can distinguish between different user types—at least between the ones who actively participate in the content co-creation and the ones who passively observe. Shao [2] divides users of services that support user-generated content into producers, participants, and consumers. Since Jodel also represents a service with user-generated content, this division is adapted in this study. Producers actively participate in the community and mainly publish their own content while using the service, whereas consumers behave completely passive and use the service only to consume the existing content without reacting in any way. Participants are actively involved in the community, but without creating their own and "new" content. For example, they participate by commenting on existing content. In the case of Jodel, it is only possible for a participant to either comment a posting or vote it up or down. Since we consider commenting to be more demanding than simply clicking on an up- or downwards-facing arrow, the user role which Shao [2] refers to as "participants" was split into commenter and rater. This way four different user roles are considered in this study: producer, commenter, rater, and consumer.

In order to detect which users take on which user roles as well as to verify whether other user types taking on different combinations of user roles can be found, we formulate the following research questions:

RQ1a: Who are Jodel's producers, consumers, and participants (i.e., commenters and raters)?
RQ1b: How do these different user roles intertwine?
RQ2: Which other user types can be detected based on the frequency of different usage activities?

1.3 Uses and Gratifications Theory

In order to investigate the motivations of the Jodel users, this study refers to the Uses and Gratifications Theory. The beginning of the Uses and Gratifications Theory can be traced back to Katz and Foulkes [22], who asked the question "What do people do with the media?" instead of the popular question "What does the media do with people?". Arising from this question the theory of Uses and Gratifications [1] was developed to better understand people's motivations to use the media. According to Katz, Blumler, and Gurevitch [23], people behave active, goal-oriented, and purposive when selecting media. The theory is based on the idea that media consumers desire to meet certain needs or gratifications with their media usage [24]. According to McQuail [25] those needs can comprise the wish for entertainment, information, self-presentation, and social interaction. The question of whether these sought gratifications can be obtained by the use of media has a major impact on user satisfaction [22]. With regard to anonymous social networks, the question arises whether real social interactions are even possible on such platforms, but Nowak et al. [8] as well as Johann et al. [14, 15] ascertained in their investigations that social interactions take place and are actively sought by the users on Jodel. In order to detect the motivations of Jodel's users we formulate the following research questions:

RQ3a: What is the motivation of users assuming different roles (producer, consumer, commenter, and rater) to apply Jodel?
RQ3b: What user groups can be detected based on their motivation to apply Jodel?

1.4 Gamification

Gamification can have a great influence on the motivation to use a service. Deterding, Dixon, Khaled, and Nacke [26, p. 10] define gamification as "the use of game design elements in non-game contexts," while Zichermann and Cunningham [27, p. XIV] describe it as "the process of game-thinking and game mechanics to engage users and solve problems." Both definitions imply that not complete games are created, but elements of these are accessed and used for other purposes [28]. Those game design elements can comprise among others point systems, level systems, challenges, virtual goods, leaderboards, and so-called quests [29]. Nicholson [30] argues that the term "gamification" has become synonymous with "rewards," since the purpose of gamification is to reward people for a certain behavior. Further reason to implement such game mechanics in non-game contexts is to increase usage motivation, activity, and engagement [31, 32] in non-game services and applications [33]. Appropriate incentives are therefore often used to encourage people to use a certain system or service [34].

Regarding Jodel, the most conspicuous gamification element is the karma point system. Its intention is to motivate the users to participate in the community in a positive way, such as writing appropriate postings and answers as well as supporting funny, helpful, or otherwise positive postings with up-votes. As already mentioned before, users get karma points for receiving and giving up-votes, while the amount of points for up-voting is much smaller than for receiving up-votes. Receiving down-votes (and since an update in 2018 also the act of giving down-votes) is penalized with a loss of karma points. The update was an answer to the problem with a so-called "down-vote mafia" [35], a collective term for users randomly distributing down-votes. The category "loudest" represents another gamification element, since it can be understood as a kind of leaderboard. It shows the current postings which received the most up-votes in a descending order. It is meant to motivate users to publish postings, which are likely to be positively rated by other users and this way have a chance of bringing the own posting on a high position in the leaderboard. Jodel therefore uses two of the game elements mentioned by Knautz et al. [29], namely a point system and a leaderboard. In order to detect the attitudes towards gamification elements of Jodel's users we formulate the following research questions:

RQ4a: What is the attitude towards gamification elements of users assuming different roles (producer, consumer, commenter, and rater) on Jodel?

RQ4b: What user groups can be detected based on their attitude towards gamification elements on Jodel?

2   Methods

2.1   Quantitative User Survey

The user survey contained sets of statements about users' motives to apply Jodel as well as socio-demographic questions. The personal assessments of the participants were rated on a Likert scale [36] from 1 ("I totally disagree") to 7 ("I totally agree"). The first question "Why do you use Jodel?" included nine Likert items describing the motivations entertainment, information, social interaction, and self-presentation, based on the Uses and Gratifications Theory [25].

The second statement block "gamification and incentives" dealt with the extent of motivation created by gamification elements. Here, Karma points, the voting function and the category "loudest" were considered.

The third set of Likert items was used to divide the participants into the user roles: producer, commenter, rater, and consumer. In order to assign the participants to the four user roles, they were asked how often they publish a posting, how often they write a comment, how often they vote on content, and how often they use Jodel only for reading content. The scale reached from 1 ("Never") to 7 ("Every time I use Jodel"). Finally, the users were asked about their gender, birth year, nationality, current activity, and highest educational achievement. The survey was distributed in Germany between October 2016 and March 2017 primarily via Jodel and Facebook and ended with a total of 874 participants who finished the survey.

2.2   Data Preparation and Evaluation

Only three of the 874 Jodel users who participated in the survey were born before 1980. Since these three users provided a sample that is too small to generate insightful results about the so-called generation of "Silver Surfers" and Generation X, this study was limited to the 871 users who belong to Generation Y and Z and are therefore born between 1980 and 2010 [37].

The collected data was evaluated using the statistics software IBM SPSS Statistics. In order to divide the participants into the four user roles, an ordinal scaled variable (on a scale from 1 to 3) for each user type was computed from the appropriate 7-point frequency scale. Those users who rated the corresponding statement with 1 ("Never") were assigned to group 1 while users who responded with a value between 2 and 4 were assigned to group 2. Those who answered with a value between 5 and 7 were assigned to group 3. This third group defined the user role in each case and was examined more closely within the scope of this study. This means that the users who answered the question "how often do you publish a posting?" with a value between 5 and 7 were assigned to the user role "producer." The same principle was applied to the other three user roles. The four individual groups are more interwoven on Jodel compared to e.g., social live-streaming services [38], where usually a clearer separation between producers (streamers) and consumers (viewers) can be observed. Therefore, it was possible for participants to be a member of several of these groups based on their answers. The classification was made to examine how the motivations differ for each user role.

In order to investigate whether there is a connection between different user groups, e.g. a producer is usually also a rater or commenter, or in contrary a consumer rarely acts as a producer, we conducted Spearman's rank correlation. Furthermore, possible correlations between the user roles and the usage reasons were examined in order to see whether different roles were characterized by different usage motivations. Finally, to find out whether the different user roles react differently to the gamification elements, the correlations between the user roles and the importance of various gamification elements were tested.

In order to analyze the existing relations between different user types in more detail and without predefined classification by the authors, a k-means cluster analysis was conducted. In a cluster analysis, each participant was assigned to exactly one cluster, therefore, unlike the assignment of the different user roles, there was no overlap between the clusters. An initial hierarchical cluster analysis showed that the optimal amount of clusters lied between 3 and 5. Consequently, several variations of k-means cluster were tested and, finally, the most suitable number of clusters was chosen for each investigated aspect. Initially, five clusters were created with regard to the user roles to verify whether they correspond with our initial user role classification. Furthermore, four clusters were created regarding the usage motivations in order to see if similar motivations, e.g. "exchange with others" and "reach people in the vicinity," performed similarly within one cluster. Concerning the gamification elements, five clusters were created in order to show which groups of gamification elements were regarded as important.

3   Results

3.1   Different User Roles on Jodel

RQ1a: Who are Jodel's producers, consumers, and participants (i.e., commenters and raters)?

The online survey was completed by 874 active Jodel users, however, after excluding three participants born before 1980, the sample consisted of 871 participants. Out of these 871 participants, 66% were female and 34% were male (see Table 1). Around 95% of the survey participants were born between 1990 and 1999. The mean birth year is

1995, whereas the peak is at 1997. There is only a very small deviation regarding the mean birth year between the user roles. Commenters are averagely the oldest (1994.83) and consumers the youngest users (1995.12). At the time of the survey most of the respondents were between 19 and 25 years old. The majority (72%) were students, 10% were in training, 9% were employed, and 6% attended school. Regarding the four user roles, raters are the most represented with 91% of all survey participants. This is followed by consumers (62%), commenters (48%), and producers (24%). In terms of percentage distribution, it should be considered that users can belong to multiple user roles. The greatest difference in the distribution of the genders can be seen among the producers. Here, only 21% of female users are producers, compared to 31% of male users. Also, the male users are more often commenters (52% compared to 45%). The female users are more represented among the raters (92% to 87%) and consumers (63% to 59%).

Table 1. Demographic information. N = 871.

		Producer (N = 212)	Commenter (N = 416)	Rater (N = 791)	Consumer (N = 538)	Total (N = 871)
Gender	Female	120	262	533	364	575
	Male	92	154	258	174	296
Birth year	Mean	1995.10	1994.83	1995.03	1995.12	1995.00
Current occupation	Pupil	20	25	49	32	53
	Student	140	291	564	389	623
	Trainee	29	38	78	56	84
	Employed	18	47	71	39	79
	Other	5	15	29	22	32

In the following, the results of the user survey are examined by means of Spearman's correlations with regard to significance gradations conforming to Bortz and Döring [39]. Correlations between user roles, usage motivations, and gamification are considered. The effect sizes are interpreted according to Cohen [40], which means that 0.1 represents a small effect size, 0.3 a moderate effect size, and 0.5 a high effect size.

RQ1b: How do these different user roles (producer, consumer, commenter, and rater) intertwine?

There is a high correlation (0.510***) between being a producer and a commenter (see Table 2). In addition, there is a linear relationship of small effect between raters and producers (0.139***) and between raters and commenters (0.212***). In contrast, the more the users act as consumers, the less active they are regarding producing any content. These negative correlations are on a similar level (small to moderate), whereas it is most pronounced for consumers and commenters (−0.319***).

Table 2. Spearman's rank correlations between the different user roles. N = 871.

	(1)	(2)	(3)	(4)
(1) Producer	1			
(2) Commenter	.510***	1		
(3) Rater	.139***	.212***	1	
(4) Consumer	−.254***	−.319***	−.224***	1

*** $p < 0.001$, ** $p < 0.01$, * $p < 0.05$.

3.2 Detecting New User Types

In the following, the results of k-means cluster analysis including the frequency of different user behaviors (in order to detect different user roles), usage motivations and gamification will be presented.

RQ2: Which other user types can be detected based on the frequency of different usage activities?

Table 3. K-means cluster analysis ($k = 5$) for different user behaviors (by frequency). N = 871, Scale = 1-7.

		Frequency of producing	Frequency of commenting	Frequency of rating	Frequency of use without interacting
1	Mean (SD)	2.29 (0.991)	2.65 (1.042)	4.24 (1.117)	5.93 (0.779)
N = 153	Med (IQR)	2 (1)	3 (1)	5 (1)	6 (1)
2	Mean (SD)	2.68 (1.004)	3.20 (1.072)	6.62 (0.568)	6.11 (0.711)
N = 209	Med (IQR)	3 (1)	3 (2)	7 (1)	6 (1)
3	Mean (SD)	4.29 (1.033)	5.53 (0.803)	6.52 (0.833)	5.16 (0.965)
N = 254	Med (IQR)	4 (1)	5 (1)	7 (1)	5 (2)
4	Mean (SD)	4.54 (0.895)	5.83 (0.876)	6.82 (0.485)	2.04 (0.793)
N = 139	Med (IQR)	5 (1)	6 (2)	7 (0)	2 (2)
5	Mean (SD)	2.80 (0.847)	3.61 (1.036)	6.60 (0.603)	2.73 (1.090)
N = 116	Med (IQR)	3 (1)	4 (1)	7 (1)	3 (2)

Regarding the frequency and type of use, there are five clusters that contain between 116 and 254 respondents (see Table 3). The means of production behavior (frequency) reach from 2.29 to 4.54, of commenting behavior from 2.65 to 5.83, of rating behavior from 4.24 to 6.82, and of consumption behavior (of users who do not create any content) from 2.04 to 5.93. In the first cluster (N = 135), the frequency of producing and commenting content is weakly pronounced. The frequency of rating is on a medium level, while consumption behavior is most prominent. In the second cluster (N = 209), the frequency of producing, commenting, and consuming is only slightly more pronounced than in the first cluster. The frequency of rating, however, is very high. The third cluster (N = 254) presents a medium occurrence of production behavior. The frequency of commenting and consuming content is on a medium high level, while the mean value of the frequency of rating postings is very pronounced. In the fourth cluster (N = 139), the frequency of producing, commenting, and rating are most pronounced in the whole cluster analysis, while the sole consumption behavior is the least frequent. The fifth cluster (N = 116) shows similar results to cluster number 2 in terms of the frequency of producing, commenting, and rating content. The difference is that the frequency of use without any interaction is on a lower level.

3.3 Motivations of Jodel's Users

RQ3a: What is the motivation of users assuming different roles (producer, consumer, commenter, and rater) to apply Jodel?

Table 4 shows that there are consistently positive linear relationships at low to medium level between producers and the motivation being social interactions, e.g. asking questions anonymously (0.308***), exchanging with others (0.280***), finding friends (0.183***), finding a partner (0.125***), or reaching people in the vicinity (0.206***). The commenters behave similarly regarding the usage motivations. Here, exchanging with others (0.393***) and reaching people (0.280***) show remarkably higher correlations. For raters, these correlations (except for finding friends or a partner) are also present, albeit only to a lesser extent (e.g. exchange with others: 0.150***). It is noticeable that the consumers behave contrarily to the other three user roles. For example, there is a negative correlation with a small effect size with the motivation being exchanging with others (−0.158***) or asking questions anonymously (−0.117**). Using the app out of boredom correlates positively only with consumers. However, the effect size here is very small (0.083*). The more users are looking to collect karma points, the more likely they are producers (0.303***), followed by commenters (0.207***). Here, raters exhibit a correlation with only low effects (0.141***), whereas for consumers the correlation is even negative (−0.134***). Hating and trolling is mostly favored by commenters (0.145***) and producers (0.109**). There are no linear relationships with raters as well as consumers.

RQ3b: What user groups can be detected based on their motivation to apply Jodel?

In the following, four clusters which contain between 80 and 280 respondents were computed for the different usage motivations (see Table 5). The first cluster (N = 278) consists of people who mainly use Jodel out of boredom and for entertainment reasons, but also to ask questions and to exchange with others. Not at all relevant in this group is finding friends or even a partner or hating and trolling. For the second user group (N = 280), all social reasons to use Jodel do not matter. They use the app exclusively out of boredom and to read funny postings. The survey participants of the third cluster (N = 80) are very balanced in their motivation to use Jodel. Except for hating and trolling, there is

Table 4. Spearman's rank correlations between user roles and usage motivations. N = 871.

	Boredom	Read funny postings	Ask questions	Exchange with others	Collect karma points	Find friends	Find a partner	Reach people	Hating and trolling
Producer	−.077*	.038	.308***	.280***	.303***	.183***	.125***	.206***	.109**
Commenter	−.064	−.030	.346***	.393***	.207***	.141***	.087*	.280***	.145***
Rater	−.031	.000	.091**	.150***	.141***	.061	.000	.151***	.030
Consumer	.083*	−.019	−.117**	−.158***	−.134***	−.087*	−.039	−.139***	−.023

*** $p < 0.001$, ** $p < 0.01$, * $p < 0.05$.

no motivation below the mean of 3.8, which is roughly the middle of the 7-point Likert scale. Social reasons are very strong, to find friends or a partner even on a medium level. It should be noted, however, that the standard deviation here is very high at some points, for example concerning the usage motivation to collect karma points (1.951). The fourth cluster consists of 233 participants. For this group, karma points are the most important reason to use the app compared to the other clusters (mean equals 4.91). In addition, the usage motivations are primarily boredom and entertainment. The means for social motivations are below the medium. For all users of the four clusters the motivation to use Jodel out of boredom and due to entertainment was similarly pronounced, as well as the irrelevance of hating and trolling. There are differences exclusively in terms of social activities.

3.4   Impact of Gamification on Jodel's Users

RQ4a: What is the attitude towards gamification elements of users assuming different roles (producer, consumer, commenter, and rater) on Jodel?

In terms of motivating effects of Jodel's gamification elements, consumers behave distinctively different than the other three user types (see Table 6). Producers are least likely to use the service without karma points (-0.136^{***}). In addition, the motivational impact of karma points on voting is the most pronounced for this group as well (0.208^{***}). Consumers are the only group that seems not to be motivated by karma points (0.110^{**}), however, in their role, it is not possible to collect many points since they do not create any content or vote. Producers are slightly more pleased with creating a successful posting (0.209^{***}) than people with other user roles, e.g. commenters (0.193^{***}). The strongest positive effect is given for the correlation between the joy about having the "loudest" posting (which means the one with the most up-votes) in the vicinity and, therefore, reaching the leading position in this category, and being active as producer (0.226^{***}). However, consumers do not care about being among the "loudest" (-0.168^{**}), which is not surprising as they do not post any content. All in all, the correlations between motivational impact of gamification elements and the different user types being producers and participants (commenters and raters) are mostly very similar.

RQ4b: What user groups can be detected based on their attitude towards gamification elements on Jodel?

With regard to the importance of gamification elements for the usage of Jodel, there are five clusters consisting of between 29 and 326 survey participants (see Table 7). The users of the first cluster (N = 326) would use the app without karma points. The joy about their own posting being successful is extraordinarily great. The voting function is important to them, but the influence of karma points on voting is on the other hand considered to be trivial. Although the second cluster consists of only 29 survey participants, it offers a characteristic that distinguishes it from the other clusters: the users do not care whether their own posting succeeds or not. In addition, karma points are unimportant to them, as is the voting function. The users of the third cluster (N = 211) perceive the

Table 5. K-means cluster analysis (k = 4) for usage motivations. N = 871, Scale = 1-7.

Cluster		Boredom	Read funny postings	Ask questions	Exchange with others	Collect karma points	Find friends	Find a partner	Reach people	Hating and trolling
1 N = 278	Mean	5.37	6.02	5.58	5.20	2.72	1.74	1.20	4.02	1.44
	SD	1.482	1.227	1.198	1.312	1.533	1.057	0.632	1.638	1.125
	Med (IQR)	6 (3)	6 (2)	6 (2)	5 (2)	2 (2)	1 (1)	1 (0)	4 (2)	1 (0)
2 N = 280	Mean	5.83	5.84	2.20	2.63	1.75	1.19	1.09	2.04	1.40
	SD	1.158	1.217	1.158	1.346	1.039	0.502	0.382	1.200	1.025
	Med (IQR)	6 (2)	6 (2)	2 (2)	2 (2)	1 (1)	1 (0)	1 (0)	2 (2)	1 (0)
3 N = 80	Mean	5.14	5.56	5.64	5.94	4.13	4.15	3.81	5.55	2.31
	SD	1.366	1.533	1.512	1.173	1.951	1.468	1.758	1.231	1.953
	Med (IQR)	5 (2)	6 (2)	6 (2)	6 (2)	4 (3)	4 (2)	4 (2)	6 (2)	1 (2)
4 N = 233	Mean	5.45	6.08	2.99	3.63	4.91	1.67	1.27	3.98	1.81
	SD	1.326	1.014	1.353	1.451	1.294	1.003	0.699	1.560	1.480
	Med (IQR)	6 (2)	6 (1)	3 (2)	4 (3)	5 (2)	1 (1)	1 (0)	4 (2)	1 (1)

Table 6. Spearman's rank correlations between user roles and motivating effects of gamification elements. N = 871.

	Usage without karma points	Usage without voting function	Joy: posting among the "loudest"	Joy: posting is the "loudest"	Impact of karma points on voting
Producer	−.136***	−.136***	.209***	.226***	.208***
Commenter	−.115**	−.144***	.193***	.211***	.116**
Rater	−.110**	−.176***	.197***	.205***	.089**
Consumer	.110**	.101**	−.168***	−.196***	−.059

*** $p < 0.001$, ** $p < 0.01$, * $p < 0.05$.

gamification elements of Jodel very similar to those of the first cluster, with the difference that here the influence of karma points on voting is considered important. This is a unique attribute compared to all the other clusters. Cluster number four contains 97 users of Jodel. The means regarding the enjoyment about creating a successful posting and the assessment of the relevance of the voting function are at a medium level. Karma points are not relevant to the survey participants in this cluster, as well as the influence of these points on voting. On the one hand, the users of the fifth cluster (N = 208) would forego karma points and the voting function of the app. On the other hand, the joy about a successful posting (and the result in the ranking list is based on the voting function) is decidedly greater. In addition, the influence of karma points on voting other postings is stated to be relatively low. All clusters reiterate that karma points are not important for the use of the app, regardless of how the other gamification elements in the clusters are affected.

Table 7. K-means cluster analysis (k = 5) based on importance of gamification elements. N = 871, Scale = 1–7.

		Usage without karma points	Usage without voting function	Joy: posting among the "loudest"	Joy: posting is the "loudest"	Impact of karma points on voting
1	Mean (SD)	5.88 (1.386)	2.42 (0.966)	6.75 (0.517)	6.78 (0.516)	1.54 (0.730)
N = 326	Med (IQR)	6 (2)	2 (1)	7 (0)	7 (0)	1 (1)
2	Mean (SD)	6.34 (1.471)	4.86 (2.065)	1.34 (0.670)	1.31 (0.604)	1.07 (0.258)
N = 29	Med (IQR)	7 (1)	5 (4)	1 (1)	1 (1)	1 (0)
3	Mean (SD)	5.18 (1.668)	2.82 (1.449)	6.76 (0.596)	6.77 (0.600)	5.67 (1.131)
N = 211	Med (IQR)	5 (3)	3 (2)	7 (0)	7 (0)	6 (2)
4	Mean (SD)	6.66 (0.675)	4.03 (1.571)	4.46 (0.751)	4.43 (0.749)	1.72 (1.018)
N = 97	Med (IQR)	7 (0)	4 (2)	4 (1)	4 (1)	1 (1)
5	Mean (SD)	6.69 (0.647)	5.74 (0.968)	6.82 (0.400)	6.82 (0.431)	2.50 (1.725)
N = 208	Med (IQR)	7 (0)	6 (2)	7 (0)	7 (0)	2 (3)

4 Discussion

RQ1a: Who are Jodel's producers, consumers and participants (i.e., commenters and raters)?

As expected, most respondents are students, as the app was originally developed for this user group. According to Palfrey and Gasser [41], the birth year 1980 represents an appropriate border between generations of digital natives and digital immigrants. Since 95% of the participants were born between 1990 and 1999, it becomes clear that the respondents represent digital natives [42]. Furthermore, the survey participants belong to Generation Y and Z. Since the number of participants is quite high and they mainly became aware of the survey directly via Jodel, it is reasonable to assume that these results can be transferred to the Jodel community and that therefore Jodel is mainly represented by digital natives of Generation Y and Z. The percentage distribution regarding the user roles shows that the male users are slightly more prone to active user behavior on Jodel (producing and commenting postings) than the female users.

RQ1b: How do these different user roles (producer, consumer, commenter, and rater) intertwine?

It is noticeable that in particular the roles of the producer and the commenter correlate very strongly with each other. However, the active roles, i.e. producer, commenter, and rater, all have clearly identifiable interrelationships. The role of the consumer is very distinctive, because the more strongly the participants have assessed themselves as consumers, the less the active roles apply to them. This is plausible, since the consumer, in opposition to the active roles, has a contrary, passive mode of use. It is interesting to note that the strongest negative correlation is between the consumer and the commenter and not, as intuitively assumed, between the consumer and the producer, although the differences between the negative correlations are marginal. The correlations between the user roles clearly show how strongly the individual roles overlap on Jodel.

RQ2: Which other user types can be detected based on the frequency of different usage activities?

The most striking aspect which the cluster analysis showed is that voting is very popular in all clusters and is carried out extremely frequently. This is also in accordance with the high number of participants assigned to the user role "rater." The first cluster tends towards the user role "consumers," since there are less postings and comments produced, but instead there is mainly content consumed. It is noticeable here that despite the passivity of the user group, rating is still highly frequented. However, the value is still the weakest, compared to the other four clusters, which all achieved the highest possible median value regarding the frequency of voting. The second cluster shows similar characteristics as the first one, except for a slightly higher tendency to produce content and a more pronounced voting behavior. It is interesting at this point that the members of this cluster classify themselves as just as passive as the members of the first cluster, despite the increased willingness to interact. The third and largest cluster is particularly striking as it shows trends in all four user roles. Based on the median, the members of this cluster would be assigned to all four user roles. It has already been demonstrated that the three active user roles overlap strongly. It is unusual, however, that there are (quite a few) users who feel associated with both the user role producer and consumer, even though they strongly contradict each other and showed highly contradictory tendencies in their answers. In addition, the cluster as a whole is very active, since own content is published, comments are written and ratings are given, yet the value of pure consumption is hardly lower than in the previous two clusters. In comparison, the fourth cluster has the strongest tendency to produce its own content and is at the same time the least passive. Compared to the other clusters, commenting is most pronounced here, while voting also shows the highest possible median. The last and smallest cluster is very similar to the second one. The members tend to comment a little more frequented, but assess themselves much less passively. The cluster analysis shows the strong promiscuity between the four user roles. The voting function seems to be an integral part of usage for most Jodel users, because voting is by far the most popular usage behavior. In addition, the assumption arises that many users regard themselves as rather passive participants despite regular use of the voting function. The assumption arises that there are virtually no pure consumers on Jodel, since even the first cluster, which seems to represent the consumers very well, showed a strong use of the voting function.

RQ3a: What is the motivation of users assuming different roles (producer, consumer, commenter, and rater) to apply Jodel?

Within the scope of this investigation, the producers in particular showed striking correlations in terms of social usage motivations, such as asking questions, exchange with others and reaching people in the vicinity. However, karma points also seem to play a significant role for producers on Jodel. Among the commenters, the coherences with social motivations are even more pronounced, while they place a little less importance on karma points. In addition, the commenters have the highest tendency to hating and trolling, while the correlation is very significant, but the effect size is rather low. The connection seems meaningful, because hating and trolling is a phenomenon that mostly occurs in comments. Overall, producers and commenters are resembling each other in their motivations, which could be due to the fact that the two user roles themselves correlate strongly. The reason for this is probably the similarity of the roles, as both actively publish content in their own way. It could be assumed that someone who publishes content of the one type (postings) also publishes content of the other one (comments) and vice versa. Among the raters, the usage motivations are weaker. Significant correlations exist at a low level only for exchanging with others, collecting karma points, and reaching people in the vicinity. However, the connection to the social motivations is surprising, since raters act as passive roles and do not even have the opportunity to perform social interactions with rating postings on Jodel. The relationships can be explained by the fact that raters also correlate with the user roles producers and commenters. Since participants can be assigned to multiple user roles based on their responses, the relationships are probably attributable to the other two roles. The consumers stand out with their usage motivations, since there are very significant negative correlations to the usage reasons exchange with others, collecting karma points and reaching people in the vicinity. Consumers generally differ strongly from the other user roles as they are negatively related to producers, commenters, and raters. They exclude the other roles the most because they are behaving in a completely passive way on Jodel.

RQ3b: What user groups can be detected based on their motivation to apply Jodel?

Regarding the usage motivations, the cluster analysis revealed four different user groups. At first it can be recorded that boredom plays a (major) role in all clusters, as does the wish to read funny postings. At the same time, there is no group emerging that is inclined towards hating and trolling. The first cluster is strongly interested in exchange, but the search for social interaction seems to be limited to the online environment, as the members are not interested in new contacts such as friends or a partner. Karma points are of no interest to the members of this group. The second cluster is also the largest and shows characteristics of a consumer. The members are hardly socially motivated or interested in exchanging ideas with others. At the same time they show the highest value regarding boredom as a usage motivation. Karma points do not matter at all for the members and (at a very small distance) the cluster shows the lowest value for hating and trolling. Both can be explained by low activity and interaction. This suggests that the members of this cluster are mainly looking for entertainment and hardly for social interaction. The third and smallest cluster differs significantly from the other three. It is highly socially motivated and seeks exchange and contacts both online and offline, as members also tend to be looking for friends or a partner. This user group also shows the highest value regarding hating and trolling, probably due to the strong interaction with other users. Interestingly, karma points are not unimportant to these members. The last cluster is moderately interested in exchange and social aspects, but comparatively strongest in karma points. The karma affinity, the moderate interest in social exchange as well as the high (relatively highest) interest in funny postings suggests a producer character of this group.

RQ4a: What is the attitude towards gamification elements of users assuming different roles (producer, consumer, commenter, and rater) on Jodel?

Regarding the gamification elements, the producers have the highest affinity to karma points. It can be observed that the less active the user role is, the less important are the karma points. The voting function is, as expected, most important for the raters. The three user roles producer, commenter, and rater have a resembling positive correlation to the joy about postings being among the category "loudest," while the producer shows the strongest one. Interestingly, the impact of karma points on the voting behavior is highest among the producers. There is no considerable correlation among the raters. Here again, the correlations among the consumers are contrary to those of the other user roles. They tend to use Jodel even without karma points and voting function, because consumers are not using these features anyway. Since they do not create their own content, there is a negative correlation to the joy caused by successful postings.

RQ4b: What user groups can be detected based on their attitude towards gamification elements on Jodel?

Within the scope of the cluster analysis, five different user groups emerged based on their attitude towards Jodel's gamification elements. Overall, it can be seen that all clusters would tend to use Jodel even without karma points, while opinions on the voting function vary widely. The members of the first and largest cluster would apply the service without karma points, but not without the voting function. The points also have no influence on their voting behavior. Achieving the "loudest" posting causes great joy among the members. This user group attaches great importance to the voting function and based on the great joy about successful own postings it can be assumed that it is not only about voting on content of others, but also about receiving votes. The second cluster is quite small and differs greatly from the other ones. There is no doubt about interest in the service without karma points and the voting function is also less important to the members. Their voting behavior is not influenced by karma points and joy about successful postings is not noticeable in this user group. Based on these aspects it can be concluded that this user group represents consumers who do not use these functions anyway and do not publish own content. None of the five clusters attaches great importance to karma points, whereas members of the third cluster appear to slightly respond to this function. For them, the voting function seems to be rather important. In turn, the feeling of joy about successful postings is very important. Interesting is the discrepancy between the importance of karma points and the voting behavior. Although the members would principally use Jodel without the points, they readily use the voting function with the underlying motive to earn karma points. Karma points do not play any role in the rather small fourth cluster, nor do they regarding the voting behavior. The members show a neutral attitude towards the voting function and the joy about successful postings. It is reasonable to assume that the members of this user group behave less interactive, but occasionally publish their own content and rate others. The karma points are also unimportant in the fifth cluster and do not really play a role in voting. It is noticeable that the voting function has no relevance for use in this cluster. Nevertheless, the members react with great joy on successful own postings, for which the voting function is essential. This suggests that the members of the last user group hardly use the voting function themselves, but still like to have their own postings rated by other users.

5   Implications and Limitations

The study has shown that Jodel would be used even without karma points, but for some users the points definitely represent an incentive to use the service. A more detailed investigation of why exactly Jodel's users find the virtual points so attractive, would have gone beyond the scope of this study, but remains a highly interesting aspect to investigate in the future. The karma points can neither be compared (e.g., on a leaderboard) nor used (e.g., for any add-ons or hidden functions) in any way and nevertheless, they seem to have a strong attraction for quite a few users. Another interesting aspect that was revealed by this study is that there is a user group that is interested in finding friends or even a partnership through the app. An investigation of the transition from a completely anonymous platform to a real friendship or partnership could certainly provide valuable insights, as such networks are usually used precisely because of their anonymity and are often associated with alternative behavior [3]. In the study, the three active user roles often showed similar tendencies, but it still became clear that motivations, incentives, and opinions differ according to the user role. Especially the consumers mostly had a contrary behavior. Jodel's developers could use this insight to conduct a study on satisfaction and user needs based on these user roles. In this way, it might be possible to determine which of the roles are probably less satisfied and therefore need special attention regarding new features and future innovations.

Should the findings of this study be used for future research, some limitations should be considered in order to avoid misleading conclusions. At first, there is an unequal distribution between female and male participants, almost exactly 2/3 of the participants were female. In addition, Jodel has become a popular anonymous social network in many countries, but the online survey was only distributed and conducted in Germany. Should there be regional differences within Germany regarding the users' opinions, it cannot be guaranteed that these are completely covered, as the survey was mainly distributed in the vicinity of North Rhine-Westphalia and sporadically in more distant German cities. At the time of the survey, Jodel still had the status of being a student app, which is why the majority of survey participants also reflect this target group. The planning of an expansion to other target groups has already been announced in an interview with the founder of the app [8] and is already going ahead. For this reason, a sample of users may present different demographic data within a short period of time and therefore express different views and opinions.

References

1. Blumler, J.G., Katz, E.: The Uses of Mass Communications: Current Perspectives on Gratifications Research. Sage, Newbury Park (1974)
2. Shao, G.: Understanding the appeal of user-generated media: a uses and gratification perspective. Internet Res. 19(1), 7–25 (2009). https://doi.org/10.1108/10662240910927795
3. Joinson, A.: Social desirability, anonymity, and Internet-based questionnaires. Behav. Res. Methods Instru. Comput. 31(3), 433–438 (1999). https://doi.org/10.3758/BF03200723
4. Berthold, O., Federrath, H., Köhntopp, M.: Project "anonymity and unobservability in the Internet". In: Proceedings of the Tenth Conference on Computers, Freedom and Privacy: Challenging the Assumptions, pp. 57–65. ACM, New York (2000). https://doi.org/10.1145/332186.332211
5. Christopherson, K.M.: The positive and negative implications of anonymity in Internet social interactions: "On the Internet, Nobody Knows You're a Dog". Comput. Hum. Behav. 23(6), 3038–3056 (2007). https://doi.org/10.1016/j.chb.2006.09.001
6. Kang, R., Brown, S., Kiesler, S.: Why do people seek anonymity on the internet?: informing policy and design. In: Proceedings of the SIGCHI Conference on Human Factors in Computing Systems, pp. 2657–2666. ACM, New York (2013). https://doi.org/10.1145/2470654.2481368
7. Kasakowskij, R., Friedrich, N., Fietkiewicz, K.J., Stock, W.G.: Anonymous and non-anonymous user behavior on social media. J. Inf. Sci. Theory Pract. 6(3), 25–36 (2018)
8. Nowak, P., Jüttner, K., Baran, Katsiaryna S.: Posting content, collecting points, staying anonymous: an evaluation of jodel. In: Meiselwitz, G. (ed.) SCSM 2018. LNCS, vol. 10913, pp. 67–86. Springer, Cham (2018). https://doi.org/10.1007/978-3-319-91521-0_6

9. Graham, J.: Yik Yak, The once popular and controversial college messaging app, Shuts Down. USA Today, 28 April 2017. https://www.usatoday.com/story/tech/talkingtech/2017/04/28/yik-yak-shut-down/101045670/. Accessed 02 Oct 2021

10. Scherkamp, H.: Warum Studenten die App Jodel lieben - und Promi-Investoren auch. Gründerszene, 25 August 2015. https://www.gruenderszene.de/allgemein/jodel-app-erfolg. Accessed 02 Oct 2021

11. Caffier, J.: Community-Feedback und Verhalten in sozialen Medien: Eine empirische Analyse subjektiver und objektiver Faktoren am Beispiel der App Jodel (bachelor's thesis) (2015). https://books.google.de/books/about/Community_Feedback_und_Verhalten_in_sozi.html?id=SDM9DwAAQBAJ&redir_esc=y. Accessed 02 Oct 2021

12. Schlenk, C.T.: Studenten-App Jodel erhält sechs Millionen – und will in die USA expandieren. Gründerszene, June 7, 2017. https://www.gruenderszene.de/allgemein/jodel-studenten-app-usa-millionen. Accessed 2021/10/02

13. Kreuter, S.: Frust und Fun für alle. Frankfurter Allgemeine Zeitung, 7 August 2017. http://www.faz.net/aktuell/stil/leib-seele/jodel-app-anonym-lokal-und-lustig-kommunizieren-15126386.html. Accessed 02 Oct 2021

14. Johann, M., Wiedel, F., Tonndorf, K., Windscheid, J.: Anonymous online communication between disinhibition, self-disclosure and social identity. a complementary mixed-method study. In: Presentation on the ICA Annual Conference, 9–13 June 2016, Fukoka, Japan (2016)

15. Johann, M., Wiedel, F., Tonndorf, K., Windscheid, J.: #jodlerhelfenjodlern - Enthemmung, Devianz und prosoziales Verhalten in anonymen Kommunikationsräumen. In: Poster session presented at the Annual Convention of the DGPuK, Leipzig, Germany (2016)

16. Böhm, A., Taubmann, B., Reiser, H.P.: Geographic localization of an anonymous social network message data set. In: 2016 11th International Conference on Availability, Reliability and Security (ARES), pp. 844–850. IEEE Computer Society, Washington, D.C. (2016). https://doi.org/10.1109/ares.2016.47

17. Schumann, L., Stock, W.G.: The information service evaluation (ISE) model. Webology 11(1), 1–20 (2014). https://doi.org/10.3233/ISU-140759

18. O'Leary, K., Murphy, S.: Moving beyond Goffman: the performativity of anonymity on SNS. Eur. J. Mark. (2018). https://doi.org/10.1108/EJM-01-2017-0016

19. Wombacher, K., Reno, J.E., Williams, G.A., Johnson, L.: Does Yik Yak promote risky health behavior on college campuses? Health Commun. 33(4), 372–378 (2018). https://doi.org/10.1080/10410236.2016.1266577

20. Seigfried-Spellar, K.C., Lankford, C.M.: Personality and online environment factors differ for posters, trolls, lurkers, and confessors on Yik Yak. Pers. Indiv. Diff. 124, 54–56 (2018). https://doi.org/10.1016/j.paid.2017.11.047

21. Lane, D.S., Das, V., Hiaeshutter-Rice, D.: Civic laboratories: youth political expression in anonymous, ephemeral, geo-bounded social media. Inf. Commun. Soc. 1–16. https://doi.org/10.1080/1369118x.2018.1477973

22. Katz, E., Foulkes, D.: On the use of mass media as "Escape": clarification of a concept. Pub. Opin. Quart. 26(3), 377–388 (1962). https://doi.org/10.1086/267111

23. Katz, E., Blumler, J.G., Gurevitch, M.: Uses and gratifications research. Pub. Opin. Quart. 37, 509–523 (1973)

24. Rubin, A.M.: Uses and gratifications perspective on media effects. In: Bryant, J., Oliver, M.B. (eds.) Media effects: Advances in theory and research, 3rd edn., pp. 165–184. Routledge, New York, NY (2009)

25. McQuail, D.: Mass Communication Theory. Sage, London (1983)

26. Deterding, S., Dixon, D., Khaled, R., Nacke, L.: From game design elements to gamefulness: defining "Gamification". In: Lugmayr, A., Franssila, H., Safran, C., Hammouda, I. (eds.) Proceedings of the 15th International Academic MindTrek Conference: Envisioning Future Media Environments, pp. 9–11. ACM, New York (2011). https://doi.org/10.1145/2181037.2181040

27. Zichermann, G., Cunningham, C.: Gamification by Design: Implementing Game Mechanics in Web and Mobile Apps. O'Reilly Media Inc, Sebastopol (2011)

28. Deterding, S.: Gamification: Designing for Motivation. Interactions **19**(4), 14–17 (2012). https://doi.org/10.1145/2212877.2212883

29. Knautz, K., Göretz, J., Wintermeyer, A.: "Gotta catch 'em all" - game design patterns for guild quests in higher education. In: Kindling, M., Greifeneder, E. (eds.) IConference 2014 Proceedings, pp. 690–699. iSchools, Illinois (2014). https://doi.org/10.9776/14010

30. Nicholson, S.: A RECIPE for meaningful gamification. In: Reiners, T., Wood, Lincoln C. (eds.) Gamification in Education and Business, pp. 1–20. Springer, Cham (2015). https://doi.org/10.1007/978-3-319-10208-5_1

31. Knautz, K.: Gamification im Kontext der Vermittlung von Informationskompetenz. In: Gust von Loh, S., Stock, W.G. (eds.) Informationskompetenz in der Schule. Ein informationswissenschaftlicher Ansatz, pp. 223–257. De Gruyter Saur, Berlin, Boston (2012)

32. Scheibe, K., Göretz, G., Meschede, C., Stock, W.G.: Giving and taking gratifications in a gamified social live streamin service. In Proceedings of the European Conference of Social Media, 21–22 June 2018, Limerick, pp. 264–273. Academic Conferences and Publishing International Limited, Reading, UK (2018)

33. Deterding, S., Sicart, M., Nacke, L., O'Hara, K., Dixon, D.: Gamification: using game design elements in non-gaming contexts. In: Proceedings of the 2011 Annual Conference Extended Abstracts on Human Factors in Computing Systems, pp. 2425–2428. ACM, New York (2011). https://doi.org/10.1145/1979742.1979575

34. Blohm, I., Leimeister, J.M.: Gestaltung IT-basierter Zusatzdienstleistungen zur Motivationsunterstützung und Verhaltensänderung. Wirtschaftsinformatik **55**(4), 275–278 (2013). https://doi.org/10.1007/s11576-013-0368-0

35. Karma Reform. https://jodel.com/blog/karma-reform/. Accessed 02 Oct 2021

36. Likert, R.: A technique for the measurement of attitudes. Arch. Psychol. **22**(140), 5–55 (1932)

37. Fietkiewicz, K.J.: Jumping the digital divide: How do "silver surfers" and "digital immigrants" use social media? Netw. Knowl. **10**(1), 5–26 (2017)

38. Zimmer, F., Scheibe, K., Stock, Wolfgang G.: A model for information behavior research on social live streaming services (SLSSs). In: Meiselwitz, G. (ed.) SCSM 2018. LNCS, vol. 10914, pp. 429–448. Springer, Cham (2018). https://doi.org/10.1007/978-3-319-91485-5_33

39. Bortz J., Döring N.: Forschungsmethoden und Evaluation. Springer, Berlin, Heidelberg (2006). https://doi.org/10.1007/978-3-540-33306-7

40. Cohen, J.: A power primer. Psychol. Bull. **112**(1), 155–159 (1992). https://doi.org/10.1037/0033-2909.112.1.155

41. Palfrey, J.G., Gasser, U.: Born Digital: Understanding the First Generation of Digital Natives. Basic Books, New York (2008)

42. Prensky, M.: Digital natives, digital immigrants. On the Horizon **9**(5), 1–6 (2001)

A Study on Influencing Factors on Internet Banking Usage During the SARS-CoV-2 Pandemic in Romania

Valentin Mihai Leoveanu[✉], Mihaela Cornelia Sandu, and Adela Coman

University of Bucharest, Bucharest, Romania
{valentin.leoveanu,mihaela.sandu,adela.coman}@faa.unibuc.ro

Abstract. The purpose of this research is to present and analyze the evolutions of Internet Banking in the conditions of the SARS-CoV-2 pandemic crisis in Romania throughout 2020 considering the typology of respondents in correlation with their needs and requirements for the characteristics and types of Internet Banking services available.

The research design was based on a statistical analysis both quantitative and qualitative, following the motivational and attitudinal changes in the use of Internet Banking services as a result of the manifestations of the SARS-CoV-2 pandemic crisis. As a primary tool, it was a questionnaire consisting of a series of questions of a general nature, but also directed to the purpose of the research, in a total of 25 questions. The questions asked to achieve the purpose of the research concerned: the influencing factors regarding the use of Internet Banking before and during the pandemic, the restrictions imposed by the bank as a result of the pandemic crisis that influenced the use of Internet Banking, the types of Internet Banking services most often used before and during the pandemic, as well as the level of money spent on Internet Banking and electronic devices used for this purpose.

The results presented by the authors as a result of the research undertaken highlighted as factors with a positive influence on the use of Internet Banking during the SARS-CoV-2 pandemic crisis in Romania in 2020 as: avoiding the queues at the bank counter, availability 24/7 of this service, time economy, and restrictions imposed by the banks while as factors with negative influence were shown to be the problems related to access to this type of service: limited internet access, technical problems, long time to complete transactions, security issues.

Keywords: Internet banking services · SARS-CoV-2 · Customer' financial behavior · Pandemic crisis restrictions · Payment methods · Electronic devices

1 Introduction

The multitude and magnitude of the transformations encountered by human society in all fields of activity as a result of the manifestation of the SARS CoV-2 pandemic crisis were also reflected in the banking field, mainly through the amplified use of remote electronic devices and the related banking interface, on short, the Internet Banking.

© Springer Nature Switzerland AG 2021
G. Meiselwitz (Ed.): HCII 2021, LNCS 12774, pp. 74–86, 2021.
https://doi.org/10.1007/978-3-030-77626-8_5

As a result of such evolutions, the authors of the present research aimed to highlight the influencing factors and particularities associated with the use of Internet banking in order to highlight the intensification of human interaction with banking institutions in the electronic environment following the constraints.

The study considered the realization and application of a questionnaire addressed to the general public, which included students from the University of Bucharest, Romania, as well as the processing of data and information collected by concretizing a quantitative analysis in statistical terms, which comes to add a qualitative analysis, to explain and understand the results obtained.

It is widely acknowledged that with the manifestations of the SARS CoV-2 health crisis, banks have begun to adapt and adapt their business to new challenges by adopting new digital business models. They tried to meet the requirements of customers as they changed their habits of payment and financial transactions and needed more support from banks in choosing financial instruments. At the same time as the introduction of new facilities and tools adapted to customer requirements, banks had to deal with the growing needs for protection of customers' personal data, as well as the security of banking transactions and the identification of suspicious or fraudulent operations in the field. Banks also faced adjusting to new health regulations and combating the spread of the SARS CoV-2 virus, so they had to adjust their actions in accordance with national and international banking laws and regulations.

The factors pursued by the authors in the research refer on the one hand to the ways of accessing and using banking services on the Internet, but also to the way in which the use of these services has led to increased consumption of goods and services through the Internet due to quarantine and social distancing in various areas and localities in Romania.

The corollary of the study in question comes to emphasize, along with the main factors involved in stimulating the use of Internet banking services, the importance of decisions taken at the level of banking management regarding banking services and products offered to Internet customers in unfavorable economic conditions caused by SARS-CoV- 2.

At the same time, the highlighted research results come to offer an image on the way in which the users of internet banking services relate to them. In this sense, banks must recognize the importance of these influencing factors and take them into account in further adapting their services to ensure customer satisfaction.

The purpose of this research is to present and analyze the evolutions of Internet Banking in the conditions of the SARS-CoV-2 pandemic crisis in Romania throughout 2020 considering the typology of respondents in correlation with their needs and requirements for the characteristics and types of Internet Banking services available.

The research design was based on a statistical analysis both quantitative and qualitative, following the motivational and attitudinal changes in the use of Internet Banking services as a result of the manifestations of the SARS-CoV-2 pandemic crisis. As a primary tool, it was a questionnaire consisting of a series of questions of a general nature, but also directed to the purpose of the research, in a total of 25 questions. The questions asked to achieve the purpose of the research concerned: the influencing factors regarding the use of Internet Banking before and during the pandemic, the restrictions imposed by the bank as a result of the pandemic crisis that influenced the use of Internet Banking, the types of Internet Banking services most often used before and during the pandemic, as well as the level of money spent on Internet Banking and electronic devices used for this purpose. Also, the payment methods most often applied in Internet Banking before and during the pandemic of 2020 in Romania were taken into account, as well as the problems encountered by users in accessing services. The qualitative research aimed at highlighting the connection between the influencing factors thus highlighted and the motivational and attitudinal aspects of the responding clients, aspects that led to the use of Internet Banking during the SARS-CoV-2 pandemic crisis in Romania in 2020.

The results presented by the authors as a result of the research undertaken highlighted as factors with a positive influence on the use of Internet Banking during the SARS-CoV-2 pandemic crisis in Romania in 2020 as: avoiding the queues at the bank counter, availability 24/7 of this service, time economy, and restrictions imposed by the banks while as factors with negative influence were shown to be the problems related to access to this type of service: limited internet access, technical problems, long time to complete transactions, security issues.

The originality of the study undertaken by the authors is reflected by the investigation directions chosen to highlight the evolutions regarding the use of Internet Banking in the periods before and during the pandemic crisis and by sizing the factors that significantly influenced the behavior of banking clients in relation to restrictions. or leisure. The obtained results constitute working premises for other researches both in the field and interdisciplinary, having an impact on the ways in which banks will focus in the future on facilitating the use of Internet Banking services.

The authors were limited in their research by the size of the respondents to the applied questionnaire, which implies in the future the consideration of a much larger number of respondents to validate and better appreciate the research done. Also, a limitation is highlighted by the time of investigation available and by restricting the number of motivating factors possible to have an impact on the use of Internet Banking services.

2 Literature Review

A review of literature regarding the adoption of Internet Banking by bank customers was offered by Anukool Manish Hyde (2015) from which the authors of this paper have selected some paragraphs: "The rise of Internet Banking is [...] due to its number of benefits for both the provider and the customer as well. From the bank's perspective these are mainly related to cost savings (Sathye, 1999; Robinson, 2000) and internet banking remain one of the cheapest and more efficient delivery channels (see Pikkarainen et al., 2004). Other rationales for the adoption of such services are also related to competition as internet banking strategy has been an interesting way to retain existing customers and attract new ones (Robinson, 2000) and to the numerous advantages to banks for instance, mass customization, more effective marketing and communication at lower costs amongst others (Tuchila, 2000). Benefits for the end users are numerous as well and include mainly conveniency of the service (time saved and globally accessible service), lower cost of transaction and more frequent monitoring of accounts among others (Pikkarainen et al., 2004). However, it should also be noted that there are still customers who fear to make use of Internet banking, as they are concerned with security aspects of such a system" [6].

Other research in this regard is highlighted in the following paragraphs: "Centeno (2004) argues that speed, the convenience of remote access, 24/7 availability and price incentives are the main motivation factors for the consumers to use internet banking. Durkin et al. (2008) notes that the simplicity of the products offered via internet banking facilitates the adoption of internet banking by consumers. Calisir and Gumussoy (2008) compare the consumer perception of internet banking and other banking channels and report that internet banking, ATM and phone banking substitute each other. Maenpaa et al. (2008) examine the consumer perceptions of internet banking in Finland and their findings indicate that familiarity has a moderating role in the perception. Guerrero et al. (2007) examine the usage of internet banking by Europeans and their results indicate that ownership of diverse financial products and services, attitude towards finances and trust in the internet as a banking channel influence clients "usage of internet banking" [6].

In their paper entitled "The factors influencing customer usage of Mobile Banking services in Jordan" the authors reveal the elements that determine the adoption of mobile banking services in Jordan with reference to two groups of factors: "the first represents the motivating factors that drive customers to use mobile banking services, it includes five factors: (Assurance, ease of use, communication, speed of transaction, pursuance), the second are the factors impeding the use of mobile banking services, which represent obstacles that prevent the use of mobile banking services, it also includes five factors: (Personal desires, knowledge, habit, resistance to innovations, experience)" [3]. The research consisted in developing a study model "made up of six dimensions with six developed hypotheses one per each corresponding dimension, with the exception of the sixth hypothesis which has been divided into two sub-hypotheses" [3]. Conclusions of the study shows that the motivating factors have a considerable influence on the use of banking services, and explain "that the effect of motivating factors is more significant than the effect of impeding factors" [3].

Another paper studies "the factors that affect the adoption of Internet banking by Tunisian bank customers" [13] by using the well-known patterns regarding the technology acceptance model (TAM) associated to the theory of planned behavior (TPB) and considering factors like "security and privacy, self-efficacy, government support, and technology support, in addition to perceived usefulness, perceived ease of use, attitude, social norm, perceived behavior control and intention to use Internet banking" [13]. The analysis thus performed by the authors allows the decision makers within the banks to better understand the mechanisms of attracting the clientele to the use of Internet Banking and to take the inspired decisions accordingly.

In the study "Factors Affecting E-Banking Adoption and Its Impact on Customer Satisfaction: A Case Study of Ethiopian Banks" the authors tried "to identify current customers of e-banking by predicting their intention to use and its acceptance and impacts on customer satisfaction in selected banks of Ethiopia" [8]. The results show that "the perceived ease of use and perceived usefulness were significantly influences the intentions of e-banking users, intentions of e-banking were significantly influences the actual usage of e-banking services and lastly actual usage of electronic banking affect customer satisfaction" [8].

A study of Musiime and Ramadhan (2011) on Internet Banking "focused on consumer adoption and customer satisfaction especially in the African setting" and "was conducted to determine the factors that influence consumer adoption of Internet banking service as well as examine the relationship between Internet banking service, customer adoption and customer satisfaction" [11]. An interesting conclusion of this paper is that "Internet banking service providers ought to look out for indicators of innovative ways of creating awareness about the service through participation in trade organizations, exhibitions as well as adoption of new technologies of Internet banking" [11].

The authors Montazemi & Qahri-Saremi (2015) appealed to "the Grounded-Theory Literature Review method to review the online banking literature" in order to "identify factors affecting pre-adoption and post-adoption of the online banking" [10]. The analysis was based on "two-stage random-effects MASEM to assess our theoretical models" and the results expose that "ten factors affect consumers' adoption of the online banking"and "the relative importance of ten factors depends on the stage of adoption" [10].

The paper "Factors Influencing the Adoption of Internet Banking in Tunisia" aimed "to determine those factors that influence the adoption of internet banking services in Tunisia" shows "that use of internet banking in Tunisia is influenced most strongly by convenience, risk, security and prior internet knowledge. [...] The results also propose that demographic factors impact significantly internet banking behavior, specifically, occupation and instruction" [12].

The main purpose targeted in the research of Ahmed E. & Phin G.S. (2016) was to inquire "on how demographic characteristics, social factors, and consumer perceptions and attitudes towards internet banking influence the adoption of internet banking in an emerging economy like Malaysia" highlighting "that social factors were strongly influence the adoption of internet banking in [...] Malaysia" [1].

Important results are shown in the work of Ming-Chi Lee (2009) revealing "that the intention to use online banking is adversely affected mainly by the security/privacy risk, as well as financial risk and is positively affected mainly by perceived benefit, attitude and perceived usefulness" [9].

The study conducted by Shaikh F.M., Kazi Z.H., Khaskheley A. (2014) shows "that demographic factors [...] impact significantly on online banking" and "that an understanding the factors affecting intention to use internet banking is very important to the practitioners who plan and promote new forms of banking in the current competitive market" [15].

The author of the paper "Measuring E-Service Quality and Customer Satisfaction with Internet Banking in India" had as research objectives "to explore the critical factors of e-service quality of internet banking in India and to measure the customers' satisfaction of internet banking on the identified e-service quality dimensions" and in this regard he presented "three factors of e-service quality, namely, 'Responsiveness', 'Efficiency', and 'Perceived Credibility' in order to identify "that there is a positive relationship [...] between e-service quality dimensions and customer satisfaction of internet banking" [16].

Al-Qeisi K., Hegazy A. (2015) analysed in their paper "whether information technology adoption/usage is ubiquitous, especially technology imported into non-industrial nations" and their analysis reveals that "facilitating conditions were not strong determinants of usage behavior and social influences were weak determinants of behavior intentions. However, performance expectancy and effort expectancy were found to be key determinants of internet banking usage behavior" [2].

In the research of Vinayek R, Jindal P. (2011) are presented "key antecedents of e-service quality that can lead customer preference towards internet banking offerings of a particular bank" and authors carried on "discriminant analysis to screen the perception of customers towards public sector bank and private sector bank internet banking service quality and to find out which variables are relatively better in predicting customers' preference towards internet banking offerings of a particular bank" [17].

A research conducted by Omar A., Sultan N., Zaman K., Bibi N., Wajid A. and Khan K. (2011) investigating "the customer perception, preferences, problems and suggestions about online banking in Pakistan" has shown "that mostly customers prefer internet banking (IB) services over branch banking due to reliability, convenience, speed, safety and security, cost effectiveness, user-friendly, and error free system. In contrast the parallel finding shows that security problems, lack of trust and knowledge, ATM machine problems etc. affect the adoption decision of customers of internet banking services" [14].

A recent work of Anouze, A.L.M. & Alamro, A.S. (2019) evidenced "that several major factors, including perceived ease of use, perceived usefulness, security and reasonable price, stand out as the barriers to intention to use e-banking services in Jordan" [4]. The study highlighted as original features "a series of implications on intention to use e-banking. It draws the attention of Jordanian banks to the full functionality of their e-banking systems, emphasizing positive safety features, which could contribute to changing negative customer perceptions. It also contributes to eliciting the theory of customer value among banks by focusing on how they should properly enhance their use of shared value" [4].

In a scientific paper of Ege Oruç Ö., Tatar Ç. (2017), the authors developed an analysis using a structural equation model which conduct to the conclusions "that 'Benefits of Internet Banking', 'Communication' and 'Convenience' significantly influence customers' Internet banking use" and that "the model helps to increase our understanding of how these factors interact to influence Internet banking use, which can help in the design of Internet banking" [5].

An important review on Mobile Banking as an instrument of Internet Banking was done by Kelly A.E., Palaniappan S. (2019) and shows that "security remains one of the principal constructs that hinder users in adopting and post-adoption of mobile banking. The research also showed that the most used model in mobile banking was TAM. Again, trust, perceived usefulness, perceived ease of use, perceived risk, compatible, and performance and effort expectation constructs remain the most studied variable in the mobile banking literature" [7].

3 Analysis of Influencing Factors on Internet Banking Usage During the SARS-CoV-2 Pandemic in Romania

3.1 Research Design

The purpose of this research is to present and analyze the evolutions of Internet Banking in the conditions of the SARS-CoV-2 pandemic crisis in Romania throughout 2020 considering the typology of respondents in correlation with their needs and requirements for the characteristics and types of Internet Banking services available.

The research design was based on a statistical analysis both quantitative and qualitative, following the motivational and attitudinal changes in the use of Internet Banking services as a result of the manifestations of the SARS-CoV-2 pandemic crisis. As a primary tool, it was a questionnaire consisting of a series of questions of a general nature, but also directed to the purpose of the research, in a total of 25 questions. The questions asked to achieve the purpose of the research concerned: the influencing factors regarding the use of Internet Banking before and during the pandemic, the restrictions imposed by the bank as a result of the pandemic crisis that influenced the use of Internet Banking, the types of Internet Banking services most often used before and during the pandemic, as well as the level of money spent on Internet Banking and electronic devices used for this purpose. Also, the payment methods most often applied in Internet Banking before and during the pandemic of 2020 in Romania were taken into account, as well as the problems encountered by users in accessing services. The qualitative research aimed at highlighting the connection between the influencing factors thus highlighted and the motivational and attitudinal aspects of the responding clients, aspects that led to the use of Internet Banking during the SARS-CoV-2 pandemic crisis in Romania in 2020.

The set of questions attached to the questionnaire by the authors included the following:

- Which of the following factors have influenced your use of Internet Banking?
- To what extent did the restrictions imposed by the COVID-19 pandemic crisis influence your use of Internet Banking?
- What restrictions imposed by banks following the COVID-19 pandemic crisis have influenced your use of Internet Banking?
- How often do you use Internet Banking services in general?
- Do you use Internet Banking services more often now than before the COVID-19 pandemic crisis?
- What types of Internet Banking services do you use?
- What Internet Banking services did you use most often during the COVID-19 pandemic crisis?
- What is your approximate monthly amount when you use Internet Banking services?
- Did you spend more during the pandemic than before using Internet Banking services?
- What devices do you use to access Internet Banking services? (Multiple answer)
- What devices have you used more in the pandemic period than before for access to Internet Banking services?
- What is the payment method you use in Internet Banking? (Multiple answer)

- What payment methods offered by Internet Banking did you use more during the pandemic period than before?
- What problems did you encounter when using Internet Banking services? (Multiple answer)
- Did you save more during the pandemic than before using Internet Banking?
- Have you used more pandemic lending than before using Internet Banking?

The analysis is based on data obtained from respondents based on the application of the questionnaire and is discussed below.

3.2 Data and Sample

The sample was formed by 241 respondents. From total respondents there were 77.59% female and 22.41% male (Fig. 1). Majority of the respondents, 59.34%, were 21–30 years old, 20.75% were 18–20 years old, 11.62% were 31–40 years old, 4.15% were 41–50 years old, 2.90% were 51–65 years old, 0.83% were over 65 years old and 0.41% were 18–20 and 21–30 years old.

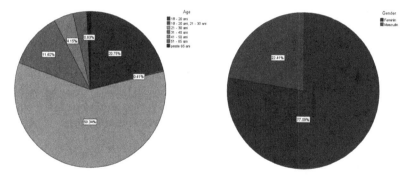

Fig. 1. Age & gender (Source: authors calculations by using SPSS)

With a majority of 69.71% they have residence in Bucharest, 15.77% were from Muntenia (south-east of Romania), 6.22% were from Oltenia (south-west of Romania), 4.15% were from Moldova (east of Romania), 2.07% were from Dobrogea (south-south-east of Romania), 1.24% were from Ardeal (centre of Romania), 0.41% were from Crisana (west of Romania) and 0.41% were from Moldavian Republic (Fig. 2).

In terms of income, majority, 30.71%, declared they earn over 3500 lei, then 14.94% said they earn 501–1000 lei, 13.69% earn 0–500 lei, 10.79% earn 2501–3000 lei, 8.71% earn 1001–1500 lei or 1501–2000 lei, 7.05% earn 2001–2500 lei and 5.39% earn 3001–3500 lei (Fig. 2). Regarding the occupation of the respondents, 41.1% are students, 7.1% are students and are also working, 0.8% don't have a job in this moment and the rest of respondents work in different branches of the economy or are retired. In terms of income source, 1% said social aid, 5% said scholarship, 5% said scholarship and parents, 2% said scholarship and parents, 4% said salary and parents, 19% said parents and the rest of respondents said only salary or pension.

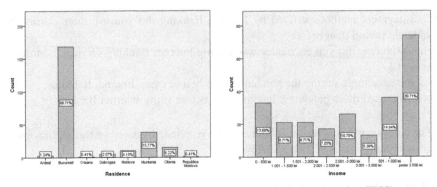

Fig. 2. Residence & income (Source: authors calculations by using SPSS)

Majority of respondents said they are using internet banking services, 87.97% (Fig. 3). The reasons why people who answered no to this question do not use internet banking are familiarity with internet banking and security. Almost a half of people who are not using internet banking said that it is likely or very likely to use it in the future. Because we are interested in the opinion of users regarding internet banking services, further we will consider only the people who answered yes to this question. The main reasons for using internet banking are avoiding the queues at the bank counter, availability 24/7, time economy, rapidity and safety of the transactions. In terms of the influence of pandemic SARS-COV-2 on internet banking usage, 33.96% said they were not influenced, 19.81% said they were very little influenced, 15.06% said they were little influenced, 14.15% said they were a lot influenced and 4.72% said they were very much influenced. We can see from respondents answers that a small part of them were influenced by pandemic SARS-COV-2 to use internet banking (Fig. 3).

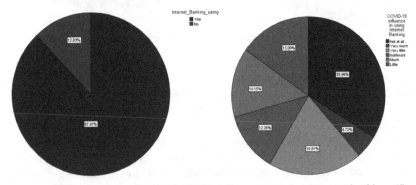

Fig. 3. Internet banking using & SARS-COV-2 influence on using Internet banking. (Source: authors calculations by using SPSS)

In terms of internet banking frequency, majority of respondents, 34.43%, said once at 2–3 days; 19.81% said they use it daily, 18.40% once a week, 14.15% two times a month, 7.08% once a month and 5.66% several times a day (Fig. 4). It seems that pandemic SARS-COV-2 didn't have a significant impact on frequency of internet banking using, 48.10% respondents said they don't use it more often, 40.10% said the frequency increased and 11.8% said they don't know if they use it more often or not. All the respondents said they use internet banking to check the balance, 98.6% use internet banking for payments, more than a half use internet banking for bank transfer, saving or investment. The reasons why people use internet banking services more often because of pandemic SARS-COV-2 are payments, checking the balance, saving; a new category has emerged in this case, lending. In terms of monthly amount spent using internet banking, almost a half said 0–500 lei or 501–1000 lei and almost a quarter of respondents said 1001–1500 lei or over 3500 lei (Fig. 4).

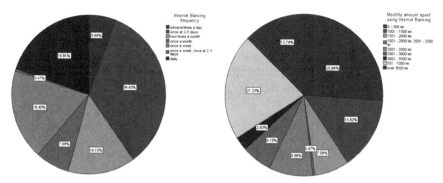

Fig. 4. Internet banking frequency & monthly amount spent using internet banking. (Source: authors calculations by using SPSS)

In a percentage of 33.5% the respondents said that they spent more using internet banking in period of pandemic SARS-COV-2 then before, 41% said they didn't spend more. In terms of device used for using internet banking services, 74.5% said smartphone. From the answers received it seems that the payment method used in internet banking is bank card and bank transfer; also, it seems that pandemic SARS-COV-2 determined people to use bank card more often than before. The problems encountered by the respondents when they used internet banking during the pandemic were limited access to the internet, technical problems and problems in monitoring transactions in real time. Respondents said in equal percentage of 45.8% that they are inclined toward saving and consumption from own money. Almost a half of them said they didn't save more during the pandemic SARS-COV-2.

4 Results: Interpretation and Discussions

The analysis made in the present study revealed a series of important results in the context of following the evolution of the use of Internet Banking services before and during the SARS-CoV-2 pandemic crisis in Romania in 2020.

A first result is shown by the fact that most of the respondents said they are using internet banking services regulary by using smartphone devices. The main reasons for using internet banking are exemplified to be: avoiding the queues at the bank counter, availability 24/7 of this service, time economy, rapidity and safety of the transactions.

A second result highlight that pandemic crisis of SARS-CoV-2 didn't have a major impact on using internet banking, most of the people used this service with the same frequency before pandemic period.

Regarding the frequency of use, most of the people declared they use internet banking once at 2–3 days and pandemic SARS-COV-2 didn't have a significant impact on frequency of internet banking using. Internet banking services are used to check the balance, for payments, bank transfer, saving or investment. The SARS-CoV-2 Pandemic Crisis has motivated the increased use of Internet Banking in order to solicit and achieve a new reason for the use of Internet banking, loans.

Another result shown that people who used internet banking declared they spent more during pandemic SARS-COV-2 than before and even they are inclined toward saving they couldn't save money during pandemic SARS-COV-2. It seems also that pandemic SARS-COV-2 determined people to use bank card more often than before. Limited access to the internet, technical problems and problems in monitoring transactions in real time are the main problems faced by users of internet banking during pandemic SARS-COV-2.

5   Conclusions

The results presented by the authors as a result of the research undertaken highlighted as factors with a positive influence on the use of Internet Banking during the SARS-CoV-2 pandemic crisis in Romania in 2020 as: avoiding the queues at the bank counter, availability 24/7 of this service, time economy, and restrictions imposed by the banks while as factors with negative influence were shown to be the problems related to access to this type of service: limited internet access, technical problems, long time to complete transactions, security issues.

5.1   Original Contribution

The originality of the study undertaken by the authors is reflected by the investigation directions chosen to highlight the evolutions regarding the use of Internet Banking in the periods before and during the pandemic crisis and by sizing the factors that significantly influenced the behavior of banking clients in relation to restrictions. or leisure. The obtained results constitute working premises for other researches both in the field and interdisciplinary, having an impact on the ways in which banks will focus in the future on facilitating the use of Internet Banking services.

5.2   Limitations

The authors were limited in their research by the size of the respondents to the applied questionnaire, which implies in the future the consideration of a much larger number of respondents to validate and better appreciate the research done. Also, a limitation is highlighted by the time of investigation available and by restricting the number of motivating factors possible to have an impact on the use of Internet Banking services.

5.3 Future Approach

Subsequent research to be undertaken by the authors will need to take into account certain types of limitations that have been highlighted in current research, as well as the possibility of approaching the TAM (Technology Acceptance Model) for a clearer and more comprehensive determination of factors. which influences the use of Internet Banking with targeted addressability to decision makers at the banking level.

References

Ahmed, E., Phin, G.S.: Factors influencing the adoption of internet banking in Malaysia. J. Internet Bank. Commerc. **21** (2016). https://www.researchgate.net/publication/301678545_Factors_I nfluencing_the_Adoption_of_Internet_Banking_in_Malaysia/citation/download

Al-Qeisi, K., Hegazy, A.: Consumer online behaviour: a perspective on internet banking usage in three non-western countries. Procedia Econ. Financ. **23**, 386–390 (2015). https://doi.org/10. 1016/S2212-5671(15)00347-0

Vinayek, R., Jindal, P.: An empirical investigation of key antecedents of customer preference of internet banking in Indian context. Asia Pacif. Bus. Rev. **7**(3), 63–71 (2011). https://doi.org/ 10.1177/097324701100700306

Alsamydai, M.J., Yassen, S.G., Alnaimi, H.M., Dajani, D.M. Al-Qirem, I.A.: The factors influencing customer usage of mobile banking services in Jordan. Int. J. Bus. Manage. Res. (IJBMR) **4**(2), 65–80 (2014). https://www.academia.edu/7339939/THE_FACTORS_INFL UENCING_CUSTOMER_USAGE_OF_MOBILE_BANKING_SERVICES_IN_JORDAN

Anouze, A.L.M., Alamro, A.S.: Factors affecting intention to use e-banking in Jordan. Int. J. Bank Mark. **38**(1), 86–112 (2019). https://doi.org/10.1108/IJBM-10-2018-0271

Ege, O.Ö., Tatar, Ç.: An investigation of factors that affect internet banking usage based on structural equation modeling. Comput. Hum. Behav. **66**, 232–235 (2017). https://doi.org/10. 1016/j.chb.2016.09.059

Hyde, A.M.: E-Banking: review of literature. Prestige e-J. Manage. Res. **2**(2), 19–28 (2015). https://www.pimrindore.ac.in/vol2,issue2/Dr.Hyde.pdf

Kelly, A.E., Palaniappan, S.: Survey on customer satisfaction, adoption, perception, behaviour, and security on mobile banking. J. Inf. Technol. Softw. Eng. **9**(2)(259), 1–15 (2019). https://www.longdom.org/open-access/survey-on-customer-satisfaction-adoption-perception-behaviour-and-security-on-mobile-banking.pdf

Lamore Bambore, P., Singla, V.: Factors affecting e-banking adoption and its impact on customer satisfaction: a case study of ethiopian banks. Int. J. Mark. Bus. Commun. **6**(1), 16–28 (2017). https://www.academia.edu/40419248/Factors_Affecting_E_Banking_Adoption_and_ Its_Impact_on_Customer_Satisfaction_A_Case_Study_of_Ethiopian_Banks

Lee, M.-C.: Factors influencing the adoption of internet banking: an integration of TAM and TPB with perceived risk and perceived benefit. Electron. Commerc. Res. Appl. **8**(3), 130–141 (2009). https://doi.org/10.1016/j.elerap.2008.11.006

Montazemi, A.R., Qahri-Saremi, H.: Factors affecting adoption of online banking: a meta-analytic structural equation modeling study. Inf. Manage. **52**(2), 210–226 (2015). https://doi.org/10. 1016/j.im.2014.11.002

Musiime, A., Malinga, R.: Internet banking, consumer adoption and customer satisfaction. Afr. J. Mark. Manage. **3**(10), 261–269 (2011). https://www.researchgate.net/publication/260302412_ Internet_banking_consumer_adoption_and_customer_satisfaction/citation/download

Nasri, W.: Factors influencing the adoption of internet banking in Tunisia. Int. J. Bus. Manage. **6**, 143–160 (2011). https://doi.org/10.5539/ijbm.v6n8p143

Nasri, W., Charfeddine, L.: Factors affecting the adoption of Internet banking in Tunisia: an integration theory of acceptance model and theory of planned behavior. J. High Technol. Manage. Res. **23**(1), 1–14 (2012). https://doi.org/10.1016/j.hitech.2012.03.001

Omar, A., Sultan, N., Zaman, K., Bibi, N., Wajid, A., Khan, K.: Customer perception towards online banking services: empirical evidence from Pakistan. J. Internet Bank. Commerc. **16**(2) (2011). https://ssrn.com/abstract=2035807

Shaikh, F.M., Kazi, Z.H., Khaskheley, A.: Factors that influence the adoption of online banking services in Hyderabad. Rom. Stat. Rev. Suppl. Rom. Stat. Rev. **62**(11), 49–63 (2014). https://ideas.repec.org/a/rsr/supplm/v62y2014i11p49-63.html

Singh, S.: Measuring e-service quality and customer satisfaction with internet banking in India. Theoret. Econ. Lett. **9**, 308–326 (2019). https://doi.org/10.4236/tel.2019.92023

Vinayek, R., Jindal, P.: An empirical investigation of key antecedents of customer preference of internet banking in Indian context. Asia Pac. Bus. Rev. **7**(3), 63–71 (2011). https://doi.org/10.1177/097324701100700306

Empirical Modeling of e-Participation Services as Media Ecosystems

Yuri Misnikov[1]([✉]) [iD], Olga Filatova[2] [iD], and Dmitrii Trutnev[1] [iD]

[1] ITMO University, Kronverksky Pr. 49, Bldg. A, St. Petersburg 197101, Russia
{misnikov,trutnev}@egov-center.ru
[2] St. Petersburg State University, Universitetskaya Emb. 7/9, St. Petersburg 199034, Russia
o.filatova@spbu.ru

Abstract. The presented research demonstrates that e-participation can be viewed and studied not only as technical tools but also in terms of the underlying mediums in which the act of participation unfolds. Informed by the real-world empirical evidence collected with the help of a number of case studies at the level of local municipalities in Russia, we build a model of e-participation ecosystem bringing together three technically different types of communication mediums: Internet websites, social networking media and mobile applications. We begin with the literature review to discuss the changes in the media beyond the web-based Internet itself. After that we describe an ecosystem approach and apply its principles to e-participation, followed by characterizing briefly e-participation research in Russia. In the following chapter we present the research methodology, discuss the obtained results and propose an e-participation ecosystem model. Limitations of the research are also covered.

Keywords: e-Participation · Ecosystem · Media ecology · Modelling

1 Introduction

Typical e-democracy and e-participation research is about assessing the performance of online platforms (and tools) from transactional, technical, functional and design perspectives. It is also about the end-user phenomenological experience, acceptance and trust. The terms 'electronic' or 'online' usually mean the website-based Internet as the main e-participation medium. Other digital mediums are rarely considered. After the two decades of voluminous e-participation research, there is still lack of clarity about the impact of the medium type on participatory efficacy in conceptual and technical sense. This is in contrast, for example, with deliberation and media studies that have benefited from the ecosystem approach resulting in such constructs as 'deliberation systems' and 'media ecology'. Against these theoretical advancements, e-participation scholarship lacks sufficient conceptual consolidation to reflect upon the fundamental changes in digital technology occurred over the past decade or so. However, '…the Internet is not a fixed entity with pre-determined effects' [1, p.vii], as governments and citizens continue exploiting diverse technological innovations and mediums to communicate more democratically and effectively.

© Springer Nature Switzerland AG 2021
G. Meiselwitz (Ed.): HCII 2021, LNCS 12774, pp. 87–104, 2021.
https://doi.org/10.1007/978-3-030-77626-8_6

Informed by the real-world empirical evidence collected with the help of a number of case studies at the level of local municipalities in Russia, we include other mediums to build a model of e-participation ecosystem consisting of Internet websites, social media pages and messenger-enabled mobile applications.

The paper is structured as follows. We begin with the literature review to discuss the changes in the media beyond the Internet itself. After that we describe an ecosystem approach and apply its principles to e-participation, followed by the chapter characterizing briefly e-participation research in Russia. In the following chapters we present the research methodology, explain the case studies, discuss the obtained results and propose an e-participation ecosystem model.

2 Beyond the Web Media: Literature Review

In the 1990s and early 2000s, the Internet as a novel communication medium dominated much of the scholarship interested in understanding the role of digital technologies in modern society. It was metaphorically imagined through a number of disguises and discourses, such as the information and network society [2–4]; cyberspace, cybersociety, information superhighway [5–10]; virtual community and Internet galaxy [11, 12]; and cyberdemocracy, when applied to politics [13]. Patrice Flichy terms such discourses as *imaginaire*, i.e., a 'collective vision' that surrounds the Internet as a new communication technique arguing that similar discourses accompanied other innovative communication mediums prior to the Internet [14, p. 4]. Understanding the Internet from the *imaginaire* perspective can explain 'how an entire society is tilting into a new technological era' [14, p. 2].

Studying and comparing the impact of the Internet web-based medium on politics, democracy and governance in varied contexts have become an essential topic of measuring such 'tilting'. Initially, comparative research across countries, regions and political regimes highlighted the importance of the relationship between the 'digital divide' and civic engagement, as the scholarship in the broad field of Internet democracy started to proliferate [15]. Much of the research and practice focused on benchmarking citizen engagement instruments deployed on the Internet by governments and civil society through website evaluation [16]. Typically, such research was – and still is – realized at the meso level of government agencies, political and civic organizations in the attempt to understand how the Internet is used by staff and activists to perform their functions and advance political agendas by exploiting such Internet properties as interactivity and networking [17–19].

The arrival in the mid-2000s of the social networking services (SNS) – or social (new) media – substantially increased interest in this new communication medium thanks to its personalization property, as if reaffirming Flichy's claim that 'Communication techniques are like some department stores: there's always something new' [14, p. 1]. The new media's engagement and interaction effects captured the imagination of e-participation scholars and practitioners who discovered in it a potential to make liberal democracy more participatory, deliberative and attentive to citizens' needs through stronger localization and personalization [20–29]. There is evidence gathered at the local municipal level that reveals a more positive attitude of citizens towards engagement through social media [30].

Today, much of the newest medium is smartphone-based mobile applications thanks to the reborn instant messaging services in particular. That changes the networking landscape, as 'mobile messaging apps and news aggregators are becoming increasingly central to people's media use" [31]. There is a shift to a distributed media environment that reconfigures communication channels to seek information and discover new ways of political participation due to the rapid increase in popularity of groups on messaging applications [32]. For example, there is evidence that young people under 35 in Europe spend daily almost five hours (284 min) on different media mobile apps, of which 1.5 h (92 min) spent on social media platforms (Instagram, Facebook, Snapchat, WhatsApp, Twitter) and only 13 min on other traditional media, such as Internet websites, with the smartphone being the main device used for accessing news for 69% of them [32]. Other research reveals that the use of smartphone and social networking services has a positive impact on various aspects of social capital and political participation [33]. Moreover, it is argued that software applications dominate the digital media environment making it a place for significant sociocultural transformations across the board [34].

These socio-cultural and technical changes prompt looking at e-participation through the lens of the media ecosystem approach. Evaluating and comparing e-participation platforms and tools against one another by applying certain metrics can reveal important insights about their individual comparative advantages. However, such platform-based approach reduces opportunities for better understanding the utility of e-participation instruments as distinct mediums from the end-user perspective of media consumption preferences. Different mediums differ substantially in their ability to convey e-participation content, processes, features, usage experience, as people may accept or reject certain instruments due to the underlying medium's form and format. This is to say that some mediums might meet specific e-participation demands better than others in the same context.

Below we describe how we build an e-participation ecosystem model to link specific participation techniques with specific media environments.

3 Applying an Ecosystem Approach to e-Participation

The term media ecology coined by Marshall McLuhan in the 1960s, means today complex, often hybrid communication systems defined as both visible and invisible environments where technologies interact with human cultures, values, opinions, languages, behaviors, i.e., with us; or, rather, how we use and consume such technologies in specific, local contexts. Recently, there has been a renewed interest in the study of media ecologies as systems [35–37]. Extending the media ecosystems' principles to studying e-participation might appear conceptually productive to understand why for example, citizens more readily discuss politics on nonpolitical forums whereas many official e-participation initiatives fail [1, 38, 39]. The underlying media would potentially matter no less than the participation practice itself, as Marshal McLuhan's slogan 'The media is the message' would suggest.

A similarly conceptualized and related notion of information ecology advanced by Bonnie Nardi and Vicki O'Day in their book *Information Ecologies: Using Technology with Heart* places a special emphasis on local contexts – localities. They argue that information ecologies 'have a sense of *locality'* in which 'different parts of ecology *coevolve,* changing together according to the relationships in the system' where the change is systemic [40, pp. 50–51]. Technologies in unique local contexts acquire unique identities through the process of *habitation,* which means the location of a technology within a network of relationships in the local information ecology.

4   e-Participation Research in Russia

The idea of applying the ecosystem approach in the field of open government and citizen participation is not entirely novel [41, 42]. However, the ecosystem-based approach is usually used here as 'a metaphor to make sense of interdependent systems and their components, as well as social systems with intensive use of information and communication technologies' rather than a pre-designed plan of ecosystem modeling [41, p. 94]. The ecosystem models developed for St. Petersburg in Russia and New York in the USA are based on a set of 'dynamic relationships among this wide range of social and technical factors that affect the nature and performance' of Open Government Data programmes [43, p. 18]. However, there are no studies known to the authors of this paper that explicitly integrate the media ecosystem dimension into the overall research agenda and design.

Typical research investigates the quality of e-participation platforms, channels, tools independently from one another. This includes, for example, the applicability of various assessment metrics to examine e-participation portals from the institutional design and performance angles [44–47], presence of government institutions on social media [48, 49]. In 2019, there has been a large-scale study to assess e-participation resources at regional and municipal levels (205 and 155 resources accordingly) of several types [50]. The typology covers such topics as open and participatory budgeting, citizens' feedback, electronic initiatives, voting and crowdsourcing. As a rule, local governments develop their e-participation tools to complement the resources deployed centrally by other government agencies. However, it is not unusual that similar instruments co-exist in parallel. Overall, instruments for engaging citizens in open and participatory budgeting clearly dominate accounting for at least two-thirds of all the resources available at each level, followed by the FixMyStreet type of resources (around 12–15%). There are few tools facilitating crowdsourcing at both levels (3–5%). Interestingly, the proportion of the electronic voting instruments at the municipal level is twice as much compared with the regional level (13% against 7%).

5   Methodology

5.1   Research Hypothesis and Questions

Our chief hypothesis claims that by applying the media ecosystem principles to e-participation, it can be possible to elaborate its holistic systemic model to reveal the relationship between citizen engagement processes and the underlying mediums.

Our key research questions concern the potential for empirically modeling an e-participation ecosystem at the local level as opposed to the currently dominant focus on unconnected platforms and tools. The research seeks to answer the following four questions:

RQ1. What is the structure and composition of e-participation services in relation to their respective mediums and ownership?

RQ2. Can e-participation services be translated into ecosystem elements?

RQ3. How complete and systemic the model of the e-participation ecosystem can be?

5.2 Description of Case Studies

There are 85 federal units (subjects) in Russia (46 regions, 22 republics, nine territories, three federal cities, four autonomous districts and one autonomous region) possessing executive, legislative, and judicial governance powers. The latter are divided between the federal and local (municipal) authorities. A municipality is a territory, which is administered by an elected assembly that forms local government to manage municipal property and budget. Municipalities may be represented by a diverse set of localities, such as rural and urban settlements, municipal districts of urban settlements, inner territories of federal city to name a few.

The research is based on three case studies representing three distinctively different localities (municipalities) in the Russia's North West federal region to test e-participation ecosystem modeling, namely (Fig. 1):

- Gatchina municipal district
- Moskovskaya Zastava (municipal district in St. Petersburg)
- Suojarvi municipal district

Fig. 1. Location of case studies

The population of Gatchina municipal district (*rayon*) is near 250,000 within Leningrad region (*oblast*), of which the city of Gatchina as an administrative centre of the district accounts for almost 100,000 residents. This is the largest city in the region, which is one of the reasons of choosing it as a case study. The other is the participation in a European international project with a focus on participatory budgeting.[1] The second case study is Moskovskaya Zastava – one of 111 municipal districts of St. Petersburg with the population of some 55,000. It is governed by a municipal council and local administration. Being part of the Russia's second largest city was an argument to select this municipality as a case study. Municipality Suojarvi is the third case study. It is an urban settlement in the Republic of Karelia housing over 15,000 residents (out of the total of 618,000 people living in Karelia). The municipality's small size and remote location were the main justification to include it into the research.

5.3 Ecosystem elements

Three groups of ecosystem's elements were defined to enable modeling by intertwining them on the assumption of their mutual dependence. These were:

- Type of ownership status of e-participation instruments.
- Category of e-participation services.
- Type of online mediums (environment) that house e-participation services.

The ownership status stemmed from the logic of technology habitation and included the following actors that deploy, own, or operate particular instruments:

- Official government authorities.
- Public (independent civil society organizations).
- Private persons (individuals).

The service category included

- Design, functionality.
- Information provision, dissemination.
- Cooperation, interaction.
- Direct participation in decision-making.

The choice of these categories was informed by the recognized international e-participation research and practice. This is a blend of public participation categories (levels, spectrum) developed by the United Nations Department of Economic and Social Affairs (UNDESA) responsible for biannual e-Government Surveys and the International Association of Public Participation (IAP2). Each category consisted of specific e-participation instruments, such as websites, portals, platforms, tools, applications. As many as 43 specific e-participation techniques were compiled drawing on the above-mentioned e-participation monitoring study (a full list is presented in Appendix 1). In addition, six features related to design and functionality were included bringing the total number of instruments to 47.

Finally, the type of online mediums covered

---

[1] Empowering Participatory Budgeting in the Baltic Sea Region – EmPaci (Interreg Baltic Sea Region Programme), see more here http://www.empaci.eu/photo/Files/EmPAci%20GoA%202. 1.1%20Status%20Quo%20Analysis%20final-18112020.pdf.

- Presence in the Internet via websites (pages, portals, blogs, forums).
- Presence on social media environment via respective pages.
- Presence in mobile environment (platforms) via messenger applications.

5.4 Examples of e-Participation Instruments

Information provision, dissemination services

- Publication of regulations, rules on participatory budgeting on official local government website in Suojarvi http://suojarvi-gp.ucoz.ru/index/narodnyj_bjudzhet_2020/0-1693.
- Publication of news on official local government website of Gatchina http://radm.gtn.ru/activity/finance/budget_people/.
- Official website to promote accessibility of urban environment in Moskovskaya Zastava via website http://www.mo44.net/.

Cooperation, interaction services

- Official online application to propose and compete for participatory budgets in Suojarvi via website https://moi-suoyarvi.ru/.
- Official government mobile chatbot platform apps@Moi_Suoyarvi_bot.
- Possibility for Suojarvi residents to send their complains, suggestions, enquiries on local issues (roads, transport, ecology, housing and communal services, buildings, culture, sports, etc.) via social media https://vk.com/nash.gorod.suoiarvi (official), https://vk.com/club33208954 (newspaper).
- Public social media page Our City Suojarvi community https://vk.com/nash.gorod.suoiarvi.
- Official social media page of Gatchina municipality head https://vk.com/id396209574.
- Official social media page of a municipal deputy in Moskovskaya Zastava https://vk.com/deputat_vorobyov.
- Public social media page Beautiful St. Petersburg – Moskovskiy rayon in Moskovskaya Zastava https://vk.com/kp_moskovskiy.

6   Results

Each locality was studied in terms of the availability of e-participation instruments that were classified according to ownership, service category and the medium type Tables 1 through 9 below contain the number of instruments identified for each ecosystem element and locality.

6.1   Gatchina Municipality

(See Tables 1, 2 and 3).

Table 1. Number of services by service domain and online medium

Service domain	Type of online environment			
	Internet websites	Social media pages	Mobile platforms, apps	Total
Design, functionality	9	0	0	9
Information provision, dissemination	21	2	4	27
Cooperation, interaction	12	20	0	32
Direct decision-making	0	0	0	0
Total:	42	22	4	68

Table 2. Number of services by online medium and ownership

Type of online environment	Type of instrument ownership			
	Official governmental	Unofficial public	Private (individual)	Total
Internet websites	29	12	1	42
Social media pages	0	19	3	22
Mobile platforms, apps	4	0	0	4
Total:	33	31	4	68

Table 3. Number of services by service domain and ownership

Service domain	Type of instrument ownership			
	Official governmental	Unofficial public	Private (individual)	Total
Design, functionality	6	3	0	9
Information provision, dissemination	20	5	2	27
Cooperation, interaction	7	23	2	32
Direct decision-making	0	0	0	0
Total:	33	31	4	68

6.2 Moskovskaya Zastava Municipality

(See Tables 4, 5 and 6).

Table 4. Number of services by service domain and online medium

Service domain	Type of online environment			
	Internet websites	Social media pages	Mobile platforms, apps	Total
Design, functionality	2	1	0	3
Information provision, dissemination	6	3	2	11
Cooperation, interaction	5	8	1	14
Direct decision-making	0	0	0	0
Total:	13	12	3	28

Table 5. Number of services by online medium and ownership

Type of online environment	Type of instrument ownership			
	Official governmental	Unofficial public	Private (individual)	Total
Internet websites	13	0	0	13
Social media pages	1	10	1	12
Mobile platforms, apps	3	0	0	3
Total:	17	10	1	28

Table 6. Number of services by service domain and ownership

Service domain	Type of instrument ownership			
	Official governmental	Unofficial public	Private (individual)	Total
Design, functionality	2	1	0	3
Information provision, dissemination	9	2	0	11
Cooperation, interaction	6	7	1	14
Direct decision-making	0	0	0	0
Total:	17	10	1	28

6.3 Suojarvi Municipality

(See Tables 7, 8, 9).

Table 7. Number of services by service domain and online medium

Service domain	Type of online environment			
	Internet websites	Social media pages	Mobile platforms, apps	Total
Design, functionality	4	0	0	4
Information provision, dissemination	24	2	0	26
Cooperation, interaction	21	24	2	47
Direct decision-making	3	0	0	3
Total:	52	26	2	80

Table 8. Number of services by online medium and ownership

Type of online environment	Type of instrument ownership			
	Official governmental	Unofficial public	Private (individual)	Total
Internet websites	46	3	3	52
Social media pages	9	12	5	26
Mobile platforms, apps	2	0	0	2
Total:	57	15	8	80

Table 9. Number of services by service domain and ownership

Service domain	Type of instrument ownership			
	Official governmental	Unofficial public	Private (individual)	Total
Design, functionality	3	1	0	4
Information provision, dissemination	25	0	1	26
Cooperation, interaction	26	14	7	47
Direct decision-making	3	0	0	3
Total:	57	15	8	80

7   Discussion of Results and Conclusions

7.1   Modeling e-Participation Ecosystem

Data cubes have been used as a visualization technique to establish the relationship between the main ecosystem elements: service domain, medium type and ownership. Figure 2 presents three models for each municipality by combining three ecosystem elements in the form of a cube.

The cubes' vertical and horizontal sides reveal the relationship between two elements. The left vertical side connects service domain and online medium; the horizontal side of

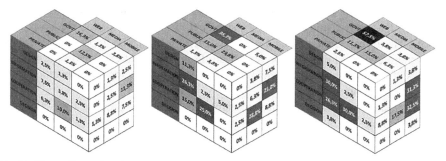

Fig. 2. Three-dimensional ecosystem model for Gatchina (left cube), Moskovskaya Zastava (middle cube) and Suojarvi (right cube)

the cube demonstrates the interconnection between medium and ownership, whereas the right vertical plain show how service domain and ownership are interrelated. Each side consists of several quadrants (cells) that display percentages of the respective instruments in relation to their total number; each side equals 100%. The quadrants are differently shaded to visualize the percentage according to a five-point scales, as illustrated below in Fig. 3.

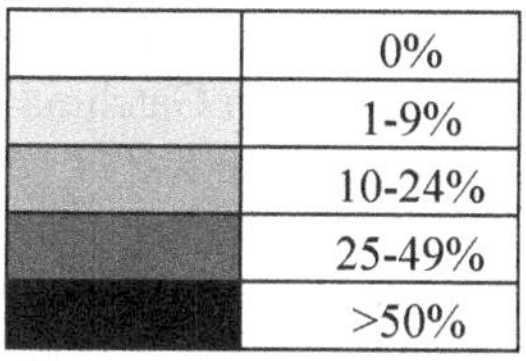

	0%
	1-9%
	10-24%
	25-49%
	>50%

Fig. 3. Visualization scheme

7.2   Validation of Hypothesis and Research Questions

The results of e-participation ecosystem modeling allow making the following claims as the research's two key takeaways. Firstly, we can cautiously confirm the research hypothesis about a possibility of building a model of e-participation media ecosystem. We have been able to distinguish three types of such media environments as the form of online presence on (a) the Internet, (b) social media and (c) mobile applications. While we realize that these forms might overleap (for example, it is possible to access and use mobile apps via website), these are still distinguishable in terms of user experience, as the research results demonstrate.

   Secondly, we have found the concept of technology habitation and locality, as part of the broader information ecology, theoretically and practically fruitful to expand the scope and breadth of e-participation enquiry. Linking e-participation technologies with unique local contexts help advance the new concept of digital identity of local communities by asking 'To whom does it belong? To whom and to what is it connected? Through what relations?' [40, p. 55]. Introducing the ownership aspect of e-participation service as an element of the ecosystem, helps better understand local e-participation landscapes as a whole. Yet to realize the potential of the technology habitation approach to a fuller extent, more emphasis needs to be placed on discovering and examining the hidden networks of relationships in the local information ecology by being more specific about e-participation actors.

With regard to the asked earlier research questions, we propose the following answers.

RQ1. What is the structure and composition of e-participation services in relation to their respective mediums and ownership?

We note that all the studies municipalities have deployed dozens of e-participation instruments ranging from 28 in the smallest Moskovskaya Zastava to 68 and 80 in substantially larger Gatchina and Suojarvi respectively. Since Moskovskaya Zastava is part of St. Petersburg and thus benefits from the city-wide services available there, it is therefore more reasonable to have a closer look at similar (size-wise) Gatchina and Suojarvi. Even though we have not assessed the effectiveness and quality of e-participation instruments, their sheer quantity points at the existence of sufficient opportunities for citizen engagement in both cities. Most likely this is the result of the city authorities' effort who are the main owners of all the instruments available – between 49% in Gatchina and 71% in Suojarvi. The websites occupy the lion share of e-participation instruments developed by local governments – 43% in Gatchina and 58% in Suojarvi, with social media pages and messengers lagging behind by a large margin (6–14%). The role of independent public owners is much stronger in Gatchina being almost on par with official authorities (46%) thanks to the pro-active use of social media. While the role of independent e-participation resources is smaller in Suojarvi (19%), they focus on social networking services and much less interested in the website-based medium. Privately owned instruments account for negligible 6–10% in both municipalities.

Between half and two-thirds of services provided by governments in Gatchina, Suojarvi and Moskovskaya Zastava are informational and interaction-oriented (split in almost equal halves). This is an interesting observation showing that the two-way type of cooperation is well represented these days, as a one-way mode of information provision has dominated until recently as the main way of engaging with the public. The independent civil society sector demonstrates much stronger interest in cooperation and interaction services that constitute between three-forths in Gatchina and over nine-tens in Suojarvi (Moskovskaya Zastava is also high enough with 70%). This trend corroborates logically with the observation showing that public e-participation resources are largely imbedded in social networking as the medium of choice, in contrast with the officially owned instruments that are mainly web-based.

The weakest service across the board is participation in decision-making. There are only three instruments available in Suojarvi related to voting and provided by local government via its official website. The design and functionality aspects of e-participation, such as the availability of the highly visible invitation to get involved on the main menu or an opportunity to become a registered member are quite weak as well.

When it comes to mobile applications, only local governments use them to a limited extent – just nine instruments found in all three municipalities out of the total 176 for both information provision and interaction.

Having described these relationship patterns, we do not overestimate them due to the limited number of case studies that prevent from confident generalizations. Nonetheless, there is certain logic in the discovered linkages between e-participation services, their owners and the underlying media.

RQ2. Can e-participation services be translated into ecosystem elements?

First of all, the research results suggest that it is theoretically possible to justify the inclusion of the medium and ownership as ecosystem elements to characterize e-participation resources. Empirical evidence can be found to support engaging with the media and information ecology theories. Second of all, it's been also technically feasible to represent these elements empirically by using the data cube technique as one of the modelling and visualization options. Other techniques should also be tested to demonstrate advantages and weaknesses of the ecosystem approach beyond its use as a metaphor. The limited number of localities can be seen as a serious limitation to draw informed conclusions. On the other hand, the research design did not intend to collect a representative set of data, placing instead the chief emphasis on testing the idea of researching e-participation from the ecology point of view as a systemic model.

RQ3. How complete and systemic the model of the e-participation ecosystem can be?

The model's content (elements) is far from complete, with many blank cells (0%). The visualized data cubes show that the white and light grey colours clearly dominate, which means either a limited presence (low percentages) or the absence of some elements all together. In the same vein, too many dark cells would reveal the unhealthy domination of some elements at the expense of others. To strike a better balance, the more evenly distributed dark grey cells would be preferable. However, in the real-world setting there always be imbalances. The main point is to detect them.

8 Conclusion

In conclusion, we would like to point at another problematic area that this research has faced, namely: the classification of e-participating instruments across service domains. Due to the lack of the agreed criteria, it is sometimes not only challenging to categorize specific instruments under particular domain. Establishing such domains convincingly in the first place is a complicated task. The available classification schemes, such those of the United Nations or the International Association of Public Participation are driven by practice lacking thereby more fundamental scholarly justifications. Experimenting with different schemes and criteria would help generate more educated cues about how public participation works in different online media environments as coherent ecosystems.

Acknowledgment. The research has been supported by the Russian Science Foundation (RSF) as part of a project №18-18-00360 «E-Participation as Politics and Public Policy Dynamic Factor».

Appendix 1. List of e-Participation Instruments

Service domain: Design, functionality

1. Availability of a personal user account on the main page (via login-password) to manage interaction with authorities (sending requests, paying taxes, correspondence, voting, obtaining personal information, etc.).
2. Availability of an easily visible item in the main menu as a single entry point for interaction between citizens and authorities.
3. Links to the federal portal of state e-services
4. Links to the federal portal of e-petitions
5. Links to other federal resources for interaction/ consultation with citizens (for example, discussion of draft federal laws, etc.)
6. RSS subscription

Service domain: Information provision, dissemination

7. Publication of news, announcements by the administration
8. Provision of information explaining the rules and procedures for submitting complaints by residents to the administration, including receiving responses
9. Publication of reports on complaints (complaints, suggestions) sent by residents, including information on the measures taken
10. Publication of information on the planned agenda for public consultations organized by the local executive body
11. Publication of information on the results of public hearings organized by the local legislature
12. Publication of results of deliberations by the local legislature
13. Publication of minutes of deliberations by the local legislature
14. Live video streaming of the local legislature meetings
15. Publication of information explaining the rules and procedures for filing electronic petitions, including conditions for accepting petitions for consideration
16. Publication of reports containing information on the results of the consideration of local petitions and the decisions taken on them
17. Publication of information on local referenda (voting procedures, voter lists, etc.)
18. Publication of information on local opinion polls
19. Publication of information on local elections (voting procedures, constituencies, voter lists, etc.)
20. Preliminary disclosure of information on planned purchases from the local budget
21. Publication of regulations, laws on access to local open data (public information)
22. Publication of local open data (public information)
23. Publication of information on the rules for publishing and protecting local open data (public information)
24. Advance publication of the planned annual budget
25. Publication of information on the actual execution of the annual budget
26. Publication of regulations, rules on the competition of local participatory budgets

27. Publication of submitted applications for participation in the competition of participatory budgets
28. Publication of submitted (registered, accepted) applications for participation in the competition of participatory budgets
29. Publication of information on development plans (strategies, roadmaps) by economic sectors
30. Publication of reports on the actual implementation of plans (strategies, roadmaps) for local development

Service domain: Cooperation, interaction

31. Possibility of addressing residents on local issues (roads, transport, ecology, housing and communal services, buildings, culture, sports, etc.)
32. Possibility to participate in public hearings organized by the local legislature
33. Possibility to participate in public consultations organized by the administration
34. Possibility to participate in local polls
35. Possibility to participate in local referendums
36. Possibility to ask questions and provide comments during live video broadcasts of local legislature meetings
37. Possibility to apply for participation in the competition of participatory budgets
38. Possibility of online discussion of submitted applications
39. Possibility to send appeals (questions, complaints, suggestions) online (feedback "window")
40. Possibility to publish local news, announcements by residents
41. Possibility to submit electronic petitions related to local development issues
42. Possibility to view completed and ongoing public consultations, public hearings
43. Possibility to participate in deliberations on local issues based on certain procedures and rules

Service domain: Direct participation in decision-making

44. Possibility to vote online in local elections
45. Possibility to vote online in local referenda
46. Possibility to vote online to select best participatory budgets
47. Possibility to vote online find best solutions to local problems

References

1. Coleman, S.: Can the internet strengthen democracy? p. vii. Polity (2017)
2. Castells, M.: The Rise of the Network Society. Blackwell, Oxford (1996)
3. van Dijk, J.: The Network Society: Social Aspects of New Media. Sage, London (2006)
4. Webster, F.: Theories of Information Society, 3rd edn. Routledge, London (2006)
5. Jones, S.G.: CyberSociety 2.0: revisiting computer-mediated communication and community. Sage, Thousand Oaks, London, New Delhi (1998)

6. Nunes, M.: What space is cyberspace? The Internet and virtuality. In: Holmes, D. (ed.) Virtual Politics: Identity and Community in Cyberspace, pp. 163–178. Sage, London (1997)
7. Wilhelm, A.: Democracy in the Digital Age: Challenges to Political Life in Cyberspace. Routledge, London (2000)
8. Resnick, D.: Politics on the internet: the normalization of cyberspace. In: Toulouse, C., Luke, N.W. (eds.) The Politics of Cyberspace, pp. 48–68. Routledge, New York (1998)
9. McConnaughey, J.: Access to the information superhighway. In: Kubicek, H., Dutton, W.H., Williams, R. (eds.) The Social Shaping of Information Superhighways: European and American Roads to the Information Society, pp. 221–31. St. Martin's Press, New York (1997)
10. Miller, S.E.: Civilizing Cyberspace: Policy, Power and the Information Highway. ACM, New York (1996)
11. Rheingold, H.: The Virtual Community: Homesteading on the Electronic Frontier (Revised Edition). The MIT Press, Cambridge (2000)
12. Castells, M.: The Internet Galaxy: Reflections on the Internet, Business and Society. Oxford University Press, Oxford and New York (2001)
13. Poster, M.: Cyberdemocracy: the internet and the public sphere. In: Holmes, D. (ed.) Virtual Politics: Identity and Community in Cyberspace, pp. 212–228. Sage, London (1997)
14. Flichy, P.: The Internet Imaginaire. MIT Press, Cambridge, London (2007)
15. Norris, P.: Digital Divide: Civic Engagement, Information Poverty, and the Internet Worldwide. Cambridge University Press, Cambridge (2001)
16. Gibson, R., Ward, S.: A proposed methodology for studying the function and effectiveness of party and candidate web sites. Soc. Sci. Comput. Rev. **18**, 301–319 (2000)
17. Bach, J., Stark, D.: Technology and transformation: facilitating knowledge networks in Eastern Europe. In: UNRISD. Technology, Business and Society. Programme Paper Number 10. UNRISD, Geneva (2003)
18. Bach, J., Stark, D.: Link, search, interact: the co-evolution of NGOs and interactive technology. Theor. Cult. Soc. **21**(3), 101–117 (2004)
19. Rafaeli, S., Sudweeks, F.; Networked interactivity. J. Comput. Mediat. Commun. **2**(4) (1997)
20. Kaigo, M., Okura, S.: Exploring fluctuations in citizen engagement on a local government Facebook page in Japan. Jpn. Telematics Inf. **33**(2), 584–595 (2016)
21. Hofmann, S., Beverungen, D., Räckers, M., Becker, J.: What makes local governments' online communications successful? Insights from a multi-method analysis of Facebook. Gov. Inf. Quart. **30**, 387–396 (2013)
22. Hemphill, L. Roback, A.: Tweet acts: how constituents lobby congress via Twitter. In Proceedings of the 17th ACM Conference on Computer Supported Cooperative Work & Social Computing, pp. 1200–1210. ACM, New York (2014)
23. Rainie, L., Smith, A., Schlozman, K., Brady, H., Verba, S.: Social media and political engagement. Pew Research: Internet Project (2012)
24. Marquart, F., Ohme, J., Möller, J.: Following politicians on social media: effects for political information, peer communication, and youth engagement. In: Media and Communication, 8, 2, 197-207, Youth Digital Participation: Opportunities, Challenges, Contexts, and What's at Stake; PRT (2020)
25. Coleman, S., Moss, G.: Under construction: the field of online deliberation research. J. Inf. Technol. Polit. **9**(1), 1–15 (2012)
26. Gil de Zúñiga, H.: Social media use for news and individuals' social capital, civic engagement and political participation. J. Comput. Mediat. Commun. **17**(3), 319–336 (2012)
27. Sæbø, Ø., Rose, J., Nyvang, T.: The role of social networking services in eParticipation. In: Macintosh, A., Tambouris, E. (eds.) ePart 2009. LNCS, vol. 5694, pp. 46–55. Springer, Heidelberg (2009). https://doi.org/10.1007/978-3-642-03781-8_5
28. Charalabidis, Y., Loukis, E.: Transforming government agencies' approach to e-participation through efficient exploitation of social media (2011)

29. Wahid, F., Sæbø, Ø.: Affordances and effects of promoting eParticipation through social media. In: Tambouris, E., Panagiotopoulos, P., Sæbø, Ø., Tarabanis, K., Wimmer, Maria A., Milano, M., Pardo, Theresa A. (eds.) ePart 2015. LNCS, vol. 9249, pp. 3–14. Springer, Cham (2015). https://doi.org/10.1007/978-3-319-22500-5_1

30. Alarabiat, A., Sá Soares, D., Estevez, E.: Municipalities e-Participation initiatives through Facebook: citizens perspective. In: ICEGOV 2020: Proceedings of the 13th International Conference on Theory and Practice of Electronic Governance, September 2020, pp. 551–559 (2020)

31. Kalogeropoulos, A., Fletcher, R., Nielsen, K.: News brand attribution in distributed environments: do people know where they get their news? New Media Soc. **21**(3), 583–601 (2019)

32. Newman, N., Fletcher, R., Nielsen, K., Kalogeropoulos, A.: Reuters Institute Digital News Report 2019, Reuters Institute for the Study of Journalism, Oxford University (2019)

33. Park, K.G., Han, S., Kaid, L.L.:.Does social networking service usage mediate the association between smartphone usage and social capital? New Media Soc. **15**(7), 1077–1093 (2013)

34. Light, B., Burgess, J., Duguay, S.: The walkthrough method: an approach to the study of apps. New Media Soc. **20**(3), 881–900 (2018)

35. Strate, L.: A media ecology review. Commun. Res. Rev. **23**(2), 3–48 (2004)

36. Scolari, C.: Media ecology: exploring the metaphor to expand the theory. Commun. Theor. **22**(2), 204–225 (2012)

37. Cali, D.: Mapping Media Ecology: Introduction to the Field. Peter Lang, New York, Bern, Frankfurt, Berlin, Brussels, Vienna, Oxford, Warsaw (2017)

38. Graham, T.: Beyond "political" communicative spaces: talking politics on the "Wife Swap" discussion forum. J. Inf. Technol. Polit. **9**(1), 31–45 (2012)

39. Alarabiat, A., Sá Soares, D.: Electronic Participation through Social media. In: ICEGOV 15–16: Proceedings of the 9th International Conference on Theory and Practice of Electronic Governance, March 2016, pp. 191–194 (2016)

40. Nardi, B., O'Day, V.: Information Ecologies: Using Technology with Heart. MIT Press, Cambridge (2000)

41. Santos, L.G.M.: Toward the Open Government Ecosystem: Connecting e-Participation Models and Open Government to Analyze Public Policies. Springer Nature Switzerland AG (2019)

42. Ju, J., Liu, L., Feng, Y.: Design of an O2O citizen participation ecosystem for sustainable governance. Inf. Syst. Front. **21**, 605–620 (2019)

43. Dawes, S.S., Vidiasova, L., Parkhimovich, O.: Planning and designing open government data programs: An ecosystem approach. Gov. Inf. Quart. **33**(1), 15–27 (2016)

44. Vidiasova, L.: The applicability of international techniques for e-participation assessment in the russian context. In: Chugunov, Andrei V., Bolgov, R., Kabanov, Y., Kampis, G., Wimmer, M. (eds.) DTGS 2016. CCIS, vol. 674, pp. 145–154. Springer, Cham (2016). https://doi.org/10.1007/978-3-319-49700-6_15

45. Vidiasova, L., Tensina, I., Bershadskaya, E.: Social efficiency of e-participation portals in russia: assessment methodology. In: Alexandrov, Daniel A., Boukhanovsky, Alexander V., Chugunov, Andrei V., Kabanov, Y., Koltsova, O. (eds.) DTGS 2018. CCIS, vol. 858, pp. 51–62. Springer, Cham (2018). https://doi.org/10.1007/978-3-030-02843-5_5

46. Chugunov, A.V., Kabanov, Y.: Evaluating e-participation institutional design. a pilot study of regional platforms in Russia. In: Edelmann, N., Parycek, P., Misuraca, G., Panagiotopoulos, P., Charalabidis, Y., Virkar, S. (eds.) ePart 2018. LNCS, vol. 11021, pp. 13–25. Springer, Cham (2018). https://doi.org/10.1007/978-3-319-98578-7_2

47. Chugunov, A.V., Kabanov, Y., Misnikov, Y.: Citizens versus the government or citizens with the government: a tale of two e-participation portals in one city-a case study of St. Petersburg, Russia. In: Proceedings of the 10th International Conference on Theory and Practice of Electronic Governance, pp. 70–77 (2017)

48. Karyagin, M.: Russian large cities authorities' pages in social media: a platform for expert communication? In: Chugunov, Andrei V., Bolgov, R., Kabanov, Y., Kampis, G., Wimmer, M. (eds.) DTGS 2016. CCIS, vol. 674, pp. 14–21. Springer, Cham (2016). https://doi.org/10.1007/978-3-319-49700-6_2

49. Bodrunova, S., Litvinenko, A., Blekanov, I.: Please follow us: media roles in Twitter discussions in the United States, Germany, France, and Russia. J. Pract. **12**(2), 177–203 (2018)

50. ITMO University Monitoring of e-Participation resources in Russia 2020 (2020). https://news.egov.itmo.ru/documents/eparticipation_index_ru_2020.pdf

Optimal Community-Generation Methods for Acquiring Extensive Knowledge on Twitter

Yuichi Okada[1]($\boxtimes$), Naoya Ito[1], and Tomoko Yonezawa[2]

[1] Graduate School of Informatics, Kansai University, Takatsuki, Osaka 569-1095, Japan
k393424@kansai-u.ac.jp
[2] Faculty of Informatics, Kansai University, Takatsuki, Osaka 569-1095, Japan
yone@kansai-u.ac.jp

Abstract. This paper proposes a method to generate an optimal community on Twitter by grouping users using a solution to the knapsack problem. Most past studies have proposed methods to recommend one user or some candidates, rather than recommending multiple users as candidates. It is quite difficult to recommend candidates as a single group that considers the balance of user characteristics, because grouping in terms of relationships among users is a combinatorial problem, especially on Twitter, as a huge number of users must be handled, so combinatorial explosion occurs easily. Although the combination optimization problem is difficult, with the knapsack problem, it is possible to obtain a solution of good quality within a practical calculation time. In this paper, we calculate the combination of users whose total amount of knowledge is maximized by using "amount of knowledge acquired" as a community evaluation item. In addition, we conduct a subject experiment to evaluate the information obtained from the generated community and the performance of the proposed method.

Keywords: Twitter · Knapsack problem · Word2vec

1 Introduction

1.1 Motivation

Twitter is one of the largest social networking sites (SNSs) in the world, with an average of 187 million daily active users in the third quarter of 2020, according to Twitter Inc. [12]. Fatigue caused by information overload has been studied in large social networks [11]. Recently, the worldwide spread of the new coronavirus has led to more active communication, business, and political activities using online systems. As a result, SNSs have become places where negative elements such as human desires, hatred, and anger are expressed, rather than a place for simple information gathering and casual communication. In other words, users have to worry not only about information overload, but also about fatigue caused by emotional overload. Therefore, the question of what kind of users to connect with and how to collect high-quality information is becoming more and more important every year. Building a community by connecting with users while

© Springer Nature Switzerland AG 2021
G. Meiselwitz (Ed.): HCII 2021, LNCS 12774, pp. 105–120, 2021.
https://doi.org/10.1007/978-3-030-77626-8_7

maintaining a balance of information content and quantity will have a positive impact on Twitter users' experience.

However, this is difficult to achieve on a service such as Twitter with a huge number of users due to the combinatorial explosion problem. To solve this problem, we used the knapsack problem, which is a combinatorial problem. Because an exact solution to the knapsack problem has been discovered, we computed an approximate solution based on it.

1.2 Related Research

In research on Twitter, predictions through machine learning are popular, because information about users and tweets can be obtained in large quantities. Studies using machine learning [5] to predict tweets that tend to be retweeted and [6] to predict users' personalities have reported that machine learning works well. Because Twitter has a large number of users, it is important to study the handling of large-scale data. Graph theory is used to treat large amounts of data in recommendation systems [8] based on users' past tweets and Wikipedia link information, as well as in studies [9] focusing on scalability in user recommendations. In this study, we use the solution of the knapsack problem to realize the optimum connection with the user, but there is a research example using the knapsack problem to efficiently collect Twitter data in other contexts [7].

2 Basic Scheme

2.1 Overview

To find the optimal group of users, the combinatorial optimization problem must be solved. The combinatorial optimization problem belongs to a problem class generally called NP-hard in the theory of computational complexity, and it requires enormous computation time, even if it is computable in theory. It is almost impossible to exactly obtain an optimal solution for a large problem such as determining a group of users on Twitter. However, an approximate solution method has been developed for the knapsack problem among the combinatorial optimization problems, and a good quality solution can be obtained within a practical calculation time. This section describes the types of knapsack problems and their approximate solutions.

2.2 Knapsack Problem

The knapsack problem is a problem of finding a way to fill a knapsack with goods that have two elements, size and value, so that the value of the goods is as large as possible within the given capacity. When there is a single constraint, the size of the goods, and each good is expressed in two states, put in or not put in the knapsack, it is called a single-constraint 0–1 knapsack problem. The knapsack problem has been extended in various ways, including a two-constraint problem in which the size of an item has two different values, such as volume and weight; a multiple-choice knapsack problem in which two or more items of each type are considered; and a multiple-choice (nonlinear) knapsack problem in which one item is selected from among multiple items.

2.3 Solutions to the Knapsack Problems

The study of the 0–1 knapsack problem with a single constraint has a long history, and the exact solution can be obtained even at a scale of over 10,000 variables [13]. In addition, the greedy method can be applied to this type of problem, so that a suboptimal solution can be obtained quickly.

When a knapsack problem has multiple constraints, not only is it difficult to obtain an exact solution, but the greedy method cannot provide a good quality solution. The surrogate constraint method [1] is a method to replace the knapsack problem with a single-constraint knapsack problem (surrogate problem) by weighting each constraint. A method to calculate the optimal weights has also been established [2].

In this method, there are cases where the solution of the surrogate problem does not satisfy the constraints of the original problem (resulting in a surrogate gap). In this case, an improved surrogate constraints (ISC) method was invented to obtain a feasible solution by enumerating the neighboring solutions [3].

However, the algorithm of the ISC method is complicated and difficult to implement. In addition, it requires a high cost, even if the software is optimized for speed. In practical applications, it is not necessary to obtain an exact optimal solution, so a speedy suboptimal solution method is effective. In this study, we developed a program based on the surrogate constraint method to find a feasible solution by tightening the constraint condition when the solution does not satisfy the constraint.

2.4 Proposed Method for Optimized Multiple User List

A user list is generated through the following procedure. In the field of psychological measurement, the objective variable corresponds to the objective function of the knapsack problem, and the dependent variable corresponds to the constraint function of the knapsack problem. The overall image is shown in Fig. 1.

- Step 1 Establish group settings for similar users (optional)

When the number of users is large, it is possible that there are multiple users with high similarity. In such a case, we can prevent bias in the data by grouping the similar users. When creating data that allows for bias, this process is skipped, and one group consists of one user.

- Step 2 Set up objective and constraint functions

The evaluation items of the hypothesis are the objective function and the constraint function. For the constraints, it is necessary to establish the constraint value (the value on the right side of the constraint inequality), so it is recommended to standardize it or use an easy-to-understand value such as an ordinal statistic to make it easier to set.

- Step 3 Generate the knapsack problem and calculate the solution

A knapsack problem is generated from user group lists and objective and constraint function definitions. In the case of the solver using the approximate solution method,

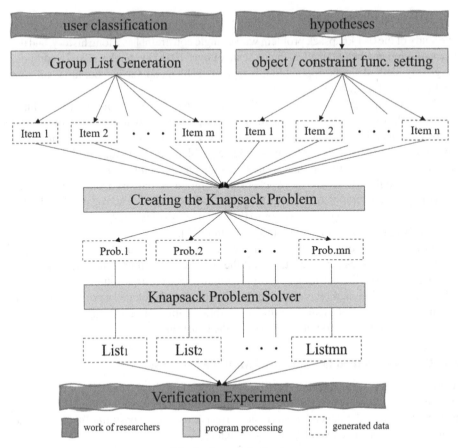

Fig. 1. Image of scheme

the solution can be obtained in a moment, and even if it takes time, it takes only several seconds at most.

- Step 4 Generate a user list

A user list is created based on a solution to a knapsack problem. When a user who tweets in Japanese is the object of the research, all tweets must be morphologically analyzed because Japanese sentences do not have explicit separators such as spaces in English. In this study, the morphological analysis library MeCab [4] was used to analyze Japanese tweets.

3 Community Evaluation Method

3.1 System Overview

In this study, we aimed to connect with people who had information on a certain topic. The number of accounts analyzed was about 6000. Such accounts had tweeted the names of several sports and had more than 50 tweets written in Japanese. For each account, the content of tweets, the number of tweets, and the number of days elapsed from the first tweet to the latest tweet were collected using the Twitter API. The maximum number of tweets that can be obtained using the Twitter API is 3200. Therefore, for accounts with more than 3200 tweets, the most recent 3200 tweets were considered for analysis. The proposed system aims to connect with users in such a way that the total amount of knowledge on a topic is maximized.

3.2 Word2vec

Word2vec was used to define words representing the knowledge of each sport. Word2vec is a group of models developed by Mikolov et al. [10]. They can vectorize a distributed representation of a word from a corpus of text and predict words with high similarity to another word. In this study, the top 50 words that were similar to keywords were defined as surrounding words. Additionally, multiple data were used as a text corpus.

3.3 Knowledge Volume

The amount of knowledge for each account was determined using the frequency of tweets including surrounding words. The amount of knowledge is defined by the following equation:

$$\sum_{i=1}^{n} similar * log(count_i + 1)$$

"*similar*" denotes the similarity value, and "*count$_i$*" denotes the frequency of the surrounding words. The logarithmic function was used to prevent an excessive increase of knowledge by one surrounding word.

3.4 Generating Knowledge Area Clusters

When a user connects with several other users, the range of knowledge the user can obtain is wider if the information they have does not overlap. For this reason, clustering was performed using the frequency information of surrounding words, and users with similar knowledge were grouped in the same cluster. By selecting users from several clusters, we can create a community where there is little overlap of information.

3.5 Optimization

To create a group of users in which the amount of knowledge was maximized, we defined a multi-constraint nonlinear knapsack problem, as follows.

$$[P]: \max. f(x) = \sum_{n \in N} f_n(x_n)$$

$$s.t \ g(x) = \sum_{n \in N} g_{mn}(x_n) \leq b_m, \ (m = 1, \ldots, M)$$

$$x_n \in A_n$$

where $N = \{1, 2, \ldots, n\}$ is a set of variable numbers and $A_i = \{1, 2, \ldots, a_i\}(i \in N)$ is a set of items for each variable. The objective function is the amount of knowledge. As constraint functions, we defined the average number of tweets per day, the density, and the number of connected people. Density is the ratio of idioms or foreign words in one tweet. By changing the upper limit of density, we can expect to reduce the frequency of meaningless sentences in tweets. By setting the average number of tweets as a constraint, the frequency of posts is limited, so users can communicate and use the SNS at the speed they expect. In our experiments, we set the upper limit of the average number of tweets per day to 80, the upper limit of the density to 16, and the number of connections to 8.

3.6 Improving the Accuracy of Thesaurus Lists by Upper-Level Concept Filtering

To improve the similarity of surrounding words, we used the upper-level concept of words. Word2vec calculates the variance of words appearing in the training data and determines that words with close variance are highly similar. The accuracy of the variance calculation is reduced because many words that do not fit the context appear on Twitter compared with texts that have a clear theme, such as blogs and news articles. As a preprocessing step, we filtered the training data by upper-level concept words for keywords. This eliminates words that are conceptually distant and is expected to improve the accuracy of the thesaurus. To further improve the accuracy, we calculated the frequency of occurrence of each generated thesaurus in the training data, and the words with the highest frequency rank were considered official thesauri.

4 Verification of the Effectiveness of the Proposed System Through Subject Experiments

4.1 Experiment 1: Validation of Surrounding Words

Purpose and Overview. For a given target topic, if the surrounding words represent the topic, the frequency of occurrence of the surrounding words is a valuable factor. In this experiment, to observe the differences depending on the word2vec input data, the participants saw 50 surrounding words for some target topics and responded to a questionnaire. We analyzed the responses and investigated the validity of the surrounding words.

Hypothesis. We hypothesized that the participants would feel as follows:

(1) Surrounding words obtained from tweets containing the word "sports" indicate knowledge of the topic.
(2) Surrounding words obtained from tweets containing the name of a sport contain a lot of noise.

Condition. This experiment had a within-subjects design with the following factor and four conditions: If a sports name was included in the surrounding words obtained from word2vec, 50 surrounding words excluding the word were presented to the participants. We used about 200 sports names obtained from [14].

a1: Surrounding words obtained from tweets containing the name of the sport
a2: Surrounding words obtained from web articles
a3: Surrounding words obtained from academic papers
a4: Surrounding words from tweets containing the word "sports"

We chose four sports as target topics: soccer, baseball, basketball, and tennis. For each target topic, we created a set of surrounding words from a1 to a4. Each condition was presented in consideration of counterbalancing.

Participants. Sixteen university students aged 19 to 27 participated in the experiment.

Experimental Procedure. First, the participants were given a paper with 50 random words for practice, and the flow of the experiment was explained. It was explained that the participants would confirm the question item and that the experiment would be carried out using the following procedure.

The participants proceeded according to the following flow.

(1) Sign the consent form
(2) Listen to the explanation of the experiment
(3) View the test paper
(4) Respond to sports names
(5) Check the correctness of sports names
(6) Review the test paper
(7) Answer questions

The participants were allowed to view the surrounding words twice, in steps (2) and (6). The participants were instructed to return the list of surrounding words to the executor of the experiment when they felt that they had sufficiently browsed the list. If the participants had any questions, they could ask the experimenter at any time.

Evaluation Procedure. The participants answered the following questions on a 5-grade scale, where $1 = $ disagree, $2 = $ disagree slightly, $3 = $ neither agree nor disagree, $4 = $ agree slightly, and $5 = $ agree. The mean opinion score (MOS) was obtained from their responses, and for Q0, they answered in a descriptive form. A one-factor analysis of variance (significance level $\alpha = 0.05$) was conducted on the MOS obtained.

Q0 What sports-related words do you think are in this group?
Q1 I feel that there are many words related to the sport.
Q2 I feel that many of the words are associated with that sport.
Q3 I feel that many of the words are not related to that sport.
Q4 Many of the words do not remind me of the sport.

In addition, participants evaluated each of the 50 words they viewed in one of the following four ways

- I think it is related to the sport.
- I don't think it is related to the sport.
- I don't know the meaning of the word.
- I don't know whether the word is related to the sport or not.

Results. Figure 2 shows the means and standard errors of the responses to each of the question items from Q1 to Q4, and Table 1 shows the results of the analysis of variance and multiple comparisons. To evaluate each word, a χ-square test was conducted on the data from which the responses for each condition were aggregated. To compare the number of correct answers for the sports names in Q0, Fisher's exact test was conducted based on the Cochran rule. For Q0, Table 3 shows the results of the correct and incorrect answers, and Table 4 shows the results of the Fisher test.

For *1 to *4 in Table 2, *1: likely to be related, *2: not likely to be related, *3: not sure if related, *4: do not know the meaning of the word.

For Q1, a2 > a1, a4 > a1, and the mean value was significantly higher. This indicates that when the input data was a web article or a tweet containing the word "sport," the words related to the sport were more frequent than when the input data was a tweet containing the name of the sport. There was no significant difference between Q2 and Q4. In the χ-square test for each word evaluation, a2 and a3 were significantly higher for "related to the sport," and a1 was significantly higher for "not related to the sport"; a4 was significantly higher for "don't know if the word is related or not".

Discussion for Results. Participants often judged that surrounding words obtained from tweets containing sports names were not related to the target sport. Although it was verified that the reinforcement of surrounding words by adopting upper-level concepts was effective, the number of participants who did not know whether the words were related to the target sport increased. This may be due to the fact that the number of specialized words, such as the names of teams or players, increased in the surrounding words, and the participants were faced with information that was beyond their knowledge. For example, when the target sport was soccer, the word "Mallorca" appeared as a surrounding word, but Japanese participants who were not familiar with soccer were not likely to understand that it was a professional soccer club team in Spain. In this case,

Table 1. Exp. 1: results of one-factor analysis of variance

	F	P	Multiple comparison
Q1	4.361	0.0089	a2, a4 > a1
Q2	2.937	0.0433	–
Q3	1.413	0.2514	–
Q4	1.689	0.1828	–

Table 2. Exp. 1: evaluation of individual surrounding words (chi-square test)

	*1	*2	*3	*4
a1	307▽	329▲	129	35▽
a2	433▲	211▽	128	28▽
a3	402▲	271	106	21▽
a4	342▽	224▽	128	106▲

(▲Significantly more, ▽significantly less, $p < .05$)

Table 3. Number of responses of subjects in each condition

	a1	a2	a3	a4
Correct	5	13	12	16
Incorrect	11	3	4	0

Table 4. P value of Fisher test

	a1: a2	a1: a3	a1: a4	a2: a3	a2: a4	a3: a4
Correct: incorrect	0.056	0.127	0.000	1.000	0.451	0.303

if the user knows that the words are related to the target sport, the user's knowledge will increase. In addition, surrounding words gathered from web articles are also considered to have good efficiency, but they are difficult to match with words appearing on Twitter due to the large number of abbreviations on Twitter.

4.2 Experiment 2: Validation of Optimized Communities Using Surrounding Words

Purpose and Overview. In this experiment, we examined how participants perceived community information depending on the presence or absence of surrounding words and on whether they were optimized. We optimized by maximizing the amount of information, and we verified that the participants could detect the knowledge of the target topic from the generated community tweets.

Hypothesis. We hypothesized that the participants would feel as follows:

(1) The community tweets obtained through the optimization include more knowledge about soccer than tweets in the other conditions.
(2) The community tweets including the surrounding words have more knowledge and information about soccer than tweets of the randomly selected community.

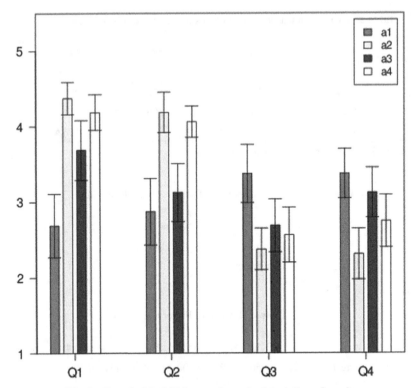

Fig. 2. Exp. 1: Q1–Q4 Mean and standard deviation of results

Condition. This experiment involved a within-subjects design with the following factor and three conditions. Soccer was chosen as the target sport, and the list of surrounding words was based on the tweet data with upper-level concept enhancement.

b1: Community selected by optimization
b2: Randomly selected community
b3: Randomly selected community from users who tweeted the surrounding words

In b1, the community with the largest amount of knowledge is selected by optimization; in b2, a community of randomly selected users is generated; in b3, the community is randomly selected from users who have tweeted surrounding words of "soccer." Each condition was presented with counterbalancing.

Materials. In all conditions b1 to b3, the number of community members was set to 8. The community members were labelled as a through h, and the names were displayed together with the contents of their statements. The community members each posted 15 tweets, and the tweets were presented to the participants in a random order. The frequency of the surrounding words in the 15 tweets was adjusted to be almost the same as the frequency of the surrounding words in all the tweets from that user. In addition, each tweet was given a unique text color to make it easier to identify to whom the tweet belonged.

Participants. Twenty-four university students aged 19 to 27 participated in the experiment.

Experimental Procedure. The participants proceeded with the experiment according to the following flow.

(1) Sign the consent form
(2) Listen to the explanation of the experiment
(3) Read tweets by community members
(4) Answer the questions

As in Experiment 1, the participants responded with the name of the sport represented by the community tweet, and then the correct sport was presented to them. The participants were allowed to ask questions during the experiment. When the participants answered the questions, they were told in advance that they were not allowed to read the tweets again. Therefore, they were instructed to consider the different sports that might be chosen as topics when viewing the content of the tweets. We also asked them to answer based on their impressions of the tweets as a whole, rather than focusing on individual tweets.

Evaluation Procedure. For the following questions (Q1–Q9), we used the same evaluation and analysis methods as in Experiment 1.

Q0 What sport did you think the community was talking about?
Q1 I felt that they were talking about something related to soccer.
Q2 I felt that there were many people who seemed to be interested in soccer.
Q3 I felt that I could gain knowledge about soccer.
Q4 I felt that I could gain knowledge about soccer by interacting with people in the community.
Q5 The people in the community had core conversations about soccer.
Q6 I felt close to the community.
Q7 I was able to be interested in soccer.
Q8 I felt that the people in the community had a lot of information to share about soccer.
Q9 I felt that the community as a whole had a lot of information about soccer.

Result. Figure 3 shows the means and standard errors of the responses to each questionnaire item. Table 5 shows the results of the analysis of variance and multiple comparisons: In Q0, 23 out of 24 participants answered soccer in all conditions, and the remaining one answered futsal in b1.

The results of the analysis of variance showed that there were significant differences in all the questions except for Q6. The multiple comparisons of all the questions that showed significant differences confirmed that b1 > b2, b3 in relation. In Q3, Q7, and Q9, the b3 > b2 result was not found. The b1 mean in Q7 was significantly higher than that in the other conditions. However, because the mean of b1 was 2.958, it could not be said that the participants were interested in soccer.

However, in Q5, the mean of the b1 responses was close to 4, indicating that the participants were able to feel that the community was talking about core content.

Discussion for Results. In this study, communication among users who form a community was not considered, so participants might not have felt familiarity to the community from the tweets. However, the significant trend of Q6 suggests that familiarity might occur in communities with a large amount of knowledge.

The tweets of the users optimized by the proposed method were evaluated as including more knowledge about soccer and talking about more core contents. Tweets containing surrounding words were perceived as somewhat more knowledgeable than those that did not. Therefore, hypotheses 1 and 2 were supported.

4.3 Experiment 3: Verification of Knowledge Spread Using Knowledge Domain Clusters

Purpose and Overview. We examined whether users could perceive extensive knowledge when they were clustered according to the knowledge domain based on surrounding

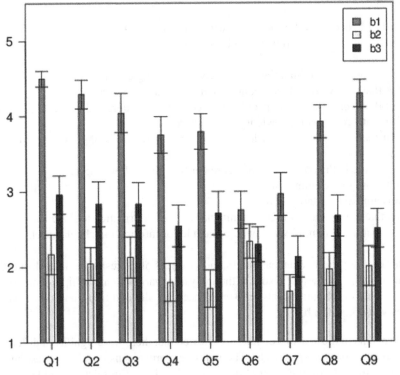

Fig. 3. Exp. 2: Q1–Q9 Mean and standard deviation of results

Table 5. Exp. 2: results of one-factor analysis of variance

	F	P	Multiple comparison
Q1	41.917	0.0000	b1 > b3 > b2
Q2	24.456	0.0000	b1 > b3 > b2
Q3	18.007	0.0000	b1 > b2, b3
Q4	22.864	0.0000	b1 > b3 > b2
Q5	19.366	0.0000	b1 > b3 > b2
Q6	2.846	0.0683	–
Q7	11.431	0.0001	b1 > b2, b3
Q8	19.806	0.0000	b1 > b3 > b2
Q9	30.646	0.0000	b1 > b2, b3

words. When clustering is based on the frequency of occurrence of surrounding words, the knowledge domains of users in each cluster should be similar. Therefore, rather than selecting multiple users from the same cluster, we expected that selecting users from several different clusters would result in less overlap of knowledge and more extensive knowledge. In this experiment, we compared the optimization data using a user list clustered by the k-means method and a randomly clustered user list.

Hypotheses. We hypothesized that the participants would feel the following:

(1) Tweets from communities optimized using clusters formed by the k-means method have larger knowledge extension than those that are not.

Condition. We chose "baseball" as the target topic (sport name) in this experiment. For clustering, we used the frequency of occurrence of 50 surrounding words to quantify the users' knowledge domain.

To examine whether users perceived expansive knowledge depending on whether they were clustered by surrounding words, we set the experimental condition as a within-subjects design with the following factor and two conditions:

c1: Cluster classification by the k-means method, using the frequency of occurrence of surrounding words as the feature value
c2: Cluster classification by randomly dividing the total data into 10 clusters

In c1, 10 clusters were generated by the k-means method according to the frequency of occurrence of surrounding words. In c2, user data was randomly arranged and divided into 10 clusters. A community of 8 members was generated.

Participants. Twenty-four university students aged 19 to 27 participated in the experiment.

Experimental Procedure. The participants proceeded with the experiment according to the following flow.

(1) Listen to the explanation of the experiment
(2) Read the tweets of community members
(3) Answer the questions

The content of the instructions given to the participants was the same as in Experiment 2.

Evaluation Procedure. For the following questions Q1–Q6, we used the same evaluation and analysis methods as in Experiment 1, and participants answered Q0 in the same way.

Q0: What kind of sports did you think this community was talking about?
Q1 I felt that people in the community had common knowledge.
Q2 I felt that people in the community mentioned baseball.
Q3 I felt that there was variation in the information in the community.
Q4 I felt that people in the community were engaged in conversation.
Q5 I felt that people in the community were exchanging information.
Q6 Each tweeter seemed to have a different area of special interest.

Results. Figure 4 shows the means and standard errors of the responses to each questionnaire item. Table 6 shows the results of the t-test. 24 out of 24 subjects answered baseball in all conditions for Q0.

The results of the t-test are shown in Table 6. In Q3, the mean response values for each condition were the same and exceeded 4, suggesting that variation was felt in both conditions. In the case of Q4 and Q5, the mean values were lower than 3 in both conditions without showing any significant difference, suggesting that the subjects did not feel as if they were having a conversation or exchanging information only when the contents of each user's post were presented.

Discussion for Results. In Q6, the mean of c_1 was significantly higher than that of c_2, indicating that hypothesis 1 was supported. In Q3, it was indicated that the variation of information in the community as a whole was the same in both groups. The reason could be that the participants could not perceive differences in the breadth of information and specialties because the optimization calculations were performed in both conditions. The high mean value of c_1 responses in Q6 indicated that there seemed to be differences in the specialty areas of the speakers in the community. Therefore, the clustering of users using the frequency information of surrounding words by the k-means method is considered to have been effective. If the surrounding words were given characteristic information such as location, player name, team name, etc., and if the number of noisy words were reduced, we might see more variation in the community information.

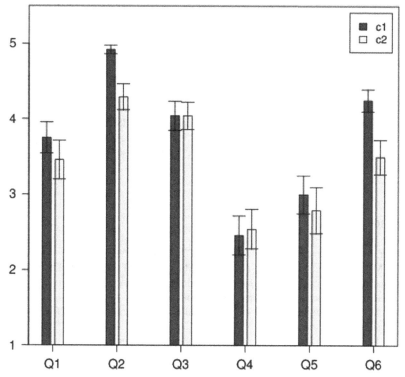

Fig. 4. Exp. 3: Q1–Q6 Mean and standard deviation of results

Table 6. Exp. 3: results of the t-test

	t	p
Q1	0.86708	0.3904
Q2	3.3874	0.0021
Q3	0	1.0000
Q4	−0.22181	0.8254
Q5	0.51607	0.6083
Q6	2.7029	0.0064

5   Conclusion

In this paper, we proposed a system to compute optimal connections for knowledge acquisition on Twitter, and we validated its effectiveness through subject experiments. However, due to the nature of the knapsack problem, it is difficult to quantify the dynamic interrelationships among users. As a future research project, we intend to tackle these problems, observe the long-term changes in the user groups, and develop a dynamic system. We have shown the effectiveness of our optimization system in terms of the amount of knowledge, but it remains to be examined whether our system can work effectively when more sentimental evaluation items are set. In this study, we used an easy-to-understand upper-level concept of "sports" for sports names. To establish a more general method, we need to develop a method to find upper-level concepts from certain words, or simply increase the amount of training data.

Acknowledgements. This research is supported in part by JSPS KAKENHI 19H04154, 18K11383, and 19K12090. We would like to thank Dr. Yuji Nakagawa for discussing the optimization method using non-linear knapsack problem. We would also like to thank the participants in the experiments.

References

1. Glover, F.: Surrogate constraints. Oper. Res. **16**, 741–749 (1968)
2. Dyer, M.E.: Calculating surrogate constraints. Math. Program. **19**(1), 255–278 (1980)
3. Nakagawa, Y.: An improved surrogate constraints method for separable nonlinear integer programming. J. Oper. Res. Soc. Jpn. **46**(2), 145–163 (2003)
4. Kudo, T.: Mecab: yet another part-of-speech and morphological analyzer (2006). https://sourceforge.net/projects/mecab/
5. Hong, L., Dan, O., Davison, B.D.: Predicting popular messages in Twitter. In: Proceedings of the 20th International Conference Companion on World Wide Web (2011)
6. Golbeck, J., et al.: Predicting personality from twitter. In: 2011 IEEE Third International Conference on Privacy, Security, Risk and Trust and 2011 IEEE Third International Conference on Social Computing. IEEE (2011)
7. Kumar, S., Carley, K.M.: What to track on the Twitter streaming API? A knapsack bandits approach to dynamically update the search terms. In: Proceedings of the 2019 IEEE/ACM International Conference on Advances in Social Networks Analysis and Mining (2019)
8. Lu, C., Lam, W., Zhang, Y.: Twitter user modeling and tweets recommendation based on Wikipedia concept graph. In: Workshops at the Twenty-Sixth AAAI Conference on Artificial Intelligence (2012)
9. Karidi, D.P., Stavrakas, Y., Vassiliou, Y.: Tweet and followee personalized recommendations based on knowledge graphs. J. Ambient Intell. Humaniz. Comput. **9**(6), 2035–2049 (2018)
10. Le, Q., Mikolov, T.: Distributed representations of sentences and documents. In: International Conference on Machine Learning (2014)
11. Dhir, A., et al.: Antecedents and consequences of social media fatigue. Int. J. Inf. Manage. **48**, 193–202 (2019)
12. Twitter, Inc.: Q3-2020-Shareholder-Letter (2020). https://s22.q4cdn.com/826641620/files/doc_financials/2020/q3/Q3-2020-Shareholder-Letter.pdf
13. Pisinger, D.: A minimal algorithm for the 0-1 knapsack problem. Oper. Res. **45**(5), 758–767 (1997)
14. Sasakawa Sports Foundation: Sports Dictionary - List of About 200 Sports - Sasakawa Sports Foundation (2018). https://www.ssf.or.jp/dictionary/tabid/884/Default.aspx

Being Part of an "Intermediate Community" and Aggressive Behavior on the Net: A Study on Cyberbullying Inside the Contrade of Siena in Italy

Oronzo Parlangeli[(⊠)] [ID], Enrica Marchigiani, Margherita Bracci, Maurizio Boldrini, Ileana Di Pomponio[ID], and Paola Palmitesta[ID]

Department of Social, Political and Cognitive Sciences, University of Siena, P.zzo san Niccolò, via Roma 56, Siena, Italy
{oronzo.parlangeli,enrica.marchigiani,margherita.bracci,
maurizio.boldrini,ileana.dipomponio,paola.palmitesta}@unisi.it

Abstract. The study investigates cyberbullying within the *Contrade* (singular *"Contrada"*) of Siena. The objective is to explore whether and how intermediate communities such as the *Contrade* of Siena, social bodies which are intermediate between the individual and the State, with their own rules and values, can play a protective role or increase the risk of detrimental behavior on the Net. Adolescents (N = 304) aged between 11 and 16 years completed an online questionnaire on moral disengagement [1], their relations with the *Contrada*, the values attributed to the *Contrada*, the use of social media [2], cyberbullying and cyber-victimization [3]. The study highlights that intermediate communities can have a protective function, through the values they manage to convey and represent, both to those who are part of them and to those who perceive them from the outside.

Keywords: Cyberbullying · Cybervictimization · Social media disorder · Intermediate communities

1 Introduction

1.1 Cyberbullying

Cyberbullying manifests itself with aggression perpetrated online and repeated over time that may involve the use of different media: e-mail and instant-messaging systems, social media, video channels. Bully's behaviors may be different, sometimes more aimed at threatening, others at making ridicule, while others take the form of offenses [4–15]. Cyberbullying is a phenomenon that correlates first and foremost with time spent online but can also manifest itself differently depending on the type of device used. There is evidence that especially younger people are prone to suffer behaviors that can be qualified as cyberbullying if they use cell phones more, which is not the case for those who use other media [16]. The greater propensity of girls/teenagers to use cell phones and

© Springer Nature Switzerland AG 2021
G. Meiselwitz (Ed.): HCII 2021, LNCS 12774, pp. 121–135, 2021.
https://doi.org/10.1007/978-3-030-77626-8_8

connect to the Internet probably exposes them more to the risks of aggressive behavior. In fact, among 11–17 years old girls, there is a higher proportion of victims compared to boys of the same age. There is also a greater risk for girls and boys between 11 and 13 years old than for older adolescents. However, some studies that focus on high school students highlight that the rate of cyberbullying can reach very high percentages in these populations as well, from 21 to 30% [17, 18]. In Italy, a study recently conducted on a sample of high school students reports that 23% of research participants have offended at least once by posting or writing embarrassing messages through social networks [8].

Cyberbullying is not only related to the socio-demographic characteristics of those who suffer it or to the way in which social networking systems are used. Many studies have shown that cyberbullying is a particularly complex phenomenon and that it is related to factors that affect individuals in their complexity, and that may be mediated by relational skills, as well as by the characteristics of the familiar, school and social contexts of reference [19, 20].

At an individual level, bullies and cyberbullies demonstrate extensive use of cognitive mechanisms aimed at diminishing the negative consequences of offending acts [1, 21] and at preserving an adequate level of self-esteem [22, 23]. This may also be related to the difficulties that bullies have in dealing with ethical issues [22]. But again, as demonstrated in other contexts [24], ethical behaviors can be influenced by factors at a higher level than the individual and refer to moral values that characterize social groups or communities. Some studies highlight how cyberbullying behavior decreases as a consequence of greater adherence to moral values: non-aggressive behavior is correlated with higher appreciations of values such as friendship and respect [22, 23], the same values that, among others, are the foundation of participation in social groups.

A sense of belonging to a community can convey positive values and the ability to establish relationships within groups are critical to developing social skills and preventing both acts of bullying and victimization [9, 19, 20, 25]. Conversely, the need to belong to a group and the fear of social exclusion also represent one of the major motivations that may drive adolescents to perpetrate bullying [26, 27].

To date, however, the role that "intermediate communities" may have on these types of phenomena has not been analyzed. These are groups of individuals (associations, cooperatives, unions, parishes, clubs, parties, bodies of any kind, etc.) that can freely aggregate to develop each individuality and that are located between the State and the individual level. Intermediate communities represent a value for democracy and are acknowledged for the growth and the well-being of the individual [28].

In the panorama of any other European city, the *Contrade* of Siena are a unique example of an intermediate community. Descended from the ancient military companies that in the 13th century had the task of defending and patrolling the city walls, the *Contrade* have survived to this day as particular forms of association strongly tied to the city's territory, bodies endowed with legal personality, distinct and autonomous among themselves, representing small municipalities within the larger city of Siena[1]. *The Contrade* of Siena are 17 areas of the historical center of the city that, over the centuries, have each been identified with a name, a coat of arms, a flag, precise boundaries and

---

[1] IPSOS 2020 Survey of Intermediate Bodies in http://www.astridonline.it/static/upload/b359/b35 97ecdb5c4f12ab0ca061ab895a742.pdf.

their own administration. The *Contrade* are regulated by a "statute" that establishes the general aims, but also the activities and the internal organization. To be a member of a *Contrada* means to be a *Contradaiolo* (plural *Contradaioli*), a person who belongs to the *Contrada*, a supporter and a sympathizer with its cause. A person who, in most cases, has assumed and developed from the earliest periods of his or her existence an identity linked to the *Contrada*.

Each *Contrada* has within it a set of facilities and premises such as the church and the museum where its history is kept and where the drapes of the *Palio* won are kept. In fact, the objective that most characterizes the *Contrada* is to win the horse race, the "*Palio*", which is run twice a year and gives glory and supremacy to the winning *Contrada* over the rest of the city. Within the *Contrade*, special attention is dedicated to the younger members of the community. The "Gruppo Piccoli" (The Youngest Group - to 12 years of age) and the "Giovani *Contradaioli*" (Young *Contradaioli* - from 12 to 16 years of age) are run by adults from the same *Contrada* who voluntarily organize events and transmit the values and knowledge of their *Contrada*. The *Contrada*, therefore, is not only an area of the city, but primarily a place of relationships and a set of values and meanings to which one adheres with one's individual and collective history, with one's thoughts, with one's affections [29].

Studying the phenomenon of cyberbullying within the *Contrade* allows us to understand if and how intermediate communities, with their own relationships, rules and values can modulate the risk of cyberbullying by creating protective circumstances or, on the contrary, as a consequence of the dynamics of opposition between *Contrade*, represent a danger to the children and adolescents who are part of them.

2   Method

2.1   Aim of the Study

The main objective of the study was to consider individual and socio-relational variables in relation to a sample of adolescents that are part of the *Contrade*, in order to understand if these communities, with their strong sense of identity and longstanding traditional culture, may affect the behavior of adolescents with respect to cyberbullying and cybervictimization phenomena.

The variables taken into consideration ranged from the use of social media to the time spent and the activities carried out within the *Contrada* premises, the values attributed to the *Contrada* and the sense of belonging to it. The individual characteristics relating to moral disengagement were also analyzed and bully or victim behaviors were explored.

The research was part of the "Salute in *Contrada*" Project promoted by the University of Siena and the "*Magistrato delle Contrade*" of Siena (the representative and protection body of the *Contrade* and of the *Palio* di Siena). The Project aimed at investigating the extent of the cyberbullying phenomenon in the *Contrade* of Siena.

The protocol of the study was approved by the Ethics Committee for Research in the Human and Social Sciences (CAREUS) of the University of Siena.

Table 1. Socio-demographic variables and social network usage.

Variable	N	%
Participants	304	100.00
Male	110	36.18
Female	194	63.82
Age		
11–13	48	15.79
14–16	256	84.21
School attended		
Middle school	40	13.20
High school	180	59.41
Institutes	83	27.39
Social network usage		
Less than 1 h a day	27	8.91
1 to 3 h a day	191	63.04
4 to 5 h a day	68	22.44
More than 5 h a day	17	5.61
Social I use mostly		
Instagram	280	9.11
Whatsapp	302	99.34
Youtube	152	50.00

2.2 Measures

The questionnaire consisted of 59 questions and was divided into 6 sections.

The first one, consisting of 6 questions, collected general information about the sample: place of birth, age, gender, school attended. The second section (13 questions) collected information on the type, frequency and experience of use of social networks, in order to detect the possible pathological use through the SMDS - Social Media Disorder Scale [30]. Moreover, participants were asked information about the type, frequency and experience of use of social networks: "Which social networks do you use mainly", "How long have you been using social networks" and "What is the frequency of use of social networks" (Table 1). The third section (21 questions) aimed at collecting information with respect to time spent in the *Contrada*, activities performed, values attributed to the *Contrada*, and friendships in the *Contrada*. This section had also some open questions, such as "For me the *Contrada* is…". The fourth and fifth sections were structured to obtain information on any aggressive behavior on the network, enacted and/or suffered (cyberbullying and/or cybervictimization, 11 questions).

Finally, the last section (8 questions) collected information in relation to the different cognitive mechanisms that can be put in place to justify misbehavior through the Moral Disengagement Scale [1].

Each of the participants was asked to answer the questionnaire without a specific time limit.

SMDS – Social Media Disorder Scale. A growing number of studies highlights how addiction and compulsive use of social networks is qualified as a mental disorder [31, 32] that is becoming increasingly common, especially among adolescents [33], and how this can be associated with cyberbullying behaviors [8].

To evaluate the degree to which adolescents are addicted to social media, the SMDS - Social Media Disorder Scale [30] was translated and used. The scale consists of 9 questions aimed at evaluating the presence or absence of certain purposes or needs related to the use of social media (e.g., "Have you tried to use social media less but failed?" or "Have you often used social media to escape negative feelings?") and corresponding to 9 criteria such as worry, forbearance, abstention, persistence, neglect, discussion, deception, escape, and confrontation. The scale involves Yes/No responses, which are then summed, where 5 or more "Yes" responses indicate compulsive social media use.

Scales of Cyberbullying and Cybervictimization. This part of the questionnaire (11 questions) is preceded by a brief description that defines cyberbullying [13]. It includes three questions about the perceived frequency of occurrence of disparaging behavior, perpetrated through the use of social networks, i) within one's own *Contrada*, ii) in other *Contrade*, and iii) outside of *Contrade* (responses are collected on a 5-point scale where never = 1 and 5 = always). The section also includes two questions about any direct experiences of cyberbullying, perpetrated ("Have you experienced posting embarrassing photos, or disparaging images, hurtful words, or confidential and personal information of someone from your *Contrada* or other *Contrade* so that other people could read it?") or suffered ("Have you experienced being publicly mocked through the publication of photos, or disparaging images, hurtful words, or by means of the dissemination of confidential and personal information, blocked on a social group?"). Responses are collected on a 5-point scale (from 1 = never to 5 = always).

It is also asked, with two questions, to assess the perception of seriousness of the act possibly committed or suffered on a 5-point scale (1 = very little and 5 = very much).

It is then asked with two other questions if the denigrating act, acted or suffered, concerns boys or girls of their own district. Here too the scale used is a 5-point scale where 1 = never and 5 = always.

Moral Disengagement Scale. As evidenced by recent studies, individuals more prone to moral disengagement are more likely to have aggressive and antisocial behaviors [8].

Bandura [1] described 8 mechanisms that act on 4 areas of the moral self-regulation process (the behavior, the agent, the victim, and the effect of the behavior) that function to downplay the seriousness of the behavior enacted (euphemistic labeling, advantageous comparison, moral justification…) relieve the perpetrator of the behavior of his responsibility (diffusion of responsibility and displacement of responsibility), make the victim deserving of the treatment suffered (dehumanization of the victim, attribution of guilt) positively reinterpret the effect caused by the behavior enacted as something positive (distortion of consequences).

The moral disengagement rating scale that we used [2] includes 8 statements, one for each of the mechanisms involved. For each statement, the participant has to express the degree of agreement/disagreement according to a 5-point Likert scale from $1 = $ not at all agree to $5 = $ fully agree.

In this study 5 items (1, 2, 3, 5 and 8) of the original scale were adapted to refer to the *Contrade*, such as the item: "It is okay to come to blows to protect your friends" was changed to: "It is okay to come to blows if someone bullies one of your friends in the *Contrada*", or the item: "People who are mistreated usually deserve it" has been replaced by "People who are mistreated in the *Contrada* usually deserve it".

3   Results and Discussion

3.1   Experience Using Social Media

Social media use experience data (SMDS) showed that 44 (14.5%) of the adolescents participating in the study met five or more of the criteria for hypothesizing addiction and/or compulsive use of social networks, in accordance with the cut-off for IGD in the DSM-5 [30, 34].

Victims show more problematic social media use behavior than their aggressors (cyberbullies: mean $= 2.09$, SD $= 1.78$; cybervictims: mean $= 3.22$, SD $= 1.64$; $F_{(1, 62)} = 6.626$, $p < .05$).

The Chi-square test on responses to the SMDS scale items showed significant differences between: victims, bullies, neither victims nor bullies, or both (see Table 2). In particular, victims reported, to a greater extent than others: feelings of dissatisfied because they would have liked to spend more time on social networks ($Chi^2_{(3)} = 8.300$, $p < .05$), and that they often tell lies to parents or friends about how much time they were spending on social media ($Chi^2_{(3)} = 13.740$, $p < .05$). On the other end bullies reported, less than others of having tried to use social media less but failing to do so ($Chi^2_{(3)} = 9.378$, $p < .05$).

About the type, frequency and experience of use of social networks, there were some differences between bullies and non-bullies. Bullies (36%) use Tik Tok significantly more than non-bullies (16%) ($Chi^2_{(1)} = 4.752$, $p < .05$). As expected, Tik Tok is one of the social networks with a high risk for cyberbullying [35].

Bullies (20%) reported using social media for less than 1 year, significantly less than what reported by non-bullies (5%) ($Chi^2_{(3)} = 6.603$, $p < .05$). As confirmation, this percentage of bullies belongs to the youngest age group (14 years). However, bullies (44%) use social media significantly for more hours per day (4 to 5 h per day) than non-bullies (20%) ($Chi^2_{(3)} = 6.603$, $p < .05$).

Analysis of variance on the two items related to social use in *Contrada* showed a significant effect on time spent on social media outside and inside the *Contrada* (Wilks' Lambda$_{(1, 298)} = .236$, $p < .05$). Participants reported that when they are inside the *Contrada* they spend significantly less time on social media (inside the *Contrada*: mean

Table 2. SMDS - social media disorder scale

During the last period	Neither victims nor bullies (n = 224)		Bullies (n = 23)		Victims (n = 41)		Both (n = 13)	
	n.	%	n.	%	n.	%	n.	%
I have used social media as a way to escape negative feelings	113	50.4%	12	52.2%	26	63.4%	8	61.5%
I have tried to use social media less. but have not been able to do so	87	38.8%	3*	13.0%	20	48.8%	7	53.8%
I have had social media as a fixed thought	61	27.2%	9	39.1%	15	36.6%	5	38.5%
I had arguments about how I used social media	58	25.9%	12	52.2%	17	41.5%	8*	61.5%
Often lied to parents or friends about how much time he/she was spending on social media	59	26.3%	2	8.7%	20*	48.8%	5	38.5%
I had a serious confrontation with parents or siblings/sisters because of my use of social media	42	18.8%	3	13.0%	14	34.1%	4	30.8%
I neglected other activities such as sports. hobbies. etc.	26	11.6%	2	8.7%	6	14.6%	2	15.4%
Often felt bad because I couldn't use the Internet	25	11.2%	3	13.0%	5	12.2%	1	7.7%
I felt dissatisfied because I would have liked to spend more time on social networks	17	7.6%	2	8.7%	9*	22.0%	1	7.7%

Note. The "both" column refers to participants who reported both engaging in cyberbullying behaviors and being cybervictimized. *Standardized residual greater than |1.96|, significant Chi^2 for $p < .05$.

$= 1.84$, SD $= .831$; outside the *Contrada*: mean $= 3.49$, SD $= .857$, $F_{(1,298)} = 966.088$, $p < .05$). The *Contrada* could therefore have a positive effect in limiting virtual aggressive behaviors, perpetrated or suffered, since, as already highlighted in the literature, the importance of being less connected to the network emerges as a protective factor for both victims and bullies [8, 9, 36].

Consistent with data reported in the literature [8, 31, 36, 37], girls appear to have a greater dependence on social networks than males, using the network more both inside (females: mean $= 1.97$, SD $= .839$; males: mean $= 1.62$, SD $= .770$; $F_{(1,433)} = 9.199$, $p < .05$) and outside the *Contrada* (females: mean $= 3.59$, SD $= .853$; males: mean $= 3.31$, SD $= .837$; $F_{(1,296)} = 12.596$, $p < .05$) (Wilks' Lambda$_{(2, 296)} = .953$, $p < .05$).

3.2 Life and Values of the *Contrada*

The answers to the question ("For me the *Contrada* is...") were divided according to their semantic value into two categories, the affective-relational and the values.

From an affective-relational point of view, the *Contrada* is felt primarily as: a family or a second home (43.06%), a place where one can meet friends or make friends (5.83%), a place of fun and carefree living (4.17%), of passion (2.78%), happiness (1.39%).

Answers referring to values say that the *Contrada* represents "life" (21.11%), "one's everything" or "a very important place" (10.56%), where one learns respect and humanity.

Just 3% of the answers concerns subjects who say they are not part of a *Contrada* while 4.5% perceive it as a non-inclusive place or with a negative meaning.

Participants believe that the values of the *Contrada* can be learned at a young age, both by living in the *Contrada* with peers (mean $= 4.13$, SD $= .949$) and by observing adults (mean $= 3.82$, SD $= 1.108$) rather than thinking that the values cannot be learned at all because a "true *Contrada* member has them inside" (mean $= 2.44$, SD $= 1.406$; Wilks' Lambda$_{(4, 293)} = .405$, $p < .05$).

There were no significant differences in perception of *Contrada* values between bullies and non-bullies (Wilks' Lambda$_{(1, 293)} = .985$, $p = .282$) and between cybervictims and non-cybervictims (Wilks' Lambda$_{(1, 293)} = .970$, $p = .119$).

3.3 Perception and Experiences of Cyberbullying and Cybervictimization

The results regarding cyberbullying behaviors perpetrated or suffered are in line with other studies [3, 8, 17]: 12.4% of the sample claims to have misbehaved online and 27.3% to have been publicly mocked through social media.

Bullies believe their misbehavior is not particularly serious, in line with the responses of those who are neither bullies nor victims (bullies: mean $= 2.95$., SD $= 1.203$; non-bullies and non-victims: mean $= 3.43$, SD $= 1.728$; $F_{(1, 88)} = 1.422$, $p = .236$). Conversely, victims felt that the misbehavior they experienced was more severe than those who were neither bullies nor victims (victims: mean $= 3.82$, SD $= 1.393$; non-bullies and non-victims: mean $= 3.11$, SD $= 1.545$; $F_{(1, 73)} = 4.372$, $p < .05$).

The bullies declare that they direct their offensive behaviors above all towards people from a different *Contrada* than their own (other *Contrada*: mean $= 3.09$, SD $=$

1.571; own *Contrada*: mean = 1.59, SD = .909; Wilks' Lambda$_{(1, 21)}$ = .616, p < .05). Victims, likewise, believe that the abusive behaviors they experienced came primarily from persons belonging to a different *Contrada* than their own (other *Contrada*: mean = 2.95, SD = 1.301; own *Contrada*: mean = 1.87, SD = 1.301; Wilks' Lambda$_{(1, 38)}$ = .803, p < .05). Cyberbullying is therefore perceived, both by the perpetrator and the recipient, as a more frequent behavior outside of the *Contrada* of belonging.

The data on the perception of the phenomenon of cyberbullying inside and outside of the *Contrada* show that these are considered, compared to the outside world, a safer place. Bullies report feeling much more *Contradaioli* ("How *Contradaiolo* do you think you are?" mean = 4.50, SD = 1.021) than they feel perceived as such by others in the *Contrada* ("How much do others in the *Contrada* think you are *Contradaiolo*" mean = 4.25, SD = 1.11), significantly (Wilks' Lambda$_{(1, 23)}$ = .750, p < .05).

Similarly, victims perceived themselves as much *Contradaioli* ("How *Contradaiolo* do you feel?" mean = 4.46, SD = .636) and think they are perceived as less *Contradaioli* by those who belong to their own *Contrada* ("How much do others in the *Contrada* think you are *Contradaiolo*" mean = 3.66, SD = 1.131), significantly (Wilks' Lambda$_{(1, 40)}$ = .604, p < .05).

In summary, the framework of the analyses again shows a protective effect of *Contrada*: those who are not perceived as *Contradaiolo* or belong to another *Contrada* may be more likely to be exposed to cyberbullying behavior.

3.4 Moral Disengagement

The mean of the scale on moral disengagement is overall 1.88 (SD = .695) on the agreement scale ranging from 1 = not at all agree to 5 = completely agree.

The results of the study highlight the use of the mechanisms of moral justification ("It is okay to come to blows if someone bullies one of your friends in the *Contrada* " mean = 2.45, SD = 1.330); attribution of guilt ("People who are mistreated in the *Contrada* usually deserve it" mean = 2.21, SD = 1.312), thus shifting blame onto the victim; diffusion of responsibility ("Teens who cyberbully other teens because their friends push them to do so should not be blamed for what they do," mean = 1.99, SD = 1.405), thus shifting blame onto others (see Fig. 1).

The results of the study highlight a greater reliance on moral disengagement mechanisms by those who experienced aggressive online behaviors than those who did not (bullies: mean = 2.36, SD = .748; non-bullies: mean = 1.84, SD = .669; F$_{(1, 253)}$ = 13.781, p < .05). More specifically, a multivariate analysis of variance on the moral disengagement items showed a significant effect of the cyberbullying variable on 4 of the 8 factors (Wilks' Lambda$_{(8, 246)}$ = .203, p < .05). Bullies, compared to non-bullies, were found to have higher scores on: distortion of responsibility, dehumanization of the victim, attribution of guilt and moral justification (see Table 3).

It is interesting to examine the relationship between moral disengagement and perceptions about *Contrada* values. Those with high moral disengagement scores, i.e., those who tend to inhibit feelings of guilt for actions that are transgressive of standards to which the individual refers, believe that *Contrada* values are learned as children from parents (high disengagement: mean = 3.84, SD = 1.214; low disengagement: mean = 3.26, SD = 1.158; F$_{(1, 251)}$ = 14.484, p < .05) or by living in the neighborhood, observing adults

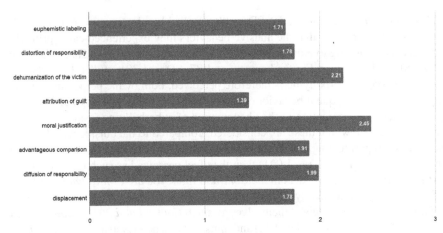

Fig. 1. Mean of moral disengagement subscales.

Table 3. Moral disengagement subscales in bullies compared to non-bullies

	Bullies (n = 23)		Non bullies (n = 229)			
	Mean	SD	Mean	SD	F	P
Euphemistic labeling	2.08	0.935	1.69	1.129	2.768	0.097
Distortion of responsibility	2.42	1.172	1.69	1.065	10.709	**0.001**
Dehumanization of the victim	2.81	1.601	2.13	1.253	6.408	**0.012**
Attribution of guilt	1.92	1.294	1.33	0.802	10.946	**0.001**
Moral justification	3.04	1.311	2.35	1.304	6.596	**0.011**
Advantageous comparison	2.19	1.386	1.84	1.044	2.435	0.120
Diffusion of responsibility	2.35	1.325	1.93	1.398	2.132	0.145
Displacement	2.08	1.324	1.76	0.937	2.500	0.115

(high disengagement: mean = 4.11, SD = 1.096; low disengagement: mean = 3.65, SD = 1.095; $F_{(1, 251)}$ = 10.451, p < .05).

3.5 Predictive Factors of Cyberbullying and Cybervictimization

To analyze whether and which variables might be predictive of bully and/or victim behavior, and whether a sense of belonging to the *Contrada* and living the *Contrada* might be a protective factor, regression analyses of cyberbullying and cybervictimization were conducted.

A first multiple logistic binomial regression analysis examined the predictive power of some socio-demographic factors on cyberbullying: age, gender, being born and living in Siena, degree of social media dependence, degree of moral disengagement with respect to bullying behaviors towards one's own and other *Contrade*, having been a victim of cyberbullying. Overall, the model was significant ($R^2 = .197$, $p < .05$; see Table 4). Significant predictors were moral disengagement ($B = .66$) and having been a victim of cyberbullying ($B = .50$).

Table 4. Predictive factors of cyberbullying: logistic regression

	B	S.E.	Wald	gl	Sig.	Exp(B)
Gender	0.173	0.558	0.096	1	0.756	1.189
Age	−0.387	0.361	1.149	1	0.284	0.679
Native of Siena	0.922	0.796	1.345	1	0.246	2.515
Living in Siena	−1.391	0.809	2.957	1	0.086	0.249
Moral disengagement	**0.657**	0.216	9.285	1	**0.002**	1.929
Cybervictimization	**0.500**	0.237	4.439	1	**0.035**	1.648
Social media disorder	−0.036	0.253	0.02	1	0.887	0.965

Note. Predictors: Gender (0 = f, 1 = m), Age, Native of Siena (0 = non, 1 = yes), Living in Siena (0 = non, 1 = yes), Moral disengagement, Cybervictimization, Social media disorder scale (SDMS). Nagelkerke's $R^2 = .197$, $Chi^2_{(3)} = 19.811$, $p < .05$. Predictors variables were standardized to facilitate the interpretation of B coefficients.

Participation and involvement in *Contrada* life could have indirect protective effects toward cyberbullying, as revealed by the framework of the data analyses already presented.

A second regression analysis examined the predictive power of the same factors on cybervictimization: age, gender, being born and living in Siena, degree of social media use/dependence, sense of belonging to the *Contrada* and being perceived by others as *Contradaioli*. Overall, the model was significant ($R^2 = .209$, $p < .05$; see Table 5).

Social media addiction and compulsive use of social media turns out to be a very strong predictor ($B = .72$) of being a victim of aggressive behavior. The *Contrada* once again play a significant role, in fact both being perceived by others as *Contradaioli* (item: "How much do others in the *Contrade* think you are *Contradaiolo*?", $B = -.62$) and the sense of belonging to the *Contrada* ($B = .82$) turn out to be a protective factor towards acts of cyberbullying.

In this context, therefore, the use and dependence on social media have a decisive weight only on the victims, while the perception of the *Contrada*, or rather "being *Contradaiolo*" is confirmed as a protective factor. Being born in Siena is a protective factor too.

Table 5. Predictive factors of cybervictimization: logistic regression

	B	S.E.	Wald	gl	Sig.	Exp(B)
Participants born in Siena	**−1.765**	0.814	4.703	1	**0.030**	0.171
Living in Siena	0.186	0.461	0.163	1	0.687	1.204
Social media disorder	**0.721**	0.177	16.701	1	**0.000**	2.057
Perceiving yourself as *Contradaiolo*	**0.816**	0.369	4.885	1	**0.027**	2.262
Being perceived as *Contradaiolo*	**−0.617**	0.287	4.634	1	**0.031**	0.539

Note. Predictors: Participants born in Siena (0 = non, 1 = yes), Living in Siena (0 = non, 1 = yes), Social media disorder scale (SDMS), "How much do you feel *Contradaiolo*", "How much do others in the *Contrade* think you are *Contradaiolo*?" ". Nagelkerke's $R^2 = .209$, $Chi^2_{(3)} = 31,466$, $p < .05$. Predictors variables were standardized to facilitate the interpretation of B coefficients.

4 Conclusions

One finding worthy of further reflection is that 12.4% of the sample says they have misbehaved online and 27.3% say they have been publicly abused through social media. In addition, 38.2% of the participants say that they have tried in the previous year to use social media less, but have not succeeded, while 31.9% have had social media as a fixed thought. In relation to these statements about uncontrolled use of social media, the *Contrade* appear to have a positive function by inducing less use of these media. This may be due to the activities that are carried out in the *Contrada*. At the same time, the *Contrade* are also considered a place where relationships are based on respect and values are learned, a place that interacts with one's sense of identity. It is evident how much the adolescents who participated in the study consider their *Contrada* as a protective community. But it is interesting to note that, if one takes into consideration the aggressive behaviors that can be perpetrated online, even the other *Contrade* are considered a safer place.

Above all, however, two pieces of evidence of particular interest emerge that seem to suggest a protective function that intermediate communities like the *Contrade* can provide to those who are part of them. The first refers to the positive role of the values transmitted to the individual by the community and that limit the implementation of reprehensible behaviors. The second refers to the protective, almost shielding role that the individual receives from "being part of" something that, from the outside, is perceived as a strong, positive, valuable community and that limits the risk of being the object of aggression. It can be assumed that perceptual factors, not only the visual ones [38, 39], but also those that can change the representation of social relations [40] can be managed to decrease the risk of the implementation of deplorable behavior among individuals.

Finally, although not directly concerning the main objectives of this study, it is worth noting the result that relates the use of Tik Tok by younger users with aggressive behavior. In previous studies a relationship between social networks such as ASK.fm and Snapchat and cyberbullying had been highlighted [8]. Now it is evident that younger people, evidently more naive and less mature from a psychological point of view, are focusing their online relational world on this new social media. As has already been indicated, however, it does not appear that Tik Tok's managers are yet building on previous social media experience to organize conditions of use that limit the possibility of enacting aggressive behavior [35].

In addition to an increased focus on determining proper terms of use by the managers of these platforms, it is possible to claim that in order to prevent these forms of aggressive behavior, it is necessary to promote programs of digital education. These should be addressed not only to adolescents, but also to older generations, such as parents or those who take care of children, in schools, in the sporting environment, and in contexts of socialization, such as in the city of Siena, *Contrade* can be. A further possibility of intervention seems to emerge from this study, which refers to the promotion of forms of aggregation within intermediate communities that carry shared moral values.

Acknowledgements. The authors are very grateful to the *Contrade* of Siena, in particular to the *Magistrato delle Contrade*, to the adults who take care of children and teens and to the young *Contradaioli* who, with their participation, made this study possible.

References

1. Bandura, A., Barbaranelli, C., Caprara, G.V., Pastorelli, C.: Mechanisms of moral disengagement in the exercise of moral agency. J. Pers. Soc. Psychol. **71**(2), 364–374 (1996). https://doi.org/10.1037/0022-3514.71.2.364
2. Meter, D.J., Bauman, S.: Moral disengagement about cyberbullying and parental monitoring: effects on traditional bullying and victimization via cyberbullying involvement. J. Early Adolesc. **38**(3), 303–326 (2018). https://doi.org/10.1177/0272431616670752
3. Calvete, E., Orue, I., Estévez, A., Villardón, L., Padilla, P.: Cyberbullying in adolescents: modalities and aggressors' profile. Comput. Hum. Behav. **26**(5), 1128–1135 (2010). https://doi.org/10.1016/j.chb.2010.03.017
4. Smith, P.K., López-Castro, L., Robinson, S., Görzig, A.: Consistency of gender differences in bullying in cross-cultural surveys. Aggress. Violent Behav. **45**, 33–40 (2019). https://doi.org/10.1016/j.avb.2018.04.006
5. Slonje, R., Smith, P.K.: Cyberbullying: another main type of bullying? Scand. J. Psychol. **49**(2), 147–154 (2008). https://doi.org/10.1111/j.1467-9450.2007.00611.x
6. Vandebosch, H., van Cleemput, K.: Cyberbullying among youngsters: profiles of bullies and victims. New Media Soc. **11**(8), 1349–1371 (2009). https://doi.org/10.1177/1461444480934 1263
7. Bracci, M., Duguid, A.M., Marchigiani, E., Palmitesta, P., Parlangeli, O.: Digital discrimination: an ergonomic approach to emotional education for the prevention of cyberbullying. In: Bagnara, S., Tartaglia, R., Albolino, S., Alexander, T., Fujita, Y. (eds.) IEA 2018. AISC, vol. 826, pp. 723–731. Springer, Cham (2019). https://doi.org/10.1007/978-3-319-96065-4_76
8. Parlangeli, O., Marchigiani, E., Bracci, M., Duguid, A.M., Palmitesta, P., Marti, P.: Offensive acts and helping behavior on the internet: an analysis of the relationships between moral disengagement, empathy and use of social media in a sample of Italian students. Work **63**(3), 469–477 (2019). https://doi.org/10.3233/wor-192935
9. Kowalski, R.M., Limber, S.P., Agatston, P.W.: Cyberbullying. Bullying in the Digital Age, 2nd edn. Wiley, Malden (2012)

10. Cassidy, W., Faucher, C., Jackson, M.: Introduction: context, framework, and perspective. In: Cassidy, W., Faucher, C., Jackson, M. (eds.) Cyberbullying at University in International Contexts, pp. 1–6. Routledge, London (2018)
11. Bauman, S., Toomey, R.B., Walker, J.L.: Associations among bullying, cyberbullying, and suicide in high school students. J. Adolesc. **36**(2), 341–350 (2013). https://doi.org/10.1016/j.adolescence.2012.12.001
12. Corcoran, L., Guckin, C., Prentice, G.: Cyberbullying or cyber aggression?: a review of existing definitions of cyber-based peer-to-peer aggression. Societies **5**(2), 245–255 (2015). https://doi.org/10.3390/soc5020245
13. Olweus, D., Limber, S.P.: Some problems with cyberbullying research. Curr. Opin. Psychol. **19**, 139–143 (2018). https://doi.org/10.1016/j.copsyc.2017.04.012
14. Hinduja, S., Patchin, J.W.: Bullying, cyberbullying, and suicide. Arch. Suicide Res. **14**(3), 206–221 (2010). https://doi.org/10.1080/13811118.2010.494133
15. Hinduja, S., Patchin, J.W.: Cyberbullying: an exploratory analysis of factors related to offending and victimization. Deviant Behav. **29**(2), 129–156 (2008). https://doi.org/10.1080/016396 20701457816
16. Athanasiou, K., et al.: Cross-national aspects of cyberbullying victimization among 14-17-year-old adolescents across seven European countries. BMC Public Health **18**(1), 800 (2018). https://doi.org/10.1186/s12889-018-5682-4
17. Beran, T., Li, Q.: Cyber-harassment: a study of a new method for an old behavior. J. Educ. Comput. Res. **32**(3), 265–277 (2005). https://doi.org/10.2190/8yqm-b04h-pg4d-bllh
18. Gámez-Guadix, M., Orue, I., Smith, P.K., Calvete, E.: Longitudinal and reciprocal relations of cyberbullying with depression, substance use, and problematic internet use among adolescents. J. Adolesc. Health **53**(4), 446–452 (2013). https://doi.org/10.1016/j.jadohealth.2013.03.030
19. Baldry, A.C., Farrington, D.P., Sorrentino, A.: "Am I at risk of cyberbullying"? A narrative review and conceptual framework for research on risk of cyberbullying and cybervictimization: the risk and needs assessment approach. Aggress. Violent Behav. **23**, 36–51 (2015). https://doi.org/10.1016/j.avb.2015.05.014
20. Zych, I., Farrington, D.P., Ttofi, M.M.: Protective factors against bullying and cyberbullying: a systematic review of meta-analyses. Aggress. Violent Behav. **45**, 4–19 (2019). https://doi.org/10.1016/j.avb.2018.06.008
21. Bandura, A.: Social Foundations of Thought and Action: A Social Cognitive Theory. Englewood, Prentice-Hall (1986)
22. Menesini, E., Nocentini, A., Calussi, P.: The measurement of cyberbullying: dimensional structure and relative item severity and discrimination. Cyberpsychol. Behav. Soc. Netw. **14**(5), 267–274 (2011). https://doi.org/10.1089/cyber.2010.0002
23. Büyükyıldırım, I., Dilmaç, B.: Investigation of cyber victimization in terms of humanitarian values and socio-demographic variables. J. Values Educ. **13**(29), 7–40 (2015)
24. Parlangeli, O., Guidi, S., Marchigiani, E., Bracci, M., Liston, P.M.: Perceptions of work-related stress and ethical misconduct amongst non-tenured researchers in italy. Sci. Eng. Ethics **26**(1), 159–181 (2020). https://doi.org/10.1007/s11948-019-00091-6
25. Slaten, C.D., Rose, C.A., Ferguson, J.K.: Understanding the relationship between youths' belonging and bullying behaviour: an SEM model. Educ. Child Psychol. **36**(2), 50–63 (2019)
26. Twenge, J.M., Baumeister, R.F., Tice, D.M., Stucke, T.S.: If you can't join them, beat them: effects of social exclusion on aggressive behavior. J. Pers. Soc. Psychol. **81**(6), 1058–1069 (2001). https://doi.org/10.1037/0022-3514.81.6.1058
27. Underwood, M.K., Ehrenreich, S.E.: Bullying may be fueled by the desperate need to belong. Theory Pract. **53**(4), 265–270 (2014). https://doi.org/10.1080/00405841.2014.947217

28. Rosboch M.: Le comunità intermedie tra storia e istituzioni. In: Rosboch M. (ed.) Le comunità intermedie e l'avventura costituzionale. Un percorso storico-istituzionale, pp. 11–69. Heritage Club, Rome (2017)
29. Weber, M.: Economia e Società. Comunità. Donzelli Editore, Rome (2016)
30. Van Den Eijnden, R.J.J.M., Lemmens, J.S., Valkenburg, P.M.: The social media disorder scale: validity and psychometric properties. Comput. Hum. Behav. **61**, 478–487 (2016). https://doi.org/10.1016/j.chb.2016.03.038
31. Pantic, I.: Online social networking and mental health. Cyberpsychol. Behav. Soc. Netw. **17**(10), 652–657 (2014). https://doi.org/10.1089/cyber.2014.0070
32. Ryan, T., Chester, A., Reece, J., Xenos, S.: The uses and abuses of facebook: a review of facebook addiction. J. Behav. Addict. **3**(3), 133–148 (2014). https://doi.org/10.1556/jba.3.2014.016
33. Van Rooij, A.J., Schoenmakers, T.M.: Factsheet: het (mobiele) gebruik van sociale media en games door jongeren. Cent. Behav. Internet Sci. (2013). https://doi.org/10.13140/rg.2.1.3396.8486
34. Lemmens, J.S., Valkenburg, P.M., Gentile, D.A.: The internet gaming disorder scale. Psychol. Assess. **27**(2), 567–582 (2015). https://doi.org/10.1037/pas0000062
35. Weimann, G., Masri, N.: Research note: spreading hate on TikTok. Stud. Confl. Terror., 1–14 (2020). https://doi.org/10.1080/1057610x.2020.1780027
36. Parlangeli, O., Marchigiani, E., Guidi, S., Bracci, M., Andreadis, A., Zambon, R.: I do it because i feel that…moral disengagement and emotions in cyberbullying and cybervictimisation. In: Meiselwitz, G. (ed.) HCII 2020. LNCS, vol. 12194, pp. 289–304. Springer, Cham (2020). https://doi.org/10.1007/978-3-030-49570-1_20
37. Blangiardo, G.C.: Indagine conoscitiva su bullismo e cyberbullismo (2019). https://www.istat.it/it/archivio/228976
38. Parlangeli, O., Roncato, S.: Draughtsmen at work. Perception **39**(2), 255–259 (2010). https://doi.org/10.1068/p6500
39. Guidi, S., Parlangeli, O., Bettella, S., Roncato, S.: Features of the selectivity for contrast polarity in contour integration revealed by a novel tilt illusion. Perception **40**(11), 1357–1375 (2011). https://doi.org/10.1068/p6897
40. Blake, E., Gannon, T.: Social perception deficits, cognitive distortions, and empathy deficits in sex offenders: a brief review. Trauma Violence Abus. **9**(1), 34–55 (2008). https://doi.org/10.1177/1524838007311104

Fake News Detection via English-to-Spanish Translation: Is It Really Useful?

Sebastián Ruíz[1], Eliana Providel[1,2], and Marcelo Mendoza[2(✉)]

[1] Escuela de Ingeniería Civil Informática, Universidad de Valparaíso,
Valparaíso, Chile
`sebastian.ruiz@alumnos.uv.cl`, `eliana.providel@uv.cl`
[2] Departamento de Informática, Universidad Técnica Federico Santa María,
Santiago, Chile
`marcelo.mendoza@usm.cl`

Abstract. Social networks are used every day to report daily events, although the information published in them many times correspond to fake news. Detecting these fake news has become a research topic that can be approached using deep learning. However, most of the current research on the topic is available only for the English language. When working on fake news detection in other languages, such as Spanish, one of the barriers is the low quantity of labeled datasets available in Spanish. Hence, we explore if it is convenient to translate an English dataset to Spanish using Statistical Machine Translation. We use the translated dataset to evaluate the accuracy of several deep learning architectures and compare the results from the translated dataset and the original dataset in fake news classification. Our results suggest that the approach is feasible, although it requires high-quality translation techniques, such as those found in the translation's neural-based models.

Keywords: Fake news · English-to-Spanish translation · Statistical Machine Translation · Deep learning · Twitter

1 Introduction

Today there are many different communications media, among which we can found social networks such as Twitter where the users can share news, express their opinions, resend information, or follow other users. A defining feature of social networks is that when a message is post, it is quickly propagated through the network, reaching many users in a short time.

In various situations, social networks have taken a leading role in being a communication media that makes it possible to inform about different events, such as natural disasters, and where people have been able to send alerts and request help [22,26,30]. However, there are also cases where social networks have been used to spread disinformation on the population, which on many

© Springer Nature Switzerland AG 2021
G. Meiselwitz (Ed.): HCII 2021, LNCS 12774, pp. 136–148, 2021.
https://doi.org/10.1007/978-3-030-77626-8_9

occasions has caused damage [4,11]. Given that all the information published on social networks cannot always be verified by specialists in real-time, by the amount of information published daily by different users, sometimes the spread of information corresponds to *fake news*. We consider the general concept of fake news as the intentional propagation of false information [2,16]. In this context, a false rumor is a specific type of fake news.

Fake news detection has become an active topic of research, with practical applications [19,38] related to news verification and fact-checking. This type of analysis uses different techniques such as user profiling, sentiment classification, and stance classification. On the other hand, these works are usually made with datasets extracted from social media, mostly from the Twitter platform. As a consequence, most of the results associated with fake news detection are available and applicable only for English, which hampers other applications or generalization of the results to other languages, such as Spanish.

To avoid the effort involved in the development of a new dataset in Spanish, we present an empirical evaluation of the application of *Statistical Machine Translation* (SMT) applied to the **Twitter16-EN** [19] dataset. First, we train the SMT model based on the available training corpus. Then, we use the model to automatically translate **Twitter16-EN** [19] dataset from English to Spanish. We use this new dataset to train different neural network architectures, following our previous methodology [27]. We consider various architectures including recurrent, convolutional, and feed-forward networks.

The main research questions of this paper are:

- Which is the optimal architecture of deep learning for the classification of fake news, based on the new dataset?
- What differences exist between the results obtained with **Twitter16-EN** and the results with **Twitter16-ES**, when applied to the same deep learning architectures?

The rest of this work is structured in the following way. First, we present related work in Sect. 2. Then we introduce the design of this study in Sect. 3. Experimental results are presented in Sect. 4. Finally, we conclude in Sect. 5.

2   Related Work

Existing literature on this research topic is pervasive. We organize this section into two parts covering machine translation and fake news detection work.

2.1   Machine Translation

Main Approaches. Machine translation has been approached from different languages and, in general, it is based on two main approaches: *Statistical Machine Translation (SMT)*, and *Neural Machine Translation (NMT)*. While the neural network approach has demonstrated better results, they usually require large amounts of data and high computer processing costs. On the other hand, the statistical approach can work with more limited data and lower computational requirements. These lower requirements are part of the motivation for using SMT in this work. More specifically, translation efforts can be evaluated using metrics, among which we highlight those used in this work:

- *Bi-Lingual Evaluation Understudy (BLEU)* [24]: It is a metric that measures the correspondence between automatic translation and human translation. The score is calculated based on the evaluation of individual text segments, usually sentences, compared with a set of reference translations made by human experts.
- *Metric for Evaluation of Translation with Explicit ORdering (METEOR)* [3]: It is a metric that aims to improve BLEU deficiencies, considering synonyms and other lexical forms. It also seeks to measure the correlation between the performance of automatic translation and human translation.

Recent Studies. SMT has been studied in different application domains. Costa-Jussa et al. [8] address the translation of texts between European and Brazilian Portuguese language, using an NMT model, with a BI-LSTM neural network that includes an attention mechanism. The results are compared with the performance of phrase-based SMT, where NMT shows the best results. For testing, they use a corpus of subtitle films, extracted from Opus[1] [32]. Lohar et al. [17] study the translation of texts from English to Serbian in a low-resource setting and where the Serbian language's complexity is morphologically rich. This language has a free enough word order and is bi-alphabetic (with Latin and Cyrillic characters). They use the dataset of Ma et al. [21] that has 50000 user reviews from IMDB films in English, using only 200 reviews. They also create a synthetic IMDB for translating the reviews from English to Serbian. For the experiments, they use (*phrase-based machine translation (PBMT)*, using the Moses [14] tool and other four NMT models implemented in OpenNMT [13]. Their results show that the morphology and syntax were better handled with neural approaches than with phrase-based approaches. Regarding the translation between Arabic and English, Bensalah et al. [23] use an encoder/decoder with recurrent bidirectional neuronal networks (BI-RNN). Specifically, one BI-LSTM encodes English sentences as vectors that are used in an LSTM decoder, using a sequence-to-sequence model.

Tweet Translation. One pioneering work [12] studies the translation of tweets from German to English using SMT. The authors show that when training with a formal language style, they do not have good results due to the informal nature of Twitter messages, which results in many Out-Of-Vocabulary (OOV) words. However, the results can improve using preprocessing techniques and domain adaptation. For training, they use the data of the European parliament[2]. Vathsala et al. [35] use a recurrent neuronal network (RNN-LSTM) for translating

---

[1] http://opus.nlpl.eu/.

[2] https://www.statmt.org/europarl/.

Twitter data in Hindi. In their work, the preprocessing of data plays an important role given by the colloquialisms of expressions. As a baseline, they use a system based on SMT at the level of sentences [31].

2.2   Fake News Detection

Based on Machine Learning. The detection of fake news has been studied from different approaches, with a primary focus on the English language. A seminal work in the field was presented by Castillo et al. [6] where they classify tweets as *credible* and *not credible*, based on text, user, and message propagation-based features. Similarly, Qazvinian et al. [28] work with three variants of features, content, network, and Twitter-specific stylometric features. They use Bayesian networks to solve the classification task. Kwon et al. [15] use user, linguistic, temporal, and network features for rumor detection tasks.

Based on Deep Learning. Ma et al. [18] use three types of neural architectures: RNN, LSTM/GRU, and multilayer GRU. In a later work, Ma et al. [20] propose two recursive neuronal models based on the propagation structure of messages. For the classification the labels used are *no-rumor, false rumor, true rumor,* and *unverified rumor.* Other approaches based on deep learning appear in the works of Yu et al. [37], where they use convolutional networks, Wang et al. [36] with adversarial networks, and Ajao et al. [1] with a hybrid model that includes LSTM and CNN, among others. Finally, Deepak et al. [9] combines the messages and the source of an article to characterize news spread. They use feed-forward and LSTM networks the check the veracity of the news.

Focused on the Spanish Language. Among the works that address the task of fake news detection in Spanish, we found the proposal of Posadas-Duran et al. [25], where many classical algorithms are studied. They represent the text using stylistic features, bag-of-words, character n-grams, and POS-tag n-grams. Boididou et al. [4] present a multimedia system for the detection of messages labeled as *real* and *fake* considering three languages: Spanish, English, and German. The tweets are represented using a set of features from the text along with user-profile features.

Datasets in Spanish. There are only a few datasets in Spanish for fake news detection. Among the existing datasets in Spanish, we found the proposal of Posadas-Duran et al. [25], that in total has 971 news[3]. The news are classified into nine categories. There is also a dataset used by Boididou et al. [4] related to the *MediaEval-2015 Verifying Multimedia Use (VMU)* task. The dataset comprises around 15500 tweets related to a set of images corresponding to real and fake news. Finally, Caled and Silva [5] developed the *FTR-18* dataset[4] containing newsworthy football tweets in different languages, where 747 labeled tweets are written in Spanish.

---

[3] https://github.com/jpposadas/FakeNewsCorpusSpanish.
[4] https://github.com/dcaled/FTR-18.

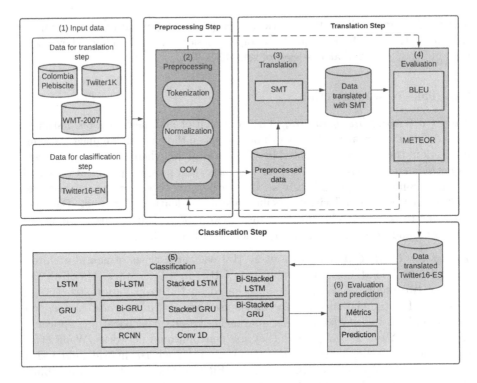

Fig. 1. General overview of our system.

3   Study Methodology

The study methodology considers three steps: data preprocessing, text translation, and classification, as is depicted Fig. 1. The datasets used are described
below, as well as each of the phases of this study.

3.1   Data Description

The study considers different datasets, allowing us to train the translation modules and the tweets used in the classification. The datasets used by the SMT
translator are:

– **WMT-2007** [33][5]: We use the partition "News Commentary Training Corpus" of this dataset, which comprises 238872 English-Spanish paired sentences. We also use the "Language Model Data" partition, using only the
   sentences in Spanish. The first partition was used to train the translation
   module, while the second was used to train the language model. Both datasets
   have a formal language in contrast to the colloquial language usually found
   in Twitter.

---

[5] http://opus.nlpl.eu/News-Commentary.php.

- **Colombia Plebiscite** [29]: This dataset was used to train the language model. It comprises more than 3000 tweets related to the 2016 Colombian plebiscite. We use this dataset due to its colloquial language, which is similar to the target language to be translated.
- **Twitter1K**: It corresponds to a set of 1000 tweets extracted from the **Twitter16-EN** dataset. These 1000 tweets were manually translated to be used as validation and testing partitions.

Once the translator is validated, we use the following dataset to study rumor verification:

- **Twitter16-EN** [19]: The dataset comprises a set of rumors and propagation threads, including responses, comments, and retweets, thus forming a conversational structure. There are 818 propagation trees, labeled either as *non-rumor, false rumor, true rumor* o *unverified rumor*. These trees correspond to 21741 individual tweets. Retweets were discarded in order to diminish overfitting risk.

Table 1. Variants of the SMT translator explored in this study.

	Datasets	Preprocessing, no hashtags	Preprocessing, with hashtags
W/o domain adaptation	WMT Bilingual WMT Spanish	Poor performance	BLEU: 16.91 METEOR: 0.4899
W domain adaptation	WMT Bilingual WMT Spanish Colombian Plebiscite	Poor performance	**BLEU: 17.43 METEOR: 0.4897**

3.2 Preprocessing Step

During the preprocessing step, the text was tokenized and normalized. For the normalization process, we use lemmatization and stemming. Then, we removed whitespaces, setting the text to lowercase, removing accents and punctuation symbols. Finally, we remove all words or characters that do not add content to the sentences to be translated, such as URLs, emojis, and usernames.

3.3 Translation Step

The translation step consists of the construction and evaluation of a SMT translator, using the Moses [14] tool. The SMT was trained by observing the *alignment* between a bilingual corpus, in this case, the corpus **WMT-2007 Bilingual News Corpus** (Sect. 3.1), and a monolingual corpus, using only the Spanish section of **WMT-2007**.

To evaluate translations, we use the BLEU [24] and METEOR [3] metrics. In this step, we evaluate if the obtained score has an acceptable value; if it does not, we return to the translation step and tune some of the parameters to retrain the model. In particular, and as we show in Table 1, we experiment with the use of domain adaptation [12] and the inclusion of hashtags.

In this regard, it is interesting to mention that domain adaptation is essential, mainly due to the bilingual corpus's formality. When we incorporate colloquial and informal language, the efficiency of the translator improves. Also, hashtags' inclusion is relevant since they are generally used as nouns or subjects in sentences. We show some examples to illustrate the effect of these processes in the translation:

- *Without special character, without hashtags*: correspond to standard preprocessing (Sect. 3.2), where we also eliminate the hashtags. For example:
  - *damn there and there. Tired already*
  - *f** hell, I know you forgot to finish some stadiums, but did you also forget to train your team?*
- *Without special characters, with hashtags*: correspond to standard preprocessing (Sect. 3.2) but without removing hashtags. For example:
  - *damn #worldcup there and #worldcup there. Tired already*
  - *f** hell #Brazil, I know you forgot to finish some stadiums, but did you also forget to train your team? #WorldCup #BrazilvsMexico*

3.4   Classification Step

The classification step receives as input the **Twitter16-ES** dataset that corresponds to the translated **Twitter16-EN** dataset. This dataset considers three partitions with the 75%, 10%, and 15% of the instances for training, validation, and testing, respectively. The experimental design is similar to the one used in [27]. We consider the following three empirical factors for the study:

- **Word Embeddings**: we work with word2vec [34], and also with BETO [7], an adaptation of BERT [10] trained with a very large Spanish corpus.
- **Neural networks**: We use the following architectures: LSTM, Stacked LSTM (S-LSTM), GRU, Stacked GRU (S-GRU), Bidirectional LSTM (Bi-LSTM), Stacked Bidirectional LSTM (S-Bi-LSTM), Bidirectional GRU (Bi-GRU), Stacked Bidirectional GRU (S-Bi-GRU), Convolutional 1D (Conv1D), and Recurrent Convolutional Neural Networks (RCNN).
- **Number of neurons**: based on previous results [27], we work with 256 and 512 units for the hidden layers, which showed the best results for classification on English datasets.

All the architectures are fed with the propagation tree for each source tweet represented using one of the word embeddings already described. The output of each network is connected to a softmax layer. Four classes are considered during training, *non-rumor, false rumor, true rumor*, and *unverified rumor* [19]. For training, we use standard cross-validation with stratified k-folds, $k = 5$. We use *categorical cross-entropy* as loss function while seeking to maximize the model's accuracy in all training settings. We used 200 epochs to train each model.

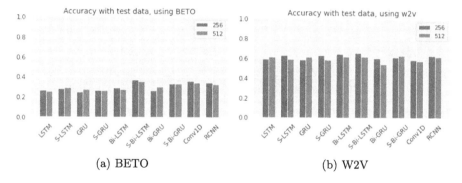

(a) BETO   (b) W2V

Fig. 2. Experimental results in terms of accuracy in the testing partition.

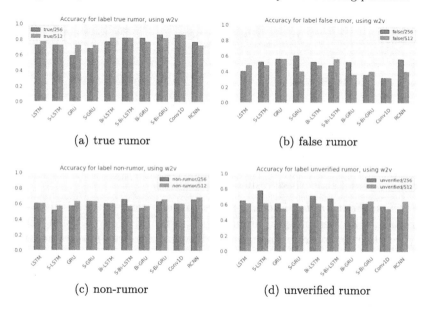

(a) true rumor   (b) false rumor

(c) non-rumor   (d) unverified rumor

Fig. 3. Experimental results per class using W2V.

4   Results

4.1   Performance on Twitter16-ES

We evaluate the performance of the different neural network architectures in the testing partition using *accuracy*. In addition to the architecture of the network itself, the embedding used to represent each tweet also influences each model's potential performance. We report these results in Fig. 2 both for the BETO embedding (Fig. 2(a)), and for the word2vec (W2V) embedding (Fig. 2(b)). We observe that in some cases, the best results correspond to 256 units. However, in other cases, the best results are obtained using 512 units. In general, the models

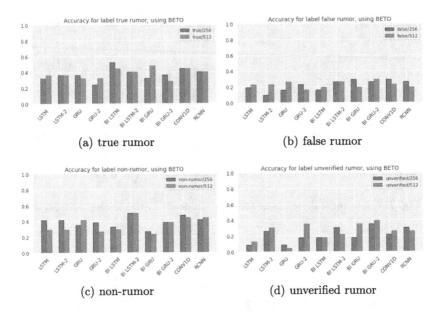

Fig. 4. Experimental results per class using BETO.

that use BETO do not exceed the 40% of accuracy, while the models that use W2V are around 60% of accuracy.

Figures 3 and 4 show these results per each class.

W2V Classification by Label. The best results were obtained in the *true rumor* class, with performance around 80% using the Convolutional 1D network (Conv1D). In contrast, the most challenging class was *false rumor*, never exceeding the 60% of accuracy. The other classes have an average performance of around 60%. S-LSTM achieves salient performances in unverified rumors and RCNN in non-rumor.

BETO Classification by Label. The results using BETO present low accuracy. We can see that the best results are obtained in the *true rumor* and *non-rumor* classes, where BI-LSTM and Stacked BI-LSTM reach around 50% of accuracy. For these classes, the other models get around 40% accuracy. On the other hand, the performance in *false rumor* and *unverified rumor* classes is quite deficient and does not exceed the 40% of accuracy.

4.2   Comparison Between Twitter16-EN and Twitter16-ES

The comparison between the best results obtained in **Twitter16-EN** presented by Providel and Mendoza [27], and **Twitter16-ES**, obtained in this paper, are shown in Table 2. The table shows the best models for each dataset and each embedding. Although it can be observed that the results for **Twitter16-EN** are quite superior to the results obtained with **Twitter16-ES**, it is interesting to observe that:

Table 2. Comparison of results between **Twitter16-EN** and **Twitter16-ES**.

Dataset	Embedding	Best model	Unit	Acc
Twitter16-EN	BERT	Bi-GRU	512	0.73
Twitter16-EN	w2v	Stacked Bi-GRU	512	0.83
Twitter16-ES	BETO	Stacked Bi-LSTM	256	0.37
Twitter16-ES	w2v	Stacked Bi-LSTM	256	0.65

– For both datasets, the best results are obtained using W2V. This result can be explained by the informal vocabulary used in the messages, which can cause out of vocabulary challenges for the models.
– For both datasets, the best models are based on stacked networks. Stacked networks tend to encode information at different abstraction levels, suggesting that this task needs a hierarchical representation of the text to succeed.
– The best models for **Twitter16-ES** use 256 hidden units while the best models for **Twitter16-EN** use 512 units.

This last observation regarding the number of hidden units allows us to hypothesize the possibility that, unlike for **Twitter16-EN**, the representation captured by the embeddings is not so informative. Notwithstanding the above, it is essential to highlight that the best results for **Twitter16-ES** achieve 65% of accuracy, being an interesting result if we consider the threats and limitations of our approach. Main limitations of this study are:

– We use an SMT translator based on low-cost computational resources whose results are not competitive.
– We evaluate the translator with BLEU and METEOR using only 100 tweets translated by hand. In the ideal case, and with access to more resources, an extensive validation might help find a better SMT translator.

That is, it is possible to consider that improvements to the translation step can expose more relevant semantic information that would also improve the accuracy of neural models used in the classification step.

5 Conclusions

This paper shows a systematic way to evaluate a machine translation performance that aims to expand the limited quantity of datasets available to verify fake news in Spanish. Following the experimental design introduced by Providel and Mendoza [27], we inquire about the usefulness of translating available datasets, mainly in English, to Spanish. This study indicates that although the best results obtained in Spanish show at least 20% worse accuracy than their English counterpart, this difference does not appear to be intrinsic to the approach is taken, but rather to the limitations of the machine translator used.

We want to improve the translation step by modifying the SMT translation schema and incorporating neural machine translation models. These extensions will require many efforts, mainly in obtaining expert translations to maximize the translator's BLEU and METEOR scores. We believe the results presented in this paper encourages further exploration in this research line.

Acknowledgements. Mr. Mendoza acknowledge funding from the Millennium Institute for Foundational Research on Data. Mr. Mendoza was also funded by ANID PIA/APOYO AFB180002 and ANID FONDECYT 1200211.

References

1. Ajao, O., Bhowmik, D., Zargari, S.: Fake news identification on Twitter with hybrid CNN and RNN models. In: Proceedings of the 9th International Conference on Social Media and Society, SMSociety 2018, pp. 226–230 (2018)
2. Allcott, H., Gentzkow, M.: Social media and fake news in the 2016 election. J. Econ. Perspect. **31**, 211–36 (2017)
3. Banerjee, S., Lavie, A.: METEOR: an automatic metric for MT evaluation with improved correlation with human judgments. In: Proceedings of the ACL Workshop on Intrinsic and Extrinsic Evaluation Measures for Machine Translation and/or Summarization, pp. 65–72 (2005)
4. Boididou, C., Papadopoulos, S., Zampoglou, M., Apostolidis, L., Papadopoulou, O., Kompatsiaris, Y.: Detection and visualization of misleading content on Twitter. Int. J. Multimedia Inf. Retrieval **7**(1), 71–86 (2017). https://doi.org/10.1007/s13735-017-0143-x
5. Caled, D., Silva, M.: FTR-18: Collecting rumours on football transfer news. In: Conference on Information and Knowledge Management Workshops, CIKM, vol. 2482. CEUR-WS (2019)
6. Castillo, C., Mendoza, M., Poblete, B.: Information credibility on Twitter. In: Proceedings of the 20th International Conference on World Wide Web, WWW, Hyderabad, India, pp. 675–684 (2011)
7. Cañete, J., Chaperon, G., Fuentes, R., Ho, J.-H., Kang, H., Pérez, J.: Spanish pre-trained BERT model and evaluation data. In: PML4DC at ICLR 2020 (2020)
8. Costa-jussà, M.R., Zampieri, M., Pal, S.: A neural approach to language variety translation. In: Proceedings of the Fifth Workshop on NLP for Similar Languages, Varieties and Dialects, pp. 275–282. Association for Computational Linguistics (2018)
9. Deepak, S., Bhadrachalam, C.: Deep neural approach to fake-news identification. Procedia Comput. Sci. **167**, 2236–2243 (2020)
10. Devlin, J., Chang, M., Lee, K., Toutanova, K.: BERT: pre-training of deep bidirectional transformers for language understanding. In: Proceedings of the 2019 Conference of the North American Chapter of the Association for Computational Linguistics: Human Language Technologies, NAACL-HLT 2019, USA, vol. 1. (Long and Short Papers), pp. 4171–4186 (2019)
11. Ferrara, E.: Manipulation and abuse on social media. ACM SIGWEB Newsletter, pp. 1–9 (2015)
12. Jehl, L.: Machine Translation for Twitter. Master's thesis, University of Edinburgh (2010)

13. Klein, G., Kim, Y., Deng, Y., Senellart, J., Rush, A.: OpenNMT: open-source toolkit for neural machine translation. In: Proceedings of ACL, System Demonstrations, pp. 67–72 (2017)
14. Koehn, P., et al.: Moses: open source toolkit for statistical machine translation. In: Proceedings of the 45th Annual Meeting of the Association for Computational Linguistics Companion Volume Proceedings of the Demo and Poster Sessions, pp. 177–180 (2007)
15. Kwon, S., Cha, M., Jung, K.: Rumor detection over varying time windows. PLOS One **12**, e0168344 (2017)
16. Liu, Y.: Early detection of fake news on social media. PhD thesis, New Jersey Institute of Technology (2019)
17. Lohar, P., Popović, M., Way, A.: Building English-to-Serbian machine translation system for IMDb movie reviews. In: Proceedings of the 7th Workshop on Balto-Slavic Natural Language Processing, pp. 105–113 (2019)
18. Ma, J., et al.: Detecting rumors from microblogs with recurrent neural networks. In: Proceedings of the Twenty-Fifth International Joint Conference on Artificial Intelligence, IJCAI2016, pp. 3818–3824 (2016)
19. Ma, J., Gao, W., Wong, K.-F.: Detect rumors in microblog posts using propagation structure via kernel learning. In: Proceedings of the 55th Annual Meeting of the Association for Computational Linguistics (Volume 1: Long Papers), pp. 708–717, (2017)
20. Ma, J., Gao, W., Wong, K.-F.: Rumor detection on Twitter with tree-structured recursive neural networks. In: Proceedings of the 56th Annual Meeting of the Association for Computational Linguistics (Volume 1: Long Papers), pp. 1980–1989 (2018)
21. Maas, A.L., Daly, R.E., Pham, P.T., Huang, D., Ng, A.Y., Potts, C.: Learning word vectors for sentiment analysis. In: Proceedings of the 49th Annual Meeting of the Association for Computational Linguistics: Human Language Technologies, pp. 142–150 (2011)
22. Mendoza, M., Poblete, B., Castillo, C.: Twitter under crisis: can we trust what we RT? In: Proceedings of the 1st Workshop on Social Media Analytics, SOMA, Washington, USA, pp. 71–79 (2010)
23. Nouhaila, B., Habib, A., Abdellah, A., Abdelhamid, I.E.F.: Arabic machine translation using bidirectional LSTM encoder-decoder (2018)
24. Papineni, K., Roukos, S., Ward, T., Zhu, W.-J.: Bleu: a method for automatic evaluation of machine translation. In: Proceedings of the 40th Annual Meeting of the Association for Computational Linguistics, pp. 311–318 (2002)
25. Posadas-Durán, J.-P., Gomez-Adorno, H., Sidorov, G., Escobar, J.: Detection of fake news in a new corpus for the Spanish language. J. Intell. Fuzzy Syst. **36**(5), 4868–4876 (2019)
26. Pourebrahim, N., Sultana, S., Edwards, J., Gochanour, A., Mohanty, S.: Understanding communication dynamics on Twitter during natural disasters: a case study of hurricane sandy. Int. J. Disaster Risk Reduct. **37**, 101176 (2019)
27. Providel, E., Mendoza, M.: Using deep learning to detect rumors in Twitter. In: Meiselwitz, G. (ed.) HCII 2020, Part I. LNCS, vol. 12194, pp. 321–334. Springer, Cham (2020). https://doi.org/10.1007/978-3-030-49570-1_22
28. Qazvinian, V., Rosengren, E., Radev, D.R., Mei, Q.: Rumor has it: identifying misinformation in microblogs. In: Proceedings of the 2011 Conference on Empirical Methods in Natural Language Processing, pp. 1589–1599 (2011)
29. Ramírez, V.: Plebiscito Colombia 2016 (2016). https://data.world/bikthor/plebiscito-colombia-2016

30. Sakaki, T., Okazaki, M., Matsuo, Y.: Earthquake shakes Twitter users: real-time event detection by social sensors. In: Proceedings of the 19th International Conference on World Wide Web, WWW 2010, pp. 851–860 (2010)
31. Sen, S., Banik, D., Ekbal, A., Bhattacharyya, P.: IITP English-Hindi machine translation system at WAT 2016. In: Proceedings of the 3rd Workshop on Asian Translation (WAT2016), pp. 216–222, Osaka, Japan (2016)
32. Tiedemann, J.: Parallel data, tools and interfaces in OPUS. In: Proceedings of the Eighth International Conference on Language Resources and Evaluation (LREC2012), pp. 2214–2218 (2012)
33. Tiedemann, J.: Parallel data, tools and interfaces in OPUS. In: Proceedings of the Eight International Conference on Language Resources and Evaluation (LREC2012) (2012)
34. Mikolov, T., Chen, K., Corrado, G., Dean, J.: Efficient estimation of word representations in vector space. In: 1st International Conference on Learning Representations, ICLR 2013, Scottsdale, Arizona, USA, 2–4 May 2013, Workshop Track Proceedings (2013)
35. Vathsala, M., Holi, G.: RNN based machine translation and transliteration for Twitter data. Int. J. Speech Technol. **23**, 499–504 (2020)
36. Wang, Y., et al.: EANN: event adversarial neural networks for multi-modal fake news detection. In: Proceedings of the 24th ACM SIGKDD International Conference on Knowledge Discovery & Data Mining, KDD 2018, pp. 849–857 (2018)
37. Yu, F., Liu, Q., Wu, S., Wang, L., Tan, T.: A convolutional approach for misinformation identification. In: IJCAI2017, pp. 3901–3907 (2017)
38. Zubiaga, A., Aker, A., Bontcheva, K., Liakata, M., Procter, R.: Detection and resolution of rumours in social media: a survey. ACM Comput. Surv. **51**, 1–36 (2018)

The Presumed Happiness of the Smiling Pile of Poo – How Emojis are Perceived by People

Simon André Scherr[✉], Frauke Neugebauer, Yannika Egler, and Frank Elberzhager

Fraunhofer Institut für Experimentelles Software Engineering, Fraunhofer Platz 1, 67663 Kaiserslautern, Germany
{simon.scherr,frauke.neugebauer,yannika.egler, frank.elberzhager}@iese.fraunhofer.de

Abstract. Emojis are widely used in digital communication, especially on phones. This makes them an important part of our multimedia experience. While most emojis are equally perceived among people, some are not. Using such emojis in UIs might lower the user experience. Furthermore, they should be used with care in communication. To get a better understanding of how people perceive emojis, we performed a survey on 15 emojis that potentially cause misunderstandings in digital communication. The responses from 1,811 participants help to interpret emojis used in online texts, as well as in text-based communication. In this article, we provide an experience report about the creation and performance of our survey as well as the results. The detailed discussion of 15 emojis provides future directions for research on how these are used. This forms the foundation for more detailed and specific future analyses aimed at exploring the potential causes of digital miscommunication.

Keywords: Emoji · Emotion · Mobile computing · Communication · Survey

1 Introduction

In face-to-face communication among human beings, emotions can be expressed by one person and detected by others. This is done through several mechanisms, e.g., watching the person's face or analyzing their vocal range or the specific words used. However, this is a challenge in digital communication because it is hard for humans to detect emotions in communication based solely on text [1], as the non-verbal aspects and cues are missing [2]. In the attempt to compensate for this lack, people use emojis in their digital and mobile communication. These emojis add visual hints that bring back non-verbal aspects of communication. According to the Oxford Dictionary, an emoji can be defined as "a small digital image or icon used to express an idea or emotion" [3]. Aside from this definition, emojis can also show objects, nature, or activities. Again, according to the Oxford Dictionary, the word "emoji" itself comes from the Japanese language and combines the word "e" meaning picture and "moji" meaning letter or character [3]. Emojis are the latest evolution of the goal to express emotions and sentiments within texts. Furthermore, they help to express sentiment and emotion and to clarify a text's

© Springer Nature Switzerland AG 2021
G. Meiselwitz (Ed.): HCII 2021, LNCS 12774, pp. 149–166, 2021.
https://doi.org/10.1007/978-3-030-77626-8_10

hidden meaning, especially in cases of irony or sarcasm [4]. As emojis provide hints for understanding texts, they are now widely in use for digital communication.

Studies [5, 6] have shown that altering messages by adding, removing, or changing emojis influences the perception of the messages substantially. This gives them power over the modern digital society. Whether and how equally emojis are perceived by humans in terms of emotions has only been analyzed by a few studies. Considering the great relevance of emojis in our digital communication, it is beneficial to investigate how they are perceived. The results can then be used to ensure that professional communication, e.g., in the field of social media, is not ambiguous or even causes significant issues for some readers. Hints for interaction designers might also lead to better user interfaces that consider emojis.

Emojis are a relevant part of the user experience of modern communication. We collected emojis that, according to several studies (e.g. [7–9]), are hard to understand. Reasons for this include, for instance, that there is no clear understanding of what the pictograph is showing or that the use of the emoji depends on different contextual situations within the communication. Our goal is to get more insights about what people associate with emojis and why. Therefore, we performed a survey with the following research questions:

- RQ1: Which contextual information about the perception of these emojis can we gather by creating and analyzing a survey?
- RQ2: Which of these emojis can be classified by the contextual information and which new research directions arise for the remaining ones?

The remainder of this work is structured as follows: Sect. 2 gives an overview of related work on the perception of emojis. Section 3 describes our study design, followed the explanation of the study execution (Sect. 4) and our analysis procedure (Sect. 5). Section 6 describes our results, followed by the identified threats in Sect. 7. The future investigations we propose for these emojis are described in Sect. 8, followed by the conclusion in Sect. 9.

2   Foundation and Related Work

2.1   Emotions

Emotions can be divided into primary or basic emotions and secondary emotions. Primary ones are considered to be universal across cultures [9], whereas secondary ones require social experience as they depend on the cultural background [11]. There is no final consensus on how to classify emotions into these categories [10, 11]. There are multiple ways to relate emotions to each other. Typically, emotion models can be distinguished into models using emotional categories and models using emotional dimensions. Models using emotional categories try to divide emotions into discrete elements, like the model of Ekman [12]. In contrast to that, models using emotional dimensions try to relate them as values in two- or three-dimensional spaces, like the Circumplex Model of Affect [13]. Both types can also be combined, as in the Wheel of Emotions by Plutchik [14].

A concept that is related to emotion detection is sentiment. Sentiment analysis defines something on the scale between being fully positive or fully negative [15]. This makes emotion more differentiated than sentiment, as there is a difference between sadness and fear, but both would represent a negative sentiment. Therefore, knowing the emotion of communication is more precise than knowing the sentiment.

2.2 Emojis

The development of modern emojis was predated by the use of emoticons. Emoticons can be defined as "a representation of a facial expression such as a smile or frown, formed by various combinations of keyboard characters and used to convey the writer's feelings or intended tone" [3]. The word itself is a combination of the two English words "emotion" and "icon" [3]. One of the earliest modern ancestors of emojis was typographical art printed in an issue of the US magazine Puck in 1881. They proposed several symbols representing faces and emotional states, which were created through combinations of dots, lines, arches, rectangles, and squares [16].

With increasing popularity of typewriters, people thought about ways to express emotions with the characters present on the machine. Even in the early days of computers with Internet access, only typewriter characters could be used due to technical limitations. In 1982 Scott Fahlman proposed the use of the characters ":-)" and ":-(" for expressing emotions [17]. Since then, more and more combinations of ASCII (American Standard Code for Information Interchange) characters available at the time have been proposed for this purpose.

Parallel to the development of expressing emotions within typewriter and computer texts, the development of the smiley face, which had been invented by Harvey Ball in 1963 [18], was picked up by the IT industry around the year 2000, as computers increased their graphics power. Messenger applications started to replace certain emoticons with yellow smile faces expressing emotions. Also new icons were created that do not have a common equivalent in ASCII.

For a long time, it was assumed that the term "emojis" was first used in 1999 for a set of icons created by Shigetaka Kurita [19]. However, this assumption was incorrect, as it turned out that the telecommunications group SoftBank had already launched a phone supporting 90 different emojis in 1997 [20]. Subsequently, more and more companies started using such characters.

From 2010 onwards, emojis became standardized, as Unicode began to also consider emoji characters [21]. Unicode is an encoding standard for characters on computers. Within Unicode, a section was dedicated to emojis with Unicode 6. Most emojis in the standard have a graphical and a textual representation. Since then, the Unicode standard for emojis presents guidelines about how to design emojis [22]. One of the goals of the standard, besides having a common set of emojis, is to have rendering among systems so that emojis look alike. The standard categorizes emojis into Smiles & Emotion, People & Body, Component, Animals & Nature, Food & Drink, Travel & Places, Activities, Objects, Symbols, and Flags. The standard is currently at version 13 and proposes a total of 3,304 emojis [23]. This number includes variations of an emoji in terms of gender and skin color [24].

Emojis also reached global popularity in 2011, when iOS introduced a worldwide emoji keyboard. Other operating systems followed and using emojis became a widespread phenomenon. Later, their use spread beyond the digital world. Oxford University Press selected "Face with Tears of Joy" (😂) as Word of the Year 2015 [25]. In 2017, "The Emoji Movie" also brought them to the cinema [26].

After the establishment of worldwide emoji keyboards and the increasing popularity of emojis [25, 27], McDonald's started using emojis on physical billboards and in TV ads in 2017 [28, 29].

Today, we cannot even draw a clear line between emojis and emoticons, as some software automatically convert traditional emoticons like these ":-)" into black and white pictographs (☺) or colorful emojis (🙂). Emojis occur "at highly predictable and linguistically significant positions" [30]. According to Hogenboom et al. [31], emojis are used to simply express sentiment, to intensify the sentiment indicated by the text, or to clarify the sentiment of the text. This is especially done to clarify irony or sarcasm, which can be misunderstood easily.

Nevertheless, more effort has to be put into studying emojis from a scientific perspective, as Ljubešić and Fiser summarize the status of emoji research as a "poorly researched communication phenomenon" [32].

2.3 Studies on Emojis

The question of whether emojis are perceived equally by humans, or to what extent, and how emojis are related to emotions, requires establishing a link between emotions or at least sentiments and the human perception of emojis. Currently there exist only a few studies that focus on the perception of emojis. As traditional emoticons are older than emojis more studies are available that focus on their perception. Many studies only focus on a few emoticons or emojis or give no classification in terms of the emotions of a larger group of humans. Researchers often use classifications they chose themselves based on interviewing very few participants or based only on sentiments and not on emotions.

In general, we can classify the studies into studies investigating the use of emojis and studies attempting to classify emojis according to sentiment or emotion.

Studies focusing at least to some extent on the peculiarities of emojis mostly apply quantitative measures to their usage and do not check how they are understood by humans. Examples are the studies by Ljubešić and Fiser [32], who investigated several million Twitter posts, and by Zhao et al. [33] who focused on the popularity of emojis. The fact that SwiftKey was used for the keyboard data and not data acquired from a single web source like Ljubešić and Fiser [32] or Novak et al. [9] makes their picture of emoji distribution more independent of concrete usage scenarios than a specific service.

Novak et al. conducted a study on the sentiment of emojis on Twitter [9]. The study derives a sentiment for emojis from the written text of labeled Twitter posts. However, the study did not consider to what extent the participants might have been influenced by the emojis used within the tweet. The studies by Wibowo et al. [5] and Riordan [6] show that messages with emojis are understood differently, after the emojis have been removed and that the choice of emojis can alter the interpretation of a message substantially.

Hogenbom et al. [17] analyzed 2,080 tweets containing emoticons. Their study only focuses on sentiments and does not consider emotions. In addition, they performed no external validation of their classification, but created the mapping between emoticons and sentiments on their own. Similarly, Zhao et al. [34] labeled 95 emoticons – including some smiley characters – into four sentiment categories.

Wibowo et al. [5] investigated the role of emojis in online communication. For this purpose, they formed three groups, whose participants were given the same chat to read. One group was given the actual conversation without emojis, another group with smiling emojis, and the third with unamused emojis. Afterwards, the participants evaluated the conversation on the basis of various parameters, such as friendliness, intellect, etc.

Even though this study does not provide an understanding of emoticons, the highly varying interpretations of the respective groups confirmed that emoticons strongly influence conversation perception by conveying non-verbal information.

Similarly, Riordan [6] investigated emojis not showing faces and their relationship to how we interpret online communication. It turned out that emojis decrease the ambiguity of a message if the textual information is ambiguous. Furthermore, she found out that emojis might alter the perception of the message. In two studies, Gesselmann et al. examined the extent to which the use of emojis is associated with more successful intimate relationships with potential partners [35]. The group found that the use of emojis does convey affective information and that study participants who used emojis more often were more likely to establish an intimate relationship with potential partners, even over a longer period of time. However, the study did not investigate which emojis were used and how they were perceived by both sides.

A comprehensive study on the perception of emojis was executed by Scherr et al. [8] in the form of a survey performed in 2017. This study is also one of the rare examples classifying emojis in terms of sentiment and emotion. They evaluated 612 emojis up to the Emoji 4 standard, concluding that – for most emojis – people have a similar perception of emojis in terms of sentiment and emotion. Although the study was performed with real participants and a large set of emojis, there are some shortcomings. First, the number of participants does not allow a generalized picture of the perception of emojis. Second, even though they followed an elaborated emotion model, disgust as an emotion, which is a basic emotion according to Ekman et al. [12], Lu et al. [36], and Plutchik et al. [14], was not considered.

3 Study Design

To answer the first research question, we performed a survey on emojis. In our study, we investigated not only the usage, but also the perception of emojis, considering the differences between sentiment and emotion based on answers received from a large number of participants.

We focused on 15 emojis that might not be clearly assignable to either sentiment or emotion. We identified these emojis by considering the work of Scherr et al. [8], Miller et al. [7], and Novak et al. [9]. As these works also made use of emoticons as a similar but older communication mechanism, we included both emojis and emoticons in our study.

The emojis we studied are listed in Table 1. We clustered them into two groups. Scherr et al. [8] especially distinguished them into those undecidable according to sentiment and those undecidable in terms of emotion.

Table 1. Emojis under investigation

Group	Emojis
Identification of a sentiment	* * 💥 😊 🙊 🙀 💩 😼
Identification of an emotion	😵 🔪 🙂 😌 |-O 😧 ;-) 🕺

To execute the study, we created an online survey with LimeSurvey[1], an open-source online survey-tool, which allows creating question groups, random question order, random question selection, and multi-language surveys. The survey could be answered in less than five minutes. To ensure that each emoji was displayed in the same way, we used the emoji font EmojiOne[2] (see Fig. 1 for an excerpt of our survey).

The study design was our first step to answering RQ 1. We created four question groups (see Table 2), distributed over four pages or groups.

The first two groups consisted of general questions about the participants, including questions about age, gender, and origin (group I) as well as questions about the usage of emojis (group II). The questions aimed at getting a better understanding of the general emoji use of our participants. Therefore, they served as context about the participants and their use and knowledge of emojis.

Group III included three out of 30 and group IV three out of 16 potential questions. The goal of these two groups was to get better insights on what people think about those emojis that could not be clearly assigned to sentiment and emotion in previous studies; for example, what people associate with them or whether they even know them. These two groups were to deliver a potential context of use for each emoji. While question group III was aimed at getting more insights into the sentiment of the different emojis, group IV focused on the emotions. To conduct an optimal evaluation, we formulated open questions in question group III and IV with free text answers for every question.

Group III contained two free text questions for each emoji: "What do you think about when you see this emoji?" and "Which feeling, or emotion does this emoji convey?". In contrast, in group IV, there was only one question for each emoji where a free text answer was possible: "What do you think about when you see this emoji?" This allowed the participants to openly think about the emoji.

In addition, group III contained the questions "In what mood is the person who writes the following message to you: That's my opinion too! [emoji]" and "In what mood is the person who writes the following message to you: That's exactly what I thought! [emoji]". For both questions, the survey participants had the following answer options: "He or she is happy", "He or she is annoyed", "The message does not convey any emotion at all", and "No answer".

Furthermore, there were two more questions referring to the emoji 💩 (pile of poo). The first was: "When would you most likely use this emoji 💩?" with the answer options "When you are happy", "When you are annoyed", "When you want to make a joke", and "No answer". The second question was "Does the facial expression of this emoji 💩

---

[1] https://www.limesurvey.org/.

[2] http://emojione.com.

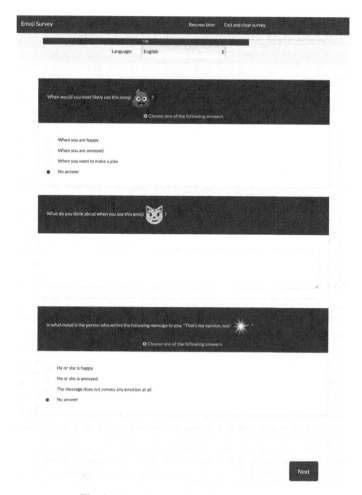

Fig. 1. Example questions from our survey

have an influence on its emotion or meaning?" with the answer options "Yes, because ...", "No, because ...", and "No answer", and a comment field for free text.

In group IV, the survey participants had to answer two different questions depending on whether the emoji conveys a positive or a neutral sentiment. For those conveying a positive sentiment, the question was: "In which context do you mostly use this emoji [emoji]?" with the potential responses "When you want to make a joke, or in a humorous message", "In a happy message", and "No answer".

For those emojis that had been classified as emojis with neutral sentiment, the question was "Which emotion does this emoji [emoji] convey?" with the answer options "It conveys an unambiguous emotion", "That depends on the context", "It does not convey any emotion at all", and "No answer".

After filling out the survey, the participants were redirected to a thank you site showing fun facts about emojis. We set a cookie to prevent them from participating again.

Table 2. Question groups

	Group description	Page
I	Participant information	1
II	Usage of emojis	2
III	Undecided emojis regarding sentiment	3
IV	Undecided emojis regarding emotion	4

4   Study Execution

We executed the survey between June and November 2018 as an anonymous survey. To promote our survey, we applied a mixture of physical and digital actions. All actions used our survey CI and our individually designed signature emoji to attract people's attention. We printed flyers, postcards, and posters in different sizes in German and English (see Fig. 2). The flyers and postcards were distributed on different days on the tables at the cafeteria of various universities, libraries and other places. The posters were distributed in different buildings in several universities, cafeterias, and companies. We placed flyers in smaller shops and gave them to people we got in touch with personally, e. g., at conferences.

In addition, we also took digital actions to promote the survey. We designed a multi-language website, double-blind.de, which provided a glimpse about the fun facts people would get rewarded with after filling out the survey. This was intended to motivate the participants to fill out the survey. Furthermore, people were able to share the website as well as the survey via social media. We sent the website link via e-mail to coworkers, collaborating companies, and students from multiple universities. The link was also shared on different social media platforms. In addition, we mentioned the survey at public speeches and on business trips. This was also done to get a more international audience for our survey. Furthermore, we created social media profiles for our survey. This was done to acquire more participants but also to keep the existing participants up to date with facts on emojis.

Fig. 2. Flyer for the survey

5   Analysis Procedure

We applied the following analysis procedure. The first two groups of questions were used to statistically classify our participants.

The questions in groups III and IV were a mixture of open and closed questions. We analyzed the results of the closed questions statistically. Due to the large number of responses (119–386 per question) the open questions were more challenging.

Therefore, we applied a workshop format where we built mind maps with all answers per question. The detailed process and the differentiated division of the answers into different categories and sub-categories is shown in Fig. 3. The goal was to get insights into the free text answers in our dataset and see how the answers could be clustered. The workshop participants were the four researchers involved in designing the study and four students. All of the participants were familiar with emojis. The workshop was executed as a group. We had two groups working on a question. The results were presented, discussed, and refined with the other group.

Our strategy for analyzing the responses was to cluster similar answers together and build initial categories. Afterwards, we sorted these categories into sentiment categories (positive, neutral, negative). In addition, we added major categories for "Object descriptions", where people just described what they saw without any emotional connotation. As a fifth group, we added "Other" for elements about which the participants said that they had no clue or for answers that we did not understand. As subcategories, we used either the emotions from the emotion set or custom elements derived from our cluster.

We applied the rule that a new subcategory had to be created if there were at least three similar answers. Furthermore, we grouped very similar elements into one subcategory if at least three of them occurred. In the "explosion" subcategory, for example, we had a group formed of people just writing the word explosion. In addition, we added connectors if a response could fit into two categories or groups. For the above example, we had a connector between the subcategory "explosion" and the subcategory "fireworks" for people writing about both. The categorization process was done in the form of an iterative discussion, where we first placed the answers into or between the categories and then added the subcategories and groups as well as the relations.

Afterwards, we connected the results for the different questions regarding one emoji. This especially included drawing connections between the open questions and the questions with a fixed set of answers.

Fig. 3. Clustering workshop

6   Results

6.1   Overview of Our Participants

We stopped our data collection phase in November 2018 after getting 1,811 responses – including 295 incomplete responses. This means that 16.29% dropped out while filling out the survey. 44.62% (n = 808) of our participants were female and 48.15% male (n = 872). 7.23% (n = 131) did not report their gender. Considering only the complete responses (n = 1516), 51.58% (n = 782) were male and 48.42% (n = 734) female.

6.2   Usage of Emojis

To get a better initial understanding, we asked our participants how often and where they use emojis. Figure 4 shows that only 26.3% of our participants used four emojis or less per day. 39.7% used between five and 14 emojis. The remaining 34% used 15 or more emojis per day. This shows that many participants must be familiar with this digital way of communication.

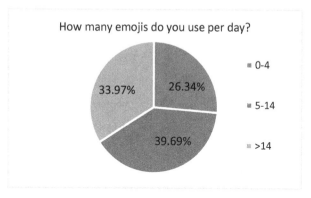

Fig. 4. How many emojis do you use per day?

Figure 5 shows in which activities emojis are used. Based on this information, it is possible to determine in which areas of communication the highest number of misunderstandings can arise through using emojis. For most of our participants, using emojis in messaging is a daily activity. More than half of them used emojis on a weekly or daily basis for their social media activities. They used them less often in online reviews, forums or emails. In addition, we offered everyone the possibility to write in a free text field where else they use emojis.

Many people reported also using emojis in handwritten letters or notes, while some mentioned using emojis for writing postcards or greeting cards, too.

6.3 Emojis with Sentiments Under Investigation

Starting with the emojis from group III "Undecided sentiment", the emoji 💥 (collision) was often perceived as an explosion with either no reference to an emotion or just an ambiguous emotion. The participants classified the emotion of this emoji as excited, surprised, angry, or even depending on the context; 61.07% of our participants reported that the person using this emoji at the end of the message "That's my opinion, too!" is annoyed.

The 😳 (flushed face) was often perceived as a surprise; many participants also perceived it as a negative surprise, e.g., as a shock. The answers revealed that the usage of this emoji is very popular and that it also shows sentimental character. But 60.78% of the people using this emoji at the end of the message "That's my opinion, too!" and 60.33% of the people using 😳 at the end of the message "That's exactly what I thought!" said that it expresses being annoyed.

We also listed two emojis from the "Three Wise Monkeys" – the 🙈 (see-no-evil monkey) and the 🙊 (speak-no-evil monkey). A total of 48.52% of the answers received

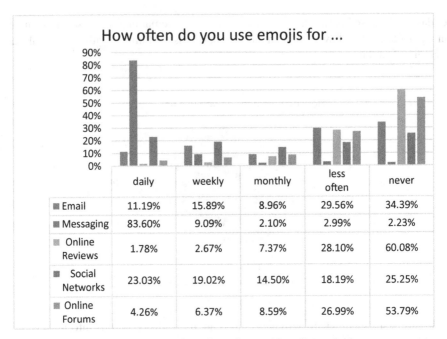

Fig. 5. Frequency of emoji use for specific online activities

for the 🙊 revealed that this emoji caused mainly negative emotions, such as embarrassment. Furthermore, it is not possible to assign this emoji to a specific sentiment, even though the sentimental character was affirmed by the participants of the survey. Most people stated that people using this emoji at the end of the two example sentences "That's my opinion, too!" (48.39%) and "That's exactly what I thought!" (59.56%) were happy. 🙊 seems to be not classifiable into a positive or negative direction and requires further investigation as it might be positive and negative depending on the context.

The answers for the emoji 🙈 concerning emotion were mainly negative (55.34%). Only a few answers classified this emoji as a positive emotion. The reason for this may be a wrong interpretation of "said something wrong". A funny and therefore positive context of utilization may also be possible. However, from the analysis of the replies, it emerged that the participants recognized the emoji for what it is. The analysis of the mood of a person using this emoji at the end of the sentence "That's my opinion, too!" does not show a clear preference, but in the opinion of most participants (45.99%), the person using 🙈 at the end of the message "That's exactly what I thought!" is happy. The analysis of the two emojis 🙊 and 🙈 shows that about half of the people associate negative emotions with them and half of the people would associate messages with these emojis in it as positive. Because of these inconsistent results, it is not possible to classify this emojis either in sentiment or in emotion.

It was remarkable that these two emojis are perceived in so many different ways, even though they show only slight differences optically (either the mouth or the eyes are covered).

The first question regarding the 💩 (pile of poo) referred to the emotional context in which people use this emoji. However, the evaluation of the three answers available did not allow drawing a clear conclusion about the emotion.

The only emotion mentioned was "funny". Regarding sentiment, we can state that this emoji is either associated with a positive emotion (e.g., "funny" or "happy") or with a negative sentiment (e.g., "disgusting"), whereas the survey participants did not associate it with a neutral sentiment. In our analysis, more than 60% mentioned that somebody using this emoji at the end of the first sentence is in an annoyed mood, and in the opinion of more than half of our participants, a person using this at the end of the second sentence is annoyed, too. It is also possible that this emoji is often misinterpreted as "gone wrong". Another possible context in which the "pile of poo" may be used is a funny one. We also came to the conclusion that for most people (68.42%), the facial expression of this emoji has an influence on its emotion or meaning.

For the emoji 😼 (cat with wry smile), 48 participants answered the questions regarding the emotion associated with "cat". These answers indicate that people recognized the emoji correctly. In summary, we can say that this emoji tends to evoke a positive sentiment. While 50% stated that somebody who uses this emoji at the end of the second sentence "That's exactly what I thought!" is in happy mood, the analysis of the first question yielded the result that 43.2% thought that people using this emoji in combination with the sentence "That's my opinion, too!" were happy, but for 40.8%, the person writing this message was annoyed. All in all, the participants gave very broad answers, suggesting that everyone has a clear but individual view of this emoji.

The emoji "*_*" is generally associated with positive emotions, such as a positive surprise or excitement. In contrast with this, we recognized that the sentiment of this emoji was mostly rated negative. Analyzing the mood of somebody using this emoji at the end of the two sentences "That's my opinion, too!" and "That's exactly what I thought!" led us to the conclusion that the author of this message was considered happy (58.78%, resp. 60.78%). Furthermore, it turned out that many participants did not know this emoji.

6.4 Emojis with Emotions Under Investigation

In the category of emojis identifying an emotion, the survey revealed that the ☐ (dizzy face) has an emotional character tending towards the emotion "confused". In the opinion of 54.8% of our participants, the emotion depends on the context.

The indicated sentiment for the 🎉 (party popper) was clearly positive. The principal emotion associated with this emoji was "happy" (94.01%), but not "funny".

The answers for 🤤 (drooling face) revealed that the questions raised in our survey did not relate to all relevant contexts. However, the answers showed that this emoji is well-known among the participants. More than 72% claimed using this emoji mostly for making jokes or writing humorous messages.

With regard to the emoji 🤑 (money-mouth face), the tendency of a positive emotion in perception could be observed and nearly ¾ claimed using this emoji to make jokes or in humorous messages.

Concerning the emoji "l-O", 27% of the participants responded with "No answer" for both questions. This emoji did not evoke positive emotions and 55.88% stated that this emoji does not convey any emotion at all.

The survey participants associated ";-)" with a positive sentiment and used it in funny messages (82.56%), often perceiving it for what it is: a winking eye.

The answers for the emoji 😣 (person pouting), which is often displayed differently, revealed that this emoji causes a negative sentiment as well as the emotion "angry". All in all, 83.33% of our participants claimed that the emotion of this emoji is unambiguous.

Concerning the emoji 🕺 (person dancing), we found that this emoji is mainly used in happy messages (79.9%).

7   Threats to Validity

In the following, we list potential issues threatening the validity of our results.

First, the study might not represent a fully global view on how emojis are perceived, as most participants had lived in Europe for some time at least, which might have influenced their view of emojis. There are reports claiming that emojis have become a lingua franca, e.g., [37, 38]. This lowers this threat.

Moreover, we only used the emoji design of EmojiOne. People's perception might be influenced by the emoji design, as some of them might differ so much that users might attribute different meanings to them [7]. This risk was lowered, as in recent years, emoji fonts have become more similar [39]. The analysis we performed in our workshop and the results and the classification of items might be biased. However, we did that as group work and discussed open issues. Furthermore, one question in the survey was how often the participants use emojis for certain online activities. In this context, the comparison of email and messaging is only suitable to a limited extent, since emails are increasingly used for business communication, whereas messaging is primarily for private use. In addition, we did not ask how often each participant performs the activity at all, which limits the validity of the answers.

8   Concept for an Additional Investigation

The insights gathered from our workshops show that some of the emojis seem to have a tendency towards a single emotion or at least a sentiment. For other emojis, the results show that there might be two directions depending on the contextual information. Furthermore, the analysis shows that there is a fourth group of emojis, which could not be classified by previous studies due to the lack of popularity. This is especially the case for the more complex emoticons.

This yields several implications for future studies on emojis (RQ2) We suggest that, before asking any questions, the survey should check for each emoji whether the participant knows the emoji or not. Such a question would provide several benefits. First, the study could track the popularity of an emoji. In addition, it could be checked how intuitive an emoji is perceived, as the answers from people knowing the emoji and those not knowing the emoji could be compared. A subsequent question could be to ask how often and in what context the emoji is seen by a participant. This would allow asking dedicated questions depending on the usage. As the studies mentioned in the Background section tried to relate certain emojis to emotions or at least sentiments, we recommend asking for each of these emojis whether it can be related to a mood or not.

As the mind maps showed that many emojis are used differently depending on the context, it might be a good idea to ask the participants with which other emoji a particular emoji could be combined. We also suggest asking them to write a message containing a certain emoji.

For some of the emojis under investigation, immediate subsequent research directions came to our mind. It turned out that many people do not directly connect them with an emotion. If the participants were to relate these to an emotion, we saw no clear direction. Many people intuitively connected the emoji 💥 with fireworks instead of a collision or explosion, which is what should be portrayed. This is an interesting finding, as the emoji standard also contains two fireworks emojis, namely 🎇 and 🎆. The two alternatives might be either too unpopular or not famous enough.

After evaluating the open questions "What do you think about when you see this emoji?" and "Which feeling or emotion does this emoji convey?" for the see-no-evil-monkey and for the speak-no-evil-monkey, we observed a slightly negative tendency for 🙈 (48.52%). In contrast to that 🙊, received fewer positive statements. This gives a slightly more negative tendency for 🙊 with 55.34% compared to 🙈 (48.52%). As we saw many statements related to seeing something wrong or saying something wrong, it might be good to explore these contexts more thoroughly.

The work of Scherr et al. [8] lists 🙊 as a positive emoji expressing funny situations. It might be a good starting point to try to distinguish the use of the three monkeys a bit more. Researchers should try to delimit the use of the three monkeys from each other and from usage scenarios.

Regarding the role of 🐱, it became obvious that people see a cat. As the answers, except for seeing a cat, were pretty diverse, we cannot see any communication patterns yet. We can just say that 😏 (smirking face) is perceived differently according to previous studies. A possible future investigation could be to let people compare these two.

As the emojis "*_*" and 😳 showed a clear sentiment, future questionnaires could directly address the identified sentiments.

One limitation of our study is that it does not cover newer emojis released after emoji 4.0, i.e., those from 2017 onwards. Therefore, such a study must be repeated with newer emojis.

It would also be interesting to analyze our data with respect to the age and cultural background of the participants. A future study could investigate the extent to which these factors cause differences in the perception of emojis.

9   Conclusion and Future Work

We conducted a large-scale survey on the perception of potentially hard-to-understand emojis. Getting better insights into how they are perceived is beneficial for digital communication and user interfaces making use of emojis. For this purpose, we acquired more than 1,800 participants for our study (RQ1). The study contained many open questions where the participants could express what they associate with each emoji. Furthermore, we captured the context through neutral sentences enriched with emojis and some usage questions. With these results, we were able to start the analysis of how well the participants agreed on the perception of several different emojis. For a subsequent survey, however, the differentiation of users according to their communication behavior in terms of frequency could also prove useful. This could help to determine whether and to what extent the frequency of communication influences the perception of emojis.

Due to the large number of responses, we received in our survey, it became a challenge to get an understanding of the qualitative responses provided in the free text fields.

Therefore, we established a workshop format to get better insights into our data. We created mind maps around each open question and performed a clustering of the answers. With the help of this approach, we were able to discuss the emojis. This led to new trigger questions for a subsequent survey. As the understanding of some of the emojis is so diverse, it is important to identify how many people recognize them. Especially "|-O" seems not to be recognized by many people. Based on this workshop, we also gained new insights into how these emojis can be perceived (RQ2). Most insights are related to a subsequent investigation, like for 🐱. But for other emojis, we could clearly identify a direction, e.g., 😲 expressing surprise or "*_*" showing a positive expression. Similarly, ";-)" showed a funny tendency and 😠 an angry one. The results will lead to a better understanding of how emojis are perceived by people. Establishing a shared understanding of emojis will lead to better digital communication, as many misunderstandings can be avoided.

Acknowledgments. The research described in this paper was performed in the project Opti4Apps (grant no. 02K14A182) of the German Federal Ministry of Education and Research and EnStadt: Pfaff (grant no. 03SBE112D and 03SBE112G) of the German Federal Ministry for Economic Affairs and Energy (BMWi) and the Federal Ministry of Education and Research (BMBF). We would like to thank Selina Meyer and Lisa Müller for their extensive contribution to this study. We thank Sonnhild Namingha for proofreading.

References

1. Park, J., Barash, V., Fink, C., Cha, M.: Emoticon style: interpreting differences in emoticons across cultures. In: 7th International AAAI Conference on Weblogs and Social Media, Cambridge, Massachusetts, USA (2013)
2. Rezabek, L., Cochenour, J.: Visual cues in computer-mediated communication: supplementing text with emoticons. J. Vis. Literacy **18**(2), 201–215 (1998). https://doi.org/10.1080/237 96529.1998.11674539
3. Oxford University Press: Oxford Dictionary of English. Oxford University Press (2010, 2017)
4. Tauch, C., Kanjo, E.: The roles of emojis in mobile phone notifications. In: Proceedings of the 2016 ACM International Joint Conference on Pervasive and Ubiquitous Computing Adjunct, UbiComp 2016, Heidelberg (2016)
5. Wibowo, M., Ats-Tsiqoh, R., Sangadah, S., Komala, E., Utomo, A.: The effect of emoji on person perception. In : Universitas Indonesia Psychology Symposium for Undergraduate Research (2016)
6. Riordan, M.A.: The communicative role of non-face emojis: affect and disambiguation. Comput. Hum. Behav. **76**, 75–86 (2017). https://doi.org/10.1016/j.chb.2017.07.009

7. Miller, H., Thebault-Spieker, J., Chang, S., Johnson, I., Terveen, L., Hecht, B.: "Blissfully happy" or "ready to fight": varying interpretations of emoji. In: International AAAI Conference on Web and Social Media (2016)
8. Scherr, S.A., Polst, S., Müller, L., Holl, K., Elberzhager, F.: The perception of emojis for analyzing app feedback. Int. J. Interact. Mob. Technol. (iJIM) **13**(02), 19 (2019). https://doi.org/10.3991/ijim.v13i02.8492
9. Novak, P.K., Smailović, J., Sluban, B., Mozetič, I.: Sentiment of emojis. PLoS ONE **10**(12), e0144296 (2015). https://doi.org/10.1371/journal.pone.0144296
10. American Psychological Association: primary emotion. https://dictionary.apa.org/primary-emotion
11. American Psychological Association: secondary emotion. https://dictionary.apa.org/secondary-emotion
12. Ekman, P.: An argument for basic emotions. Cogn. Emot. **6**(3–4), 169–200 (1992)
13. Russell, J.A.: A circumplex model of affect. J. Pers. Soc. Psychol. **39**(6), 1161–1178 (1980). https://doi.org/10.1037/h0077714
14. Plutchik, R.: A general psychoevolutionary theory of emotions. In: Theorie of Emotions, pp. 3–33 (1980)
15. Giachanou, A., Crestani, F.: Like it or not: a survey of twitter sentiment analysis methods. ACM Comput. Surv. **49**(2), 1–41 (2016). https://doi.org/10.1145/2938640
16. Keppler & Schwarzmann: Typographical Art. Puck, vol. IX, no. 209, p. 65 (1881)
17. Hogenboom, A., Bal, D., Frasincar, F., Bal, M., de Jong, F., Kaymak, U.: Exploiting emoticons in sentiment analysis. In: Proceedings of the 28th Annual ACM Symposium on Applied Computing, Coimbra, Portugal (2013)
18. Silzer, K.: Artsy. https://www.artsy.net/article/artsy-editorial-staying-power-smiley-face. Accessed 15 Aug 2019
19. Sternbergh, A.: Smile, you're speaking emoji. The rapid evolution of a wordless tongue (2014). https://nymag.com/intelligencer/2014/11/emojis-rapid-evolution.html. Accessed 2014
20. Emojipedia Blog. https://blog.emojipedia.org/correcting-the-record-on-the-first-emoji-set/. Accessed 8 Mar 2019
21. Unicode: The Unicode Blog: Unicode Version 6.0: Support for Popular Symbols in Asia. http://blog.unicode.org/2010/10/unicode-version-60-support-for-popular.html. Accessed 12 Oct 2010
22. Unicode: Unicode Emoji. http://www.unicode.org/emoji/. Accessed 9 May 2018
23. Emojipedia: Emojipedia. https://emojipedia.org/faq/#how-many. Accessed March 2020
24. Unicode: Emoji Count. https://www.unicode.org/emoji/charts/emoji-counts.html
25. Oxford University Press: Word of the Year 2015. https://en.oxforddictionaries.com/word-of-the-year/word-of-the-year-2015. Accessed 2015
26. BBFC. https://www.bbfc.co.uk/releases/emoji-movie-2017. Accessed 25 Jul 2017
27. Emoji: 2015 Emoji Report (2015)
28. Haysom, S.: British graffiti artist pranks McDonald's emoji billboard. https://mashable.com/2015/07/15/mcdonalds-emoji-advert-trolled-graffiti-artist/?europe=true. Accessed 15 Jul 2015
29. Spary, S.: Do you think this McDonald's ad that turns people into emojis is creepy? https://www.campaignlive.co.uk/article/think-mcdonalds-ad-turns-people-emojis-creepy/1360121. Accessed 14 Aug 2015
30. Provine, R., Spencer, R., Mandell, D.: Emotional expression online. J. Lang. Soc. Psychol. **26**(3), 299–307 (2007)
31. Hogenboom, A., Bal, D., Frasincar, F., Bal, M., de Jong, F., Kaymak, U.: Exploiting emoticons in sentiment analysis. In : Proceedings of the 28th Annual ACM Symposium on Applied Computing, SAC 2013 (2013). https://doi.org/10.1145/2480362.2480498

32. Ljubešić, N., Fiser, D.: A Global Analysis of Emoji Usage. In : Proceedings of the 10th Web as Corpus Workshop, Berlin (2016)
33. SwiftKey: SwiftKey Emoji Report (2015)
34. Zhao, J., Dong, L., Wu, J., Xu, K.: MoodLens: an emoticon-based sentiment analysis system for Chinese tweets. In: Proceedings of the 18th ACM SIGKDD International Conference on Knowledge Discovery and Data Mining, Beijing, China (2012)
35. Gesselman, A.N., Ta, V.P., Garcia, J.R.: Worth a thousand interpersonal words: Emoji as affective signals for relationship-oriented digital communication. PLoS ONE **14**(8), e0221297 (2019). https://doi.org/10.1371/journal.pone.0221297
36. Lazarus, R.: Emotion & Adaptation (1991)
37. Lu, X., et al.: Learning from the ubiquitous language: an empirical analysis of emoji usage of smartphone users. In: Proceedings of the 2016 ACM International Joint Conference on Pervasive and Ubiquitous Computing, UbiComp 2016 (2016). https://doi.org/10.1145/297 1648.2971724
38. Lo, J.: Medium. https://medium.com/language-insights/emoji-as-a-lingua-franca-69ef08 cb820c. Accessed 25 Aug 2018
39. Emojipedia: The Year of Emoji Convergence? (2018). https://blog.emojipedia.org/2018-the-year-of-emoji-convergence/. Accessed 13 Feb 2018

Commenting or Discussing? Comment Sections of German Russian-Speaking News Media on Facebook

Anna Smoliarova[(✉)] [ORCID], Svetlana S. Bodrunova [ORCID], and Ekaterina Ivantey

St. Petersburg State University, Universitetskaya nab. 7/9, 199034 St. Petersburg, Russia
a.smolyarova@spbu.ru

Abstract. Implementation of user comments created a new phase in audience participation. However, high expectations on rational, responsible, and civil user commenting have quickly vanished. Online, people want to interact with others, to express their opinion on the problem, and to teach others. Thus, recent studies criticize the quality of discussions formed in the comment sections on Facebook pages of news media as well as on the news websites. High-quality discussions demand from the participants to actively connect with other participants' comments. This research aims at exploring the interactivity of discussions that are formed through comments under FB posts published on the news media FB pages. We focus on the media for migrants and, of them, upon those for Russian-speaking migrants in Germany. This group of Internet users tend to be excluded from the public sphere of the host country, but migrant media allow them to join public debate. Thus, two German news FB public pages in Russian with more than 25,000 subscribers in the spring of 2019 were selected for analysis: German News and Germany24. The level of interactivity is measured as the ratio of comments posted in response to another user's comment to the total number of comments under the post. On average, every third comment to the most commented posts was published as an answer to the comment of another user. Due to the criticism towards comments sections and evidence of absence of a real dialogue, we might seem this average level as a significant one.

Keywords: Deliberation · Comment sections · News media on Facebook

1 Introduction

'Discussion among citizens has long been identified as a necessary condition for a healthy and functioning democracy' [35: abstract]. However, high expectations on rational, responsible, and civil user commenting have quickly vanished. Online, people want to interact with others, to express their opinion on the problem, and to teach others [see review in 23]. In many cases, users' exchange of opinion was of such low quality that various news outlets closed comment sections on their websites and outsourced discussions among their audience to SNS [42]. The ongoing discussion tends to criticize the quality of discussions formed in the comment sections on a Facebook page even harder than for the news websites [20, 46].

© Springer Nature Switzerland AG 2021
G. Meiselwitz (Ed.): HCII 2021, LNCS 12774, pp. 167–178, 2021.
https://doi.org/10.1007/978-3-030-77626-8_11

As deliberative framework constitutes one of the most influential paradigms in online communication research, studies of user comments on SNS refer to deliberative norms as a normative tool to assess the quality of online discussions [9, 32]. Deliberation is a politically and mentally demanding type of communication that is characterized by the norms of inclusiveness, civility, rationality, and interactivity. In this study we focus on one parameter, interactivity [32], and explore it on the migrant media on Facebook. This parameter allows us to measure the level of user engagement into a dialogue with other users, thus, the potential of engagement in meaningful political deliberation. Paraphrasing Edda Humprecht, Lea Hellmueller and Juliane A. Lischka, commenting on a Facebook page of a migrant news media 'is important to analyze, as these comments may reveal the opinions of those who are willing to engage in public debates and attempt to influence public opinion' among people with migration background that [15:1].

The largest number of Russian speakers in Europe lives in Germany. In 2015, the rapid intensification of migration processes led to a significant increase in social and interethnic tensions in Germany. Russian-language media in Germany cover the ongoing process involving their audiences into the national political debates of the host country. Interactivity of the discussions in their comment sections might serve as an important factor increasing involvement of Russian-speaking residents into political deliberation, and therefore, into civic engagement [12].

The remainder of the paper is organized as follows. Section 2 elaborates on a theoretical framework for the research on online comments and their interactivity. Section 3 describes data sampling. In Sect. 4, we provide the research results and discuss them in Sect. 5.

2   Theoretical Framework

2.1   Online Comments in the Deliberation Process

'Only in the freedom of our speaking with one another does the world ... emerge in its objectivity and visibility from all sides,' Hanna Arendt stated in her essay 'Introduction into Politics' [2: 128–129]. Dialogic exchange is crucial for deliberation, when the reciprocal speaking and listening of other discussants takes place [50]. According to one model of democratic engagement [25], willingness to argue belongs to three prerequisites of engagement in meaningful political deliberation [27]. Deliberation as a process emerges when individuals discuss issues they are concerned about or consider important for the society they belong to [11]. Different issues 'are inextricably political' [17: 2] and require citizens who will deliberate on them and through this 'achieve political objectives applies to a wide range of social topics' [17: 2].

Scholars consider user comments as one of the most popular form of online participation, if not the most popular one [29, 49]. While criticizing Facebook reactions and the feed's algorithm for not exhibiting 'the two specific characteristics of a political realm' [10: 18], namely not serving as a common world and providing spaces of appearance, Jennifer Forestal, however, argues that comments constitute a possible digital space for constructing a public realm. For mass deliberation, online discussion forums provided a practical solution [47]. Scholars have argued that comment sections could constitute deliberative public spheres [33]. Anne Schuth, Maarten Marx and Maarten de Rijke stressed the importance of user-to-user interactions under the news items back in 2007 [36].

Other studies confronted these optimistic beliefs revealing incivility, homophily, and polemics in user discussions [1]. Researchers were concerned about the low quality of comments (offensive nature, lack of relevant discussion) on the news websites [43], on textual social media [41], and on video hosting platforms like YouTube [6]. Financial reasons for the media business [19] or negative attitude of journalists to the comment sections [7] led to the closure of the comment sections on the websites of news media. As shown by a comparative study of news user behavior in six countries, the number of users commenting and sharing news items in social media is higher than in the websites [18].

Recent studies raised questions about the radical evil nature of aggressive comments, one of the main points in the criticism towards the quality of online discussions [6, 50]. Scholars also called to pay more attention on the structures of the discussions in the 'commentosphere' [36]. As Marc Ziegele, Timo Breiner and Oliver Quiring noted in 2014, there is active research on comments, but the question 'why some online news discussions are more interactive than others' is still under-researched [49].

Although an online news discussion can be defined as a sequence of user comments on a particular news item [33], these 'comment conglomerates' not necessarily should constitute a discussion, as it was recently proven for YouTube [6]. The formal criteria only that the comments reply to the content publish by a media outlet or an Internet user are not sufficient. Comments need to be interconnected, that is, the user should address at least one message posted by another user [45]. In this case, communication can be classified as reciprocal.

'Responding to a user comment can be considered as the first necessary step to initiate an interpersonal discussion' [49:1114]. This interpersonal discussion is needed to let the commenting as an Internet activity 'to evolve into a meaningful discussion' [6: 183]. The empirical evidence about how widespread are such meaningful interactions is contradictive. According to some results, up to 50% of the comments are posted in response to a previous comment and not to the news item the comment thread belongs to, despite the criticism towards comment sections, [33, 37]. Other studies revealed the exceedingly small share of repeated commenting [6]. The cumulative character of deliberation [5] manifests itself in the fact that even users' expressive 'shouts to the air' take part in an asynchronous inter-action potentially influencing the online behavior or even perception of the commented item. This research aims to measure the level of the user engagement in the discussions that are formed through comments under FB posts published on the news media FB page. We focus on the media for migrants, since this group of Internet users tend to be excluded from the public sphere of the host country, but migrant media allow them to join the deliberation process.

2.2 Why Some Comments Threads Are More Interactive?

The ongoing research explores three major groups of factors that might influence commenting behavior – the cognitive responses of users, the content of the news item and the previous comments.

Commenting is associated with negative emotions and a sense of disagreement [1, 21]. Not every person is ready to interact with another user facing disagreement, thus, scholars assume that there are significant psychological predictors on commenting behavior [4]. Commenters might be driven by social-interactive motives and not be deliberatively motivated [39]. A study of US commenters has shown that the likelihood of an unemployed and unmarried man posting a comment online is around 35% [3].

At the same time, the contradictive evidence of the level of interactivity measured by scholars in different cases [32, 33] confirms that the nature of news items and the comments of other users play an important role and users' behavior cannot be explained only with personal traits. Marc Ziegele, Timo Breiner and Oliver Quiring even states that 'users reading comments behave similarly and respond in particular to comments that include specific discussion factors' [49: 1112]. They developed a model of interactivity of online discussions that is based on the discussion factors from both news items and previously posted user comments. Thus, the willingness of the users not only to comment but to discuss a news item in a mediatized interpersonal communication that takes place in public is affected by the news item itself and the comments published previously below the news item [49].

Comments with controversial statements, addressing directly other users, containing questions, and suggesting an unexpected perspective on the issue are more likely to receive response comments. To evaluate the potential of a news item to provoke an interpersonal communication in the comment section, Marc Ziegele and Oliver Quiring applied the criteria known as news values. According to their findings, the more a news item fits the model of news values, for example, controversy and conflict, the more it increases the probability of users' cognitive and affective involvement [48]. A prognostic model developed on the data from eight online news websites from Netherlands in 2008–2009 also supports the idea of news values as an important predictor, at least, of the volume of comments on an online news story [44]. Geographical remoteness or local scale of an event decrease the probability of being heavily commented, while emotional content generates more comments.

This paper develops the approach that was suggested by Marc Ziegele and his colleagues with a special focus on the unique features of migrant media in relation to news values. According to our knowledge, comment sections of migrant media are underresearched, in particular from the deliberative perspective. We aim to partly close the gap through studying comment sections of Facebook pages of German Russian-language news media.

2.3 Migrant Media in a Mediatized Public Sphere

Since topic-centered discussions are important in the research on deliberation processes [40], in this paper we focus on the question whether topics special for the audience with migration background increase the engagement of users into the interpersonal communication in the comment section. Media for migrants, first and foremost, cover the general agenda in the immigrant's native language. They also provide access to an alternative agenda since the information needs of their audience differ from the needs of the media audience of the host society or not fulfilled by the mainstream media. Finally, media for migrants might have an alternative coverage of news that is also in agenda of the mainstream media in the country of residence.

Media for migrants can differ in their agenda priorities. Matthew D. Matsaganis, Vikki Katz and Sandra Ball-Rokeach suggested among others the following criteria for classification: local ethnic community; country of residence; country of origin (or 'mythical homeland'); members of the ethnic community dispersed in the country of residence; people identified as members of the same ethnic community and living in different countries [24].

Wan-Ying Lin and Hayeon Song introduced the concept of 'geo-ethnic storytelling' [22], by which they mean the production of culturally relevant and locally relevant information for audiences with migration background. Texts with the elements of geo-ethnic storytelling might cover the local news of the immigrant community (alternative agenda), pay special attention to the news from the home countries or to the issues related to the regulation of immigration (alternative agenda or alternative coverage).

In this paper we explore whether the posts on the Facebook pages of Russian-language news media in Germany that contain elements of geo-ethnic storytelling got more comments in general and increase the number of response comments.

2.4 Russian Speaking Residents in Germany

The number of German residents having their roots in the successor states of the Soviet Union exceeds 3 million. Russian-speaking residents in Germany do not form a homogeneous community. They are united by the Russian language and post-Soviet heritage but differ in terms of time and reasons for moving, legal statuses and prosperity, and language competencies. Estimates of the Russian-speaking population in Germany vary from source to source because statistics on different groups – Russian Germans (Spätaussiedler), Jews from post-Soviet countries, those who moved under an employment contract, through marriage or for educational purposes – are kept by several institutions [28].

"The internal communication and ethnic solidarity between Russian speakers is disturbed by various migration statuses, ethnic, professional differences and geographic distance. Perhaps the periodical local Russian-language press is the only collective product representing migrants as a group" [8]. In this context we assume that the normative criteria of transparency and quality of online deliberation in the mediatized European public sphere seem worth considering [31]: discussion of the same topics at the same levels of attention (regardless of the boundaries between groups) and the recognition of each other as legitimate participants in a common discourse.

According to the report of the Centre for East European and International Studies [13], the majority of residents from post-Soviet countries use Russian social networks and consume information on the Internet not only in German, but also in their native language. Many migrants tend to actively participate in politically engaged groups created on the platform of Russian social networks, while occupying a pro-Russian position, despite their migrant status [26]. A significant share of Russian-speakers share negative attitudes towards refugees and associate them with criminality and terrorism [34]. These attitudes are also typical for Russian-language media in Germany [16, 38].

3 Data Sampling

Russian-language media landscape in Germany is well-established. Diverse media, from German public state-owned international broadcaster (Russian-language version of Deutsche Welle) and TV (Ostwest TV) to the newspapers and magazines (Russkaja Germanija, Partner) with their online versions, or online-only news media (Germania.one, Germany24), might be part of the media repertoire of a Russian speaker residing in Germany. We did not include in our sample Ostwest TV or Deutsche Welle due to the fact that the significant part of the audience of both media resides outside Germany. The audience size of a Facebook page was measured by the number of followers, since these users receive news updates in their own feeds. The data about number of followers is publicly available on each page and was collected in May 2019. Thus, Facebook pages of three Russian language news media in Germany were selected: German News in Russian with 26836 followers, Germany24 with 26653 followers and Russkaja Germanija with 15233 followers by May 2019.

German News in Russian is the official Facebook page of the online magazine Germania.one. The magazine publishes news about politics, economy, society, culture and sports throughout Germany, as well as foreign news. Germany24 is the official page of the online publication "Our DEU. German News", which also covers a broad spectrum of news, prom politics to culture. Russkaja Germanija is one of the oldest German newspapers in Russian that is published weekly since 1996.

The posts were download with the Netvizz application in May 2019. The application was elaborated specially for scientific research on publicly available Facebook pages and was closed after significant changes in the social network privacy policy [30]. The dataset contains for each post following information: time of publication, text of the post, number of likes, number of comments, number of comments written in response to a comment of another user. Netvizz collected data in a strictly anonymous way: the name or link to the commenter's FB page was replaced with random numbers and letters (Table 1).

Table 1. German Russian-language news media on Facebook.

Media	Number of FB followers	Number of FB posts	Comments per post
German News in Russian	26836	1021	3,54
Germany24	26653	842	5,76
Russkaja Germanija	15244	432	1,19

Since the activity on the page of Russkaja Germanija is significantly lower – as for posting frequency, as well for commenting, we decided to exclude it from the sample. Thus, the final dataset contains 1863 posts on two Facebook pages and 8468 comments to these posts.

4 Findings

4.1 RQ1. How Often the Posts Get Commented?

Our findings suggest that two news media Facebook pages differ in terms of their followers' activity (see Fig. 1). Followers of Germany24 tend more than followers of German News to comment the news posts. Only every third post on the page of Germany24 remains without comments, while more than half of posts on the page of German News were not commented. Interestingly, the share of posts that got only one comment is almost similar for both media – roughly 15%.

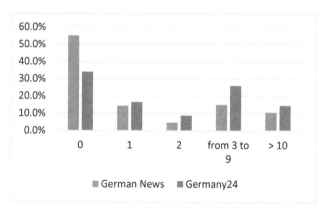

Fig. 1. The share of posts according to the number of comments they received.

A discussion between followers might take place when at least two comment were left under the post, and on the page of Germany24 it happens twice as often as on the page of German News. Still, the share of posts with only two comments does not exceed 9% and 5% accordingly. Every fourth post on the Facebook page of Germany24 collected 3 to 9 comments, while only sixth post on the Facebook page of German News was likely to be commented the same number of times. Based on the previous research, we have studied more closely those posts under which more than 10 comments were left. 106 posts with 1161 comments were selected for German News and 123 posts with 1679 comments for Germany24.

4.2 RQ2. Does the Geo-Ethnic Storytelling Lead to More Interactive Commenting?

For each post that was commented more than ten times we measured the level of the interactivity as the ratio of comments posted in response to another user's comment to the total number of comments under the post. The data whether the comment was posted in response or independently is provided by a special algorithm operated by Netvizz.

A median value of interactivity for the Facebook page of German News is 0,38, for Germany24 it is slightly higher – 0,42. More detailed distribution of interactivity in the comments is visualized on the Fig. 2.

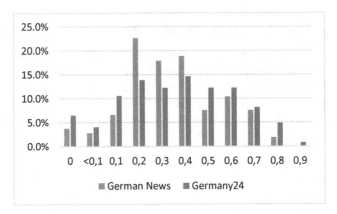

Fig. 2. The share of posts with a given interactivity value from 0 to 0.9.

As shown on Fig. 2, followers of the Facebook page of Germany24 tend more to interact in the comments and respond to the comments of other users. The value of interactivity of every fifth post on the page of Germany24 exceeds the level of 0,66, which means that two thirds of the comments were posted in response to another comment. The share of posts with the same value of interactivity on the Facebook page of German News is smaller – 12,2%.

To answer RQ2, each post was coded accordingly whether it contains any mentions of post-Soviet countries, or immigration, or refugees. In these cases, posts were coded as implying principles of geo-ethnic storytelling. The code scheme was binary (0 – post without geo-ethnic storytelling, 1 – post with the elements of geo-ethnic storytelling) (Table 2).

Table 2. Spearman's rho correlating the geo-ethnic character of the post to …

	Geo-ethnic storytelling
Number of comments	0,452
Level of interactivity	0,118

The correlation between the geo-ethnic character of the post and the number of comments left under the post is weak and positive. This finding suggests that the posts with the elements of geo-ethnic storytelling tend to be slightly more commented. The correlation between the geo-ethnic character of the post and the level of interactivity is very weak, thus, we cannot argue that the level of interactivity tends to be higher among comments to the posts with the elements of geo-ethnic storytelling.

Still, among 13 most interactively discussed (value of interactivity > 0,66) posts on the Facebook page of German news two posts cover stories related to immigration experience and refugees, and the third one relates to a tragic event in Russia. Among 24 most interactively discussed posts on the Facebook page of Germany24 the stories about immigration experience and refugees are covered by 5 posts, events in Russia and Ukraine by 4 posts.

5   Conclusion

Affordances for public discussion on the Internet were long considered as possibilities for users to gain greater control over who can speak to an expanded media audience [14]. Despite the increasing criticism towards the quality of online discussions, the ongoing scholar debate has shown that reciprocal communication in the comment sections can be considered as a sign of meaningful political deliberation. In this paper we explored interactivity of discussions that are formed through comments under FB posts published on the news media FB pages. As a case study, Russian-language news media in Germany were selected.

Russian-speaking population residing in Germany represents a significant and heterogenous minority that has been politicized during last six years [26]. The media landscape targeting these audiences is diverse and includes a plenty of news media created in Germany in Russian. Besides the German public state-owned international broadcaster Deutsche Welle and Ostwest TV that is produced for the larger European audience, two news media outlets reached the audience on Facebook by May 2019 over 25 000 users: German News and Germany24.

The followers of these two news media are relatively active commentors: from November 2018 to May 2019, they left 3,54 and 5,76 comments per post accordingly. Followers of Germany24 were more likely to leave a comment than users on the Facebook page of German news. Followers of Germany24 also tend more to interact in the comments and respond to the comments of other users. A median value of interactivity for the Facebook page of German News is 0,38, for Germany24 it is slightly higher – 0,42. Taken into consideration to the criticism towards comments sections and evidence of absence of a real dialogue, we might consider this average level as a significant one.

Since the media for migrants might differ from mainstream media in terms of news values, we tried to adapt the model developed by Marc Ziegele and his colleagues. According to our findings, the coverage of topics that are considered to be of special interest of the audience with migration background, namely issues related to the immigration policy or events in the home countries, tends to slightly increase the likelihood that a follower will comment the post. Hence, the correlation between the value of interactivity and the migration-related agenda is very weak. Even in case when media for migrants cover specific agenda, followers with migration background might not interact with other users around the issues they consider important for the community.

Commenting means engagement but does not imply a digital footprint of a publicly performed dialogue between Internet users. Without such a footprint of an interaction between humans, we cannot assess whether a dialogue has occurred as an intrapersonal communication. The reaction on the comments might be asynchronous and even invisible for the researchers if the person will send a link to the news item and discuss it in a closed messenger or share some information in a kitchen conversation. The inextricable nature of involvement in politicized discourse poses challenging goals for future research.

References

1. Anderson, A.A., Brossard, D., Scheufele, D.A., Xenos, M.A., Ladwig, P.: The "nasty effect:" online incivility and risk perceptions of emerging technologies. J. Comput. Med. Commun. **19**(3), 373–387 (2014)
2. Arendt, H.: Introduction into politics. In: Kohn, J. (ed.) The Promise of Politics, pp. 93–200. Schocken Books, New York (2005)
3. Artime, M.: Angry and alone: demographic characteristics of those who post to online comment sections. Soc. Sci. **5**(4) (2016)
4. Boczkowski, P.J., Mitchelstein, E.: How users take advantage of different forms of interactivity on online news sites: clicking, e-mailing, and commenting. Hum. Commun. Res. **38**, 1–22 (2012)
5. Bodrunova, S.S., Blekanov, I.S., Maksimov, A.: Public opinion dynamics in online discussions: cumulative commenting and micro-level spirals of silence. In: Meiselwitz, G. (ed.) HCII 2021. LNCS, vol. 12774, pp. 205–220. Springer, Cham (2021)
6. Bodrunova, S.S., Litvinenko, A., Blekanov, I., Nepiyushchikh, D.: Constructive aggression? Multiple roles of aggressive content in political discourse on Russian YouTube. Media Commun. **9**(1), 181–194 (2021)
7. Curran, J., et al.: Internet revolution revisited: a comparative study of online news. Media Cult. Soc. **35**(7), 880–897 (2013). https://doi.org/10.1177/0163443713499393
8. Darieva, Ts.: Manipulation of identity: a view on Russian-language press in Berlin (2000). (in Russian)
9. Esau, K., Fleuß, D., Nienhaus, S.-M.: Different arenas, different deliberative quality? Using a systemic framework to evaluate online deliberation on immigration policy in Germany. Policy Internet **13**, 86–112 (2020)
10. Forestal, J.: Constructing digital democracies: Facebook, arendt, and the politics of design. Polit. Stud. (2020)
11. Friess, D., Eilders, C.: A systematic review of online deliberation research. Policy Internet **7**, 319–339 (2015)
12. Gil de Zúñiga, H., Jung, N., Valenzuela, S.: Social media use for news and individuals' social capital, civic engagement and political participation. J. Comput. Med. Commun. **17**(3), 319–336 (2012)
13. Golova, T.: Postsowjetische Migranten in Deutschland und transnationale Social Media-Öffentlichkeiten. ZOiS Report 2 (2018)
14. Hille, S., Bakker, P.: Engaging the social news user: comments on news sites and Facebook. Journal. Pract. **8**(5), 563–572 (2014)
15. Humprecht, E., Hellmueller, L., Lischka, J.A.: Hostile emotions in news comments: a cross-national analysis of Facebook discussions. Soc. Media Soc. **6**(1), 2056305120912481 (2020)
16. Ivanova, E.O.: Intercultural discourse in ethnically oriented Russian-language news media in Germany. MediaAlmanac **1**, 182–193 (2019)
17. Jennings, F.J., Suzuki, V.P., Hubbard, A.: Social media and democracy: fostering political deliberation and participation. West. J. Commun., 1–21 (2020)

18. Kalogeropoulos, A., Negredo, S., Picone, I., Nielsen, R.K:. Who shares and comments on news? A cross-national comparative analysis of online and social media participation. Soc. Media Soc. **3**(4) (2017)
19. Karlsson, M., Bergström, A., Clerwall, C., Fast, K.: Participatory journalism—the (r)evolution that wasn't: content and user behavior in Sweden 2007–2013. J. Comput. Med. Commun. **20**(3), 295–311 (2015)
20. Kim, J., Lewis, S. C., Watson, B.R.: The imagined audience for and perceived quality of news comments: exploring the perceptions of commenters on news sites and on Facebook. Soc. Media Soc. **4**(1), 2056305118765741 (2018)
21. Larsson, A.O.: Diversifying likes. Journal. Pract. **12**(3), 326–343 (2018)
22. Lin, W.-Y., Song, H.: Geo-ethnic storytelling: an examination of ethnic media content in contemporary immigrant communities. Journalism **7**(3), 347–373 (2006)
23. Lischka, J.A., Messerli, M.: Examining the benefits of audience integration: does sharing of or commenting on online news enhance the loyalty of online readers? Digit. Journal. **4**(5), 597–620 (2016)
24. Matsaganis, M.D., Katz, V.S., Ball-Rokeach, S.J.: Understanding Ethnic Media Producers, Consumers, and Societies. Sage, Los Angeles (2011)
25. McLeod, J.M., Scheufele, D.A., Moy, P.: Community, communication, and participation: the role of mass media and interpersonal discussion in local political participation. Polit. Commun. **16**(3), 315–336 (1999)
26. Mitrokhin, N.: 'The case of the girl Lisa': Putin's Russian-speaking supporters in Germany and German right-wing radicalism. Neprikosnovennyi zapas **3**, 132–146 (2017). (in Russian)
27. Moy, P., Gastil, J.: Predicting deliberative conversation: the impact of discussion networks, media use, and political cognitions. Polit. Commun. **23**(4), 443–460 (2006)
28. Panagiotidis, J.: Postsowjetische Migration in Deutschland: eine Einführung. Beltz Juventa, Weinheim (2021)
29. Reich, Z.: User comments: the transformation of participatory space. In: Singer, J.B., et al. (eds.) Participatory Journalism: Guarding Open Gates at Online Newspapers, pp. 96–117. Wiley-Blackwell, Malden (2011)
30. Rieder, B.: Studying Facebook via data extraction: the Netvizz application. In: Proceedings of the 5th Annual ACM Web Science Conference, pp. 346–355. ACM, New York (2013)
31. Risse, T.: An emerging european public sphere? Theoretical clarifications and empirical indicators. In: Proceedings of the Annual Meeting of the European Union Studies Association (EUSA), Nashville, TN (2003)
32. Rowe, I.: Deliberation 2.0: comparing the deliberative quality of online news user comments across platforms. J. Broadcast. Electron. Media **59**, 539–555 (2015)
33. Ruiz, C., Domingo, D., Micó, J. L., Díaz-Noci, J., Meso, K., Masip, P.: Public sphere 2.0? The democratic qualities of citizen debates in online newspapers. Int. J. Press Polit. **22**, 463–487 (2011)
34. Russians in Germany. Report by Boris Nemtsov Foundation. 14.11.2016. https://nemtsovfund.org/en/2016/11/boris-nemtsov-foundation-s-survey-russian-speaking-germans/. Accessed 30 Jan 2021
35. Scheufele, D.A.: Talk or conversation? Dimensions of interpersonal discussion and their implications for participatory democracy. Journal. Mass Commun. Q. **77**(4), 727–743 (2000)
36. Schuth, A., Marx, M., De Rijke, M.: Extracting the discussion structure in comments on news-articles. In: Proceedings of the 9th Annual ACM International Workshop on Web Information and Data Management, pp. 97–104 (2007)
37. Singer, J.B.: Separate spaces: discourse about the 2007 Scottish elections on a national newspaper web site. Int. J. Press Polit. **14**, 477–496 (2009)
38. Smoliarova, A.S.: Immigrant news media about refugees: refugees in the headlines of the newspaper 'Russkaja Germanija'. Journal. Yearb. **6**(C), 12–18 (2017). (in Russian)

39. Springer, N., Engelmann, I., Pfaffinger, C.: User comments: motives and inhibitors to write and read. Inf. Commun. Soc. **18**(7), 798–815 (2015)
40. Stromer-Galley, J., Martinson, A.M.: Coherence in political computer-mediated communication: analyzing topic relevance and drift in chat. Discourse Commun. **3**(2), 195–216 (2009)
41. Stroud, N.J., Scacco, J.M., Muddiman, A., Curry, A.L.: Changing deliberative norms on news organizations' Facebook sites. J. Comput. Med. Commun. **20**(2), 188–203 (2015)
42. Stroud, N. J., Van Duyn, E., Peacock, C.: News commenters and news comment readers. Engaging News Proj. 1–21 (2016)
43. Toepfl, F., Litvinenko, A.: Transferring control from the backend to the frontend: a comparison of the discourse architectures of comment sections on news websites across the post-Soviet world. New Media Soc. **20**(8), 2844–2861 (2018)
44. Tsagkias, M., Weerkamp, W., de Rijke, M.: News comments: exploring, modeling, and online prediction. In: Gurrin, C., et al. (eds.) ECIR 2010. LNCS, vol. 5993, pp. 191–203. Springer, Heidelberg (2010). https://doi.org/10.1007/978-3-642-12275-0_19
45. Walther, J.B., Jang, J.-W.: Communication processes in participatory websites. J. Comput. Med. Commun. **18**, 2–15 (2012)
46. Winter, S.: Do anticipated Facebook discussions diminish the importance of argument quality? An experimental investigation of attitude formation in social media. Media Psychol. **23**(1), 79–106 (2020)
47. Wright, S., Street, J.: Democracy, deliberation and design: the case of online discussion forums. New Media Soc. **9**(5), 849–869 (2007)
48. Ziegele, M., Quiring, O.: Conceptualizing online discussion value: a multidimensional framework for analyzing user comments on mass-media websites. Ann. Int. Commun. Assoc. **37**(1), 125–153 (2013)
49. Ziegele, M., Breiner, T., Quiring, O.: What creates interactivity in online news discussions? An exploratory analysis of discussion factors in user comments on news items. J. Commun. **64**(6), 1111–1138 (2014)
50. Ziegele, M., Quiring, O., Esau, K., Friess, D.: Linking news value theory with online deliberation: how news factors and illustration factors in news articles affect the deliberative quality of user discussions in SNS' comment sections. Commun. Res. **47**(6), 860–890 (2020)

Queermuseu – Frameworks in Social Network

Rodolfo Ward[1]([⊠]) [iD] and Suzete Venturelli[2] [iD]

[1] MediaLab/UnB, Brasilia University – UnB, Brasilia, Federal District, Brasilia, Brazil
rodolfoward@unb.br
[2] Medialab/AM, Anhembi Morumbi University, São Paulo, Brazil

Abstract. This work intends to collaborate with the discussions on digital activism and collective mobilizations through social platforms in cyberspace. It is intended to work on questions about framework and mobilization strategies used by political groups on the social networking platforms of the internet, more specifically on Facebook.

Keywords: Digital culture · Cyberspace · Cyberculture

1 First Section

This work intends to collaborate with the discussions on digital activism and collective mobilizations through social platforms in cyberspace. Its goal is to address questions related to the framework and mobilization strategies used by political groups on the social networking platforms of the Internet, more specifically on Facebook.

The starting point of this research is the questioning of how the use of social media enabled the organization and mobilization of social groups across Brazil and contributed to the closing of the exhibition Queermuseu – Cartographies of Difference in Brazilian Art. The artistic exhibition aimed to explore the diversity of art and contemporary culture through a set of works by renowned artists, such as Adriana Varejão, Lygia Clark, Candido Portinari, Flávio de Carvalho, Alair Gomes, and Alfredo Volpi, presented at Santander Cultural, in the city of Porto Alegre, Rio Grande do Sul, in 2017.

Queermuseu was the first exhibition on the subject held in Brazil and the first of its magnitude in Latin America. Its contribution to a history of exhibitions in the global context is worth highlighting, as it joined a small number of exhibitions on the subject in the global context, particularly the exhibitions "Queer British Art 1861–1967" at Tate, the museum United Kingdom's national art gallery in London, or those taking place at Leslie-Lohman, the New York City-based LGBTQ museum, Hide/Seek: Difference and Desire in American Portraiture, by the National Portrait Gallery of the Smithsonian institution, in Washington, D.C., and Ars Homo Erotica, by the National Museum of Poland in Warsaw, both held in 2010.

This work was funded by the State Secretariat of Culture and Creative Economy - SECEC / DF through the Programa Conexão Cultura DF and by the notice of the Pos Graduate Decanate of the University of Brasilia DPG / UnB N ° 01/2021.

G. Meiselwitz (Ed.): HCII 2021, LNCS 12774, pp. 179–189, 2021.
https://doi.org/10.1007/978-3-030-77626-8_12

The research shows that, through the use of social networking platforms, it was possible to organize a populist campaign with a biased narrative in opposition to the artistic exhibition, in a way that contributed to the closing of the Queermuseu exhibition on the Santander premises one month prior to the scheduled date. The mobilization strategies were enmeshed, disseminated and promoted by social movement activists from the new Brazilian right, which is an "heir to the political capital of parties that supported the Military Dictatorship," or the "religious right," which is regulated "by conservative moralism, often with a religious bias" (Kinzo 1988Apud Holanda, p. 1). According to Codato, Bolognesi and Roeder (2017), it emerges as a political-electoral response to the old right and in opposition to the rise of the left, becoming popular since 2014 with the first anti-Workers' Party demonstrations in Brazil (Malini 2017, ONLINE), and which Madeira and Tarouco (2010) referred to as the "right."

Discussions on the facts related to the artistic exhibitions of the Queermuseu exhibition were a trending topic on social media for several weeks, in the period between August and October 2017, on social media platforms. The controversies between those who were in favor and those who were against the exhibition branched out in a rhizomatic manner through social media platforms, causing public disturbance and collective attraction to the topic, which instigated a number of individuals to generate opinions and participate in the debate, initially in cyberspace, and subsequently and consequently, in the physical space.

The general purpose of this work is to analyze how digital activists create framing strategies and collective mobilization in cyberspace, in addition to contributing to a better understanding of the digital strategies of groups to the right of the political spectrum. For this purpose, the case of the Queermuseu will be assessed, focusing on the digital activism of the Movimento Brasil Livre[1] (MBL).

Given their rhizomatic characteristics, the debates do not follow a logical sequence or a hierarchy. What is visibly perceived is where the controversy starts and who starts it. After the posting of the video originally published on the Facebook page of the "Terça Livre" channel, on September 9, with the title *"Exposição criminosa no Santander criminal"* ("Criminal exhibition at the criminal Santander"), the publication was reproduced over 1.2 million times" (Mendonça 2017). The post was shared and promoted by MBL, which contributed to the spread of the attack on exhibition on social media platforms.

Also noteworthy is the influence of conservative members of Congress in this debate, which, alongside MBL, created a narrative and a framework to place the public opinion against the exhibition, in addition to promoting more political instability in the post-impeachment period and possibly targeting the 2018 elections. These stakeholders take advantage of the strong engagement they have on social media platforms to turn the debate into a dispute for ideological and political power.

MBL, supported by the conservative representatives, began a defamatory campaign on the Queermuseu Exhibition, which had an exponential growth in interaction on its official Facebook page, in a viral manner, as stated by Malini (2017): "The increase in number of active users was a direct consequence of turning a fact into a polarized

---

[1] The Movimento Brasil Livre ("Free Brazil Movement") group is a political group of the Brazilian new right which claims a liberal background and works alongside the evangelical members of Congress.

political debate." This debate leads us to believe that everything was planned and pre-meditated by the groups mentioned. MBL and evangelical and the law enforcement members of Congress, and conservative and moralistic groups are positioned "to the right of the political-ideological spectrum in Brazil" (Tatagiba; Trindade; Teixeira 2015, p. 198, Apud Dias, 2017, p. 1). Using populism, half-truths and a mix of facts, MBL created fictional narratives and collective action frameworks that were absorbed by the population that is present on social media platforms.

The political mobilization of Brazilian society through social media platforms reached its peak in Brazil during the impeachment of former President Dilma Rousseff, "which was marked by high political and economic instability, influenced by corruption scandals investigated by Operation Car Wash and which lasts to this day" (Dias 2017, p. 3). Digital platforms are located where organizations build frameworks based on facts and political situations (Vicari 2014, Apud Dias 2017), so that discourses and practices on social media can inspire and motivate street demonstrations (Gerbaudo 2012, Apud Dias 2017). The empirical object for this analysis will be the posts about the Queermuseu Exhibition on the official page of the Movimento Brasil Livre group on Facebook.

Currently, groups of digital activists use real facts to create fictional stories and publicize them as real. MBL created frameworks and narratives in order to convince and mobilize social groups for real actions. They negatively framed what they intended to combat and created narratives to persuade individuals into actions, which were presented as necessary to defend current social structures, such as family, homeland, religion, morals and everything that forms and structures a traditional society. In the discourse developed by the conservative groups, it is understood that there is a left-wing group that wishes to corrupt society and that, the individuals fail to "fight" for certain facts, there will be a change for the worse. In this discourse, the Exhibition is included, being considered degrading because it promotes pedophilia, zoophilia, incest, homosexuality and other frameworks considered taboo.

Pinheiro-Machado (2017, Online) argues that the new conservative right engages in populism and the narrative of easy resolutions to complex problems in order to change the current regimes of truth about humanity, while seeking to legitimize, through rhetoric, a new direction for global society according to its interests. According to Rech and Schutz (2017), the Brazilian arts curriculum is hampered by the lack of arts education in the twenty-first century, which was reflected in the Queermuseu case. Additionally, the intellectual project of the new right (which has been applied at a global level) consists of reducing the workload and disciplines of humanities in school curricula. Looking at the recent history, it is observed that this is not a new project. In the 1970s, Lyotard (1986, p. 84) already developed this thinking when claiming that "power legitimizes science," when studying how developed nations fostered science and technology.

2   Second Section

Online social networks allow people, wherever they are and in any manner, to interact and keep in touch with friends and acquaintances, as well as allowing individuals to express themselves and be heard by a local or even global audience and, increasingly, becoming the target of marketing and advertising campaigns, as well as the stage for political and ideological disputes. Social movements on the Internet seek to create identities that distance them from old movements while giving a new guise or proposing a new approach to old problems.

Attracting these diverse groups creates political capillarity, which greatly favors the expansion of ideas and group dominance. Nevertheless, this expansion also fragments the group due to a series of factors that are explained by the dilemma of cohesion and expansion. Cohesion considers the unity of the group through identity, the identification that people have with a cause, group, action, topic, or framework. In turn, the expansion concerns the flexibility of indemnity commitments to reach a greater number of individuals (Gobbi 2016, p. 42).

We understand that there are factors of extreme complexity for the leaders of social movements to keep a group cohesive and engaged while expanding the group's territory and scope. Tarrow (2009) states that the power to promote collective actions is not the same as the power to continue them. Leadership control and strategy is required to balance internal disputes in organizational processes and to keep the group cohesive, while utilizing the Internet on political processes (Vön Bullow 2016 apud Gobbi 2016).

As seen below, right-wing groups have managed to maintain cohesion and expansion during the effective attack on the Queermuseu Exhibition, which lasted approximately two months, but it only took four days to reach its peak and impose defeat on the Exhibition organizers and the Santander Bank. Bennet and Segerberg (2012) divide actions into networks into three main topics: organically negotiated networks; organizationally activated networks; and crowd-activated networks. In the three cases, individuals have a certain degree of freedom and autonomy over their actions – "customizable action frameworks" – which differ from the logic of collective action. What interests us in this study is the first topic, in which organizations of social movements coordinate actions on social media to achieve their goals. It is quite clear in the case of the Queermuseu that MBL employed its mobilization power to attack the Exhibition and contribute to its closure.

Online activism has brought about changes in political culture and guided the fight against various forms of oppression of gender, sexuality, race, creed, or class. "It consists of an engagement that aims not only to confront or connect to the formal mechanisms of politics, but which mainly manages to generate and foster behavioral changes in society" ' (Teixeira et al. 2017). In turn, Gerbaudo (2016) analyzes this activism as "moments of digital enthusiasm" generated by the synergy between the page manager, who creates narratives and frames, and the followers, who play the role of a type of prosumer when receiving, reinforcing, and sharing content. The author also reflects suffers the liquidity of social media, in which events are fleeting and movements decline when they leave the "live" environment, becoming ephemeral and replaced by others, which are very characteristic of the society of consumption and the society of the spectacle.

3   Methodology

This work makes a case study of a campaign mobilized on Facebook. In order to achieve the proposed objectives, a qualitative research was carried out on the posts of the administrators of the MBL Facebook page during the period of greatest mobilization and interaction: from August 9 to October 8, 2017. Fonseca (2008, p. 280) states that "content analysis, in a broad conception, refers to a method of human and social sciences aimed at the investigation of symbolic phenomena through various research techniques". In addition, the engagement metric of the posts aims to quantify the number of people who voluntarily participated in the confrontation.

Data capture was performed using the Netvizz[2] application, on the Google Chrome browser, which provided us with a set of zipped (compacted) computer files, in tab format, which we downloaded and later tabulated on Microsoft Excel. According to Rieder (2013), the Netvizz tool produces raw data linked to Facebook, extracting it into three different sections: personal user networks, open groups that have up to 5,000 members, and pages, retrieving the last 999 publications made. As of 2015, Facebook removed the collection of data relating to users' personal networks, in accordance with a new policy for accessing information on the social network. Based on the texts, a manual search was carried out on Facebook and YouTube using the title of the videos.

This work is based on previous studies on the topic of digital activism, based on the content analysis of the populist frameworks presented in the posts, as well as on the content of the videos posted during the date specified earlier. The populist language categories proposed by Engesser et al. (2017) were used: simplification, emotionalization, and negativity.

Twenty-two (22) posts were collected from the administrators of the MBL Facebook page in the interval of thirty days, which accounted for 2.46 million engagements. The engagement metric was chosen for this work, as it comprises an index of the sum of likes, comments and shares, i.e., it represents the sum of quantifiable interaction data.

4   Data Analysis

Based on the theoretical analysis presented, it becomes easier to understand why MBL attacked the Queermuseu Exhibition and transformed the media campaign into an interactive spectacle that was widely accepted by the population. MBL's plot consisted of projecting in the collective imagination the narrative of topics that are taboo for Brazilian society, such as diversity of gender, sex, religion, zoophilia, and incest, among others, and from this framework, to link the image of the Queermuseu Exhibition to something harmful to the common good and which hurts the ethical, moral and religious principles of Brazilian society. Bandeira and Batista (2002) state that Brazilian society was marked for centuries by the condition of prejudiced and discriminatory practices exercised by a "political elite" that monopolized the power of the state and acted against certain groups identified according to their ethnicity, race, religion, sex, region, etc., denying them the legitimacy to exist and to express themselves. According to IBGE data released by journalist Lira Souza (2017), from Folha de São Paulo, 93% of Brazilians have never visited an art exhibition and 92% have never been to a museum. Most of the people who participated in the online discussion about the Queermuseu exhibition probably did not visit the exhibition to express their own opinion on the topic they set out to discuss, whether due to geographical factors, time, or personal interest. Part of the Internet users

---

[2] URL for Netvizz: https://apps.facebook.com/107036545989762/.

expressed their anger based on the content of the narrative presented by MBL on social networks. These are extremely important factors to analyze.

MBL mobilized masses from a distance, creating discussions between people in the cyberspace, which then branched out to physical spaces across all regions of Brazil. These discussions in many cases presented repetitive, programmed speech, based on hatred, prejudice or discrimination against the other or against ideological, belief, or sex differences. The debates were fueled partly by robots (FGV DAPP 2018), partly by people who are neither consumers nor art or museum goers, and partly by an artistically educated minority. Nevertheless, arts education in Brazilian schools is linked to the Enlightenment concept of beauty and symmetrical proportions, not addressing contemporary art, or 21st-century conceptual art, which ends up being taught only in university courses and graduate programs, i.e., a tiny part of the population has access to it. Thus, the population is not prepared for art that causes strangeness, disgust, or social criticism.

The data collected on MBL's Facebook will be presented below (Table 1).

The controversy surrounding the Queermuseu Exhibition started on social media after the posting of the video originally published on the Facebook page of the "Terça Livre" channel, on September 9, with the title *"Exposição criminosa no Santander criminal"* ("Criminal exhibition at the criminal Santander"). The publication was reproduced over 1.2 million times "(Mendonca, 2017 ONLINE). The post was shared and Promoted by Movimento Brasil Livre (MBL), which contributed to the spread of the attack on exhibition on social media platforms, reaching an engagement of 1.6 million. We opted to bring the engagement metric to this work, as it clarifies and quantifies the number of people who voluntarily participated in the action through comments, likes, or shares.

The analysis of the engagement in publications is important because, as Massuchin and Tavares (2016) say, "the high degree of engagement allows the content to reach users' subnets (Recuero 2009), having a significant impact on the propagation of this content (Zago; Bastos 2013), allowing more people to have access to this type of information."

The initial attack employs populist language targeted and planned to be easily assimilated by the followers of the pages, implying that the frameworks presented were a desire initiated by the people. This type of language and approach seeks an approximation with the agendas and struggles of the people and proposes to fight against the agendas of the elites. Bennett and Segerberg (2012, p. 22) suggest that groups that use populist language create their framing and mobilization actions in a flexible way, not just based on frames of personal action in established social groups, associations and ideologies, but also in situations broader approaches that can reach a wide variety of recipients.

Bennett and Segerberg (2012) contrasted a logic of collective action associated with organizations and collective identity to a logic of joint action involving customized and inclusive content, such as "personal action frameworks" (p. 744), and media as a means of distribution (Engesser et al. 2017, p. 7).

With the advent of new technologies and the expansion of networks and social media, populists have created their agendas and shared them without the filters of gatekeepers, journalists, and mass media professionals. This relationship between politics, social media and populism is referred to in the study by Bimber (1998, p. 137; Engesser et al. 2017), which clarifies the potential to promote unmediated communication between politicians and citizens and, thus, "restructure political power in a populist direction."

Table 1. Publication of the MBL page admins on Facebook in the period from 9/9/2017 to 10/8/2018

Date	Publication content	Engagement
9/9/2017	"Criminal exhibition at the criminal Santander," repost from "Terça Livre"	1.6 million
9/11/2017	"Santander canceled an art exhibition with material containing pedophilia and zoophilia aimed at school children after pressure from MBL and other right-wing groups"	20,605
9/11/2017	"MBL NEWS LIVE: The controversial Santander exhibition"	2,174
9/11/2017	"Via: Fernando Holiday associating pedophilia and zoophilia with the LGBT cause is one of the most offensive things I have ever seen"	9,336
9/11/2017	"HELP US SPREAD THE WORD! SHARE IT! DON'T LET THE PRESS TWIST THE TRUTH!"	9,742
9/11/2017	"Good one, Kim Kataguiri" (video about the Exhibition)	3,291
9/11/2017	"The mobilization of Brazilian society successfully managed to boycott an art exhibition with pedophilia and zoophilia content. The success of the process outrages the Brazilian left outraged. Militants and…"	76,595
9/12/2017	"LIVE: Mamãefalei and Paula Cassol from MBL – Movimento Brasil Livre RS on a debate with the curator of the controversial Queermuseu exhibition, Gaudêncio Fidelis"	27,330
9/12/2017	"Kim Kataguiri sends a message about those who defend Santander's zoophilia and pedophilia exhibition Queermuseu. Check it out: Help MBL: https://goo.gl/y9SXRp Visit our store"	6,016
9/12/2017	"Filipe Barros comments on the repercussions on the case of the Santander Queermuseu and videos deleted from Facebook. YouTube channel: Filipe Barros"	7,923
9/12/2017	"MBL is being cowardly attacked by leftist militants and by the press, which frighteningly confuses boycott with censorship. One of the lowest attacks came from Marco Antonio from Kiss FM. The radio gave us the right of reply. Congratulations to the radio for opening this space for us"	11,452
9/12/2017	"Unlike what leftists are trying to suggest, making popular pressure and promoting a boycott have nothing to do with censorship. Facebook is the one doing the censoring"	2,150
9/12/2017	"Deputy Sóstenes Cavalcante supports the campaign to pressure Santander to donate to NGOs that help children victims of abuse. SIGN HERE: https://www.change.org/p/grupo-santander-popula%C3%A7%C3%A3o-exige-retrata%C3%A7%C3%A3o-do-santander-contra-a-pedofilia"	3,180

(*continued*)

Table 1. (*continued*)

Date	Publication content	Engagement
9/13/2017	"In a heated debate, Mamãefalei hits back at Gaudêncio Fidélis, curator of the Queermuseu exhibition. CHECK IT OUT! Help MBL: https://goo.gl/y9SXRp. Visit our store: http://loja.mbl. org.br./ Join us: http://platform.mbl.org.br/"	79,386
9/13/2017	"The attack was against all Brazilians who were outraged by a pornographic exhibition aimed at children and financed with public funds. If we lose the right to speak out against what we think is wrong, what rights will be further curtailed later?"	3,104
9/14/2017	Deputy Elizeu Dionizio challenges Banco Santander to donate R$800,000 to an entity that takes care of children victims of sexual abuse in order to revert the social damage it caused. Watch and sign the petition for..."	2,370
9/14/2017	"We would like to thank Marco Feliciano for his support in the Chamber of Deputies against the cowardly attacks by part of the press that supports the public funding pedophilia and zoophilia for children"	8,548
9/14/2017	"The debate on the Santander case has ceased to be about the works exhibited and has become one about freedom: the left has always boycotted companies and has never been bothered by it; now that non-leftists wanted to boycott a bank, the press is calling us Nazis. Attacking a portion of society for questioning the use of public money will demote it to a type of non-citizen. This is not the practice of a democracy – they are dictatorial practices"	13,197
9/29/2017	"Arthur from Mamãefalei destroys this bizarre art supported by the left and exhibited to children with public funds"	58,637
9/29/2017	"Via Filipe Barros: A naked man with children touching him? Queermuseu? An apology of incest and pedophilia? You won't believe this"	26,090
9/29/2017	"What are these people so obsessed with involving children in pornographic exhibitions?"	38,734
10/8/2017	"Mamãefalei DESTROYS Caetano Veloso and artists from Globo who started a campaign against MBL and in defense of the Queermuseu for children"	46,031

When analyzing the political growth in social media and the expansion of the populist language for social mobilization, Bartlett (2014, p. 94), reiterates that "the bitter and short-lived nature of populist messages works well in this medium," which contributes to the analysis of the frameworks created by MBL against the Exhibition.

Chart 1 highlights the short, easily understandable and sensationalist phrases used by the administrators of the MBL page, in most cases, with an aggressive and emotional position. This study analyzed the frameworks promoted by MBL through three categories of language style proposed by Engesser et al. (2017): simplification, emotionalization, and negativity.

The video "Criminal exhibition at the criminal Santander" appears amateur and intimate, being recorded by three members of the group Terça Livre, who converse colloquially with the public, filming carefully selected works that make up the Exhibition and vociferating personal, biased, and moralistic analyses with the aim of denigrating and defaming the Exhibition, in addition to inciting people's hatred towards the Exhibition and against Banco Santander. They declare right at the beginning of the video that the works are "filthy," "pornographic," "in favor of pedophilia and zoophilia and against the Christian family." In the video, one of the commentators claims that "not even a transvestite would agree to do this to a child." At one point, one of the authors of the video, just before being expelled from the exhibition, films a child who is visiting the exhibition accompanied, hand in hand, by their guardians, and shouts, "That is pedophilia! There is a child here. That is pedophilia." The entire frame of the footage is composed of a negative narrative that incites hatred while moving people in favor of the cause they are defending.

The oral narrative easily assimilated by the public is used in the personal interpretations of the authors of the video during the presentation of the Exhibition to the public. The authors constantly used words to show that they were outraged with the content of the exhibition, explaining to the public that they were cursing because they were angry with everything they were seeing there, as it "hurt the traditional Christian family." This oral and visual narrative, which combined several feelings, the main one being indignation, captivated the audience with the intention of continue to promote the attack. The populist language style used in the videos is clarified by Engesser et al. (2017, p. 4), when they say that "populist stakeholders seek to maintain a close relationship with the people. They consider people's needs and demands to be inviolable and place them above all in society."

On August 11, the day when Santander Cultural decreed the Exhibition to be closed through its Facebook profile, MBL published six posts related to the Queermuseu, which recorded 121,743 engagements (see Chart 1) from Internet users on MBL's Facebook posts. The clear demonstration of the group's use of the populist language is seen in the frames used in all posts that contained a sentimental, sensationalist and negative appeal, such as the post published on August 11: "The mobilization of Brazilian society successfully managed to boycott an art exhibition with pedophilia and zoophilia content. The success of the process outrages the Brazilian left outraged."

August 12 also featured six posts – with the one referring to the debate between Arthur do Val, from the YouTube channel Mamãefalei; Paula Cassol, from MBL Rio Grande do Sul, Gaudêncio Fidelis, Municipal Secretary of Culture of Rio Grande do Sul and Lygia Clark's son for the Guaíba radio station, which generated the most public engagement, with 27,330 interactions (see Chart 1). In this debate, Cassol distorts information about the historical context of the works, claiming that they were works to encourage pedophilia and zoophilia.

A few meetings were held between right-wing leaders and Gaudêncio Fidélis, curator of the exhibition, to discuss the Exhibition. Some politicians took advantage of the great repercussion and took a position on it, mainly Marcos Feliciano and Magno Malta. The latter calls for a Parliamentary Investigation Commission (CPI) so that Fidélis could provide an explanation on the issue.

5   Conclusions

After researching and analyzing the data, we concluded that the Queermuseu exhibition was closed due to pressure from groups of digital activists who began a virtual attack on the cyberspace that took nationwide proportions and promoted actions of social movements in the physical field. Misrepresented and fictional frameworks, of a populist nature, were created regarding the works featured on the Exhibition, which were widely disseminated and shared on social media platforms by groups located to the right of the Brazilian political spectrum. The closing statement was released by Banco Santander Cultural on its Facebook profile even before a meeting with the organizers of the exhibition, which demonstrates the density and engagement that activists achieved with the attack.

One of the main stakeholders was Movimento Brasil Livre (MBL), which explored the possibilities and potential offered by social media to spread its messages by creating mobilization and engagement among Internet users in a type of joint action against the subject of the Exhibition. The group took advantage of the population's lack of knowledge about the issues addressed by the Queermuseu Exhibition, which are mostly taboo topics, in addition to taking advantage of the population's lack of knowledge about subaltern movements, studies on art, communication, and political science, which have been discussed in the academic field.

When analyzing the data collected in this work, we observe a well-planned strategy applied by the groups of the new right wing, which summoned the population to the debate, featuring sensationalist and populist frameworks created by them, achieving a high level of population engagement in a short period of time, thereby contributing to keeping the attack cohesive and achieving the result expected by the group, i.e., the closing of the Exhibition and, in the background, the political strengthening of the group itself. We notice the short, easy-to-understand and sensationalist phrases used by the administrators of the MBL website – in most cases, featuring an aggressive and emotional positioning. It is also important to note that these groups have become more professional in the use of social media platforms to create truths through fictions and to promote a broad dissemination of content without the traditional filters of professional journalists or the traditional media.

We suggest the transdisciplinary study for future research and discussions in the academic field so that it is possible to develop methodological studies on the subject and promote a real democratization of knowledge and a probable decrease in the manipulation of the population on topics already covered by university chairs.

References

Bennett, L., Segerberg, A.: The logic of connective action. Inf. Commun. Soc. **15**, 1–30 (2012). https://doi.org/10.1080/1369118X.2012.670661

Benevenuto, F.: Redes sociais on-line: técnicas de coleta, abordagens de medição e desafios futuros. Tópicos em Sistemas Colaborativos, Interativos, Multimídia, Web e Banco de Dados, pp. 41–70 (2017)

Bimber, B.: The internet and political transformation: populism, community, and accelerated pluralism. Polity **31**(1), 133–160 (1998). https://doi.org/10.2307/3235370

_____. **A era da informação**: economia, sociedade e cultura. **A sociedade em rede**, vol. 1. Paz e Terra, São Paulo (2000)

Dias, T.: **"É uma batalha de narrativas"**: os enquadramentos de ação coletiva em torno do impeachment de Dilma Rousseff no Facebook. http://repositorio.unb.br/handle/10482/24344

Engesser, S., Fawzi, N., Olof, A.: Populist online communication: introduction to the special issue. Inf. Commun. Soc. **20**(9), 1279–1292 (2017). https://doi.org/10.1080/1369118X.2017.1328525

Fonseca, W.C.J.: Análise de conteúdo. In: Duarte; B. (Org.). Métodos e técnicas de pesquisa em comunicação. São Paulo: Atlas (2008)

Kinzo, M.D.G.: **Oposição e autoritarismo ¾ Gênese e trajetória do MDB**, pp. 1966–1979. São Paulo, Idesp/Vértice (1988)

Gobbi, D.: **Identidade em ambiente virtual**: uma análise da Rede Estudantes Pela Liberdade (2016). http://repositorio.unb.br/handle/10482/22245

Holanda, M.F.: As Duas Direitas No Brasil: Uma Análise Sobre O Espectro Ideológico Dos Partidos Políticos Brasileiros. X Encontro da Associação Brasileira de Ciência Política Ciência Política e a Política: Memória e Futuro Belo Horizonte – 30 de agosto a 2 de setembro (2016)

Malini, F., Cancian, A.: **A nova cara da direita no Brasil**: um estudo sobre o grupo político MBL – Movimento Brasil Livre. Trabalho apresentado no 1o Simpósio Direitas (Da Redemocratização ao Governo Temer, Faculdade de Filosofia, Letras e Ciências Humanas da Universidade de São Paulo.

Massuchin, M.G., Tavares, C.Q.: Cobertura da greve paranaense no Facebook: engajamento dos leitores na página da Gazeta do Povo. Revista FAMECOS: Mídia, Cultura e Tecnologia [en linea] 2016, 23 (mayo-agosto). http://www.redalyc.org/articulo.oa?id=495553927011. Accessed 30 May 2018. ISSN 1415–0549.

Rieder, B.: Studying facebook via data extraction: the Netvizz application. In: Proceedings of WebSci 2013, The 5th Annual ACM Web Science Conference, pp. 346–355 (2013)

Tarrow, S.: Ballots and Barricades: On the Reciprocal Relationship between Elections and Social Movements (2009)

Websites.

FGV, Dapp. http://dapp.fgv.br/pesquisa-da-fgv-dapp-identifica-uso-de-robos-em-13-debate-nas-redes-por-boicote-exposicao-queermuseu/

Lira, S.: http://www1.folha.uol.com.br/colunas/lira-neto/2017/09/1919101-caso-da-queermuseu-confirma-atual-cenario-de-obscurantismo-no-pais.shtml?loggedpaywall

Human-Machine Interaction for Autonomous Vehicles: A Review

Jiehuang Zhang[1,2(✉)], Ying Shu[1,2(✉)], and Han Yu[1(✉)]

[1] School of Computer Science and Engineering, Nanyang Technological University, Singapore, Singapore
{jiehuang001,ying005}@e.ntu.edu.sg, han.yu@ntu.edu.sg
[2] Alibaba-NTU Singapore Joint Research Institute, Singapore, Singapore

Abstract. The rate of advancement in autonomous systems has been increasing and humans rely on such systems for every aspect of daily life. This is especially true in the area of autonomous vehicles, where new techniques and discoveries have been uncovered and Society of Automotive Engineers (SAE) Level 5 self-driving might be a reality in a few years. Despite the significant body of work on self driving technology, many people are still sceptical about the idea of riding in a fully autonomous vehicle (AV). There is a need to build trust between humans and vehicles for successful adoption of AVs. In this paper we complement existing surveys by describing 3 active research areas that are key for enhancing trust in autonomous vehicles, namely 1) Trust in Autonomous Vehicles, 2) Human Machine Interfaces, and 3) Driver Activity Detection. We discuss and highlight the key ideas and techniques in recent research works of each field, and discuss potential future directions.

Keywords: Autonomous vehicles · Human Machine Interface · Human machine interaction · Trust · Artificial Intelligence · Driver activity recognition

1 Introduction

A direct result of the exponential growth in technology is that autonomous systems are becoming more common in our daily lives. From industrial machines to autopilot functions, computing systems assist humanity in performing the repetitive, dull and tedious tasks [33]. Specifically, AI (Artificial Intelligence) has the potential to accelerate breakthroughs in many fields, especially in the area of AVs (Autonomous Vehicles). Consequently, AVs are one of the most widely investigated technologies within the automotive field [7] as intelligent features such as adaptive cruise control and lane keeping aid are introduced.

As these technological advances improve at a breakneck pace, the importance of trust in the human machine partnership takes centre stage. This synergy between man and machine is highlighted in [19,20,25] and demonstrated in

ⓒ Springer Nature Switzerland AG 2021
G. Meiselwitz (Ed.): HCII 2021, LNCS 12774, pp. 190–201, 2021.
https://doi.org/10.1007/978-3-030-77626-8_13

more recent work [37], where an end-to-end learning strategy can be harnessed to improve the combined performance of human-automation teams by considering the distinct abilities of both people and automation respectively. The authors show that the human-machine teams outperform both the individual performances of the human and machine.

The benefits of autonomous vehicles have been widely recognized (e.g., reducing traffic fatalities, improving navigation efficiency and reducing human error). Before these visions can be realised, a certain level of trust must be built between users and AVs such that societies are comfortable with adoption on a large scale. Yu et al. 2018 [39] briefly discusses the role of trust in the ethics of human AI interaction, highlighting the importance of facilitating the cooperation of humans when using AI systems. The authors also explored the ethical dilemmas involving AVs, such as the moral machine project [5]. Based on feedback from the public, it is clear that different regions prioritize a different set of values due to cultural and societal norms.

In order to promote trust in autonomous systems, it is imperative to begin considering the opinions and preferences of natives before designing any interface or system that interacts with them, directly or indirectly. While safety and trust are major issues concerning autonomous vehicles, other considerations such as clarity and effectiveness of communication are also key factors [13]. We discuss both the internal and external interfaces that are being designed to face both passengers and road users. In this paper, we survey recent advances in the techniques for building trust, human machine interfaces as well as driver activity recognition in AVs. We then discuss these techniques and propose several potential trajectories for these fields going forward. Finally, we conclude the paper and reiterate our vision for the field of AVs as a whole.

2   Building Trust in Autonomous Driving Systems

In order to design autonomous vehicles that are effective at communication, we need to investigate how trust is built between users and machine. Trust is a term that is differently defined in any different contexts, such as psychology, human-computer interaction (HCI), economics, and computer science. Most research works of trust in HCI aims to establish a quantifiable model of trust so that the level of trust and can be monitored. According to [18], there is still noticeable scepticism in society regarding AVs and their use. Furthermore, one of the most challenging barriers to entry is the average's consumer's significant distrust in fully autonomous vehicles. Public trust is essential to the success and adoption of new technology such as automated driving, and it should be a key focus during the design process.

Uggirala et al. 2004 [35] postulates that uncertainty is more easily quantifiable compared to trust, and used this concept to compare the participants' judgement of the performance of autonomous vehicles. The results conclude that trust in the system scale with the understanding of how it works. This finding has implications on the required transparency of AVs, that some basic understanding of the inner workings of self driving might be conducive for human machine cooperation.

Kyriakidis et al. 2015 [22] conducted a crowd-sourced online study on the public opinions of partial, highly and fully automated vehicles. The authors discovered that despite significant support of the benefits of AVs, participants were most concerned about the software hacking or misuse as well as legal and safety issues. These concerns may extent towards data security and privacy issues that are part of the backdrop of the conversations among the wider public. Nevertheless, these findings enable AV manufacturers deeper insight as to how to address doubts in order to streamline adoption.

Wagner et al. 2015 [36] postulates that advancing autonomous driving technology has rendered traditional software safety techniques inadequate, and a new software safety philosophy is required. This new philosophy is vital in the process of deciding whether the software in control of an autonomous vehicle is safe and trustworthy or not. The process should include testing for the potential of the AV to be trustworthy enough to be on the road driving itself and to develop its trust with the passenger over time. The authors also highlighted that there are significant expectations that the algorithms behind self driving technology achieve close to 100% accuracy, however this is beyond the performance of most machine learning and image processing methods. As the accuracy and demands of AI improve, we may see a paradigm shift whereby the self driving AI techniques outperform humans by a large enough margin that it no longer makes sense for humans to drive vehicles, considering the large number of accidents due to human errors.

Akash et al. 2017 [2] presents a model of the dynamic levels of trust between AVs and their passengers. The authors recommend that this data can then be integrated into a feedback control system for improving the AV's response to human trust. The online crowd-sourced study involves 581 human participants judging whether they trust a computer vision based obstacle detection system. As expected, trust decreased significantly during faulty scenarios, while the rebuilding of trust slightly takes place after 8 to 10 performing trials by the system. This study also considered the effects of nationality, culture and gender on trust. Americans usually are less trusting of AVs compared to Mexicans and Indians, while women tend to have a larger rate of change of trust compared to men.

Shahrdar et al. 2019 [34] extends the literature by studying how trust can be eroded, rebuilt or enhanced in the context of a passenger riding in a fully autonomous vehicle. The authors argue that in most situations, trust can be rebuilt after a reasonable time frame despite prior faulty behaviour. In the case of pedestrians, they are unlikely to encounter the same AVs multiple times in a short duration. However, prolonged exposure to negative experiences with AVs tends to erode trust and amplify negative emotions associated with these AVs.

Alvarez et al. 2019 [3] studies pedestrian behaviour when a slow moving AV with a "eye contact" eHMI communicates with them. The findings of the study concludes that the implementation of visual cues in eHMIs was not specifically necessary in a shared space where informal traffic rules are used. They are more likely to help when the ORUs and AV have potential that cause danger. This can be inferred that for commonplace, low risk interactions, pedestrians have high trust in AVs that may cause them to act normally regardless of whether a vehicle has a driver or not.

Olaverri et al. 2020 [27] suggests that it is paramount to understand the actions of different road users and their reactions to AVs. Initially, the interaction of the public and AVs will lead to some unexpected situations that can affect the level of trust. In order to develop confidence in the technology, manufacturers of AVs can consider the expectations and user experience of the average road user. Promoting trust between AVs and ORUs can seem like a daunting task, but AVs have the potential to change transport as we know it. Hence it is worthy of our effort to help facilitate society to widely embrace AVs.

3   Human Machine Interface on Autonomous Vehicles

The human machine interface (HMI) is the collection of hardware and software systems used for communication between AVs and humans such as passengers and road users. Well designed HMIs help to instil effective communication and in turn trust in this dynamic relationship, by presenting information, commands and intention to individuals inside and outside the vehicle. As full self driving SAE Level 5 [10] is being developed, it is critical that we take a look at the human factor aspects of AV communication methods.

Currently, drivers and road users communicate using either vehicle centric cues or driver centric cues to signal to road users. Subsequently, as Autonomous Vehicles (AVs) and full self-driving are being developed, it is becoming more important and urgent to develop proper communication systems between AVs and other road users. AVs are poised as having the potential to reduce the overall frequency and severity of crashes and bodily injury, ultimately to help achieve the vision of eliminating deaths from traffic fatalities [10].

However, to achieve this vision, the knowledge gap of how AVs communicate and interact with Other Road Users (ORU) needs to be addressed. Furthermore, the complexity of this issue is compounded by many factors, such as the diversity of road/traffic conditions, the visibility, weather and the fact that the AV might not even have a passenger in it. These problems have spurred new methods of communication approaches that can replace the traditional long-established ways of communication. We discuss 2 main types of HMI, the external human machine interface and automotive user interface that communicates with external road users and passengers within the AV respectively.

3.1   External Human-Machine Interfaces

In this section, we briefly present the plethora of external Human-Machine Interface (eHMI) designs, which have been effective at facilitating communication between AVs and ORUs. Most of the current systems involved some sort of external Human Machine Interface (eHMI), which is a device on the vehicle that uses light, sounds or other sensory methods to send messages to pedestrians. eHMIs need to be effective and reliable for the general public to gain trust and acceptance, for adoption in the long term.

eHMI designs are an ongoing field of research that is rapidly gaining attention. This section contributes to the line of research to enable a recent overview of the current eHMI solutions. Numerous reviews outline the state of the field which have been categorised, we outline the most relevant recent papers. Dey et al. 2020 [13] proposes a unified taxonomy that allows a systematic comparison of the eHMI designs across 18 dimensions, covering their physical characteristics and communication aspects from the perspective of human factors and human machine interaction.

Bazilinskyy et al. 2019 [6] discusses the effect of factors like text, color and perspective on the clarity and perceived to be better by road users via a crowdsourcing study. Rouchitsas et al. 2019 [31] provides a comprehensive survey of empirical work done in the field of eHMIs. Despite the number of surveys documenting the variety of eHMI designs, there has yet to be a consensus that which aspects of an eHMI constitute an effective usable one. Furthermore, most of the work in the field do not agree on a ceteris paribus approach when conducting experiments to verify their hypothesis. Fridman et al. 2017 [16] presents a crowdsourced insight from 200 qualified participants regard their preferences for eHMI display concepts, providing a scalable methodology to assess early prototypes. Eisma et al. 2020 [14] identifies the need for an assessment of the location of the eHMI impact on the crossing intention of ORUs, using eye tracking techniques to determine their preferred and situational behaviour.

Interestingly, besides visual communication cues, researchers have been experimenting with unique modes of communication such as Virtual Reality (VR) and synthetic motor sounds. Asha et al. 2020 [4] contributes a method of using VR eHMIs to provide visualisations that share context and user-specific information for enhanced vehicle-pedestrian interaction. The VR prototypes were shown to participants in the Unity game engine, where they were relatively positive about the potential of VR eHMIs being used in various traffic scenarios. The silent operation of electric vehicles has proven problematic for vulnerable road users (VRUs), especially the visually impaired group. As a matter of fact, due to the safety hazard the United States and European Union has mandated that electric vehicles are required to augment their motor sounds [1].

The authors of [26] conducted an online study to assess the appropriateness and preference of synthetic vehicles sounds on Amazon Mechanical Turk. Subsequently, a Wizard of Oz stimulated driver-less car was used to test the chosen sounds in real life scenarios in Stanford University. The findings from this study encouraged the implementation of synthetic sounds both for pedestrians to detect EVs, and also for them to decipher their intentions. Colley et al. 2020 [9] extends the scenarios where eHMI are evaluated beyond simple crossings to the realm of trucks. The authors imagined future automated trucks being parked on sidewalks, where pedestrians have to negotiate around the trucks safely. Participants in this study feed-backed that while some modes of communication such as auditory cues were rather intrusive, they generally agreed that having information from the eHMI to indicate safe to cross was appreciated.

These are just a few of the research works in the domain of eHMIs. While the magnitude of work in the field is substantial, there are many considerations that are yet to be discovered until AVs are adopted on a large scale.

3.2   Automotive User Interfaces

Next, we take a look at the interior of a AV and how the user interface can be optimised for interaction with passengers and to promote trust. Increasing attention in the optimisation of user interfaces (UI) for user experiences in AVs has inspired multiple research studies in this domain.

Alpers et al. 2020 [32] conducted a study where participants were driven in a Wizard of Oz mock AV, and each were subjected to either a human-like or opposite non-human-like digital assistant. As expected, the study concluded that the anthropomorphic interaction of the digital assistant was crucial in improving passenger's user experience and confidence in the AV. Additionally, participants subjected to the human like digital assistant were also more willing to ride in an AV again in the future. These findings point towards the inclusion of human traits such as humour, personality etc. into future digital assistants, whether they are used in AVs or other devices.

Lee et al. 2020 [23] studied the type and amount of information that should be presented to drivers during the manual and autonomous driving. The authors also placed an emphasis on the differences between men and women when it comes to the level of information they prefer. They found that women preferred more information in both manual and autonomous driving, while men preferred more information only in the autonomous mode. These findings along with AI techniques such as driver identity and activity can allow interfaces to be customised automatically according to the driver's preferences.

Hannah et al. 2020 [17] investigated the visual demand required by vehicle displays by considering the amount of glance time across various heads up display (HUD) locations. The study's objective was to specify how long it took before inappropriate or unsafe driving happens when the driver needs to make a long glance at the HUD. The authors found that the glance times can actually be longer than the current guidelines prescribed by the National Highway Traffic Safety Administration. The findings recommend that design of HUDs within the vehicle interior can be more visually demanding or require longer glances from drivers without impacting driving performance. This is generally encouraging news for AVs that may require human intervention from time to time to deal with emergency situations. Furthermore, the type and quantity of data to be shown on the automotive interface to the driver needs to be further refined. The right data can help to make AVs safer and provide high quality user experience for the passengers, in turn reducing the barriers of adoption.

4   Driver Activity Detection

In the case of an AV, since the driving task has been delegated to the vehicle, the passenger can either be engaged in monitoring the driving or distracted activities such as using handheld devices or reading. Despite full self driving capabilities, it is still within reasonable expectation that humans can overwrite or takeover the driving task from AVs in exceptional situations or emergencies. Since driver decisions and behaviours are essential factors, it can be worth the effort to install driver activity recognition systems for the additional margin of safety. Dang et al. 2020 [12] provides a recent overview of sensor and vision based human activity recognition (HAR). While not specific to driving related applications, the authors show that HAR is a promising field that potentially can be enhanced by the improving performance of deep neural networks.

Braunage et al. 2015 [8] contributes a novel method of driver activity recognition, using eye tracking and head movement data. The data was gathered from 85 test subjects driving in a driving simulator, then applied to an algorithm consisting of a Bayesian online mixture model, feature extraction and selection methods. The authors achieve an improvement from 53% to 77% compared to related work with the proposed method.

In recent years due to the rise of deep learning, the techniques employed in driver activity recognition is increasingly based on deep convolutional neural networks (CNN). Xing et al. 2019 [38] presented such an approach based on computer vision and transfer learning, using a neural network that can identify seven common driving activities such as mirror checking. The images were collected using a camera, then fed into pretrained classic computer vision-based neural networks in order to perform the classification into normal driving and distracted states.

Martin et al. 2020 [24] investigates the use of graph neural networks (GNN) for pose based driver activity detection. In this work, the camera captures the 3D body pose of the driver as well as the interior elements of the vehicle interior such as smartphones or laptops. The raw image data is passed to a novel graph representation and subsequently into a GNN to classify the activity of the driver. The authors argue that the object is critical to determining the state of the driver is much as their body pose.

Pan et al. 2020 [28] explores an alternative perspective by using graph convolutional networks (GCN) as well as long short term memory for temporal motion feature learning. They employ the same method using on board monocular cameras to capture image data, focusing on the upper body of the driver, before feeding the data into a proposed neural network architecture that proceeds to classify the driver activity. Due to the merits of transfer learning, the authors opted to use pretrained neural networks in order to optimise the training.

Roitberg et al. 2020 [30] highlights the common obstacles for using computer vision techniques on driver activity detection, such as the dynamic nature of the surrounding environment. As such computer vision techniques are trained to recognise the recurring patterns in the dataset, in the event of an unforeseen situation, the algorithm might prove ineffective at inferring that situation. The author suggests that closed sets that assume all situations and categories are known a prior is actually causing a bottleneck as driver observation algorithms are intended to handle the uncertainty of driving in dynamic conditions. A benchmark named Open-Drive&Act is proposed to address this issue by modelling and identifying behaviours previously unseen by the computer vision classifier.

In the light of advancing computer vision and deep learning techniques, we expect driver activity recognition to become more accurate. Coupled with a feedback system from the automotive user interface, this system can potentially be even more well performing and might be the key to preventing accidents.

5   Discussion

After providing a broad overview of the state of work in human AV interaction, we will discuss the trends, trajectories and our direction for future work. Most of the work in building trust belong to a mock up experimental setup, such as a Wizard of Oz where the driver is disguised as the car seat. There is no guarantee that the study participants believe that the vehicle they are riding in is truly autonomous, the relatively more perceptive ones may figure it out early in the experiment. Using real autonomous vehicles seems to be fairly risky and therefore are unlikely to obtain the approval of most institution's internal review boards. Until researchers are allowed to conduct experiments in real autonomous vehicles, we are in the dark on the differences of the results compared to mock AVs. Furthermore, it has been explored that self reported preferences often do not align well with user's actual behaviours [40]. It remains to be seen if the findings from existing and past work contributes to significant improvements in the design and operation of AVs. Several companies such as Tesla and Waymo have reportedly achieved SAE Level 4 AVs and we may witness the adoption of AVs on a large scale.

There are still many unanswered questions such as the trolley problem [39]. When we allow AVs on the roads, they are essentially given the power to make decisions of life and death during emergencies. Although the process of a passenger takeover exists, we still expect that in some situations the self driving system has to reach a time sensitive decision on its own. Researchers from interdisciplinary fields are encouraged to engage with each other in order to collect more data on various ethical dilemmas within the context of diverse cultural and social norms. Besides AVs, other Artificial Intelligence technologies such as autonomous weapons, and surveillance systems are becoming a reality and have a real impact on society. This calls for a global and unified AI regulatory framework that needs to be established in the short term to address the ethical issues [15].

Other issues that many have highlighted is privacy concerns and security issues [21]. AVs on the road today use sensors, complex algorithms and other tools such as lidar. These vehicles share sensitive data which could include passenger's personal data. Although having interconnected vehicles can optimise traffic conditions, privacy and cybersecurity issues are still a reality. An AV is still a computing device that can be hacked, and the hacker can potentially takeover the vehicle's steering, acceleration and other controls. Although the consequences of a hacked AV are dire, paying attention to the security architecture can potentially address this issue. It also requires cooperation between automakers, cybersecurity experts and government agencies to reach a concerted effort. It is necessary for us to build up the defense before we enjoy the benefits of a AV powered traffic network.

From this survey, we envision the possible future research directions which can impact the field. Currently, the field of communication between AVs and pedestrians is still in the nascent stage compared to the other mature research areas such as machine learning. While there is already a large body of work, there are several areas that are still largely unexplored. We point to specific scenarios where additional research attention is required, such as:

1. Emergency vehicles (police cars, ambulances, fire engines etc.);
2. eHMI behaviour in accidents or unusual circumstances;
3. Communicating with visually or auditory impaired or other disabled communities;
4. Internal user automotive interface for disabled passengers; and
5. User experience with robotaxis.

We also need to take into consideration the impact of self-driving systems under different social, cultural and political settings [11]. Advanced AI systems cannot be analysed or regulated by a simple one size fits all solution, due to the diversities in cultural and social norms. As we advance towards a vision of AI enabled society, we must consider the revision of current social contracts. Parker et al. 2019 [29] highlights the notion of a revealed right - a right that is only meaningfully revealed in certain technological contexts. Novel situations may arise out of this new method of mobility in the age of AVs, and there is a need to establish regulations and transparency on the responsible party when things malfunction. The AI systems we use on a regular basis needs to be able to explain or show how did things go wrong in a manner that humans can understand. However, not all situations and decision making can be reasonably programmed into a self driving system despite best efforts.

6   Conclusions

Human transport has come a long way since the steam engine, and we are now just around the corner of the age of fully autonomous vehicles. While the breakneck pace of scientific innovation and technological advancement continues, researchers and other groups need to look at the human side of the equation. AVs should be positioned as an extension of the basic human need for mobility, ensuring that our commuting experience is elevated while also reducing our impact on the environment. It is key that we put the focus on people when designing AVs, because technology should be pursued for the betterment of humanity. We envision that future research can be help improve drivers' trust and user experience in AVs, thereby enabling harmonious integration of future autonomous vehicles into our societies.

Acknowledgement. This research is supported, in part, by Nanyang Technological University, Nanyang Assistant Professorship (NAP); Alibaba Group through Alibaba Innovative Research (AIR) Program and Alibaba-NTU Singapore Joint Research Institute (JRI) (Alibaba-NTU-AIR2019B1), Nanyang Technological University, Singapore; the RIE 2020 Advanced Manufacturing and Engineering (AME) Programmatic Fund (No. A20G8b0102), Singapore; and the Joint SDU-NTU Centre for Artificial Intelligence Research (C-FAIR).

References

1. Administration, N.H.T.S.: Federal motor vehicle safety standards; minimum sound requirements for hybrid and electric vehicles (2016)
2. Akash, K., Hu, W.L., Reid, T., Jain, N.: Dynamic modeling of trust in human-machine interactions. In: 2017 American Control Conference (ACC), pp. 1542–1548. IEEE (2017)
3. Alvarez, W.M., de Miguel, M.Á., García, F., Olaverri-Monreal, C.: Response of vulnerable road users to visual information from autonomous vehicles in shared spaces. In: 2019 IEEE Intelligent Transportation Systems Conference (ITSC), pp. 3714–3719. IEEE (2019)
4. Asha, A.Z., Anzum, F., Finn, P., Sharlin, E., Costa Sousa, M.: Designing external automotive displays: VR prototypes and analysis. In: 12th International Conference on Automotive User Interfaces and Interactive Vehicular Applications, pp. 74–82 (2020)
5. Awad, E., et al.: The moral machine experiment. Nature **563**(7729), 59–64 (2018)
6. Bazilinskyy, P., Dodou, D., De Winter, J.: Survey on eHMI concepts: the effect of text, color, and perspective. Transp. Res. Part F: Traffic Psychol. Behav. **67**, 175–194 (2019)
7. Beiker, S.A.: Legal aspects of autonomous driving. Santa Clara L. Rev. **52**, 1145 (2012)
8. Braunagel, C., Kasneci, E., Stolzmann, W., Rosenstiel, W.: Driver-activity recognition in the context of conditionally autonomous driving. In: 2015 IEEE 18th International Conference on Intelligent Transportation Systems, pp. 1652–1657. IEEE (2015)
9. Colley, M., Mytilineos, S.C., Walch, M., Gugenheimer, J., Rukzio, E.: Evaluating highly automated trucks as signaling lights. In: 12th International Conference on Automotive User Interfaces and Interactive Vehicular Applications, pp. 111–121 (2020)
10. Committee, S.O.R.A.V.S., et al.: Taxonomy and definitions for terms related to on-road motor vehicle automated driving systems. SAE Stan. J. **3016**, 1–16 (2014)
11. Crawford, K., Calo, R.: There is a blind spot in AI research. Nat. News **538**(7625), 311 (2016)
12. Dang, L.M., Min, K., Wang, H., Piran, M.J., Lee, C.H., Moon, H.: Sensor-based and vision-based human activity recognition: a comprehensive survey. Pattern Recogn. **108**, 107561 (2020)
13. Dey, D., et al.: Taming the eHMI jungle: a classification taxonomy to guide, compare, and assess the design principles of automated vehicles' external human-machine interfaces. Transp. Res. Interdiscip. Perspect. **7**, 100174 (2020)

14. Eisma, Y.B., van Bergen, S., Ter Brake, S., Hensen, M., Tempelaar, W.J., De Winter, J.C.: External human-machine interfaces: the effect of display location on crossing intentions and eye movements. Information **11**(1), 13 (2020)

15. Erdélyi, O.J., Goldsmith, J.: Regulating artificial intelligence: proposal for a global solution. In: Proceedings of the 2018 AAAI/ACM Conference on AI, Ethics, and Society, pp. 95–101 (2018)

16. Fridman, L., Mehler, B., Xia, L., Yang, Y., Facusse, L.Y., Reimer, B.: To walk or not to walk: Crowdsourced assessment of external vehicle-to-pedestrian displays. arXiv preprint arXiv:1707.02698 (2017)

17. Hannah Topliss, B., Harvey, C., Burnett, G.: How long can a driver look? exploring time thresholds to evaluate head-up display imagery. In: 12th International Conference on Automotive User Interfaces and Interactive Vehicular Applications, pp. 9–18 (2020)

18. Hengstler, M., Enkel, E., Duelli, S.: Applied artificial intelligence and trust-the case of autonomous vehicles and medical assistance devices. Technol. Forecast. Soc. Change **105**, 105–120 (2016)

19. Hoc, J.M.: From human-machine interaction to human-machine cooperation. Ergonomics **43**(7), 833–843 (2000)

20. Hoc, J.M.: Towards a cognitive approach to human-machine cooperation in dynamic situations. Int. J. Hum. Comput. Stud. **54**(4), 509–540 (2001)

21. Kim, Y., Kim, I.: Security issues in vehicular networks. In: The International Conference on Information Networking 2013 (ICOIN), pp. 468–472. IEEE (2013)

22. Kyriakidis, M., Happee, R., de Winter, J.C.: Public opinion on automated driving: results of an international questionnaire among 5000 respondents. Transp. Res. Part F: Traffic Psychol. Behav. **32**, 127–140 (2015)

23. Lee, J.M., Park, S.W., et al.: Drivers' user-interface information prioritization in manual and autonomous vehicles. Int. J. Automot. Technol. **21**(6), 1355–1367 (2020)

24. Martin, M., Voit, M., Stiefelhagen, R.: Dynamic interaction graphs for driver activity recognition. In: 2020 IEEE 23rd International Conference on Intelligent Transportation Systems (ITSC), pp. 1–7. IEEE (2020)

25. Millot, P.: Toward human-machine cooperation. In: Filipe, J., Cetto, J.A., Ferrier, J.L. (eds.) Informatics in Control, Automation and Robotics. LNEE, vol. 24, pp. 3–20. Springer, Berlin (2009). https://doi.org/10.1007/978-3-540-85640-5_1

26. Moore, D., Currano, R., Sirkin, D.: Sound decisions: how synthetic motor sounds improve autonomous vehicle-pedestrian interactions. In: 12th International Conference on Automotive User Interfaces and Interactive Vehicular Applications, pp. 94–103 (2020)

27. Olaverri-Monreal, C.: Promoting trust in self-driving vehicles. Nat. Electron. **3**(6), 292–294 (2020)

28. Pan, C., Cao, H., Zhang, W., Song, X., Li, M.: Driver activity recognition using spatial-temporal graph convolutional LSTM networks with attention mechanism. IET Intell. Transport Syst. **15**(2), 297–307 (2020)

29. Parker, J., Danks, D.: How technological advances can reveal rights. In: Proceedings of the 2019 AAAI/ACM Conference on AI, Ethics, and Society, p. 201 (2019)

30. Roitberg, A., Ma, C., Haurilet, M., Stiefelhagen, R.: Open set driver activity recognition. In: 2020 IEEE Intelligent Vehicles Symposium (IV), pp. 1048–1053. IEEE (2020)

31. Rouchitsas, A., Alm, H.: External human-machine interfaces for autonomous vehicle-to-pedestrian communication: a review of empirical work. Front. Psychol. **10**, 2757 (2019)

32. Alpers, S., et al.: Capturing passenger experience in a ride-sharing autonomous vehicle: the role of digital assistants in user interface design. In: 12th International Conference on Automotive User Interfaces and Interactive Vehicular Applications, pp. 83–93 (2020)

33. Shahrdar, S., Menezes, L., Nojoumian, M.: A survey on trust in autonomous systems. In: Arai, K., Kapoor, S., Bhatia, R. (eds.) SAI 2018. AISC, vol. 857, pp. 368–386. Springer, Cham (2019). https://doi.org/10.1007/978-3-030-01177-2_27

34. Shahrdar, S., Park, C., Nojoumian, M.: Human trust measurement using an immersive virtual reality autonomous vehicle simulator. In: Proceedings of the 2019 AAAI/ACM Conference on AI, Ethics, and Society, pp. 515–520 (2019)

35. Uggirala, A., Gramopadhye, A.K., Melloy, B.J., Toler, J.E.: Measurement of trust in complex and dynamic systems using a quantitative approach. Int. J. Ind. Ergon. **34**(3), 175–186 (2004)

36. Wagner, M., Koopman, P.: A philosophy for developing trust in self-driving cars. In: Meyer, G., Beiker, S. (eds.) Road Vehicle Automation 2. LNM, pp. 163–171. Springer, Cham (2015). https://doi.org/10.1007/978-3-319-19078-5_14

37. Wilder, B., Horvitz, E., Kamar, E.: Learning to complement humans. arXiv preprint arXiv:2005.00582 (2020)

38. Xing, Y., Lv, C., Wang, H., Cao, D., Velenis, E., Wang, F.Y.: Driver activity recognition for intelligent vehicles: a deep learning approach. IEEE Trans. Veh. Technol. **68**(6), 5379–5390 (2019)

39. Yu, H., Shen, Z., Miao, C., Leung, C., Lesser, V.R., Yang, Q.: Building ethics into artificial intelligence. arXiv preprint arXiv:1812.02953 (2018)

40. Zell, E., Krizan, Z.: Do people have insight into their abilities? a metasynthesis. Perspect. Psychol. Sci. **9**(2), 111–125 (2014)

Social Network Analysis

Public Opinion Dynamics in Online Discussions: Cumulative Commenting and Micro-level Spirals of Silence

Svetlana S. Bodrunova[1]($\boxtimes$) (iD), Ivan S. Blekanov[2] (iD), and Alexey Maksimov[2] (iD)

[1] School of Journalism and Mass Communications, St. Petersburg State University, 7-9 Universitetskaya nab., St. Petersburg 199004, Russia
s.bodrunova@spbu.ru

[2] Faculty of Applied Mathematics and Control Processes, St. Petersburg State University, 7-9 Universitetskaya nab., St. Petersburg 199004, Russia

Abstract. Objectives: Social media have become a place where the bulk of grass-roots political discussion takes place. Today, the growing body of research is dedicated to cumulative patterns on online deliberation, the predecessors of which were the concept of the spiral of silence, the silent majority hypothesis, and influencer studies. However, when applied to the dissonant, disruptive, and discontinued online discussions of today where gatewatching is much less predictable and cumulation of support is often accompanied by communicative aggression, these concepts need to be reconsidered and re-tested. Also, the current public communication online is much more multi-level than before; even within one platform, several communication layers may be defined, and their inter-relations in terms of public opinion aggregation remain under-studied. *Research goal.* This paper aims at discovering patterns of cumulative deliberation in online communication. We first discuss the umbrella concept of cumulative deliberation. Then, we test the dynamics of the discussion on Belarusian oppositional YouTube in terms of impact of cross-account commenting on growth of commenting within the cross-account community and the overall discussion. *Method and sampling.* We have collected the data by YouTube crawling. The data include all user comments of 2018 for six salient Belarusian oppositional accounts. To define the cross-account commenters, we used Gephi-based web graph reconstruction. We manually coded user posts for interactivity, aggression, and criticism. Dependencies in the dynamics of the discussion were tested by correlational and cluster analysis. *Results.* We have discovered that users diverged into two mutually exclusive modes of expression, namely aggressive-dialogical and (self-)critical. Of the cross-account commenters, several users demonstrated 'cumulative' behavior and personal opinion bubbles. While there were nearly no dependencies discovered in the dynamics of user posting, criticism and self-criticism show capacity of spurring/diminishing the dynamics of public communication online, even if commenting on the whole is cumulative, not dialogical.

Keywords: Communication · Networked discussions · Deliberation · Cumulative deliberation · Granger test · Belarus · YouTube · Political protest

© Springer Nature Switzerland AG 2021
G. Meiselwitz (Ed.): HCII 2021, LNCS 12774, pp. 205–220, 2021.
https://doi.org/10.1007/978-3-030-77626-8_14

1 Introduction

Social media have become a place where the bulk of grassroots political discussion takes place. Social networking sites, online platforms, and messengers have become a focus of scholarly attention in their relation to public opinion formation and spread, which, in its turn, directly affects the quality of offline democratic deliberation.

The models that described opinion formation in the era of traditional media have been applied to online discussions, with varying degree of proof and support. Thus, the idea of opinion leaders [1] has been re-interpreted to describe the practices of influencers [2, 3, 4], and the older idea of echo chambers [5] has transformed into filter bubbles [6].

Along with this, today's public spheres are, in general, described as dissonant [7] and discontinued [8]. The dynamics of formation of dominant opinions have been conceptualized in several theoretical models, among them, most famously, in the idea of spiral of silence [9]. In this conceptualization, under pressure of fear to be excluded, supporters of one candidate become gradually silenced by the supporters of the other one, and the latter are capable of doing this just by expressing their opinion more massively.

However, when applied to the dissonant and disruptive online discussions of today where cumulation of support is often accompanied by communicative aggression [10, 11], Noelle-Neumann's concept and similar conceptualizations needs to be reconsidered and re-tested. This is especially because there is growing evidence that online discussions are the place where silent majority flourishes [12–15].

Today, instead of dialogue and polylogue in the forms of opinion exchange, we witness cumulative modes of discussion prevail [11]. To re-conceptualize the ways public communication exists and develops in online milieus, we suggest the idea of *cumulative deliberation* on which we elaborate below (see Sect. 2). Our previous works, as well as many works before ours, have shown that cumulation may be regarded as a universal mechanism of public opinion growth and polarization [16]. E.g., in the form of echo chambering, it works on many levels in globalized discussions, such as language, hashtagging, and sentiment [17]. We have also demonstrated that, on Russian oppositional YouTube, users hardly form what might be called 'a discussion'; they, rather, express themselves *urbi et orbi* without entering any dialogue with particular users, despite their high polarization in political terms and an extremely high level of aggressive and hate speech discovered [11].

The current paper further fosters the idea of discovering patterns of cumulative deliberation in oppositional discourse and, this time, uses a year-long dataset from Belarusian oppositional YouTube of 2018. We have collected comments left by users under the videos of six salient Bealrusian oppositional accounts (one of which, Nexta, has become world-renowned during the Belarusian protest of 2020). We have identified users who linked these accounts by posing to at least five of them, and have analysed this core of commenting for the features important for the deliberative process, namely orientation to dialogue [18], aggression [11, 19], and political criticism. In the latter we have taken in mind the difference between uncritical, policy-critical, and leadership critical publics, as it was suggested and explained for authoritarian societies [20].

In particular, we focus on two research questions. First, we ask whether (and how exactly) the deliberative features mentioned above accumulate in the discussion and affect its dynamics in the core of the discussion (which is, in the Belarusian case, the cross-commenter conglomerate) on various time spans. Second, we look at whether the deliberative feature of the discussion core affect the bulk of the discussion. This paper is only a trial that shows the necessity of further exploration of cumulative patterns of online discussions and points out to possible bigger cumulative effects that deserve exploration and explanation.

The remainder of the paper is organized as follows. Section 2 elaborates on cumulative deliberation as a concept and suggests how dynamics of the discussions might be affected by cumulative patterns of opinion formation. Section 3 poses the research questions. Section 4 describes sampling, data collection, dataset limitations, and methods of data assessment. Section 5 provides the results; Sect. 6 discusses them and concludes the paper.

2   Cumulative Foundations and Deliberative Features of Online Opinion Formation

2.1   Cumulative Patterns in Online Opinion Formation

As already stated above, the idea of cumulation as a basic principle of how online public opinion forms has come from two streams of literature.

Cumulative Effects in Online Opinion Formation. The first one focuses upon patterns of winning the public debate – that is, majority/minority formation in public opinion and electoral research. In political sociology, the works that have demonstrated that people may change opinion just knowing or supposing what others might think have been numerous [21], and they have posed a question of whether opinion change is a result of persuasive external arguments, including mediated ones.

However, despite their evident high impact upon the rational choice debate, relatively few important works linked individual/public opinion shifts to communication and deliberation patterns on aggregated levels. Well-known are, e.g., the works on 'spiral of silence' by Elizabeth Noelle-Neumann [9] or Latané's social impact theory that emerged, i.a., from studying interaction patterns [21, 22]. But it was not before the advent of social media that the scholars have received a chance to study the multi-level communicative interactions.

There is one significant factor that distinguishes the pre-Internet era from today's communication. In online communication, the iceberg of what could previously remain an oral utterance exchange and disappear forever after being pronounced, remains written and accessible by the newcomers who join the communicative milieu later in time. Potentially, this casts impact upon the newcomers and their personal, seconds-long opinion formation, in accordance with the social impact theory; this remains highly understudied. At the same time, there is a substantially bigger corpus of works upon various discussion-level effects of opinion cumulation, such as echo chambering and filter bubbles studies or research on influencers who become such by cumulation of user support. (Of these studies, we will focus on user comments studies – see below).

Thus, cumulative effects in communication have long been demanding generalization and systematization – or at least a proper acknowledgement of the role of cumulation in opinion formation online.

Dissonant Public Spheres: Getting Rid of Excessive Normativity. The second stream of literature is that on public sphere as a normative space of (arguably) consensus-oriented discussion of conflictual issues in public domain, as well as on deliberation as a special form of public communication, an imagined round-table process of collection and adjustment of individual, group, and institutionalized opinions that leads to decision on a given issue. For several decades, public sphere studies have almost exclusively, either adhering or critically, oriented to the works by Juergen Habermas.

The Habermasian view on deliberation is known for its high normativity, as communicative actions need to be rational, consensus-oriented, and civil in order to count for public decision-making. Despite the overwhelming amount of academic criticism from both left and right parts of the political spectrum, as well as the shifts in Habermas's own conceptualization of public sphere and deliberation, the normative notion of orientation to consensus (or to struggle, in the leftist view [23]) and high *deliberative quality* of public communication was not challenged.

Again, it was not before the advent of blogs and social networking sites that the scholars questioned the belief that people come into a discussion either 'to agree or to argue' [24] – that is, with a certain deliberative goal. Today, this notion has been shaken by description of online public spheres as dissonant – that is, not aiming to consonance and consensus; public spheres where myriads of actors express themselves simultaneously [7]. There are also works that describe public spheres as discontinued, whose actors constantly change and re-aggregate [8], and, in general, disrupted [25].

Moreover, recent research suggests that users might participate in dialogical forms of communication much more rarely than deliberation theory suggests [11], and that their motivation is neither to agree nor to argue in order to come to a conclusion, but more to express themselves, solidarize with an earlier opinion or negate it without having in mind any longer-term effects. Yet, even such communicative activity, 'irrelevant, aggressive, and stupid' [26: 659], seemingly aimless in deliberative terms and dismissed as slacktivism [27] and 'sofa warrior' behavior, acquires importance if seen from the cumulative-effects viewpoint.

The plea for finding new grounds for assessment of public spheres influenced by massive micro-level communication, united with the view upon cumulation as an overarching pattern of how opinion aggregates and dissipates online, has led us to the concept of *cumulative deliberation*. This concept is, in essence, an alternative vision on public deliberation that covers by one umbrella many cumulative effects scattered around academic works on older and newer media and opinion formation via them. Cumulative deliberation allows for a closer-to-reality look at how people talk online, as it lets avoid the excessive normativity and merit the smallest forms of online user activity: each individual comment, like, share, or mention matters for cumulative deliberation. It also aims at discovering patterns of opinion aggregation on various levels and explaining/predicting critical thresholds in cumulative communication. And the patterns of opinion cumulation, not only user intentions, should be subjected to critical assessment within the democratic perspective of public communication.

2.2 User Comments on YouTube and Other Social Media: The Issue of Deliberative Quality of Communicative Micro-action

Thus, user commenting seen as deliberative activity may be put into the cumulative deliberation perspective – that is, cumulative patterns and their effects in user commenting need to be detected and assessed, without putting the blame to users for not being rational or purposeful. Previous research shows that users' comment 'exchange is socially and not deliberatively motivated', and, in reading comments, 'entertainment dimension – a dimension that is not usually considered to be linked to deliberation processes – is the more stable one' [28: 798]. This points out to the necessity for the academe to move towards accepting these motivations as normal and assessing the cumulative effects of such online posting.

Close enough to this notion, computational social scientists have tried to detect statistical effects in comment threads and discussion graph structure, such as various types of distributions like lognormal [29], negative binomial [30], Zipf's law [31], or power law [32]. However, cumulative effects may be of a more nuanced nature, as they combine statistical features of communication flows and contents of user utterances (for a short review on early works that include content features into statistical modelling of commenting dynamics, see [33]). Even successful modelling of discussion growth [33] often sees comments as discreet items, not cumulative conglomerates, and fails to encompass deliberative features of comments (sometimes focusing on one selected). On the other hand, communication scholars who focus on deliberative quality of commenting [34] are less attentive to various formal levels on which cumulation might shape the discussion, as well as to statistical features of discussions linked to platform affordances and human capacities that define posting and reading.

In our current research, we do not aim at creating overarching models of user commenting; we just want to demonstrate easily discoverable impact of deliberative features of user posts upon various structural levels and temporal fragments of online discussions. In previous studies, several user-dependent features of comments and their deliberative potential have been discussed. In a more systematic view, assessment of democratic quality of deliberation online moves from evaluating the constellation of major institutional discussants to single user and features of their statements.

Orientation to Dialogue. Addressing the other is an inevitable pre-requisite for any sort of dialogue, public or private. Interactivity has been conceptualized as capable of 'contribut[ing] to shaping a democratically valuable and vivid interpersonal discourse on topics of public interest' [35: 1112]; see also [36–38]. However, user comments do not necessarily have this feature. Thus, an important division has been introduced between user-to-content (e.g., news video) and user-to-user orientation in commenting [39], and user-to-content comments, as a rule, do not involve other users to interaction.

While we praise this important distinction, we prefer to see formal interactivity (often marked by user mentions) as just a part of wider orientation to dialogue. Thus, our earlier study [11] shows that, on Russian-speaking YouTube, 'discussion' in the form of dialogue hardly takes place at all, despite the political topicality of the assessed videos, and formal and substantial markers of dialogue may not correspond. E.g., even when users formally reply to other users' comments, they construct the phrases the way that does not invite their correspondents to answer; they just solidarize with the expressed opinion or share their own experience that, in most cases, supports the view in the primary post. Or, vice versa, a comment may be openly dialogical in substance (interrogative, sarcastic, or denialist) without any formal interactivity features. In normative view, dialogue features should oppose.

Aggression. When a dialogue does take place, it may easily take an anti-normative direction, as users attach each other aggressively, rather than interact in civil manner. Studies of user sentiment, emotions, affect, and aggression in social media content are overwhelming in number. Of emotional substance of comments, various types of aggressive speech are the sharpest; this, i.a., includes hate speech, obscene and tabooed lexicons, politically motivated offence, calls for violence, cyberbullying, humiliation, and harsh shaming. However, we have demonstrated [11, 40] that communicative aggression may play constructive roles in online discussions, such as influencing its dynamics and performing individual- and group-level psychological functions.

Today, surprisingly few works focus on how aggressive and emotional speech relates to opinion aggregation and fueling discussions. This is especially true for languages like Russian and Belarusian where obscene lexicon has grown into a highly developed sub-language.

Criticism. Aggression needs to be distinguished from criticism, another pragmatic dimension of user speech. Critical assessment of reality has for centuries been acknowledged as a pre-requisite for substantial debate on nearly any issue. Political criticism may be directed to individual/group ideological opponents, as well as to the state, public bodies, persons, and policies. Recently, three types of publics have been defined for authoritarian public spheres, based on what is subjected to criticism [20], namely uncritical, policy-critical, and leadership-critical publics. Criticism to policies is expected to be milder, more discussion-oriented, and perhaps a bit more toothless, as it follows from the paper. Criticism towards the authorities brings more dangers to the speaker and, thus, demands passing a certain psychological threshold. This might imply that leadership-critical users could use aggressive speech and be less willing to take part in meaningful discussion. Both critical stances, however, may foster cumulative effects in discussions, as earlier critical comments may help diminish participation thresholds for users who comment later, and thus create avalanche effects.

Taken together, these three deliberative features may work on various levels of online discussion architectonics, from single comments to platform-based publics. We will look at their potential to foster cumulative effects in online communication on Belarusian YouTube.

3   Research Questions

Having said that, we have formulated the research questions for our study.

RQ1. Are the three deliberative features relate to each other in the discussion, and how?

RQ2. Do the three deliberative features influence the discussion dynamics, and on what levels and time spans?

RQ3. Are there any distinctive patterns of cumulative deliberation that we can point to, and on what levels and time spans?

We do not pose any exact hypotheses, as our study is exploratory; below, we will summarize our findings according to the RQs stated above.

4 Data Collection and Methods

4.1 Case Description: Belarusian Oppositional YouTube

To address the research questions, we have used the dataset of comments published within the year of 2018 to six YouTube accounts from Belarus, all of them politically oppositional, most salient on Belarusian political YouTube in 2018–2019.

This choice is explainable in many respects. First, Belarus remains one of most understudied media landscapes of Europe; as a recognized autocracy, it represents a case for analysis of authoritarian public sphere. Second, the dataset is not hashtag-based, which allows for avoiding the dissipative and affective effects [41] in how it develops; the dataset represents a 'chronic' discourse on the oppositional YouTube. Its oppositional orientation allows for comparing the results with our earlier work on Russia [11]; the pre-set political standing of channels sets the conditions for potentially conflictual and polarized opinion exchange. At the same time, the volume of discussion is by an order of magnitude smaller than in Russia and the most studied Western countries, due to lower levels of YouTube consumption and smaller populace in general; thus, a year-long dataset remains feasible for both automated and manual research. In this respect, Belarusian YouTube is sort of an 'ideal gas' of studying online political communication in autocracies. To this, we add that, to avoid geographical echo chambering, we have focused not only on the accounts based in Minsk but also on those produced in other Belarusian regions. The accounts are Belsat (Belarusian oppositional satellite TV channel sponsored from abroad), Nexta (by 2021, a world-famous Belarusian blogger and protest facilitator), Garantiy NET ('No guarantee', Gomel; by 2021, the videos of 2018 are deleted), Narodny Reporter ('Popular reporter', Brest region), The Belarusian Experimental Field (positioned as all-Belarusian), and Rudabelskaya pakazuha ('Window dressing in Rudabelka', Gomel region).

It is worth mentioning that, in 2020, Belarus has lived through a months-long political protest unprecedented in the newest Belarusian history. The data of a year and a half before the protests erupted demonstrate the mood of Belarusians and are relatively highly politicized.

4.2 Data Collection and the Dataset

YouTube crawling was performed by the web crawler created and patented by our research group [42]. The overall number of user comments in the dataset is 120,412 posted by 3000 + users.

4.3   Research Procedures and Methods Used

The logic of our research demanded several steps of working upon the dataset.

Defining the Discussion Core. After preliminary studying of comment structure and their appearance on actual YouTube pages, we have divided the dataset into the core and periphery. The core users were those who performed an important deliberative function of cross-account commenting, thus transforming the accounts and the discussion into one discursive field. Reconstructing the web graph of the discussion by the YifanHu Gephi algorithm, we have identified users who posted in at least five of six accounts (76 users with 8,610 comments). Answering the RQs was linked to both the discussion core itself and to relations between the core and the periphery of the discussion.

Forming Sub-Datasets. We have identified the levels on which we search for cumulative patterns. We have used seven levels/time spans formed from the bulk data. The logic of it is to 'zoom in' from the whole discussion to the level of one particular day

Table 1. Sub-datasets of the project

#	Time span	Unit of analysis / Granger test increment	Type of data	N of comments
(1)	Year	Any	The whole discussion bulk (used to detect the core and form other datasets)	120,412
(2)	Year	Week	The whole discussion core	8,610
(3)	5 weeks, February 26 to April 1	24 h	The most rapidly growing discussion segment around a key event	(3a) 1,164 – core vs (3b) 17,222 – bulk
(4)	Week, March 26 to April 1	6 h	The most commented week around a key event	287
(5)	Day, March 26	1 h	The day next to the key event	(5a) 113 – core vs. (5b) 1,269 – bulk
(6)	Year	Year	Comment conglomerates by each cross-commenter	8,610
(7)	Year	Year	Comments under a particular video of March 25	127

Note. The sub-datasets (3a), (4), (5a) are formed out of the sub-dataset (2) and, thus, were coded within the coding process for the sub-dataset (2).

(step-by-step via other time spans), one video, and one user. The sub-datasets used for this paper include the following (see Table 1).

Zooming in was performed after detecting the most actively growing segment of the year-long discussion. This segment was 5 weeks from February 26 to April 1, 2018, structured around an event of high importance to the opposition, namely the celebration of 100 years of the so-called 1918 Belarusian Republic (March 25, most active commenting taking part on March 26).

Coding Deliberative Features of Comments. The contents of the sub-datasets (2) including (3a), (4), and (5a), as well as (6) and (7), were coded for the three deliberative features described above, that is, orientation to dialogue ('dialogue' from now on), aggression, and criticism.

For the latter, we have introduced additional variables after preliminary reading of the data and following Toepfl's argument [20]. Thus, three more coding variables were added: criticism towards authorities/security services (corresponding to 'leadership-critical public'), and self-criticism. We have discovered this phenomenon of Belarusians criticizing themselves and self-blaming for the political situation in the country and have coded this as a separate variable. Thus, 'criticism' was coded as comprising the three types of critique found in the comments.

The coding was performed by two coders (Cohen's kappa = 0,81), both speaking native Russian and Belarusian, as the discussion was bilingual.

Testing the Dependencies. For testing the inter-relation between the variables, descriptive statistics (Cramer's V) were used. For demonstration of discursive divergence of the cross-commenters, k-means clustering with silhouette quality metric was applied. For assessment of the possible impact of the deliberative features to discussion dynamics, Granger testing was used.

5   Results

RQ1. *Inter-relation between the deliberative features and their impact to discussion structure.* After we have coded the data, it became evident that dialogue, aggression, and criticism were inter-related in our data in specific ways that might relate to cumulation of support or criticism during the discussion.

From the first correlation tests we have seen that, counter-intuitively, aggression is linked not to criticism but to dialogue, and, moreover, this inter-relation intensifies on the most intense commented days (see Tables 2 and 3 for year-long and day-long spans, respectively). Dialogue and aggression correlate strong enough, while none of criticism types correlates with dialogue or aggression, and criticism to power and self.

Based on this finding and on the insights from the coding process, we have tested whether the discovered correlations matter on the user level – that is, whether there are distinct discursive clusters that would diverge, e.g., the 'dialogical and aggressive' users and critical users. For this, we have used k-means clustering and silhouette as a quality metric (see earlier accounts on this method used for social media data in [16]).

Indeed, we have discovered that two clusters form well enough (S > 0,6; see Fig. 1); however, the two clusters diverged only on aggression (p = 0.000) and dialogue (p = 0.001), not on criticism (p = 0.3). The best clustering option (of over two dozen probed, from 2 to 5 clusters, from 3 to 5 variables) is presented on Fig. 2, it has three clusters and is based on the three initial variables (for all variables, p < 0.0002). On Fig. 2, the aggressive-dialogical Cluster 3 is formed by 4 users only, with the rest of the users distributing nearly equally between two 'calm' clusters with varying level of criticism. However, if we use another sorting option (with observations taken as fixed intervals), their number grows to 15.

This supports what we have seen during coding. There are two modes used by cross-commenters of our dataset. Mostly, users self-express 'urbi et orbi' or, more rarely, address their comments to the authors of the discussed videos. There were nine users among 76 who never addressed anyone and just commented by expressing themselves; for 42 of 76 users (55%), dialogue-oriented comments were fewer than 10%. Such users seem to form a personal 'opinion bubble' which they stretch across the YouTube channels they comment in. The dialogue appears to 'belong' to other users that enter aggressive interrogations with other users (whom they often dismiss as trolls), and these micro-skirmishes evolve into microscopic 'spirals of silencing' one of the opponents.

Table 2. Inter-relation between deliberative features in the comments of cross-commenters on the year-long span (Cramer's V, N = 8,610)

Deliberative feature	Dialogue	Aggression	Criticism	Criticism power	Criticism policy	Criticism self
Dialogue	1.000					
Aggression	0.289***	1.000				
Criticism	−0.177***	−0.074***	1.000			
CriticismPower	−0.151***	−0.014	n/a	1.000		
CriticismPolicy	−0.048***	−0.052***	n/a	−0.107*	1.000	
CriticismSelf	−0.043***	−0.076***	n/a	−0.156***	−0.054***	1.000

Another interesting, even if intuitively understandable, finding is that self-criticism is inversely proportional to criticism to authorities, as well as to policy criticism (despite the fact that all options could be coded for one comment). However, unlike criticism on the whole, self-criticism does not help users diverge. We have tested self-criticism in various combinations of variables for 2, 3, and 4 clusters, and self-criticism was never significant. Thus, this modus is spread all over the discussion core, but in small proportions which are not enough to influence individual user strategies; only 12 of 76 users (circa 16%) have not expressed self-criticism in their comments.

Table 3. Inter-relation between deliberative features in the comments of cross-commenters on a weekly span, March 26 to April 1 (Cramer's V, N = 287)*

Deliberative feature	Dialogue	Aggression	Criticism	Criticism power	Criticism self
Dialogue	1.000				
Aggression	0.470***	1.000			
Criticism	−0.347***	−0.243***	1.000		
CriticismPower	−0.299***	−0.205**	n/a	1.000	
CriticismSelf	−0.153*	−0.095	n/a	−0.143*	1.000

*Note. The correlations between criticism to policy and other variables was not tested due to scarcity of data.

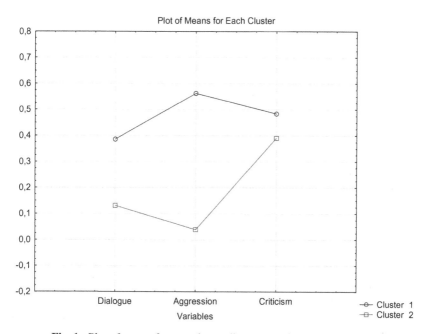

Fig. 1. Plot of means for two-cluster divergence of cross-commenters

RQ2. *Impact of the deliberative features to the discussion dynamics.* To assess whether the deliberative features cast impact upon the discussion dynamics, we have tested the relations between the overall number of posts and the number of posts with deliberative features for various time spans (see Table 1). After our findings for the Russian YouTube of 2019 [11] where we have seen that aggression highly influences discussion dynamics, as well as vice versa, we expected this to be also true for the Belarusian YouTube.

However, of all the Granger tests we have conducted for weekly, daily, 6-h, and hourly spans, only two cases detected dependencies. Thus, by Granger tests, dynamics of self-criticism shaped the dynamics of the discussion core in 6-h increment, both for

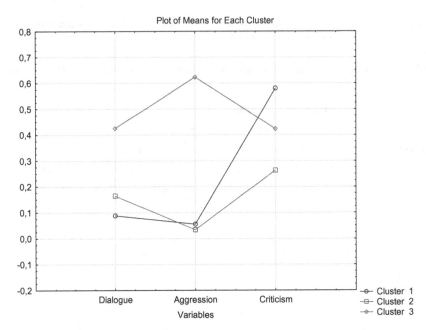

Fig. 2. Plot of means for three-cluster divergence of cross-commenters

the overall number of posts (6.3*, p = 0.021) and for the posts with self-critical ones excluded (5.64*, p = 0.03). In its turn, criticism in the discussion core affects the number of comments in the whole dataset within one day (1-h increment). This may point out to a cumulative pattern of core-to-periphery influencing: when criticism in the core discussion grows or diminishes, intensity of the whole discussion changes accordingly. This, of course, needs more testing to detect stricter patterns of influence; however, for the discussion under scrutiny, we see that the macro-levels (yearly and monthly spans) are too loose in terms of number of posts to create meaningful patterns of cumulation, while, within hours, the discussion fluctuates depending on how critical it is.

Another interesting finding, perhaps, is that neither the overall number of comments casts impact upon the number of comments with distinct deliberative features, which is counter-intuitive. We think that this effect is related to the fact that the discussion is too loose in terms of number of posts in time. In non-dense discussions, each week and day start anew: what was said before, even immediately before, neither spurs nor slows down the pace of dispersed user commenting. This is also supported by how the number of comments in the core and the whole discussion inter-relate: their correlation is very high (R Pearson 0.880***), but Granger test does not show any mutual impact (which was expected, at least in terms of impact of the whole discussion upon its core).

This, combined with the knowledge of low orientation to dialogue, creates a picture of dispersed, self-expression-oriented, and non-deliberative *cumulative commenting*. Despite formally present user-to-user comments, they do not involve users into opinion argumentation and (dis)agreement. What they do is perhaps lowering entry thresholds for those who would like to express their dissent towards authorities and the country.

RQ3. *Qualitative assessment of the results.* Thus, what we have seen as cumulative patterns are the following:

(1) The personal bubbles of opinion expression. Such users do not enter any dialogue with other commenters; when put into the position of influencing, they may spread their influence to others who reply them in various YouTube accounts.
(2) Micro-spirals of silencing. The aggressive-dialogical users enter discussion episodes and silence their opponents in skirmish-like communication. Due to this, a bigger 'spiral of support' forms and grows under particular videos.
(3) Micro-impact of criticism expressed by users. While the level of aggression was low enough not to cast any significant impact upon the dynamic of user talk, criticism took its place and cast impact within 1-h and 6-h time spans.
(4) Cumulative commenting. This might as well describe what happens on the macro-level of the discussion bulk. Cumulative commenting happens when comments are relatively rare and dispersed, previous talk does not shape the current one even within several days, and dialogue does not form. However, opinion (in this case, clearly oppositional, critical towards the authorities, and self-critical to a large extent) forms anyway, which points out to the cumulative effects of how we perceive comments online.

6 Discussion and Conclusion

In the discussion on Belarusian oppositional YouTube of 2018, we have discovered two modes of expression that were mutually exclusive – namely, the aggressive-dialogical and (self-)critical ones. This was true on both the level of a single post and user deliberative strategy. We have seen that these discursive strategies play a role in formation of cumulative patterns within the discussion, forming personal opinion bubbles and micro-spirals of silencing. Both strategies deserve further exploration, as they, e.g., contradict conventional view on filter bubbles as formed by many users. Opinion bubbles of the users that stand in the middle of discussions may involve other users (who respond to their comments) into their orbits, thus forming hardly detectable but clearly important influence spreading patterns. Proving this goes beyond the immediate goal of this paper, but definitely deserves exploring.

We have also shown that Toepfl's theory [20] needs to be amplified by the notion of self-critical public. Criticism and self-criticism have become the only deliberative features of the discussion under our scrutiny that, at least to some extent, shaped the overall / core discussion dynamics.

We have spotted patterns of cumulative nature that work each on its own level of the discussion. Thus, micro-spirals of silencing happen within small interactions, and thanks to this a bigger 'spiral of support' forms easier under individual videos; personal opinion bubbles exist on the user level; multiple deliberative posts affect the immediate development of the discussion; and cumulative commenting is how it looks in general.

Unlike in Russia [11], aggression, due to its non-saliency, did not play a meaningful role in discussion dynamics. This points out to cultural differences in how authoritarian public spheres work, even in countries as culturally close as Russia and Belarus.

References

1. Katz, E., Lazarsfeld, P.F.: Personal Influence. Free Press, Glencoe (1955)
2. Gillin, P.: The New Influencers: a Marketer's Guide to the New Social Media. Linden Publishing, California (2007)
3. Bakshy, E., Hofman, J.M., Mason, W.A., Watts, D.J.: Everyone's an influencer: quantifying influence on twitter. In: Proceedings of the Fourth ACM International Conference on Web Search and Data Mining, pp. 65–74. ACM (2011)
4. Bodrunova, S.S., Litvinenko, A.A., Blekanov, I.S.: Comparing influencers: activity vs. connectivity measures in defining key actors in Twitter ad hoc discussions on migrants in Germany and Russia. In: International conference on social informatics, pp. 360–376. Springer, Cham (2017). https://doi.org/10.1007/978-3-319-67217-5_22
5. Key, V.O.: The Responsible Electorate. Harvard University Press, Cambridge (1966)
6. Bruns, A.: Are Filter Bubbles Real? Wiley, Hoboken (2019)
7. Pfetsch, B.: Dissonant and disconnected public spheres as challenge for political communication research. Javnost Public 25(1–2), 59–65 (2018)
8. Smoliarova, A.S., Bodrunova, S.S., Blekanov, I.S., Maksimov, A.: Discontinued Public Spheres? Reproducibility of User Structure in Twitter Discussions on Inter-ethnic Conflicts. In: Stephanidis, C., Antona, M., Ntoa, S. (eds.) HCII 2020. CCIS, vol. 1293, pp. 262–269. Springer, Cham (2020). https://doi.org/10.1007/978-3-030-60700-5_34
9. Noelle-Neumann, E.: The spiral of silence a theory of public opinion. J. Commun. 24(2), 43–51 (1974)
10. Sidorov, V.A.: Communicative aggressions of the 21st century: definition and analysis of the prerequisites. Vestnik Sankt-Peterburgskogo universiteta, series 'Language and Literature', 15(2), 300–311 (2018)
11. Bodrunova, S.S., Litvinenko, A., Blekanov, I., Nepiyushchikh, D.: Constructive aggression? Multiple roles of aggressive content in political discourse on Russian YouTube. Media Commun. 9, 181–194 (2021)
12. Mustafaraj, E., Finn, S., Whitlock, C., Metaxas, P.T.: Vocal minority versus silent majority: Discovering the opionions of the long tail. In: 2011 IEEE Third International Conference on Privacy, Security, Risk and Trust and 2011 IEEE Third International Conference on Social Computing, pp. 103–110. IEEE (2011)
13. Chen, X., Li, X., Yao, D., Zhou, Z.: Seeking the support of the silent majority: are lurking users valuable to UGC platforms? J. Acad. Mark. Sci. 47(6), 986–1004 (2019)
14. McKeever, B.W., McKeever, R., Holton, A.E., Li, J.Y.: Silent majority: childhood vaccinations and antecedents to communicative action. Mass Commun. Soc. 19(4), 476–498 (2016)
15. Mai, F., Shan, Z., Bai, Q., Wang, X., Chiang, R.H.: How does social media impact Bitcoin value? A test of the silent majority hypothesis. J. Manag. Inf. Syst. 35(1), 19–52 (2018)
16. Bodrunova, S.S., Blekanov, I., Smoliarova, A., Litvinenko, A.: Beyond left and right: real-world political polarization in Twitter discussions on inter-ethnic conflicts. Media Commun. 7, 119–132 (2019)
17. Bodrunova, S.S., Blekanov, I.S., Kukarkin, M.: Multi-dimensional echo chambers: language and sentiment structure of Twitter discussions on the Charlie Hebdo Case. In International Conference on Human-Computer Interaction, pp. 393–400. Springer, Cham (2018). https://doi.org/10.1007/978-3-319-92270-6_56

18. Ksiazek, T.B.: Commenting on the news: explaining the degree and quality of user comments on news websites. J. Stud. **19**(5), 650–673 (2018)
19. Ksiazek, T.B., Peer, L., Zivic, A.: Discussing the news: civility and hostility in user comments. Digit. Journal. **3**(6), 850–870 (2015)
20. Toepfl, F.: Comparing authoritarian publics: the benefits and risks of three types of publics for autocrats. Commun. Theory **30**(2), 105–125 (2020)
21. Nowak, A., Szamrej, J., Latané, B.: From private attitude to public opinion: a dynamic theory of social impact. Psychol. Rev. **97**(3), 362 (1990)
22. Latané, B.: The psychology of social impact. Am. Psychol. **36**, 343–365 (1981)
23. Mouffe, C.: Radical democracy or liberal democracy. Soc. Rev. **20**(2), 57–66 (1990)
24. Yardi, S., Boyd, D.: Dynamic debates: An analysis of group polarization over time on twitter. Bull. Sci. Technol. Soc. **30**(5), 316–327 (2010)
25. Bennett, W.L., Pfetsch, B.: Rethinking political communication in a time of disrupted public spheres. J. Commun. **68**(2), 243–253 (2018)
26. Schultes, P., Dorner, V., Lehner, F.: Leave a comment! an in-depth analysis of user comments on YouTube. Wirtschaftsinformatik **42**, 659–673 (2013)
27. Morozov, E.: The Brave New World of Slacktivism. Foreign Policy, 19 May 2009. http://net effect.foreignpolicy.com/posts/2009/05/19/the_brave_new_world_of_slacktivism.
28. Springer, N., Engelmann, I., Pfaffinger, C.: User comments: motives and inhibitors to write and read. Inf. Commun. Soc. **18**(7), 798–815 (2015)
29. Gomez, V., Kappen, H., Kaltenbrunner, A.: Modeling the structure and evolution of discussion cascades. HT (2011)
30. Tsagkias, M., Weerkamp, W., De Rijke, M.: Predicting the volume of comments on online news stories. In: Proceedings of the 18th ACM conference on Information and knowledge management, pp. 1765–1768 (2009)
31. Kumar, R., Mahdian, M., McGlohon, M.: Dynamics of conversations. KDD (2010)
32. Bodrunova, S.S., Blekanov, I.S.: Power laws in ad hoc conflictual discussions on Twitter. In: International Conference on Digital Transformation and Global Society, pp. 67–82. Springer, Cham (2018). https://doi.org/10.1007/978-3-030-02846-6_6
33. Wang, C., Ye, M., Huberman, B.A.: From user comments to on-line conversations. In: Proceedings of the 18th ACM SIGKDD International Conference on Knowledge Discovery and Data Mining, pp. 244–252 (2012)
34. Rowe, I.: Deliberation 2.0: comparing the deliberative quality of online news user comments across platforms. J. Broadcast. Electron. Media **59**(4), 539–555 (2015)
35. Ziegele, M., Breiner, T., Quiring, O.: What creates interactivity in online news discussions? An exploratory analysis of discussion factors in user comments on news items. J. Commun. **64**(6), 1111–1138 (2014)
36. Boczkowski, P.J., Mitchelstein, E.: How users take advantage of different forms of interactivity on online news sites: Clicking, e-mailing, and commenting. Hum. Commun. Res. **38**, 1–22 (2012)
37. Freelon, D.G.: Analyzing online political discussion using three models of democratic communication. New Media Soc. **12**, 1172–1190 (2010)
38. Ruiz, C., Domingo, D., Micó, J. L., Díaz-Noci, J., Meso, K., Masip, P.: Public sphere 2.0? The democratic qualities of citizen debates in online newspapers. Int. J. Press/Politics **22**, 463–487 (2011)
39. Ksiazek, T.B., Peer, L., Lessard, K.: User engagement with online news: conceptualizing interactivity and exploring the relationship between online news videos and user comments. New Media Soc. **18**(3), 502–520 (2016)

40. Bodrunova, S.S., Nigmatullina, K., Blekanov, I.S., Smoliarova, A., Zhuravleva, N., Danilova, Y.: When Emotions Grow: Cross-Cultural Differences in the Role of Emotions in the Dynamics of Conflictual Discussions on Social Media. In: Meiselwitz, G. (ed.) HCII 2020. LNCS, vol. 12194, pp. 433–441. Springer, Cham (2020). https://doi.org/10.1007/978-3-030-49570-1_30
41. Papacharissi, Z.: Affective publics: Sentiment, technology, and politics. Oxford University Press, Oxford (2015)
42. Blekanov, I.S., Sergeev, S.L., Martynenko, I.A.: Constructing topic-oriented web crawlers with generalized core. Sci. Res. Bull. St. Petersburg State Politechnic Univ. 5(157), 9–15 (2012)

Global Agendas: Detection of Agenda Shifts in Cross-National Discussions Using Neural-Network Text Summarization for Twitter

Svetlana S. Bodrunova[1]($\boxtimes$) ![ORCID], Ivan S. Blekanov[2] ![ORCID], and Nikita Tarasov[2]

[1] School of Journalism and Mass Communications, St. Petersburg State University,
7-9 Universitetskaya nab., St. Petersburg 199004, Russia
s.bodrunova@spbu.ru
[2] Faculty of Applied Mathematics and Control Processes, St. Petersburg State University,
7-9 Universitetskaya nab., St. Petersburg 199004, Russia

Abstract. Agendas in online media have become a scholarly focus nearly two decades ago, leading to shifting conceptualizations of what we see as agenda. Thus, agendas and agenda shifts *inside* online discussions have shown its potential to influence offline deliberation, aggregate support, fuel protest, passing through and/or bypassing traditional media's gatekeeping. Real-time (or nearly-real-time) learning about quick agenda movement inside globalized public debate might be particularly important for international organizations like UN or EU. However, we today lack both knowledge on how agendas move in such discussions and instruments on such analysis. In particular, we are next-to-unaware of to what extent globally relevant themes get contextualized within language-based discussion segments, as well as to what extent the latter depend on each other and lag behind each other in developing agendas and public opinion on quickly evolving issues or conflicts. In this paper, we propose a method of agenda detection based on neural-network text summarization and compare summaries of tweet packages across three languages within the Twitter hashtag #jesuischarlie. We show that sentiment detection may allow for quality assessment of the text summaries, as compared to aggregated sentiment to the original tweets. We show that, outside France, agendas were more interpretational, abstract, and non-contextualized. The pattern of news changing to 'issue outburt' was simultaneous in dense discussion segments and lagged behind in a sparser one. We also show that, globally, main issues of the discussion may be spotted within the first hour.

Keywords: Agenda · Topic detection · Text summarization · Charlie hebdo · Neural networks · Longformer · Cross-national agendas · Twitter

1 Introduction

The spread of agendas in online media has been a focus of scholarly attention for nearly two decades [1]. However, for social media, the meaning of agendas transform; scholars discuss smaller-scale agendas and their shifts [2] within particular online discussions, including hashtagged ones. Despite its seemingly smaller impact, in-discussion agendas

© Springer Nature Switzerland AG 2021
G. Meiselwitz (Ed.): HCII 2021, LNCS 12774, pp. 221–239, 2021.
https://doi.org/10.1007/978-3-030-77626-8_15

may spill over to traditional media and thus press public bodies, gather support, call for action, or fuel protest. Also, affect-based discussions [3] help identify immediate popular reaction to trigger events and issues behind them.

Global-scale discussions caused by events of international relevance may evoke varying interpretations in different national contexts. And yet, evidence on cross-cultural, especially multilingual, dynamics of agendas in large-scale public discussions is still highly under-explored. In particular, we lack knowledge on whether affect-based agendas develop concurrently in various languages and to what extent they become contextualized within language-bound discussion segments, while knowing it would be relevant for elaborating quicker institutional response by, e.g., UN, EU, or other international and macro-regional organizations. Knowing how people perceive ongoing conflicts might help incorporate this knowledge into political decision-making.

Computational methods of textual analysis allow for automated detection of agendas in user talk, agenda being reinterpreted as topicality, and agenda research reconceptualized as topic detection and modeling [2]. Earlier, we have shown that it is possible to detect pivotal points in debate on social media by assessing the saliency of detected topics within the time of discussion [4]. However, classic topic models like LDA or BTM demand data processing which is often multi-run [5, 6] or unfeasible due to longevity of procedures or scarcity of instruments. They also demand reading top words and interpreting topics by human assessors, which might be tricky, and the results might be misleading. Thus, close-to-real-time agenda detection remains an unreached goal, and this often leaves potential industrial, political, and academic consumers of topicality assessment frustrated.

In this paper, we propose a method of topicality detection based on text summarization produced by neural network models. And, as we aim at agenda detection in general as well as cross-language agenda shifts and comparisons, we will try to define one topic per short time slot or fixed number of user posts, to be able to follow how the agendas move. To test the method we propose, we use the Twitter discussion on the infamous *Charlie Hebdo* massacre of 2015 and exploit tweets in English, French, and German that were posted under #jesuischarlie within 24 h after the massacre (which makes thousands of tweets from all around the world).

The remainder of the paper is organized as follows. In Sect. 2, we shortly review the existing literature on agenda detection on social media and use of topic modeling and text summarization for this task. In Sect. 3, we tell of the case under scrutiny and our research questions. In Sect. 4, we describe the methodology, formation of sub-datasets and their processing, as well as quality checks by application of sentiment analysis. In Sect. 5, we provide the results of text summarization and assess the cross-language agenda shifts. In Sect. 6, we discuss the findings and reflect on methodological limitations of our research.

2   Agenda Detection vs. Topicality Detection: Current Approaches

2.1   Public Agendas on Social Media: Do They Matter?

As stated above, agendas in online media have been a focus of scholarly research for nearly two decades [1, 7]. From the very beginning, the major attention has been put to how agendas of online media, then blogs, and then social media ('mediated public agen-das') built into the exiting agenda-setting infrastructures. Reverse and cross-platform agenda-setting, as well as other types of interplay between older and newer agenda-setting actors, were suggested. The focus on 'who sets the agendas', however, provoked a certain inertia in understanding of the nature of public agendas and processes of their formation – not only regarding the topics that people discuss but also the features of 'agenda building blocks' and discursive localization of agendas.

Gradually, computational research has entered agenda studies [8, 9, 10], and, follow-ing the works on methods of textual analysis, 'public agendas' were in several influential works reconceptualized via topicality and explored with the help of topic modeling and similar techniques [11], thanks to the capability of probabilistic text clustering to capture the themes in large text corpora.

These studies, though, had a double-edged impact upon how we understand public agendas that emerge on social media platforms. On one hand, topicality studies have highlighted the importance of *in-discussion* topicality and agenda shifts, while, earlier, agendas were seen as belonging to the highest level of content generalization, e.g., the whole content of public debate. On the other hand, the scholarly attention massively moved to methodological aspects of topic detection, and, due to early-stage method-ological limitations, the topics could not be discovered in real time and were substituted by the post-factum evaluations. Later works have tackled this problem in various ways (see below) but, till today, we lack approaches that would be relatively easy solutions for assessment of agenda shifts in near-to-real time.

This is especially relevant for the areas where cross-country comparisons are neces-sary. The 2020–2021 COVID-19 pandemic has shown how crucially important it was to trace local public reactions to global-scale events and issues; earlier, European migra-tion crisis, the 2008–2209 global recession, and globalized military conflicts like the one in Syria have demanded for advancement of methodologies of agenda detection in multilingual online environments.

We cannot help mentioning, of course, that there is also a substantial corpus of academic and analytical writing that emphasizes trivial nature and unimportance of public agendas [12, 13]. Indeed, empirical research suggests provides mixed evidence on whether social media and microblogs can well play an indicator role in terms of agenda shifts. Partly, it is due to social non-representativity of platform use. But it is also true because the Twitter population has its own substantial agendas, as compared to traditional media and survey results [14], while Twitter agendas of politicians my closely correlate with their offline deliberative agendas [15]. This proves again that 'patterns of societal activity observed through the lens of Twitter research are… dependent on a range of additional variables' and need to be assessed case-to-case [16: 4].

2.2 Automated Agenda Detection

Automated means of topicality detection has been a rapidly growing area of research, and its relations with agenda studies, being truly multi-faceted, have not escaped certain meaningful limitations.

Agendas vs. Topics: The Issue of Simultaneity. One of the biggest limitations of topic modeling for agenda detection is that the models work with text corpora as if the texts they contain were created simultaneously; the posting time is not calculated in. Thus, in classic models, it is impossible to see how agendas (topic diversity and substance) change in time. However, tracking the agenda shifts is basically the essential task of agenda setting studies. Several studies have used Granger causality testing and vector autoregressions (VAR) to detect agenda dependence either across platforms [8] or across actor groups on Twitter [17]. Both studies, even if successfully detected dependencies in cross-platform impact, issue attention, and prediction by groups of Twitter users, did not focus on agendas themselves and how they evolved, seeing agenda issues as constant. Another work [18] assessed political spin and party discipline in the US Democrat and Republican tweets with the help of topic modeling, autoregressive distributed-lag modeling, and n-gram assessment; the authors have detected time lags between the party agendas and differences in 'discourse ownership' in terms of lexicons; the authors also used data slicing into varying time spans to detect agenda cycles. But the very agendas and time shifts between them were not discussed.

This, in effect, does not allow us to learn about *the pace of public agendas* on social media – how quickly they change, i.e., what time or number of posts is needed to significantly shift them. While media are still, even if to a much-decreased extent, subjected to their news production cycle which takes hours and days, social media can potentially shift agendas in minutes during (and within!) outbursts of public reaction.

Topic Evolution Studies. Scholars have tried to overcome this limitation by developing topic evolution studies – the area of research that models emergent and evolving topics within social media data. But the general intention of this group of studies is looking at how the identified topics evolve in time within themselves (see, e.g., [19, 20] and also [21] for short texts), including how they evolve all in parallel, not how the public shifts from one dominant theme to another. This idea, though, has been amplified in various ways that come closer to the idea of representing agendas. Thus, by focusing on both evolving themes and emergent topics, researchers have introduced emergence regularization for topic detection, which may potentially be used to detect emerging agendas [22], as well as metrics for measuring novelty and fading of topics [23]. However, the focus on emergent topics still blurs from view the detection of the *main* topics in each period of time.

Several studies [24], including ours [4], have focused on relative saliency of the topics found throughout the dataset. By such studies, we can see *what* (of the topics discovered) is discussed more and *when*; but we do not see *how* the themes look like and what their substantial features are, which is essential in agenda studies. Another pack of research papers focusses on topic-sentiment relation over time (for a short review and original results, see [25]). In this work, again, the authors receive results within the pre-discovered topics.

Thus, paradoxically, in the works dedicated to modeling topic evolution, we do not see the evolving topics themselves, only the model on the whole and its quality. The same goes for trending topics detection [26]: except for Twitter itself, we practically do not see how exactly the new trending topics look and how they are thematically or otherwise connected/different from the existing topics.

This is why it remains important to look at what people actually talk about in dynamics and, moreover, learn it in the quickest possible way.

Cross-Language Agenda in Online Discussions: Putting Topics in Context. Another issue in social media agenda studies is the (alleged) global character of the discussions and, thus, the extent to which the agendas related to the same issues or events and discussed in various language-bound segments of discussions get contextualized and 'nationalized.'

First of all, it needs to be stated that the discussions that are seen as global by conventional wisdom demonstrate, in reality, high inequalities in language (and, thus, country, culture, and values) representation. This is true for the case we assess further in the text, namely the discussion hashtagged #jesuischarlie of 2015 [27]. However, such discussions are involving enough cross-nationally to pose questions of whether the topicality and agendas that emerge can be compared across countries and what their substance is in comparative perspective; how and via what means they get contextualized in national discussion segments; and whether there are time lags between the rising waves of compassion, shock, or outrage.

Till today, cross-country studies in general social media remain relatively rare [28]. At the same time, the issue of context as the discussion definer is one of those of acute importance [29, 30] – and, despite this, remains a significant research gap. Context for Twitter studies is understood in varying ways: it is defined via the hashtag distribution/hashtag clusters [19], in some cases, Twitter itself is seen as provider of social context for interpreting news agendas in traditional media [31]. The closest to the agenda-tracking idea seems to be the evolutionary clustering approach called Recurrent Chinese Restaurant Process (RCRP) [32], as it has been developed to involve contextual variability by capturing temporal dynamics and local semantic sequential dependencies [33]. The only problem with this method is that it demands complicated layer-introduction procedures.

Thus, we are looking for a method that would allow for tracking the current (or immediately previous) agenda/topicality of online discussions that would allow for showing the agenda in a quick enough and accessible way in comparative cross-language perspective.

2.3   Text Summarization in Agenda Detection Studies

For resolving this task, we suggest to use another method of topic formulation, which is text summarization. Successfully used in computational studies of text corpora, text summarization allows to 'summarize the text documents in order to obtain a brief overview of a large text document or a set of documents on a topic' [34: 4] and 'to produce a concise and fluent summary conveying the key information in the input' [35: 44]. Summarizations may be of extractive and abstractive nature; in the latter case, the machine provides a textual summary of a text (sub-)corpus that may contain words that were not found in the initial data. They may also be indicative (providing a very brief indication summary) and informative (providing more information on the text); and be executed over single or multiple documents [35]. Previous research also shows that summarization may depend on the text subject and the nature of the dataset (e.g. news texts, documents, or social media posts) [36].

Today, advanced text summarization studies are conducted with the use of neural networks (for an early account, see [37]; for a later one on abstractive summarization, [38]). Neural networks are employed for both extractive [39] and abstractive summarization [40] for Twitter. Earlier, several successful instruments for Twitter text summarization have been proposed, like TweetMotif [41]. Later models employ BERT [40] and USE [42] architectures. In 2019–2020, new transformer-based architectures such as Longformer [43] and t5 [44], have been proposed and tested; we see them as most suitable for our tasks.

In our research, we use the existing text summarization models; their quality has been tested multiple times. This is why we do not use traditional quality metrics assuming that the models produce sustainable results. However, we provide additional checks oriented to our research questions and use sentiment analysis for detecting the quality of summarization. Even if, as a rule, sentiment analysis is used in combination with summarization in order to reach substantial goals, there is also evidence that sentiment detection can be used as a quality indicator for topics [45] and summarizations.

3   Research Questions and the Datasets

3.1   The Case Under Scrutiny and the Language-Based Datasets

Thus, in this study, we focus on detecting agendas and agenda shifts in various language-bound segments within one globalized discussion. For that, we use the dataset we have collected in 2015 by the hashtag #jesuischarlie that gathered much of the user reaction to the *Charlie Hebdo* massacre in Paris, France. The dataset was collected using our own patented web crawler [46], comprised the three first days of the discussion and, after cleaning and preprocessing, contained 420,080 tweets.

This dataset of over five years ago was chosen, as it was much less bot-infested than today's data. It contained a discussion that, to a large extent, reproduced the language structure of Twitter itself [47], with circa 50% of posts being in English [27].

This dataset allows for looking at two languages – English and French – as similarly dense, which makes it possible to juxtapose the 'global' (Eng-lang) and 'local' (Francophone) reaction of the Twitter populace. We have also chosen a third language, in order to see how the discussion differs in a much looser discussion segment. We have chosen German based on the number of tweets on main languages of the discussion (see Fig. 1 and Table 1). The language of tweets was detected by using the FastText algorithm [48].

As a result, we have received three datasets: English (213,558 tweets), French (133,671 tweets), and German (7,430 tweets).

3.2   Research Questions

Our research questions relate to both methodology of text summarization and to the substance of our study of agenda shifts.

RQ1. How well does the neural-network-based text summarization capture agendas from tweets in three languages?

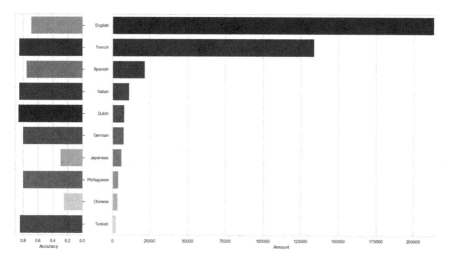

Fig. 1. Language distribution in the #jesuischarlie discussion

Table 1. Sub-datasets of the project

Language	Accuracy	N of tweets	% of total
English	0.6961355805397034	213,558	0.51
French	0.8610345721244812	133,671	0.32
Spanish	0.7578563690185547	21,604	0.05
Italian	0.8599529266357422	11,251	0.027
Dutch	0.8691623210906982	7,699	0.018
German	0.8065633773803711	7,430	0.018
Japanese	0.30159252882003784	5,946	0.014
Portuguese	0.8060423731803894	3,874	0.009
Chinese	0.2554042339324951	3,423	0.008
Turkish	0.8499038219451904	2,261	0.005

H1. Summarized sentiment of the tweet conglomerates is reflected by the sentiment of summarizations.

RQ2. Do agendas develop simultaneously in the global and local segments of a Twitter discussion?

H2. Agendas shift simultaneously (within very short timing) in the local and global discussion segments. There is no detectable time lag between the same agendas in the local and global segments of discussions if they develop with comparable density.

H3. In looser discussion segments, agendas shift more radically thematically.

RQ3. Are Twitter agendas within one discussion get contextualized in various language segments?

H4. Text summarizations represent local context in a negligible percentage of cases (less than 5%) for all the three cases.

4 Methods and Data Processing

4.1 Application of Text Summarization

The Choice of Summarization Models. Based on the latest literature, we have chosen two models mentioned above, namely Longformer and t5, for text summarization.

Pretrained Longformer model was used to summarize subset in the English language. Longformer is a language model with a unique attention mechanism that scales linearly with sequence length (as opposed to the quadratic scaling of traditional models), making it easy to process documents of thousands of tokens or longer [43]. The resulting summarization is obtained using the longformer-large-4096 pretrained model.

For French and German, t5 model was used with t5-base-fr-sum-cnndm and mt5-small-german-finetune-mlsum pretrained models, respectively. T5 is an encoder-decoder model and converts all NLP problems into a text-to-text format. T5 is an encoder-decoder model and converts all NLP problems into a text-to-text format. While providing a very general and well-built structure with unified framework for a variety of NLP tasks, authors achieve state-of-the-art results on many benchmarks covering summarization, question answering, text classification, and more. T5 uses a standard encoder-decoder Transformer with a baseline model designed so that the encoder and decoder are each similar in size and configuration to a BERT. Specifically, both the encoder and decoder consist of 12 blocks (each block comprising self-attention, optional encoder-decoder attention, and a feed-forward network with ReLU nonlinearity) [44].

The Choice of Increment. As we have stated above, three languages were chosen based on the models' accessibility, peer review potential, identification quality, and the sample structure and volume.

The most problematic issue for us was the choice of the 'step' for agenda shifts, or the increment, that would fit both our RQs and the tweet distribution. And it was not the timing itself. The matter was that both summarization models had a limitation, as they worked best with certain number of texts. To find the optimal number of tweets for summarization, we have constructed diagrams of tweet distribution in time in each sub-set. We have constructed them for 1-h, 3-h, and 6-h increments (see Fig. 2, 3, and 4 for 1-h increments for French, English, and German, respectively).

Our decision-making in choosing the increment for summarization was, in the end, based on two circumstances. First, the limitation of the model showed circa 300 tweets to be the optimal number to be summarized; second, the German model as the most sparce showed that 300 tweets would comprise 1 to 2 h in the most sparce case, which suits our goal. But, to make the pace comparable, we should have either used an increment based on tweets or the one based on hours.

We have opted for the number of tweets, even if it looks counter-intuitive. This was because: (1) the hourly number of tweets varied highly in 24-h cycles, and thus the

French - 1 hour

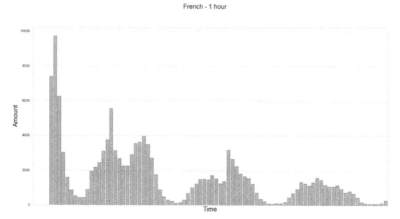

Fig. 2. The French-language tweet distribution, 1-h increment

English - 1 hour

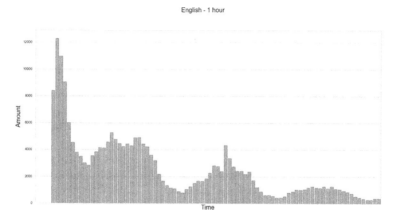

Fig. 3. The French-language tweet distribution, 1-h increment

summarizations would be incomparable; (2) the 300-tweet samples allow for a more fine-grained study, and several 300-tweet summarizations may reflect an hourly time span; but an hourly time span that comprises several thousand tweets might be too general and non-informative.

Thus, we have chosen 300-tweet increments for summarization. They allow to trace hourly dynamics of agenda for the German case (daytime) and for more fine-grained gaze into the English and French cases.

Summarization Results. However, the models we have received were not satisfactory at the first trials. While the English-language one was clearly understandable, with only rare non-comprehensible inclusions, the German and French versions returned understandable but broken sentences with loose endings (for examples, see Table 2, marked in bold). Additional runs did not bring better results; later, we will check the model with other datasets to find out why the sentences were broken.

German - 1 hour

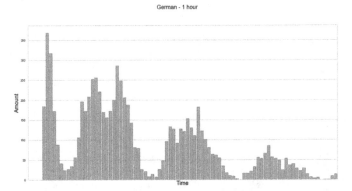

Fig. 4. The German-language tweet distribution, 1-h increment

Despite the loose endings, the produced summarizations were comprehensible enough for our goals. They were for English, 422 for French, and 22 for German.

Table 2. Text summarizations: examples for the three languages

English	French	German
2015–01-07 12:26:00 the terrorist attack on the offices of the satirical magazine Charlie Hebdo has left 12 dead	2015–01-07 12:03:00 Le mardi, à Bruxelles, il y a une minute de silence **pour**	2015–01-07 12:24:00 RT und klingt nicht nur ähnlich.. **Du caricaturiste haitien Bousiko**
2015–01-07 12:31:00 this is a tribute to the 12 people who were killed in the attack on the satirical magazine **@xmath0**	2015–01-07 12:28:00 Le hashtag #suischarlie est le plus utilisé de toute l'histoire**de**	2015–01-07 15:20:00 Anschlag auf Satire-Zeitung: Dieter Nuhr rettet sich in Bunker
2015–01-07 12:33:00 the attack on the offices of the satirical magazine Charlie Hebdo has left 12 people dead and 12 others wounded	2015–01-07 12:29:00 Le dessin de Cabu s'éteint en hommage aux 12	2015–01-07 21:17:00 Der Pariser Anschlag ist auch auf Facebook und Twitter das grosse Thema. Irr
2015–01-07 12:34:00 this is a tribute to the 12 people killed in the terrorist attack on the satirical magazine on the 12th of january 2015	2015–01-07 12:30:00 Charlie Hebdo est mort dimanche à Brest. **Les kiosques**	2015–01-07 23:52:00 Hollande hat in der Hand, ob Frankreichs Demokratie Anschlag überlebt- **zu**
2015–01-07 12:36:00 we are all Charlie	2015–01-07 12:32:00 Nouveau: hommage à Stéphane Charbonnier **et**	2015–01-08 01:27:00 Cartoonist Jean Jullien:. "Wir trauern um Frankreichs **bedeuten**

4.2 Quality Assessment of Summarization by Sentiment Detection

Given that the models, despite their high reputation, have provided results that were not fully satisfactory, we have introduced additional checks of the model quality. As we mentioned above, we have used sentiment detection to construct a quality metric. A BERT model [49] pretrained for multilingual sentiment analysis was used for each summarization to analyze summaries in the context of generalised sentiment.

In general, the idea was to compare sentiment of the original tweet samples to that of the respective summarizations. First, we have compared the mean sentiment of 300 tweets to the sentiment of the summarizations. We have seen that, in the overwhelming majority of cases, the sentiment of the 300 tweet samples tends to neutral (see Fig. 5 for English). This is why we have introduced another way of measurement that aimed at highlighting the positive/negative difference in the samples. We have labeled the tweets: 'negative' $- 0 \leq k < 0.4$; 'neutral' $- 0.4 \leq k < 0.6$; 'positive' $- 0.6 \leq k \leq 1$. Then we eliminated the neutral tweets and calculated the difference between the positive and negative tweets, to see which sentiment dominated in the sample. We compared the sentiment of the samples to that of the summarizations (see Fig. 6, 7, and 8 for English, French, and German, respectively).

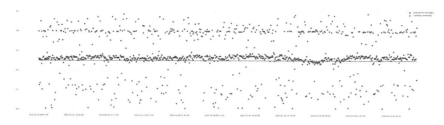

Fig. 5. Representation of sentiment distribution in time, the English sub-dataset, mean sentiment score: tweet samples, blue; summarizations, red. (Color figure online)

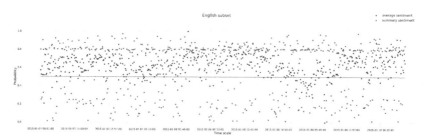

Fig. 6. Representation of sentiment distribution in time, the English sub-dataset, positive/negative difference, blue; summarizations, red. (Color figure online)

By manual assessment of over 100 tweet samples vs. summarizations, we have established that good correspondence in the pair 'sample – summarization' is when the distance between them is circa 0.25. To measure the quality of the model, we calculated

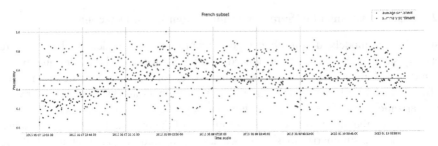

Fig. 7. Representation of sentiment distribution in time, the French sub-dataset, positive/negative difference, blue; summarizations, red. (Color figure online)

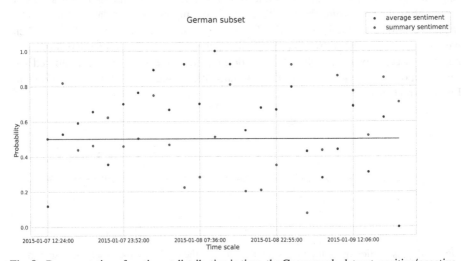

Fig. 8. Representation of sentiment distribution in time, the German sub-dataset, positive/negative difference: tweet samples, blue; summarizations, red. (Color figure online)

Table 3. Quality measurement of the models

Language	Metric by average score	Metric by difference score
English	27%	51%
French	69%	61%
German	58%	48%

the percentage of the pairs 'sample – summarization' with the distances of 0.25 or less for both types of sentiment measurement. The received values are shown in Table 3.

Our measurements show that, despite the broken sentences in French and German, the sentiment scores for these models are relatively high. The graphs show, though, that the 'movement' of summarizations does not follow the positive/negative dynamics of tweet samples. Thus, in future, more manual assessment needs to be done for short-text data to understand how well the summaries capture the tone of public speak in a particular moment.

5   Results: Global Interpretational Agendas vs. Local News Agendas in a Global Twitter Discussion

5.1   RQ1: Quality of Representation of Agendas by Tweet Summaries

As we have seen from Table 3, the models work moderately well in terms of overall performance, when sentiment is measured as the difference between positive and negative tweets. However, when we have given a look to the original texts vs. summaries, we have noticed that the English ones summarized the user sentiment and contents much better. Thus, in our future work, we will use Longformer and train it to be used for German and French. As for now, H1 may be partly proven but needs more studies.

The two other RQs are based on our additional coding of the summarizations (see Table 4). We coded them for being (1) news or opinion/issue and (2) local/global. Combining (1) and (2) and stating keywords for the issues found, we have received the agendas and could judge their nature and shifts.

Table 4. Agendas in the sub-datasets, first 50 summarizations of January 07 (English and French)/full list (German)

Time	English	Time	French	Date time	German
8:51	news	12:03	news	07.01 12:24	*uninterpretable*
12:26	news	12:25	**news: local**	07.01 13:20	media
12:28	freedom of expression	12:26	tribute	07.01 14:10	news: French
12:29	freedom of expression	12:28	hashtag	07.01 15:20	**news: local**
12:31	news	12:29	**tribute: local**	07.01 21:17	hashtag
12:33	news	12:30	news	07.01 23:52	Francois Hollande
12:34	news	12:32	**news: local**	08.01 1:27	mourning: French
12:36	solidarity	12:33	news	08.01 2:52	solidarity: French
12:38	news	12:35	news	08.01 4:06	opinion
12:40	news	12:36	**news: local**	08.01 5:45	mourning: global
12:42	deadliest in history	12:38	**news: local**	08.01 7:36	news: French
12:43	news	12:39	**news: local**	08.01 9:09	news: French

(continued)

Table 4. (*continued*)

Time	English	Time	French	Date time	German
12:45	religion	12:40	tribute	08.01 10:26	media
12:47	solidarity	12:42	media	08.01 11:57	opinion
12:48	pacifism	12:43	news	08.01 13:58	opinion
12:50	freedom of expression	12:45	**tribute: local**	08.01 22:55	Mohammad cartoons
12:51	freedom of expression	12:46	armistice over ChEbdo	09.01 1:43	opinion
12:53	freedom of expression	12:47	**news: local**	09.01 4:32	solidarity
12:55	impact	12:49	**France is rising**	09.01 6:51	opinion
12:57	news	12:50	news	09.01 8:58	solidarity
12:59	news	12:52	**news: local**	09.01 12:06	war on terrorism
13:00	freedom of expression	12:53	news	10.01 0:44	news: French
13:02	freedom of expression	12:55	**solidarity: local**	10.01 5:52	opinion
13:04	mourning	12:56	Fidel Castro	10.01 13:36	mourning: French
13:06	news	12:58	**Death of the Republic**		
13:08	solidarity	13:00	**news: local**		
13:10	freedom of expression	13:01	**news: local**		
13:12	cartoons control the world	13:03	Muslims oppose murder		
13:14	world's fury	13:04	**mourning: local**		
13:16	freedom of expression	13:06	*irrelevant*		
13:18	news	13:07	hostages		
13:20	solidarity	13:09	hashtag		
13:22	solidarity	13:11	**news: local**		
13:24	mourning	13:12	freedom		
13:26	**Banksy**	13:14	media		
13:28	solidarity	13:16	**mourning: local**		

(*continued*)

Table 4. (*continued*)

Time	English	Time	French	Date time	German
13:30	news	13:18	**news: local**		
13:32	freedom of expression	13:19	news		
13:34	news	13:21	**tribute: local**		
13:36	news	13:23	**tribute: local**		
13:38	freedom of expression	13:24	**tribute: local**		
13:41	freedom of expression	13:26	**tribute: local**		
13:43	news	13:28	**news: local**		
13:45	solidarity / pacifism	13:30	hashtag		
13:47	news	13:32	**news: local**		
13:50	war on Islam	13:34	news		
13:51	solidarity	13:36	*irrelevant*		
13:54	solidarity	13:38	**news: local**		
13:56	news	13:40	freedom of expression		
13:58	news	13:42	solidarity		

Note. Highlighted: local; red: new; grey: news; black: previously mentioned issues

5.2   RQ2: Agenda Nature and Agenda Shifts

H2. *Agenda shifts.* In the English sub-dataset, we clearly see a globalized agenda which is constructed as interpretational: news on the 12 killed change to globally-relevant issues of freedom of expression, solidarity, and mourning, as well as the non-omnipresent pacifism ('the pen is mightier than the sword'). These issues appear within the first 40 min from the start of the active discussion (January 7, 12:26). The dynamics show that news spread through the discussion, as well as the issue of freedom of expression, and other issues rise each 6 to 8 min in the discussion within the first hour. As to the French agenda, it is shallower and more local in focus. However, we see that the first 'issue outburst' appears nearly simultaneously on 12:40/12/45 to 12:49/12:52, and then issues start to dominate. The issues of freedom of expression and solidarity, though, appear relatively late in France where local tribute and news play an expectedly bigger role. Thus, we can make several conclusions for equally dense discussion segments: (1) active discussion starts the same moment, and news change to interpretation within one hour of active discussion, with very similar timing; (2) after the 'issue outburst', both agendas exist in the form of issues with news popping up between them; (3) the array of issues is practically the same; (3) however, in the global discussion, the leading issues appear 1 to 1,5 h earlier and (5) understanding of issues is more general, abstract, and detached from realities of the event, more commentative and rhetoric, while the national agendas are much more focused on local events and context, which puts the same issues on another level and turns them into news. E.g., in France, mourning was mostly expressed via spreading news on who mourns (cartoonists, students etc.). Thus, H1 is confirmed in terms of discussion timing, but rejected in terms of depth and generalization of issues and the time of appearance of the leading issues.

H3. *The German agenda.* The German-language discussion looks like incomparable with the two other sub-datasets. What differentiates German-language summaries is that many of them look as personal opinions ('Can't wait...', 'I was asked...'), and this effect needs to be investigated. However, we definitely see a similar pattern of news changing to interpretations from the midnight of January 8 on, and the issues of mourning, solidarity, and hashtag impact similarly arise. For national agendas, the issue of media behavior is important. Thus, we see the 'lagging effect': in sparser discussions, the shift from news to interpretations is stretched in time.

5.3 RQ3. Contextualization of Agendas

H4: *Low presence of local context.* Two of the three discussions, indeed, have shown the lowest number of summaries where local context played a role (in Table 4, 1 in English and 1 in German). France, however, involved local context in 50% of summaries. This shows that local segments of Twitter other from those where the event 'belongs' do not tend to put the discussion into local context, and it is limited to globalized interpretations and news from the country where the event happened. The English discussion is purely global, with Banksy being the only 'local context' which is, though, already a global artist, too. Thus, H4 is proven for contexts other than France.

6 Discussion and Conclusion

In this paper, we have tried to show how the agendas within one globalized discussion on Twitter shift and differ. We have seen that there is a pattern of changing news to stable issues that may stretch in time; that topicality shifts take minutes. We have seen that public agendas are *interpretational* and abstract everywhere except for the place of the event, while in the country of the event agendas are much more news-oriented and contextualized. We show that interpretation first outbursts and then takes a stable pace with some stable topics and interpretations repeating, thus pointing out to cumulative effects in socially-mediated discourse. Such stable topics may be detected within hours in the global segment of the discussion and do not change much within days, and the global (Eng-lang) discussion might be an indicator of what shows up in other languages.

Methodologically, the paper has demonstrated serious shortcomings of the t5 model for German and French, including uninterpretable summaries, broken endings, and mismatches with tweet substance. Also, we have seen that sentiment is not a very good instrument for assessing the model quality, as summaries may capture the factual side of the tweets but not sentiment. This demands both searching for more adequate quality metrics and for improving the quality of text summarization models.

Acknowledgement. This research has been supported in full by Russian Science Foundation, grant 21-18-00454.

References

1. McCombs, M.: Setting the agenda: the mass media and public opinion. Polity, Malden (2004)
2. Koltsova, O., Nagornyy, O.: Redefining media agendas: topic problematization in online reader comments. Media Commun. **7**(3), 145–156 (2019)
3. Papacharissi, Z.: Affective Publics: Sentiment, Technology, and Politics. Oxford UP, Oxford (2015)
4. Smoliarova, A.S., Bodrunova, S.S., Yakunin, A.V., Blekanov, I., Maksimov, A.: Detecting pivotal points in social conflicts via topic modeling of Twitter content. In: Bodrunova, S.S., et al. (eds.) INSCI 2018. LNCS, vol. 11551, pp. 61–71. Springer, Cham (2019). https://doi.org/10.1007/978-3-030-17705-8_6
5. Koltcov, S., Koltsova, O., Nikolenko, S.: Latent Dirichlet allocation: stability and applications to studies of user-generated content. In: Proceedings of the 2014 ACM Conference on Web Science, pp. 161–165. ACM (2014)
6. Bodrunova, S.S., Koltsova, O., Koltcov, S., Nikolenko, S.: Who's bad? Attitudes toward resettlers from the post-Soviet south versus other nations in the Russian blogosphere. Int. J. Commun. **11**, 3242–3264 (2017)
7. Kim, S.-T., Lee, Y.-H.: New functions of Internet mediated agenda-setting: agenda-rippling and reversed agenda-setting. Korean J. Commun. Stud. **50**(3), 175–205 (2006)
8. Russell Neuman, W., Guggenheim, L., Mo Jang, S., Bae, S.Y.: The dynamics of public attention: agenda-setting theory meets big data. J. Commun. **64**(2), 193–214 (2014)
9. Guo, L.: Media agenda diversity and intermedia agenda setting in a controlled media environment: a computational analysis of china's online news. J. Stud. **20**(16), 2460–2477 (2019)
10. Koltsova, O., Bodrunova, S.S.: Public discussion in Russian social media: an introduction. Media Commun. **7**(3), 114–118 (2019)
11. Koltsova, O., Koltcov, S.: Mapping the public agenda with topic modeling: the case of the Russian Livejournal. Policy Internet **5**(2), 207–227 (2013)
12. Fuchs, C.: Social Media: A Critical Introduction. Sage, Thousand Oaks (2017)
13. Martin, S., Grüb, B.: Towards a process of agenda setting driven by social media. Int. J. Energy Sect. Manage. **10**(1), 38–55 (2016)
14. Posegga, O., Jungherr, A.: Characterizing political talk on Twitter: a comparison between public agenda, media agendas, and the Twitter agenda with regard to topics and dynamics. In: Proceedings of the 52nd Hawaii International Conference on System Sciences, pp. 2590–2599 (2019)
15. Casas, A., Morar, D.: Different channel, same strategy? Filling empirical gaps in Congress literature. In: Paper presented at the 2015 Annual Meeting of the American Political Science Association (APSA), San Francisco (2015)
16. Bruns, A., Stieglitz, S.: Twitter data: what do they represent? IT Inf. Technol. **56**(5), 240–245 (2014)
17. Barberá, P., et al.: Who leads? Who follows? Measuring issue attention and agenda setting by legislators and the mass public using social media data. Am. Polit. Sci. Rev. **113**(4), 883–901 (2019)
18. Tsur, O., Calacci, D., Lazer, D.: A frame of mind: using statistical models for detection of framing and agenda setting campaigns. In: Proceedings of the 53rd Annual Meeting of the Association for Computational Linguistics and the 7th International Joint Conference on Natural Language Processing, vol. 1: Long Papers, pp. 1629–1638. ACL (2015)

19. Alam, M.H., Ryu, W.-J., Lee, S.: Hashtag-based topic evolution in social media. World Wide Web **20**(6), 1527–1549 (2017). https://doi.org/10.1007/s11280-017-0451-3

20. Zhang, Y., Mao, W., Lin, J.: Modeling topic evolution in social media short texts. In: 2017 IEEE International Conference on Big Knowledge (ICBK), pp. 315–319. IEEE (2017)

21. Zhang, Y., Mao, W., Zeng, D.: Topic evolution modeling in social media short texts based on recurrent semantic dependent CRP. In: 2017 IEEE International Conference on Intelligence and Security Informatics (ISI) (pp. 119–124). IEEE (2017)

22. Saha, A., Sindhwani, V.: Learning evolving and emerging topics in social media: a dynamic nmf approach with temporal regularization. In: Proceedings of the Fifth ACM International Conference on Web Search and Data Mining, pp. 693–702. ACM (2012)

23. Huang, J., Peng, M., Wang, H., Cao, J., Gao, W., Zhang, X.: A probabilistic method for emerging topic tracking in microblog stream. World Wide Web **20**(2), 325–350 (2017)

24. Deng, Q., Cai, G., Zhang, H., Liu, Y., Huang, L., Sun, F.: Enhancing situation awareness of public safety events by visualizing topic evolution using social media. In: Proceedings of the 19th Annual International Conference on Digital Government Research: Governance in the Data Age, pp. 1–10 (2018)

25. Dermouche, M., Velcin, J., Khouas, L., Loudcher, S.: A joint model for topic-sentiment evolution over time. In: 2014 IEEE international conference on data mining, pp. 773–778. IEEE (2014)

26. Wang, Y., Agichtein, E., Benzi, M.: TM-LDA: efficient online modeling of latent topic transitions in social media. In: Proceedings of the 18th ACM SIGKDD international conference on Knowledge discovery and data mining, pp. 123–131. ACM (2012)

27. Bodrunova, S.S., Smoliarova, A.S., Blekanov, I.S., Zhuravleva, N.N., Danilova, Y.S.: A global public sphere of compassion? #JeSuisCharlie and #JeNeSuisPasCharlie on Twitter and their language boundaries. Monitoring Obshchestvennogo Mneniya: Ekonomicheskie i Sotsial'nye Peremeny **1**(143), 267–294 (2018)

28. Bodrunova, S.S., Blekanov, I., Smoliarova, A., Litvinenko, A.: Beyond left and right: real-world political polarization in Twitter discussions on inter-ethnic conflicts. Media Commun. **7**(3), 119–132 (2019)

29. Bodrunova, S.S.: When context matters. analyzing conflicts with the use of big textual corpora from Russian and international social media. Partecipazione e conflitto **11**(2), 497–510 (2018)

30. Bodrunova, S.S.: The boundaries of context: contextual knowledge in research on networked discussions. In: Antonyuk, A., Basov, N. (eds.), Proceedings of the Fifth Networks in the Global World Conference (NetGloW2020). Springer, Cham (2021)

31. Kalyanam, J., Mantrach, A., Saez-Trumper, D., Vahabi, H., Lanckriet, G.: Leveraging social context for modeling topic evolution. In: Proceedings of the 21st ACM SIGKDD International Conference on Knowledge Discovery and Data Mining, pp. 517–526 (2015)

32. Ahmed, A., Xing, E.: Dynamic non-parametric mixture models and the recurrent Chinese restaurant process: with applications to evolutionary clustering. In: Proceedings of the 2008 SIAM International Conference on Data Mining, pp. 219–230. Society for Industrial and Applied Mathematics (2008)

33. Lu, Z., Tan, H., Li, W.: An evolutionary context-aware sequential model for topic evolution of text stream. Inf. Sci. **473**, 166–177 (2019)

34. Aggarwal, C.C., Zhai, C. (eds.): Mining Text Data. Springer, Cham (2012). https://doi.org/10.1007/978-3-319-14142-8_13

35. Nenkova, A., McKeown, K.: A survey of text summarization techniques. In: Aggarwal, C.C., Zhai, C. (eds.) Mining Text Data, pp. 43–76. Springer, Boston (2012). https://doi.org/10.1007/978-1-4614-3223-4_3

36. Tas, O., Kiyani, F.: A survey automatic text summarization. PressAcademia Proc. **5**(1), 205–213 (2007)

37. Ferreira, R., et al.: A context based text summarization system. In: 2014 11th IAPR International Workshop on Document Analysis Systems, pp. 66–70. IEEE (2014)
38. Kaikhah, K.: Automatic text summarization with neural networks. In: 2004 2nd International IEEE Conference on Intelligent Systems. Proceedings (IEEE Cat. No. 04EX791), vol. 1, pp. 40–44. IEEE (2004)
39. Nallapati, R., Zhou, B., Gulcehre, C., Xiang, B.: Abstractive text summarization using sequence-to-sequence rnns and beyond. arXiv:1602.06023 (2016)
40. Celis, L.E., Keswani, V.: Dialect Diversity in Text Summarization on Twitter. arXiv:2007. 07860 (2020)
41. Li, Q., Zhang, Q.: Abstractive Event Summarization on Twitter. Companion Proceedings of the Web Conference **2020**, 22–23 (2020)
42. Mottaghinia, Z., Feizi-Derakhshi, M.R., Farzinvash, L., Salehpour, P.: A review of approaches for topic detection in Twitter. J. Exp. Theor. Artif. Intell. (2020). https://doi.org/10.1080/095 2813X.2020.1785019
43. Asgari-Chenaghlu, M., Nikzad-Khasmakhi, N., Minaee, S.: Covid-transformer: Detecting trending topics on twitter using universal sentence encoder. arXiv:2009.03947 (2020)
44. Beltagy, I., Peters, M.E., Cohan, A.: Longformer: The long-document transformer. arXiv: 2004.05150 (2020)
45. Raffel, C., et al.: Exploring the limits of transfer learning with a unified text-to-text transformer. arXiv:1910.10683 (2019)
46. Bodrunova, S.S., Blekanov, I.S., Kukarkin, M.: Topics in the Russian Twitter and relations between their interpretability and sentiment. In: 2019 Sixth International Conference on Social Networks Analysis, Management and Security (SNAMS), pp. 549–554. IEEE (2019)
47. Blekanov, I.S., Sergeev, S.L., Martynenko, I.A.: Constructing topic-oriented web crawlers with generalized core. Sci. Res. Bull. St. Petersburg State Polytech. Univ. **5**(157), 9–15 (2012)
48. Mocanu, D., Baronchelli, A., Perra, N., Gonçalves, B., Zhang, Q., Vespignani, A.: The Twitter of Babel: Mapping world languages through microblogging platforms. PLoS ONE **8**(4), e61981 (2013)
49. Joulin, A., Grave, E., Bojanowski, P., Mikolov, T.: Bag of tricks for efficient text classification. arXiv:1607.01759 (2016)
50. Devlin, J., Chang, M.W., Lee, K., Toutanova, K.: Bert: Pre-training of deep bidirectional transformers for language understanding. arXiv:1810.04805 (2018)

Identifiability as an "Antidote": Exploring Emotional Contagion and the Role of Anonymity in Twitter Discussions on Misinformation

Chen (Crystal) Chen$^{(\boxtimes)}$ (iD), Hao Yuan, and Mike Z. Yao

University of Illinois at Urbana-Champaign, Champaign, IL 61820, USA
{chenc4,haoyuan4,mzyao}@illinois.edu

Abstract. Misinformation carries both distorted facts and sophisticated emotional signals. Comparing to facts that could be labeled as true or false, we are more concerned about contaminative negative emotions transferring digitally among users. In this study, we explored an emotional contagion effect among misinformation discussion participants on Twitter. We analyzed the sentiment of 573 tweets in 192 discussion threads. Our result revealed that highly emotional tweets do not have a universal effect on the online discussions, but it affects those individuals with limited social and personal identity cues (i.e., being anonymous). We found that anonymous members of the online discussion are more susceptible to emotional contagions than those are not. We also suggest coping strategies that protect social media users' emotional well-being during the era COVID-19.

Keywords: Emotion contagion · Anonymity · SIDE · Sentiment analysis

1 Introduction

The proliferation of social media communication allows users to engage in conversations and exchange opinions related to various topics, but little validation of online information and the careless use of social media also lowers the bar for misinformation propagation. The spread of misinformation has been a concern since the beginning of coronavirus pandemic (COVID-19). Distorted facts and misinformation not only deepen users' misunderstandings of the virus and the pandemic, but they also often carry negative emotional signals that may affect Internet users' emotional well-being. Online discussions that contain misinformation or involve accusations of misinformation are often contentious and heated. Such discussions divide the online community and spread negative sentiment. There has been initial evidence indicating global emotional contagion in the era of COVID-19. For instance, Kabir and Madria [11] identified an increasing number of aggressive sentiments in tweet threads compared to positive counterparts since the beginning of COVID-19. Medford and colleagues' [17] exploratory study showed that anger and fear are the top two emotions identified in users' COVID-19 twitter posts.

The current study starts with exploring emotional contagion within discussion threads about misinformation on Twitter. Emotional contagion refers to individuals'

G. Meiselwitz (Ed.): HCII 2021, LNCS 12774, pp. 240–252, 2021.
https://doi.org/10.1007/978-3-030-77626-8_16

tendency to automatically mimic and synchronize others' emotions [9] While different emotions can transfer digitally among users, negative emotions are particularly contaminative [13]. Previous studies found that when reducing positive content in Facebook's News Feed, participants posted more negative words in their own posts. In a similar way, we expect to observe an emotional contagion effects in discussions threads about COVID-19 and misinformation on Twitter.

In this study, we first examine whether the emotional signals carried by an initial tweet would influence the valence and sentiment of subsequent replies. We then explore the moderating effect of online anonymity on the emotional contagion effect. Following principles of the Social Identity model of Deindividuation Effects (SIDE) [22, 24, 25], we speculate that anonymous participants in an online discussion group might be particularly susceptible to negative emotion contagions. The SIDE model proposes that online anonymity obscures social and personal identity cues and interpersonal differences, thereby diminishes the relative importance of interpersonal concerns in online groups [24]. Under such conditions, depersonalized individuals become susceptible to group influence [22, 33]. For instance, past research has found that when participants were exposed to an aggressive group discussion in which their peers spoke aggressively to each other, anonymous participants were more susceptible to the influence of negative emotions and behave in a similar fashion; in contrast, identified participants seemed to be immune from such influence [26]. As such, we are particularly interested in exploring identifiability as an "antidote" for the emotional contagions in negative online discussion groups.

We collected twitter posts and replies discussing COVID-19 misinformation from January to June using a web crawler and applied a pre-trained sentiment analysis model "VADER" [10] for language analysis. By applying the SIDE model to a more natural user generated content on Twitter, this exploratory study aims to contribute to a better understanding of factors that affect users' emotional well-being during COVID-19 and come up with a proper coping strategy that sets the stage for a better mediated communication environment.

2 COVID-19 Misinformation and Negative Emotion

Since the beginning of the quarantine and execution of social distance, individuals' increasing dependence on social media also raises concerns of misinformation exposure. Previous studies have identified an enormous amount of misinformation on twitter. For instance, Sharma and colleagues [27] using keywords related to COVID-19 collected tweets from 182 countries, resulting in a subset of 4.58M English tweets with external links. Among this dataset, 150.8K (3.29%) tweets were identified as misinformation source tweets, carrying unreliable, conspiracy, or biased news sources. Although different websites used fact-checkers and took quick actions to remove or attach warnings to these pieces of misinformation, the effectiveness of these actions varies among companies [2]. According to Brennen and colleagues' [2] study, about 24% of the COVID-19 misinformation remains up without warning labels on Facebook. On YouTube, this number rises about 3%, with 27% of the misinformation remaining unchecked. Twitter has the worst condition, with about 59% of misinformation remaining unchecked.

Misinformation creates misleading guidance in the face of COVID-19, but it also carries sophisticated emotional signals, particularly negative emotions such as anger and fear [4]. The worst part is that the more anger a fake news source carries, the more likely it becomes viral, leading to a higher exposure to normal social media users. Recent research collected the fake news from both Weibo and Twitter and investigated the emotion carried by misinformation across platforms. When compared to real news, fake news from both platforms contained significantly higher proportions of anger and lower proportions of joy. Also, researchers found a positive association between proportion of anger in the fake news and the number of retweets. If a piece of misinformation contains more anger, it has a higher chance to spread out and infect the vulnerable general public. We are concerned that the prevalence of misinformation that carries negative emotion may contaminate social media users' emotional well-being and mental health during COVID-19. This concern is related to emotional contagion, a well-established finding from social psychology.

2.1 Emotional Contagion

Emotional contagion refers to individuals' tendency to automatically mimic and synchronize others' expressions, vocalizations, postures, and movement, and consequently, to converge emotionally [9]. For instance, when showing human pictures with varying facial expressions to viewers, happiness and sadness expressions significantly and repeatedly evoke the same emotion among viewers, even when the presentation duration lasts only 500 million seconds [36].

Recent work has indicated that emotional contagion does not always require in-person interaction and non-verbal cues; rather, emotional contagion can happen through social networks [13]. An experiment conducted on Facebook showed that, when reducing positive content in the News Feed, participants posted more negative words and less positive words in their own posts. When reducing negativity in the News Feed, the opposite pattern occurred [13]. Further, another study pointed out that when one user gets affected by one particular emotion on social media, this emotion is likely to transmit to friends in their social network [5]. In their study, researchers collected data from millions of Facebook users and found that bad weather negatively influences the emotional content of posters who experienced bad weather, but also, that this negative emotion additionally contaminates the status content of posters' friends who did not experience bad weather.

2.2 Emotional Contagion in the Era of COVID-19

Different emotions appear to be contagious, including anger, happiness, and anxiety [1], but negative emotions appear to be the most influential [21]. The effect of negative emotional contagion has received some evidence in studies conducted during the recent pandemics (i.e., during SARS: [37]; during H1N1:[31]; during COVID-19: [20, 35]). For instance, Wheaton and colleagues [35] conducted a survey among 600 students during COVID-19 and found high COVID-19 media consumption was associated with high anxiety among participants. For those who are more susceptible to emotional contagion, COVID-19 media consumption had a higher impact on their elevated obsessive-compulsive disorder (OCD) symptoms. In this case, reading misinformation containing anger and fear may also elicit more negative emotions among users.

Indeed, when facing COVID-19 misinformation, not everyone is a passive recipient. Social media empowers users to debunk misinformation and clarify misleading content. However, those who intend to debunk misinformation also have a high chance to get infected with negative emotion [18]. In a recent study, researchers found that susceptibility to and severity of misinformation induced negative emotions among vaccine supporters, including anticipated guilt and anger [30]. In this case, even though misinformation per se did not distort users' understanding of vaccines, it negatively impacted users' emotions.

That being said, when it comes to discussion related to negatively emotional misinformation, regardless of communicators' role as a misinformation disseminator, debunker, or reader, their emotions are likely to be contaminated during the interaction. Their negative emotions will be reflected in the linguistic valence of their responses and further influence more users. Emotional contagion happening digitally and transmitting via social networks may magnify the intensity of emotional synchronization, which is particularly sensitive to social media users' emotional well-being and mental health in the era of COVID-19 [32]. As such, we propose the following:

H1. Linguistic valence of the lead post in an online discussion thread will transmit to its replies, such that a negative post will more likely be followed by negative replies.

2.3 The SIDE Model: Depersonalization Versus Deindividualization

Following the SIDE model, we speculate that that users' online anonymity may modify the impact of negative emotion contagions. The SIDE model states that online anonymity obscures *personal features* and *interpersonal differences* but heightens one's sensitivity to the situational and group norms [24, 33]. More specifically, the model attributes individuals' heightened norm sensitivity to the influence of depersonalization, a tendency to perceive the self and others not as individuals with a range of idiosyncratic characters and ways of behaving but as representatives of social groups or wider social categories that are made salient during interaction [22].

The idea of depersonalization is different from deindividuation, a concept that was developed to explain antisocial behavior in crowds [6, 39]. Deindividuation theory proposes that, with reduced social cues (i.e., high visual anonymity or uniform representation of group members) in a crowd, individuals have a *decreased sense of self identity*, and consequently, exhibit a deregulation of social behavior [12, 39]. On the other hand, depersonalization from the SIDE model suggests conformity happens not because individuals lose self-identity. Rather, it happens because of a *reduced awareness of group member differences*, an increased salience of social identity among group members, and consensus of group norms. Further, crowd behavior is not always antinormative. Rather, depersonalization is the result of conformity to norms, which could be either positive or negative, depending on the nature of the group. Postmes and Spears [25] conducted a meta-analysis with 60 empirical studies and found weak support for the deindividuation theory, suggesting that being anonymous is not the only factor that contributes to individuals' anti-normative behavior.

Although the SIDE model rejects the process account of antisocial behavior in the deindividualization theory, it builds on previous theory's distinctions between two aspects of anonymity, high visual anonymity and uniform representation of group members, and formed cognitive and strategic dimensions of the SIDE model [29]. The cognitive dimension of the SIDE model refers to "anonymity of" and how the anonymity of/within the group can enhance the salience of group identity. The strategic dimension of the SIDE model refers to "anonymity to", the reduced accountability to others. The reduced accountability allows group members to nominate in group behaviors that may otherwise be sanctioned by the outgroup.

2.4   The Influence of Anonymity Based on the Cognitive Dimension of the SIDE Model

Previous research has collected empirical evidence in favor of the cognitive dimension of the SIDE model (i.e. [14, 16, 26, 28, 38]). For instance, Spears, Lea, and Lee [28] conducted a study in which participants were directed to discuss a range of controversial topics using a text-based synchronous CMC system. Researchers manipulated participants' visual anonymity by arranging them to co-present in the same room or separating them into different rooms. Researchers also provided participants with norm references where participants could know their groups' preferred solution for each topic. The results revealed that participants show shifts in the direction of group norms when their social identities are salient, and they are isolated (and therefore anonymous).

In addition, when aggressiveness becomes the group norm, researchers found participants in an anonymous condition are more likely to adopt similar ways of communication styles, when compared to participants in a non-anonymous condition. For instance, Rosner and Kramer [26] conducted a lab experiment investigating the moderating role of anonymity on the effect of aggressive group norms on individuals' commenting behavior. Researchers manipulated anonymity by two measures: on one hand, participants could reply using their registered Facebook account (identified) or reply without registration. On the other hand, participants could see peer comments either with or without the author's identifiable information (i.e., name, profile). The result revealed that, when peer comments include more aggressive wording, participants who perceive commenters have a high anonymity also use more aggressive expressions in their comments, but those who perceive commenters have a low anonymity are not influenced by aggressive comments. Further, there were studies zoomed in on specific information process [15]. For instance, Lee [15] extended the depersonalized effect by showing that identified users paid more attention to and influence of the strengths and weakness of specific arguments, while among those who were not individually identifiable, they paid less attention to the argument quality, but more were susceptible to the group influence.

These studies shed light on our current situation and suggest that when joining an online discussion thread, if users are anonymous or perceive other commenters as anonymous, they may be vulnerable to emotional contagion and will reply in a similar fashion to the lead post. However, if they are identified or perceive other commenters as more identified, their personal identity may remain salient. In this case, they will be less susceptible to the influence of the affective comments in misinformation discussion. The current study proposed the following hypotheses:

H2. In an online discussion thread, a) when repliers are anonymous, they are more susceptible to the emotional contagions in the environment. b) On the other hand, the effect of emotional contagion from the lead post will diminish among identified repliers.

3   Method

3.1   Data Collection

We started with an existing COVID-19 misinformation tweet dataset (CMU-MisCov19) [19]. The original dataset was collected based on hashtags and keywords in conjunction with "coronavirus" and "covid" on three days: 29th March 2020, 15th June 2020, and 24th June 2020 (Table 1). Each of these collections extracted a set of tweets from their corresponding week. The original dataset contained 4573 tweets, comprising 3629 users.

This dataset helped us to identify a list of tweets that posted topics related to COVID-19 misinformation. We collected the tweet IDs from this dataset and further scraped the webpage. We applied the python Selenium package and mimicked real visits to each tweet in this dataset. During the web scrape, we found that twitter blocked some original posts and replies due to policy violation and misinformation dissemination, so some content was not retrievable. In addition, we did not collect posts that do not have replies. The final dataset contained a total of 573 tweets, including 192 posts and 381 replies. We further used the python Beautiful Soup package to parse and extract relevant variables, including posters' and repliers' profile images, usernames, ids, posting timestamps, and their tweets.

Table 1. Keywords and Hashtags used in the data collection [19]

Type	Terms
Keywords	Bleach, vaccine, acetic acid, steroids, essential oil, saltwater, ethanol, children, kids, garlic, alcohol, chlorine, sesame oil, conspiracy, 5G, cure, colloidal silver, dryer, bioweapon, cocaine, hydroxychloroquine, chloroquine, gates, immune, poison, fake, treat, doctor, senna makki, senna tea
Hashtags	#nCoV2019, #CoronaOutbreak, #CoronaVirus, #CoronavirusCoverup, #CoronavirusOutbreak, #COVID19, #Coronavirus, #WuhanCoronavirus, #coronaviris, #Wuhan

3.2   Measure

Sentiment Analysis. In this study, we intended to use sentiment analysis to *estimate* individual posts' and replies' emotions (as indicated by language valence). This is because affective comments often carry emotion-expressive functions, which are reflected in their language valence [7]. In this study, we chose a pre-trained model "VADER" over human raters to measure language valence due to its convenience and accuracy. The training of the model started with examining existing sentiment word banks (LIWC, ANEW, and GI) and incorporating lexical features common to emotional expressions in CMC, including a full list of Western-style emoticons. Then researchers collected intensity ratings on each lexical feature candidate from 10 independent coders, ranging from "−4 extremely negative" to "4 extremely positive." In addition, the model also incorporated five generalizable heuristics based on grammatical and syntactic cues that further changed the sentiment intensity. The heuristics included punctuation (i.e., the exclamation mark "!"), capitalization, degree modifiers (i.e., degree adverbs such as "extremely"), contrastive conjunctions (i.e., "but" stands for a shift in sentiment polarity), and tri-grams preceding sentiment-laden lexical features (i.e., "The food here isn't really all that great"). Researchers also conducted two quantitative studies and found that the trained model outperformed individual human raters [10].

The VADER provided an output in the following form: { 'neg': 0.267, 'neu': 0.662, 'pos': 0.072, 'compound': −0.9169}. This means there is a 26.7% possibility that the sentence is negative, a 66.2% possibility that the sentence is neutral, and a 7.2% possibility that the sentence is positive. The final "compound" score is a normalized, weighted, and composite score, indicating the sentence carries negative emotion. Our calculation of valence is based on the compound score. We grouped posts with their replies and ended up with a total of 192 groups.

Post/Reply Valence. The posts' and replies' emotions were estimated by sentiment analysis and indicated by their valence. If the post or reply had a negative valence (valence < 0), we regarded it as having a negative emotion. If the post or reply had a positive or neutral valence (valence >= 0), we regarded it as having a neutral or positive emotion.

Anonymity. Individuals' anonymity was measured based on the user's first and last name identification. First, username identification was completed by matching usernames with an existing open-source name database[1]. The database included approximately 160k first names and 100k last names. We coded 0 for each identified first name and last name and 1 for cells with no name. For each reply, we combined first name and last name scores and formed their name anonymity scores, with a higher score indicating a higher level of anonymity (N[both names|0] = 79, N[one name|1] = 126, N[no name|2] = 176). We regarded replies with no name as an anonymous group and combined replies with one name or both names to form an identified group (N[anonymous] = 176, N[identified] = 205).

4 Result

Hypothesis 1 predicted that the emotion of a post, as reflected by its language valence, will transmit to its replies, such that a negative valence post will be followed by negative valence replies. A simple linear regression model was conducted to test this hypothesis, with the valence of the post as the independent variable and valence of the reply as the dependent variable. The result showed that the valence of the post does not significantly

---

[1] https://github.com/philipperemy/name-dataset.

influence the valence of the reply (b = 0.01, t = 0.15, p >,05). As a result, H1 was not supported.

Hypothesis 2 proposed the valence of the post by the replier's anonymity interaction. We proposed different patterns of commenting behavior among repliers classified as anonymous or identified when they are exposed to posts with positive or negative valence. Because we believe that the valence of the replies is influenced by factors from an individual level (between person difference: anonymous or identified) and factors from a group level (between group/thread difference: the valence of the post), we fitted a multilevel model with cross-level interaction. At Level 1, we modeled the valence of the post as a predictor of the valence of the reply across groups/threads. At Level 2, we examined the individual anonymity (anonymous = 0, identified = 1) as predictors of the intercept of repliers' language valence (i.e., average replies' language valence across all misinformation threads) and the level 1 random slope. The cross-level interaction between the estimated slope at level 1 and replies' anonymity (anonymous or identified) assessed whether the association between the valence of the reply and the valence of the post differed as a function of the replier's individual anonymity. All variables were mean-centered (i.e., individual's raw score minus group mean) prior to model tests.

To test our hypotheses, we fit a series of models in SPSS using maximum likelihood estimation. The intercept-only model indicated significant variability in replies' language valence at both the level 1 (.16) and level 2 (.03); the ICC was 16.93%, indicating that 17% of the variation in reply valence was between persons, whereas 83% was between groups (threads). Results from the conditional multilevel model are summarized in Table 2. At level 1, the random linear slope was not significant, such that the valence of the posts did not predict the valence of replies (B = .03, SE = .04, t = 0.64, p > .05). At level 2, the cross-level interaction between anonymity (level 2) and valence of the post (level 1) in the prediction of the valence of replies was significant, indicating that the influence of group norm on valence of replies differed depending on users' anonymity (B = −.16, SE = .08, t = −1.97, p < .05) (See Fig. 1).

To probe this significant cross-level interaction, we examined the influence of posts' valence for the identified and the anonymous groups respectively. Because the anonymous group was coded as 0 in the main model reported in Table 2, the level 1 slope represents the simple slope for the anonymous group. To obtain the simple slope for the identified group, we fit an identical multilevel model with the anonymity variable reverse coded (i.e., identified = 0, anonymous = 1). As shown in Fig. 1, simple slope tests revealed a significant positive association between the valence of anonymous reply and the valence of the post (B = 0.11, SE = .06, t = 1.92, p = .05), and an insignificant negative association between the valence of identified reply and the valence of the post (B = −0.05, SE = .04, t = −.80, p > .05). The result suggested that individual's anonymity modified replies' language valence in the twitter thread. For anonymous users, the emotions in posts have a positive effect on their replies, and this effect is significant (H2a supported). For identified users, the emotion carried in the post has a negative effect on their replies, but the influence is not significant (H2b supported).

Table 2. Results of hierarchical linear modeling

Variables	Null	Model 1: adding Level 1 predictors		Model 2: effect of level 1 and level 2 predictors		Model 3: cross-level interaction effects	
Level 1		Coefficient	SE	Coefficient	SE	Coefficient	SE
Intercept		.00	.02	.03	03	.04	.03
Post valence		.03	.04	.03	.04	.11	.06
Level 2							
Anonymity				−.06	.04	−.06	.04
Cross-level							
Post valence* Anonymity						−.16*	.08
Additional information							
ICC	0.17						

Note. *p < .05

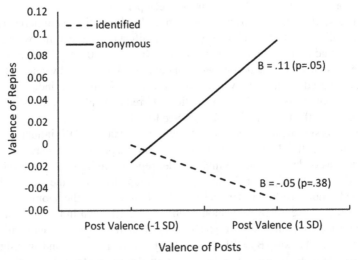

Fig. 1. Associations between valence of the posts and valence of the replies given identified or anonymous users.

5   Discussion

Misinformation is more likely to transmit among social media users in highly uncertain emergencies, such as disease outbreaks and pandemics [3]. Increasing exposure to misinformation may not only deepen users' understanding of the disease but also immerse users in unnecessary anxiety, anger, and fear. A recent survey conducted by the National

Center for Health Statistics (NCHS) in January 2021 estimated that 35.8% of adults have symptoms of anxiety disorder, which is 27.6% higher than estimates in 2019. Empirical evidence suggested that these negative emotions are associated with excessive social media exposure [35], and that negative emotions could transmit digitally across social networks [5]. As a result, the current study starts with exploring emotional contagion among misinformation discussion participants on Twitter. We then investigated the moderating effect of online anonymity on the emotional contagion effect under the guidance of the SIDE model.

The result showed that highly emotional tweets do not have a universal effect on online discussions, but it affects those individuals with limited social and personal identity cues (i.e., being anonymous). We found that anonymous members of the online discussion are more susceptible to emotional contagions than those are not. When users being anonymous, they are more susceptible to emotional contagion. When users being identified, they are more immune to emotional contagion. This finding is aligned with the prediction of the SIDE model that users tend to be more susceptible to group influence when they have less personal identity cues.

By further looking into group differences, we found that anonymous and identified users responded to posts carrying positive emotion differently, with anonymous users replying in a more positive tone. Anonymous and identified users did not differ significantly when replying to a post carrying negative emotion. However, the result revealed a trend that anonymous users reply in a negative tone to posts with negative emotion. The reason that we did not see a significant difference between groups when they replying to a negative post may be due to the sample bias. Twitter has enforced a stricter regulation to remove potentially harmful information since last March, and the automated systems have challenged more than 1.5 million accounts targeting COVID-19 discussions with spammy or manipulative behaviors [34]. As a result, a number of posts and replies containing sensitive or improper contents may have been removed by Twitter.

This study also suggests coping strategies that protect social media users' emotional well-being during the era of COVID-19. The result showed that users are more immune to the influence of emotional contagion when they are identified with names. This finding complies with the prediction of the SIDE model, except that our goal is to reduce (negative) social influence by maintaining one's personal identity and refusing the social influence (the null hypothesis in the SIDE model). Our study suggests that being identified with names in social media may be one way to reduce negative social influence, but it is not the only way. Previous experimental findings suggested that visual identification, such as unique profile pictures/avatars, also highlights one's personal identity and inhibit social identity [16]. That being said, we encourage users to find their own way (i.e., create unique profile avatar, use meaningful pseudonyms) to highlight their personal identities and reduce negative social influence.

6 Limitations and Future Research

This study is a timely piece of research that investigates the effect of emotional contagion and suggests coping strategies for users during the era of COVID-19, but it is limits in its nature as a cross-sectional design that precludes causal inferences. For example, we cannot determine if there is a third variable outside of this observational dataset that contributes to users' sensitivity to emotional contagion. A more powerful design would be a controlled lab experiment that manipulates the valence of the lead post and compares group differences given different levels of individual identity salience and group uniformity. Also, as a study applying the SIDE model, it does not have a strict manipulation of the group or a salient group identity. In the current study, a group is regarded as nodes in communication networks [23], such that a post and its subsequent replies are treated as one group. Although this approach defines a group structurally rather than psychologically, users' posting and reacting to COVID-19 misinformation topics indicated a common interest and some shared social identity. Previous research also indicated that a conformity to a form of communication (such as humor, verbal aggression) is an indication of social identity influences [8]. Regardless, a better measure of the group would be to apply network analysis and identifying users who interact most within all misinformation conversations.

7   Conclusion

Notwithstanding these limitations, the present observational study highlights the group difference between users who are anonymous versus identified in their sensitivity to the emotional contagion coming from misinformation discussions. The findings indicated that users with a reduced sense of depersonalization through having an identified name are more immune to the emotional contagion. Based on the finding, we proposed coping strategies for inhibiting global emotional contagion.

References

1. Behnke, R.R., Sawyer, C.R., King, P.E.: Contagion theory and the communication of public speaking state anxiety. Commun. Educ. **43**, 246–251 (1994)
2. Brennen, J.S., Simon, F., Howard, P.N., Nielsen, R.K.: Types, sources, and claims of COVID-19 misinformation. Reuters Inst. **7**, 3–1 (2020)
3. Carey, J.M., Chi, V., Flynn, D.J., Nyhan, B., Zeitzoff, T.: The effects of corrective information about disease epidemics and outbreaks: evidence from Zika and yellow fever in Brazil. Sci. Adv. **6**(5), eaaw7449 (2020)
4. Chuai, Y., Zhao, J.: Anger makes fake news viral online. arXiv:2004.10399 (2020)
5. Coviello, L., et al.: Detecting emotional contagion in massive social networks. PLoS ONE **9**(3), e90315 (2014)
6. Festinger, L., Pepitone, A., Newcomb, T.: Some consequences of de-individuation in a group. J. Abnorm. Soc. Psychol. **47**, 382–389 (1952)
7. Foolen, A.: Word valence and its effects. In: Lüdke, U. (ed.) Emotion in Language, pp. 241–256. John Benjamins, Amsterdam (2015)
8. Giles, H., Coupland, N., Coupland, J.: Accommodation theory: communication, context, and consequence. In: Giles, H., Coupland, J. (eds.) Contexts of Accommodation: Developments in Applied Sociolinguistics, pp. 1–68 (1991)
9. Hatfield, E., Cacioppo, J.T., Rapson, R.L.: Emotional contagion. Curr. Dir. Psychol. Sci. **2**, 96–100 (1993)

10. Hutto, C., Gilbert, E.: Vader: A parsimonious rule-based model for sentiment analysis of social media text. In: Proceedings of the International AAAI Conference on Web and Social Media, vol. 8, No. 1 (2014)

11. Kabir, M., Madria, S.: Coronavis: a real-time covid-19 tweets analyzer. arXiv:2004.13932 (2020)

12. Kiesler, S., Siegel, J., McGuire, T.W.: Social psychological aspects of computer-mediated communication. Am. Psychol. **39**, 1123–1134 (1984)

13. Kramer, A.D., Guillory, J.E., Hancock, J.T.: Experimental evidence of massive-scale emotional contagion through social networks. Proc. Natl. Acad. Sci. **111**(24), 8788–8790 (2014)

14. Kugihara, N.: Effects of aggressive behavior and group size on collective escape in an emergency: a test between a social identity model and deindividuation theory. Br. J. Soc. Psychol. **40**(4), 575–598 (2001)

15. Lee, E.J.: When are strong arguments stronger than weak arguments? Deindividuation effects on message elaboration in computer-mediated communication. Commun. Res. **35**(5), 646–665 (2008)

16. Lee, E.J.: Effects of visual representation on social influence in computer-mediated communication: experimental tests of the social identity model of deindividuation effects. Hum. Commun. Res. **30**(2), 234–259 (2004)

17. Medford, R.J., Saleh, S.N., Sumarsono, A., Perl, T.M., Lehmann, C.U.: An "infodemic": Leveraging high-volume Twitter data to understand early public sentiment for the coronavirus disease 2019 outbreak. Open Forum Infect. Dis. **7**(7), 258 (2020)

18. Melissa, H.: Misinformation about the coronavirus abounds, but correcting it can backfire". Los Angeles Times (2020). https://www.latimes.com/science/story/2020-02-08/coronavirus-outbreak-false-information-psychology

19. Memon, S.A., Carley, K.M.: Characterizing covid-19 misinformation communities using a novel twitter dataset. arXiv:2008.00791 (2020)

20. National Center for Health Statistics: Mental health household pulse survey (2020). https://www.cdc.gov/nchs/covid19/pulse/mental-health.htm

21. Paukert, A.L., Pettit, J.W., Amacker, A.: The role of interdependence and perceived similarity in depressed affect contagion. Behav. Ther. **39**, 277–285 (2008)

22. Postmes, T., Spears, R., Lea, M.: Breaching or building social boundaries? SIDE-effects of computer-mediated communication. Commun.Res. **25**(6), 689–715 (1998)

23. Postmes, T., Spears, R., Lea, M.: The formation of group norms in computer-mediated communication. Hum. Commun. Res. **26**, 341–371 (2000)

24. Postmes, T., Spears, R., Sakhel, K., de Groot, D.: social influence in computer-mediated communication: the effects of anonymity on group behavior. Pers. Soc. Psychol. Bull. **27**(10), 1243–1254 (2001)

25. Postmes, T., Spears, R.: Deindividuation and antinormative behavior: a meta-analysis. Psychol. Bull. **123**(3), 238–259 (1998)

26. Rösner, L., Krämer, N.C.: verbal venting in the social web: effects of anonymity and group norms on aggressive language use in online comments. Soc. Media + Soc. **2**(3), 1–13 (2016)

27. Sharma, K., et al.: Coronavirus on social media: analyzing misinformation in Twitter conversations. arXiv:2003, p. 12309 (2020)

28. Spears, R., Lea, M., Lee, S.: De-individuation and group polarization in computer-mediated communication. Br. J. Soc. Psychol. **29**(2), 121–134 (1990)

29. Spears, R., Postmes, T.: Group identity, social influence, and collective action online. In: Sundar, S.S. (ed.) The Handbook of the Psychology of Communication Technology (2015)

30. Sun, Y., Chia, S.C., Lu, F., Oktavianus, J.: The battle is on: factors that motivate people to combat anti-vaccine misinformation. Health Commun. 1–10 (2020)

31. Tausczik, Y., Faasse, K., Pennebaker, J.W., Petrie, K.J.: Public anxiety and information seeking following the H1N1 outbreak: blogs, newspaper articles, and Wikipedia visits. Health Commun. **27**(2), 179–185 (2012)
32. Trautmann, S., et al.: Susceptibility to others' emotions moderates immediate self-reported and biological stress responses to witnessing trauma. Behav. Res. Ther. **110**, 55–63 (2012)
33. Turner, J. C.: The analysis of social influence. In: Turner, J.C., Hogg, M.A., Oakes, P.J., Reicher, S.D., Wetherell, M.S. (eds.) Rediscovering The Social Group: A Self-Categorization Theory, pp. 68–88 (1987)
34. Twitter Inc. Staying safe and informed on Twitter (2021). https://blog.twitter.com/en_us/top ics/company/2020/covid-19.html#definition
35. Wheaton, M.G., Prikhidko, A., Messner, G.R.: Is fear of COVID-19 contagious? The effects of emotion contagion and social media use on anxiety in response to the coronavirus pandemic. Front. Psychol. **11** (2020)
36. Wild, B., Erb, M., Bartels, M.: Are emotions contagious? Evoked emotions while viewing emotionally expressive faces: quality, quantity, time course and gender differences. Psychiatry Res. **102**(2), 109–124 (2001)
37. Xie, X.F., Stone, E., Zheng, R., Zhang, R.G.: The 'typhoon eye effect': Determinants of distress during the SARS epidemic. J. Risk Res. **14**(9), 1091–1107 (2011)
38. Yao, M.Z., Flanagin, A.J.: A self-awareness approach to computer-mediated communication. Comput. Hum. Behav. **22**(3), 518–544 (2004)
39. Zimbardo, P.G.: The human choice: Individuation, reason, and order vs. deindividuation, impulse and chaos. In: Arnold, W.J., Levine, D. (eds.) Nebraska Symposium on Motivation, vol. 17, pp. 237–307. University of Nebraska Press, Lincoln, NE (1969)

Citizen Analytics: Statistical Tools for Studying Multicultural Environments and Distributed Cognition on Social Media

Nick V. Flor(✉) (iD)

University of New Mexico, Albuquerque, NM 87131, USA
nickflor@unm.edu

Abstract. People of all cultures depended largely on the mainstream media to report the details and the progress of the 2019 novel coronavirus disease (COVID-19). Such reports caused anxiety, depression, and helplessness. I attribute these negative attitudes partly to the lack of ability in citizens to self-analyze the current and the projected state of the virus, both locally and globally. This paper explores the research question: What skills do citizens need to self-analyze the current and projected state of a pandemic, and to report their analyses to the public? I use a data ethnography of my experience analyzing the JHU CSSE Data repository to report on five categories of key analytic skills: preparation, visualization, comparison, prediction, and socialization along with the details of their code implementation.

Keywords: Data ethnography · Exploratory data analytics · Covid-19

1 Introduction

The existential threat that the novel coronavirus of 2019 (technically, "SARS-CoV-2", but commonly and hereafter "COVID-19") posed to all cultures, left people feeling fearful, anxious, and helpless. Citizens relied primarily on the mainstream media—includes broadcast, cable, and print news for information about the progress and the trajectory of the virus, and then used social media to voice and ultimately amplify their frustrations. This reliance on the mainstream media for information is partly responsible for the negative feelings the public held. If citizens had the ability to self-analyze COVID-19 and to share their analyses with others on social media, they would be empowered, which would lessen their negative attitudes. That is a hypothesis I will leave for psychologists and sociologists to explore. But to help with that hypothesis, in this paper I explore the research question: *What analytic skills do citizens need to self-analyze pandemic data, and to share the results of their analyses?*

To help answer this question I perform a data ethnography on the COVID-19 Data Repository by the Center for Systems Science and Engineering (CSSE) at Johns Hopkins University, or "JHU CSSE COVID-19 Data" for short. Similar to anthropologists describing their experiences living in another culture (ethnography), in a data ethnography an exploratory data analyst reports his or her experience analyzing a data set.

© Springer Nature Switzerland AG 2021
G. Meiselwitz (Ed.): HCII 2021, LNCS 12774, pp. 253–267, 2021.
https://doi.org/10.1007/978-3-030-77626-8_17

2 The Data: JHU CSSE COVID-19 Data

The Center for Systems Science and Engineering (CSSE) at John Hopkins University (JHU) created a data repository for the 2019 novel coronavirus [1]. This repository contains data sets that provide daily updates of both new cases and deaths for COVID-19 and is the most popular and widely used repository [2] by researchers and the media. It is available open access at https://github.com/CSSEGISandData/COVID-19 [3], and the CSSE labels the repository the *JHU CSSE COVID-19 data*.

There are many datasets in the repository, but there are four main ones located in the folder *csse_covid_19_data/csse_covid_19_time_series/*. The files are:

- time_series_covid19_confirmed_US.csv
- time_series_covid19_confirmed_global.csv
- time_series_covid19_deaths_US.csv
- time_series_covid19_deaths_global.csv

Figure 1 depicts how the data sets look within the GitHub repository. The first column is a data set's file name. The second column is a "commit message", which the CSSE must add each time they update the data set. It indicates that the CSSE updated the files based on delayed data received from the United States. The last column is the time of the update, "4 h ago". Based on this information, an analyst can decide whether to download the data sets. I will cover the contents of these files in the skills section.

time_series_covid19_confirmed_US.csv	Automated update for delayed data for US	4 hours ago
time_series_covid19_confirmed_global.csv	Automated update for delayed data for US	4 hours ago
time_series_covid19_deaths_US.csv	Automated update for delayed data for US	4 hours ago
time_series_covid19_deaths_global.csv	Automated update for delayed data for US	4 hours ago

Fig. 1. The four main datasets in the JHU CSSE

An important piece of information in the file name is the extension ".csv". Short for *comma separated values,* it signals that the different categories of information in the file are separated by commas and that, typically, the first line of the file contains the header labels. Many office apps such as Microsoft Excel and Libre Office Calc can open.csv files directly and display them as tables. The major data science languages—Python, Julia, and R—provide libraries that read.csv files in a single statement.

3 The Analysis Tools: R and R Studio

To analyze the JHU-CSSE COVID-19 data, I used R [4] and R Studio [5].

R is a programming language for statistical computing and data visualization. I choose it for several reasons. First, it is free, open source, and has an active community of contributors that are continuously creating packages containing commands for the latest statistical, machine learning, and graphical techniques. Second, it runs on a variety of computer operating systems including, MacOS, Windows, Linux, and Unix systems like FreeBSD. Lastly, and more importantly, I choose R because I am an instructor for non-technical undergraduate and graduate students. These students all have experience with Excel and have found R to be an easy transition. The general consensus among my students is that "R is like Excel, but without the visual interface, and the commands are like Excel macros". Figure 2 depicts the user interface for the R app.

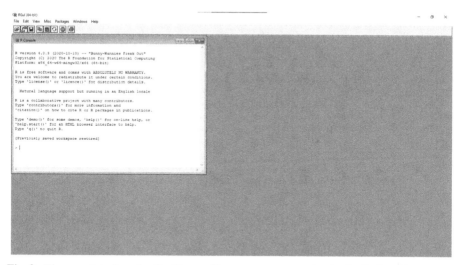

Fig. 2. The user interface for the R app. Users enter commands via the R Console window (displayed), which may open other windows to display results.

The R user interface can be difficult for beginning users to navigate. RStudio is an integrated development environment (IDE) that makes it easier for both beginners and experts to interact with the R language and with R packages.

For example, the default RStudio user interface displays four windows on a single screen. The windows are (refer to Fig. 3): source code (upper left), variables & values (upper right), an R Console (lower left), and a plot window (lower right). For the sake of brevity, I use R to refer to the programming language, the packages, and RStudio collectively.

4   Analysis Skills

Given a data set and R for analyzing the data set, how do you make sense of the data? During my analysis of the JHU CSSE COVID-19 data, from February 1, 2020 to the present day, I have found several skills that I repeatedly use.

4.1   Skill Proposition 1: Citizens Need the Ability to Read in a Data Set

Before analyzing a data set you need the ability to open it inside your analysis app. In office software like Microsoft Excel or Libre Office Calc, this is a simple menu operation: File > Open (click on file). In R, the general command syntax is:

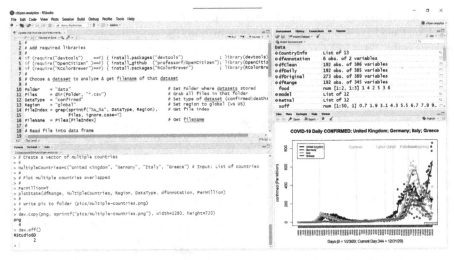

Fig. 3. The RStudio default user interface. See text for explanation.

```
dataframe = read.csv(filename) # data frame === worksheet
```

For example, to read in the data set for the number of confirmed covid-19 cases in the United States, you could enter into the R console:

```
df = read.csv("time_series_covid19_confirmed_US.csv")
```

RStudio then allows you to click on the variable (*df*) to see the contents of the csv file. Figure 4 depicts the contents of the data set.

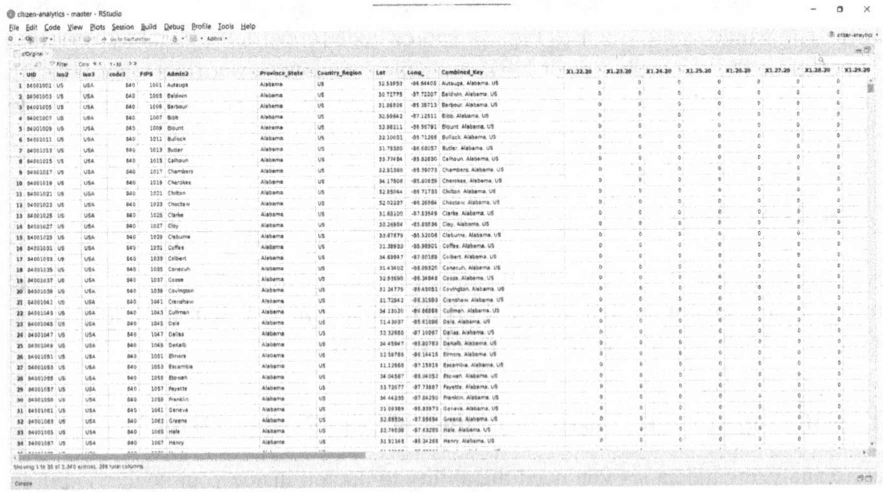

Fig. 4. The contents of time_series_covid19_confirmed_US.csv

Unlike Microsoft Excel or Libre Office Calc, you cannot edit the cells directly. You must enter commands to view specific cells, columns, and rows. But the ability you lose to manipulate the data directly, is often more than offset by the ability you gain to run statistics, model, and graph the data.

The data set contains eleven columns of categorical data: *UID, iso2, iso3, code3, FIPS, Admin2, Province_State, Country_Region, Lat, Long_, Combined_Key.* The remaining columns are dates labeled with the syntax X*Date.* For example, X.1.22.20, denotes January 1, 2020, and the cell values represent the accumulated values for that date. It's important to note that the cell values are cumulative for that date, e.g., a cell value of 100 is not the number of new cases for that day, but the total for that day along with all previous days. Note: although this is the time series data for confirmed cases in the US, the format for the global data sets, and for the death case data sets are similar.

4.2   Skill Proposition 2: Citizens Need the Ability to Clean the Data

When I first started analyzing the JHU CSSE COVID-19 data, I only wanted to know how my state, New Mexico, was performing—in terms of daily new cases and deaths—relative to other states in the United States. But the data set did not provide daily totals for a given state. Instead, the data set distributed state totals across counties, e.g., see Alabama in Fig. 4, and you needed to sum up all the columns for the rows of a specific state to get its daily cumulative totals.

In short, you must clean the information. Visually and mathematically cleaning is a simple operation. In Microsoft Excel, you could copy and paste the cells for a State into a new worksheet. If C represents the number of counties in a state, and D represents the number of day columns, then you would have a new worksheet with C rows and D columns. You could then find the state totals by simply running the SUM macro on across all the columns. Mathematically, you have a $C \times D$ matrix, M with elements m_{ji}, and the resulting state vector, S, is:

$$S : \{s_i = \sum_{j=1}^{C} m_{ji} | i \in 1 : D\}$$

Cleaning operations for the JHU CSSE COVID-19 data generally consists of two suboperations: filtering and collapsing. In filtering, one keeps only the columns of interest, e.g., dates and not latitude & longitudes. In collapsing, one reduces the extracted columns for a given category (state) into a single row.

I implemented the filtering operation in R across all states in the following code fragment:

```
#
# Get a list of unique states
#
States=unique(dfOrig[,ColName])
#
# For each State's rows, sum all columns
#
StateTotals=sapply(States, function (x) {
   # Extract the county rows for a given state x
   rows=which(dfOrig[ColName]==x)
   # Extract just the date cols for a county
   cols=grep("^X", colnames(dfOrig))
   # Results: matrix w/rows as counties & cols as dates
   rect=dfOrig[rows,cols]
   # Sum all columns to get the totals for a given state
   totals=colSums(rect)
})
# Transpose and add row & column names
StateTotals=t(StateTotals)
cols=grep("^X", colnames(dfOrig))
colnames(StateTotals)=names(dfOrig)[cols]
rownames(StateTotals)=States
#
# Create a dataframe (df) of the collapsed state values.
#
df=data.frame(State=States,StateTotals)
```

Admittedly, for non-technical citizens this is a complex bit of programming to learn. Fortunately, one can place this and other complex programming into a package of functions—analogous to a library of macros in an office app—which one can invoke using a single function call. In fact, the main reason R is widely used by researchers in the social sciences is because complex algorithms can be reduced to a single function call, eliminating the need for expert programming skill.

The result of the filtering operation is depicted in Fig. 5. It is a new data frame with just the fifty states in the United States along with US territories like American Samoa and Guam. One can now plot any given state with R code similar to the following:

```
StateRow=which(State=="New Mexico")
StateData=as.integer(df[StateRow,2:length(df)])
barplot(StateData)
```

The code displays a bar plot of daily cumulative covid-19 new cases for the state of New Mexico, from January 22, 2020 through February 11, 2021 (see Fig. 6).

The slope of the graph represents how fast covid-19 is spreading, with a zero slope indicating the desirable condition of no spreading. With cumulative data it is difficult

Fig. 5. The filtered data set with state-county data collapsed into a single state row.

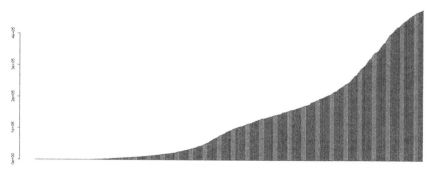

Fig. 6. A bar plot of cumulative new cases of covid-19 for the state of New Mexico from January 22, 2020 to February 11, 2021.

to determine daily progress. Questions like "How did our state do today?" or "How did our state do this week?" are best answered with a graph of daily differences.

4.3 Skill Proposition 3: The Ability to Transform Daily Cumulative Data to Daily Difference Data

To transform the JHU CSSE COVID-19 data from daily cumulative totals to daily differences, you need to subtract two consecutive days. If C, with individual elements c_i, represents a vector of N cumulative days, then we can define a daily difference vector, D, as

$$D : \{d_i = c_{i+1} - c_i | i \in 1 : N - 1\}$$

In R, we can create a function that does all the states in the data frame as follows:

```
createDaily=function(df, StartCol=3) {
    NumCols = length(colnames(df))
    NumRows = length(df$State)
    Deltas  = sapply(1:NumRows, function (row) {
        Delta   = sapply(StartCol:NumCols, function (col) {
                    df[row,col]-df[row,(col-1)]
                  })
    })
    Deltas=t(Deltas)
    colnames(Deltas)=colnames(df)[StartCol:NumCols]
    States  = unique(df$State)
    dfd=data.frame(State=States,Deltas)
    dfd
}
```

This function returns a new data frame, e.g., *dfd,* where each item in a vector is now the total number of new cases (or deaths) for a particular day, rather than a running-total of all previous days.

4.4 Skill Proposition 4: The Ability to Graph the Data

Given a data frame of daily values, the next important skill is the ability to graph those values. Conceptually, you must: (1) find the row corresponding to a particular state in the data frame of differences; (2) extract all the data starting from the second column (the first column is the state name); and (3) plot the data. The R code is straightforward:

```
StateRow=which(State=="New Mexico")
StateData=as.integer(dfd[StateRow,2:length(dfd)])
plot(StateData, type="l")
```

Figure 7 depicts the results of the plot.

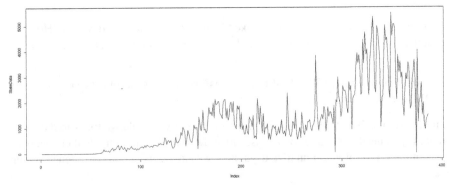

Fig. 7. Daily new cases of covid-19 in the State of New Mexico for the dates January 23, 2020 thru February 11, 2021

4.5   Skill Proposition 5: The Ability to Calculate and Plot a Moving Average

When the data is choppy and changing rapidly, it helps to smooth out the graph by calculating and then plotting a moving average, where each point is an average of N sequential points. Typically $N = 7$ and is known as a 7-day moving average. Given a vector of length L, the moving average is a vector M with individual elements m_i, and defined formally as:

$$M : \left\{ m_i = \frac{\sum_{j=i}^{j=i+N-1} d_j}{N} \, | \, i \in 1 : (L - N + 1) \right\}$$

The R code for implementing this moving average is:

```
N=7
MovingAverage=sapply(N:length(StateData), function(x) {
    mean(StateData[(x-(N-1)):x])})
```

Finally, the R code to plot this moving average over the existing plot is:

```
lines(N:length(StateData), MovingAverage, col="green")
```

Yielding both the plot and the 7-day moving average super-imposed (see Fig. 8).

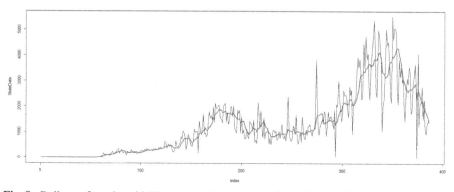

Fig. 8. Daily confirmed covid-19 new cases for the state of New Mexico from January 23, 2020 until February 11, 2021, with a 7-day average super-imposed.

4.6   Skill Proposition 6: The Ability to Label and Annotate the Graph

A graph of just the daily data and a moving average is helpful for tracking covid-19 in a specific state or region. Such a graph indicates when the spread of covid-19 is increasing or decreasing. But details of the exact dates, and possible events that may be causing the increase or decrease require labeling the graph and overlaying annotations on the graph.

R provides four main commands in the basic plot package that are helpful in labeling and annotating graphs. They are:

```
title
text
legend
axis
```

It is beyond the scope of this paper to cover the numerous options for these commands. Suffice it to say, they allow you to position text throughout the graph in different fonts, colors, and orientations. Figure 9 depicts the state of New Mexico with the axes labeled and specific events overlayed as vertical lines topped by an event label.

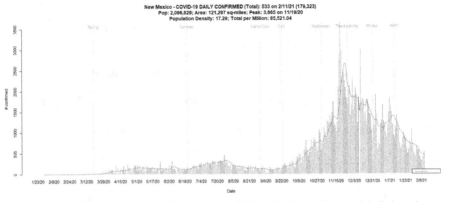

Fig. 9. Daily confirmed new cases for the state of New Mexico, with axes labeled, and event markers overlayed. The events show covid-19 cases increasing in the Fall and decreasing rapidly after the World Health Organization (WHO) gave updated guidelines for counting cases.

With a graph labeled and annotated, one can share it on social media and have a discussion about its interpretation. Figure 10 depicts a posting on Twitter, with 15 replies.

4.7 Skill Proposition 7: The Ability to Compare Different Regions

Using the skills above along with R's ability to overlay graphs you can compare how your state or region is doing relative to other states. Figure 11 compares new cases of covid-19 in New Mexico with those in New York, Texas, Florida, and California.

Such direct comparisons of state values can be misleading because states with a bigger populations will have more deaths than states with smaller populations. A fair comparison between states requires that you at least adjust for population. Given a vector of state values V, and a scalar population P, one adjustment is to calculate per million values, A, and is defined formally as is simply:

$$A = \frac{V}{P} \times 1,000,000$$

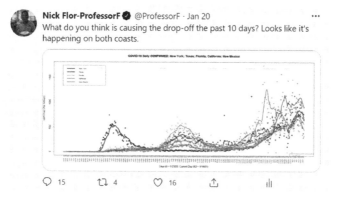

Fig. 10. Posting an annotated graph on social media for feedback. 15 users responded.

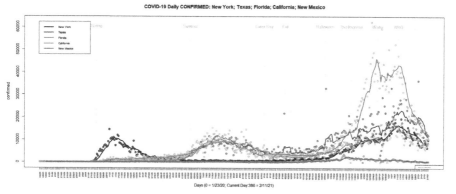

Fig. 11. New cases of covid-19 for the states of New Mexico, New York, Texas, Florida, and California. The values are not adjusted for population.

The R code is equally straightforward:

```
Values=Values/StateInfo$StatePopulation*1000000
```

Adjusted for population, we get the unexpected result that New Mexico had the highest maximum number of daily cases (see Fig. 12).

4.8   Skill Proposition 8: The Ability to Predict Future Values

The spread of biological viruses and viral messages on social media both follow log-normal distributions. Typically, analysts use the natural log as a base to model the probability distribution function (PDF):

$$f(x) = \frac{1}{x\sigma\sqrt{2\pi}}exp\left(-\frac{1}{2\sigma^2}(\ln(x) - \mu)^2\right)$$

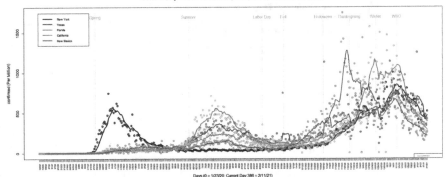

Fig. 12. New cases of covid-19 for the states of New Mexico, New York, Texas, Florida, and California. The values are adjusted for population (c.f., previous figure).

However, one can use other bases as well with rescaled parameters [6]. I use base 10 because it is easier for students to understand. My simplified log-normal PDF is:

$$f(x) = \frac{peak}{10^{(\log_{fat} \frac{x}{shift})^2}} + lift$$

The variable *peak* controls the highest point of the log-normal curve, *fat* controls its breadth, *shift* controls the position of the curve on x-axis, and *lift* is a kind of error term that denotes all other non-log-normal factors that shift the curve up the y-axis.

Given a range of dates for a state, e.g., 9/1/2020 – 12/31/2020, my prediction algorithm first calculates initial guesses for *peak* and *shift*. The initial guess for *peak* is the maximum value in the date range. The initial guess for *shift* is the offset from the starting date to the date that the maximum value occurs. I empirically determined the initial guess for the *fat* = 2, and *lift* = 0.

With initial guesses set for the control variables, I use the R non-linear least squares function to determine the actual control variables:

```
CurveModel    = nls(y~peak/10^((log(x/shift)/log(fat))^2)
+ lift, dfCurveToFit,start=list(peak=StateInfo$MaxDayVal,
shift=iMaxDay,fat=2,lift=0), trace=T)
```

Where *dfCurveToFit* is a data frame containing a specific date range of values. I then use the *CurveModel* to generate additional points past the end of the date range, e.g., 12/31/2020, to a future date, e.g., 3/1/2021.

Figure 13 depicts the predicted the level of new cases on March 1, 2021 based on data from September 1, 2020 through December 31, 2020 fit to a log-normal distribution. The model predict that on March 1, 2021, the number of new cases should drop from 1,678 to 262. One can experiment with different date ranges as input and future dates for predictions.

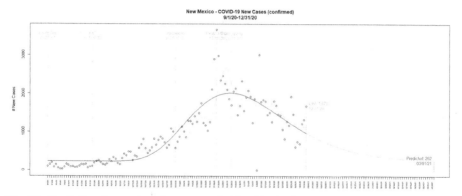

Fig. 13. Predicting the number of new cases in New Mexico based on a log-normal distribution, using September 1, 2020 through December 31, 2020 as input.

5   Summary and Conclusion

The anxiety and helplessness that people experience due to covid-19, derives partly from a lack of information about the virus. One kind of information deficiency concerns the spread of the virus locally, nationally, and globally. Citizens must wait for reports from the mainstream media and for predictions from experts, when the main data set used by both the mainstream media and experts is publicly available, namely the JHU CSSE COVID-19 data.

In this paper I describe eight skills that citizens must acquire to create meaning from covid-19 data sets. I summarize these skills using use-case diagram terminology in Fig. 14. Aside from data cleaning, the coding requirements are not onerous to learn.

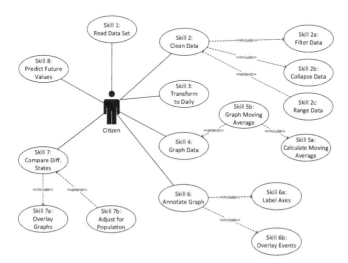

Fig. 14. Key skills citizens need to analyze pandemic data, modeled as a use-case diagram.

Armed with these skills, citizens can generate their own graphs and predictions that they can share on social media. This kind of sharing can lead to a distributed cognitive system for reasoning about possible events that precede rises and falls in the trajectory of the virus, which can then lead to more detailed research on specific causes associated with the events. Furthermore, knowing states and regions that have lower incidences compared to one's own state can suggest further research on specific policies enacted by those states that may be applied to one's own state.

The more important point is that citizens need not be passive consumers of pandemic information. Rather, with the proper set of analytical skills they can be pro-active producers of information and can engage other citizens on social media to reason and to perform further research on the virus. This kind of empowerment, at minimum, may alleviate the anxiety and fears associated with the unknown, and at best engage the power of distributed users to discover policies and procedures that minimize the spread of the virus.

To assist citizens in acquiring these exploratory data analytics skills, I have created an open-source R package, *OpenCitizen* [7], that streamlines many of the skills outlined in this paper into a single R function call. The source code for the package is at:

```
http://github.com/professorf/OpenCitizen
```

Load the package into R with the following commands:

```
install_github("professorf/OpenCitizen")
library(OpenCitizen) }
```

Finally, I have created an open-source repository of vignettes, *Citizen-Analytics* [8], that illustrate how to use the *OpenCitizen* package to visualize, to compare, and to predict the trajectory of the virus, at the county, state, national, and global levels. The repository is at:

```
https://github.com/professorf/citizen-analytics
```

References

1. Dong, E., Du, H., Gardner, L.: An interactive web-based dashboard to track COVID-19 in real time. Lancet Infect. Dis. **20**, 533–534 (2020). https://doi.org/10.1016/S1473-3099(20)30120-1
2. Guo, C., et al.: Meteorological factors and COVID-19 incidence in 190 countries: an observational study. Sci. Total Environ. **757**, 143783 (2021)
3. JHU CSSE: COVID-19 Data Repository by the Center for Systems Science and Engineering (CSSE) at Johns Hopkins University (JHU CSSE COVID-19 Data) (2020). Retrieved from 12 Feb 2021. https://github.com/CSSEGISandData/COVID-19.
4. R Core Team: R: A language and environment for statistical computing. R Foundation for Statistical Computing, Vienna, Austria (2020). https://www.R-project.org/
5. RStudio Team: RStudio: Integrated Development for R. RStudio, PBC, Boston, MA (2020). http://www.rstudio.com/
6. Limpert, E., Stahel, W.A., Abbt, M.: Log-normal distributions across the sciences. Bioscience **51**, 341–352 (2001)

7. Flor, N.: OpenCitizen: An R Package for Pandemic Citizen Analytics. GitHub (2021). https://github.com/professorf/OpenCitizen
8. Flor, N.: Citizen Analytics: Vignettes for the R OpenCitizen Package. GitHub (2021). https://github.com/professorf/Citizen-Analytics

Investigating the User Experience in the Process of Text Mining in Online Social Networks

Jésyka M. A. Gonçalves⬤, Maria L. B. Villela$^{(\boxtimes)}$⬤, Caroline Q. Santos⬤, and Marcus V. C. Guelpeli⬤

Universidade Federal dos Vales do Jequitinhonha e Mucuri, Diamantina, MG, Brazil
marcus.guelpeli@ufvjm.edu.br

Abstract. With the advancement of technologies and the spread of the internet, online social networks have become increasingly popular. Associated with this growth, the volume of digital data made available by these media has significantly increased. In this context, there is an interest on the part of researchers to increasingly use online social networks as a source of data to obtain knowledge and develop important research in all scientific areas. Thus, this work aimed to investigate, through an exploratory and qualitative study, the difficulties and needs of researchers related to the data collection and the other steps of the text mining process in online social networks. The Underlying Discourse Unveiling Method was used to collect and analyze the data. The results show that users are dissatisfied with the existing tools that support them in this process. In addition, the results also highlight the needs of data researchers in order to create a tool that provides them a better user experience during text mining on online social networks (OSN), making this process more effective.

Keywords: Data collection · Text mining · Online social networks

1 Introduction

The great advances of technologies and the popularization of the internet have stimulated the proliferation of social networking. People connected to the network started to replace traditional forms of socialization by digital ones. According to Recuero [15:6], "social networks represent a new and complex universe of communicative, social and discursive phenomena.

In this virtual environment, people freely interact, produce, disseminate and locate information, leaving it up to internet users to judge what is or is not in their interests [7]. Every day, large amounts of content are shared and millions of users interact through social links [2]. This dissemination has enabled the generation and the increasing storage of large amounts of data.

Glimpsing this new place of interaction, researchers from different areas began to use it as a source of information in their studies. Costa [7] justifies this reality when stating that the OSN, in addition to having the social character for which they were developed,

G. Meiselwitz (Ed.): HCII 2021, LNCS 12774, pp. 268–283, 2021.
https://doi.org/10.1007/978-3-030-77626-8_18

also became channels for scientific and empirical studies, serving as a means for data collection and dissemination of results.

In order to extract relevant information from this extensive database, professionals use techniques of extraction and analysis of textual data, which involve the application of computational algorithms that process texts and identify useful and implicit information [4]. This process consists of initially defining the data to be collected, followed by how the collection will be carried out and, finally, how it will be processed and presented. These steps are considered the basis for obtaining data, information and knowledge that aid analysis and decision making [17].

To carry out this process, researchers use different computational tools, which may often have limitations. They do not allow efficient use by their users and also do not take into account the specific needs of their different user profiles. Thus, it is important that system designers and programmers seek to understand how to develop tools that meet those needs, in order to provide a positive user experience to their users [3].

In this work we investigate, through an exploratory study, the experiences and the needs of researchers during the text mining process in OSN, when using tools that support them in this process, more specifically in data collection.

This study was conducted through semi-structured online interviews, with the participation of nine respondents, who carry out scientific research based on data extracted from social media. For the analysis of the collected data, the Underlying Discourse Unveiling Method (UDUM) was used, which is a qualitative research method developed by Nicolaci-da-Costa [12].

Such analysis made possible to extract the main difficulties faced by the respondents when interacting with tools and/or scripts that allow them to perform text mining in OSN. It was also possible, through the analysis of the collected data, to identify their needs during that process.

This research is part of a larger research, which proposes the development of a framework, called *Oráculo* [9], which integrates, in a single tool, the different activities of the text mining process, such as the collection, treatment and visualization of the data. The proposed tool should allow data researchers to schedule collections in OSN, and then treat the collected data, so that they can be used in the most diverse types of analysis, in order to extract knowledge from them. Thus, the results obtained here contribute to the construction of the user layer of the framework *Oráculo*.

Therefore, the knowledge obtained from this research is important for the areas of Text Mining (TM) and Human–Computer Interaction (HCI), because it can be applied in the generation of interaction models and tool interfaces that meet the needs of users, in the collection, treatment, visualization and analysis of OSN data. With this, it is envisioned to provide data researchers with a better experience with the use of tools that assist them in text mining, and, consequently, give them greater effectiveness in this process.

This work is organized as follows: the next section presents concepts related to text mining in OSN, followed by the works related to the present study. Then, the methodology used is presented and, later, the results obtained and the discussion about them are shown. Lastly, the conclusions and the next steps of this research are described.

2   Text Mining in Online Social Networks

With the growth in the number of users and the content generated by them, OSN, such as Facebook, Twitter, Foursquare, Instagram and others, have become a very rich source of information for companies, governments and researchers. Understanding the immense scope and advantages of this new form of communication, can bring great benefits [11]. Currently, there are refined computational techniques that allow the analysis of this massive volume of data in order to obtain useful knowledge from them.

Such techniques lie within a process known as text mining. This process consists of a set of activities that include the use of techniques, based on models, capable of finding patterns, summarizing data or making predictions, in order to extract new knowledge based on large volumes of data [19].

Text mining in OSN covers the stages of collection, pre-processing, indexing, mining, visualization and analysis, as it can be seen in Fig. 1.

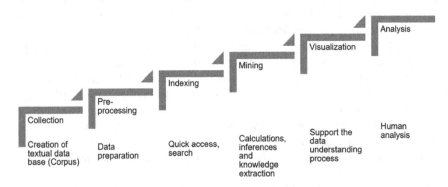

Fig. 1.   Text mining process. adapted from [1]

In this process, the initial stage is the collection and it aims to form a textual database, known in the literature as Corpus. Basically, in this stage the data that will be analyzed are collected. The pre-processing stage aims to improve the quality of the collected data and organize it, promoting some formatting and representation of the textual mass obtained in the previous stage. In this stage, all irrelevant terms in the text are removed, which should not be considered in the mining process, known as stopwords. Then, in the indexing stage, all acquired terms are organized and recognized, facilitating their access and retrieval, and ensuring agility to the data localization process. In the mining stage, techniques for the extraction of knowledge are applied, through calculations, inferences and algorithms whose objective is the discovery of important patterns and behaviors to be observed [1]. In the visualization stage, data are represented in a language that is easier for users to understand, such as graphics and visual concepts [20]. And finally, there is the stage of analysis and interpretation of data. This stage is performed through the search for patterns and/or analysis of the previously obtained views, in order to support concerned parties in their decision making [1].

3   Related Studies

Text mining in online social networks is an area of research that has considerably grown in recent years. Numerous researches have focused on developing and improving computational techniques that support the different activities that compose text mining. However, there are still few studies that explore this process, either as a whole or with a specific focus on any of its activities, considering the experience and needs of those concerned.

In this regard, Brooks [3] investigated, through an ethnographic study, how researchers work with data collected from social media, seeking to better understand the analysis process. Based on the ethnographic study, the author discusses the implications of using a new technology to expand the scope of the analysis. In addition, two design proposals to support this activity are discussed: one considers the visual exploration of data and the other makes use of collaboration in online data analysis.

Still aiming to understand the needs of social media data researchers, Santos et al. [18] focused specifically on visualization, when investigating whether data analysts know and use visualization and how important they consider it. Through semi-structured interviews, the authors collected information that allowed them to discover that social media data analysts know the concept of data visualization and believe that its use can significantly improve the analysis process. In a second study, Santos et al. [17], also through a qualitative exploratory study, sought to understand how visualization can help social media data analysts understand the data and make decisions. The results reveal that social media analysts are aware of the existing visualization tools and highlight their needs, in order to provide a basis for the design of new tools for this purpose.

Chen et al. [6] also conducted a formative study, based on interviews with social scientists, to understand their needs, practices and restrictions in working with social media data. Based on the results obtained, the authors developed an exploratory visual analysis tool for social media data, which supports the construction and visualization of categories, in order to help researchers discover and refine important categories of content, and also compare and analyze categories with visualizations and statistical summaries.

There are also studies that aim to describe or understand stages of the text mining process on social media, considering that data researchers who perform these steps may be from different areas of knowledge. In this sense, Chen et al. [5] describe the characteristics, elements and chronological process of analyzing social media data from the perspective of an academic in the field of mass communication. The objective is to present the chronological process in which a researcher deals with social media data in the form of case studies. Marques and Vidigal [10] verified, through semi-structured interviews with professionals from different companies, how social networks are used in the data collection phase, with a focus on competitive intelligence as a fundamental tool for a company to stand out from its competitors.

Cribbin et al. [8] propose a set of methodologies to support the analysis of social media data. To implement these methodologies, the authors present a software tool that illustrates a data visual analytical approach, by using data visualizations from Twitter as an instrument for the formation and hypothesis search by analysts.

The studies mentioned above explore the activities and needs of data researchers, as well as the use of OSN, in specific stages of the text mining process, such as collection

[10], visualization [6, 8, 17, 18] and analysis [3, 5, 6, 8]. However, we have not found researches that address the experiences and needs of data researchers, with regard to data collection, but also taking into account the other activities of the text mining process in OSN, in an integrated manner, as it is the case of this work. The research described in [10], while also focusing on data collection, deals specifically with the use of OSN at this stage, rather than the collection process itself and the experience it provides to data researchers.

4 Methodology

This study was guided by the following research question: "How is the experience of data researchers in the process of text mining in social media, taking data collection as a starting point?". In order to direct the discussion of the results, this research question was divided into the following specific questions: "What are the **difficulties** faced by data researchers during text mining in OSN, taking data collection as a starting point?" (Q1) and "What are the **needs** of data researchers in the text mining process in OSN, taking data collection as a starting point?" (Q2).

In order to answer these questions, an in-depth exploratory study was carried out, by conducting semi-structured interviews, applying the Underlying Discourse Unveiling Method (UDUM) [12].

UDUM is a qualitative research method, which allows systematic analysis of discursive material. This method does not start from a pre-defined hypothesis, but from an open question. Its use is more appropriate than a quantitative method, when one wishes to understand a question still unknown. It is qualitative, so it is also characterized by the fact that it seeks greater depth and detail than a quantitative method, which favors general knowledge. To reach this depth, it involves a laborious process, which is why it uses small samples [12].

The steps established by UDUM were rigorously applied in this research. They are: 1 - Outline of the objectives to be achieved; 2 - Recruitment of participants, determining the sample of people who participated in the study, to which an invitation was sent by email; 3 - Preparation for data collection, which consisted of defining the topics to be addressed during the interviews, as well as preparing the Consent Term, contemplating the ethical guidelines of the research to be clarified to the respondents; 4 - Data collection, which consisted of conducting semi-structured interviews with the respondents; 5 - Preparation for data analysis, when the transcription and organization of the audios of the interviews occurred, for later analysis; 6 - Analysis of the collected data, when the analysis of the respondents' discourse was performed; and, finally, the last step, 7 - Interpretation of the results, when the categories that emerged from the speeches of the respondents were determined.

The steps mentioned above are described in more detail below, grouped into two topics: Preparation and Conducting interviews.

4.1 Preparation

For the collection of data for the research, nine participants were recruited, whose profiles are described in Table 1.

Table 1. Participants profiles

ID	Age	Occupation	Study field
P1	50	Higher education teacher	Computing
P2	34	Information technology analyst	Computing
P3	33	High school/technical teacher	Education
P4	28	Developer	Computing
P5	28	Technical support scholarship holder	Social communication
P6	28	Developer	Computing
P7	34	Higher education teacher	Social communication
P8	26	Scientific initiation scholarship holder	Journalism
P9	40	Higher education teacher	Computing

Participants were selected from the contact network of the authors, with researchers working with social media data collection and analysis, in different higher education institutions in Brazil. The recruited participants should know the text mining process in OSN and have performed data collection in scientific research to participate in this study. This requirement was established as a way to standardize the profile of the participants and reduce the external factors that could influence their responses, following the recommendations on high definition profiles, described by UDUM.

The script[1] of the semi-structured interview addressed 20 open and closed questions, divided into three thematic blocks: the first block brought questions about the information of the educational and professional profile of the participant; the second block asked about the computational experience; and, finally, the third block sought to collect information about the experience and satisfaction of users when carrying out their data collection activities in the text mining process in OSN. The last block of questions had more specific questions on the research topic, such as questions about how participants perform collections in OSN and whether they are satisfied with the way they perform those collections. There were questions about how they proceed with the data collected, in the execution of the text mining process, and what their difficulties they face when carrying out these activities. There were also questions that aimed at explicitly identifying the needs and recommendations of the participants for the interface of a possible new tool that would allow them to carry out their activities more efficiently and effectively.

4.2 Conducting Interviews

The interviews were conducted in March 2019, online, and had an average duration of 34 min. The decision to conduct the interviews online was made because most of the participants, six of them, were located in different cities from the one where the researcher who conducted the interviews was.

---

[1] Available at: https://drive.google.com/file/d/1nr6rLSDgBRlZrie_ichFimEHMysXadCZ/view? usp=sharing.

Before starting the interviews with the selected participants, a pilot test was carried out with a university professor who fit the same profile as the participants. The participation was voluntary, with prior acceptance of the invitation sent. All the participants read the Informed Consent sent by e-mail and returned it duly signed, before the beginning of the interview.

After conducting the interviews, as a stage of preparation for data analysis, the transcription of the audios of the interviews was carried out.

The stage of data analysis, as guided by UDUM, was carried out through the analysis of inter-subjects and intra-subjects [12]. The first consisted of analyzing the responses given by the group as a whole, where all the responses of all participants to each of the questions were analyzed systematically and rigorously. The second part of the analysis consisted of analyzing each interview individually, with the responses of each of the interviewees being approached as a single set, being analyzed possible conflicts of opinion, contradictory feelings, inconsistency between responses and others. After performing these two parts iteratively, it was possible to identify common recurrences in the participants' statements, described in the next section.

5   Results

UDUM is based on the assumption that the more recurrent an idea is identified, the more likely it is to have been socially constructed. Therefore, the categories for analysis are established based on the common recurrences presented in the participants' discourses. Therefore, five categories were identified, presented below. In this paper, all participants' quotations were translated from Portuguese into English.

5.1   The Interfaces of Existing Tools for Collecting Social Media Data are Difficult to Use

We sought to find the perception and contentment of the interviewees in relation to the existing data collection tools in OSN, in order to verify whether they used them and what their experience was like. Thus, it was observed that the participants present, in general, difficulties not only to use such tools, but also to install and configure them, which leads to an ineffective use.

Most participants reported that they had difficulty using the tools due to unfriendly interfaces, as can be seen in the statement of participant P3: "*the difficulty exists because all tools lack a friendlier graphic interface, so that the users can identify exactly where they can search and collect more objectively*". Participant P6 agrees by stating that: "*the interface of the tools in general were just search and filter fields with some loose, undocumented and quite confusing buttons*".

Therefore, the use of the resources made available by the collection tools is compromised, because little information is transmitted to users through its interface, and, when they are, it is often done in a confusing way.

Some respondents even talked about it, showing dissatisfaction, as can be seen in the statements of participant P4: "In the free tools I have used, there is not a part of the interface that I liked, because they were very simple, but not as neat and intuitive. There are some very confusing options on the collection screen, and there is no menu option". Participant P7 also reports this difficulty: "*I think the information clutter can create some barriers. There are several tab information that can be accessed, and because of that the information is very loose on the screen and we have to try and find exactly what works for us. Not all the resources found on the screen will always be used in a data collection, then this is the greatest difficulty*".

Difficulties also occur during installation and configuration of the tools. Participant P6 expresses this perception: "*The interface is not friendly, so it creates a distance, a tension when you open it, because you need a server, and you need to connect and set this server up and you need to know how to do it. I get very lost when I have to do it by myself. Its information does not lead you, in fact you have to know where you are going to insert everything before you start the collecting phase*". This difficulty is also clear in the statements of participant P7: "*the main difficulty I faced, I even needed help from a colleague, is the configuration. Since we are often from areas that do not have a lot knowledge in the programming area, we end up being held hostage by the basic settings of the platform, and when we need to do any type of modification or adaptation for our project, we have a huge difficulty in doing it*".

It is known that data collection tools have complex functionalities, and such complexity is recognized by the participants. However, the low quality of the interfaces of these tools prevents users from performing data collection efficiently, driving them frustrated and discontent, as can be seen in the statement of participant P7: "*I understand the degree of complexity of the platforms and that is why we really need help with the processing of this data there, but I find it very complicated and frustrating when I work with a tool that requires a couple of complementary tutorials for understanding its functioning to really get to the result I would like. The tool's interface should provide me with more information, be more intuitive*".

This usage difficulty contributes to the ineffectiveness of data collection on social media, by not allowing the user to use the tool to fully achieve its objective. This can be seen in the statement of participant P3: "*The user does not know what the tool offers, if it had a friendly interface it would be possible to use all the resources available*".

5.2 Collecting Data from Social Media is a Task Aimed More at Professionals in the Field of Computing, With Knowledge in Computer Programming

When asked about which tools they use most to perform the collections, most participants reported that they often prefer not to use any. Thus, the development of scripts was mentioned as one of the most used ways of collecting data from social media.

As the creation of scripts requires specific knowledge related to logic and programming languages, lay users in computing, who need to collect data from OSN to carry out their research, are hampered in the execution of this type of task.

The participants expressed their understanding that social media data collection is currently more focused on people who have at least intermediate knowledge in computer programming and other approaches related to computer science. This can be confirmed by the statement of participant P9: "*I believe that what I did during my doctorate would not be feasible for a person who did not have the training and knowledge in computing and programming (...) it would be necessary to create an interface and simpler ways for a lay person in computing to carry out the collections*". The speech of participant P5 also reflects the need for specific knowledge in programming to make use of scripts in data collection: "*When working with scripts we have typical script problems, like installing a library, missing pieces of code (...) in short, programming things, even though not everyone has knowledge*".

From the participants' answers, we could observe that the use of scripts for data collection is precisely a consequence of the low quality of use of the existing tools. P5 highlights this in his statement: "*So, in the end, for the bulk of the research I ended up using a handful of Python scripts that I developed with a friend, because I needed data that the tool didn't provide me*".

Some participants went beyond data collection, mentioning that they also use scripts in the other stages of the text mining process, as can be seen in the statement of P9: "*The data was collected using scripts, and through scripts I also cleaned the collected data that were invalid, incomplete, useless or unrelated to the research. Then I used some technique to process the data, such as Machine Learning, Text or Data Mining, Natural Language Processing and others, but in none of these I used a tool, I did everything through code*".

5.3   The Use of Different Tools for the Different Stages of the Social Media Text Mining Process Makes It More Complex

Usually, different tools are used for the collection, mining, treatment, visualization and analysis of data from social media, in order to extract valid knowledge from the information collected. Participant P7, for example, illustrates this by saying: "*I take the data and when I want graphs of relationships from this data I use Tableau; but when I want graphs that are references between colored dots, I use Gephi*".

In the text mining process, when using different tools, the participants reported that they encounter several difficulties. In addition to the problems with the low quality of the interfaces of these tools, there is still incompatibility between the different tools. This is due to the different formats of data to be exported and imported by them, which often allows only experienced professionals, with specific knowledge in Computing, to execute the process, returning to what was exposed in the previous category.

Participant P1 clearly presents this difficulty in his statement: "*we treated data, but not with tools; we collected and did it through spreadsheets or external tools, separately. We fell into that problem of having to use a lot of tools to reach a result*". Participant P6, who has a background in computing and works supporting other researchers in the text mining process in OSN, reveals this difficulty by saying: "*Converting the tabulated data into data that could be imported and visualized required a lot of technical knowledge that some people, who are not in a STEM related field of study, had a lot of difficulty to do, so it was very up to me to convert this data so that they could do the part they were familiar with*".

Such difficulties point to the importance of creating unique tools, which allow the researcher to perform all the steps of the text mining process, which consist of collecting, visualizing and analyzing data from social media, in an integrated way and in a single location. Which is glimpsed in the statement of P1: "*I think this part is essential, being able to use the same tool that we collect to see the results is very interesting. Grouping everything in one place (…) even for people who have knowledge in this area, assembling all these tools, and getting a result from it, is very difficult".*

5.4 New Features Should Be Added to the Tools to Provide Greater Precision in Data Collection and Other Activities of the Text Mining Process, in Addition to Greater Flexibility to Users

When asked about what they consider essential in tools that support the process of collecting and mining texts in OSN, most respondents pointed out the integration of features that would suit them more fully in their research in these environments.

The main and most mentioned functionality by most respondents was related to the temporality of collections, in other words, the possibility of carrying out collections in real time and retroactive collections using the same tool. This is shown in the statement of participant P1: *"For the collection area in social networks, the functionality that I think is essential (…) is collection time, in real time or retroactive. This functionality is very important".* In addition to this feature, the possibility of providing a preview of the data for analysis, still in the collection time, was also mentioned a lot. Participant P6, for example, talks about this: *"(…) it would provide some types of analysis already in real time, for example displaying graphs or the number of words".*

Another feature widely mentioned for a new tool was the possibility of making different settings for the collection, from options offered to the users on the data they aim to collect, providing them with greater flexibility in this process. Participant P7, for example, aims to use several different types of terms for the collection: *"I often use extraction via keywords or hashtags, so it is very much important to be able to collect, within the same collection, several configurable options for hashtags and keywords".* Participant P9 mentions the possibility of working with different languages: *"I would like to be offered the option of choosing the language of the text I want to collect, for example, only tweets in Portuguese or English, or in any other language".* P7 envisions the possibility of carrying out broader research: *"for me it is very much important to be able to collect, within the same collection, hashtags and keywords and have the possibility of placing an intersection or union between collection terms".* Participant P5 talks about the possibility of the user being able to direct the collection to a specific subset of the data: *"(…) you can select, for example, which part of the database you want, this is very interesting, because it allows you not to use the entire database, if you don't need to".*

In addition to the flexibility in data collection, another need pointed out by the participants for a new tool was the addition of pre-processing the terms and treating the collected data, in order to provide greater precision in the data collection and analysis. The pre-processing of collection terms refers to obtaining versions of these terms without accent, cedilla, etc., and then submitting them into the collection. Participant P4 highlights this need: *"treating the terms for the collection, as a pre-processing, for example, accentuation of words, re-tweets, cedilla, tilde and others, already being solved during the collection".* Regarding the treatment of the collected data, the most mentioned functionality was the organization of the data at the time of extraction, as shown by the statement of participant P6: *"(…) extract these tabulated data and also extract others, such as word cloud and different types of graphs, or even organized in directories".*

5.5   Improvements in the Interface of Social Media Text Mining Tools to Provide Better Interaction with the User

When asked about what improvements they would make to the interface of the tools that support the text mining process in OSN, the participants were unanimous in stating that they would make them easy to use, clean and intuitive, characteristics that are essential for them to be more effective in their researches. That happened because of the difficulties when using the existing tools used for data collection, pointed out by the participants and described in category 5.1. The statements of participants P3 and P4 summarize what was said by the others: *"The improvements would really be an interface that facilitates the use of the tool"* (P3) and *"improvements related to the design of the screen, would make it more clean and intuitive, with fewer paths to follow to reach a configuration or to perform the collection itself"* (P4).

Participant P9 mentions an interesting feature, regarding the availability of help options and better elaborated documentation: *"In the existing interfaces there are practically no icons, but also with a certain frequency when placing icons it is difficult to understand its purpose. Having a better documentation and some aesthetic improvements would be interesting, since some tools are quite odd to use"*.

6   Discussion

From the analysis of the data collected through the interviews, we were able to identify the main difficulties and needs of the participants about the tools used in the text mining process in OSN.

Initially, it was possible to observe that the participants know the available tools and understand how important they are to support them in the collection process. It was noticed that all participants know what they want to collect and what they intend to analyze in a set of data, which leads them to have a more critical view on such tools.

Therefore, answering Q1 ("What are the difficulties faced by data researchers during text mining in OSN, taking data collection as a starting point?"), we identified that the difficulties are primarily related to the low quality of use of tool interfaces, which negatively impact user interaction.

This fact leads data researchers to even give up using such tools, often opting to use scripts to carry out their activities, which is not easy either, especially for those who have no computer training. The participants report that they think the cost of learning about programming languages and some specific aspects of computing, necessary to use scripts, even though it is high, it is still less than the cost of using the existing tools.

Using scripts can also turn the activities of the text mining process on social media restricted to professionals with more specific knowledge of programming and computing. It is more difficult for professionals in other areas to carry out such activities, as it is the case with journalists and advertising professionals, among others, who have the need to analyze data from social media. In addition, considering the entire text mining process in OSN, compatibility issues between the tools used in the different stages make it even more difficult for users to interact. Such difficulties frustrate data researchers, negatively impacting the effectiveness of their research, which generates dissatisfaction in relation to the way the data are collected and analyzed.

In order to address this dissatisfaction and overcome the difficulties of researchers in the process of collecting and analyzing data from OSN, we sought to identify their needs, answering Q2 ("What are the needs of data researchers in the text mining process in OSN, taking data collection as a starting point?"). The answer to this question is presented in a similar way to the presentation of the results in [17]. The needs of the participants were summarized in a figure, in addition to the creation of personas to represent groups of users of text mining tools, focusing on data collection.

Thus, from the discourses of the participants in this study, we identified four needs, shown in Fig. 2, which must be met in order to make the activities of the text mining process in OSN more effective: (1) Use unique tools to treat, in an integrated manner, all stages of the text mining process; (2) Provide greater precision in the collection and analysis of data; (3) Provide data researchers with greater flexibility in the process of collecting and analyzing social media data; and (4) Quality in user interaction.

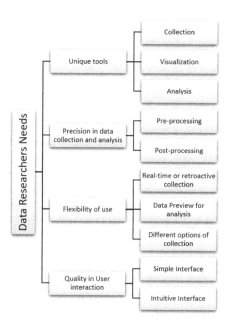

Fig. 2. Data researchers' needs for social media data collection tools

We can see that such needs reflect the importance of considering usability aspects in the design of tools to be used by researchers in the text mining process.

Specifically, the development of unique tools to meet all the activities of this process, the precision in the collection and analysis of data and the flexibility of use refer to "efficiency of use". This usability factor is related to the productivity of the users when using the system to carry out their activities [13].

Therefore, by offering the user a single tool that allows them to perform all the tasks of the text mining process in an integrated manner, they will be able to achieve their goals more quickly, once that they will not have to make use of different tools and, consequently, will not have the cost of learning or converting data to deal with incompatibility issues between tools.

In addition, by offering users automated ways of pre-processing collection terms and processing the collected data, the accuracy of data collection and analysis will be ensured by the tool itself, saving the user from having to perform these tasks manually. This will allow the user to also perform their tasks in a more efficient way.

By providing greater flexibility to the data researcher in the phase of setting how the collection will be carried out, the tool also provides greater control to the user in order to obtain the data in a broader or more specific way, as necessary, without having to manipulate it or make additional collections to meet their specific needs.

The quality of the interaction with the user of these tools, provided by simple and intuitive interfaces, refers to the usability factors "easy to learn" and "easy to remember how to use it" [13]. That is quite evident, because when interacting with a friendly interface, the user will not have difficulties to learn how to use the tool or to remember how to access its functionalities, after not using it for a while.

Finally, meeting the needs of the researchers, shown in Fig. 2, will provide them greater satisfaction in their use. Usability will lead to a positive user experience, related to the emotions and feelings aroused while interacting with the system [16]. The importance of considering the user experience in the design of tools that support the activities of the text mining process in OSN can be justified by the difficulties, identified during interviews, users faced while using existing tools.

Based on the identified needs and the profile information of the participants in this study, two personas were created [14]. They represent the groups of users of the tools used in the text mining process in OSN, according to their perceptions, usage experiences and needs. As in [17], the personas are divided into two groups: 1) users who are proficient in the text mining process, with knowledge of techniques and tools for that purpose; and 2) lay users, with little or no skills with such tools.

Persona 1, shown in Table 2, represents data researchers from Computing areas, with knowledge in programming languages. They have knowledge about the computational tools that support the text mining process in OSN, but, in most cases, they prefer to develop scripts to carry out their activities. Their main needs are related to having greater precision in the collection and analysis of data and greater flexibility of use when performing these activities. However, they also want to have a quality interaction with the tools that support them in their work.

Persona 2, shown in Table 3, represents researchers who have little or no computer knowledge, but need to obtain information from social media to carry out their work. They have difficulty using the existing tools and need the help of professionals in the Computing area to perform the configuration of the tools, and even to assist them in the process of data collection. Their needs are basically the ones shown in Fig. 2.

It is worth noting, as a limitation of the present study, the size of the sample, as well as its non-randomness, which may compromise its generalization potential. However, the balance between the number of participants from the Computing area (5) and from other areas (4) means that the sample is properly diversified in relation to the different backgrounds of data researchers.

Table 2. Persona 1

Name: Caetano Leite	Age: 36

Caetano has a degree in Computer Science. He works at a university and does research from textual databases, collecting and analyzing data on online social networks to discover knowledge in different areas. He is proficient in carrying out activities of the text mining process on these systems and he also helps colleagues who work with the same purpose. Data collection is carried out, most of the time, through scripts that he develops himself. In each collection, Caetano needs to go to the university laboratory, either to develop scripts or to make some configuration in tools to visualize or treat the collected data. He understands the complexity of the activities involved in the text mining process, and does not mind having to make settings to adapt the tools to his needs, but he would like them to have a more intuitive interface, thus allowing the process to be carried out efficiently and pleasantly.

Table 3. Persona 2

Name: Paula Braga	Age: 32

Paula has a degree in journalism and currently holds a master's degree in social communication. She conducts research based on textual databases, collecting and analyzing data on social networks. Paula does not use tools for the data collection and visualization process, as she considers them very difficult to use. Sometimes, she uses textual tools only to assist her in the analysis process, which she considers an obstacle. In each collection, she needs to go to the university laboratory, to find a colleague to help her with the settings or even with the development of scripts so that she can continue with her research. She is really frustrated because she depends on other people to do her job. Thus, she would like to learn how to configure and use the existing tools, because she believes that she could complete her master's research with greater agility and confidence.

The analysis and interpretation of the data collected in this study allowed a greater understanding of the universe of research and the needs of researchers who work with text mining in OSN, in relation to the tools that support them in this process. It was possible to understand that, even though it is a complex approach, everyone believes that the process would be facilitated if unique and intuitive tools were made available.

The results indicated that professionals who work using already available tools are unsatisfied with them. This fact often leads them to use strategies for data collection and analysis that require more specific knowledge in the area of Computing, which not all of them have.

In addition, the study also highlights the needs of data researchers in order to create a tool, whose design can provide users with greater effectiveness during the collection, visualization and analysis of data from online social networks. We discussed the results by considering the relationship between the difficulties faced by the participants in this study and the low quality of use of the interfaces of the existing data collection tools. We also discussed their needs of tools that have high usability and provide them with a better user experience.

The results obtained contribute to the areas of HCI and text mining, since they bring considerations about relevant aspects for the design and evaluation of tools for collecting, visualizing and analyzing data from OSN. The difficulties faced by data researchers, especially in the data collection process, as well as their needs, are a first step towards creating a tool that allows them to be more effective in their text mining work in OSN, proposed in the context of the framework *Oráculo* [9].

Thus, the next step of this research will be to design a tool, focusing on its interaction with the user, in a way that addresses the needs of data researchers, pointed out in this paper. In addition, it is intended to evaluate such design with its users, through a functional prototype, in order to verify whether their needs will in fact be met by the tool.

Acknowledgements. We acknowledge all participants in the study conducted for this paper, for their collaboration and contributions.

References

1. Aranha, C., Passos, E.: A tecnologia de mineração de textos. Revista Eletrônica de Sistemas de Informação, **5**(2) (2006) https://doi.org/10.21529/RESI.2006.0502001
2. Benevenuto, F.: Redes Sociais Online: Técnicas de Coleta e Abordagens de Medição. Sociedade Brasileira de Computação (2010)
3. Brooks, M.: Human centered tools for analyzing online social data (Doctoral dissertation) (2015)
4. Cardoso, O.N.P., Machado, R.T.M.: Gestão do conhecimento usando data mining: estudo de caso na Universidade Federal de Lavras. Revista de administração pública **42**(3), 495–528 (2008). https://doi.org/10.1590/S0034-76122008000300004
5. Chen, P.L., Cheng, Y.C., Chen, K.: Analysis of social media data: an introduction to the characteristics and chronological process. In: Chen, S.H. (ed.) Big Data in Computational Social Science and Humanities. Computational Social Sciences. Springer, Cham (2018). https://doi.org/10.1007/978-3-319-95465-3_16.
6. Chen, N.C., et al.: Lariat: a visual analytics tool for social media researchers to explore Twitter datasets. In: Proceedings of the 50th Hawaii International Conference on System Sciences (2017). https://doi.org/10.24251/HICSS.2017.228.
7. Costa, B.R.L.: Bola de neve virtual: O uso das redes sociais virtuais no processo de coleta de dados de uma pesquisa científica. Revista Interdisciplinar de Gestão Social **7**(1) (2018). https://doi.org/10.9771/23172428rigs.v7i1.24649.
8. Cribbin, T., Barnett, J., Brooker, P.: Doing social media analytics. Big Data Soc. **3**(2) (2016). https://doi.org/10.1177/2053951716658060
9. de Oliveira, H.B., Guelpeli, M.V.C.: Performance analysis of the Oráculo framework for data collection from Twitter. Brazilian J. Dev. **6**(12), 100969–100986 (2020)
10. Marques, L.K.D.S., Vidigal, F.: Prosumers e redes sociais como fontes de informação mercadológica: uma análise sob a perspectiva da inteligência competitiva em empresas brasileiras. Transinformação **30**(1), 1–14 (2018). https://doi.org/10.1590/2318-08892018000100001
11. Martins, R.F., Pereira, A., Benevenuto, F.: An approach to sentiment analysis of web applications in portuguese. In: Proceedings of the 21st Brazilian Symposium on Multimedia and the Web, pp. 105–112 (2015). https://doi.org/10.1145/2820426.2820446.
12. Nicolaci-da-Costa, A.M., Leitão, C.F., Romão-Dias, D.: Como conhecer usuários através do Método de Explicitação do Discurso Subjacente (MEDS). VI Simpósio Brasileiro sobre Fatores Humanos em Sistemas Computacionais, IHC, pp. 47–56 (2004).

13. Nielsen, J.: Usability Engineering. Morgan Kaufmann, San Francisco, CA, USA (1994)
14. Pruitt, J., Adlin, T.: The Persona Lifecycle: Keeping People in Mind Throughout Product Design. Elsevier (2010)
15. Recuero, R.: Contribuições da Análise de Redes Sociais para o estudo das redes sociais na Internet: o caso da hashtag# Tamojuntodilma e# CalaabocaDilma. Fronteiras-estudos midiáticos **16**(2), 60–77 (2014). https://doi.org/10.4013/fem.2014.162.01
16. Rogers, Y., Sharp, H., Preece, J.: Interaction Design: Beyond Human-Computer Interaction. John Wiley & Sons (2011)
17. Santos, C.Q., Silveira, M.S.: What do social media data analysts want? An analysis from the perspective of data visualization. In: Proceedings of the 17th Brazilian Symposium on Human Factors in Computing Systems, pp. 1–4 (2018). https://doi.org/10.1145/3274192.3274246.
18. Santos, C.Q., Silveira, M.S., Manssour, I.H.: Visualization and Social Media Data Analysis: preliminary studies about data analysts' perception. In: Proceedings of the 15th Brazilian Symposium on Human Factors in Computing Systems, pp. 1–4 (2016). https://doi.org/10.1145/3033701.3033737.
19. Tan, A.H.: Text mining: tthe state of the art and the challenges. In: Proceedings of the PAKDD 1999 Workshop on Knowledge Disocovery from Advanced Databases, vol. 8, pp. 65–70. Sn (1999)
20. Ward, M.O., Grinstein, G., Keim, D.: Interactive Data Visualization: Foundations, Techniques, and Applications. CRC Press (2010)

Analysis of User Relationships on Cooking Recipe Site Using Network Structure

Yuzuki Kitajima[1]([✉]), Kohei Otake[2], and Takashi Namatame[3]

[1] Graduate School of Science and Engineering, Chuo University, 1-13-27 Kasuga, Bunkyo-ku, Tokyo 112-8551, Japan
a16.tdsm@g.chuo-u.ac.jp
[2] School of Information and Telecommunication Engineering, Tokai University, 2-3-23 Takanawa, Minato-ku, Tokyo 108-8619, Japan
otake@tsc.u-tokai.ac.jp
[3] Faculty of Science and Engineering, Chuo University, 1-13-27 Kasuga, Bunkyo-ku, Tokyo 112-8551, Japan
nama@indsys.chuo-u.ac.jp

Abstract. User Generated Contents (UGC) is one of representative tools to grow and make popular internet. In many UGCs, some influential users and groups exists, and various studies focused on these users. In recent years, "user-generated cooking recipe sites" have also been populated, and many consumers can post their own recipes. Many studies on recipe sites focus on evaluation of recipes, such as the number of evaluators and average scores. However, there are few studies focused on user relationships on cooking recipe site. In this study, we assume that cooking recipe sites have a user relationship structure similar to social media. Then, we aim to identify the relationship among users on cooking recipe site. Specifically, we use network analysis to visualize the relationship between recipe contributors and Reviewers on Japanese recipe sites. In addition, we used Modularity for community detection to identify similar groups and influential users.

Keywords: Customer review · Cooking recipe · Network analysis · PageRank

1 Introduction

Since the appearance of smartphones, our lives became more convenient. In recent years, various digital platforms have been emerging along with the popularization of internet. In Japan, Amazon and Yahoo! Japan are known as representative shopping platforms in Japan. Similarly, Spotify and Apple Music also known as famous music streaming platforms. In the same way, Cookpad and Rakuten Recipe Site are known as popular cooking recipes platforms in Japan. These cooking recipe sites are one of the most visited User Generated Contents (UGC).

UGC is a general term for media in which content is posted by ordinal consumers, not professionals or entertainers. It has characteristic the content is activated by interaction

© Springer Nature Switzerland AG 2021
G. Meiselwitz (Ed.): HCII 2021, LNCS 12774, pp. 284–300, 2021.
https://doi.org/10.1007/978-3-030-77626-8_19

among users. There are various types of UGC. Social Networking Services (SNSs) and video sharing services are also UGC. In addition, Blog is also a typical service of UGCs.

In this study, we target a cooking recipe site in Japan. We think cooking recipe site has similar structure as blog. About blog, some studies focused on link structure. Taniguchi et al. [1] investigated that Japanese blog community using PageRank. Iida et al. [2] performed community detection using Modularity, they used the Japanese Wikipedia and visualized human connections from page links. Besides, they suggested that community detection could identify users who influence other people, such as who influence a famous blogger.

As research on cooking recipe sites, there are many studies focusing on "recipes", for example, what recipe has high evaluation or what similar recipes are [3, 4]. On the other hand, few studies have focused on relationship among users on cooking recipe site. We assumed that there are popular users and community with similar cooking preferences in cooking recipe site.

2   Purpose of This Study

In this study, we aim to identify the relationship between cooking recipe post side (Reciper) and user who makes it (Reviewer), or the persons who does both of posted recipe and made the other Reciper's recipe. Then we identify the good recipe creator and and key user for the users on the cooking recipe site. Key user is those who influence popular Recipers.

Specifically, using the Rakuten recipe dataset, which is one of the user-generated recipe sites, the connections among recipe contributors and review contributors are represented by a network by cooking genre, and the relationships between users in each cooking category. We also consider the top users having influence in each category.

3   Data Summary

We aim to identify the relationship between Recipers and Reviewers on cooking recipe site. In this chapter, we explain the "Rakuten Recipe Datasets" used in this analysis.

In this research, we used "Recipe Data" and "Review Data" from "Rakuten Datasets" [5] (Tables 1 and 2).

Table 1. Recipe dataset

Dataset name	Rakuten recipe data
Data period	July 1, 2010–Oct 1, 2015
Users	1,059 (Users)
Recipes	37,092 (Recipe posts)
Columns	Recipe ID, Reciper ID, Recipe Title, Category, Subcategory, Date (upload)

Table 2. Review data

Dataset name	Rakuten recipe review data
Data period	Aug 27, 2010–Oct 2, 2015
Users	6,012 (Users)
Reviews	115,337 (Reviews)
Columns	Recipe ID, Reviewer ID, Comments (from Reviewer), Comments (from Reciper), Date (reviewed)

The target user of the recipe data is the person who posted the recipe with at least one review. In this data, 334 users in Tables 1 and 2 were duplicate users. This indicates some users post not only recipes but also review.

In addition, we analyzed by category in this study. There are 43 main cooking categories on cooking recipe site. We selected major 6 cooking categories that can be treated as the main cooking category and that have more than 1,000 recipes posted. These category tags were added by Recipers. Table 3 shows our selected cooking categories list.

Table 3. Details for each select cooking categories

Category name	Number of recipes	Details
Vegetable	6,931	More detailed tags are added by the user such as tomatoes, cucumbers, and potatoes
Bread	2,936	For example, hot sandwiches and yeast bread
Rice dish	2,821	Rice is indispensable for Japanese food. This category includes rice balls, sushi, etc
Meat	2,508	Includes Japanese classic meat dishes. For example, Pork cutlet, Chicken nanban
Dessert	2,241	Various dessert, cookies, chocolate, donuts, etc
Fish	1,389	Includes Japanese fish dishes using horse mackerel and saury

4 Analysis of User Relationships on Cooking Recipe Site

In this study, we identify the user relationships between Recipers and Reviewers using network analysis. In this section, we explain the analysis procedure. Specifically, we describe the PageRank algorithm used to identify users with high importance and the weights used to calculate the PageRank. Next, we explain the modularity used for community detection. Finally, we introduce the flow of analysis.

4.1 Most Popular Users for Each Cooking Category

PageRank is used as an indicator of user importance, in this study. PageRank is one of the Search Ranking Algorithms invented by Page and Brin [6] in 1998.

In general, the PageRank is that each page randomly selects another page with a certain probability. The value is called PageRank which obtained by repeating. For example, we consider a network structure with N web pages as nodes and links among pages as edges. In this situation, PageRank value of web page node $i(\in N)$ is calculated by Eq. (1).

$$p(i) = (1 - c)Ap + cq \tag{1}$$

p is PageRank vector. A is the adjacency matrix. When O_i is the number of links coming out of the node i, element A_{ij} represent by $\frac{1}{O_i}$. c is the probability of randomly jump to arbitrary node generality c is set to 0.15. q is $\sum_{j \in M(i)} \frac{PR(j)}{L(j)}$. $M(i)$ that is the set of pages that link to page i, and $L(j)$ is the total number of links to pages that are neither i nor j in page j.

In this analysis, we weighted the initial pages of PageRank. As a rule, on a cooking recipe site, we assumed that the more recipes Recipers posted, the more they tended to get reviews (because the population parameter is larger). If the number of co-occurrences that have been created were set as the weight, the PageRank of the users with a large number of recipe posts will simply increase. In this analysis, to avoid this, we weighted as shown in Eq. (2).

$$weight_{(Rec_j \, from \, Rev_i)} = co - occurence(Rev_i, Rec_j) \times support(Rev_i \Rightarrow Rec_j)$$

$$(i = 1, \ldots n, j = 1, \ldots m) \tag{2}$$

Rev_i, Rec_j means Rev_i stands for Reviewer i and Rec_j stands for Reciper j. $co - occurence(Rev_i, Rec_j)$ is the number of times Rec_j has created a recipe for Rec_j in a particular cooking category. $support(Rev_i \Rightarrow Rec_j)$ is number of times a Rev_i has made a Rec_j's recipe divided by number of Rev_i's reviews in a particular cooking category.

We based on the idea that multiplying the number of co-occurrences by the approval rating from Reviewers, increase the importance of Recipers who have strong support from Reviewers. We calculated PageRank using these values assigned as the PageRank weight.

4.2 Community Detection for Each Cooking Category

Community detection is a method of clustering to cut out that the edge density in the subgraph higher than the edge density outside the subgraph. In this study, we detected community using Modularity to clarify similar subgroup for each cooking category.

Modularity is one of the indicators how well communities are indicated [7]. In general, it is better that the cutout subgraph is the different from random graph. Modularity

Q can be expressed as Eq. (3) by the number of edges inside the divided community and the number of edges between communities.

$$Modularity\ Q = \frac{1}{2m} \sum_{vw} \left[A_{vw} - \frac{k_v k_w}{2m} \right] \delta(c_v, c_w) \tag{3}$$

In Eq. (3), consider two nodes v and w. m represents the number of edges. A_{vw} is the (v, w) component of the adjacency matrix. k_v and k_w represents the degree of node v and the degree of node w. Also δ is Kronecker delta, c_v and c_w refers to the community including nodes v and w, respectively.

In this study, we screened edges to make users community. As the index value, we used the Jaccard Index. The Jaccard index in the set A containing one node and the set B containing another node are expressed by Eq. (4). Jaccard index represents the common ratio of the elements contained in the two sets.

$$Jaccard(A, B) = \frac{|A \cap B|}{|A \cup B|} \tag{4}$$

The number of nodes and communities in each cooking category were shown in Table 4. The original number of nodes was adjusted using the number of co-occurrence. This is because that the greater the number of co-occurrence, the strong support for users.

Table 4. Number of nodes and communities in each cooking category

Cooking category	Number of nodes	Number of communities
Vegetable	314	25
Bread	327	20
Rice dish	314	23
Meat	268	25
Dessert	286	33
Fish	312	34

5   Results of Analysis

In this section, we explain the results of analysis. Our analysis flow is as follows. First, we summarized the recipes with reviews in the specified genre. Second, we extracted Reviewers for each recipe genre. Third, we calculated the number of times the Reviewer reviewed each Reciper's recipe. Next, we visualized users network each cooking category. Then, we detected community using Modularity.

The size of the nodes in the network represents the size of PageRank. The edge thickness represents the weight of Eq. (2). For visualization, we used "Fruchterman and Reingold Model" [8]. The indicators used in this chapter are as follows.

- Average of PageRank is average PageRank of nodes belonging to the community.
- Average of degree centrality is average degree centrality of nodes belonging to the community.
- Community density is density of nodes belonging to the community.

5.1   Vegetable Category

Figure 1 is the result of community detection for vegetable category. Q-value was 0.66. Table 5 is the result of index values each community on vegetable category network. Among the communities, the number of nodes in the community including the maximum number of nodes was 21. In addition, since the average PageRank for each community is divided into a community of 0.007 or higher and a community of around 0.005, it can be seen that it takes the form of a distributed community derived from multiple users.

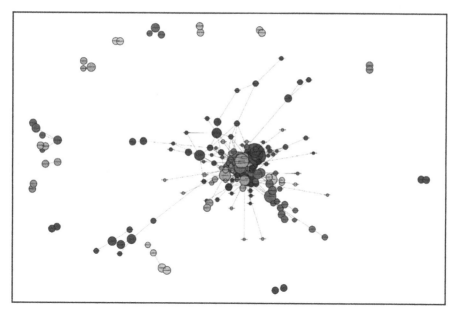

Fig. 1. Vegetable category's community (Overall density = 0.02)

From the community density, community number 2 has a high value of 0.89, and the others are 0.5 or less, indicating that only community 2 has a strong two-way connection.

5.2   Bread Category

Q-value in this category was 0.60. Figure 2 and Table 6 are the result of community detection and each index value for bread category. The number of nodes in community (community number 6) with the largest number of nodes was 45, while the number of nodes in other upper communities was around 20.

Table 5. Each index value by vegetable category's community (Number of nodes > 5)

Cluster	Average of PageRank	Number of nodes	Average of degree centrality	Community density
5	0.0074	21	0.030	0.25
7	0.0055	20	0.019	0.17
11	0.0042	18	0.020	0.20
14	0.0078	17	0.024	0.25
9	0.0040	15	0.021	0.26
3	0.0043	13	0.028	0.39
1	0.0081	12	0.031	0.48
2	0.0053	8	0.037	0.89
24	0.0056	7	0.011	0.31

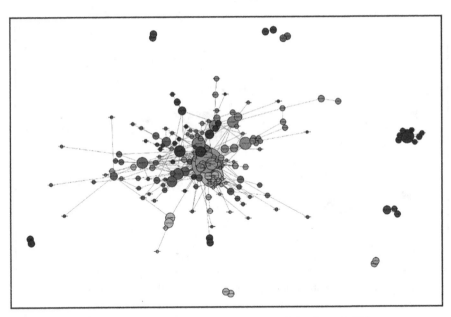

Fig. 2 Bread category's community (Overall density = 0.018)

From the average of PageRank, community number 1 had a high value of 0.0123, and other communities had a high value of about 0.004 to 0.007. From the density value of each community, the overall density was low. Furthermore, the results for communities with 3 or less nodes were very small compared to the community results for other cooking categories. Therefore, we found that the bread category had a hierarchical structure in which one community was divided into multiple communities.

Table 6. Each index value by bread category's community (Number of nodes > 5)

Cluster	Average of PageRank	Number of nodes	Average of degree centrality	Community density
6	0.0033	45	0.019	0.08
12	0.0047	23	0.015	0.13
5	0.0052	22	0.021	0.18
11	0.0037	21	0.018	0.17
1	0.0123	19	0.035	0.36
13	0.0073	18	0.020	0.22
2	0.0054	8	0.009	0.25

In addition, we found that this category had a completely different and independent community that had no involvement with other communities.

5.3 Rice Dish Category

Figure 3 and Table 7 are the results of Rice Dish's community. Q-value was 0.63. In this category, from Fig. 3, we found that there are core nodes for each community. In addition, from Table 7, the average PageRank of communities (community number 14 and community number 1) were high, and there was no big difference in other

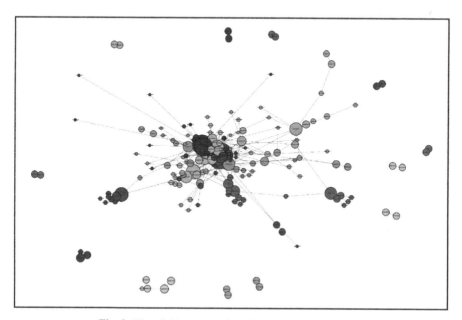

Fig. 3 Rice dish's community (Overall density = 0.019)

Table 7. Each index value by rice dish category's community (Number of nodes > 5)

Cluster	Average of PageRank	Number of nodes	Average of degree centrality	Community density
6	0.0041	23	0.015	0.12
15	0.0053	20	0.033	0.31
16	0.0041	20	0.018	0.17
10	0.0060	18	0.025	0.27
1	0.0069	16	0.024	0.29
9	0.0054	16	0.015	0.18
14	0.0098	16	0.022	0.26
22	0.0047	12	0.013	0.20
2	0.0038	9	0.024	0.53

communities, indicating that this category has a hierarchical community structure derived from the core nodes.

Furthermore, we found that the community with the largest number of nodes in this category (community 6) has a lower density than other higher-ranking communities.

The average degree centrality of each community tends to be low as a whole, indicating that it is a sparse community structure.

5.4 Meat Category

Q-value of meat category was 0.76. From the average page ranks in Table 8, we found that the average PageRank of communities (community number 2 and 11) tend to be higher than those of other communities, and that the other communities have almost the same values (Fig. 4).

On the other hand, this category had a low degree centrality of the community and a low density, which indicates that it is a distributed community with multiple core nodes. In addition, in multiple communities, a hierarchical structure was also found within the communities.

5.5 Dessert Category

Q-value was 0.70 in dessert category. From Table 9, the community with the highest average PageRank (community 4) was 0.008, and the others were 0.003 to 0.006.

In Fig. 5, it can be seen that one community is hierarchically derived from another community. In addition, there were very small communities with 3 or less nodes compared to other categories. Furthermore, the maximum density is 0.64, and most of them are around 0.2, so we found that nodes are softly connected in this community.

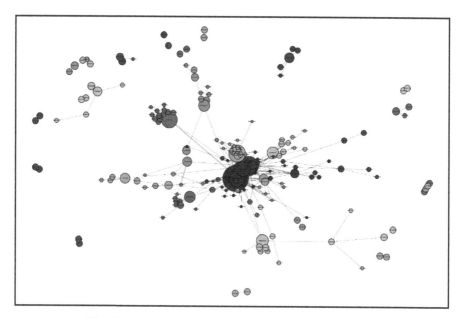

Fig. 4 Meat category's community (Overall density = 0.014)

Table 8. Each index value by meat category's community (Number of nodes > 5)

Cluster	Average of PageRank	Number of nodes	Average of degree centrality	Community density
1	0.0048	29	0.019	0.13
3	0.0042	29	0.021	0.15
13	0.0050	25	0.011	0.09
12	0.0048	16	0.013	0.17
22	0.0051	15	0.011	0.15
2	0.0072	14	0.016	0.24
11	0.0084	14	0.019	0.27
17	0.0047	7	0.012	0.38

5.6   Results of Top User and User Network for Fish Category

Figure 6 is a community detection result of the fish category. Q-value was 0.82. This category has the largest number of clusters among all categories, even though the number of nodes is almost the same as the vegetable category.

From Table 10, there was no community with an extremely high average PageRank, so we found the fish category was a distributed community. Since the average degree centrality and the density are low as a whole, it can be seen that there are many sparse communities in which multiple users exist at the center of each community.

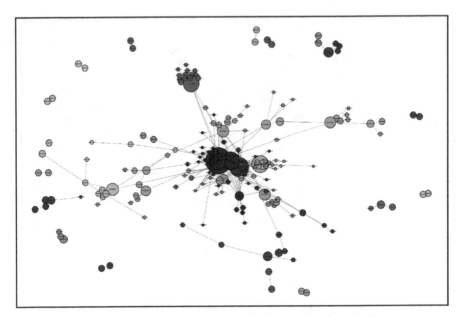

Fig. 5 Dessert category's community (Overall density = 0.01)

Table 9. Each index value by dessert category's community (Number of nodes > 5)

Cluster	Average of PageRank	Number of nodes	Average of degree centrality	Community density
3	0.0058	27	0.016	0.13
28	0.0042	22	0.011	0.11
14	0.0052	20	0.022	0.24
7	0.0048	15	0.015	0.22
16	0.0043	15	0.010	0.15
9	0.0046	14	0.010	0.16
4	0.0080	11	0.023	0.47
13	0.0040	10	0.011	0.27
26	0.0037	10	0.010	0.23
2	0.0030	7	0.018	0.64
5	0.0032	6	0.015	0.63

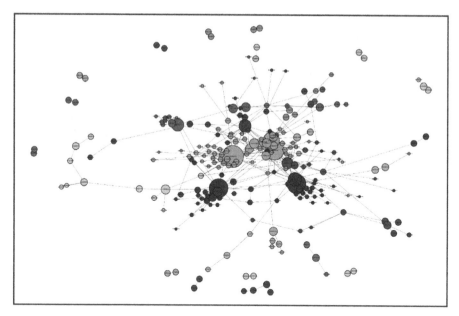

Fig. 6 Fish category's community (Overall density $= 0.01$)

Table 10. Each index value by fish category's community (Number of nodes > 5)

Cluster	Average of PageRank	Number of nodes	Average of degree centrality	Community density
0	0.0036	37	0.011	0.08
5	0.0044	24	0.011	0.11
8	0.0043	24	0.012	0.12
10	0.0051	18	0.015	0.21
15	0.0034	15	0.012	0.21
17	0.0038	12	0.011	0.24
12	0.0066	11	0.017	0.40
32	0.0041	11	0.009	0.22
21	0.0035	10	0.016	0.42
20	0.0035	9	0.009	0.26
26	0.0045	8	0.009	0.30

6 Discussions

First, from the results of the entire network, the community network revealed a low density for all cooking categories. We found scale-free structures that some nodes were connected to many nodes in all cooking categories, most of nodes connected to only a few. On the other hand, it was confirmed that there are differences in the way users from communities depending on the cooking category. Figure 7 shows directed graph for each category. From Fig. 7, it showed that some nodes were densely overlapped, while others had weak connections and scattered.From Fig. 7 and results of the analysis, the community structure of each cooking category was discussed as follows.

- Distributed Community: Vegetable Category, Meat Category, Fish Category
- Hierarchical Community: Bread Category, Rice Dish Category, Dessert Category

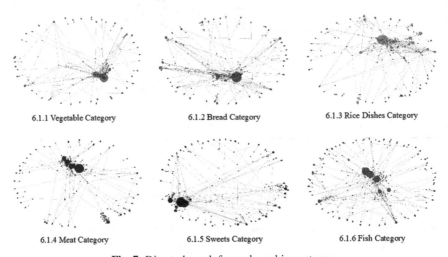

6.1.1 Vegetable Category   6.1.2 Bread Category   6.1.3 Rice Dishes Category

6.1.4 Meat Category   6.1.5 Sweets Category   6.1.6 Fish Category

Fig. 7 Directed graph for each cooking category

In the distributed community structure, there were very small communities with 3 or less nodes. On the other hand, there tended to be few very small communities in the hierarchical communities. The bread and dessert categories were considered to have such hierarchical structures because there were users who post new recipes with reference to the recipe of the user in the center. In addition, the distributed community structure supported multiple core people with high PageRank, as each community did not have an intermediate Reciper or Reviewer. Furthermore, due to the structure of the entire network, there was a community with a hierarchical structure, not limited to cooking categories. Users who connect the community and those who were in the middle of the hierarchy between the communities should be considered as growing users who supported by other users by referring to the top Recipers.

Next, we focused on the results of top rank users of each cooking category. Table 11 shows the top 10 users who had the highest PageRank of each cooking category. The user has been masked. Among them, user A, B, C, E, and G were the 5 users included in the top 10 users in more than half of the cooking categories. Therefore, these 5 users are considered to be the top Recipers in the recipe site used in this analysis. In addition, the popular users who ranked high in only one category were considered to be the top Recipers in a specific category, and this resulted in different results for each category.

Table 11. Top 10 users with high PageRank for each cooking category

Vegetables	Bread	Rice dish	Meat	Dessert	Fish
A	A	B	U	E	F
B	B	P	E	A	E
C	I	Q	B	C	S
D	K	G	H	B	C
E	G	A	A	X	B
F	L	K	G	Y	AB
G	M	R	C	D	R
H	H	S	F	Z	AC
I	N	E	V	AA	A
J	O	T	W	S	G

Most of the users in Table 11 were supported by many people with 20 or more, but some users had a single digit. Therefore, this single digit user is considered to be a "fan type" who has received enthusiastic support from some people.

Moreover, in this research, we focused on identifying influence users a certain person from the structure of the community in the previous research. Table 12 extracts the users most referred by the top users for each cooking category.

As the weight described in Eq. (2) was used as the index value for whether or not it was the most referenced. The number of co-occurrence represents how many created the user recipes. From Table 12, we identified that use A and C refer recipes to each other in many times. Additionally, in bread and rice dish categories, we found the same tendency in user B and G. Therefore, these users are considered to be active users of the recipe sites that influenced each other. Hyphens in Table 12 indicate that they are complete Recipers who have not posted reviews. In other words, they have posted only their own recipes without any reference. We found such Recipers in 4 of the 6 cooking categories.

In addition, since this complete Reciper had a high PageRank result even though they didn't receive support from other high-ranking users. Because of this, we assumed that they were supported from the low PageRank Reviewer a lot.

Furthermore, if we didn't consider the interconnection, G and H in the vegetable category, M in the bread category, C and AD in the rice dish category, C, F, and G in the meat category, A and G in the dessert category and AB in the fish category we could think of it as users who is influencing the top users.

In the visualization of communities, one community was not located in one place, but was displayed across multiple communities. This was especially common in low-density figures throughout the network (especially community graphs with densities of 0.14 or less). The Fruchterman and Reingold Model used when deciding the arrangement of nodes is adjusted not by the community unit but by the relationship between the nodes,

Table 12. Most referenced users from the top recipers for each cooking category (Top 5)

Category	Reviewer	Reciper	Number of co-occurence	Weight
Vegetable	A	C	48	16
	B	G	161	94.6
	C	A	41	10.1
	D	C	154	89.5
	E	H	8	1.9
Bread	A	B	48	28.4
	B	G	226	131.6
	I	A	568	485.9
	K	M	21	6.49
	G	B	221	218
Rice Dish	B	G	161	94.6
	P	–	–	–
	Q	AD	43	5.59
	G	B	67	35.1
	A	C	48	16
Meat	U	–	–	–
	E	F	5	1.67
	B	G	37	25.4
	H	E	4	2.67
	A	C	10	3.13
Dessert	E	A	3	0.4
	A	C	31	10.9
	C	A	52	32.6
	B	A	20	5.3
	X	–	–	–
Fish	F	B	6	1.1
	E	AB	26	18.3
	S	–	–	–
	C	B	7	2
	B	G	13	5

and if it is related to the node of another community, it is pulled to that side as well. It is thought that this is the cause. Therefore, if there is a connection with another community, it is possible that the communities also have similarities.

7 Conclusion

In this study, we performed network analysis and community detection using PageRank and Modularity for the purpose of identifying the community structure for each cooking category. In the analysis, we selected users using data from a Japanese recipe sites, visualized the network for each cooking category. In addition, we have detected a user community for each cooking category.

As results of analysis, we founded that there were differences in the structure of the community for each cooking category. Cooking categories, which mainly consists of meat, vegetables, and fish ingredients, had distributed structures that surrounds multiple Recipers within each community. On the other hand, it was clear that cooking categories, which mainly consists of dessert, rice dish, and bread had hierarchical structures and that derives from the community consisting of core users. The scale-free nature of the entire community was confirmed, and it was not clear that the majority users were active. In addition, regardless of structure of the entire network, since identified communities with a hierarchical structure regardless of the entire network, it became possible to identify key persons within the community located in the middle layer.

Furthermore, we identified the top Recipers for the entire recipe site from the top 10 users of PageRank. At the same time, we also identified the top Recipers for each cooking category.

As a future work, the node arrangement by the dynamic model did not work especially in the cooking categories low density. This is thought to be due to the fact that the nodes are arranged by the connections between the nodes, so it is necessary to arrange the nodes using the index of similarity and connection in each community.

Acknowledgements. In this paper, we used "Rakuten Dataset" provided by Rakuten, Inc. via IDR Dataset Service of National Institute of Informatics. This work was supported by JSPS KAKENHI Grant Number19K01945.

References

1. Taniguchi, T., Matsuo, Y., Ishizuka, M.: Detecting and analyzing community in BLOGs. In: Proceedings of the 6th Semantic Web and Ontology Research, p. 6. Japanese Society for Artificial Intelligence Study Group (2004). (in Japanese)
2. Iida, Y., Kishimoto, Y., Fujiwara, Y., Shiokawa, H., Onizuka, M.: Finding communities and ranking for large-scale graphs –fast algorithms and applications–. J. Jpn. Soc. Artif. Intell. **29**, 472–479 (2014). (in Japanese)
3. Sato, A., et al.: Estimating the attractiveness of a food photo using a convolutional neural network. Inst. Electron. Formation Commun. Eng. Tech. Rep. IEICE **117**, 107–111 (2017). (in Japanese)
4. Hanai, T., Namba, E., Takimoto, A.: Presentation method of closely resembles recipe clusters on a user-generated recipe site. In: Proceedings of the 17th International Conference on Information Integration and Web-based Applications and Services, p. 5 (2015)
5. Rakuten, Inc.: Rakuten Recipe data. Informatics Research Data Repository, National Institute of informatics (2020). https://doi.org/10.32130/idr.2.4

6. Page, L., Brin, S., Motwani , R., Winograd, T.: The PageRank citation ranking: bring order to the web. Technical Report of the Stanford Digital Library Technologies Project (1998)
7. Newman, M.E.J.: Modularity and community structure in the networks. Proc. Nat. Acad.Sci. U.S.A. **103**, 8577–8582 (2006)
8. Fruchterman, T.J., Reingold, E.M.: Graph drawing by force-directed placement. Softw. Pract. Exp. **21**, 1129–1263 (1991)

Multimodal Emotion Analysis Based on Acoustic and Linguistic Features of the Voice

Leon Koren and Tomislav Stipancic[✉]

Faculty of Mechanical Engineering and Naval Architecture,
University of Zagreb, Zagreb, Croatia
`tomislav.stipancic@fsb.hr`

Abstract. Artificial speech analysis can be used to detect non-verbal communication cues and reveal the current emotional state of the person. The inability of appropriate recognition of emotions can inevitably lessen the quality of social interaction. A better understanding of speech can be achieved by analyzing the additional characteristics, like tone, pitch, rate, intensity, meaning, etc. In a multimodal approach, sensing modalities can be used to alter the behavior of the system and provide adaptation to inconsistencies of the real world. A change detected by a single modality can generate a different system behavior at the global level.

In this paper, we presented a method for emotion recognition based on acoustic and linguistic features of the speech. The presented voice modality is a part of the larger multi-modal computation architecture implemented on the real affective robot as a control mechanism for reasoning about the emotional state of the person in the interaction. While the audio is connected to the acoustic sub-modality, the linguistic sub-modality is related to text messages in which a dedicated NLP model is used. Both methods are based on neural networks trained on available open-source databases. These sub-modalities are then merged in a single voice modality through an algorithm for multimodal information fusion. The overall system is tested on recordings available through Internet services.

Keywords: Emotion recognition · Affective robotics · Multimodal information fusion · Voice analysis · Speech recognition · Learning · Reasoning

1 Introduction

Sources of social signals treated as single modalities and then fused can be used in a form of computation mechanisms to control the behavior of the robot. For the purposes of this study, a voice modality control algorithm is developed and tested under laboratory conditions. This algorithm is a part of the bigger computation architecture composed of four distinct sources of social signals, including the following: face emotion recognition, level of loudness in the room, the intensity of body movements, and sentiment analysis applied on speech (sound modality). These modalities can be understood as weak classifiers used for emotion recognition tasks during human-robot interaction. Each of these modalities is used to generate a strong hypothesis about the emotional status of

© Springer Nature Switzerland AG 2021
G. Meiselwitz (Ed.): HCII 2021, LNCS 12774, pp. 301–311, 2021.
https://doi.org/10.1007/978-3-030-77626-8_20

the person in interaction through the emotion fusion procedure. Based on those insights the robot can respond with non-verbal communicational responses modeled using information visualization techniques and projected to the face of the robot to establish and maintain the common ground process [1, 2]. A common ground approach enables the robot to adapt its behavior where environmental perspectives change constantly through interaction based on newly acquired, insufficient or partial information. The following figure (Fig. 1.) depicts a robot PLEA where the described control mechanism is used.

  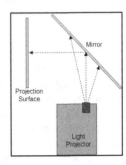

Fig. 1. Robot head design solutions: (1) PLEA - physical robot design, (2) light *pico* projector fixed at the robot base, and (3) light projection solution.

Built-in functionalities of the robot can provide a degree of situational embodiment, self-explainability, and context-driven interaction, as explained in [3, 4]. The overall architecture is designed to provide the adaptation-to-changes capability to the system instead of controlling them, as explained in [5]. As a proof-of-concept, the sound modality is implemented and tested in a couple of testing scenarios. The overall research can show in what way and to what extent a cognitive robot can be truly effective in technology-enhanced interaction.

2   Related Work

Nowadays artificial speech analysis is a highly researched area of artificial intelligence. Most commonly research is based on a multimodal approach. In this approach, researchers use more modalities and information fusion algorithms to achieve better sentiment recognition. A common goal of all researches is to achieve better social interaction between virtual agents and humans.

2.1   Acoustic Sentiment Recognition

The subfield of acoustic sentiment recognition uses recordings or live audio to recognize the emotional state of the interlocutor during an interaction. The base of recognition is the detection of prosodic features in speech like shown in Koolagudi et al. [6]. Commonly, audio sentiment recognition is divided into two distinct categories: (1) speaker-independent and (2) speaker-dependent. The main difference is in the working environment of the recognition algorithm. While speaker independent can work with many speakers it's less accurate comparing to speaker dependent [7].

The latest research is using LSTM (Long-Short Term Memory) algorithm to get temporal characteristics from an audio recording. This approach shows promising high accuracy results. In work of Zhao et al. [8] is shown that using the 2D CNN LSTM algorithm outperforms commonly used DBN (Deep Belief Network) and standard CNN (Convolutional Neural Network). Yet another approach is shown by Uddin et al. [9]. They use MFCC (Mel Frequency Cepstrum Coefficients) obtained through fast Fourier transformation to train a neural network.

2.2 Linguistic Sentiment Recognition

Linguistic sentiment recognition is commonly known as natural language processing which task is to extract sentiment from written language. One of the best-known algorithms is designed by Perikos et al. [10]. Authors use a Naïve Bayes and Maximum Entropy learner for statistical algorithm paired with a knowledge-based system. Naïve Bayes relies on a bag of words approach and analyzes each word. Also, the algorithm is concentrated on the occurrence of words in a whole document but not on inter-word relations. In contrast, the Maximum Entropy learner uses word relations and extracts features from these relations. To extract sentiment from a text in a more human-like way a knowledge-based system is used. It analyzes the sentence structure, position of each word, and its grammatical role. More, the system analyses lexical resources of the knowledge base to detect subtle differences in emotions. Combining these three methods accuracy of the system rises to nearly 90%.

Another method is relying on deep learning neural networks to recognize the sentiment. This kind of approach is shown in Kratzwald et al. [11]. Authors are using hand-crafted architecture composing of a recurrent neural network, traditional machine learning, feature extraction through bag-of-words, word embeddings, and custom-crafted transfer learning. The transfer learning approach applies knowledge from sentiment analysis to emotion recognition. In the holistic analysis, a proposed system outperformed others by as much as 23.2%. Combining a deep learning approach with Big Data showed yet another good approach to the problem. As shown in the work of Halim et al. [12] such a system achieves 83% accuracy on the real-world data.

2.3 Information Fusion

As state of the art demonstrates [13], generally better results are achieved using algorithms that are based on a fusion of more than one modality. Nowadays these algorithms are divided into few categories based on the fusion type. Feature level algorithms fuse features before recognition. Opposing to them, decision level algorithms fuse beliefs of modalities to give a decision [14]. Also, there is a hybrid fusion, which combines even more fusion algorithms [15] and a model level fusion where modalities are fused at the model level [16].

3   Algorithm

The algorithm comprises of acoustic and linguistic modalities. Those two modalities are combined through the information fusion algorithm based on weight factors. Acoustic modality uses *Mel-scale Frequency Cepstral Coefficients* and spectrogram to extract features from an audio recording. With these features, the convolutional neural network used in this work is trained. Linguistic modality is created from a hand-crafted feature extractor based on the bag-of-words approach. Recognition is achieved with a *Long-Short Term Memory* neural network. Additionally, a speech-to-text algorithm is used to accomplish linguistic sentiment recognition from audio recordings. The whole algorithm was implemented in a Python language and tested with real-world data. A graphical representation of the algorithm can be seen in Fig. 2.

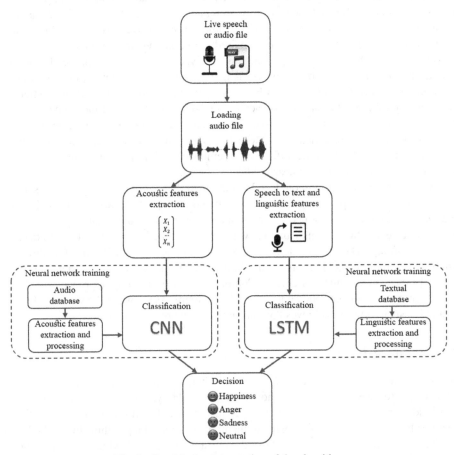

Fig. 2. Graphical representation of the algorithm

3.1 Acoustic Sub-modality

Acoustic sub-modality is based on the CNN architecture comprised of eight dedicated layers. Each layer has a *ReLu* activation function. Prevention of over-learning is achieved by two additional Dropout layers. To normalize features and improve stability, two Batch Normalization layers were added. As for output, the network has eight outputs to distinguish between male and female speakers and classify under four possible emotions. Audio processing and feature extraction was done with the *LibRosa* library. Feature extraction was based on *Fast Fourier Transformation* for both used features. To additionally improve their stability all features were averaged for the length of the whole recording. Training of the neural network was done on open-source data corpus: (1) SAVEE [17], (2) CREMA-D [18], (3) RAVDNESS [19], (4) TESS [20] and (5) Emo-DB [21]. From databases were extracted four emotion labels: anger, happiness, neutral, and sadness. The number of labels for each emotion is shown in Table 1.

Table 1. Number of database labels by emotion

Emotion	Number of labels
Female angry	1163
Female happy	1140
Female sad	1133
Female neutral	1000
Male angry	887
Male happy	854
Male sad	852
Male neutral	782

Data were divided into training and validation sets with a ratio of 4 to 1 (20% validation). The learning process was optimized with *RMSprop*, which is the popular and robust optimization algorithm for adaptive learning procedures. All results were analyzed with validation accuracy and confusion matrix.

3.2 Linguistic Sub-modality

Linguistic sub-modality is based on a recurrent LSTM architecture comprising of 4 dedicated layers. Conversion from the numeric representation to a vector space is done with an embedding layer. The second layer is a bidirectional LTSM layer which improves better learning of long strings. Also, this layer has a dropout function to achieve better over-learning protection. After that two layers network has two dense layers. The first of them has a *ReLu* activation function and the second has a *Softmax* function with four outputs. In contrast to the acoustic sub-modality, this algorithm doesn't need 8 outputs because we cannot distinguish a male from a female in a written text. For a faster and more optimized process of learning an Adam optimizer was used.

Training data was taken from the open-source database named *DailyDialog*. Similarly, to the acoustic sub-modality from the database were extracted four labels. The number of the statements was equalized to 1550 per label to prevent the algorithm from learning one label better than the others.

In a normal human speech, many words don't convey a sentiment, so these words were removed from the labeled data. Also, all statements were stripped of all interpunction and converted to a lower case. Because neural network prefers fixed and defined inputs all the statements were tokenized. The process of tokenization goes as follows:

1. Count frequency of the words in a given text
2. Give each word a unique identifier based on the frequency
3. Put the first N words to the vocabulary
4. Check the statements for out-of-vocabulary words, change them to the " $< OOV >$" token
5. Convert the statements to fixed-width arrays with the identifiers instead of words

   - If a statement is shorter than the length of an array add zeros to the end of a statement
   - If a statement is longer than the length of an array truncate the excess

After a feature extraction and processing, data is divided into the training and the validation sets in a ratio of 4 to 1 (20% validation). Lastly, the labels are encoded into the binary array representation using One-Hot Encoding.

With the process of training finished, results were analyzed using validation accuracy and confusion matrix.

3.3 Information Fusion

The algorithm makes a decision based on both sub-modalities. To achieve that, the decisions of both neural networks must be fused. For this, weighted factor decision level fusion was used. The algorithm took both decisions from the neural networks and multiplied them with a constant. Depending on the various parameters of sub-modalities this constant can determine which sub-modality we trust more. This sub-modality gets larger a constant. In our case, both sub-modalities get 0.5 so both decisions are weighted equally. After weighting, the results were summed up and the final decision was made. The algorithm for fusion is shown in Table 2.

4 Results

After training both sub-modalities F1-score, accuracy, and confusion matrices were generated. A full algorithm was evaluated on the audio recordings from the popular TV series Office. All the results are presented below.

4.1 Linguistic Sub-modality

Linguistic sub-modality scored 0.753 F1-score and 0.754 accuracy on validation data. The confusion matrix for this case is depicted at Fig. 3.

Table 2. Information fusion algorithm

1: $d(t) \leftarrow LinguisticModality(f(t))$	Decision making in both modalities
2: $d(a) \leftarrow AcousticModality(f(a))$	
3: $Procedure\ Information\ Fusion(T, A)$	Procedure for information fusion where N is the number of
4: $for\ i\ in\ 1\ to\ N\ do :$	labels used in sentiment recognition
5: $F(T, A)_i = W_t * T_i + W_a * A_i$	
6: $return F(T, A)$	
7: $Procedure\ Clasification(X)$	Classification based on a result from a fusion
8: $return\ (label(max(X)))$	
9: $F \leftarrow Information Fusion(d(t), d(a))$	Fusion
10: $C \leftarrow Clasification(F)$	Classification

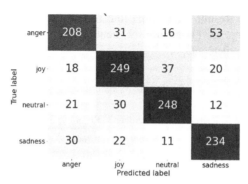

Fig. 3. Linguistic sub-modality confusion matrix

4.2 Acoustic Sub-modality

Acoustic sub-modality scored 0.7304 on F1-score and 0.7306 on the accuracy score. The confusion matrix which explains part of the problem of low accuracy score is depicted at Fig. 4.

The confusion matrix shows that the sub-modality can differentiate between a female and a male. On the other hand, when trying to recognize different emotions we see a similar pattern as with the linguistic sub-modality. Most of the time modality confuses emotions for no emotion both for a male and a female. On the other hand, given relatively small data sets, the results are better than expected.

4.3 Multi-modal Fusion

Finally, we test the whole system on the audio recordings downloaded from the internet. Audio recordings are taken from the popular TV sitcom Office and made available on the repository [22]. All the recordings have only one speaker which speaks only one full sentence. There is a total of eight recordings that are prelabeled. Labeling was done manually.

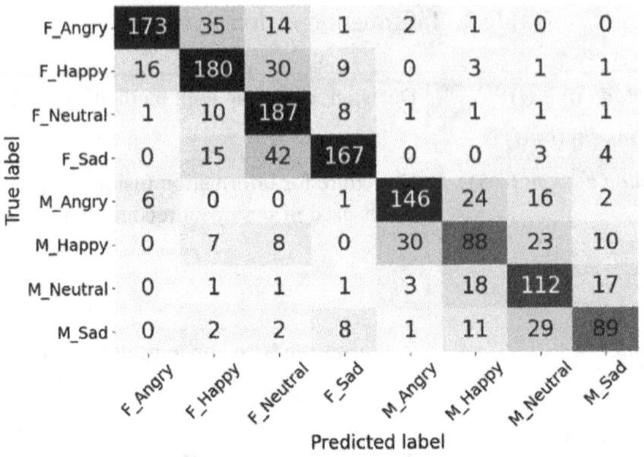

Fig. 4. Acoustic sub-modality confusion matrix

Audio recording 1–4. Results for the first four recordings are shown in Table 3. The labels for the recordings are (1) neutral, (2) neutral, (3) angry, and (4) sad. Decision certainties are shown in percentage.

Table 3. Results for recordings 1–4

Emotion	Recording 1	Recording 2	Recording 3	Recording 4
Anger	0.0226	0.0299	**0.9666**	0.0030
Happiness	0.0106	0.2122	0.0185	0.0245
Neutral	0.3025	**0.4976**	0.0014	0.1063
Sadness	**0.6643**	0.2603	0.0135	**0.8662**

From the results of the first four recordings can be seen that the algorithm makes accurate decisions in most of the cases. The first recording proved to be hard to label, so this kind of poor performance was expected.

Audio recording 5–8. Results for the second four recordings are shown in Table 4. The labels for the recordings are (5) sad, (6) sad, (7) happy, and (8) angry. Decision certainties are shown in percentage.

Table 4. Results for recordings 5–8

Emotion	Recording 5	Recording 6	Recording 7	Recording 8
Anger	0.0003	0.0472	0.0424	**0.6270**
Happiness	0.0051	0.0092	**0.7561**	0.1160
Neutral	0.4042	0.0906	0.1980	0.1343
Sadness	**0.5903**	**0.8530**	0.0036	0.1228

5 Discussion and Conclusion

The main goal of this work is to show how combining acoustic and linguistic sub-modalities with decision fusion based on weight factors can give good results on real-world data. This work is also representing just a step in a development of the larger reasoning architecture used to control the behavior of the new affective robot.

The performed research demonstrated some interesting results. For example, if results (e.g. accuracy) are analyzed when labelled input data is neutral, it can be seen a decrease in the certainty of decision. The possible reason for increase in uncertainty towards neutral sentiment can be found within the definition of it. In the presented system, a neutral sentiment can be no emotion at all or all other emotions for which the network was not trained for.

Secondly, humans change sentiment in interaction fluidly, from one to other, frequently passing this so-called neutral sentiment. This also can be caught by algorithms and lower belief in primary sentiment. To better answer this enigma, additional research is needed.

The benefit of the proposed system is the ability to create and train it on a standard personal computer with minimal time loss compared to other works. The difference between this approach and recent state of the art algorithms is in the usage of near real-world data for validation.

Nevertheless, methods shown in this paper could be additionally improved to score more accurate results. For example, some state-of-the-art projects use advanced speech-to-text algorithms. Moreover, advances could be achieved on the side of features extraction methods, both in linguistic and acoustic sub-modalities. Finally, the state-of-the-art also reported efficient algorithms for multimodal information fusion.

The main direction of this work is to provide an adaptive behavior of the system under uncertainties of the real world where deterministic chaos is a rule. When the created algorithm is implemented with interaction strategy, it will modify and improve beliefs of both sub-modalities. Also, interaction strategy would change weight factors depending on the beliefs of the whole system. Deterministic chaos is a characteristic of the real world where the existence of living beings depends mostly on their capability to adapt to changes instead of controlling them. Deterministic chaos inevitably obstructs absolute expectations, always producing slightly changed situations. Therefore, to alter the uncertain situations in the real world, conventional automation methods tend to create a technical system that can function only in a perfectly defined world. It seems that such an approach is definitely hopeless and often leads to complex, expensive, or inefficient systems resulting in a lack of space or rigid system. Further work will therefore be concentrated on the acquisition of new information through interaction and adaptation. In this vision, the presented sub-modalities are just weak classifiers and part of the larger multimodal algorithm used to recognize a human sentiment through interaction. In a case of a lower certainty of the sound modality, other available modalities will strengthen or weaken the main reasoning hypothesis. In this way, the general multimodal algorithm becomes more resistant to mistakes in reasoning or changes within the real environment.

Acknowledgements. This work has been supported in part by Croatian Science Foundation under the project "*Affective Multimodal Interaction based on Constructed Robot Cognition (UIP-2020-02-7184)*".

References

1. Nathan, M.J., Alibali, M.W., Church, R.B.: Making and breaking common ground: how teachers use gesture to foster learning in the classroom. In: Why Gesture? How the Hands Function in Speaking, Thinking and Communicating, Gesture Studies, vol. 7, pp. 285–316. John Benjamins Publishing Company, Amsterdam (2017). https://doi.org/10.1075/gs.7.14nat
2. Stipancic, T., Ohmoto, Y., Badssi, S.A., Nishida, T.: Computation mechanism for situated sentient robot. In: Proceedings of the 2017 SAI Computing Conference (SAI), London (2017)
3. Jerbic, B., Stipancic, T., Tomasic, T.: Robotic bodily aware interaction within human environments. In: SAI Intelligent Systems Conference (IntelliSys 2015), London (2015). https://doi.org/10.1109/IntelliSys.2015.7361160
4. Stipancic, T., Jerbic, B., Curkovic, P.: Bayesian approach to robot group control. In: International Conference in Electrical Engineering and Intelligent Systems, London (2011). https://doi.org/10.1007/978-1-4614-2317-1_9
5. Stipancic, T., Jerbic, B.: Self-adaptive vision system. In: Camarinha-Matos, L.M., Pereira, P., Ribeiro, L. (eds.) Emerging Trends in Technological Innovation, DoCEIS 2010, IFIP Advances in Information and Communication Technology, vol. 314. Springer, Heidelberg (2010). https://doi.org/10.1007/978-3-642-11628-5_21
6. Koolagudi, S.G., Kumar, N., Rao, K.S.: Speech emotion recognition using segmental level prosodic analysis. In: 2011 International Conference on Devices and Communications (ICDeCom) (2011). https://doi.org/10.1109/ICDECOM.2011.5738536
7. Yogesh, C.K., et al.: A new hybrid PSO assisted biogeography-based optimization for emotion and stress recognition from speech signal. Expert Syst. Appl. **69**, 149–158 (2017). https://doi.org/10.1016/j.eswa.2016.10.035
8. Zhao, J., Mao, X., Chen, L.: Speech emotion recognition using deep 1D & 2D CNN LSTM networks. Biomed. Signal Process. Control **47**, 312–323 (2019). https://doi.org/10.1016/j.bspc.2018.08.035
9. Uddin, M.Z., Nilsson, E.G.: Emotion recognition using speech and neural structured learning to facilitate edge intelligence. Eng. Appl. Artif. Intell. 9 (2020). https://doi.org/10.1016/j.engappai.2020.103775
10. Perikos, I., Hatzilygeroudis, I.: Recognizing emotions in text using ensemble of classifiers. Eng. Appl. Artif. Intell. **51**, 191–201 (2016). https://doi.org/10.1016/j.engappai.2016.01.012
11. Kratzwald, B., Ilic, S., Kraus, M., Feuerriegel, S., Prendinger, H.: Deep learning for affective computing: Text-based emotion recognition in decision support. Decis. Support Syst. 24–35 (2018). https://doi.org/10.1016/j.dss.2018.09.002
12. Halim, Z., Waqar, M., Tahir, M.: A machine learning-based investigation utilizing the in-text features for the identification of dominant emotion in an email. Knowl.-Based Syst. (2020). https://doi.org/10.1016/j.knosys.2020.106443
13. Jiang, Y., Li, W., Hossain, M.S., Chen, M., Alelaiwi, A., Al-Hammadi, M.: A snapshot research and implementation of multimodal information fusion for data-driven emotion recognition. Inf. Fusion 53, 209–221 (2020)
14. Poria, S., Cambria, E., Howard, N., Huang, G.-B., Hussain, A.: Fusing audio, visual and textual clues for sentiment analysis from multimodal content. Neurocomputing 50–59 (2016). https://doi.org/10.1016/j.neucom.2015.01.095

15. Qian, Y., Zhang, Y., Ma, X., Yu, H., Peng, L.: EARS: Emotion-aware recommender system based on hybrid information fusion. Inf. Fusion 141–146 (2019). https://doi.org/10.1016/j.inffus.2018.06.004

16. Gkoumas, D., Li, Q., Lioma, C., Yu, Y., Song, D.: What makes the difference? An empirical comparison of fusion strategies for multimodal language analysis. Inf. Fusion 184–197 (2021). https://doi.org/10.1016/j.inffus.2020.09.005

17. Haq, S., Jackson, P.: Speaker-dependent audio-visual emotion recognition. In: AVSP (2009)

18. Cao, H.W., Cooper, D.G., Keutmann, M.K., Gur, R.C., Nenkova, A., Verma, R.: CREMA-D: Crowd-sourced emotional multimodal actors dataset. IEEE Trans. Affect. Comput. **5**, 377–390 (2014). https://doi.org/10.1109/taffc.2014.2336244

19. Livingstone, S.R., Russo, F.A.: The Ryerson Audio-Visual Database of Emotional Speech and Song (RAVDESS): a dynamic, multimodal set of facial and vocal expressions in North American English. PLoS ONE 13 (2018). https://doi.org/10.1371/journal.pone.0196391

20. Pichora-Fuller, M.K., Dupuis, K.: Toronto Emotional Speech Set (TESS), Toronto Emotional Speech Set (TESS), Toronto (2020)

21. Burkhardt, F., Paeschke, A., Rolfes, M., Sendlmeier, W., Weiss, B.: A database of German emotional speech. In: 9th European Conference on Speech Communication and Technology, Lisabon (2005)

22. Daniels, G., Gervais, R., Merchant, S.: The Office US (2005–2013). https://github.com/LAPISLab-FSB/HCII_21/tree/main/Recordings

Evaluation of Cooking Recipes Using Their Texts and Images

Mei Nonaka[1]($\boxtimes$), Kohei Otake[2], and Takashi Namatame[3]

[1] Graduate School of Science and Engineering, Chuo University, 1-13-27, Kasuga, Bunkyo-ku, Tokyo 112-8551, Japan
a16.kyp4@g.chuo-u.ac.jp
[2] School of Information and Telecommunication Engineering, Tokai University, 2-3-23, Takanawa, Minato-ku, Tokyo 108-8619, Japan
otake@tsc.u-tokai.ac.jp
[3] Faculty of Science and Engineering, Chuo University, 1-13-27, Kasuga, Bunkyo-ku, Tokyo 112-8551, Japan
nama@indsys.chuo-u.ac.jp

Abstract. Many people are using smartphone applications and websites with respect to cooking recipes in almost everyday life. By using cooking recipe sites, we easily search the cooking recipe for dishes that we want to eat and cook the dish based on the recipe. When we search cooking recipes, we refer to the two information that are pictures of cooked food and texts of cooking recipe. In this study, to investigate good cooking recipes, we built a multimodal coupled network to use these two kinds of information of cooking recipe sites. In this multimodal coupled network, as pre-learning, we learned images and texts separately. To learn texts, we first used word2vec to vectorize for each text, and then we use the deep averaging network to identify the objective function. To learn images, we performed transfer learning of images using VGG16 which is a famously trained model. We combined these two kinds of 300-dimensional feature vectors extracted from the final layer of the two models obtained by pre-learning, and then we learned a total of 600-dimensional feature vectors. As a result, the multimodal coupled network that combines image and text data has the best accuracy.

Keywords: Multimodal coupled network · Cooking recipes · Deep learning

1 Introduction

Many people are using smartphone applications and websites with respect to cooking recipes in everyday life. By using cooking recipe sites, we easily search the cooking recipe for the dish that we want to eat and cook the dish based on the recipe. When we search cooking recipes, we refer to the two pieces of information that are pictures of cooked food and texts of cooking recipe. From the images of cooking recipe, we get information about how the food looks when using this recipe. From the texts of cooking recipe, we get information about difficulty of cooking, ingredients, cooking time and so on. Therefore, it is necessary to consider the image information and text

© Springer Nature Switzerland AG 2021
G. Meiselwitz (Ed.): HCII 2021, LNCS 12774, pp. 312–322, 2021.
https://doi.org/10.1007/978-3-030-77626-8_21

information of food in combination. In cooking recipe sites, users are classified into two types: recipe contributors and recipe viewers. For recipe contributors and recipe viewers, estimating notable cooking recipes is useful information for each other. When we propose recipes with good conditions for recipe viewers, we will be able to apply recipe recommendation/search, advertisement placement, etc.

2 Purpose of This Study

There are many studies using cooking recipes and text data and picture data. For example, Nakaoka et al. [1] and Maruyama et al. [2] analyzed cooking recipe to recommend effective recipes to users. However, in these studies, cooking recipes are recommended using only image data or text data. As a research that combines text data and image data, Ito et al. [3] investigated a method for estimating the taste of cooking recipes in consideration of cooking procedures by learning together image features, ingredients features, and features related to procedural verbs that appear in cooking procedure sentences. They show the usefulness of combining text data and image data. Also, Sanjo et al. [4] estimated the popularity of cooking recipes using deep learning architecture. However, because we are using access logs, we have not yet identified the cooking recipes that are reflected in the results of actually cooking and posting on the cooking recipe site from among the popular recipes.

As shown in the previous section, it is necessary to use the two information of pictures of cooked food and texts of cooking recipe when estimating recipes that are easy to refer to. However, to analyze cause and effect among complex and big data, we expect that conventional analyzing technologies using only either images or texts are not suitable. Therefore, in this study, we use a combination of text and image features to estimate a notable cooking recipe. Specifically, first, we learn a deep neural network to calculate features in texts and images. Next, we combined the feature vectors of each final layer and obtain the multimodal feature vectors. After the end, we learned a new network by inputting multimodal features. The objective function in the all model is the presence or absence of a photo and comment report for the recipe named "Tsukurepo" posted by the recipe viewer. "Tsukurepo" is a representative cooking recipes site in Japan, and Rakuten is the operating company.

3 Dataset

In this chapter, we explain the dataset in this model.

In this paper, we used "Rakuten Dataset" provided by Rakuten, Inc. via IDR Dataset Service of National Institute of Informatics [5]. This dataset includes about 796,028 cooking recipes which posted by ordinal users from October 2010 to April 2012. Each recipe had a cooking image and title, description, ingredients, and report of the recipe viewers. In this study, we targeted six categories in large category about cooking recipe. The six categories are "bread", "meat", "sweet", "soup", "egg" and "pasta". Because we used the objective function about the presence or absence of a photo and comment report for the recipe named "Tsukurepo" posted by the recipe viewer, we show the number of recipes that have "Tsukurepo" in each category in Table 1.

Table 1. The number of recipes that have "Tsukurepo" of six categories

Category	The number of recipes in "Tsukurepo"
Bread	2936
Meat	2263
Sweet	2241
Soup	1939
Egg	1016
Pasta	640

We undersampled the recipes without "Tsukurepo" by category according to the number of recipes with "Tsukurepo" shown in Table 1. For that reason, we used 22056 cooking recipes in the model. In this model, we use texts about title, the trigger for the cooking recipe, the introducing the cooking recipe and ingredients. We performed morphological analysis used Mecab [6] and the dictionary of NEologd [7] which are Japanese dictionaries for morphological analysis, because the language of this dataset is Japanese. We focus on nouns, adjectives and verbs as part of texts. In order to normalize the Japanese writing system, we unified all kanji, hiragana, and katakana into katakana using the reading information of MeCab. As for the image data, since the shapes of images are different, we paint the parts that are not enough to form a square in black and perform preprocessing to make the sizes uniform. Table 2 shows the frequently occurring words in the dataset. The total number of words was 544647, and the number of unique words was 7339.

Table 2. The frequently occurring words in the dataset

Words Katakana : English	Number of Words
シオ : salt	9383
タマゴ : egg	7950
カンタン : easy	6207
オイシイ : delicious	5528
サトウ : sugar	5450
チーズ : cheese	5155
ミズ : water	5145
ツクリ : making	5035
コショウ : pepper	4995
ショクパン : Plain bread	4751

4   Method

In this section, we explain how to estimate a notable cooking recipe. We show the schematic diagram of the proposed method in Fig. 1. We combine two kinds of multi-modal features about texts and images and we learn the network that has multimodal features. First, we explain word2vec to transform from texts to feature vector which is used to and pre-learning of texts. Next, we explain pre-learning of images. Finally, we learned multimodal coupled network about the feature value from texts and images.

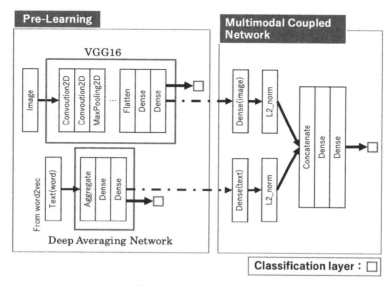

Fig. 1. Schematic diagram

4.1   Learning Texts Using Word2vec

In this study, we transformed words in cooking recipe texts into vectors using word2vec. The structure of word2vec is a simple neural network consisting of two layers, a hidden layer and an output layer. By acquiring a distributed expression, we express concept of a word by a low-dimensional dense vector. To learn word2vec, we used the skip-gram method. The skip-gram method predicts what kind of words that are likely to appear around the input word. This is defined as the Eq. (1).

$$p(w_o|w_I) = \frac{\exp\{v'^{T}_{w_o} v_{w_I}\}}{\sum_{w_v \in V} \exp(v'^{T}_{w_o} v_{w_I})} \tag{1}$$

w_I represents a specific word, and w_o represents a word located around the specific word. $v'^{T}_{w_o}$ and v_{w_I} are vectors representing words. v represents the input vector and v' represents the output vector. V is the entire vocabulary.

When we learned word2vec, we used the rest of the text data in the dataset created in Sect. 3. Therefore, we used 219,538 cooking recipes. In this model, we use texts about the title, the trigger for the cooking recipe, the introducing the cooking recipe and the ingredients. Before learning, we apply morphological analysis to the title, the trigger for the cooking recipe, the introducing the cooking recipe and the ingredients, divide it into words, and then normalize it as in Sect. 3. The output vector size, the window size, the number of epochs, and the minimum number of words is set to 300, 5, 10 and 5, respectively. We used genism [8] for learning.

4.2 Pre-learning About Texts

We used Deep Averaging Network (DAN) [9] for pre-learning about texts. DAN uses the embedded vector of each word averaged and aggregated into one vector as the input of the network. Figure 2 shows a schematic diagram of DAN in this model. The proposed method used DAN with two connected layers of 300 units and applies ReLU as the activation function for each layer. Sentence vectorization used word2vec learned in Sect. 4.1 to convert each word into a 300-dimensional vector. For learning, the mini-batch size was 64, the number of epochs was 30, and the optimization algorithm was Adam and the objective function is to determine the presence or absence of "Tsukurepo".

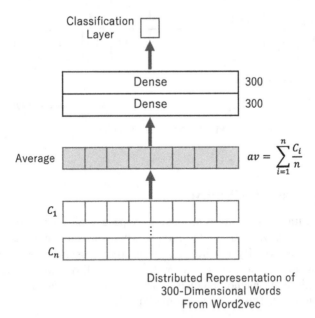

Fig. 2. Schematic diagram of DAN in this model

4.3 Pre-learning About Images

For pre-learning of images, VGG16 [10] is used. In the proposed method, we perform transfer learning using VGG16 and adapt it to recipe prediction that is easy to refer to. VGG16 is a Convolutional Neural Network (CNN) model with a 16-layer structure. Figure 3 shows a schematic diagram of VGG16. In transfer learning, we fixed the learning up to the 15th layer and tried to learn the layers after that. We added a 300-dimensional intermediate layer after the flatten layer and performed regularization and dropout. About hyper-parameter in the learning model, the mini-batch size was 128, the number of epochs was 30, and the optimization algorithm was Adam, and the objective function was to determine the presence or absence of the same "Tsukurepo" as in Sect. 4.2.

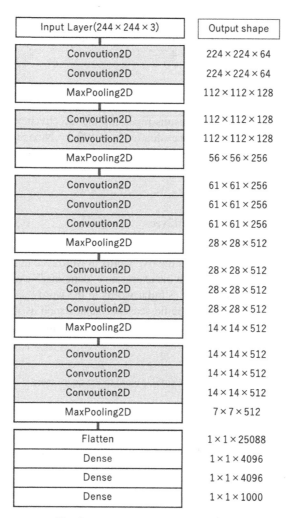

Fig. 3. Schematic diagram of VGG16

4.4 Learning Multimodal Coupled Network

After pre-learning about texts and images, we extracted the features quantity for input of DAN. We took a 300-dimensional feature vector through the final layer of each modality and then applied L2 regularization to both vectors. We combine 300-dimensional vectors to obtain 600-dimensional features and we learned the combined network. The combined network consisted of a multi-layer perceptron with 300 hidden layers and a regression unit in the output layer. As an activation function for each layer except the output layer, we apply ReLU which is one of the most effective activation function of piecewise linear shaped. For learning, the mini-batch size was 64, the number of epochs was 50, and the optimization algorithm was Adam and the objective function is to determine the presence or absence of "Tsukurepo" as in Sect. 4.2.

5 Result

This section shows the verification results regarding the effectiveness of the proposed method. First, we perform a qualitative evaluation of word2vec. Next, in order to compare the differences in the accuracy of the created models, we show the results of accuracy of pre-learning. Finally, we show the results of accuracy of learning multimodal coupled network.

5.1 Qualitative Evaluation of Word2vec

We qualitatively evaluate how well the learned word2vec can capture the semantic relevance between words. Table 3 shows the five words in word2vec that are most similar to the query word. From the results, in the expression "delicious", words with the same meaning expressed in different ways. Similar words to the word "season" in Japanese appear as words that are close to specific seasonal names such as winter and spring, and emotional words that you miss the season. In addition, with respect to ingredients, similar words indicate similar ingredients or words used in cooking at the same time.

Table 3. The most similar word to the query word

Query Word	イチゴ: Strawberry	スープ: Soup	チーズ: Cheese	オイシイ: Delicious	カンタン: Easy	キセツ: Season
Similar Words	ブルーベリー: Blueberry	コンソメ: Consommé	トロケル: Melting	ビミ: Delicious	テガル: Easy	ジキ: Season
	ラズベリー: Raspberry	ポタージュ: potage	ピザ: Pizza	オイシク: Delicious	ツクレ: Make	シュン: Season
	ストロベリー: Strawberry	シルモノ: Soup	プロセス: Process	オイシカッ: Delicious	カタテマ: One-handed	ハルサキ: Easy Spring
	ジャム: Jam	スープニ: Boiled Soup	マヨネーズ: Mayonnaise	サイコウ: Best	ササッ: Quickly	フユ: Winter
	チョコ: Chocolate	ハルサメ: Glass Noodles	クラフト: Craft	アイ: Fit	ツクレル: Can Make	コイシイ: Miss

5.2 Performance Comparison

Figure 4 shows the transition of accuracy of pre-learning about texts learned in Sect. 4.2 and Fig. 5 shows the transition of loss of the model. In Fig. 4, the vertical axis shows accuracy and the horizontal axis shows the number of epochs. In Fig. 5, the vertical axis shows loss and the horizontal axis shows the number of epochs. From Fig. 4 and Fig. 5, the loss function is approaching convergence for both train and validation data. However, in order to improve the prediction accuracy, it is considered that we need improvements when learning words.

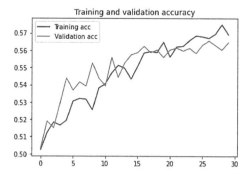

Fig. 4. Transition of accuracy of pre-learning about texts

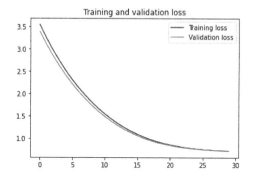

Fig. 5. Transition of loss of pre-learning about texts

Next, Fig. 6 shows the transition of accuracy of pre-learning about image model learned in Sect. 4.3 and Fig. 7 shows the transition of loss of the model. In Fig. 6, the vertical axis shows accuracy and the horizontal axis shows the number of epochs. In Fig. 7, the vertical axis shows loss and the horizontal axis shows the number of epochs. From Fig. 7, while the loss function of train data decreased, the validation data remained constant after increasing after 4 epochs. Therefore, overfitting is occurring and Fig. 6 also show the tendency of overfitting. From these reasons, it is necessary to improve the incorporation of an index that is easily referred to as an image in advance and an approach to suppress overfitting.

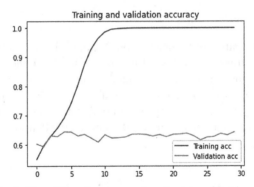

Fig. 6. Transition of accuracy of pre-learning about images

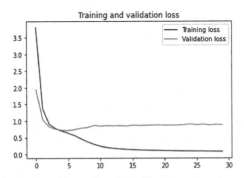

Fig. 7. Transition of loss of pre-learning about images

Figure 8 shows the transition of accuracy of learning multimodal coupled network learned in Sect. 4.4 and Fig. 9 shows the transition of loss of the model. In Fig. 8, the vertical axis shows accuracy and the horizontal axis shows the number of epochs. In Fig. 9, the vertical axis shows loss and the horizontal axis shows the number of epochs. Comparing with the result of pre-learning of only texts and images, it can be read that the validation accuracy is improved. Therefore, it was verified that the prediction accuracy can be improved by combining the two elements.

Table 4 shows verification results for test data. From Table 4, it was not possible to obtain as much accuracy as the validation accuracy of Fig. 8. Therefore, it is necessary to improve the acquisition of feature vectors from two pre-learning data and the model construction method for future models. As a result of accuracy by large category, bread had the highest accuracy, followed by soup, eggs, meat, pasta, and sweets. For dishes with many types in the category, it appeares that difficult to distinguish because the types of texts used in cooking recipes and the images expressed increase. Therefore, as an issue, it is necessary to devise pre-learning so that there is no difference between categories.

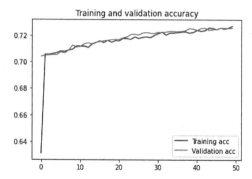

Fig. 8. Transition of accuracy of learning multimodal coupled network

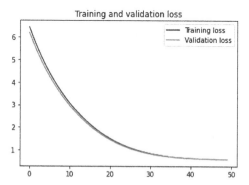

Fig. 9. Transition of loss of learning multimodal coupled network

Table 4. Verification results for test data

Model	Accuracy
Images	0.5578
Texts	0.5882
Multimodal	0.6000

6 Conclusion

In this study, we constructed a deep learning model to evaluate cooking recipes. In this model, we built the model with the presence or absence of a photo and comment report of the recipe named "Tsukurepo" posted by the recipe viewer as the objective function. Therefore, the proposed method makes it possible to estimate cooking recipes that are easy to refer to by combining image and text data. In the model, we first pre-learned photo and text data, and then trained a multimodal coupled network. As future issues, we need improvements and ingenuity to improve the accuracy of pre-learning and multimodal coupled networks. Regarding the pre-learning of images, it is necessary to pre-learn the images of other highly evaluated dishes when we transferred-learned the images, and then perform the transfer-learning. Regarding pre-learning of texts, it is necessary to learn items other than the text data used this time and learn methods. For a multimodal coupled network, it is necessary to consider the order in which images and texts are combined and the number of dimensions to be trained.

Acknowledgments. In this paper, we used "Rakuten Dataset" provided by Rakuten, Inc. via IDR Dataset Service of National Institute of Informatics. This work was supported by JSPS KAKENHI Grant Number 19K01945.

References

1. Nakaoka, Y., Satoh, T.: Strategic recipe recommendation method for cooking repertory expansion. In: The 5th Forum on Data Engineering and Information Management co-sponsored by IEICE (Institute of Electronics, Information and Communication Engineers), DEIM2013 Proceedings, D3–1 (2013). (in Japanese)
2. Maruyama, T., Akiyama, M., Yanai, K.: Recipe recommendation system using ingredient image recognition. IEICE Technical report (Institute of Electronics, Information and Communication Engineers), vol. 111, no. 478 (IE2011 133-175), pp. 43–48 (2012). (in Japanese)
3. Ito, Y., et al.: Improvement of taste estimation from a cooking recipe with an image -a study on the utilization of the cooking procedure. IEICE Technical report, vol. 117, no. 485, MVE2017-77, pp. 59–60 (2018). (in Japanese)
4. Sanjo, S., Katsurai, M.: Prediction of popularity of cooking recipes based on image and text features. In: The 10th Forum on Data Engineering and Information Management (DEIM2018) (2018). 4 pages
5. Rakuten recipe. https://recipe.rakuten.co.jp/
6. MeCab: Yet Another Part-of-Speech and Morphological Analyzer. https://taku910.github.io/mecab/
7. neologd/mecab-ipadic-neologd. https://github.com/neologd/mecab-ipadic-neologd
8. RaRe-Technologies/genism. https://github.com/RaRe-Technologies/gensim
9. Iyyer, M., Manjunatha, V., Boyd-Graber, J., Daumé III, H.: Deep unordered composition rivals syntactic methods for text classification. In: Proceedings of the 53rd Annual Meeting of the Association for Computational Linguistics and the 7th International Joint Conference on Natural Language Processing (Volume 1: Long Papers), pp. 1681–1691 (2015)
10. Simonyan, K., Zisserman, A.: Very deep convolutional networks for large-scale image recognition. In: International Conference on Learning Representations (2015). 14 pages

Readability of Posts and User Engagement in Online Communities of Government Executive Bodies

Konstantin Platonov[1]([✉]) [iD] and Kirill Svetlov[2] [iD]

[1] Center for Sociological and Internet Research,
Saint Petersburg State University, Saint Petersburg, Russia
[2] Laboratory for Research of Social-Economic and Political Processes of Modern Society,
Saint Petersburg State University, Saint Petersburg, Russia
k.svetlov@spbu.ru

Abstract. The article deals with the question of the link between readability and engagement rates on social media. On one hand, easy-to-read texts can be useful to attract and involve broader audience, but on the other hand, texts which draw attention and spark discussions often tend to be complex, controversial, even sophisticated, and consequentially less readable. Our database consisted of 115245 posts retrieved from social networking site VKontakte, the most popular SNS in Russia. The sample included all publicly available posts in online communities of 47 Russian state bodies: ministries, federal services and federal agencies published from 01.01.2017 to 16.09.2020. For each post, engagement rate (ER) and 79 other metrics of the texts were calculated. Gradient Boosted Decision Trees were used to build the regression model which took into account all the features including 10 different readability metrics and other measures, such as topics, linguistic characteristics, sentiment and so on. As a result, the most significant factors were the variables determining the presence of certain topics. All readability scores were weak predictors of engagement rate. And furthermore, our data provided no evidence that topics can help to increase ER, but only the topics causing lowering of ER. Using correlation analysis, we showed that in the case of communication strategies in online communities in social network VKontakte, the readability of posts is not directly related to engagement rates.

Keywords: Social media · Political communication · Online communities · User engagement

1 Introduction

Increasing the level of engagement is one of the main tasks for drawing attention and retaining of the audience, this goal is becoming increasingly relevant in public politics, especially in the context of social media use. Apart from the topic and the visual appearance of the message, the lexical characteristics of the texts themselves can influence the perception of posts on social networks. "Branding" of parties and political movements and "celebritization of politics" [1] trend are forcing political actors to elaborate

© Springer Nature Switzerland AG 2021
G. Meiselwitz (Ed.): HCII 2021, LNCS 12774, pp. 323–340, 2021.
https://doi.org/10.1007/978-3-030-77626-8_22

sophisticated strategies that determine the stylistics, formats and methods of presenting information.

Official texts related to politics and public life are often complex in form and content [2]. State authorities, political organizations and movements are forced to construct a language that reflects the complexity and richness of the official agenda, but also have to remain understandable to overall audience. Low readability, on the one hand, makes the news more difficult to perceive and, on the other hand, the complexity is a natural consequence of the needs of precise representation of information about the real (and objectively sophisticated) world, while overly simple language is often used in the context of sensationalism and deceptive news [3].

Some studies show that the readability of posts in blogs can decrease significantly when the online platform or service becomes more politicized and communication becomes more institutionalized [4]. In turn, other studies show that the use of simple language, such as the choice of common vocabulary and the prevalence of short words and sentences in political communication, helps individual candidates gain popularity [5].

Less readable news is easier to produce, for instance automatic algorithms can create them in proper manner, furthermore, this news can be perceived by the audience as more credible [6].

Large-scale research on online news shows that user engagement depends on the topic and these differences are varying according to platform [7]. In terms of agenda-setting theory, communication platforms, in addition to the choice of topics, also inform the reader "how to think about" a particular problem [8]. Commitment to certain rhetoric and word choices, among other things, are the tools to influence the audience on the second level agenda [9]. Some studies based on Facebook and Twitter content show that "easy-to-read posts are more liked, commented on, and shared on social media" [10, 11]. Others do not find such a connection [12].

This paper is focused on the set of factors that can influence user engagement in the context of political communication on social media. We consider the readability metrics as key variables, and additionally take into account other measures: the topics of the texts, their linguistic and sentiment characteristics. Based on the experience of previous studies, we formulate research questions. After that, a detailed description of the methods is presented. This is followed by a discussion, conclusion, and information on further work.

Research Questions. In this article we considered the content of online communities in the context of the topics it covers and its readability, as well as these metrics' relationship with the engagement level the content produces.

RQ1. How does the readability of the communities' texts influence the level of audience engagement?

RQ2. What are the other factors that influence the level of engagement? (topics, sentiment, linguistic metrics etc.)

2 Related Work

Complexity of a text has a significant impact on perception of political information and estimated political knowledge acquisition [2]. In the research by Tolochko et al. it was shown that semantic complexity affects perceived complexity [13]. In the context of political communication, the obfuscation hypothesis is also of particular interest. It is related to the effect of actors' intention to "cover" inappropriate results of some initiatives (for instance in financial activity or corporate social reliability program) with less clear, less concise and more optimistic texts [14]. Attempts to obscure the negative information behind complex textual structures can be used by official organizations for political purposes [15].

In addition to the difference between objective and perceived complexity, there is also an amount of formal metrics for evaluating complexity, which are based on syntax and semantic measures [2]. Some statistical models of sophistication include other factors, for instance, word rarity in language [16].

The political meaning of text complexity and readability is an ambiguous phenomenon. A communication strategy can rely on different approaches to balancing text accessibility and simplicity. Some studies identified the links between text complexity, quality, and its ability to establish trust [17], others linked it to the clarity of official communication and concluded that it is necessary to use concise sentences and avoid superfluous words, using 1 or 2 keywords to improve comprehensibility of texts [18].

The political effects of readability have been shown in research in an abundance of various contexts. Experimental studies show that the wording in ballots can have an impact on voting behavior [19]. Low text readability potentially leads to an overall decrease in the effectiveness of e-government institutions [20]. The problem of readability is important in practice, largely for the simple reason that the characteristics of political texts, weather press releases or laws, can indicate that their understanding requires a level of education far higher than that of a typical member of the target audience [21, 22]. At the same time, simplicity of language, often interpreted as low complexity associated with high readability, may be a sign of a certain political ideology such as populism [23] or conservatism [24].

Automated content analysis provides a broad set of methods for studying political communication, which includes various classification approaches at the levels of documents, authors, and time periods, as well as ideological scaling [25]. Readability analysis has already become a promising trend in the context of research of political texts.

The question of the possible connection between readability and engagement has been developed in the context of various practical tasks. First and foremost, consumer engagement studies that focus on the phenomena of processing fluency [10], as well as virality and the connection between enjoyment and engagement are worth mentioning [11, 26]. Another direction is related to the analysis of partisan communities, for instance pro- and anti-vaccine movements [12]. Similar studies dedicated to politics-related texts are relatively few in number. Firouzjaei & Ozdemir, in the article devoted to political tweets, showed that easy-to-read texts evoke a higher level of engagement [27]. Pancer & Poole, using Clinton's and Trump's tweets as examples, showed that features that increase perceptual disfluency lead to decrease in interactions [28]. Noguti, in a study on Reddit, showed that complexity of political posts correlated positively to the post scores (ratings) and negatively to the number of comments [29].

In addition to a variety of readability metrics, there are other measures that can influence user engagement. Therefore, it is reasonable to consider readability in the context of other potential predictors of engagement.

At first, the topics of texts, their salience, and relevance to different audiences should be mentioned. A large contribution in this direction was made by media researchers, who have shown the significant differences in engagement rates across different news topics and media outlets [7]. A study by Ebernl et al. showed that low issue salience can amplify the effect of the sentiment of the post on provoking negative reactions [30]. Gerbaudo et al. showed, using the example of the Labor Party in the UK, that a focus on positive topics, so-called "positive posting", for instance, associated with promises of a higher social spending, helps to ensure an increased level of audience engagement on social media [31].

Morphological characteristics, the ratios of certain parts of speech in texts can also have a potential impact. Thus, by measuring lexicosemantic and morphological parameters, researchers can attempt to predict the ideological orientation of a political text [32]. Shukrun-Nagar showed how "timeless verbs" are used to construct "general truth" in politicians' posts on Facebook [33]. Psycho-linguistic characteristics were also used to analyze political tweets [34].

The tone of a post can also increase engagement level, as shown, for example, in the case of "love" and "angry" reactions on Facebook [30]. Shugars & Beauchamp have shown that negative and unpleasant tweets help to ensure sustained engagement, long discussions, and reduce information bubbles [35]. There is a variety of approaches to sentiment classification, since positive, negative and neutral messages in certain conditions can provoke a strong reaction in the form of comments, likes, reposts or retweets. Regarding political texts, the distinction between attitudes in general vs. attitudes toward the content in the context is particularly important [36]. There are also more exotic factors that can influence user engagement, such as the presence of humor or reasoning in a post [37], disagreement in the comments which spark further discussion [38].

3   Method

3.1   Data

We turned to the data from the message boards ("walls") on VKontakte (the most popular SNS in Russia) in official online communities, representing the executive authorities. Our sample contains communities of 47 Russian state bodies: ministries, federal services and federal agencies. By using VK API all available posts published from 01.01.2017 to 16.09.2020 were gathered, 115245 posts in total. For all calculations linked to engagement metrics we used the subsample of 34 communities which allowed leaving comments.

3.2 Pre-processing

The pre-processing of the database included the following procedures.

1. Posts with no text (for instance ones which include only images) were discarded.
2. All letters were converted to lower case. All non-alphabetic characters, including punctuation, numbers, emoticons were removed. Stop words presented in NLTK package were excluded. All links to web resources and user mentions were deleted.
3. MyStem morphological analyzer [39] was used to transform words presented in posts into their dictionary form.
4. Posts which were detected as outliers with "1.5 IQR" rule were discarded from the final database.
5. Posts with less than 2 sentences and less than 10 words were excluded.

The final database contained 103327 posts. For each post metrics for the following parameters were calculated.

- Engagement metrics.
- Metrics of text complexity.
- Topics of posts.
- Paralinguistic Features.
- Text sentiment.

3.3 Engagement

However, if communities with different audience sizes are compared using these features, the result can be heavily biased in favor of the larger communities. In order to account for this bias, weighted measures have to be applied. The main variable is engagement rate calculated for each post.

The widely used metric of popularity of content on SNSs is Engagement rate, calculated separately for each post:

$$Eng.Rate = \frac{Likes + Comments}{Views} \cdot 1000$$

The special indicators of engagement were also added.

$$Eng.Rate_M = \frac{M}{Views} \cdot 1000$$

where $M \in \{Likes, Comments, Reposts\}$.

3.4 Text Readability

The metrics of readability [40] of the texts include a number of basic properties, e.g. its length in characters, the number of words in a post, the number of punctuation marks, etc., as well as more complex metrics [41, 42].

Following the approach described by Solnyshkina et al. [43], we calculated the metrics for each post in the database: n_sent (number of sentences in the text), n_word (number of words in the text), n_word_unique (number of unique words in the text), characters_count (number of characters in the text), letters_count (number of letters in the text), punct_count (number of punctuation marks in the text), n_syllables (number of vowels in a word; if a word does not contain vowels (for instance, some prepositions), it was "glued" to the next word in text), n_long_words (number of words longer than 4 syllables). The above metrics were calculated on unprocessed texts, the only exception was the metric n_word_unique, which was calculated on the texts that underwent the pre-processing procedure described above.

Using the above "basic" metrics, we also calculated more complex metrics.

- Average number of words per sentence, ASL = n_word/n_sent
- Average number of syllables per word, ASW = n_syllables/n_word
- Percentage of long words per sentence, PLW = n_long_words/n_word
- Total unique tokens / total tokens, TTR = n_word_unique/n_word
- Average number of punctuation marks per sentence, APS = punct_count/n_sent

Each of the above metrics characterizes the complexity of the text in a certain way, assuming that higher values of any of these metrics would correspond to more complex texts.

In addition, the following readability indices were considered [41].

- Flesch–Kincaid readability index $= (ASL) + (ASW)$
- Coleman–Liau index $= (\text{letters\_count}/\text{n\_words}) - (1/ASL)$
- SMOG grade $= \left(\sqrt{PLW \cdot ASL} \right)$
- Dale–Chall readability formula $= (PLW) + (ASL)$
- Automated readability index $= (\text{letters\_count}/\text{n\_words}) + (ASL)$

The formulae of these indices contain language-specific constants and multipliers. In particular, we took the values of the constants corresponding to the Russian language based on values calculated by Begtin [42].

3.5 Topic Modeling

The text topic definition was done with the BigARTM library, which implements the Additive Regularization of Topic Models approach [44]. Topic modeling reconstructs topic-term matrix Φ and topic-document matrix Θ from the corpus D using token dictionary W and token frequency matrix P [45]. Thus, for each document in the corpus, a vector of the topics' distribution represented by a column in the topic-document matrix Θ will be obtained and also for each topic we can obtain a vector of tokens' distribution represented by a column in the topic-term matrix Φ. We chose the number of possible topics for the texts equal to 50, which, on the one hand, is more than the number of communities in sample, and on the other hand, this helped to avoid the topics which could be excessively narrow. In the process of model building, we also used *Sparse regularizer* that provides a larger number of zero elements in matrices Φ and Θ, so that different topics contained as few common tokens as possible, and for a particular document the number of topics which produces a smaller number of topics associated. Another implemented feature was *Decorrelator regularizer* which minimizing the covariances between topics (columns of the matrix Φ), which also increases the interpretability of topics.

Resulting matrix Θ can be used to analyze topic proximity of the communities. Indeed, averaging its columns corresponding to different documents d placed in the same community c, we obtain a matrix $H = \{\eta_{tc}\}_{t,c}$ of size $|T| \times |C|$,

$$\eta_{tc} = \frac{\sum_{d \in c} \theta_{td}}{\sum_{d \in c} 1}$$

where $|C|$ is the number of analyzed communities. Matrix H also has the property that the sum of the elements of any of its columns equals 1. Column c itself can be interpreted as a vector of the topic orientation of the community. Based on such thematic representations of communities, we can compare how similar the communities are, using, for example, the cosine similarity measure.

$$cosine\_similarity(c_1, c_2) = \frac{\sum_{t \in T} \eta_{tc_1} \cdot \eta_{tc_2}}{\sqrt{\sum_{t \in T} \eta_{tc_1}^2} \cdot \sqrt{\sum_{t \in T} \eta_{tc_2}^2}}$$

This measure is calculated with the cosine of the angle between the vectors η_{c_1} and η_{c_2} in the Euclidean space $R^{|T|} = R^{50}$. Communities with similar topic distributions will have this metric close to 1 and, in contrast, communities with completely different topics will have this metric close to 0. Using this metric, we constructed a graph (Fig. 1). Its nodes are individual communities, and its edges connect those pairs of communities in which the value of this metric is greater than a certain threshold value (in this case, the threshold value was chosen as $\cos = 0.35$, which corresponds to 0.75 of the sample quantile). The resulting graph was further analyzed using Gephi application. The color in it corresponds to the main topic prevailing in the community.

3.6 Linguistic Features

For each post several measures borrowed from computational linguistics were calculated (objectiveness, qualitativeness, activeness, dynamism) [46: 148]. These indices were evaluated using the morphological analyzer pymorphy2.

The values of these indicators can give a basic understanding of the structure of the author's style, as well as what syntactic constructions used to engage the audience of social network users.

$$objectiveness = \frac{NOUN + PRO}{ADJ + VERB},$$

$$qualitativeness = \frac{ADJ + ADVB}{NOUN + VERB},$$

Fig. 1. Graph of communities' proximity

$$activeness = \frac{VERB}{n\_word},$$

$$dynamism = \frac{VERB}{NOUN + ADJ + PRO},$$

$$coherence = \frac{CONJ}{n\_sent},$$

where *NOUN* is the number of nouns in the post, *ADJ* is the number of adjectives, *VERB* is the number of verbs and participles, *PRO* is the number of pronouns, *ADVB* is the number of adverbs, *CONJ* is the number of prepositions and conjunctions. The calculation of these indices was carried out using the morphological analyzer pymorphy2.

The values of these indices can give a basic understanding of the structure of the author's style, as well as what syntactic constructions were used to attract the audience of social media audience.

Also using regular expressions, the boolean measures reflecting a presence of links, hashtags and emoji were assigned for each post.

- "has_hashtag" = presence of hashtags in the text
- "has_url" = presence of links in the text of the post
- "has_emoji" = presence of emojis

3.7 Sentiment

Using FastTextSocialNetworkModel and other models embedded in Dostoevsky library [47] each post has been matched to a particular class, such as «negative», «neutral», «positive», «skip», «speech». «Skip» is a code for unrecognized texts, «speech» means direct speech or addressing to someone.

Above mentioned model from Dostoevsky library with F1 = 0.71 in this research trained on RuSentiment [48] text corpus, which includes text from social networking site VKontakte.

3.8 Regression

To test the model performance, we split the entire data set into a training set (75%) and test set (25%). To build the regression model we used the Gradient Boosted Decision Trees, and also we built a few simpler models for comparison, such as DummyRegressor (predictor = the mean of ER in train sample), regression based on the k-nearest neighbors, and two versions of regularized linear regression: Ridge and Lasso (Table 1).

Table 1. The results of model training

	Train R^2	Test R^2	Train MAE	Test MAE
DummyRegressor	–	–	5,24	5,26
KNeighborsRegressor (n_neighbors = 50)	0,15	0,12	4,80	4,90
Ridge (alpha = 1)	0,36	0,37	3,99	4,00
Lasso (alpha = 1e−05)	0,36	0,37	3,99	4,00
GradientBoostingRegressor	0,70	0,48	2,76	3,55

GradientBoostingRegressor allowed to reach $R^2 = 0,70$ for train set and $0,48$ for test set.

4 Results

Summarizing the results of the calculations allows to construct a histogram of the significance of each of the 79 features that affect the engagement rate of the post. As can be seen, the most significant factors were the variables determining the presence of certain topics. Readability scores proved to be weak predictors of ER.

For each feature a *permutation importance* is given. This value indicates how much the quality of the model drops when the given feature is randomized in the set of parameters. For example, the model in which data from a column with the measure "topic_30" is shuffled would have R^2 lower by 0.074. If shuffling a given attribute decreases the predictive quality of the model, this attribute is important (Fig. 2).

Spearman rank correlation coefficients for the engagement and readability metrics were evaluated. All calculated coefficients reached significance level of 0.05. Although the correlation coefficients, as expected, were negative (with the exception of the TTR metric), the correlation values themselves were close to zero. The highest correlation coefficients were found for n_long_words and ind_SMOG metrics, as well as Coleman-Liau and Dale-Chall indices, that is, the absolute or relative number of "long" words in the text. High values of these metrics had a weak negative impact on user engagement (Tables 2 and 3).

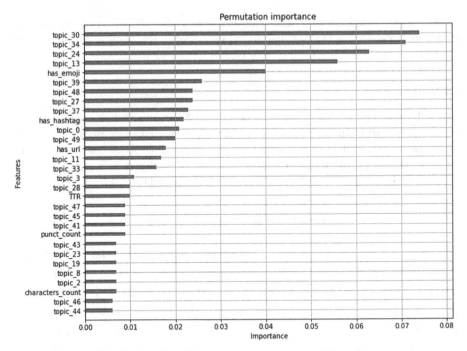

Fig. 2. Top-20 predictors for engagement rate of the posts

We selected a predominant topic for each post from our corpus of texts and then calculated the average engagement rate by topic.

The five topics with the highest engagement rate were topic_49 ("Exercises conducted by Ministry of defense"), 20 ("Marine exercises"), 39 ("Antitrust bodies' activity"), 0 ("Tactical exercises"). The same topics received the highest number of likes.

The largest number of comments per thousand of views obtained in topics about Roskomnadzor's restrictive measures against Internet sites violating copyright or related rights. Engagement measured with the number of reposts the leaders in ER were topics 28 ("Information on the Unified State Exam"), 45 ("Information about webinars, conferences, etc. hosted by authorities") and 12 ("Statistics on macroeconomic indicators published by various organizations"). Among the most significant attributes, the first were the attributes which corresponded to the share of a particular topic in post.

The topic of «Information about COVID-19» (topic_30) received low engagement score. This effect can be linked to the abundance of extremely diverse coronavirus-related posts, which can be followed by a decrease in the audience's interest in the topic and, in particular, negative attitudes dropping the number of likes. Topics related to the activities of bailiffs, debt collection had a negative impact on engagement (topic_34 + topic_13). Engagement rate in the topic relating to crises abroad (topic_24) was also significantly lower compared to other topics (Table 4).

Table 2. Spearman rank correlation coefficient

	n_sent	n_word	n_word_unique	characters_count	letters_count	punct_count	n_syllables	n_long_words
eng_rate	−0,05	−0,12	−0,11	−0,13	−0,13	−0,10	−0,13	−0,16
eng_L	−0,06	−0,12	−0,11	−0,13	−0,13	−0,10	−0,13	−0,16
eng_C	−0,01	−0,05	−0,04	−0,07	−0,06	−0,04	−0,06	−0,07
eng_R	0,04	−0,01	−0,02	−0,02	−0,02	0,03	−0,02	−0,04

Table 3. Spearman rank correlation coefficient

	ASL	ASW	PLW	TTR	APS	ind_Flesh_Kincaid_Grade	ind_Coleman_Liau	ind_SMOG	ind_Dale_Chall	ind_ARI
eng_rate	−0,12	−0,09	−0,12	0,12	−0,13	−0,12	−0,12	−0,15	−0,15	−0,13
eng_L	−0,11	−0,07	−0,11	0,13	−0,13	−0,11	−0,10	−0,15	−0,14	−0,12
eng_C	-0,06	−0,10	−0,05	0,05	−0,07	−0,10	−0,12	−0,07	−0,07	−0,12
eng_R	-0,08	−0,07	−0,08	−0,02	−0,01	−0,09	−0,10	−0,10	−0,10	−0,11

Table 4. Topics with negative affect on ER

Topics significantly affecting ER and top words	Effect
topic_34: bailiff judicial executive debtor rouble production Russia means debt FBS (Federal bailiffs service) penalty fulfillment citizen thousand debt region criminal [case]_against money	Low ER
topic_24: center Roshydromet (Federal service for hydrometeorology and environmental monitoring) department information situational crisis SCC (Rescue coordination center) flight expedition foreign assistant airport weather possible communication vessel country strike transport island station	Low ER
topic_13: bailiff service administrative Russia press UFSSP (Federal bailiffs service) employee activity reliability requirement organization executive management region work execution violation decision	Low ER
topic_30: medical care coronavirus doctor infection health care patient covid medicine pandemic center coronavirus disease health spread treatment coronavirus blood hospital specialist	Low ER

Features related to the readability of the texts proved to be much less significant. One of the most significant features in this category was the number of punctuation marks in the text.

The readability of texts has a much weaker impact on the level of engagement than topic distribution. The SMOG index corresponding to the complexity of the text had a weak inverse relation to the level of engagement.

Particular topics were presented primarily in one or few communities (Table 5).

Table 5. Topics and their presence in communities' content

Topics	Top-5 communities representing topics, share
topic_30 (COVID-19)	Federal Service for Surveillance on Consumer Rights Protection and Human Wellbeing, 0.2
	Ministry of Health of the Russian Federation, 0.19
	Federal Service for Supervision in the Sphere of Healthcare, 0.19
	Administrative Directorate of the President, 0.06
	Government, 0.03
topic_34 (Activities of bailiffs, debt collection)	Federal Bailiffs Service, 0.58
	Federal Taxation Service, 0.07
	Federal Service for Labor and Employment, 0.06
	Federal Security Service, 0.04
	Ministry of Emergency Situations, 0.02

(continued)

Table 5. (*continued*)

Topics	Top-5 communities representing topics, share
topic_24 (Crisis situations abroad)	Federal Service for Hydrometeorology and Environmental Monitoring of Russia, 0.33
	Ministry of Foreign Affairs, 0.12
	Federal Subsoil Resources Management Agency, 0.11
	Federal Service for Supervision in Education and Science, 0.09
	Federal State Statistics Service, 0.06
topic_13 (Activities of bailiffs, debt collection)	Federal Service for Labor and Employment, 0.34
	Federal Bailiffs Service, 0.22
	Federal Penitentiary Service, 0.11
	Federal Security Service, 0.07
	Federal Service for Supervision in the Sphere of Healthcare, 0.04

5 Discussion

The topics which were revealed as the most significant predictors of engagement rate were specific themes mostly presented in posts of the certain communities (such as the Ministry of Defense and Federal Bailiffs Service) whose texts are not similar to the texts in the almost all other communities. (Fig. 1).

The vast majority of the 79 metrics we used to describe texts published in online communities of government agencies proved to be uninformative for making predictions on the possibility of influencing engagement rates. Topics and communities (places of publication) were much more useful for predicting audience engagement than other factors. To a certain extent, this also indicates that differences in the audiences themselves matter, as subscribers differ in their interests in various communities.

The readability indicators that we used were quite diverse, which allows to claim that, at least in the case of automatic classification, easy-to-read posts in general do not differ from other typical posts in the communities of Russian government executive bodies in terms of provided engagement.

The question of the influence of text length on the quality of classification remains relevant, since, firstly, texts in different communities vary significantly in length and, secondly, they are still short for some metrics. It is worth to admit that classification of short texts is associated with certain limitations [49]. Moreover, some experimental studies of online communities show that quality of texts can be directly and linearly related to their length [17].

6 Conclusion

In this study, we addressed the question of the influence of text readability and other text characteristics on the level of user engagement in social media within the context of political communication. The posts in communities of Russian government executive bodies published on social networking site Vkontakte published from 01.01.2017 to 16.09.2020 were taken as a sample.

We considered engagement rate (which characterizes the level of feedback based on likes, comments, and views) as dependent variable and various characteristics of the texts, among which including 10 readability measures and 69 other metrics, as independent variables.

The set of additional features included readability metrics as well as additional variables such as topics presence, linguistic and paralinguistic metrics, and sentiment. This approach allowed to consider readability in the context of other effects to provide a comprehensive picture.

As our data showed, in the case of communication strategies in online communities in social network VKontakte, the readability of posts was not directly related to engagement rate. Much more significant factors were the topics presence and, respectively, the belonging of the posts to certain communities. Also, we got no evidence that some topics to help to ensure the increase in ER, but we revealed some topics connected with a lowering of ER.

Thus, according to our data, it is difficult to influence the growth of feedback by improving the readability; accordingly, the question arises about the possibility of influencing other factors that represent the satisfaction and engagement of the audience. Readability research is relevant in the context of fake news detection techniques [50] and improving the comprehension of different documents and reports [51]. Accordingly, the analysis of readability metrics in relation to online community posts can be useful for the overall assessment of ease of perception and fact-checking.

Limitations. The dataset used in this study represents fairly specific communities; for better representation, it would be useful to compare the results with some control sample of "neutral' communities in the future. We do not analyze or even consider the possibility of artificial (automated) influence on engagement, in particular, the number of likes and comments. The readability metrics we use are computational, and in some cases have tangible limitations comparing to subjective manual classification. Also, among the limitations are the typical assumptions that accompany regression analysis and topic modeling techniques (such as the hypothesis of the existence of topics and the independence of observations).

Further Work. This research suggests several possible directions for the development of the method used in it. First, there is interest in the scenario of a creation of more complex, comprehensive indicators of readability, which are capable of reflecting an amount of the nuances specific to publications on social networks. Second, it can also be implemented to design alternative indicators measuring other potentially important factors, such as the time of publication, the effect of community scale, attached images, videos and so on.

Acknowledgement. The reported study was funded by RFBR and EISR according to the research project № 20-011-31318.

References

1. Machiavelli, N.: Concerning the politician and the media. In: The Politician, pp. 97–102. Springer, Cham (2020). https://doi.org/10.1007/978-3-030-39091-4_19
2. Tolochko, P., Boomgaarden, H.G.: Determining political text complexity: conceptualizations, measurements, and application. Int. J. Commun. **13**, 1784–1804 (2019)
3. Dalecki, L., Lasorsa, D.L., Lewis, S.C.: The news readability problem. Journal. Pract. **3**(1), 1–12 (2009)
4. Bigi, A.: Viral political communication and readability: an analysis of an Italian political blog. J. Public Aff. **13**(2), 209–217 (2013)
5. Kayam, O.: The readability and simplicity of Donald Trump's language. Polit. Stud. Rev. **16**(1), 73–88 (2018)
6. Graefe, A., Haim, M., Haarmann, B., Brosius, H.B.: Readers' perception of computer-generated news: credibility, expertise, and readability. Journalism **19**(5), 595–610 (2018)
7. Aldous, K.K., An, J., Jansen, B.J.: View, like, comment, post: analyzing user engagement by topic at 4 levels across 5 social media platforms for 53 news organizations. In: Proceedings of the International AAAI Conference on Web and Social Media, vol. 13, pp. 47–57 (2019)
8. Balmas, M., Sheafer, T.: Candidate image in election campaigns: attribute agenda setting, affective priming, and voting intentions. Int. J, Public Opin. Res. **22**(2), 204–229 (2010)
9. Funk, M.J., McCombs, M.: Strangers on a theoretical train: inter-media agenda setting, community structure, and local news coverage. Journal. Stud. **18**(7), 845–865 (2017)
10. Pancer, E., Chandler, V., Poole, M., Noseworthy, T.J.: How readability shapes social media engagement. J. Consum. Psychol. **29**(2), 262–270 (2019)
11. Leonhardt, J.M., Makienko, I.: Keep it simple, readability increases engagement on twitter: an abstract. In: Krey, N., Rossi, Patricia (eds.) AMSAC 2017. DMSPAMS, pp. 333–334. Springer, Cham (2018). https://doi.org/10.1007/978-3-319-66023-3_116
12. Xu, Z., Ellis, L., Umphrey, L.R.: The easier the better? Comparing the readability and engagement of online pro-and anti-vaccination articles. Health Educ. Behav. **46**(5), 790–797 (2019)
13. Tolochko, P., Song, H., Boomgaarden, H.: "That looks hard!": effects of objective and perceived textual complexity on factual and structural political knowledge. Polit. Commun. **36**(4), 609–628 (2019)
14. Melloni, G., Caglio, A., Perego, P.: Saying more with less? Disclosure conciseness, completeness and balance in integrated reports. J. Account. Public Policy **36**(3), 220–238 (2017)
15. Hassan, M.K., Abbas, B.A., Garas, S.N.: Readability, governance and performance: a test of the obfuscation hypothesis in Qatari listed firms. Corporate Governance. Int. J. Bus. Soc. **19**(2), 270–298 (2019)
16. Benoit, K., Munger, K., Spirling, A.: Measuring and explaining political sophistication through textual complexity. Am., J. Polit. Sci. **63**(2), 491–508 (2019)
17. Al Qundus, J., Paschke, A., Gupta, S., Alzouby, A.M., Yousef, M.: Exploring the impact of short-text complexity and structure on its quality in social media. J. Enterp. Inf. Manag. **33**(6), 1443–1466 (2020)
18. Temnikova, I., Vieweg, S., Castillo, C.: The case for readability of crisis communications in social media. In: Proceedings of the 24th International Conference on World Wide Web, pp. 1245–1250 (2015)

19. Michalski, K.B., Guile, M.N.: Readability of simulated state question ballots affects voting behavior. Bull. Psychon. Soc. **28**(3), 239–240 (1990). https://doi.org/10.3758/BF03334014
20. King, B.A., Youngblood, N.E.: E-government in Alabama: an analysis of county voting and election website content, usability, accessibility, and mobile readiness. Gov. Inf. Q. **33**(4), 715–726 (2016)
21. Gyasi, W.K.: Readability and political discourse: an analysis of press releases of Ghanaian political parties. J. Media Commun. Stud. **9**(6), 42–50 (2017)
22. Göksu, G.G., Dumlupinar, S.: Readability analysis of laws related to public financial responsibility and state budget: a comparison of selected countries. In: Contemporary Studies in Economic and Financial Analysis, vol. 105, pp. 91–112. Emerald Publishing Limited (2021)
23. Bischof, D., Senninger, R.: Simple politics for the people? Complexity in campaign messages and political knowledge. Eur. J. Polit. Res. **57**(2), 473–495 (2018)
24. Schoonvelde, M., Brosius, A., Schumacher, G., Bakker, B.N.: Liberals lecture, conservatives communicate: analyzing complexity and ideology in 381,609 political speeches. PLoS ONE **14**(2), e0208450 (2019)
25. Grimmer, J., Stewart, B.M.: Text as data: the promise and pitfalls of automatic content analysis methods for political texts. Polit. Anal. **21**(3), 267–297 (2013)
26. Berger, J., Milkman, K.L.: What makes online content viral? J. Mark. Res. **49**, 192–205 (2012)
27. Firouzjaei, H.A., Ozdemir, S.F.: Effect of readability of political tweets on positive user engagement. In: 2020 IEEE/ACM International Conference on Advances in Social Networks Analysis and Mining (ASONAM) (2020, preprint)
28. Pancer, E., Poole, M.: The popularity and virality of political social media: hashtags, mentions, and links predict likes and retweets of 2016 US presidential nominees' tweets. Soc. Influ. **11**(4), 259–270 (2016)
29. Noguti, V.: Post language and user engagement in online content communities. Eur. J. Mark. **50**(5/6), 695–723 (2016)
30. Eberl, J.M., Tolochko, P., Jost, P., Heidenreich, T., Boomgaarden, H.G.: What's in a post? How sentiment and issue salience affect users' emotional reactions on Facebook. J. Inform. Tech. Polit. **17**(1), 48–65 (2020)
31. Gerbaudo, P., Marogna, F., Alzetta, C.: When "positive posting" attracts voters: user engagement and emotions in the 2017 UK Election Campaign on Facebook. Soc. Media+ Soc. **5**(4), 2056305119881695 (2019)
32. Preoţiuc-Pietro, D., Liu, Y., Hopkins, D., Ungar, L.: Beyond binary labels: political ideology prediction of Twitter users. In: Proceedings of the 55th Annual Meeting of the Association for Computational Linguistics, vol. 1, pp. 729–740 (2017)
33. Shukrun-Nagar, P.: Constructed general truths against specific political rivals in politicians' Facebook posts. J. Pragmat. **172**, 79–88 (2020)
34. Furini, M., Montangero, M.: On predicting the success of political tweets using psycholinguistic categories. In: 2019 28th International Conference on Computer Communication and Networks, pp. 1–6. IEEE (2019)
35. Shugars, S., Beauchamp, N.: Why keep arguing? Predicting engagement in political conversations online. SAGE Open **9**(1), 2158244019828850 (2019)
36. Liebeskind, C., Nahon, K., HaCohen-Kerner, Y., Manor, Y.: Comparing sentiment analysis models to classify attitudes of political comments on Facebook. Polibits **55**, 17–23 (2017)
37. Heiss, R., Schmuck, D., Matthes, J.: What drives interaction in political actors' Facebook posts? Profile and content predictors of user engagement and political actors' reactions. Inf. Commun. Soc. **22**(10), 1497–1513 (2019)
38. Dutceac Segesten, A., Bossetta, M., Holmberg, N., Niehorster, D.: The cueing power of comments on social media: how disagreement in Facebook comments affects user engagement with news. Inf. Commun. Soc. 1–20 (2020, ahead of print). https://doi.org/10.1080/1369118X.2020.1850836

39. Mystem on Github. https://github.com/nlpub/pymystem3. Accessed 01 Feb 2021

40. François, T., Miltsakaki, E.: Do NLP and machine learning improve traditional readability formulas? In: Proceedings of the First Workshop on Predicting and Improving Text Readability for Target Reader Populations, pp. 49–57 (2012)

41. Laposhina, N., Veselovskaya, V., Lebedeva, M.U., Kupreshchenko, O.F.: Automated text readability assessment for Russian second language learners. In: Conference: Proceedings of the International Conference on Computational Linguistics and Intellectual Technologies "Dialogue", vol. 24, pp. 403–413 (2018)

42. Begtin, I.V.: What is "Clear Russian" in terms of technology. Let's take a look at the metrics for the readability of texts: the blog of the company "Information Culture". (in Russian). http://habrahabr.ru/company/infoculture/blog/238875/. Accessed 01 Feb 2021

43. Solnyshkina, M., Ivanov, V., Solovyev, V.: Readability formula for Russian texts: a modified version. In: Batyrshin, I., Martínez-Villaseñor, M. de L., Ponce Espinosa, H.E. (eds.) MICAI 2018. LNCS (LNAI), vol. 11289, pp. 132–145. Springer, Cham (2018). https://doi.org/10.1007/978-3-030-04497-8_11

44. Vorontsov, K., Potapenko, A.: Tutorial on probabilistic topic modeling: additive regularization for stochastic matrix factorization. In: Ignatov, D.I., Khachay, M.Yu., Panchenko, A., Konstantinova, N., Yavorskiy, R.E. (eds.) AIST 2014. CCIS, vol. 436, pp. 29–46. Springer, Cham (2014). https://doi.org/10.1007/978-3-319-12580-0_3

45. Ianina, A., Golitsyn, L., Vorontsov, K.: Multi-objective topic modeling for exploratory search in tech news. In: Filchenkov, A., Pivovarova, L., Žižka, J. (eds.) AINL 2017. CCIS, vol. 789, pp. 181–193. Springer, Cham (2018). https://doi.org/10.1007/978-3-319-71746-3_16

46. Golovin, B.: Language and Statistics. Enlightenment, Moscow (1971). (in Russian)

47. Dostoevsky library. https://pypi.org/project/dostoevsky/. Accessed 01 Feb 2021

48. Rogers, A., Romanov, A., Rumshisky, A., Volkova, S., Gronas, M., Gribov, A.: RuSentiment: an enriched sentiment analysis dataset for social media in Russian. In: Proceedings of the 27th International Conference on Computational Linguistics, pp. 755–763 (2018)

49. Alsmadi, I., Gan, K.H.: Review of short-text classification. Int. J. Web Inf. Syst. **15**(2), 155–182 (2019)

50. Santos, R., et al.: Measuring the impact of readability features in fake news detection. In: Proceedings of the 12th Language Resources and Evaluation Conference, pp. 1404–1413 (2020)

51. Hadden, K.B., Prince, L.Y., Moore, T.D., James, L.P., Holland, J.R., Trudeau, C.R.: Improving readability of informed consents for research at an academic medical institution. J. Clin. Transl. Sci. **1**(6), 361–365 (2017)

Effects of Conspiracy Thinking Style, Framing and Political Interest on Accuracy of Fake News Recognition by Social Media Users: Evidence from Russia, Kazakhstan and Ukraine

Alexander Porshnev[1]([✉]) [iD], Alex Miltsov[2] [iD], Tetyana Lokot[3] [iD], and Olessia Koltsova[1] [iD]

[1] National Research University Higher School of Economics, St. Petersburg, Russia
aporshnev@hse.ru
[2] Bishop's University, Sherbrooke, Canada
[3] Dublin City University, Dublin, Ireland

Abstract. This study examines the effect of specific factors (including user features, such as propensity for conspiracy thinking, and news item features, such as news frame and news source) on the accuracy of social media users in fake news recognition. Being a part of a larger research on fake news perception, this study uses the data from an online experiment that asks social media users from three countries (Russia, Ukraine and Kazakhstan) to evaluate a set of news items constructed with specific conditions. Namely, the users receive true and fake news about the neighboring countries framed differently and ascribed to either domestic or foreign sources. We then assess users' accuracy in detecting fake news. The results of the study confirm the important role of conspiracy thinking style in false news recognition (leading to a decrease in accuracy) and users' capability for deliberation on social media more broadly. However, the influence of contextual factors is mixed. While news sources exhibit no influence on the accuracy of fake or true news detection, dominant framing tends to increase the accuracy of true news only. More predictors of news recognition accuracy are discussed in the paper. As a result, this research contributes to the theory of fake news susceptibility by revealing a rich set of individual factors and interaction effects that influence human judgment about news truthfulness and impact deliberation possibilities in socially mediated environments.

Keywords: Fake news · Accuracy · Conspiracy mentality · Frame · Thinking style

1 Introduction

The development and diffusion of digital technologies has transformed the informational environment by creating the possibility of quick dissemination of false news in social networks. Recent studies have identified several factors affecting the accuracy of fake news recognition by social media users. These factors include individual thinking styles,

© Springer Nature Switzerland AG 2021
G. Meiselwitz (Ed.): HCII 2021, LNCS 12774, pp. 341–357, 2021.
https://doi.org/10.1007/978-3-030-77626-8_23

news sources, reader attitudes, and social influence, among others. We argue that the concept of fake news detection should be divided into two related, but separate concepts. The first concept is associated with an individual's assessment of news truthfulness based on their cognitive abilities [1]. The second concerns the degree of trust towards a news item [2], based on certain cues (such as news sources or news framing) whose trustworthiness is transferred to the news item [3, 4]. These concepts are related as the usage of cues is likely to depend on individual thinking styles.

However, each concept is not only associated more closely with one group of predictors than the other (user features, including cognitive abilities, vs news features, including cues of trustworthiness). In fact, each concept constitutes a distinct phenomenon that should be measured in its own way. While news trust, or news item credibility, is the inclination to view a given news item as truthful, the accuracy of fake news detection is the ability to classify a news item correctly. Accuracy is thus higher when the trust in true news is also higher, but the trust in fakes is simultaneously lower. In this paper, we focus on the investigation of the factors influencing accuracy, although both aforementioned groups of factors are studied. News credibility is not a part of the present paper.

In our pilot study based on a sample of students [5], we discovered that conspiracy thinking affected the likelihood of false news recognition. News framing and such attitudinal factors as political views, attitude to the current government, and conflict perception were some of the other important factors. In this paper, we seek to further examine the effects of these factors based on a much broader sample from three countries: Russia, Kazakhstan and Ukraine.

1.1 Theoretical Framework

Our theoretical framework is based on the key factors that affect the accuracy of fake news recognition by social media users. First, we consider the scholarship on cognitive factors such as thinking style and conspiracy thinking, associated with an individual's assessment of news truthfulness based on their cognitive abilities. Second, we review the literature on news item features. Although they have been mostly studied as predictors of news item credibility, they matter as possible factors influencing the accuracy of fake news recognition. We begin our review by reviewing the growing literature on fake news as a concept.

Fake News

Although the concept of "fake news" has gained widespread popularity in recent years, our analysis of relevant scholarship indicates that the issue of false, inaccurate or incomplete information and its dissemination is not new [6]. The concept can be traced back to a long history of related phenomena, such as propaganda, which can be defined as information aimed at supporting certain political or ideological decisions or at denying alternative ideas [7, 8]. Propaganda usually achieves its aims through distorting information (i.e., through fake news dissemination), selective information provision and focusing attention on certain aspects of an issue (i.e., framing) [9]. Another related concept is unintentionally misleading or inaccurate information that is spread organically

[10] which is outside of the scope of our study. Our experiment, therefore, focuses on fake news as information that is deliberately created to be false [11].

Thinking Styles and Conspiracy Thinking

An analysis of the relevant scholarship reveals that one of the most important factors in determining the accuracy of fake news detection is the style of thinking. Studies by Bronstein and colleagues have shown that rational thinking largely determines the ability of fake news detection [12]. On the other hand, dogmatism and belief in various extrasensory phenomena reduce people's ability to differentiate between truth and lies [12–14]. For instance, Coe found that magical thinking heightens the susceptibility of a person towards fake news [15].

Having examined the literature related to thinking patterns and people's abilities to evaluate the credibility of information, we propose to include the concept of conspiracy thinking as one of the possible factors impacting detection accuracy. It has recently attracted considerable attention from political scientists, psychologists and sociologists [16]. In 2018, an entire issue of the European Journal of Social Psychology was devoted to the concept of conspiracy theory and its impact on decision-making processes [17]. Several studies have demonstrated the influence of conspiracy thinking on decision-making mechanisms during elections [18]; shown a negative relationship between belief in conspiracies and interpersonal trust or trust in the police [19–21]; or revealed a connection between conspiracy and authoritarian thinking [22]. Our study thus includes several variables related to social media users' cognitive abilities and thinking styles, and specific questions measuring conspiracy thinking.

News Framing

The scholarship on news framing and agenda setting is an established area in media studies, with research exploring the limits of journalistic objectivity as well as the possible impact of agenda setting and framing on public opinion [23]. The agenda-setting function refers to the media's capability to direct audience attention to a specific set of themes or issues [24], as well as to influence the audience's awareness of particular subjects or their salience. The concept of media framing [25] is related to agenda setting and is generally defined as a particular way of interpreting a particular news agenda or topic or of presenting the news item in a specific light. News framing and the construction of media frames have garnered substantial scholarly attention [9, 23, 25, 26]. Relevant scholarship has identified key factors influencing frame formation, including dominant social and political views [27] and the structure of the media industry in a given geopolitical context [28].

Our research considered a broad spectrum of approaches to frame operationalization proposed in a number of empirical studies [29, 30], as well as various methodological approaches to frame identification [31–35], their limitations and applications. Importantly, scholars have found that perceptions of news issue frame believability [36] can affect sharing intention, especially in politically polarized contexts where disinformation is known to proliferate. Because frames tend to emphasize specific "potentially relevant considerations" [37], p. 672), they can lead social media audiences to adhere to certain beliefs when forming attitudes or making judgments [38, 39]. However, there has been no research on the influence of framing on the accuracy of fake news recognition.

News Source and Related Cues

Recent studies have identified the credibility of the news source as one of several factors affecting the accuracy of fake news recognition by social network users [40, 41]. On the other hand, the potential effect of news source credibility perception on news recognition accuracy is often compounded by other relevant factors, such as prior exposure to news items or sources [13], the construction and structure of the news title and text [42], as well as a user's level of political loyalty or partisan orientation [15].

In addition, a number of factors have been found to affect fake news detection accuracy in the context of trust-based actions, including alignment of political orientation of the news author/source with that of the reader [15]; the presence of comments connected to the news story [43, 44]; the presence of hyperlinks in the news text [45]; recommendations by opinion leaders [46], as well as levels of generalized trust in other people. Our study controls for generalized trust among other variables, and includes variable conditions with regard to news frame, news source and news truthfulness.

1.2 Hypotheses

The above overview of relevant literature coupled with an analysis of experimental research on fake news perception [12, 15, 43, 44, 47, 48] and experimental studies of trust in social media networks [40, 46, 49, 50] indicate that the design of our own experimental research study would benefit from incorporating both elements that would allow us to examine factors of accuracy in news recognition and elements that would permit us to study cognitive factors of fake news detection. Combining both approaches allows for a more robust design that accounts for the complex process of fake news recognition and the multiple combinations of factors that might impact on the success of fake detection.

Based on the overview of scholarship presented in the preceding section, we formulate the following hypotheses that account for both the potential impact of thinking styles, and conspiracy thinking in particular, and the impact of news-related cues such as framing and news source, on accuracy of fake news recognition.

Thinking Styles/Conspiracy Thinking

We expect that individuals prone to thinking styles characterized by conspiracy thinking will exhibit less accuracy in recognizing fake news stories. This expectation is grounded in prior research on the connections between conspiracy thinking and trust in authority, as well as interpersonal trust, and the impact of conspiracy thinking on decision-making. We therefore formulate our first hypothesis as:

H1. Conspiracy thinking decreases the accuracy of news recognition.

News Framing

As news framing has been found to influence belief adherence, it is unlikely to influence accuracy directly – rather, it can be expected to increase believability if this frame is familiar to a user or contains the values she shares, while having an opposite effect if this framing is unfamiliar or far from a user's values. In our research, we single out two types of framing: dominant, meaning the one prevalent in the user's country, and therefore familiar and likely shared, and alternative, which is rare and thus less familiar and less likely to be shared by users. Given the aforementioned reasoning, dominant framing should increase believability of both true and fake news, while alternative should have the opposite influence; thus the influence of both on accuracy depends on the type of news the user is dealing with – either true or false. Therefore, our second hypothesis is as follows:

H2. The influence of news framing on the accuracy of news recognition is moderated by the type of news – either true or fake.

News Sources

Likewise, we discriminate between two types of news sources: sources from the country of the user and sources from the country covered in the news (as we deal only with international news). Here, however, we have a slightly different expectation. First, we assume that a foreign news source would be treated by most users with more suspicion and thus make them alert which can potentially contribute to accuracy. Domestic sources are thus expected to make the readers more relaxed and less attentive, which is why our next hypothesis is as follows:

H3. Domestic news source decreases the accuracy of fake news recognition.

2 Methodology

2.1 Research Design

This paper uses the data from a broader project on fake news perception published in a series of related papers. To collect these data, we invited users to take part in our online experiment through targeted ads on Facebook and VKontakte. From April 13, 2020 to June 23, 2020, 10,380 people from three countries (Russia, Ukraine and Kazakhstan) participated in our study. This resulted in 8,559 completed surveys, representing the population of users from three countries (across both SNSs) in eight subsamples (approx. 900 respondents in each subsample). For more details about data collection and participants' churn rate see [57].

We used a $2 \times 2 \times 2$ design for the experiment. Participants were offered eight news items that varied by the following conditions: frame (dominant or alternative); publication source – from the country of respondent or not; news truthfulness – whether the news was true or false. Respondents were asked to evaluate their perception of each news item on a 6-level Likert scale (from "False" to "True").

The control variables were: gender, age, level of education, news consumption preferences, generalized trust, and political interests. To evaluate political orientation we used the following question: "To what extent do you generally agree with the policy of your country's leadership?". Respondents' perception of the relationship between countries was measured by a question about bilateral relations between countries. To measure conspiracy thinking style, we used two questions adapted from the Conspiracy Mentality Scale [21]. To assess the validity of adaptation of the Conspiracy Mentality Scale, we tested the factor structure, and calculated its Cronbach reliability coefficient.

Next, we carried out nested and generalized linear regression analyses with mixed effects to analyze the influence of each independent variable on the overall accuracy of news recognition, the accuracy of recognition of false news and truthful news separately, and the accuracy of recognition for each news item.

2.2 News Selection

The content presented to the participants included a set of news items selected to fulfil a number of conditions. First, the news items had to correspond to the empirically justified frames for each country, while remaining realistic regardless of their true or false nature. In order to address the comparative objectives of the study, two pairs of news item sets were created: 1) a) containing news stories about Ukraine for users from Russia; b) containing news stories about Russia for users from Ukraine; 2) a) containing news stories about Kazakhstan for users from Russia; b) containing news stories about Russia for users from Kazakhstan. Each set included 24 news items and had equal numbers of combinations of false and real news stories with dominant or alternative frames. In addition, each set included an additional control news item related to the coronavirus pandemic. Thus, the total volume of stimulus materials included 100 news texts [51]).

The real news items were selected from actual media outlets with additional verification to ensure they were factually correct, whereas the fake news items were constructed by the researchers. We conducted a news agenda analysis using a substantial news data set to understand each country's news agenda regarding the other country (e.g. Russian news about Kazakhstan) in each comparative pairing (for more details see [52, 53]). We then used the results of this analysis to finalize the selection of news.

The following conditions were used as additional criteria for news item selection: 1) the news item covers a single event which is discernibly verifiable as true or false; 2) the news item can be attributed to a source from either of the two countries without contradictions; 3) the news item contains a frame (dominant or alternative) which is typical for the news agenda of the respondent's native country.

2.3 Sampling

As a result of advertisements displayed online, a total of 44,600 users from both SNSs (Facebook and VKontakte) clicked through to the app or the experiment website. Of these, 30,702 users began participation in the study, while 10,830 users participated in the post-experiment survey. It is worth noting that some demographic groups were over-represented in the sample, so after data collection, the subset of valid survey responses was additionally rebalanced so that each subsample corresponded to its general population in terms of age, gender and audience region in the SNSs. For balancing, consolidated regions were used: seven federal districts in Russia and four consolidated regions each in Ukraine and Kazakhstan based on the relevant scholarly literature. In Ukraine, Crimea, Donetsk and Luhansk regions were excluded for both technical and methodological reasons.

As a result, the number of completed surveys was reduced from 10,380 to 8,559, excluding containing incomplete information (due to database errors caused by disconnection of mobile internet) or containing discrepancies in answers to questions (e.g., a respondent stating they were 36 years old and then selecting "I am a school pupil" category). In the filtered and balanced dataset, each sample of users from each SNS in each country contains data from over 500 participants (see Table 1). From here on, unless stated otherwise, the paper refers to the sample of 8,559 respondents, refined and reflecting the distribution of VKontakte and Facebook users by region, age, and gender of the audience in Russia, Ukraine and Kazakhstan.

Table 1. Balanced sample sizes for each country and SNS.

Country and SNS	Number	Percentage
Facebook (Kazakhstan)	904	10.56%
VKontakte (Kazakhstan)	913	10.67%
Facebook (Russia)	2076	24.26%
VKontakte (Russia)	1810	21.15%
Facebook (Ukraine)	2286	26.71%
VKontakte (Ukraine)	570*	6.66%

*The VKontakte social network is blocked for users in Ukraine (though still available via VPNs), which results in a lower respondent rate in this region

2.4 Variables

Accuracy
In the experimental part we asked participants to evaluate the truthfulness of the presented news item. This allowed us to measure respondents' accuracy in identifying a particular news item (descriptive statistics presented in Appendix 1 Table A1). The largest proportion of respondents (26.67%) were able to correctly recognize five news items as either true or false. Accurate recognition of four news items was demonstrated by 24.4% of participants, and of six news items – by 18.62%. The numbers differed from country to country, but without significant anomalies. The analysis of individual participants' accuracy for specific news items recognition demonstrated that the accuracy varied from 28.35% to 86.93%. This is why we decided to use linear mixed effect models to analyze the impact of each possible factor, taking into account accuracy variance related to the content of a news item.

The accuracy of recognition of dominant and alternative news frames was similar (56.62% and 59.1% respectively). The accuracy for true news stories was slightly lower (56.83%) than for fake ones (58.89%). Participants, on average, were equally accurate in deciphering news attributed to their own (57.78%) or to a foreign country (57.94%). Since the results do not take into account the variability of accuracy in news item recognition, we cannot use them to either confirm or reject H2 and H3. At the same time, we expect that these hypotheses will be rejected in further, more refined analysis.

Conspiracy Thinking

Conspiracy thinking was measured by using two questions adapted from the Conspiracy Mentality Scale [21]: "The alternative explanations for important societal events are closer to the truth than the official story" and "The government or covert organizations are responsible for events that are unusual or unexplained." The conspiracy thinking scale showed good reliability in almost all samples with the exception of the Ukraine Facebook sample, where the scale's reliability was lower than the usual threshold of 0.70 (0.63). The sample from VKontakte in Russia demonstrated the lowest conspiracy mentality (Mean = 3.14) and the highest average was in the Ukraine Facebook sample (Mean = 3.72). However, because of the low reliability of the scale in the Ukraine Facebook sample, this result should be regarded with caution. Descriptive statistics are presented in Appendix 1 Table A2.

Double-Checking of Information

Since we administered the questionnaire online, we could not prevent our participants from using the internet to double-check the news. To account for that, for each news item, we asked participants whether they had checked this news during the experiment. Based on this information, we created the "News checked" variable. Notably, the majority of participants (7,767 – 90.75%) did not check a single news item. One story was checked by 446 respondents (5.44%), two by 101 (1.18%), three by 79 (0.92%), four by 55 (0.64%) and between five and eight news items by 36 (0.37%), and all nine news items were checked by 30 respondents (0.35%).

Table 2. Frequency distribution for "News checked" and "News seen" variables.

Number of news	News seen	News seen%	News checked	News checked%
0	5558	64.94	7767	90.75
1	1,301	15.2	466	5.44
2	599	7	101	1.18
3	466	5.44	79	0.92
4	324	3.79	55	0.64
5	159	1.86	30	0.35
6	65	0.76	15	0.18
7	33	0.39	10	0.12
8	10	0.12	6	0.07
9	44	0.51	30	0.35

All the true news stories selected for the experiment originated from publicly available sources and these news had been in circulation for a while, so it was possible that they had already been seen by our respondents. For each news item, we asked participants whether they had already seen this information. Based on these data, we created the "News seen" variable. Notably, the majority of participants (5,558 or 64.94%) indicated that they had never seen a single news item prior to the experiment (Table 2).

Although the false stories were specifically created for the purpose of the experiment and we double-checked that they did not appear on the web, 1,415 (16.53%) participants indicated that they had already seen them before. As for the true stories, they were indicated as previously seen by 1,719 (20.08%) participants. This high level of recognition of fake news may be explained by the fact that this variable measures the perception of participants that they have already encountered this information, and not the actual encounter with a news item.

News Consumption

The question about news consumption included the following answer options: TV, Print newspapers and journals, Radio, SNSs and Forums, Bloggers, News sites and News aggregators, Friends, Other. Participants were asked to indicate their top three choices. All options were recorded as individual dummy variables. Descriptive statistics are presented in Appendix 1 Table A3.

The top three sources of information for participants in our study were: SNSs and forums – 70.51%, news sites and aggregators – 46.64%, and TV – 42.70%. While Russian and Kazakhstani respondents were similar in their patterns of news consumption, Ukrainian respondents were slightly different: while SNSs were in first place (74.92%), television was second (46.91%), and news aggregators – third (36.37%). The rest of the sources received no more than 25% each. The majority of respondents (47.80%) indicated that they used three sources (the respondent could choose no more than three sources), only one source was used by 29.68%, and two sources by 22.52%.

General Trust

Prior research indicates that news perception may be related to the level of general trust in people. To measure general trust, we used three questions adapted from the World Values Survey: "Most of the time people try to be helpful", "People can be trusted", "Most people would try to take advantage of you if they got a chance" [54]. The results of combining three questions into a single scale showed low psychometric characteristics (a-Cronbach = 0.48). Therefore, during the analysis, we considered these questions separately (descriptive statistics are presented in Appendix 1 Table A4).

2.5 Strategy of Analysis

First, we conducted a correlation analysis of the variables. We then compared generalized linear regression models with the news ids as dummy variables with linear mixed models with news ids as random variables [55]. The performance of generalized linear mixed models was higher (BIC = 87187 vs BIC = 87732), and the analysis of intraclass correlation (ICC = 0.118) suggested the use of mixed generalized linear models. Thus, we decided to continue with linear mixed models in which we used recognition of each news item as a trial (with properties: truthfulness, frame, source); thus for each participant we had eight trials. The analysis of the ids of participants as a random variable was not

Table 3. Generalized linear mixed effect model for accuracy of news item recognition

Predictors	Accuracy			
	Odds Ratios	std. Beta	p	std. p
(Intercept)	1.48	1.28	**0.039**	0.178
Dominant news frame	1.23	1.23	0.430	0.428
True news items	0.55	0.55	**<0.001**	**<0.001**
News about [Russia]	1.58	1.58	**0.025**	**0.025**
News about [Ukraine]	1.68	1.68	**0.028**	**0.028**
Age	1.05	1.05	**<0.001**	**<0.001**
Male gender	1.09	1.09	**<0.001**	**<0.001**
Higher education	1.08	1.08	**<0.001**	**<0.001**
Time for news item (log)	0.95	0.97	**<0.001**	**<0.001**
News item seen before	1.19	1.05	**<0.001**	**<0.001**
Domestic news source	0.99	1.00	0.676	0.676
SNS [VK]	0.96	0.96	**0.031**	**0.031**
TV (one from main sources)	0.94	0.97	**0.001**	**0.001**
Newsaggregators (one from main sources)	1.05	1.02	**0.009**	**0.009**
Conspiracy mentality scale	0.95	0.95	**<0.001**	**<0.001**
Politics interest	0.95	0.95	**<0.001**	**<0.001**
Dominant frame *True items	2.71	2.71	**<0.001**	**<0.001**
Dominant frame * News about [Russia]	0.35	0.35	**<0.001**	**<0.001**
Dominant frame * News about [Ukraine]	0.42	0.42	**0.009**	**0.009**

Random Effects

σ^2	3.29	ICC	0.09	
$\tau_{00 \ news\_jid}$	0.33	N $_{news\_jid}$	96	
Observations		65744		
Marginal R^2 / Conditional R^2		0.037 / 0.123		

possible due to the large size of the sample (8,559) and did not converge. Analysis of the random effect associated with participants on country and SNS subsamples showed no need to use random models associated with participants (e.g. for subsample Russia VKontakte ICC = 0.009).

Next, we analyzed the effect of each of the suggested variables separately by adding them to a linear mixed effect model to see if they had a significant impact on the accuracy of fake news recognition. We found that 22 variables had significant effects (see Appendix 1 Table A5). Next we included all significant variables in one model (Marginal R2 = 0.01, Conditional R2 = 0.127, see Appendix 1 Table A4). Only several variables found to be significant at the first step showed significance in the joint model. They were: social network, age, gender, education, conspiracy mentality, do participants recall this news item (news seen); do participants mention news aggregators as one of three most important news courses; time spent on assessing the news item (logarithm), interest in politics.

The next model included only significant variables from the previous step (Marginal R2 = 0.006, Conditional R2 = 0.124, see Appendix 1, Table A5). The observed reduction in Marginal R2 indicates that there may be an important interactional effect that we miss in this model. We expected that news frame and truth might interact as well as frame and news object country (the country which the news item is about). Adding these two interactional effects increases Marginal R2 to 0.037 (see Table 3). We also tested the interaction of the source of the news with frame, truthfulness, and country, but found no interaction effects.

3   Results

The results of the GLM mixed regression modeling for accuracy are given in Table 3. They show significant influence of many unexpected predictors, while some of the expected predictors have proven to be insignificant. Thus, age (Std. Odds Ratios = 1.05), male gender (Std. Odds Ratios = 1.09), and using news aggregators (Std. Odds Ratios = 1.02) increased the odds of higher accuracy. TV as one of the primary news sources (Std. Odds Ratios = 0.97), inclination to conspiracy thinking (Std. Odds Ratios = 0.97), the use of VKontakte SNS (Std. Odds Ratios = 0.96) and, surprisingly, interest in politics (Std. Odds Ratios = 0.95) were significant in lowering the accuracy. These results confirm hypothesis H1: "Conspiracy thinking decreases the accuracy of news recognition".

When participants indicated that they had already seen a certain news item, this also increased the accuracy of news recognition (Std. Odds Ratios = 1.05). At the same time, we know from prior analysis that this perception was also observed when participants viewed fake news items created for the study. On the one hand, this could be the result of the "illusory truth effect", and some of the news items with similar properties could affect participants' perception. At the same time, this heuristic (as it increases accuracy) is ecologically rational [56].

While "news checked" was a significant predictor during the first step of the analysis, it became insignificant after adding control variables and the "news seen" variable. This supports the important role of heuristics in fake news recognition and participants' feeling that they have already seen certain news items before is more important than the fact-checking. Still, this effect may be less universal as it may depend on the levels of education or digital literacy training. Similarly, the effect of trust which is significant at the early steps of modeling disappears at the later stages.

We observe two significant interactions in the resulting model. The first and expected one is between the news frame and the truthfulness of the news item. While news frame alone predictably has no effect on the accuracy of news recognition, and while true news items have lower chances of being recognized correctly than fake stories (Std. Odds Ratios = 0.55), the dominant framing of true stories drastically increases their odds of being recognized correctly (Std. Odds Ratios = 2.71). We can explain this by stipulating that dominant framing increases believability and, in the case of the true news stories, increases accuracy. For fake news the interactions works in the opposite direction: alternative frame decreases the believability of a fake news item and this contributes to the increase of accuracy, while the dominant frame contributes to its decrease. Thus, we also confirm H2 "The influence of news framing on the accuracy of news recognition is moderated by the type of news – either true or fake". However, the influence of the frame on believability or on trust in news needs to be tested in further studies.

The second significant interaction observed was between dominant framing and the country featured in the news item. We found that news about Ukraine and Russia are recognized better than those about Kazakhstan (Std. Odds Ratios = 1.58 for news about Russia and 1.68 for news about Ukraine). Given that Russia and Ukraine are involved in an ongoing conflict, it would be logical to expect the opposite: namely, that users from both countries would be more prone to fakes that might be more intensively produced by the media of the conflicting countries. However, when packaged in the dominant framing, news about these two countries obtain much lower odds of being recognized correctly than those about Kazakhstan (Std. Odds Ratios = 0.35 for news about Russia and 0.42 for news about Ukraine). This suggests that the recognition of news about Ukraine and Russia owes its overall high accuracy to correct classification of alternatively framed news which is hard to confirm and to interpret without further in-depth research.

The results of our research do not support hypothesis H3 "Domestic news sources decrease the accuracy of fake news recognition". The news source was not significant in the regression model. One reason for this may be that the source type behaves in a way similar to that of framing: domestic sources may increase the trust in both true and fake news, while foreign sources may affect the trust in the opposite direction.

Limitations

Our analysis of how users from the two most popular social networks (VKontakte and Facebook) in Russia, Ukraine and Kazakhstan engage with news shows the importance of both socio-demographic and behavioral factors. At the same time, there may be significant differences between VKontakte and Facebook in how their users engage with news. These differences need to be explored in future research.

To further analyze the dynamics that influence fake news recognition, it is important to separate the analysis of fake and true news items when assessing accuracy. This would allow us to see whether thinking style or heuristics cues affect participants' recognition of true and fake stories differently. Furthermore, the analysis of news recognition accuracy should be combined with the analysis of news item credibility, as both these concepts and the factors influencing them are closely related, though not identical.

4 Conclusion

The results of the study confirm the important role of conspiracy thinking style in false news recognition (decreasing accuracy) and its impact on social media users' deliberation capabilities. Another significant factor is the number of news items already seen by participants (increasing accuracy). This is in line with previous research on the "illusory truth effect" [13]. We also found that generalized trust does not play an important role and becomes insignificant when other contextual factors are introduced. The role of news consumption, with TV as the main source of information, decreases accuracy, whereas news consumption primarily through news aggregators increases accuracy.

In our analysis we observe two significant interactions between news frame and truthfulness, and news frame and the country featured in the news item. Both of these interactions provide evidence that the role of news frames in fake news recognition is closely connected to the context of news. It is interesting that the perceived interest in politics decreases the level of accuracy. We associate this finding with the subjectivity of assessment, which is not necessarily related to participants' actual knowledge about politics. Higher levels of education contribute to greater accuracy, which is in line with the previous studies on the role of analytical thinking [14, 15]. It is worth mentioning that SNSs remain significant predictors of accuracy even in the presence of such control variables as age and education. It is plausible that the users of different SNSs have distinct news consumption habits. This is partially confirmed by the results of our study, which indicate that Facebook users demonstrate better ability to recognize fake news than VKontakte users.

To summarize, the main contribution of this paper is in examining the impact of different thinking styles, as well as various contextual features of the news (cues for heuristics) on the accuracy of fake news detection. Our findings also have implications for understanding how fake news susceptibility impacts user capabilities for online deliberation in the context of news consumption.

Acknowledgements. The research was implemented in the framework of the Russian Scientific Fund Grant № 19-18-00206 at the National Research University Higher School of Economics (HSE) in 2021.

The authors acknowledge the research and data collection assistance by Maxim Terpilowski, Yadviga Sinyawskaya, and Victoria Vziatysheva.

Compliance with Ethical Standards. The authors declare that they have no conflict of interest. All procedures performed in studies involving human participants were in accordance with the ethical standards of the institutional and/or national research committee (National Research University Higher School of Economics Institution Research Board decision, 23.04.2020).

Appendix 1. Supplementary Material

Supplementary tables associated with this article can be found, in the online version, at https://fakenewsproject.org/HCI2021/Appendix_1.pdf.

References

1. Buller, D.B., Burgoon, J.K.: Interpersonal deception theory. Commun. Theor. **6**, 203–242 (1996). https://doi.org/10.1111/j.1468-2885.1996.tb00127.x
2. Metzger, M.J., Flanagin, A.J., Eyal, K., Lemus, D.R., Mccann, R.M.: Credibility for the 21st century: integrating perspectives on source, message, and media credibility in the contemporary media environment. Ann. Int. Commun. Assoc. **27**, 293–335 (2003). https://doi.org/10.1080/23808985.2003.11679029
3. Colquitt, J.A., Scott, B.A., LePine, J.A.: Trust, trustworthiness, and trust propensity: a meta-analytic test of their unique relationships with risk taking and job performance. J. Appl. Psychol. **92**, 909–927 (2007). https://doi.org/10.1037/0021-9010.92.4.909
4. Gill, H., Boies, K., Finegan, J.E., McNally, J.: Antecedents of trust: establishing a boundary condition for the relation between propensity to trust and intention to trust. J. Bus Psychol. **19**, 287–302 (2005). https://doi.org/10.1007/s10869-004-2229-8
5. Porshnev, A., Miltsov, A.: The effects of thinking styles and news domain on fake news recognition by social media users: evidence from Russia. In: Meiselwitz, G. (ed.) HCII 2020. LNCS, vol. 12194, pp. 305–320. Springer, Cham (2020). https://doi.org/10.1007/978-3-030-49570-1_21
6. Flynn, D.J., Nyhan, B., Reifler, J.: The Nature and origins of misperceptions: understanding false and unsupported beliefs about politics: nature and origins of misperceptions. Adv. Polit. Psychol. **38**, 127–150 (2017). https://doi.org/10.1111/pops.12394
7. Robinson, P., Goddard, P., Parry, K., Murray, C., Taylor, P.M.: Pockets of Resistance: British News Media, War and Theory in the 2003 Invasion of Iraq. Manchester University Press, Oxford (2016)
8. Zollmann, F.: Bringing propaganda back into news media studies. Crit. Sociol. **45**, 329–345 (2019). https://doi.org/10.1177/0896920517731134
9. Nisbet, M.C., Brossard, D., Kroepsch, A.: Framing science: the stem cell controversy in an age of press/politics. Harvard Int. J. Press/Polit. **8**, 36–70 (2003). https://doi.org/10.1177/1081180X02251047
10. Berinsky, A.J.: Rumors and health care reform: experiments in political misinformation. Brit. J. Polit. Sci. **47**, 241–262 (2017). https://doi.org/10.1017/S0007123415000186
11. Allcott, H., Gentzkow, M.: Social media and fake news in the 2016 election. J. Econ. Perspect. **31**, 211–236 (2017)
12. Bronstein, M.V., Pennycook, G., Bear, A., Rand, D.G., Cannon, T.D.: Belief in fake news is associated with delusionality, dogmatism, religious fundamentalism, and reduced analytic thinking. J. Appl. Res. Mem. Cogn. **8**, 108–117 (2019). https://doi.org/10.1016/j.jarmac.2018.09.005
13. Pennycook, G., Cannon, T.D., Rand, D.G.: Prior exposure increases perceived accuracy of fake news. J. Exp. Psychol. Gen. **147**, 1865–1880 (2018). https://doi.org/10.1037/xge0000465
14. Pennycook, G., Rand, D.G.: Lazy, not biased: susceptibility to partisan fake news is better explained by lack of reasoning than by motivated reasoning. Cognition **188**, 39–50 (2019). https://doi.org/10.1016/j.cognition.2018.06.011
15. Coe, C.M.: Tell Me Lies: Fake News, Source Cues, and Partisan Motivated Reasoning, (2018)
16. Anthony, A., Moulding, R.: Breaking the news: belief in fake news and conspiracist beliefs. Aust. J. Psychol. **71**, 154–162 (2019)
17. van Prooijen, J.-W., Douglas, K.M.: Belief in conspiracy theories: basic principles of an emerging research domain. https://onlinelibrary.wiley.com/doi/abs/10.1002/ejsp.2530. Accessed 4 Sept 2019
18. Edelson, J., Alduncin, A., Krewson, C., Sieja, J.A., Uscinski, J.E.: The effect of conspiratorial thinking and motivated reasoning on belief in election fraud. Polit. Res. Q. **70**, 933–946 (2017). https://doi.org/10.1177/1065912917721061

19. Abalakina-Paap, M., Stephan, W.G., Craig, T., Gregory, W.L.: Beliefs in conspiracies. Polit. Psychol. **20**, 637–647 (1999)
20. Goertzel, T.: Belief in conspiracy theories. Polit. Psychol. **15**, 731 (1994). https://doi.org/10.2307/3791630
21. Stojanov, A., Halberstadt, J.: The Conspiracy mentality scale: distinguishing between irrational and rational suspicion. Soc. Psychol. **50**, 215–232 (2019). https://doi.org/10.1027/1864-9335/a000381
22. Uscinski, J.E., Olivella, S.: The conditional effect of conspiracy thinking on attitudes toward climate change. Res. Polit. **4**, 205316801774310 (2017). https://doi.org/10.1177/2053168017743105
23. Iyengar, S., Simon, A.: News coverage of the Gulf crisis and public opinion: a study of agenda-setting, priming, and framing. Commun. Res. **20**, 365–383 (1993)
24. McCombs, M.E., Shaw, D.L.: The agenda-setting function of mass media. Public Opin. Q. **36**, 176 (1972). https://doi.org/10.1086/267990
25. Scheufele, D.: Framing as theory for media effects. J. Commun. **20**, 103–122 (1999)
26. D'Angelo, P., Kuypers, J.A. (eds.): Doing News Framing Analysis: Empirical and Theoretical Perspectives. Routledge, New York (2010)
27. Pavik, J.V.: News framing and new media: Digital tools to re-engage an alienated citizenry. In: Reese, S.D., Gandy, O.H., Grant, A.E. (eds.) Framing Public Life: Perspectives on Media and Our Understanding of the Social World, pp. 311–321. Lawrence Erlbaum Associates, Mahwah, N.J. (2001)
28. Gitlin, T.: The Whole World is Watching: Mass Media in the Making & Unmaking of the New Left. University of California Press, Berkeley, CA (2003)
29. Dusyk, N., Axsen, J., Dullemond, K.: Who cares about climate change? The mass media and socio-political acceptance of Canada's oil sands and Northern gateway pipeline. Energy Res. Soc. Sci. **37**, 12–21 (2018). https://doi.org/10.1016/j.erss.2017.07.005
30. Kwon, K.H., Chadha, M., Pellizzaro, K.: Proximity and terrorism news in social media: a construal-level theoretical approach to networked framing of terrorism in Twitter. Mass Commun. Soc. **20**, 869–894 (2017). https://doi.org/10.1080/15205436.2017.1369545
31. Carragee, K.M., Roefs, W.: The neglect of power in recent framing research. J. Commun. **54**, 214–233 (2004). https://doi.org/10.1111/j.1460-2466.2004.tb02625.x
32. Coleman, C.-L., Dysart, E.V.: Framing of Kennewick man against the backdrop of a scientific and cultural controversy. Sci. Commun. **27**, 3–26 (2005). https://doi.org/10.1177/1075547005278609
33. Kohring, M., Matthes, J.: Trust in news media: development and validation of a multidimensional scale. Commun. Res. **34**, 231–252 (2007). https://doi.org/10.1177/0093650206298071
34. Pan, Z., Kosicki, G.: Framing analysis: an approach to news discourse. Polit. Comm. **10**, 55–75 (1993). https://doi.org/10.1080/10584609.1993.9962963
35. Semetko, H.A., Valkenburg, P.M.V.: Framing European politics: a content analysis of press and television news. J. Commun. **50**, 93–109 (2000). https://doi.org/10.1111/j.1460-2466.2000.tb02843.x
36. Su, M.-H., Liu, J., McLeod, D.M.: Pathways to news sharing: Issue frame perceptions and the likelihood of sharing. Comput. Hum. Behav. **91**, 201–210 (2019). https://doi.org/10.1016/j.chb.2018.09.026
37. Druckman, J.N.: Political preference formation: competition, deliberation, and the (ir)relevance of framing effects. Am. Polit. Sci. Rev. **98**, 671–686 (2004). https://doi.org/10.1017/S0003055404041413
38. Chong, D., Druckman, J.N.: Spanish abstract. J. Commun. **57**, 99–118 (2007). https://doi.org/10.1111/j.1460-2466.2006.00331_3.x

39. Slothuus, R.: More than weighting cognitive importance: a dual-process model of issue framing effects: a dual-process model of issue framing effects. Polit. Psychol. **29**, 1–28 (2008). https://doi.org/10.1111/j.1467-9221.2007.00610.x

40. Morris, M.R., Counts, S., Roseway, A., Hoff, A., Schwarz, J.: Tweeting is believing?: Understanding microblog credibility perceptions. In: Proceedings of the ACM 2012 Conference on Computer Supported Cooperative Work - CSCW 2012, p. 441. ACM Press, Seattle, Washington, USA (2012). https://doi.org/10.1145/2145204.2145274.

41. Pornpitakpan, C.: The persuasiveness of source credibility: a critical review of five decades' evidence. J. Appl. Soc. Pyschol. **34**, 243–281 (2004). https://doi.org/10.1111/j.1559-1816.2004.tb02547.x

42. Horne, B.D., Adalı, S.: This just in: fake news packs a lot in title, uses simpler, repetitive content in text body, more similar to satire than real news. In: The Workshops of the Eleventh International AAAI Conference on Web and Social Media AAAI (ICWSM-17) Technical Report WS-17-17: News and Public Opinion, pp. 759–766 (2017)

43. Colliander, J.: "This is fake news": investigating the role of conformity to other users' views when commenting on and spreading disinformation in social media. Comput. Hum. Behav. **97**, 202–215 (2019). https://doi.org/10.1016/j.chb.2019.03.032

44. Vendemia, M.A., Bond, R.M., DeAndrea, D.C.: The strategic presentation of user comments affects how political messages are evaluated on social media sites: evidence for robust effects across party lines. Comput. Hum. Behav. **91**, 279–289 (2019). https://doi.org/10.1016/j.chb.2018.10.007

45. Borah, P.: The hyperlinked world: a look at how the interactions of news frames and hyperlinks influence news credibility and willingness to seek information. J. Comput.-Mediat. Comm. **19**, 576–590 (2014). https://doi.org/10.1111/jcc4.12060

46. Turcotte, J., York, C., Irving, J., Scholl, R.M., Pingree, R.J.: News recommendations from social media opinion leaders: effects on media trust and information seeking. J. Comput.-Mediat. Comm. **20**, 520–535 (2015). https://doi.org/10.1111/jcc4.12127

47. Craciun, G., Moore, K.: Credibility of negative online product reviews: reviewer gender, reputation and emotion effects. Comput. Hum. Behav. **97**, 104–115 (2019). https://doi.org/10.1016/j.chb.2019.03.010

48. Graefe, A., Haim, M., Haarmann, B., Brosius, H.-B.: Readers' perception of computer-generated news: credibility, expertise, and readability. Journalism **19**, 595–610 (2018). https://doi.org/10.1177/1464884916641269

49. Chung, M.: The message influences me more than others: how and why social media metrics affect first person perception and behavioral intentions. Comput. Hum. Behav. **91**, 271–278 (2019). https://doi.org/10.1016/j.chb.2018.10.011

50. Meyer, H.K., Marchionni, D., Thorson, E.: The journalist behind the news: credibility of straight, collaborative, opinionated, and blogged "news." Am. Behav. Sci. **54**, 100–119 (2010). https://doi.org/10.1177/0002764210376313

51. Vziatysheva, V., Sinyavskaya, Y., Porshnev, A., Terpilovskii, M., Koltcov, S., Bryanov, K.: Testing users' ability to recognize fake news in three countries. An experimental perspective. In: Social Computing and Social Media. Design, Ethics, User Behavior, and Social Network Analysis. Springer, Cham (in press). https://doi.org/10.1007/978-3-030-49570-1

52. Kazun, A., Pashakhin, S.: 'Alien elections': neighboring state news on the 2018 Russian presidential elections. J. Econ. Sociol. **22**, 71–91 (2021)

53. Koltsova, O., Judina, D., Pashakhin, S., Kolycheva, A.: Coverage of Presidential Elections in Kazakhstan and Ukraine by Russian Media. POLIS (in press)

54. Inglehart, R., et al. (eds.): World Values Survey: Round Six, http://www.worldvaluessurvey.org/WVSDocumentationWV6.jsp (2014)

55. Bates, D., Mächler, M., Bolker, B., Walker, S.: Fitting linear mixed-effects models using lme4. J. Stat. Soft. **67** (2015). https://doi.org/10.18637/jss.v067.i01.

56. Gigerenzer, G., Gaissmaier, W.: Heuristic decision making. Annu. Rev. Psychol. **62**, 451–482 (2011). https://doi.org/10.1146/annurev-psych-120709-145346

57. Koltsova, O., Sinyavskaya, Y., Terpilovskii, M.: Designing an experiment on recognition of political fake news by social media users: factors of dropout. In: Meiselwitz, G. (ed.) HCII 2020. LNCS, vol. 12194, pp. 261–277. Springer, Cham (2020). https://doi.org/10.1007/978-3-030-49570-1_18

Analysis of Modality-Based Presentation Skills Using Sequential Models

Su Shwe Yi Tun[1], Shogo Okada[1(✉)], Hung-Hsuan Huang[2],
and Chee Wee Leong[3]

[1] Japan Advanced Institute of Science and Technology, Nomi, Japan
{sushweyitun,okada-s}@jaist.ac.jp
[2] The University of Fukuchiyama, Fukuchiyama, Japan
hhhuang@acm.org
[3] Educational Testing Service, Princeton, USA
cleong@ets.org

Abstract. This paper presents an analysis of informative presentations using sequential multimodal modeling for automatic assessment of presentation performance. For this purpose, we transform a single video into multiple time-series segments that are provided as inputs to sequential models, such as Long Short-Term Memory (LSTM). This sequence modeling approach enables us to capture the time-series change of multimodal behaviors during the presentation. We proposed variants of sequential models that improve the accuracy of performance prediction over non-sequential models. Moreover, we performed segment analysis on the sequential models to analyze how relevant information from various segments can lead to better performance in sequential prediction models.

Keywords: Social signal processing · Multimodal · Presentation skills · Sequence modelling

1 Introduction

Communication is one of the essential essences of human life. Verbal and non-verbal behaviors of human are used to predict the outcome of social interactions. Indeed, communication skills have been one of the important factors in affecting decisions in employment and other high-stakes situations. In the literature, there exists many studies that are focused on the training, feedback and assessment of communication skills, including those focused on monologue scenarios such as public speaking [4,20,25], business presentations [26] or social meeting [18], as well as those focused on communication skills in dyadic interaction situations, including the job interviews [5,16], group interactions [17,21] and human-computer interactions [10,23,24].

An oral presentation is a type of communication focused on a specific topic given to a potentiallylarge group of people. Intuitively, a good speaker should be articulate, organized, and purposeful to influence outcomes through the delivery

© Springer Nature Switzerland AG 2021
G. Meiselwitz (Ed.): HCII 2021, LNCS 12774, pp. 358–369, 2021.
https://doi.org/10.1007/978-3-030-77626-8_24

of the talk. While the success of presentation largely depends on the content of the talk, the speaker's verbal behavior, non-verbal (visual) cues, such as body language and gestures, also play a significant role. Nevertheless, good presenters can still adopt and practice presentation styles that differ from one another, resulting in significant challenges in modeling this variability in the assessment of presentations. To date, many studies focused on the automatic assessment of oral communication tasks [4,20,25] have relied on using features from various modalities to develop automatic assessment modelsto predict the scores assigned by human expert raters.

Automatic assessment of presentation skills can be performed using both verbal and non-verbal cues of the whole presentation or thin slices extracted from a video presentation [6,11], using different machine learning algorithms. With the exception of a few efforts [9,13], most efforts so far have relied on traditional machine learning approaches, as deep learning methods often require large amounts of *labeled* data for training, which is expensive and laborious to obtain for videos.

In our work, we use the time-series sequences from a dataset of 81 videos as input representation for training sequential models in an effort to do a comparative evaluation between sequential and non-sequential classifiers, such as SVM, when applied to the oral presentation assessment task. Sequential models, such as LSTM, are used to model a sequence of behavioral patterns over time during the presentation. Those information from time-series sequences can help improve presentation scoring accuracy. Evaluation on the presentation dataset shows that all scores of the proposed sequential models for each modality, except for the modality score of visual modality, significantly outperform non-sequential models with the best overall score (0.609) of audio modality using Stacked LSTM and best modality score (0.608) of text modality using RNN. Additionally, we analyze how each segment in a presentation can potentially contribute to improve the assessment accuracy of such presentations. Moreover, we discover which segment of presentation has more impact on the presentation assessment using sequential models and show that the presentation segments have different effectiveness to sequential models depending on the specific modality of a presentation.

2   Related Work

Previously, Haley et al. [14] collected an informative oral presentation dataset and described how information from each specific modality presented to a rater affects her judgment in the assessment of presentation tasks and investigated automatic assessment of presentation content using modality-specific machine learning features and model. They presented multi modal model prediction results on the dataset with overall and modality-score labels by fusing the modality-based features in an incremental approach (Text, Text + Audio, Text + Audio + Video). However, in their work, they did not investigate unimodal approaches as they mainly focus on the incremental fusion of modality-based features to investigate the presentation assessment improvement. They also did not explore regression modeling approaches from a deep learning perspective. In our work, we investigate each modality's effectiveness through sequential models to see how each modality affects the presentation.

In another line of work, Haider et al. [8] proposed an active data representation using audio-video segments of students' presentation and unsupervised self-organizing mapping for automatic scoring of delivery skills along with feedback generation. They described a data representation of videos using low-level audio descriptors and video descriptors (modeling body postures and movement). They created fusion models for those low-level descriptors to evaluate public speaking abilities. Additionally, they proposed a feedback method to flag presentation segments requiring improvement to users.

Kimani et al. [11] used HMM with state transition to provide feedback to the presenter and improve the presentation quality assessment results. They transform the overall presentation quality into states that represent the presenter's gaze, gesture, audience interaction, etc., and show how state-based representation improves the presentation results.

3   Data

In this section, the English oral presentation dataset [14] is used in this study, and its annotations are described.

Task and Participants. The dataset contains videos of 81 college students from the United States giving an informative presentation for high school freshman students about what to prepare when choosing and applying to colleges. Note that the participants were asked to share their knowledge and information on college preparation instead of persuading the students to apply for college. The task involved (i) preparing a checklist to consider when selecting and applying to college, (ii) preparing for the presentation, and (iii) presenting an oral presentation for three minutes. The data were collected through participants interacting with HALEF [1] via a Web page, which is an open-source, cloud-based dialog system. In addition to the presentation, the participants also answered a few background information survey questions after the presentation recording.

Annotation. The annotation of the dataset was performed by human experts scoring on each presentation using an oral communication scoring rubric. Each presentation is scored on the content dimension of the rubric using a Likert scale of 0 to 4, where 0 is 'off-topic', '1' is deficient, '2' is 'weak', '3' is 'competent' and '4' is 'proficient'. Annotation is performed by two experienced raters for each of the three modalities, i.e., audio, video, and text. If there is a discrepancy in score level of more than one, then a third rater will be asked to perform the annotation. The raters provide three types of modality scores (audio, video, text) to each presentation. Two types of scores are defined for automatic assessment:

(1) overall score, which is the rounded median of all modality scores (audio, video, text) (2) modality-specific score (modality score) for each presentation, which is judged by observing only one modality (audio or video or text). The scores are assigned from the raters.

Scores Distribution. Due to the small dataset, we use the rounded down median of the two (or rounded median of three scores) as the final score for each presentation and combine the lowest two classes into a single class, which results in a three-class distribution. Figure 1 shows the distributions of both overall and modality scores of the oral presentation dataset.

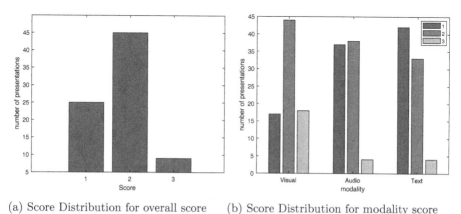

(a) Score Distribution for overall score   (b) Score Distribution for modality score

Fig. 1. Distribution of scores by (a) overall score (b) modality score

4   Multimodal Feature Extraction

Multimodal feature extraction of the dataset is performed automatically. We extracted acoustic information, facial expressions as a non-verbal aspect, and word-level features from the spoken utterances of the users as a verbal aspect. We extracted acoustic and visual features in an automatic manner and the word-level features are extracted using a cloud-based automatic speech recognition system. The following sections explain how these features are extracted.

4.1   Linguistic Features

Linguistic features are extracted from transcriptions. We extracted word embedding features for text computed using the word2vec [15] method. Firstly, we tokenized words from transcriptions and removed stop words using the Natural Language Toolkit library (NLTK) [3], and trained a word embedding model using the tokenized words via the Genism modeling toolkit [27]. The word2vec model projects our corpus with a vocabulary size of 1110 into the embedded vector space (embedding size of 200-D word2vec features). We converted each word in the transcription file into 200-D word2vec features and aggregated whole word embedding from each transcription into a single embedding input using sequential data modeling approach.

4.2 Acoustic Features

For acoustic modality, each audio file is first segmented into 5-s segments with an overlap of 1.5 s, and speech-based features are extracted using COVAREP [7]. The acoustic features set contains the prosodic features, voice quality information, and spectral information. Then, we computed the statistical values: mean, maximum, minimum, median, standard deviation, variance, kurtosis, skewness, percentile values for each feature and used them as acoustic features. Lastly, we combine all the segments of a given audio file into one feature vector, and feature selection is performed via the correlation matrix to select the top 100 features as the feature set for the model.

4.3 Visual Features

For video modality, each video file is also first segmented into 5-s segments with an overlap of 1.5 s and extracted time-series features at a sampling rate of 10 FPS using the OpenFace Toolkit [2]. We then used the 2D facial landmark data from eyes, mouth, eyebrows, and eye landmark data to calculate the velocity and acceleration of each data point and the mean value of the 18 facial AU features. Finally, we combine all the segments of a given file into one feature vector.

The transcription is annotated by timestamp per each utterance, which only contains timestamps of start and end time. Therefore, we cannot align the audio and video frame timing with each word in the transcriptions. Table 1 describe the details of features used in the experiments.

5   Experiments

In this section, the experiment is performed for each modality based on two labels: (i) overall score, and, (ii) modality score of that modality. In order to account for the variable length of input sequences, we used zero padding to normalize the length of the input sequence data. We evaluate both sequential and non-sequential models in two ways using (1) overall labels, and (2) modality-specific labels, where the labels specify performance levels based on the presentation content. For the experiments, we used the 81 samples that were obtained from the 81 participants.

Non-sequential Classification Models. For the non-sequential models: we experimented with two classification learners: Linear Support Vector Machine

Table 1. Summary of feature sets for presentation assessment

Modality	Feature names	Features
Linguistic	word2vec	200 dimension word2vec features
Audio	Prosodic	Fundamental Frequency(f0), voicing or not (VUV)
	Voice quality	Normalized Amplitude Quotient (NAQ),
		Quasi Open Quotient (QoQ),
		Amplitude difference between first two harmonics of the differential glottal source spectrum (H1H2),
		Parabolic Spectral Parameter (PSP),
		Maxima Dispersion Quotient (MDQ),
		Slope of Wavelet response (peakSlope),
		Shape parameter of LF glottal model (Rd),
		Detecting creaky voice (creak)
	Spectral	Mel-cepstral coefficient (MCEP 0–24),
		Harmonic model phase distortion mean (HMPDM 0–24),
		Phase distortion deviation (HMPDD 0–12)
Visual	2D facial landmarks	Four points from eyes,
		Four points from eyebrows,
		Four points around the mouth
	Facial action units	18 AU units

(LinearSVC) and Random Forest (RF). We use the average value of each element in a feature vector, which are extracted in Sect. 4, as an input to non-sequential models for each modality. We find the optimal hyperparameters of models using the grid search. We used SKLL[1], an open-source Python package that wraps around the sckit-learn package [19] for implementing the non-sequential learner.

Sequential Classification Models. For the sequential modeling approaches, we experimented with three models: RNN, LSTM, and Stacked-LSTM. An RNN model is composed of a single GRU layer with 128 units is used to extract

---

[1] https://github.com/EducationalTestingService/skll.

the features from input sequence data. The GRU layer was followed by a fully connected layer to learn RNN output. An output layer is used for predicting three labels. An LSTM model is composed of a single LSTM layer with 128 units is used to extract the features from the input sequence data, followed by a fully connected Layer to learn LSTM output. An output layer is used for predicting three labels. A Stacked-LSTM model is composed of two LSTM layers with 128 units is used to extract the features from the input sequence data, followed by a dropout (rate = 0.5) [22] layer. The LSTM layer was followed by 3 time-distributed dense layers to learn the LSTM output with 64, 32, and 16 for the number of units per layer, respectively. An output layer is used for predicting three labels. In our experiment, we used the Adam [12] optimizer with the learning rate of 0.001. For all models, sparse cross-entropy loss is used as the loss function with Softmax activation. We set the batch size to 16 and the number of epochs to 100. We used Keras with a TensorFlow backend for implementing the sequential models.

Evaluation Schemes. We experimented with each model using 10-fold cross-validation, and data normalization is performed using Z-normalization. We evaluated the experiments based on both average accuracy and balanced accuracy score since the dataset is imbalanced.

6   Experimental Results

Table 2 shows the comparison of average accuracy and balanced accuracy results of sequential models and non-sequential models. Since the dataset we used in this experiment was the imbalanced one, and we do not balance the data before training models in such results, we evaluated the results based on the accuracy score. We observed that except for the modality score of visual modality, all scores for other modalities achieved higher results in the sequential model than the non-sequential model. The highest accuracy for text, visual, and audio for the overall score using the sequential models were 0.590, 0.609, and 0.581, respectively, while the modality score yielded accuracies of 0.608, 0.593, and 0.497. Overall, the best accuracy (0.609) is achieved using the Stacked LSTM learner using audio modality, while the best accuracy for the text modality (0.608)is achieved using RNN.

7   Analysis of Specific Modality by Segments

In the previous section, we explored the sequential models using the full time-series data. However, the use of full data may contain irrelevant information for the presentation assessment. To address this issue, we performed manual segment analysis for finding which segments are relevant to the presentation assessment. Since we do not have the annotation for the individual segments, we define the label of all segment slices to be equal to the annotated score of the whole presentation. For this analysis, we extracted segments from the

Table 2. Experimental results for content presentation score using sequential and non-sequential models

		Overall score		Modality score	
Modality	Learner	Accuracy	Balanced accuracy	Accuracy	Balanced accuracy
Text	LinearSVC	0. 581	0. 346	0. 482	0. 327
	Random Forest	0. 528	0. 362	0. 435	0. 292
	RNN	**0. 590**	**0. 397**	**0. 608**	**0. 550**
	LSTM	0. 556	0. 376	0. 596	0. 527
	Stacked LSTM	0. 581	0. 375	0. 569	0. 511
Audio	LinearSVC	0. 491	0. 320	0. 492	0. 345
	Random Forest	0. 556	0. 342	0. 543	0. 379
	RNN	0. 441	0. 329	0. 487	0. 401
	LSTM	0. 491	0. 350	**0. 593**	**0. 562**
	Stacked LSTM	**0. 609**	**0. 514**	**0. 593**	0. 513
Visual	LinearSVC	0. 385	0. 290	0. 461	0. 354
	Random Forest	**0. 581**	0. 488	**0. 497**	**0. 414**
	RNN	**0. 581**	**0. 501**	0. 449	0. 375
	LSTM	0. 568	0. 443	0. 464	0. 390
	Stacked LSTM	0. 539	0. 408	0. 428	0. 363

presentation based on the transcription timestamps, which results in a total of three segments per presentation. We performed analysis on all three segments using the sequential models above. We train the models on (1) each segment, and, (2) all segments. Additionally, the evaluation is performed on the previous sequential models and the best score among the three models is used as a final score for analysis. The score is evaluated based on the balanced accuracy of the whole presentation. Using utterance-level timestamps, we used two segmentation approaches, described below, for comparative evaluation.

Nearest-Minute Segmentation. The data is segmented at the point closest to a minute-interval mark, which corresponds to the ending point of the last utterance in the previous segment, or the starting point of the first utterance in the next segment. The longest duration in the presentation dataset is three minutes two seconds while the shortest one is one minute and ten seconds. Because of this variable-length in presentations, we only have 79 last segments out of the initial 81 presentations.

Uniform Segmentation. The data is decomposed equally into first, middle, and last segments of equal lengths. The duration of each presentation may be different, but the duration of intra-presentation segments is always equal.

Results on Segment Analysis. Figures 2 and 3 describe the overall score and modality score for the nearest-minute segmentation and uniform segmentation approaches respectively. Table 3 shows the contributing segment that generated the best performance for each combination of modality and score metric. Regardless of segmentation approaches, we observe that the middle segments can be effective for predicting modality scores for both audio and visual modalities. Perhaps not so surprisingly, the first segment (representing first impressions) can be effective for predicting overall scores for both text and visual modalities when the uniform segmentation approach is used. Although we do not have exact annotation for each segment, the results show that not all segments are equal in their effectiveness as inputs to the models.

Table 3. Summary of segment contributions, by modality and score metric combinations

Modality	Nearest-minute		Uniform	
	Overall score	Modality score	Overall score	Modality score
Text	All	First	First	Last
Audio	All	Middle	All	Middle
Visual	Last	Middle	First	Middle

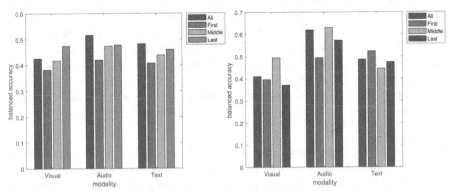

(a) Comparison of overall score between segments

(b) Comparison of modality score between segments

Fig. 2. Comparison of results obtained by nearest-minute segmentation

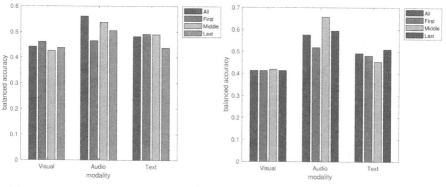

(a) Comparison of overall score between segments (b) Comparison of modality score between segments

Fig. 3. Comparison of results obtained by uniform segmentation

8 Discussions and Conclusion

In this work, we experimented with using unimodal approaches to model the performance of an oral presentation. While we did not explore any multimodal approach, we are mainly interested to employ sequential-based, unimodal models to study their efficacy against previously published approaches using non-sequential models on the same dataset. On this limited dataset of 81 videos, we achieved preliminary findings that sequential-based models are promising. As the next step, we plan to implement a fusion of the modalities using sequential models to predict human ratings on the same oral presentation task. In the future, we also plan to leverage transfer learning from a larger dataset to finetune models built for our small dataset. Moreover, given annotations on the more fine-grained, individual segments extracted from a video, it is possible that we further validate the effectiveness of our proposed segment-based, sequential approach on modeling oral presentations.

Acknowledgements. This work was partially supported by the Japan Society for the Promotion of Science (JSPS) KAKENHI Grant Numbers 19H01120, 19H01719 and JST AIP Trilateral AI Research, Grant Number JPMJCR20G6, Japan.

References

1. Halef. http://halef.org
2. Baltrusaitis, T., Zadeh, A., Lim, Y., Morency, L.: OpenFace 2.0: facial behavior analysis toolkit. In: Proceedings of the International Conference on Automatic Face and Gesture Recognition (FG), pp. 59–66 (2018)
3. Bird, S., Loper, E.: NLTK: the natural language toolkit. In: Proceedings of the ACL Interactive Poster and Demonstration Sessions, pp. 214–217. Barcelona, Spain (2004)

4. Chen, L., Feng, G., Joe, J., Leong, C.W., Kitchen, C., Lee, C.M.: Towards automated assessment of public speaking skills using multimodal cues. In: Proceedings of the International Conference on Multimodal Interaction (ICMI), pp. 200–203 (2014)
5. Chen, L., Zhao, R., Leong, C.W., Lehman, B., Feng, G., Hoque, M.E.: Automated video interview judgment on a large-sized corpus collected online. In: 2017 Seventh International Conference on Affective Computing and Intelligent Interaction (ACII), pp. 504–509. IEEE (2017)
6. Chollet, M., Scherer, S.: Assessing public speaking ability from thin slices of behavior. In: Procedings of the International Conference on Automatic Face and Gesture Recognition (FG), pp. 310–316 (2017)
7. Degottex, G., Kane, J., Drugman, T., Raitio, T., Scherer, S.: COVAREP: a collaborative voice analysis repository for speech technologies. In: Proceedings of the IEEE International Conference on Acoustics, Speech & Signal Processing (ICASSP) (2014)
8. Haider, F., Koutsombogera, M., Conlan, O., Vogel, C., Campbell, N., Luz, S.: An active data representation of videos for automatic scoring of oral presentation delivery skills and feedback generation. Frontiers Comput. Sci. **2**, 1 (2020)
9. Hemamou, L., Felhi, G., Vandenbussche, V., Martin, J.C., Clavel, C.: HireNet: a hierarchical attention model for the automatic analysis of asynchronous video job interviews. In: Proceedings of the AAAI Conference on Artificial Intelligence, pp. 573–581 (2019)
10. Hoque, M.E., Courgeon, M., Martin, J.C., Mutlu, B., Picard, R.W.: MACH: my automated conversation coach. In: Proceedings of the 2013 ACM International Joint Conference on Pervasive and Ubiquitous Computing, pp. 697–706. New York, USA (2013)
11. Kimani, E., Murali, P., Shamekhi, A., Parmar, D., Munikoti, S., Bickmore, T.: Multimodal assessment of oral presentations using HMMs. In: Proceedings of the International Conference on Multimodal Interaction (ICMI), pp. 650–654. New York, USA (2020)
12. Kingma, D.P., Ba, J.: Adam: a method for stochastic optimization. In: Bengio, Y., LeCun, Y. (eds.) 3rd International Conference on Learning Representations, ICLR 2015, San Diego, CA, USA, 7–9 May 2015, Conference Track Proceedings (2015)
13. Leong, C.W., et al.: To trust, or not to trust? A study of human bias in automated video interview assessments. arXiv preprint arXiv:1911.13248 (2019)
14. Lepp, H., Leong, C.W., Roohr, K., Martin-Raugh, M., Ramanarayanan, V.: Effect of modality on human and machine scoring of presentation videos. In: Proceedings of the International Conference on Multimodal Interaction (ICMI), pp. 630–634 (2020)
15. Mikolov, T., Chen, K., Corrado, G., Dean, J.: Efficient estimation of word representations in vector space. arXiv preprint arXiv:1301.3781 (2013)
16. Nguyen, L., Frauendorfer, D., Mast, M., Gatica-Perez, D.: Hire me: computational inference of hirability in employment interviews based on nonverbal behavior. IEEE Trans. Multimed. **16**, 1018–1031 (2014)
17. Okada, S., et al.: Estimating communication skills using dialogue acts and nonverbal features in multiple discussion datasets. In: Proceedings of the International Conference on Multimodal Interaction (ICMI), pp. 169–176. New York, USA (2016)
18. Park, S., Shim, H.S., Chatterjee, M., Sagae, K., Morency, L.P.: Computational analysis of persuasiveness in social multimedia: a novel dataset and multimodal prediction approach. In: Proceedings of the International Conference on Multimodal Interaction (ICMI), pp. 50–57. New York, USA (2014)

19. Pedregosa, F., et al.: Scikit-learn: machine learning in Python. J. Mach. Learn. Res. **12**, 2825–2830 (2011)
20. Ramanarayanan, V., Leong, C.W., Chen, L., Feng, G., Suendermann-Oeft, D.: Evaluating speech, face, emotion and body movement time-series features for automated multimodal presentation scoring. In: Proceedings of the International Conference on Multimodal Interaction (ICMI), pp. 23–30 (2015)
21. Sanchez-Cortes, D., Aran, O., Mast, M., Gatica-Perez, D.: A nonverbal behavior approach to identify emergent leaders in small groups. IEEE Trans. Multimed. **14**, 816–832 (2012)
22. Srivastava, N., Hinton, G., Krizhevsky, A., Sutskever, I., Salakhutdinov, R.: Dropout: a simple way to prevent neural networks from overfitting. J. Mach. Learn. Res. **15**(56), 1929–1958 (2014)
23. Tanaka, H., et al.: Automated social skills trainer. In: Proceedings of the International Conference on Intelligent User Interfaces (IUI), pp. 17–27. New York, USA (2015)
24. Trinh, H., Asadi, R., Edge, D., Bickmore, T.: RoboCOP: a robotic coach for oral presentations. In: Proceedings of the ACM Interactive Mobile, Wearable and Ubiquitous Technologies 1(2) (2017)
25. Wörtwein, T., Chollet, M., Schauerte, B., Morency, L.P., Stiefelhagen, R., Scherer, S.: Multimodal public speaking performance assessment. In: Proceedings of the International Conference on Multimodal Interaction (ICMI), pp. 43–50 (2015)
26. Yagi, Y., Okada, S., Shiobara, S., Sugimura, S.: Predicting multimodal presentation skills based on instance weighting domain adaptation. J. Multimod. User Interfaces 1–16 (2021). https://doi.org/10.1007/s12193-021-00367-x
27. Řehůřek, R., Sojka, P.: Software framework for topic modelling with large corpora. In: Proceedings of LREC 2010 Workshop New Challenges for NLP Frameworks, pp. 46–50. Valletta, Malta (2010)

Testing Users' Ability to Recognize Fake News in Three Countries. An Experimental Perspective

Victoria Vziatysheva$^{(\boxtimes)}$ ⓘ, Yadviga Sinyavskaya ⓘ, Alexander Porshnev ⓘ,
Maxim Terpilovskii ⓘ, Sergey Koltcov ⓘ, and Kirill Bryanov ⓘ

Laboratory for Social and Cognitive Informatics,
National Research University Higher School of Economics, Saint-Petersburg, Russia
vvzyatysheva@hse.ru

Abstract. Fake news dissemination online can negatively affect public deliberation and opinion formation as well as contribute to conflicts in society. In recent
years, the spread of misinformation has attracted ample attention of scholars who
examine why people believe fake news. Nonetheless, existing research focusing
on this phenomenon often lacks comparative perspective. This article is devoted
to the methodological aspects of designing a cross-national online experiment on
fake news perception. Based on our recent study, which tested the influence of
news frames, sources and thinking styles on the ability to recognize fake news
about foreign countries in Russia, Ukraine, and Kazakhstan, we provide a set
of methodological steps that could be taken to design such an experiment. In
particular, we demonstrate the necessity to create unique sets of stimulus material
adjusted to specific national media systems. We also discuss the operationalization
of complex variables (i.e. frames) and format of message presentation. Furthermore, we report the results of recruitment of participants through the ad campaigns
on social network sites (Facebook and VKontakte) and suggest the approaches to
creating samples representative of these platforms' populations. This article is
aimed to be a methodological toolkit, which points at the challenges that may
occur while designing a cross-national experiment on media consumption—and
provides practical recommendations to overcome them.

Keywords: Fake news · Research design · Online experiment · Comparative
methods

1 Introduction

Fake news—as a widely discussed phenomenon in the contemporary public sphere—is
commonly associated with a range of direct and indirect adverse consequences. False
messages circulating online have the potential to undermine trust in government [1], public health policies, such as vaccination [2], and in news media in general [3]. Fake news
is also harmful for opinion formation and informed decision making [4]. Furthermore,

© Springer Nature Switzerland AG 2021
G. Meiselwitz (Ed.): HCII 2021, LNCS 12774, pp. 370–390, 2021.
https://doi.org/10.1007/978-3-030-77626-8_25

some studies have found false messages to produce opinion polarization [5], contribute to hostility [6], and generally undermine the quality of online discussion.

Fake news spread is closely tied to digital communication, social media use, and recent structural transformations of news production [7]. Carrying a negative connotation and being often used in public debate, "fake news" is hard to define precisely. As its distinctive features most of the scholars emphasize the fabricated nature of fake news, intention to deceive, and news-like format [8]. Allcott and Gentzkow [9] define fake news more narrowly as "a news article that is intentionally and verifiably false".

One of the major avenues of fake news research is focused on its perception. A substantial question raised is: *Why do people believe fake news?* Scholars tested various factors in this domain including cognitive traits and message features. Yet addressing this question with the experimental design faces a number of methodological challenges.

In this article, we discuss the methodology of the cross-national experiment on misinformation perception based on our recent study testing users' ability to recognize fake news in three countries. It examines how audiences respond to fake and real political news framing a foreign country from different perspectives. Importantly, we analyze the effect of media framing in the situation of conflict between countries where fake news can be especially harmful for public deliberation.

Since, to our knowledge, this is the first experiment on fake news with such goals and methods, this task requires a specific design. Here, we describe the choices we made on both stages of designing and conducting the study—and provide tips and recommendations for future research. We intend this article to be a set of methodological guidelines for scholars who aim to conduct an experiment on fake news, specifically—on the cross-national level.

1.1 Theoretical Background

Multiple studies have examined the reasons why people trust fake news and what influences the accuracy of their judgements. They employ both qualitative (e.g. focus groups) and quantitative (e.g. surveys, analysis of the online data) methods; a large body of research addressed this question with experimental designs. Often these studies use different operationalizations of outcome variables to study misinformation perception: for example, they frequently test users' *accuracy in discernment* between real and fake news, *perceived credibility/believability* of fake news or *user engagement* (e.g. the likelihood of sharing or liking it). Factors influencing the perceived credibility of misinformation and the ability to discern between real and fake news are studies on both individual and message levels. However, we argue that these experiments contain several gaps related to the research scope and methods.

First of all, even though creation of explicitly false information, or disinformation, is considered to be one of the forms of political propaganda [10], the ability to recognize fake news about other countries (i.e. foreign reporting) is rarely studied. Many of the experiments were conducted within the US context in the aftermath of 2016 elections using domestic news as a stimulus material. Yet research suggests that media is powerful in shaping audiences' attitudes towards foreign countries—both by framing [11] and agenda setting [12]. Lewandowsky et al. [13] argue that misinformation and disinformation are not only a matter of individual cognition but it can also contribute to violent conflicts, while another study shows that public opinion can be influenced by media headlines framing social conflict in a particular way [14]. We believe that fake news, in this sense, can shape an especially biased view of other states, nations, or ethnic groups.

Secondly, we observe a lack of research examining fake news on a cross-national scale, which juxtapose differences and similarities of misinformation perception across various societies. Although there are examples of comparative studies per se [15–17], most of them do not employ experimental design while relying on other methods including surveys or content analysis.

Thirdly, a group of limitations concerns both sampling and the experimental procedure. The prevailing tool used for recruiting participants is Amazon Mechanical Turk, which, however, is suggested to be "limited in terms of the size and diversity of the sample" [18]. To our knowledge, no existing experiments on fake news employ quota targeting on social media—a tool of recruitment that provides access to the population of users and constitutes a natural environment of online news consumption. Furthermore, the observed experimental settings appear to be contextually imbalanced, as Facebook dominates among the studied platforms.

1.2 Objectives

In this article, we describe the challenges that we faced while designing a cross-national experiment with fake news and provide a set of methodological solutions that were used in this study. We discuss in detail the following stages of our research: (1) designing the experiment; (2) construction of stimulus material; (3) sampling; (4) recruitment of participants (via social media); (5) post-stratification of the obtained samples. Reflecting on the choices we made, we aim to create a methodological toolkit for the studies with similar designs or approaches.

2 Designing a Cross-National Experiment

In this section, we briefly outline the goals of our experiment and discuss the specifics of its design.

An online experiment was conducted to test the users' ability to recognize fake news about foreign countries. It was carried out in three neighboring states: Russia, Ukraine, and Kazakhstan. We examined factors that influence the perceived credibility of the news and individual accuracy in recognizing fake news. Our predominant focus was on news frames (dominant/alternative), i.e. how another country is portrayed in the media, news sources (from the user's country/from the country covered in the news), political attitudes, conflict perception, and propensity for conspiracy thinking. Overall, 10,789 people participated in the study. Each user received eight news items randomly retrieved from our database and evaluated their credibility.

We hypothesize that news frames corresponding to the dominating narrative of the nation's mainstream media will be perceived as more credible/recognized more accurately than those with the alternative frames. We also assume that news coming from the respondent's country will be perceived as more credible/recognized more accurately than those coming from the country described in the news article. These effects are expected to be stronger if the countries have conflicting relations. Some of the results—reflecting the effects of conspiracy thinking style, framing and political interest on accuracy of fake news recognition—are reported in the article by Porshnev et al. [19].

Based on Kohn's classification of comparative studies [20], nations in our experiment constitute a context of the study rather than its object or unit of analysis. Thus, we expect certain generalizability of the results, nonetheless considering national differences. The choice of the countries can be supported by several arguments. First, these post-Soviet states have strong historical, cultural, and economical ties, thus, are prominent in the media agenda of one another. Secondly, Russian is widely spoken in all three countries. Finally, such selection of countries allows us to explore the role of international conflict in misinformation perception. While Russia maintains neutral relations with Kazakhstan, it has an explicit conflict with Ukraine which started in the aftermath of Ukrainian revolution in 2014 and escalated due to the annexation of Crimea and ongoing war in Donbass.

2.1 Research Design

In our research, we employ $2 \times 2 \times 2$ experimental design with elements of both between-subject and within-subject design. Separately both approaches have their advantages and disadvantages. For instance, within-subject designs help to mitigate individual differences. However, Charness, Gneezy, and Kuhn [21] note that the results of such studies might be confounded by the order of the treatment exposure. Between-subject designs, as argued by the same authors, are statistically simpler to perform, yet their results may have substantial noise.

We use a combination of methods, which, in relation to media studies, can be defined as a message subset design (it involves multiple stimuli for each of the treatment levels— for example, several different true and fake news) [22]. Elements of the within-subject design (each participant in each condition) let us mitigate substantial differences between users. Furthermore, as argued by Reeves and Geiger [22], demonstrating messages on different treatment levels (fake and true news, in our case) holds a higher ecological validity, because in real world people are more likely to consume different types of news together and not separately. Additionally, by randomizing the order of exposure we aim to minimize the order effects and by varying sets of the stimulus between users—to isolate the effect of a specific news item. On the other hand, our experiment has elements of between-subject design as participants received different sets of stimuli. It was also necessary in our case, since we manipulated the source of the same news items, thus making it impossible to show a message in both treatment levels to the same participant.

3 Stimuli Development

The corpus of stimulus material for our experiment included 100 texts in total. We developed five sets of news items: (1) news about Russia for Kazakhstani users; (2) news about Kazakhstan for Russian users; (3) news about Ukraine for Russian users; (4) news about Russia for Ukrainian users (in Russian language); (5) news about Russia for Ukrainian users (in Ukrainian language). Each of the sets contained 24 texts which included fake and true news with dominant and alternative frames in equal proportions (Fig. 1). However, since the data collection took place during the peak of the COVID-19 pandemic (April–July, 2020), and media at the time was overfilled with the its coverage, we also included one truthful news item devoted to the outbreak of the coronavirus in each of the sets as a distractor.

<table>
<tr><td>

Russia
(news about Ukraine)
6TD
6TA
6FD
6FA
1TDis

Language: Russian
</td><td>

Russia
(news about
Kazakhstan)
6TD
6TA
6FD
6FA
1TDis

Language: Russian
</td></tr>
</table>

Kazakhstan
(news about Russia)
6TD
6TA
6FD
6FA
1TDis

Language: Russian

Ukraine
(news about Russia)
6TD
6TA
6FD
6FA
1TDis

Language:
Russian/Ukrainian

Fig. 1. Structure of stimulus material. T—true; F—fake; D—dominant frame; A—alternative frame; Dis—distractor.

To test our hypotheses we needed all of the news items to satisfy the following criteria: (1) the information can be undoubtedly verified as true or false; (2) the news describes an event related to one of the examined countries; (3) the news contains a political frame (dominant/alternative) regarding the described country; (4) an article can be credibly ascribed both to the media of the respondent's country or to the media of the country described in the news.

Selection of media stimuli for an experiment requires a clear operationalization of the reflected variables [23]. Thorson et al. [24] emphasize that it is necessary to "select the physical stimulus features considered important in the tested theory, treat them as the independent variables, and then measure psychological responses".

Message variance in experimental studies could be created by either altering one message to represent more than one level of the variable or by selecting different messages to represent different treatment levels [25]. Our study uses both of these approaches. For example, for two independent variables (source and language) the same messages were presented in different treatment levels meaning that users could see the same news article ascribed to different sources or in different language (the latter is valid only for the Ukrainian users, who could choose the language of the interface).

With regard to the frame, each message could only be allotted into one of the categories—dominant or alternative—since true articles were taken from the media without significant alterations. Thus, this parameter was fixed for each text.

3.1 Identifying Frames

Framing, as conceptualized by Entman, is "selecting and highlighting some facets of events or issues, and making connections among them so as to promote a particular interpretation, evaluation, and/or solution" [26]. According to one of the categorizations, frames can be divided into two major types: equivalency and emphasis frames [27]. While equivalency framing is based on the use of "different, but logically equivalent, words or phrases", emphasis framing highlights a particular "subset of potentially relevant considerations" [28]. Some scholars criticize the approach using emphasis frames for blurring the boundaries between framing and other media effects, such as priming or agenda-setting [29]. However, others argue that emphasis frames create contextualization—by including pieces of topic-relevant information and avoiding others [30].

In our research, we use elements of both equivalency and emphasis frames due to the substantial differences in media agendas of the studied countries. While equivalency frames in our stimuli are mostly shaped by emotional words, evaluative language, phrases with clear positive or negative attitude (e.g. "Minister of foreign affairs disgraced himself"), emphasis frames are represented by the articles highlighting issues that are rarely brought up by the media that advance an alternative political agenda.

To detect frames common for the media of all three countries, we conducted topic modelling of texts from the Russian, Kazakhstani, and Ukrainian media outlets as well as consulted with experts. However, the analysis showed that it is impossible to apply the universal approach to coding frames to all three countries. To give an example, categories "dominant" and "alternative" in Russian reporting usually can be interpreted as "pro-governmental" and "oppositional". For instance, dominant frames in reporting on Ukraine or Kazakhstan mostly reflect the state position regarding the countries' relations. Yet in Ukraine the coverage of Russia is not aligned with the attitudes towards the government; here, the dominant way of reporting on Russia is in general negative regardless of the issue, while the alternative is more neutral, which could be explained by conflicted relations between countries. Kazakhstani media also demonstrate a different type of framing: reporting on Russia is generally neutral, but the "alternativeness" can be observed in discussion of Kazakhstani politics towards Russia. In this case, neutral and moderate coverage was identified as dominant, while coverage drifting towards one of the sides (either positive or negative)—as alternative.

Generally, the process of frame determination and news selection included the following steps:

1. Identifying common topics in the reporting on the country of interest through topic modelling;
2. Selecting the most prominent and/or controversial issues;
3. Identifying the dominant and the alternative frames regarding an issue;
4. Looking for / constructing relevant news items;
5. Double-checking news items with experts (regarding its factual correctness for true news and believability for fake ones).

In summary, we argue that a cross-national experiment using frames as an independent variable requires unique sets of news for each country. Such customized approach towards stimuli selection allows to integrate specificity of different media systems and news agendas, which are crucial for the news perception.

3.2 Selecting Fake and True News

All of the news items used in the experiment were labeled as either true or false. True articles were collected from the real news outlets and verified in other sources. Fake stories were constructed by a professional journalist (member of the research team) and evaluated by the experts in terms of their believability and relevance. All fake news items were written so that they do not significantly differ in style from the real ones.

Many of the similar experiments use debunked fake news from fact-checking websites like Snopes.com, PolitiFact.com and others [31, 32]. Nonetheless, the decision to create fake articles was made based on several reasons. Firstly, prior exposure increases the perceived believability of misinformation [33], thus, it could lead to biased responses from the participants that are already familiar with particular fake news. Secondly, all items had to satisfy specific criteria listed earlier in this section. Due to the complexity of requirements, relevant items could be hardly found among a relatively small number of debunked false stories. Finally, we assumed that participants of an online experiment could search for the news during the test (although this option was not clearly suggested in the task). In this case, they could come across the headlines of published and/or debunked fake news and perceive them as true without doing a deeper research. Therefore, by constructing fake stories we ensured that it would be impossible to find similar news in search engines.

Thus, such design allowed us not only to mitigate possible effects of prior exposure and fact-checking behavior, but also to determine how often users actually check the validity of the news they consume.

3.3 Source Manipulation

In our study, we randomly manipulated the source of the news items. In order to avoid a possible effect of the particular medium/news source, concrete names of the outlets were not used. Instead, news had more general attribution: "from Russian/Ukrainian/Kazakhstani media".

However, source manipulation provided an additional restriction for the news selection because news items had to fit agendas of two countries equally compellingly. This was especially challenging in the pair Russia—Ukraine, since the conflict between the countries has a significant impact on the media coverage [34]. Above all, it reflects in the word choice: for instance, while Ukrainian media mentioning Crimea almost always adds the definition "occupied", Russian media (even the oppositional outlets) never use this particular phrasing. As a result, we had to find real (or construct fake) news items which would not contain discrepancies obvious to a respondent.

However, this challenge also arises due to the nature of domestic and foreign reporting. For example, a very local story about a foreign country is highly unlikely to appear on the media of another country. On the other hand, being aimed at a different audience, news about another country may contain specific details or excessive explanations, which would not be relevant for the local audience (e.g. "a Russian parliament called Gosduma"). In other words, such universal stimuli require a contextual balance between too specific and too general information so that it could be perceived as coming from both countries.

3.4 Language

Another important aspect of a cross-national experiment is language. In our study, three of the stimuli sets were demonstrated only in Russian and one—in Russian and Ukrainian, so that Ukrainian users could switch between the two languages. The same option, however, was not provided to the Kazakhstani users. Despite a growing expansion of Kazakh language in the post-Soviet time [35], Russian is widely used in Kazakhstan: according to the last census in 2009, nearly 94% of the population understand Russian, whereas only 74% understand Kazakh being an official language. Besides, we argue that a choice of language in Kazakhstan is by all means a less controversial issue in comparison to Ukraine.

We introduced the option of changing language to the Ukrainian users not only as a matter of convenience but also a matter of political perspective, since the issue of bilingualism in Ukraine has been especially complex. As it is noted by Bilaniuk and Melnyk [36], the choice of language is symbolic of one's political views and reflects the polarization of Ukrainian society. This discussion became even more tense since the start of the Ukrainian conflict resulting in the adoption of the language law in 2019 which requires the use of Ukrainian in most spheres of public life. Kulyk [37] views language in Ukraine as a predictor of people's attitudes and even policy preferences.

Therefore, the instrument (including stimulus material, questionnaire and interface of the app) targeted at the Ukrainian users was translated into Ukrainian with the help of native speakers and experts. From a methodological perspective, language in our study can be considered not only as a feature of the instrument but also as an independent variable indicative of people's attitudes.

3.5 Presentation Format

Media stimuli in an online experiment can be demonstrated in various forms: for instance, as a headline, as a Facebook post, as a text with picture, etc. Many experiments on fake news perception—such as studies conducted by Pennycook, Rand and co-authors [31, 33, 38]—use news headlines (mostly presented as Facebook posts). Scholars base this decision on the argument that on social media people mostly consume just headlines [39]. Another advantage of such stimuli format, in our opinion, is convenience for the participants because it may be easier to perceive and faster to evaluate.

However, headlines may also lead towards a biased perception of news. Studies showed that headlines can differ from the full articles in terms of emphasis and issue salience [40], mislead readers [41] or—if being clickbait—be perceived as less credible [42]. Furthermore, we argue that such short pieces of information may not provide enough cues and details for a reader to assess it and, on the other hand, may not fully reflect framing which, as discussed earlier, significantly varies from country to country. Therefore, we chose to expose participants to short news headlines accompanied by a small block of text (not longer than 537 characters).

Finally, we chose to demonstrate news as a plain text rather than a social media post. Mainly it was done because our primary focus is news perception in general— not only on social media. another constraining factor emerged due to the nature of the recruitment process: since we targeted our potential respondents via two social media platforms, Facebook and VKontakte, showing posts mimicking only one of them could be confusing for part of the users, and the varying format of the post depending on the platform could distort the results.

4 Data Collection

In our research we employed social media as a source of recruitment and data collection. Using the online social networks (OSN) advertisement systems for improving recruitment outcomes has several advantages over traditional offline and online recruiting methods.

First, OSN platforms brought about great opportunities for scholars to reach large and diverse audiences. The online population of the world's most popular OSN Facebook is not dominated anymore by the young adults, at least among American users [43, 44]. Moreover, our analysis revealed that Russian Facebook is occupied mainly by the middle-age group. Despite the OSN populations being not yet representative of the world's general population, it grows rapidly. For instance, in 2014 nearly 37% of America's older adults (over 65 years of age) were on Facebook while in 2019 it constitutes 46% [44, 45]. Thus, it seems that even the underrepresented populations on OSNs are relatively large.

Comparative studies showed that even at the rise of the Internet online samples were more demographically diverse than those obtained by traditional offline methods [46]. In comparison to other online recruiting methods (Google and Craigslist advertising, email invitations, market research panels, and party membership online referendums) targeting via advertisement systems on Facebook leads to higher response rate in shorter time and at reduced costs [47].

Second, being very globalized (more than 200 countries are presented at least on Facebook), large social media offer an incentive for cross-cultural comparisons that are relevant to the aims of our study.

Another reason to turn to the OSN as a recruitment source is in the very essence of our experiment, which, as it was mentioned above, focuses on online news consumption. Since the large OSNs usually aggregate news, they create the natural setting for conducting such experiments, and their users seem to be an appropriate sample to analyze.

Despite the advantages provided by OSNs, the process of recruitment and data collection via advertisement systems leads to several challenges related to designing sample or organizing and managing ad campaigns, which will be discussed further below.

4.1 Sample Construction

The existing reviews reveal that targeting is a helpful and widely used method for reaching niche and hard-to-reach populations, that it is especially popular among the public health scholars [44, 48–55].

However, most studies investigate the specific subpopulations like young adults cigarettes-smokers [49] or individuals with mental disorders [52, 53], for which by its nature no prior sociodemographic data about the general population is available. Such sampling strategies that do not rely on demographic quotas might potentially produce very non-representative samples [56]. Thornton et al. [48] showed that most studies that applied targeting recruiting design did not contain the post-hoc representativeness check. Among those who reported it, only 36% characterized the obtained samples as overall representative of the population of interest. In addition, some OSNs like Facebook apply algorithms based on the characteristics of the users who have already responded to optimize the further impressions of advertising. Such Facebook advertisement delivery optimization might potentially lead to the homogeneity of the recruited subjects.

At the same time, social media provide the opportunity to improve the external validity of non-probabilistic samples obtained from targeting river sampling by relying on platform-specific quota sampling techniques. It is possible to estimate the sociodemographic distribution of an online population of interest before the data collection and further recruit participants in correspondence with pre-established quotas. Zhang et al. [56] claim that this approach "allows quota sampling on conditional strata themselves rather than simply ensuring the sample marginals approximate the population marginals" [56].

Surprisingly, the potential of OSN to reach the nationally representative samples through quota sampling is understudied. To date, only Zhang and colleagues' [56] work was found showing that the results from the Facebook-sampled survey approximate quite accurately those obtained by the online panel through address-based probability-sampling.

In our research, we tested such an approach to recruit nationally representative samples of Facebook and VKontakte online populations. These social media platforms were chosen as the biggest in Post-Soviet region, thus providing not only the access to a wide audience of populations of interest, but also technical capabilities for targeting. As the VKontakte OSN is officially banned in Ukraine, Facebook provided us with primary access to residents of this country.

The main reason for choosing these particular social networks is the necessity to avoid sampling bias which would occur due to significant differences in social media use between different regional and age groups in the studied countries. In addition, our analysis of its audience showed that it possesses slightly different audiences in terms of sociodemographics. Thus, this provides the additional comparative perspective to our study.

As a basis for our quota samples we used the data on the overall age and gender distribution as well as data on the geographical distribution of users among the regions in all countries of interest that were available in the ad manager systems of both Facebook and VKontakte.

The question about the extent of quota specification inevitably arises on this stage. If no process of automation of targeting data collection is made as in Zhang et al. [56], the need to keep the sample representativeness clashes with the capacities to manually launch multiple campaigns at one time. In the context of our study, the simple calculation of quotas only for Russian users revealed the need for 83 distinct quotas (i.e. campaigns) for each region. Thus, the regions of each country were aggregated into larger instances like 8 officially declared federal districts in Russia and 4 districts for Ukraine and Kazakhstan which were artificially constructed based on the suggestions of local experts and the registries used at the sociological polls. In addition, we rejected the idea to represent the age and gender distribution within each region because it would also result in a very complex ads campaign design. Alternatively, these two types of quotas were managed separately but in parallel to each other. Each quota was targeted until its saturation and the special automatic checking system was created for facilitating the monitoring of quotas filling.

4.2 Creating Ad Campaigns

Two peculiarities of targeting methods require special attention. First, the targeting procedure, like other digital recruitment methods, lacks direct personal contact with a potential recruitee. At the same time, in the context of our study which touches upon such sensitive topics as political and military conflicts, participant's loyalty might be important for incentivizing trust to the study and research group itself. Second, targeting systems are implemented to the technological environment of OSNs that have their own policies. For example, both Facebook and VKontakte moderate the advertisement content before it would be allowed to be released. More importantly, usage of targeting for research activity should be also approved by moderators. Thereby, some preliminary work should be made even before starting the advertisement campaigns.

Considering VKontakte, as all ads should be targeted on behalf of the public pages of online communities, it is important to take care in advance about the content and appearance of the online public page that you refer to in your advertisement. For our research we created online public pages that were administered and filled with the content relevant to the study topic. This page contained detailed information about the research project and links to all official university bio pages of research team members. Additionally, the project public page was promoted by means of targeting in all three countries of interest in order to attract the geographically diverse audience. By the time of the moderation phase the project's VKontakte page contained around 10 posts and had around 200 subscribers. Thus, such a preparation stage helps to build the initial pool of trust with both users who click on the project page and moderators who need to quickly recognize fraudulent content. In contrast to VKontakte, which allows natively integrating the external research tool as a part of its own ecosystem, Facebook permits promoting only external standalone sites if some research apps are presented. In this case, instead of focusing on fostering some internal official project page like in VKontakte, we made the same efforts to increase the credibility of our standalone site specially created for the purposes of the study.

4.3 Constructing Ads

The process of creating ads should rely on both practical and methodological considerations. The former assumes following the technical OSN requirements and policies regulating the ad's format and content. The difficulties on the stage of ads' approval might cause, in turn, methodological issues. For example, if the campaigns are planned to launch sequentially, we strongly recommend to initiate the moderation phase of each campaign at the same time. The decision to approve or to not approve an ad might substantially vary from one moderator to another, that potentially might lead to a non-symmetrical campaign in terms of displayed ads.

The ads framing is another important issue on the stage of ads development. One of the most common types of an ad post both in Facebook and VKontakte contains a picture followed by a short text with an internal or external link to the survey. The way how people are invited to participate may affect the recruiting outcome and sample quality.

On the one hand, the interest in the topic increases the response rate that is especially relevant for studies looking for specific target groups. However, for studies aimed at representing a "global" population, leading wordings in advertising might result in a biased sample, i.e. attract people with strongly pronounced qualities or personality traits.

For our study, we prepared a set of 7 advertisements challenging users to take part in our research and test their ability to distinguish fake facts from true ones. Specifically, the application was promoted by the analogy with popular online entertainment apps like quasi-psychological tests proposing to learn something new about one's personality. It seems that this gamification of the process would be helpful for competing for the attention of users exposed to a variety of other alternatives present in OSNs environment. The ads wordings and pictures slightly varied from the stylistically neutral and emphasizing the research part to the more catchy ones.

The utility of our ads was tested during the pilot study. The testing period lasted 1 day since the campaign began, which was enough to estimate the attractiveness of each ad for the audience. In the case of VKontakte it was critically important to reduce the number of ads managed, because, unlike Facebook, it has no nested structure where each campaign might transmit different content simultaneously. As a result, 4 key ads were chosen for VKontakte and Facebook which showed high performance during the pilot stage. All supplementary materials including the ads content are available at the public GitHub repository (github.com/hse-scila/fakenews).

Overall data collection stage lasted 2 months (April-May 2020), with an additional 2-day campaign (July 21–22, 2020) for Ukrainian audiences performed due to technical issues. For all countries the sought-for datasets were successfully collected, except that for Ukrainian-speaking users in VKontakte. It could be explained by the poor presence of Ukrainian users on this social networking site which has been banned in Ukraine since 2017.

In general, there were 10 ads campaigns fielded symmetrically on Facebook and VKontakte. For Russia and Kazakhstan the audience of VKontakte that met the eligibility criteria (aged 21–65) substantively outnumbers that on Facebook (see Table 1). Ukrainian users as expected were represented more on Facebook due to the official ban of VKontakte.

Of the 323,596 Facebook users reached from overall 414,227 ads impressions, 9,4% (30,268 unique users) clicked the ads, 78% (23,659 users) reached the preview page. 35% of the latter (8477) completed the questionnaires. Thus, the unique CTR metrics traditionally used as indicator of conversion (the percentage calculated by dividing the number of unique clicks on an ad receives by the number of displays) varies from 2,7% to 12,7%, while the completion rate (the ratio of number of clicked on ads users to the number of completed questionnaires) ranged from 18 to 40%. The Facebook campaign

Table 1. Campaign performance

Campaign name[a]		RUS—KZ	RUS—UA	KZ—RUS	UA—RUS(rus)	UA—RUS(ua)[b]	Average	Total
Duration, days	VK	6	6	4	13	2	6	31
	FB	6	6	8	2	2	5	24
Unique, clicks	VK	7950	12404	7455	16757	929	9099	45495
	FB	4050	6814	3832	9852	5720	6054	30268
Landing views	VK	2603	4156	2632	2959	105	2491	12455
	FB	3437	5178	3150	7381	4513	4732	23659
Impressions	VK	828642	1178823	1052492	2707736	213882	1196315	5981575
	FB	60470	85805	138390	83767	45795	82845	414227
Reach	VK	695561	1191669	628893	1225212	159611	780189	3900946
	FB	48944	71808	81208	76624	45012	64719	323596
Unique CTR, %	VK	1.01	1.10	0.70	0.60	0.4	0.8	—
	FB	6.7	8.0	2.7	11.8	12.5	8.3	—
Spent per campaign, $	VK	511	837	304	85	129		1866
	FB	195	257	185	66	50	—	753
Cost per click, $	VK	0.06	0.36	0.05	0.13	0.2	0.15	—

(continued)

Table 1. (*continued*)

Campaign name[a]		RUS—KZ	RUS—UA	KZ—RUS	UA—RUS(rus)	UA—RUS(ua)[b]	Average	Total
	FB	0.04	0.04	0.05	0.01	0.01	0.03	—
Target population size	VK	54,495,000		4,289,000	4,334,00		—	63,118,000
	FB	8,720,000		1,976,000	13,220,00		—	23,916,000
Full questionnaires	VK	1249	1570	1324	1363	65	—	5571
	FB	1616	1850	1575	1730	1706	—	8477

[a]In the column "Campaign name," the first abbreviation stands for the name of the country to which news is shown, then goes the name of the country discussed in the news. RUS—Russia; KZ—Kazakhstan; UA (rus)—Ukraine on Russian language; UA (ua)—Ukraine on Ukrainian language.
[b]Not completed campaign in VKontakte.

lasted on average 5 days (the longest took 8 days) and cost 753$ with 0,08$ cost per completer.

To compare, the VKontakte campaigns aimed to reach the target population 2,5 times greater than FB. The overall 5,9 million ads impressions reached around 3,9 million Vkontakte users, among those only 1,2% (45,495 users) clicked on the ads and 27% of them (12,455 users) visited the preview page. The number of users who completed the survey totaled 5571. The unique CTR thereby varied from 0,4% to 1,1%, and the completion rate lay between 7 and 16%. The average duration of VKontakte campaigns was 6 days (the most time-consuming lasted 13 days) and cost 1866$ with an average cost-per-completer at 0,3$.

This comparison reveals the significant difference between Facebook and VKontakte OSNs in campaigns' performance characteristics. Facebook substantially outperforms VKontakte by the time, cost, and conversion rates. Such tangible performance gaps could be attributed primarily to the difference in marketing strategy and technological approach applied by these two OSNs. Contrary to Facebook, which automatically applies sophisticated algorithms for displaying the advertisement to the potentially more interested or look-alike audience, VKontakte seems to be randomly "screening" the users with active accounts if no additional options are specified. Predictably, Facebook's tactics result in higher response, but at the same time it might lead to more homogeneous or biased samples [54, 56] if no control under the quota filling is applied by scholars. In contrast, VKontakte advertisement system provides much more ease and transparent control over the targeting process.

Placing such results into the context of existing research, our Facebook campaigns demonstrated comparable and even higher CTR rates than in prior works that ranged from 0.05% and 4.07% [48, 49, 54, 57]. Our campaigns turned out to cost substantially less both paid overall on average and per completer than in previous research – 2407.07$ [48].

It should be noted that several considerations complicate the very possibility of comparing the campaigns across the studies. In the context of our study, as the absolute majority of prior works recruited participants through Facebook, it is impossible to compare their performance with those obtained in our VKontakte part of data collection. In addition, only one research with similar quota sample design was found while the vast majority aimed to recruit specific or hard to reach target populations with no control applied over the quota filling.

More generally, it seems problematic to compare the performance rates across the studies due to the difference in campaigns' duration, budget, size of target population, study context and many other parameters that might significantly influence the response from the users' side. To sum up, each ads campaign has unique features, and the experience of past research showed that sought-for populations might be successfully reached even with the relatively low targeting performance rates.

5   Data Pre- and Postprocessing

Preparation of data obtained for further analysis consisted of two stages. The first stage included data integrity testing, cleaning, and filtering. The respondents who did not finish the survey were excluded from the samples. Discrepancies in the answers (for example, when a person claims to be studying in secondary school while being 40 years old) were resolved using the additional filters applied to respondents' age, gender, and country data. The samples were also checked for minor mistakes in records, and the corrupted observations were dismissed.

The second stage involved post-stratification. As it was described above, we utilized a quota sampling technique for collecting the samples. However, there was a delay due to the gap between starting and completing the survey by a participant. Therefore, quotas oversampling was inevitable. In order to improve the collected samples, we applied post-stratification to them. Post-stratification is an effective method for adjusting a non-representative sample and obtaining more accurate estimates by balancing representation of the strata in a sample and also partially correcting for non-sampling error [58–61]. This approach allowed us to optimize the samples and make them less skewed and more representative of ONS populations in terms of respondents' age, gender, and regional distribution. The overall sizes of the cleaned, filtered, and post-stratified samples are given in Table 2.

Table 2. Post-stratified sample sizes for all targeted countries and social networking sites.

Targeted country	Opponent country appeared in news	Facebook	VKontakte	Total
Russia	Ukraine	1436	1201	2637
Russia	Kazakhstan	1317	983	2300
Kazakhstan	Russia	1305	1019	2324
Ukraine	Russia (in Ukrainian language)	1394	—	1394
Ukraine	Russia (in Russian language)	1326	808	2134

6   Conclusion and Discussion

In this article, we have discussed the methodology of a cross-national online experiment on fake news perception. Based on our study conducted in Russia, Ukraine, and Kazakhstan, we have outlined the main methodological and conceptual challenges that researchers can face while designing such projects. Providing a number of practical guidelines, this article can be considered as a toolkit for media and communication scholars. These tips can be relevant to different groups of research designs depending on their scope including: 1) comparative media studies; 2) online experiments; 3) experiments with fake news; 4) experiments with media content in general; 5) studies using ad targeting for data collection.

In our study, we tested how users perceive true and fake news about foreign countries depending on different factors including news frames, news source, political attitudes, the relations between countries, and thinking styles. Due to the lack of comparative studies on misinformation perception as well as the complexity of the task, our study required a novel design and methodology, which, to our knowledge, had not been used in previous experiments with fake news.

First of all, we explain the benefits of the combination of elements of between- and within-subject designs. On the one hand, it allows us to expose users to different treatment levels (e.g. true and fake news, alternative and dominant frames). On the other hand, by randomly selecting messages from a bigger subset of stimuli and varying them between different participants, we, thus, isolate the influence of particular messages or sequence effects.

Secondly, we provide a detailed description of stimuli construction. We conclude that a cross-national experiment with the focus on media messages requires different sets of stimulus material and individual approach to its selection—especially when it comes to the factors that highly depend on the news agenda of a country (e.g. framing). Nonetheless, it also leads to certain limitations by making the effects of the stimuli less comparable across the studied groups. Thus, here we face one of the crucial problems of comparative media research: as described by Livingstone [62], such studies require standardized methods to ensure comparability of the data, however methodological and theoretical universalism comes "at the cost of recognizing cultural specificity".

Thirdly, this article explores some of the methodological aspects specific to experiments with fake news in particular—for instance, constructing fake news for the research purposes instead of using "real" fake news from fact-checking websites. We argue that "made-up" fake news allows to test complex combinations of independent variables as well as to isolate the effect of prior exposure and the possibility to look up the news. On the other hand, this approach raises both methodological (lower ecological validity) and ethical concerns. Exposing people to "new" fake news may lead to memorization of false facts, as misinformation has a continued effect even after it has been retracted [63]. As a partial compensation for that, we published correct answers clearly labeled as true or false at the end of the experiment.

Fourthly, we applied the quota sampling techniques for acquiring representative samples through ad targeting recruitment in social media. Although it is also not free from certain methodological issues typical to classic recruiting methods (like non-response or self-selection bias), the control over the quota fillings seems to ease the process of data collection and prevent the bias in key demographic characteristics.

To sum up, while acknowledging that the methodology of experimental designs is highly dependent on the goals of the research, we believe our experience may provide useful practical guidelines for other scholars.

Acknowledgements. The research was implemented in the framework of the Russian Scientific Fund Grant №19-18-00206 at the National Research University Higher School of Economics (HSE) in 2021.

References

1. Huang, H.: A War of (mis)information: the political effects of rumors and rumor rebuttals in an authoritarian country. Br. J. Polit. Sci. **47**(2), 283–311 (2017). https://doi.org/10.1017/S00 07123415000253

2. Larson, H.: The biggest pandemic risk? viral misinformation. Nature **562**, 309 (2018). https://doi.org/10.1038/d41586-018-07034-4

3. Van Duyn, E., Collier, J.: Priming and fake news: the effects of elite discourse on evaluations of news media. Mass Commun. Soc. **22**(1), 29–48 (2019). https://doi.org/10.1080/15205436.2018.1511807

4. Tucker, J.A., et al.: Social media, political polarization, and political disinformation: a review of the scientific literature, pp. 1–95 (2018). https://doi.org/10.2139/ssrn.3144139

5. Nyhan, B.: Why the "death panel" myth wouldn't die: misinformation in the health care reform debate. The Forum **8**(1) (2010). https://doi.org/10.2202/1540-8884.1354

6. Lee, T., Hosam, C.: Fake news is real: the significance and sources of disbelief in mainstream media in Trump's America. Sociol. Forum **35**(S1), 996–1018 (2020). https://doi.org/10.1111/socf.12603

7. Martens, B., Aguiar, L., Gomez, E., Mueller-Langer, F.: The digital transformation of news media and the rise of disinformation and fake news - An economic perspective. Digital Economy Working Paper 2018–02; JRC Technical Reports (2018). https://doi.org/10.2139/ssrn.3164170

8. Lazer, D., et al.: The science of fake news. Science **359**(6380), 1094–1096 (2018). https://doi.org/10.1126/science.aao2998

9. Allcott, H., Gentzkow, M.: Social media and fake news in the 2016 election. J. Econ. Perspect. **31**(2), 211–236 (2017). https://doi.org/10.1257/jep.31.2.211

10. Benkler, Y., Faris, R., Roberts, H.: Network Propaganda: Manipulation, disinformation, and radicalization in American politics. Oxford University Press, New York (2018). https://doi.org/10.1093/oso/9780190923624.001.0001

11. Brewer, P.R., Graf, J., Willnat, L.: Priming or framing: media influence on attitudes toward foreign countries. Int. Commun. Gaz. **65**(6), 493–508 (2003). https://doi.org/10.1177/0016549203065006005

12. Wanta, W., Golan, G., Lee, C.: Agenda setting and international news: media influence on public perceptions of foreign nations. Journalism Mass Commun. Quart. **81**(2), 364–377 (2004). https://doi.org/10.1177/107769900408100209

13. Lewandowsky, S., Stritzke, W.G.K., Freund, A.M., Oberauer, K., Krueger, J.I.: Misinformation, disinformation, and violent conflict: from Iraq and the "War on Terror" to future threats to peace. Am. Psychol. **68**(7), 487–501 (2013). https://doi.org/10.1037/a0034515

14. Colvin, R.M., Witt, G.B., Lacey, J., McCrea, R.: The role of conflict framing and social identity in public opinion about land use change: an experimental test in the Australian context. Environ. Policy Gov. **30**(2), 84–98 (2020). https://doi.org/10.1002/eet.1879

15. Martin, J.D., Hassan, F.: News media credibility ratings and perceptions of online fake news exposure in five countries. J. Stud. **21**(16), 2215–2233 (2020). https://doi.org/10.1080/1461670X.2020.1827970

16. Humprecht, E.: Where 'fake news' flourishes: a comparison across four Western democracies. Inf. Commun. Soc. **22**(13), 1973–1988 (2019). https://doi.org/10.1080/1369118X.2018.1474241

17. Humprecht, E.: How do they debunk "fake news"? a cross-national comparison of transparency in fact checks. Digit. Journal. **8**(3), 310–327 (2020). https://doi.org/10.1080/21670811.2019.1691031

18. Chandler, J., Rosenzweig, C., Moss, A.J., Robinson, J., Litman, L.: Online panels in social science research: expanding sampling methods beyond Mechanical Turk. Behav. Res. Methods **51**(5), 2022–2038 (2019). https://doi.org/10.3758/s13428-019-01273-7

19. Porshnev, A., Miltsov, A., Lokot, T., Koltsova, O.: Effects of conspiracy thinking style, framing and political interest on accuracy of fake news recognition by social media users: evidence from Russia, Kazakhstan and Ukraine. In: Social Computing and Social Media. Design, Ethics, User Behavior, and Social Network Analysis. Springer, Cham (in press)

20. Kohn, M.: Cross National Research in Sociology. SAGE Publications. (1989)

21. Charness, G., Gneezy, U., Kuhn, M.A.: Experimental methods: between-subject and within-subject design. J. Econ. Behav. Organ. **81**(1), 1–8 (2012). https://doi.org/10.1016/j.jebo.2011.08.009

22. Reeves, B., Geiger, S.: Designing experiments that assess psychological responses to media messages. In: Lang A. (ed.) Measuring Psychological Responses to Media Messages, 1st edn., pp. 165–180. Routledge, New York (1994). https://doi.org/10.4324/9780203812853

23. Tao, C.-C., Bucy, E.P.: Conceptualizing media stimuli in experimental research: psychological versus attribute-based definitions. Human Commun. Rese. **33**(4), 397–426 (2007). https://doi.org/10.1111/j.1468-2958.2007.00305.x

24. Thorson, E., Wicks, R., Leshner, G.: Experimental methodology in journalism and mass communication research. Journalism Mass Commun. Quart. **89**(1), 112–124 (2012). https://doi.org/10.1177/1077699011430066

25. Slater, M.D.: Use of message stimuli in mass communication experiments: a methodological assessment and discussion. Journalism Mass Commun. Q. **68**(3), 412–421 (1991). https://doi.org/10.1177/107769909106800312

26. Entman, R. M.: Projections of Power: Framing News, Public Opinion, and U.S. Foreign Policy. University of Chicago Press (2004)

27. Iyengar, S.: Speaking of values: the framing of American politics. The Forum **3**(3) (2005). https://doi.org/10.2202/1540-8884.1093

28. Druckman, J.N.: On the limits of framing effects: who can frame? J. Polit. **63**(4), 1041–1066 (2001). https://www.jstor.org/stable/2691806

29. Cacciatore, M.A., Scheufele, D.A., Iyengar, S.: The end of framing as we know it … and the future of media effects. Mass Commun. Soc. **19**(1), 7–23 (2016). https://doi.org/10.1080/15205436.2015.1068811

30. D'Angelo, P.: Framing: media frames. In: Roessler, P., Hoffner, C. A., Van Zoonen, L. (eds.) The International Encyclopedia of Media Effects, pp. 1–10. Wiley, New York (2017). https://doi.org/10.1002/9781118783764.wbieme0048

31. Pennycook, G., Rand, D.G.: Lazy, not biased: susceptibility to partisan fake news is better explained by lack of reasoning than by motivated reasoning. Cognition **188**, 39–50 (2019). https://doi.org/10.1016/j.cognition.2018.06.011

32. Hameleers, M., Powell, T.E., Van Der Meer, T.G.L.A., Bos, L.: A picture paints a thousand lies? the effects and mechanisms of multimodal disinformation and rebuttals disseminated via social media. Polit. Commun. **37**(2), 281–301 (2020). https://doi.org/10.1080/10584609.2019.1674979

33. Pennycook, G., Cannon, T.D., Rand, D.G.: Prior exposure increases perceived accuracy of fake news. J. Exp. Psychol. Gen. **147**(12), 1865–1880 (2018). https://doi.org/10.1037/xge0000465

34. Koltsova, O., Pashakhin, S.: Agenda divergence in a developing conflict: quantitative evidence from Ukrainian and Russian TV newsfeeds. Media, War & Conflict **13**(3), 1–21 (2019). https://doi.org/10.1177/1750635219829876

35. Fierman, W.: Language and education in Post-Soviet Kazakhstan: Kazakh-medium instruction in urban schools. Russian Rev. **65**(1), 98–116 (2006). https://www.jstor.org/stable/3664037

36. Bilaniuk, L., Melnyk, S.: A Tense and shifting balance: bilingualism and education in Ukraine. Int. J. Biling. Educ. Biling. **11**(3–4), 340–372 (2008). https://doi.org/10.1080/13670050802148731

37. Kulyk, V.: Language identity, linguistic diversity and political cleavages: evidence from Ukraine. Nations Nationalism **17**(3), 627–648 (2011). https://doi.org/10.1111/j.1469-8129.2011.00493.x

38. Pennycook, G., Rand, D.G.: Who falls for fake news? the roles of bullshit receptivity, over-claiming, familiarity, and analytic thinking. J. Pers. **88**, 185–200 (2020). https://doi.org/10.1111/jopy.12476

39. Gabielkov, M., Ramachandran, A., Chaintreau, A., Legout, A.: Social clicks: what and who gets read on Twitter? In: Proceedings of ACM SIGMETRICS/IFIP Performance 2016. (2016). https://hal.inria.fr/hal-01281190

40. Andrew, B.C.: Media-generated shortcuts: do newspaper headlines present another roadblock for low-information rationality? Int. J. Press/Politics **12**(2), 24–43 (2007). https://doi.org/10.1177/1081180X07299795

41. Ecker, U.K.H., Lewandowsky, S., Chang, E.P., Pillai, R.: The effects of subtle misinformation in news headlines. J. Exp. Psychol. Appl. **20**(4), 323–335 (2014). https://doi.org/10.1037/xap0000028

42. Molyneux, L., Coddington, M.: Aggregation, clickbait and their effect on perceptions of journalistic credibility and quality. J. Pract. **14**(4), 429–446 (2020). https://doi.org/10.1080/17512786.2019.1628658

43. Kosinski, M., Matz, S.C., Gosling, S.D., Popov, V., Stillwell, D.: Facebook as a research tool for the social sciences: opportunities, challenges, ethical considerations, and practical guidelines. Am. Psychol. **70**(6), 543–556 (2015). https://doi.org/10.1037/a0039210

44. Nelson, E.J., Loux, T., Arnold, L.D., Siddiqui, S.T., Schootman, M.: Obtaining contextually relevant geographic data using Facebook recruitment in public health studies. Health Place **55**, 37–42 (2019). https://doi.org/10.1016/j.healthplace.2018.11.002

45. Pew Research Internet Project-2019. Social Networking Fact Sheet. http://www.pewinternet.org/fact-sheets/social-networking-fact-sheet/. Assessed 15 Jan 2021

46. Gosling, S.D., Vazire, S., Srivastava, S., John, O.P.: Should we trust web-based studies? a comparative analysis of six preconceptions about internet questionnaires. Am. Psychol. **59**(2), 93–104 (2004). https://doi.org/10.1037/0003-066X.59.2.93

47. Iannelli, L., Giglietto, F., Rossi, L., Zurovac, E.: Facebook digital traces for survey research: assessing the efficiency and effectiveness of a Facebook ad–based procedure for recruiting online survey respondents in niche and difficult-to-reach populations. Soc. Sci. Comput. Rev. **38**(4), 462–476 (2020). https://doi.org/10.1177/0894439318816638

48. Thornton, L., Batterham, P.J., Fassnacht, D.B., Kay-Lambkin, F., Calear, A.L., Hunt, S.: Recruiting for health, medical or psychosocial research using Facebook: systematic review. Internet Interv. **4**, 72–81 (2016). https://doi.org/10.1016/j.invent.2016.02.001

49. Ramo, D.E., Prochaska, J.J.: Broad reach and targeted recruitment using Facebook for an online survey of young adult substance use. J. Med. Internet Res. **14**(1), e28 (2012). https://doi.org/10.2196/jmir.1878

50. Gilligan, C., Kypri, K., Bourke, J.: Social networking versus facebook advertising to recruit survey respondents: a quasi-experimental study. JMIR Res. Protocols **3**(3), e48 (2014). https://doi.org/10.2196/resprot.3317

51. Whitaker, C., Stevelink, S., Fear, N.: The use of Facebook in recruiting participants for health research purposes: a systematic review. J. Med. Internet Res. **19**(8), e290 (2017). https://doi.org/10.2196/jmir.7071

52. Youn, S.J., et al.: Using online social media, Facebook, in screening for major depressive disorder among college students. Int. J. Clin. Health Psychol. **13**(1), 74–80 (2013). https://doi.org/10.1016/S1697-2600(13)70010-3

53. King, D.B., O'Rourke, N., DeLongis, A.: Social media recruitment and online data collection: a beginner's guide and best practices for accessing low-prevalence and hard-to-reach populations. Can. Psychol. **55**(4), 240–249 (2014). https://doi.org/10.1037/a0038087

54. Arcia, A.: Facebook advertisements for inexpensive participant recruitment among women in early pregnancy. Health Educ. Behav. **41**(3), 237–241 (2014). https://doi.org/10.1177/1090198113504414

55. Kapp, J.M., Peters, C., Oliver, D.P.: Research recruitment using Facebook advertising: big potential, big challenges. J. Cancer Educ. **28**(1), 134–137 (2013). https://doi.org/10.1007/s13187-012-0443-z

56. Zhang, B., Mildenberger, M., Howe, P.D., Marlon, J., Rosenthal, S.A., Leiserowitz, A.: Quota sampling using Facebook advertisements. Polit. Sci. Res. Methods **8**(3), 558–564 (2020). https://doi.org/10.1017/psrm.2018.49

57. Richiardi, L., Pivetta, E., Merletti, F.: Recruiting study participants through Facebook. Epidemiology **23**(1), 175 (2012). https://doi.org/10.1097/EDE.0b013e31823b5ee4

58. Smith, T.M.: Post-stratification. J. Roy. Stat. Soc. Ser. D (The Statistician) **40**(3), 315–323 (1991)

59. Little, R.J.A.: Post-stratification: a modeler's perspective. J. Am. Stat. Assoc. **88**(423), 1001–1012 (1993)

60. Heeringa, S.G., West, B.T., Berglund, P.A.: Applied Survey Data Analysis, 2nd edn. CRC Press, Boca Raton (2017)

61. Tillé, Y., Wilhelm, M.: Probability sampling designs: principles for choice of design and balancing. Stat. Sci. **32**(2), 176–189 (2017). https://doi.org/10.1214/16-STS606

62. Livingstone, S.: On the challenges of cross-national comparative media research. Eur. J. Commun. **18**(4), 477–500 (2003). https://doi.org/10.1177/0267323103184003

63. Lewandowsky, S., Ecker, U.K.H., Seifert, C.M., Schwarz, N., Cook, J.: Misinformation and its correction: continued influence and successful debiasing. Psychol. Sci. Public Interest **13**(3), 106–131 (2012). https://doi.org/10.1177/1529100612451018

Public Responses and Concerns Regarding Vape Bans on Reddit: A Longitudinal Topic Modeling Approach

Yusi Aveva Xu[1][✉][iD], Hye Min Kim[1][iD], Yunwen Wang[1][iD], Jiaxi Wu[2][iD], Traci Hong[2][iD], and Margaret McLaughlin[1,2][iD]

[1] University of Southern California, Los Angeles, CA 90089, USA
yusixu@usc.edu
[2] Boston University, Boston, MA 02215, USA

Abstract. Public responses toward vaping (i.e. electronic cigarette use) and vape bans have been hotly debated on social media. This study investigated vape-ban-related posts ($n = 6{,}547$) published between August 15, 2019 and February 15, 2020 on Reddit, a news aggregation social networking site that tolerates discussions that may be self-censored on other platforms. We conducted time series analysis and structural topic modeling to track public responses to the vape ban over a six-month period. Results showed that Google searches for vaping-related information were significantly associated with vape-ban-related posting activity on Reddit; and that eight topics emerged from the data, which included (1) Donald Trump, (2) vaping products, (3) liberty and autonomy, (4) inaccurate media reporting, (5) loopholes in state vape bans, (6) tobacco industry influence and the stupidity of ban, (7) the contrast between vaping and other more dangerous issues (e.g. school shootings, suicides), and (8) encouraging vapers to "vape on" (continue to vape). Each topic was examined in terms of their modelled longitudinal prevalence. All eight topics shared a similar theme of advocating vaping, although Redditors provided nuanced responses across time as the vaping epidemic unfolded. Social media discourse is promising to provide real-time indications of public response for diseases and epidemic surveillance, and to shed light on broader societal issues beyond the specific public health context.

Keywords: Vaping · Topic modeling · Vape ban · Reddit · Agenda setting

1 Introduction

As vaping (or e-cigarette use) becomes increasingly popular in recent years [9], the controversy associated with its use has also escalated. E-cigarette and vaping associated lung injuries (EVALI) were classified as an epidemic in the U.S. [30]. Parents and teachers were concerned about minors' use of flavored vaping products; while avid vapers considered it a healthier substitute to cigarettes [4].

© Springer Nature Switzerland AG 2021
G. Meiselwitz (Ed.): HCII 2021, LNCS 12774, pp. 391–403, 2021.
https://doi.org/10.1007/978-3-030-77626-8_26

With an increasing number of vaping-related injuries and deaths identified, public health institutions and authorities started to recommend guidelines and/or issue bans. A plethora of discussions around vaping were observed on social media and critically examined. They complemented our understanding of the social context of health behaviors in their unobtrusive environments [1,2]. This study investigates the public responses toward the vape ban over six months in 2019 and 2020, covering the time period from the first vaping-related death to the passage of a federal ban on certain flavored vaping products. Leveraging time series analysis and a longitudinal topic modeling approach, we track the estimated prevalence of post topics over time, especially in response to significant media reports of key policies, scientific findings, and vaping-related injuries.

2   Literature Review

2.1   Tracking Public Response with Social Media

Regulations on vaping or e-cigarettes have been rapidly evolving from both the state and federal levels to protect public health [5]. Examining public opinion in response to such policy changes is important for authorities and practitioners to assess the effectiveness and design of policies through a greater understanding of public needs and compliance [16]. Traditionally, public attitudes toward policy have been assessed in retrospective surveys or polling. More recently, however, an increasing number of studies (e.g. [37,41]) make use of social media discourse to monitor and analyze public attitudes and responses that may better reflect public opinion without the time-lags or recall limitations that are endemic to survey questionnaires. For instance, prior research analyzed social media discourse on contentious issues such as gun violence [29] and abortion [31,41] to investigate diverse points of views. Additionally, several studies have examined social media discourse to gauge the public responses to vaping-related policies including when the flavor ban proposal was first introduced [37] and when FDA announced the classification of e-cigarettes as tobacco products [17]. These studies demonstrated that topics discussed on social media while controlling for time and location indeed followed government policies and bans, supporting the use of social media discourse as an unobtrusive and effective way of understanding public response to policies.

2.2   Agenda Setting Theory

The core proposition of agenda setting theory is that news media is able to influence the public's perceived salience of different social agenda [22]. The seminal study of agenda setting theory demonstrated a strong correlation between the key issues on local and national news reports and that of the undecided voters' agenda [23]. Hundreds of studies have empirically tested and enriched propositions around agenda setting theory by comparing the salience of issues in the news coverage with the salience of those issues among the public to determine the correlations between the media and public agendas (e.g. [24,39]).

Recently, a symbiotic relationship has emerged between real-life news events and social media platforms. On one hand, social media have become a dominant source of breaking news and current events for users. About 71% of U.S. adults reported using social media as part of their news digest, among which Twitter, Facebook and Reddit have become the top three most popular social media sites from which people receive news [33]. In addition to being a news source, social media platforms enable individuals to exchange views about social and political issues. Much of the discussion on social media is inspired by the news, with 85% of trending topics on Twitter being news in nature [15].

With the enormous development in the Internet and communication technology, agenda setting researchers also examined the agenda-setting process and the power of news media on online communication. This interplay among news media and social media constitutes the intermedia agenda-setting theory. Inter-media agenda-setting research is concerned with the extent to which news content transfers across various media [13]. For example, a study found that newspapers influenced the online bulletin board conversation during the general election in South Korea [18]. Similarly, another study showed that the online media's coverage of three issues, immigration, health care, and taxes, stimulated the discussions of these issues on electronic bulletin boards with a time-lag influence varying between one to seven days [27]. A more recent study also found that the agenda of traditional news media was in tandem with that of Twitter feeds during the presidential election, suggesting that traditional news media indeed set and influence the public agendas on Twitter [8].

The relationship between news reports and social media discussions has been examined in various contexts, including political debates [6], police brutality [12], and heated social issues ranging from the ice bucket challenge to amyotrophic lateral sclerosis (ALS) [14]. However, the relationship of the vape ban and related vaping news to social media agenda is relatively unexplored. When new regulations or recommendations of vape products were issued, we expected news media would report more of these issues than usual. The first objective of the current study is to examine the agenda setting effects of the vape ban, EVALI, and vaping related news events on the social media agenda of the vape ban, reflected through discussions on Reddit. We ask the following research question:

RQ1. Are there associations between vaping- and vape-ban-related news media agendas and vape-ban-related social media agendas?

2.3   Reddit as a Platform for Vaping-Related Discussions

Reddit is regarded as a space where extreme words and controversial topics are relatively more tolerated than on other social media platforms [21]. It serves as an appropriate platform for studying otherwise self-censored discourse about vaping. Although a recent study [2] has examined the discourse of specific subreddit communities, there is a gap in the current literature regarding the communicative dynamics across the platform, especially in response to the rapidly evolving information about vaping risks and regulations over time.

Previous studies have examined Reddit for vaping-related discussions with various emphases, including popular e-cigarette flavors [38], motivation and limitations of vaping [32], reasons for using particular brands (e.g. JUUL, [3]), and most recently the associations between vaping flavors and health symptoms [20]. As these studies concluded, vapers shared both negative and positive sentiment toward vaping. On the negative side, they considered e-cigarettes as an unsatisfactory substitute for cigarettes and psychiatric medicines; they worried about drug interactions, nicotine addiction, risks of e-liquid, and the practical difficulties and cost of vaping [32]. Meanwhile, Redditors frequently discussed the potential associations between respiratory/throat, digestive, psychological, and cardiovascular symptoms - respectively - with the use of e-cigarettes of different flavors [20]. In contrast, the sizable "vaper" community on Reddit reported using vaping as a means to quit smoking combustible cigarettes, as self-medication for mental illnesses, in order to express freedom and control, get socially connected, or feel the "buzz," or as a hobby [3,32]. Notably, vaping is a socially motivated phenomenon: peers [3], caregivers, and online communities [32] can play a role in leading people to vape. Regardless of being intrinsically or extrinsically motivated, vaping is tied to one's identity and values.

Analyzing open discussions on Reddit, hence, can provide a naturalistic window to the lay experience of vapers in networked communities. Findings on themes of discussions can meaningfully inform regulatory decision-makers. No studies, to our best knowledge, have specifically examined public discussions about regulations and bans on vaping. A second objective of this study is thus to understand and explicate the public priorities and concerns on Reddit in the light of the evolving reports around the vape ban from a temporal perspective. Therefore, we ask:

RQ2. What topics emerged from the public responses to vaping- and vape-ban-related news during the peak of the vaping epidemic?

3   Methods

3.1   Data

Reddit Data. We used the Python Reddit API Wrapper (PRAW) and a search word of "vape ban" to scrape posts from Reddit. Among all data from February 2019 to February 2020, we selected posts ($n = 6{,}547$) that appeared between August 15, 2019 and February 15, 2020 as our final sample period for analysis. This covered the timeline of key events: from the first reported death related to vaping on August 23, 2019, to the national ban on certain flavored e-cigarette products that went into effect on February 6, 2020. The data collection ended in mid-February also due to the rise of misinformation about vaping as a preventive measure for COVID-19 around March and April 2020; at this time, "vape ban" discussion was no longer as salient as before. We believe the data from our final sample period more accurately captured the communication dynamics around vape ban. Figure 1 depicts the original time series data of Reddit posts about

"vape ban" in the dataset before detrending. The series displays a linear trend
of declining activity with periodic short-lived spikes.

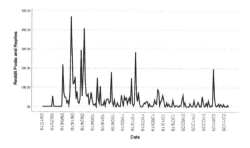

Fig. 1. Undifferenced time series of Reddit posts on "vape ban," 8/15/2019 – 2/15/2020

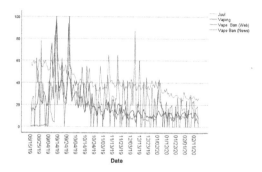

Fig. 2. Sequence charts for the time series of "Juul," "vaping," "vape ban" (Google
web searches), and "vape ban" (Google news searches)

Google Search Data. Key events regarding EVALI and the subsequent federal
and state efforts to ban the sale of vaping products were identified. Google Trends
data was used to derive a distribution of relevant keyword searches during the
same six-month period as the Reddit data set. Time series of daily search terms
were constructed where each data point represented the term's relative popularity on that day compared to all searches for the term during the designated time
frame. We constructed time series for "vape ban" on Google Web searches and
News searches, and for "vaping" and "JUUL" on Google Web searches. Figure 2
presents the sequence charts for these four time series, using the original data
prior to detrending. All time series demonstrated a linear trend of declining
activity with occasional spikes in response to relevant external events.

3.2 Data Analysis

Cross-Correlation Analysis. Cross-correlations analysis was conducted among the time series of the Google Trends search and the Reddit posts and replies. All five series were differenced to remove a linear trend before further analysis.

Time Series Analysis. To determine if key events dictate active posting on Reddit across all subreddits, we conducted ARIMA modeling in SPSS Version 26. Key events were identified from Google Trends search.

Structural Topic Modeling (STM). We used unsupervised STM to determine the prevalence of topics overtime in R [26].

4 Results

4.1 Cross-Correlation Analysis

Results of cross-correlation analysis indicated that Google News searches were not significantly associated with Reddit activity at any lag; Google Web searches for keywords "JUUL," "vape ban," and "vaping" were significantly associated with Reddit posts and replies at lag 0 and in one case lags 1 and −1. Google News searches were dropped from predictors in further considerations. Table 1 reports the lags at which the five time series were significantly correlated pairwise.

Table 1. Presence of significant cross-correlations of time series by lag

	JUUL searches	Vaping searches	Vape ban searches (Web)	Vape ban searches (News)	Reddit posts and replies
JUUL searches	−	Lag 0	Lag 0	n/a	Lag 0
Vaping searches	−	−	Lags 0, 1, 3, 4, 6, 7, −4, −7	n/a	Lag 0
Vape ban searches (Web)	−	−	−	n/a	Lags 0, 1, −1
Vape ban searches (News)	−	−	−	−	n/a
Reddit posts and replies	−	−	−	−	−

4.2 Time Series Analysis: ARIMA Modeling

We first ran the Expert Modeler function in SPSS Version 26 to find the best-fitting univariate model of Reddit activity without predictors. The best-fitting model, an ARIMA (0,0,1), with a significant moving average component at lag 1, was significantly different from the observed data (Stationary R-squared = .591, the normalized Bayesian Information Criterion was 7.839, and the

Ljung-Box statistic was 30.749, df $= 17$, $p < .021$). The Ljung-Box statistic if significant indicates that there is still structure in the observed data set, beyond the autocorrelation effects, which is not captured by the model (in the case of the univariate model, the first lag of the Reddit activity variable). In effect it is an index of badness-of-fit. Our next step was to try to improve the fit of the model by incorporating the predictors of search activity on Google.

Using the Expert Modeler, we derived a series of models with Reddit activity related to "vape ban" as the dependent variable and Google searches for "JUUL," "vaping," and "vape ban" as predictors. Variables were first differenced to remove the linear trends; results of differencing twice to remove a quadratic trend did not yield a measurable improvement in terms of stabilizing the variance of the Google series over time, nor did applying a natural log transformation. The best-fitting model incorporating predictors was an ARIMA $(0,0,2)$ model, which did not depart significantly from the data. Stationary R-squared for the model was .617, a slight improvement over the univariate ARIMA model. Normalized Bayesian Information Criterion was 7.841. The Ljung-Box statistic was 16.779 (df $= 16$, $p = .40$), indicating that values predicted by the model did not depart significantly from the observed values. The significant ($p < .001$) parameters included in the ARIMA model were the moving average of (differenced) Reddit posts at lags 1 and 2 and (differenced) Google searches for "JUUL" at Lag 0. Figure 3 displays the fit of the daily volume of Reddit activity predicted by the model, with the dotted lines representing the upper and lower confidence levels around the predicted values.

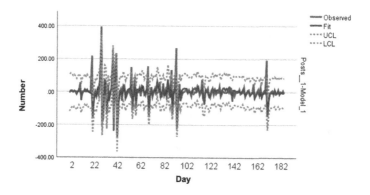

Fig. 3. Observed versus predicted (differenced) volume of Reddit activity predicted by the ARIMA $(0,0,2)$ model, with Google searches for "Juul" as an independent predictor

Through time series analysis, we found that Google search activity about the term "Juul" had a small association with the daily volume of Reddit vape-related posting, but that daily search interest in other vape-relevant terms did not improve prediction of Reddit post volume about vaping bans compared to a simple moving average model.

4.3   Structural Topic Modeling

In an unsupervised approach, STM offered topic solution statistics for different numbers of topics (K). We first ran models in increments of five with potential Ks ranging from 2 to 72, and results indicated more redundancy in models with a larger K. We then narrowed down the selection to models with K ranging from 2 to 10. As multiple scholars contended [7,19], statistical measures should be supplemented with human interpretation to yield the most meaningful model decisions. Based on both the STM diagnostic values (i.e., held-out likelihood, semantic coherence, residuals, and lower bound) per the number of topics [26] and human interpretations, we selected the eight-topic solution (see Fig. 4).

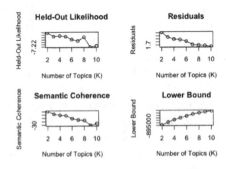

Fig. 4. STM topic solution statistics by number of topics

To best capture the semantics of the most representative posts recommended by the model, and the most representative words provided in the additional matrices: Highest Prob, FREX, Lift, and score (Roberts et al., 2014), we labeled the eight emerging topics as: (1) Donald Trump, (2) vaping products, (3) liberty and autonomy, (4) inaccurate media reporting, (5) loopholes in state vape bans, (6) tobacco industry influence and the stupidity of ban, (7) the contrast between vaping and other more dangerous issues (e.g. school shootings, suicides), and (8) encouraging vapers to "vape on" (continue to vape).

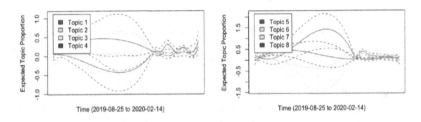

Fig. 5. Expected longitudinal topic prevalence (dashed lines indicate the 95% CI.)

Figure 5 depicts the expected prevalence of the eight topics over the observed period. All topics are plotted as a smooth function of day, holding rating at the sample median, with 95% confidence intervals indicated by dashed lines (Roberts et al., 2014). The first several weeks of the data set saw the highest topic prevalence of Topic 8 (with s(time)1 t-value $= 2.624$, $p < .01$), in which Redditors engaged in discussion of continuing vaping, or "vape on". Soon after that, Topic 5 peaked (s(time)2 t-value $= 2.939$, $p < .01$), when various state-introduced regulatory measures and narratives about "loopholes in state bans" were salient. The prevalence of Topic 4, accusations around "inaccurate media reporting", was depicted as a smooth curve with no particular peaks, yielding non-significant results. Highlighting "the tobacco industry's influence and the stupidity of vape bans", Topic 6 (s(time)8 t-value $= -2.005$, $p = .05$) was borderline significant approaching the end of our observed time period, when media reports focused on the rapid changes in policy in relation to vaping-industry response, and the evolving state and federal policy responses. Almost simultaneously, discussion centered around Donald Trump was salient during the later stage of the observed period (s(time)8 t-value $= 2.644$, $p < .001$; s(time)9 t-value $= -2.147$, $p = .03$), after he controversially retreated from the federal ban of flavored vaping products and sparked criticism from both vaping advocates and adversaries [10].

5 Discussion

As shown in this study, the eight topics emerging from the vape ban discussion on Reddit have a similar theme of advocating for vaping, although Redditors provided nuanced responses at different points during the sample period as related news reports unfolded. For example, during the early months of the observed period, when EVALI incidences were initially reported and the controversy gradually emerged, the first salient discussion topic was to encourage fellow vapers to "vape on," echoing previous scholars' findings that online communities [32] can play a role in leading people to vape. However, the tone of encouraging vapers to "vape on" became attenuated as time went by with more cases revealed and policies introduced.

Around mid-September 2019, key events about the vape ban were clustered and Google searches for "Juul" and other vaping-related terms peaked. Multiple reports about regulatory activities or adverse news toward the vaping industry were published, such as the FDA announcement of conducting a criminal probe into the 530 vaping-related illnesses and eight deaths [11], as well as Juul CEO's stepping down and the company's suspension of all advertising in the US [28]. Prevalent discussion topics moved from the previous "vape on" to more detailed and targeted discussions such as identifying loopholes in various state bans.

Meanwhile, many of the discussions on social media were inspired by news about vape products [15]. The more generic discussions questioning the accuracy of new reports persisted, suggesting to some extent that news media still set the agenda for public discussion [8,13], be that virtual or not. Such mistrust toward the media touched upon a broader societal issue [35] facing the US right now.

Later in the time period of the study, salient topics including Donald Trump and the influences of the tobacco industries underscored the media agenda regarding the inconsistent public health policies at the end of 2019 and the beginning of 2020. It was also noteworthy that as the biggest player in the vaping or e-cigarette market, "Juul" had its Google search frequency as the best predictor for Reddit activities, in comparison to Google search frequencies of "vaping" and "vape ban." Therefore we inferred that the tremendous success of "Juul" the brand led it to become synonymous with vaping such that it is often used as a generic reference for vaping. Another possible explanation could be that the vape ban intended to combat the epidemic of youth e-cigarette use, while Juul, the slim, high-tech vaping device that comes with a variety of flavors was particularly popular among youth and young adults [40] and thus received more attention from the general public.

The longitudinal topic modeling revealed that Redditors generally view vape bans, especially state vape bans, as unjustifiable policies. Although policy still seems to shape the media agenda, the public responses are only impacted partially by vaping-related news. Many posts cluster around themes to rationalize support for vaping, arguing for liberty and autonomy, claiming media reports of vape-related injuries and deaths as inaccurate, or identifying loopholes in vape bans. Our findings seem to suggest that public responses to vape ban and related news represented on Reddit are not only predominantly against vape bans but also use the vape ban related news reports to reinforce their existing attitudes, which is in favor of vape use and products, by derogating the news reports and regulations. This is also in line with the long-standing concerns that social media may serve more as an echo chamber [36] where only like-minded people interact to reaffirm their existing opinions than a public sphere with diverse and cross-cutting viewpoints, exacerbating polarization.

Lastly, our findings corroborated earlier studies that social media conversation in response to policy offers critical insights to gauging the changes in public attitudes and opinion. In particular, the focus of Redditors' rationalization of support for vaping was largely on identifying policy loopholes and questioning the integrity of media and authorities, highlighting an eroding media trust. Consequently, Redditors' disregard of other information on important public health perspectives offer practical insights for policy practitioners and future research.

We should acknowledge that this study has several limitations. Reddit users are not representative of all segments of the population [34] engaged in or impacted by vaping, as vaping content on Reddit was found to be primarily about the flavors and the purchases and the uses of vaping products [2]. The analysis of agenda setting effects of policies and external events on social media agenda were not through direct content analysis of related news reports. Instead, we operationalized the Google search data of Jull, vape ban and vaping as proxy indicators of the media agenda. Nevertheless, the correlation between news reports and search engine data has been established in previous research; specifically, news reports influenced search engine attention, while news reports are also driven by search engine attention [25].

6   Conclusions

Confirming the observation of previous researchers [34], this study demonstrated that longitudinal topic modeling of Reddit textual data is effective in identifying the temporal patterns of public response to evolving news events and in guiding targeted interventions. However, some themes stayed consistent over the observation period, which suggests that characteristics of Redditors may be different than audiences of other social media platforms. As agenda setting theory posits, news reports can shape the salience of topics of social media discussion during a particular time frame – yet topics that profoundly interest social media users may persist, and continue generating related content. In this study, Redditors' responses toward vape bans became silos that were independent from the reported key events and public health information. Yet, as the vaping epidemic unfolded, nuanced responses also emerged. Salient topics on Reddit gradually moved from generic vaping advocacy to a more detailed discussion about the loopholes in vape bans and their mistrust of media and health authorities. Hence, social media discourse may provide real-time indications of public response toward diseases and epidemic surveillance, particularly in ambiguous circumstances where such understanding provides insights into how to effectively and strategically engage the public. Public discourse on social media may also shed light on broader societal issues beyond the specific public health context.

References

1. Allem, J.P., Ferrara, E., Uppu, S.P., Cruz, T.B., Unger, J.B.: E-cigarette surveillance with social media data: social bots, emerging topics, and trends. JMIR Public Health Surveill. **3**(4), e98 (2017)
2. Barker, J.O., Rohde, J.A.: Topic clustering of e-cigarette submissions among reddit communities: a network perspective. Health Educ. Behav. **46**(2_suppl), 59S–68S (2019)
3. Brett, E.I., et al.: A content analysis of JUUL discussions on social media: using reddit to understand patterns and perceptions of JUUL use. Drug Alcohol Depend. **194**, 358–362 (2019)
4. Brown, J., Beard, E., Kotz, D., Michie, S., West, R.: Real-world effectiveness of e-cigarettes when used to aid smoking cessation: a cross-sectional population study. Addiction **109**(9), 1531–1540 (2014)
5. Center, P.H.L.: U.S. e-cigarette regulations - 50 state review (2020)
6. Ceron, A., Curini, L., Iacus, S.M.: First-and second-level agenda setting in the Twittersphere: an application to the Italian political debate. J. Inf. Technol. Polit. **13**(2), 159–174 (2016)
7. Chen, X., Zou, D., Cheng, G., Xie, H.: Detecting latent topics and trends in educational technologies over four decades using structural topic modeling: a retrospective of all volumes of computers & education. Comput. Educ. **151**, 103855 (2020)
8. Conway, B.A., Kenski, K., Wang, D.: The rise of Twitter in the political campaign: searching for intermedia agenda-setting effects in the presidential primary. J. Comput. Mediat. Commun. **20**(4), 363–380 (2015)

9. Cullen, K.A., Ambrose, B.K., Gentzke, A.S., Apelberg, B.J., Jamal, A., King, B.A.: Notes from the field: use of electronic cigarettes and any tobacco product among middle and high school students-united states, 2011–2018. Morb. Mortal. Wkly. Rep. **67**(45), 1276 (2018)

10. Ducharme, J.: Trump administration announces ban on some flavored vapes (2020). https://time.com/5758004/flavored-vape-ban/

11. FDA: Fda's forensic chemistry center playing critical role in vaping illness investigation (2020). https://www.fda.gov/consumers/consumer-updates/fdas-forensic-chemistry-center-playing-critical-role-vaping-illness-investigation

12. Freelon, D., McIlwain, C., Clark, M.: Quantifying the power and consequences of social media protest. New Media Soc. **20**(3), 990–1011 (2018)

13. Harder, R.A., Sevenans, J., Van Aelst, P.: Intermedia agenda setting in the social media age: how traditional players dominate the news agenda in election times. Int. J. Press/Polit. **22**(3), 275–293 (2017)

14. Jang, S.M., Park, Y.J., Lee, H.: Round-trip agenda setting: tacking the intermedia process over time in the ice bucket challenge. Journalism **18**(10), 1292–1308 (2017)

15. Kwak, H., Lee, C., Park, H., Moon, S.: What is Twitter, a social network or a news media? In: Proceedings of the 19th International Conference on World Wide Web, pp. 591–600 (2010)

16. Latimer, W.W., Harwood, E.M., Newcomb, M.D., Wagenaar, A.C.: Measuring public opinion on alcohol policy: a factor analytic study of a us probability sample. Addict. Behav. **28**(2), 301–313 (2003)

17. Lazard, A.J., Wilcox, G.B., Tuttle, H.M., Glowacki, E.M., Pikowski, J.: Public reactions to e-cigarette regulations on Twitter: a text mining analysis. Tob. Control **26**(e2), e112–e116 (2017)

18. Lee, B., Lancendorfer, K.M., Lee, K.J.: Agenda-setting and the internet: the intermedia influence of internet bulletin boards on newspaper coverage of the 2000 general election in South Korea. Asian J. Commun. **15**(1), 57–71 (2005)

19. Levy, K.E., Franklin, M.: Driving regulation: using topic models to examine political contention in the us trucking industry. Soc. Sci. Comput. Rev. **32**(2), 182–194 (2014)

20. Luo, J., Chen, L., Lu, X., Yuan, J., Xie, Z., Li, D.: Analysis of potential associations of JUUL flavours with health symptoms based on user-generated data from reddit. Tob. Control (2020)

21. Massanari, A.: # Gamergate and the fappening: how reddit's algorithm, governance, and culture support toxic technocultures. New Media Soc. **19**(3), 329–346 (2017)

22. McCombs, M.: Setting the Agenda: The Mass Media and Public Opinion. Polity Press, Cambridge (2004)

23. McCombs, M.E., Shaw, D.L.: The agenda-setting function of mass media. Public Opin. Q. **36**(2), 176–187 (1972)

24. McLaren, L., Boomgaarden, H., Vliegenthart, R.: News coverage and public concern about immigration in Britain. Int. J. Public Opin. Res. **30**(2), 173–193 (2018)

25. Ragas, M.W., Tran, H.L., Martin, J.A.: Media-induced or search-driven? a study of online agenda-setting effects during the BP oil disaster. J. Stud. **15**(1), 48–63 (2014)

26. Roberts, M.E., Stewart, B.M., Tingley, D.: stm: An R package for structural topic models. J. Stat. Softw. **91**(1), 1–40 (2019)

27. Roberts, M., Wanta, W., Dzwo, T.H.: Agenda setting and issue salience online. Commun. Res. **29**(4), 452–465 (2002)

28. Rushe, D., Betancourt, S.: Trump administration announces ban on some flavored vapes (2019). https://www.theguardian.com/business/2019/sep/25/juul-ceo-kevin-burns-steps-down-vaping-illnesses
29. Saha, K., De Choudhury, M.: Modeling stress with social media around incidents of gun violence on college campuses. Proc. ACM Hum. Comput. Interact. **1**(CSCW), 1–27 (2017)
30. Salzman, G.A., Alqawasma, M., Asad, H.: Vaping associated lung injury (EVALI): an explosive united states epidemic. Mo. Med. **116**(6), 492 (2019)
31. Sharma, E., Saha, K., Ernala, S.K., Ghoshal, S., De Choudhury, M.: Analyzing ideological discourse on social media: a case study of the abortion debate. In: Proceedings of the 2017 International Conference of the Computational Social Science Society of the Americas, pp. 1–8 (2017)
32. Sharma, R., Wigginton, B., Meurk, C., Ford, P., Gartner, C.E.: Motivations and limitations associated with vaping among people with mental illness: a qualitative analysis of reddit discussions. Int. J. Environ. Res. Public Health **14**(1), 7 (2017)
33. Shearer, E., Mitchell, A.: News use across social media platforms in 2020. Pew Research Center (2021)
34. Stokes, D.C., Andy, A., Guntuku, S.C., Ungar, L.H., Merchant, R.M.: Public priorities and concerns regarding covid-19 in an online discussion forum: longitudinal topic modeling. J. Gener. Intern. Med. **35**(7), 2244–2247 (2020)
35. Strömbäck, J., et al.: News media trust and its impact on media use: toward a framework for future research. Ann. Int. Commun. Assoc. **44**(2), 139–156 (2020)
36. Sunstein, C.R.: Echo Chambers: Bush v. Gore, Impeachment, and Beyond. Princeton University Press, Princeton (2001)
37. Tian, Y., Chunara, R.: Quasi-experimental designs for assessing response on social media to policy changes. In: Proceedings of the International AAAI Conference on Web and Social Media, vol. 14, pp. 671–682 (2020)
38. Wang, L., Zhan, Y., Li, Q., Zeng, D.D., Leischow, S.J., Okamoto, J.: An examination of electronic cigarette content on social media: analysis of e-cigarette flavor content on reddit. Int. J. Environ. Res. Public Health **12**(11), 14916–14935 (2015)
39. Weaver, D.H.: Media Agenda-Setting in a Presidential Election: Issues, Images, and Interest. Greenwood, Westport (1981)
40. Willett, J.G., et al.: Recognition, use and perceptions of JUUL among youth and young adults. Tob. Control **28**(1), 115–116 (2019)
41. Zhang, A.X., Counts, S.: Gender and ideology in the spread of anti-abortion policy. In: Proceedings of the 2016 CHI Conference on Human Factors in Computing Systems, pp. 3378–3389 (2016)

Experience Design in Social Computing

ECUXH: A Set of User eXperience Heuristics for e-Commerce

Camila Bascur$^{(\boxtimes)}$, Cristian Rusu, and Daniela Quiñones

Pontificia Universidad Católica de Valparaíso, Av. Brasil, 2241, 2340000 Valparaíso, Chile
{cristian.rusu,daniela.quinones}@pucv.cl

Abstract. Currently, e-Commerce users have different objectives and contexts of use, so it is essential to consider each of these cases when designing appropriate websites, so that the User eXperience (UX) would be as pleasant as possible. UX extends the usability concept. UX refers to user's perceptions and responses that result from the use and/or anticipated use of a system, product, or service. Heuristic evaluation is an inspection method that allows evaluating the usability of interfaces. A set of heuristics can be general, like Nielsen's heuristics, or specific to the area of application of the interactive software system under evaluation. Due to the specific characteristics of e-Commerce websites, general usability heuristics are not suitable, especially when evaluating UX aspects beyond usability. Specific sets of heuristics have been proposed to evaluate e-Commerce websites, but they mainly focus on usability. This article presents a set of heuristics that address not only usability, but also other UX factors. The new set of heuristics was developed, validated, and refined in three iterations, based on the methodology established by Quiñones et al. (2018). This methodology establishes 8 steps that allow obtaining a set of heuristics for a specific domain. The results obtained in the experimental validation indicate that the ECUXH set is a useful and more efficient tool than generic heuristics, when evaluating e-Commerce websites. As future work, we pretend to develop a set of retail-oriented Customer eXperince (CX) heuristics, based on ECUXH.

Keywords: User experience · e-Commerce · Usability · Heuristic evaluation · User experience heuristics

1 Introduction

At present, there has been an increase and massification in the use of the internet, this has led to the transformation that a many companies had to adapt to change, promoting the development of increasingly sophisticated applications to encourage the use of their websites [1]. Due to this, the concepts of user experience and usability have been used more and more in the development of websites [2], in which users have become the main focus for companies.

Due to the above, several researchers have proposed sets of usability heuristics to assess how user-friendly websites are. One of the best known are those of Jakob Nielsen, who proposes 10 heuristics that are used to identify usability problems of interactive

© Springer Nature Switzerland AG 2021
G. Meiselwitz (Ed.): HCII 2021, LNCS 12774, pp. 407–420, 2021.
https://doi.org/10.1007/978-3-030-77626-8_27

software products [3]. Although many of the heuristic evaluations are performed using Jakob Nielsen heuristics, and although it covers many of the principles for evaluating traditional websites, it ignores many other factors that are present on specific platforms and applications.

This article presents a set of heuristics that address not only usability issues, but also other UX factors, the e-Commerce website UX heuristics: ECUXH. The new set of heuristics was developed, validated, and refined in three iterations, based on the methodology established by Quiñones et al. (2018) [4]. This methodology establishes 8 steps that allow obtaining a set of heuristics for a specific domain. We developed ECUXH based on the Morville's UX model, which considers 7 aspects: useful, usable, desirable, findable, accessible, credible and valuable [5]. ECUXH set is also based on a set of usability heuristics for transactional websites [6], and on a set of cultural-oriented usability heuristics for e-Commerce [7].

The results obtained in the experimental validation indicate that the ECUXH set is a useful and more efficient tool than generic heuristics, when evaluating e-Commerce websites. As future work, we pretend to develop a set of retail-oriented Customer eXperince (CX) heuristics, based on ECUXH. The paper is structured as follows: Sect. 2 presents the theoretical background; Sect. 3 describes the process of developing EXUXH; finally, Sect. 4 highlights conclusions and future work.

2 Theoretical Background

2.1 Usability

According to the ISO9241–11:2018 [8], usability refers to "the degree to which a system, product or service can be used by specified users to achieve specified goals with effectiveness, efficiency and satisfaction in a specified context of use". This definition emphasizes the concept of quality of use, that is, how the user performs specific tasks in different scenarios, specifically in this paper the scenario, is through websites where products and/or services are marketed [9].

Nielsen proposes five basic attributes to understand usability [10]:

- Learnability: It describes the ease of learning the basic functionality of the system, so as to be able to correctly perform the task that the user wishes to perform. It is usually measured by the time spent in the system to be able to perform certain tasks in less than a given time (time usually used by expert users).
- Efficiency: Measured by the number of transactions per unit of time that the user can make using the system. What is sought is the maximum speed of accomplishment of user tasks. The greater the usability of a system, the faster the user is when using it, and the work is done more quickly.
- Memorability: The learning curve must be significantly less in a user who has already used the system. In this way, when the user has the need to reuse the system, it is easy to remember and does not have to spend as much time as a user who has not used the system.

- Errors: The system should generate as few errors as possible. If they occur, it is important that they make the user know quickly and clearly, while offering some mechanism to recover from that error.
- Satisfaction: This attribute refers to the subjective impression of the user regarding the system.

2.2 User Experience (UX)

The User eXperience (UX) is defined by the ISO 9241–210:2019 standard as: "The perceptions and responses of people, as a result of the use (or anticipated use) of a product, system or service" [11]. In order to better understand UX, it is necessary to identify the set of factors that define it.

In 2004, Peter Morville created a model that groups together the main factors that should be considered to create a good UX, called "The honeycomb of the user experience" [12], to explain the importance of UX and the need to go beyond usability. The author describes 7 main factors that will be described below:

- Useful: The site must be able to cover a need, in addition to having a real purpose for its construction. The content is expected to be useful and this comes with innovative solutions.
- Usable: The site must be simple and easy to use, so that its design is familiar and easy to understand, meaning that a site can be used effectively and efficiently to achieve a goal established by the product and the user.
- Desirable: Image, identity, brand and other design elements are used to evoke emotion and gratitude.
- Valuable: The site should add value for interested users.
- Findable: The information should be easy to find and easy to navigate. In case of any problem the user should be able to find a solution quickly. The navigation structure must be configured in a way that makes sense.
- Accessible: The product should be designed so that even people with disabilities can have the same user experience as others.
- Credible: The products must be reliable, so that they fulfill the function for which they were designed.

It should be noted that the UX is a much broader concept than usability, the latter concept refers to the ease of using a specific product or service, while the UX corresponds to the process of user interaction with respect to a product or service, so it represents an even more complex process.

2.3 Heuristics Evaluation

There are several methods to assess the usability of a system or software. According to the classification proposed by Andreas Holzinger, they are divided into two large groups that are described below, which are inspections and tests [13]:

- Usability inspections: they are characterized by carrying out evaluations with specialists using a set of usability guidelines without the participation of users. Among this method can be found heuristic evaluation, cognitive path and predictive models (Analysis of actions).
- The usability tests: they are characterized by a qualitative approach that involves real users, observers and experts, who evaluate a system or site in operation. There are various methods for conducting usability testing, including pencil and paper testing, thinking aloud, constructive interaction (Co-Discovery), consultation techniques, and formal experiments.

Heuristic evaluation is an expert inspection method that consists of a technical analysis, which seeks to identify usability errors on a website, guided by a set of usability criteria, known as usability heuristics [14]. It is one of the most used, efficient and accessible methods to ensure the usability of an interface. It considers that the ideal number of experts to evaluate critical systems range from three to five people, who evaluate the interface by writing down their observations regarding if they meet the usability principles.

The heuristic evaluation has four stages mainly. The first is that each evaluator independently identifies potential problems that users may have when interacting with the system. Then, a group work is carried out, which is coordinated by a supervising evaluator, where each evaluator exposes their problems, thus generating a single list of these. Then, an individual work is started again for each evaluator, where each one of these independently qualifies the severity and frequency of the problems found by each of the evaluators. Finally, we return to the group work coordinated by a supervising evaluator, in which the averages of severity, frequency and criticality are calculated for each problem found and a ranking of these is established, in this way the reader is oriented to what problems they are more serious and therefore require more attention to be solved. The results obtained are then analyzed and solutions are suggested.

2.4 Websites e-Commerce

Electronic commerce, or better known as e-Commerce websites, is defined as: "All transactions that occur digitally between organizations and individuals, through the internet and the web, which culminate in the individual's payment of the product/purchased service" [15]. Transactional websites specialize in commercial transactions, and not only in information.

There are multiple classification criteria for electronic commerce, and three of the many that exist but represent an important part of electronic commerce will be shown below [15]:

- B2C (Business to Consumer): Type of commerce where companies offer their products or services to consumers.
- B2B (Business to Business): Type of commerce where the commercial transaction is carried out between companies.
- C2C (Consumer to Consumer): Type of business where consumers interact with each other, carrying out transactions or information exchanges.

Among the many characteristics that an e-Commerce website can have, we will use the following to define the set of heuristics [16]:

- Product/service search system: Refers to the ease with which a user can search and find the product/services they wish to purchase.
- Shopping cart: It is the space where the user can add products, buy them, delete them or transfer them to other lists.
- Registration: It is a feature (may be optional) that allows the user to make their purchase more expeditiously.
- Customer service: It refers to the help that is given to the user in case there is any doubt in the navigation or use of the website.
- Description of the product/service: It refers to keeping the user informed at all times about the product/service that he wishes to purchase, includes items that help in the purchase process, such as: product name, images, price, description, option to "add to shopping cart", discounts and promotions, rating and reviews, among others.
- Recommendation system: It is the system that the sites use to suggest products/services that are similar or that are part of the complement of what the user has chosen or is choosing.
- Post-Sales Service: It is a customer support system after the purchase of the product/service, in which the detailed obtaining of the purchase made is included, through a tracking code or as a message via email, among others.
- Intelligent agents: It is a system to help the user while browsing the website, which aims to facilitate the UX within it.

3   Methodology

In this research we used the methodology to develop usability/UX heuristics for specific domains proposed by Quiñones et al. [4], its 8 stages are explained below:

1. Exploratory Stage: At this stage a review of the literature is carried out.
2. Experimental Stage: The data obtained in different experiments is analyzed to collect additional information that has not been identified in the previous stage.
3. Descriptive Stage: Select and prioritize the most important topics of all information that was collected in the previous stages.
4. Correlational Stage: At this stage, the characteristics of the specific application domain are matched with the usability/UX attributes and the existing heuristics (and/or other relevant elements).
5. Selection Stage: The existing usability/UX heuristic sets that were selected in Step 3 (and/or other relevant elements) are maintained, adapted and/or discarded.
6. Specification Stage: The new usability/ UX heuristic set is formally specified.
7. Validation Stage: The set of heuristics is validated through several experiments in terms of their effectiveness and efficiency in the evaluation of the specific application.
8. Refinement Stage: The new set of heuristics is refined and improved based on the comments obtained in Step 7.

3.1 How the Set of Heuristics was Developed

Our research included three iterations; none of these were performed the 8 stages of the methodology. Figure 1 shows how we worked in each iteration.

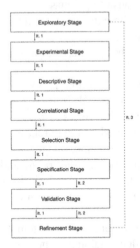

Fig. 1. Iterative process used in this research

In the first iteration, all the stages of the methodology were carried out; In the second iteration, only the last three stages of the methodology were completed, as the details of the specifications and subsequent stages had to be refined. Finally, in the stage three some initial definitions were corrected, and the stages of the methodology were revised.

Thanks to the first stage of the methodology, which included a review of the previous literature in order to find articles related to research that could be useful to create or adapt a set of heuristics focused on UX in e-Commerce. There were several investigations directly related to the domain of the problem. The main basis of this work was the set of heuristics proposed by Quiñones et al. (2016) [6], and Díaz et al. (2016) [7].

Although the sets of base heuristics provide an approach and are oriented to usability/UX and consider aspects close to e-Commerce, after analyzing them we concluded that there are certain characteristics of e-Commerce websites that are not properly covered by these two sets.

In the first instance, the base sets were adapted as indicated in Tables 1 and 2. The justification for the action that was carried out with each heuristic is presented below.

- TWH1: It is important to show the user what is happening on the website.
- TWH2: It is relevant that the user is kept informed of everything that the transaction that he is carrying out entails.
- TWH3: It is important when the user is browsing the website, the transactions on it must work as expected by the user.
- TWH4: Security must be provided when the user interacts with a website.
- TWH5: The website should be designed in a way that is as familiar to you as possible, without it you could quickly become frustrated.

- TWH6: The user should feel free to make or undo during all navigation on the website.
- TWH7: It is considered important that there is coherence in the elements and the operation of the website.
- TWH8: It is considered relevant that e-Commerce websites present similarities so that the user does not have to learn from scratch each time.
- TWH9: You must be aware of all possible errors that may occur to the user when browsing the website.
- TWH10: In navigation, the user must instinctively navigate and be able to understand the normal flow of the site, without having to study it each time he enters.
- TWH11: It is important that the website is designed so that any user can use it without difficulty.
- TWH12: It is relevant that the website shows true and truthful information, so as not to confuse the user.
- TWH13: The website must be designed to provide all the help that a user needs when navigating it.
- TWH14: In case the user needs it, there should be help that can provide autonomous learning to understand the functionality of the website.

In relation to the set of heuristics proposed by Díaz et al. [7] only the following heuristics are considered:

- ECAH2: It is relevant to consider it since it considers cultural aspects within the definition.
- ECAH4: It is important since it considers that not all users understand the same thing when they visualize a certain action.
- ECAH8: You consider cultural aspects in its definition, such as visual noise.

The other heuristics of the set were left out because they were included in the set of heuristics of Quiñones et al. (2016) [6], and some escaped the focus of the new set of heuristics that we propose.

After having selected the heuristics to work with, a preliminary version of this set was obtained (see Table 3) and a second version of the set was obtained according to the experiments carried out (see Table 4). Heuristics were formalized using the template proposed by the methodology of Quiñones et al. [4] for the specification stage.

3.2   A Set of User eXperience Heuristics for e-Commerce

Following the experiments carried out, we obtained the first version of the set of heuristics. To show this set of heuristics, we have used the work template that appears in the methodology of Quiñones et al. [4].

Table 1. Action to take, first filter – Transactional websites heuristics, Quiñones et al. (2016).

ID	Name	Action
TWH1	System visibility	Adapt
TWH2	Keep the user informed about the status of transactions	Adapt
TWH3	Expected reliability and functionality	Adapt
TWH4	Security and speed of transactions	Adapt
TWH5	Match between the system and the real world	Adapt
TWH6	Control and user freedom	Keep
TWH7	Consistency between system elements	Adapt
TWH8	Use of web standards and symbology	Adapt
TWH9	Error prevention	Adapt
TWH10	Minimize memory load to user	Keep
TWH11	Flexibility and efficiency of use	Adapt
TWH12	Aesthetic and minimalist design	Adapt
TWH3	Helps the user to recognize, diagnose and recover from errors	Adapt
TWH14	Help and documentation	Keep

Table 2. Action to take, first filter – e-Commerce with culture aspect heuriştics, Díaz et al. (2016).

ID	Name	Action
ECAH1	System visibility	Discard
ECAH2	Match between the system and the real world	Adapt
ECAH3	Control and user freedom	Discard
ECAH4	Consistency and standards	Adapt
ECAH5	Error prevention	Discard
ECAH6	Minimize memory load	Discard
ECAH7	Flexibility and efficiency of use	Discard
ECAH8	Aesthetic and minimalist design	Adapt
TECAH9	Help users recognize, diagnose, and recover from errors	Discard
ECAH10	Help and documentation	Discard
ECAH11	Information structure	Discard
ECAH12	Accurate and detailed results	Discard

Table 3. ECUXH "E-Commerce User eXperience Heuristics", preliminary version.

ID	Name	Heuristic's update
ECUXH1	System and transaction status visibility	Base heuristic is adapted
ECUXH2	Reliability, speed and security of transactions	Base heuristic is adapted
ECUXH3	Match between the system and the real world	Base heuristic is adapted
ECUXH4	User control and freedom	Base heuristic is adapted
ECUXH5	Consistency and standards	Base heuristic is adapted
ECUXH6	Error prevention, recognition, diagnosis and recovery	Base heuristic is adapted
ECUXH7	Minimize memory load to user	Base heuristic is adapted
ECUXH8	Flexibility and efficiency of use	Base heuristic is adapted
ECUXH9	Aesthetic and minimalist design	Base heuristic is adapted
ECUXH10	Help the user	Base heuristic is adapted
ECUXH11	Payment methods	New heuristic is created

Table 4. ECUXH "E-Commerce User eXperience Heuristics", version 1.

ID	Name	Heuristic's update
ECUXH1	System and transaction status visibility	Definition, explanation and checklist was improved
ECUXH2	Reliability, speed and security of transactions	Checklist was improved
ECUXH3	Match between the system and the real world	No changes
ECUXH4	User control and freedom	No changes
ECUXH5	Consistency and standards	Explanation was improved
ECUXH6	Error prevention, recognition, diagnosis and recovery	Checklist was improved
ECUXH7	Minimize memory load to user	Checklist was improved
ECUXH8	Flexibility and efficiency of use	No changes
ECUXH9	Aesthetic and minimalist design	No changes
ECUXH10	Help the user	Definition was improved
ECUXH11	Payment methods	New heuristic on the set. Add security aspect

We carry out all the pertinent changes according to the experiments carried out. According to this, the following definitions of the set of heuristics have been obtained:

- (ECUXH1) System and transaction status visibility: The system must keep the user informed within a reasonable time about: the current status of the application and the processing that is being carried out, by providing feedback to the user. In addition, the user must be informed when an operation is successful or unsuccessful.
- (ECUXH2) Reliability, speed and security of transactions: Transactions must be highly reliable, function correctly (without errors) and safely, delivering appropriate results, without altering the value of the products/services, using security measures in each of the transactions carried out by the user, this within a reasonable time.
- (ECUXH3) Match between the system and the real world: The system must speak the user's language either with words, phrases or concepts that are familiar to them and that allow them to orient themselves within the application. Showing the information in a natural and easy-to-understand way, avoiding confusion.
- (ECUXH4) User control and freedom: The system must allow undo and redo actions that have been selected by mistake by the user, exit unwanted states and grant emergency exits.
- (ECUXH5) Consistency and standards: The system must follow established conventions throughout the entire website, maintaining a consistent and standard design structure and style throughout the application. In addition, the system must follow the standards for web design, in commonly used location and structure, making use of related symbology in the function to be displayed. It is also necessary to consider that the amounts of the product/service are visible at all times and that they do not vary depending on the payment method.
- (ECUXH6) Error prevention, recognition, diagnosis and recovery: The system must prevent errors from occurring by displaying a warning before the action that will lead to the error is performed. In the event of an error, the system must display simple and clear error messages to understand, suggesting to the user a solution that will allow them to get out of the problem. In addition, the system must be able to help the user to recover from errors, indicating the most appropriate solution to get out of the problem.
- (ECUXH7) Minimize memory load to user: The system must facilitate the user's work, avoiding that he is forced to remember previously seen information to carry out a transaction in the current state of the system. Also, important options must be clearly visible and detailed.
- (ECUXH8) Flexibility and efficiency of use: The system must be designed so that any user can use it, that is, the system must be able to adapt to the needs of all users through simple and efficient use. In addition, the system must accommodate the different ways in which a user can perform the same task, either manually or through filters or search bar.
- (ECUXH9) Aesthetic and minimalist design: The system should show only the relevant information, hiding that which is not necessary. The information must be correctly distributed, without overloading elements, showing a pleasant interface to the user.
- (ECUXH10) Help the user: The system must provide some option for interaction with consumers who visit the website, so that they can communicate quickly and efficiently with the website that provides what they want to purchase. In addition, the system must provide help regarding the operation of the application. This must be easy to find and understand, it must be precise, as short as possible and focused on the tasks performed by the user.

- (ECUXH11) Payment methods: The system must grant the user a variety of payment methods for the purchase of the products/services offered.

We have defined the set of heuristics to evaluate e-Commerce website using the template of the methodology of Quiñones et al. [4]. In Table 5 we show as an example the first heuristic of the set using the mentioned template, in addition to including cases of compliance and non-compliance of this heuristic in the case study.

Table 5. Example of a complete heuristics: ECUXH1 - System and transaction status visibility

ID	ECUXH1
Priority	(3) Very important
Name	System and transaction status visibility
Definition	The system must keep the user informed within a reasonable time about: the current status of the application and the processing that is being carried out, by providing feedback to the user. In addition, the user must be informed when an operation is successful or unsuccessful
Explanation	The system should focus on the importance of informing the consumer about everything that happens in the application (that is relevant to him), rather than on the information itself. In addition, the user must know when an action is being carried out by the system and when an action is required by it
Application feature	Inform de user (general aspect)
Examples with a images	Examples of heuristic's compliance are shown in Figs. 2 and 3
Benefit	The user will feel guided and informed about the transactions carried out while using the website
Problems	-
Checklist	1. The site indicates when the user takes an action 2. The site indicates when a transaction is in process, and when it has been successful or failed 3. The site informs the user when an unavoidable delay occurs in the response of a transaction 4. The site maintains adequate feedback with the user
UX attribute	Satisfaction (Usability)
Set of heuristics related	Quiñones et al. (2016) and Díaz et al. (2016)

In Fig. 2, it can be seen that when performing a search on the ·Despegar· website, it informs the user about the status of the system, showing a message to the user that their request is being carried out.

In Fig. 3, it can be seen that when entering the "My orders" section on the ·Falabella website·, it does not issue any message that shows the user that there are no orders associated with it.

Fig. 2. Example of compliance ECUXH1

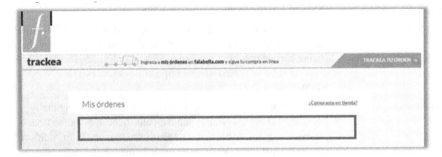

Fig. 3. Example of non-compliance ECUXH1

3.3 Preliminary Validation

The set of heuristics was preliminarily validated using three evaluation methods: heuristic evaluation, user test, and expert judgment.

Six evaluators with similar experience reviewed the same case study; three evaluatores searched for problems based on the control set [6], while the other three used the ECUXH set. Each collaborator evaluated the www.falabella.com [17] case study in its web and mobile versions individually. On this occasion, it was possible to conclude that despite the fact that there is not a great difference in terms of effectiveness, the new set of heuristics designed to evaluate eCommerce websites, was able to find more usability problems than the control heuristics, and better covers the characteristics of e-Commerce websites.

The usability tests aimed to identify from the problems identified in the heuristic evaluation, to check those that were identified by the control group, but that were not identified by the experimental group (ECUXH), guiding the user through various tasks to analyze the problems and verify if they considered them as such. There were 6 participants where the case study was evaluated through a Co-Discovery test which contained 3 tasks that were, find a camera (1), find the most economical camera (2) and simulate the purchase process of a photographic camera (3). The results obtained were analyzed, in addition to taking into account the comments and impressions of the participants.

Finally, the experiment showed that although the participants felt comfortable browsing the website, there were several problems that slowed the natural navigation of the site.

The last experiment was expert judgment involving 6 experts, all of whom had participated in at least two heuristic evaluations. The method consisted of subjecting the experts to a survey that aimed to obtain their feedback. The heuristics were evaluated in three dimensions (clarity, usefulness and ease of use). The results were mostly favorable, reflecting minimal modifications necessary for the set to be fully understood.

Finally, positive results were obtained in the use of the proposed set and only some modifications were necessary to obtain the final set of heuristics.

4   Conclusions and Future Work

Nowadays the number of people who are interested in making purchases through online stores has increased, this added to the technological advance that has occurred in recent years, we can notice that it is becoming more accessible and comfortable to buy through the internet, since various products are offered to attract your customers. However, despite being very comfortable with this new method of purchase, there are always problems when using them, which is why it was decided to evaluate the usability of this type of website.

This research was carried out using the methodology proposed by Quiñones et al. [4] for the development of usability/UX heuristics, which includes a series of steps necessary to ensure that the proposed set of heuristics is optimal when evaluating sites eCommerce web. We developed a set of 14 UX heuristics for e-Commerce (ECUXH).

The set was validated through the three experiments proposed in the aforementioned methodology, which are, heuristic evaluation, user tests and expert judgment, throughout three iterations. Validation results shows that ECUXH is an effective tool. According to the results obtained in each of the experiments, it can be concluded that the new set of heuristics is more specific than the basic sets, so it can better respond to the needs of users who use websites in where products/services are marketed.

As future work, we pretend to develop a set of retail-oriented Customer eXperince (CX) heuristics, based on ECUXH.

Acknowledgements. The authors would like to thank the School of Informatics Engineering of the Pontificia Universidad Católica de Valparaíso (PUCV), Chile, and the Agencia Nacional de Investigación y Desarrollo (ANID).

References

1. Cómo crece el Comercio Electrónico en el mundo. https://observatorioecommerce.com/como-crece-el-comercio-electronico-en-el-mundo/. Accessed 10 Jan 2021
2. Usabilidad Web y Experiencia de Usuario (UX): Todo lo que debes saber. http://www.staffc reativa.pe/blog/usabilidad-web-experiencia-usuario/. Accessed 10 Jan 2021
3. Nielsen, J.: Usability inspection methods. In: Conference Companion on Human Factors in Computing Systems, pp. 413–414. ACM (1994)

4. Quiñones, D., Rusu, C., Rusu, V.: A methodology to develop usability/user experience heuristics. Comput. Stand. Interf. **59**, 109–129 (2018)
5. Improving the User Experience. http://www.usability.gov. Accessed 10 Jan 2021
6. Usabilidad en sitios web transaccionales. http://opac.pucv.cl.pucv.idm.oclc.org/pucv_txt/txt-2500/UCE2599_01.pdf. Accessed 10 Jan 2021
7. Díaz, J., Rusu, C., Collazos, C.A.: Experimental validation of a set of cultural- oriented usability heuristics: E-Commerce websites evaluation. Comput. Stand. Interfaces **50**, 160–178 (2017)
8. ISO Standard 9241–11:2018. Ergonomics of Human-System Interaction—Part 11: Usability: Definitions and Concepts, International Organization for Standardization; ISO: Geneva, Switzerland (2018)
9. Estándares formales de usabilidad y su aplicación práctica en una evaluación heurística. https://olgacarreras.blogspot.com/2012/03/estandares-formales-de-usabilidad-y-su.html. Accessed 10 Jan 2021
10. Introduction to Usability. https://www.nngroup.com/articles/usability-101-introduction-to-usability/. Accessed 10 Jan 2021
11. ISO Standard 9241–210:2010. Ergonomics of Human System Interaction—Part 210: Human-Centred Design for Interactive System; International Standardization Organization (ISO): Geneva, Switzerland (2019)
12. Improving the User Experience. www.usability Accessed 10 Jan 2021
13. Holzinger, A.: Usability engineering methods for software developers, vol. 48(1), pp. 71–74. ACM (2005)
14. Evaluación heurística. https://www.usableyaccesible.com/recurso_glosario.php#E. Accessed 10 Jan 2021
15. Laudon, K.C., Traver, C.G.: e-Commerce, negocios, tecnología y sociedad, Naucalpan de Juaréz, Estado de México, Pearson (2009)
16. Bonastre, L.: Elaboració d'una heurística per a l'avaluació de l'Experiència d'Usuari en llocs web de comerç electrònic (Tesis magistral). Universitat de Lleida, Cataluña, España (2013)
17. Falabella. https://www.falabella.com/falabella-cl/. Accessed 10 Jan 2021

Ethical Design in e-Commerce: Case Studies

Camila Bascur[1]([☒]), Catalina Montecinos[2], and Veronica Mansilla[3]

[1] Pontificia Universidad Católica de Valparaíso, Av. Brasil 2241, 2340000 Valparaíso, Chile
[2] Universidad Adolfo Ibañez, Diagonal las Torres 2640, 7910000 Santiago, Chile
[3] Universidad del Desarrollo, Av. Plaza 680, 7550000 Santiago, Chile

Abstract. The exponential growth of electronic commerce in recent years has meant a sustainable advance in what are technologies, imposing trends. This has revealed new patterns of behavior and has brought to the fore the need to reflect on abuse, such as the indiscriminate use of private data (which gave birth to the General Data Protection Regulation, GDPR) and obscure design patterns (coercion through graphic interface elements to condition acts that a person does not want such as guarantees or coercive terms and conditions).

That is why it is necessary to raise an ethical theoretical framework that helps to identify these phenomena that seem to be unable to be regulated in terms of State policies. We believe that this lack of regulation is due to lobbies probably coming from the private sector, but in most cases to ignorance around the creation, management and maintenance of the different digital products. Which is why we have recently seen the emergence of issues such as accessibility and ethics in most international conventions and congresses on design and interaction.

The following article aims to carry out a review of basic concepts around the ethical use of interfaces. Based on this review and adaptation to the local reality, a small study will be carried out in which the ethical use of interfaces will be studied. Well, we are not only interested in being able to evaluate, but also in knowing people's perception regarding the understanding of ethics on e-commerce platforms.

Keywords: Ethics · Business ethics · Consumer ethics · e-Commerce · GDPR · Dark patterns

1 Introduction

It is important to highlight the growth that e-Commerce has had in recent times, this due to the pandemic we are experiencing (Covid). What has allowed in a certain way, accelerate the process of change of companies and access more quickly to the products/services that the client wishes to acquire. As a result of this, resources have been invested in providing better experiences to customers, who ultimately are the ones who make the final purchase decision but are also affected in the decisions of companies.

As a result of the aforementioned and the need for consumers to acquire products/services as quickly as possible, companies in favor of acting quickly (as customers do) have had to ignore various parameters ethics where both they and consumers are

© Springer Nature Switzerland AG 2021
G. Meiselwitz (Ed.): HCII 2021, LNCS 12774, pp. 421–436, 2021.
https://doi.org/10.1007/978-3-030-77626-8_28

affected. A clear example is when certain customer data is rescued or requested, ignoring requesting their consent. In general, these data are frequently used to study customer behavior, but without consent they should not be used.

Adding all of the above is that an issue arises that is relevant, both for consumers and for organizations, and that is ethics. Ethics seeks to protect in a certain way both those who are internally in the organizations, as well as the external/consumers, establishing common characteristics that allow us to live in an environment that is as harmonious and respectful as possible.

The article presents in Sect. 2: basic concepts, such as ethics, business ethics, consumer ethics, e-Commerce; In Sect. 3: it shows ethical problems that occur around e-Commerce, including indiscriminate use of data and dark patterns; in Sect. 4: ethical problems that occur in four of the largest e-Commerce in Chile are shown; and finally, in Sect. 5: the conclusions are shown, both general and specific to the case studies.

2 Theoretical Background

2.1 Ethics

Much has been written about the ethics of the Greek Ethos over the years. The Greeks already used this word to refer to custom and morals. Philosophers like Aristotle in his book Nicómano Ethics [1] dedicate a whole chapter to talk about this discipline, which addresses morality and adds that people's behavior has a purpose, pointing out that man moves for reasons [2].

Ethics, being a moral discipline, is related to politics (when addressing the "norms") and the intellect (which is the best of people), which leads to the "path of happiness" [3]. This is because man has a good life and performs good works.

But, advancing in history we arrive at the renaissance period in which this discipline lives its darkest time. Different thinkers began to question it. Among them, Tomás de Aquino stands out, a religious who follows the Aristotelian guidelines on Ethics, but there is something that changes because he points out that the "way to happiness" is Love [4].

So, we can say according to Adela Cortina and Emilio Martínez (2008) that ethics addresses: what is morality, grounding morality and, finally, bringing morality to the entire scope of our social life [5]. Meanwhile, Fraedrich and Ferrell (2010) are more specific and define ethics as "the study and philosophy of human activities, with the specific purpose of determining whether a certain action or behavior is correct or incorrect" [6].

The study of this discipline includes various edges, one of the most relevant topics being the class struggle, a topic that to this day generates controversy; in our case study due to the limited access that some users have to the internet.

As we can see, ethics is present in the entire scope of our lives, that is why it is vitally important to establish a theoretical framework that indicates the guidelines that should be followed in this area of study, because at present there is not much related philosophy behavior in the development of e-Commerce.

As we can see, there is quite a bit of literature on how ethics has been carried out over the years. Considering the time in which we are living, we can land these concepts by taking them to the pyramid "Ethical Needs of Aral Balkan and Laura Kalbag" [7]:

- Human Rights: is when a product and/or service is decentralized, private, open, secure, interoperable, accessible, safe and sustainable.
- Human Effort: functional, convenient and reliable.
- Human Experience: that a service and/or product produces delight.

Ideally, all three criteria must be met for a service and/or product to be considered ethical. If it is not complied with, even one, it falls into unethical practices.

2.2 Business Ethics

Business ethics refers to "the moral and ethical belief system that guides the values, behaviors and decisions of an organization and of the individuals within that organization" [8], that is, it is directly related to the actions of people who work within companies.

The goal of business ethics is to ensure a consistent moral attitude within the company, ensuring that all members of the company are respected and well treated. Business ethics influences the internal organization of a company in various aspects, that is, the conduct of employees, including interpersonal relationships within the company and business relationships with external clients [9].

Just as consumers have the right to know about the use of the product and they must be given all the information that is possible about it. Businesses have certain responsibilities to provide whatever they pay for, assuming the products are safe for normal use.

There are multiple cases where business ethics has not been present where consumers have been intentionally violated. In Chile we have the controversial case of La Polar retail [10], where they sought to benefit by granting loans to low-income people without their consent.

In international companies, according to what is shown in the Netflix documentary "Social Dilemma" [11], it is possible to identify how the users' data has been violated, using the information rescued by the companies to obtain a benefit from it and influence behavior. natural consumer.

We have seen that ethics have led companies to regulate their behavior to satisfy the needs of users and thus guarantee their personal and social well-being [12]. If this point is not guaranteed, people tend to punish unethical companies. [13] Considering this, it is of vital importance to have business ethics because in this way possible losses that both companies and consumers can have been avoided. So, the latter can make purchases without major misgivings.

2.3 Consumer Ethics

Consumer ethics refers to "moral principles and norms that guide the conduct of individuals or groups in their action of disposing or using goods and services" [14].

Muncy and Vitell (1992, 2005) established a Consumer Ethics Scale that examines the extent to which consumers believe that certain questionable behaviors are ethical or unethical on the Consumer Ethics Scale (CES). The scale contains five dimensions that cover different aspects [14, 15]:

1. Actively profiting from illegal activities. In this dimension, it is analyzed whether the consumer can consciously harm the seller.
2. Passively profiting from illegal activities. In this dimension, situations are compared in which the consumer passively benefits from a seller's error, benefiting from the situation unintentionally.
3. Actively profiting from questionable or disappointing practices, despite being legal. This dimension includes actions that the consumer considers questionable, but are legal practices
4. Do not engage in harmful practices. In this dimension we speak of a set of actions that do not cause harm.
5. Doing the right thing and following recycling practices. In this dimension we talk about the desire of consumers to do things well.

This scale makes it possible to identify questionable consumer practices in order to measure consumer beliefs. Taking this scale into account, it has been seen that the behavior of consumers has changed in recent years, this is due to the fact that they seek to buy in a more ethical way, both from the consumer's point of view, buying more ethical products/services or looking for businesses fairer to make purchases, which shows positive purchasing behavior. However, not all consumers can access more ethical products/services, because products with ethical characteristics tend to be more expensive than normal products, it is also impossible to assume that consumers always behave ethically [16].

2.4 E-Commerce

Electronic E-Commerce is defined as: "All transactions that occur digitally between organizations and individuals, through the Internet and the web, which culminate in the payment of the product/service purchased by the individual" [17]. E-Commerce is a type of transactional website that specializes in business transactions and not just in the delivery of information.

There are different criteria to classify electronic commerce, three that represent an important part of e-Commerce [17] will be shown below.

- B2C (Business to Consumer): Type of commerce where companies offer their products or services to consumers.
- B2B (Business to Business): Type of commerce where the commercial transaction is carried out between companies.
- C2C (Consumer to Consumer): Type of business where consumers interact with each other, conducting transactions or exchanging information.

As the use of the internet by people increases, e-Commerce is becoming more and more relevant in different markets. To better understand what e-Commerce is, the following characteristics will be used to help us give it a more holistic perspective [18].

- Interconnectedness: refers to the degree of connection that companies have with their vendors, suppliers, consumer and strategic partners, allowing them to expand their ability to provide products to their consumer. This enables them to have unlimited access to all types of global trading companies, reliably and at low cost.
- Simplicity: refers to the fact that e-Commerce provides multiple unprecedented entries at a low cost, that is, it allows large and small companies to compete at the same level.
- Speed: refers to the growth experienced by e-Commerce, in general to participate in an e-Commerce it must be extremely fast, because the time of use of the internet advances much faster than without it, being a competitive environment created by the high-speed nature of online business
- Virtuality: in an online virtual environment. It refers to the availability of services in terms of time and location. Facilitating the blurring of traditional lines between companies as they connect with their vendors, vendors, and other businesses to create virtual businesses
- Cost: refers to time and cost savings due to process automation, minor and large economies of scale. Adding to this, the convenience when consumers can access products and services at any time.

2.5 Why Are Ethics Important in e-Commerce?

You often have different issues that affect the ethics of e-Commerce. It is clear that the problems listed below are not limited solely to e-Commerce. All these problems also arise in traditional commerce (Brick-and-morta). Kracher and Corritore (2004) propose that the differences are not the issues themselves, but the manifestations and their scope. Below are the top issues in e-Commerce ethics [18]:

- Access: refers to the digital divide that exists with respect to access to computing. It is a problem because potential consumers without computer access cannot take advantage of trading opportunities, such as obtaining deeply discounted rates offered on e-Commerce sites.
- Intellectual Property: refers to when the interests of the creators are obviated by not offering them prerogatives in relation to their creations. It is a problem because it is easier to share information in electronic media.
- Privacy and Informed Consent: refers to when consumer data is shared without their consent. It is a problem because various forms of data collection are used to obtain detailed information on what consumers are doing to study their behavior.
- Protection of Children refers to how vulnerable minors are to having uncontrolled access to the internet. It is a problem since e-Commerce sites are available to any child, without subscription or censorship from their personal computers, such as pornography. These activities are facilitated by the simplicity, interconnection, and low-cost features of electronic commerce.

- Security of Information refers to the management of information and how e-Commerce handles the data collected. It is a problem as a transaction provides sensitive consumer information and a breach of information security can easily be global and affect millions of people. The scope of the consequences of security flaws often makes security a priority for e-commerce companies.
- Trust: refers to the basis of any customer-company relationship and is present in almost all commercial decisions and transactions, both in e-Commerce and in traditional commerce. It is a problem since if the e-Commerce does not give confidence to the client, the sale instance is not generated, this is why website designers try to create the impression of reliability through the design of websites, navigation systems of latest generation and seals of approval.

It is due to the aforementioned that it is necessary to have ethics in e-Commerce. As the internet advances, so does electronic commerce, that is why e-Commerce must be supported by principles that can generate confidence in consumers to provide a wider space for the fulfillment of the quality of goods/services according to the wishes and capabilities of consumers.

In turn, having ethics in the company will allow to regulate the relationship between collaborators, companies and consumers, so that all obtain a fair treatment and service feeling part of the business, this will help reduce losses, both by the consumer and the organizations and thus carry out transactions in a confident and secure manner, minimizing the fraud that frequently occurs in e-Commerce transactions.

In e-Commerce media, it is essential to be guided by an ethical framework to avoid falling into dark patterns that lead consumers/users to expect erroneous behavior from e-Commerce. This allows us to conclude that a company that ignores ethics in its day-to-day life, may "be lucky" and achieve significant short-term benefits, but will disappear from the business world in the long term, because it will not have the support of its employees or acceptance at the social level [19].

3   Problems in e-Commerce Ethics

From where or when can we identify the origin of unethical practices in digital products? It is thanks to a growing number of product-conscious professionals that they have created, improved or understood to get their work done. Uber, Facebook, Google, Amazon, among some of the greats in the industry, have seen their secrets and unethical methods of traffic and sales of people's private data exposed.

Zuboff (2020) points out "They certainly sell. To be successful in this business, you need to have great predictions. Large predictions require large amounts of data [20]". We can say that the cause of these practices is due to the current market model, where conglomerates with great purchasing power are able to buy entire companies just to be able to take over business models based on advertising profits and be sure that they continue to generate or even increase those profits.

Falbe (2018) adds "By now, most people who work in technology know and feel the deep concerns related to the surveillance capitalism promoted and supported by the tech giants. We understand that the root of the problem lies in the business model of capitalizing and monetizing user data. Stories of how people are being exploited crop up on a daily basis, such as the recent story about how Instagram withholds similar notifications from certain users, with the purpose of increasing the open rate of the application. In the same story, The Globe and Mail describe how former high-level Facebook employees are developing a conscience and telling horrible stories about how functions are being meticulously built to exploit human behavior and become addicted to social media" [7].

The problem with generating data is that said data leads us to identify behaviors and thereby create profiles with the purpose of increasing the annual net profit of a company or company. Even going further, the current data collected is not only used to manipulate, but also serves to feed predictive models through machine learning, thus giving the power to companies and companies to impact our decisions and future behavior patterns.

How many times have we not marveled at the convenience of a certain advertising or set of content oriented to what we just wanted or wanted at a certain moment, until we were horrified to notice all the interactions that we were creating until feeding the algorithm that led to that guilty purchase?

3.1 Indiscriminate Use of Private Data

For us who work with digital products, no matter the role, we start from a base where we want to contribute to their improvement. We believe that collecting data will help us provide better services. To a large extent this is true, products improve, become more intuitive and effectively make people's lives easier.

However, what happens when they influence behaviors, beliefs, or foster impulses that we try to control? Predictive models and algorithms have been shaped by a select group of professionals, where another select group of people make decisions that are applied to products and services that will affect a thousand people who make use of them.

Parakitas (2020) tells us in this regard "All this data we produce is being fed to systems that barely have human supervision. And make better and better predictions about what we are doing to do or what we are. There is this misconception that companies sell our data. This is not true. It's how they use our data. They build models that predict our actions. And whoever has that model, wins" [20].

As an example, Falbe (2018) adds "Data trade and data tracking is big business. According to the report "Corporate Surveillance in Everyday Life", Oracle provides access to 5 billion unique user ID's (this is confirmed on Oracle's website). "

In this regard, it should be noted that so far, the most complete and detailed corpus of laws on the use and handling of private data is the "GDPR" (General Data Protection Regulation) [7]. Regulation born in the European Union as a directive in 1996. And that exists as a milestone in 2012 as a reform to strengthen privacy rights and the digital economy, adding several milestones between 2015 and 2016, and that is finally officially applied on 25 May 2018 [22].

The GDPR in essence is one of the most robust corpus of laws in terms of data protection, it not only watches over European citizens in European territory, but also all European citizens independent of the physical territory. It protects the privacy of citizens and their institutions, but also forces suppliers and third parties to comply with these regulations. This implies any service, product and/or website that is used by European citizens, regardless of where they are located. Failure to comply with regulations, update privacy policies, as well as report exposure of databases, among others, can incur fines of up to 4% of a company's global net profit [23].

Although Chilean legislation is a little behind in relation to the efforts of the EU, Law 21.096 is aiming to achieve the standards of the European Union, APEC, OECD [23]. However, currently the only institution that protects consumers who make use of digital platforms, products and/or services is the SERNAC (National Consumer Service). Likewise, there is no or little audit regarding the ethical uses of information in Chilean digital retail, and it is generally the consumers themselves who are responsible for reporting such bad practices/abuses through complaints and / or reports to the service channels or to the SERNAC.

In foreign products, services and/or platforms it is common to come across pop-ups to authorize cookies, the most advanced ones even point out, explain and differentiate between the basic ones (operation) and the accessory ones (experience or advertising, for example).

In most Chilean cases, the basic provisions of the legislation are usually met, that is: the terms and conditions of the service and the privacy policies. In terms of interface, they are usually checkboxes next to a top-notch button [24].

3.2 Dark Patterns

We previously pointed out that the economic model is the great cause and motive of unethical practices in digital products. From the exploitation and use of millions of data to feed algorithmic predictions, to the manipulation of opinion and the growing "misinformation" of the population when consulting alternative "truths" sites, which, using design methods to generate trust and truthfulness, are taken as true [25].

"Dark patterns" are a type of unethical design practice that consists of using visual and content patterns that encourage behaviors and/or thoughts that we do not necessarily want to believe or carry out. These actions can range from buying something, signing up for a news list, to taking out insurance that only appears when they are seen on the payment chart.

Brignull (2010), notes that dark patterns work because they take advantage of weaknesses in human cognition [26]. For example, it is common for people to not read every word when faced with a digital experience. The text is simply scanned quickly, and assumptions are generated about what it indicates. If a company wants to push you to do something, it is enough to understand this advantage and design a site that pretends to say something but actually points out the opposite. Practices such as "Privacy Zuckering" (a practice that consists of tricking people into publishing more personal data than they really wanted to publicly) or "Hidden Costs" (a practice that shows unforeseen costs in the last step of the checkout without them have been noted before).

4   Problems in Chilean e-Commerce Ethics

For this analysis, we will focus clearly on the creation of a user account and how privacy policies are addressed in the following platforms: Falabella [27], Paris [28], Ripley [29] and Mercado Libre [30]. We focus on Indiscriminate use of private data (see Sect. 3.1) and dark patterns (see Sect. 3.2).

4.1   Indiscriminate Use of Private Data

In this section we review the indiscriminate use of data in the following sections "account creation", "Treatment of terms and conditions", "Privacy statement" and "Control over privacy ".

- Account creation: Mercado Libre and Ripley request as basic mandatory fields: name, surname, RUT, email and password; Paris and Falabella additionally request code and telephone. Only Paris asks to confirm password.
- Treatment of "terms and conditions" and "Privacy Statement":

  o Mercado Libre has a checkbox where both are authorized, the continue button is only activated when you click on the checkbox (see Fig. 1).
  o Falabella breaks down two checkboxes. We can notice that the button seems to be "inactive" in both situations (see Fig. 2).
  o Ripley does not have a checkbox so the "Terms and Conditions" as well as the "Privacy Policies" are accepted by submitting the form (and subsequent account creation) (see Fig. 3).
  o Paris does not indicate the "Terms and Conditions" or the "Privacy Policies" (see Fig. 4).

Fig. 1. Terms and conditions and privacy statement – Mercadolibre

- Control over privacy

  o Mercado Libre it allows a person to have control over the use of their data for personalized advertising, download a report on the use of the data and details of the operations carried out. It also allows you to delete the account and personal data. (see Fig. 5).
  o Falabella, Ripley y Paris grants their users power and control over their private and personal data. Less delete account.

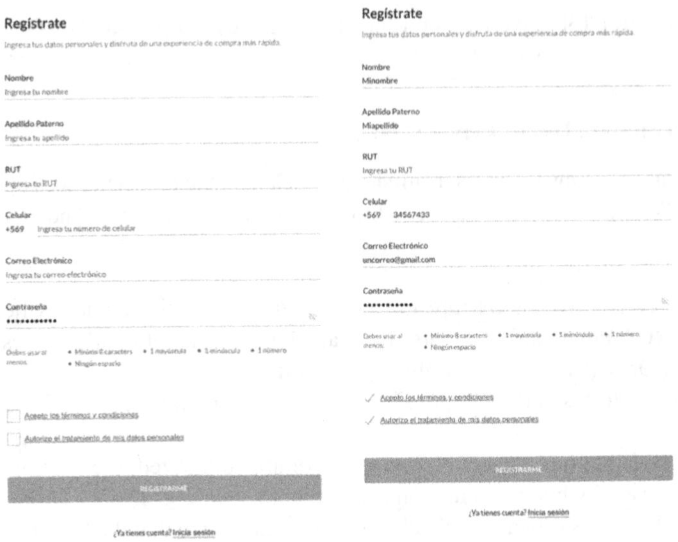

Fig. 2. Terms and conditions and privacy statement – Falabella

Fig. 3. Terms and conditions and privacy statement – Ripley.

Fig. 4. Terms and conditions and privacy statement – Paris

4.2 Dark Patterns

The main dark pattern discovered was that of "Bypass" of information, that is, it takes advantage of the known phenomenon of "scanning type reading" to present long blocks

Fig. 5. Control over privacy – Mercado Libre

of text, difficult to read or using technical language. This causes the behavior of omission on the part of a user and will make them accept the "terms and conditions" and/or "privacy policies" by simply checking the checkbox or clicking on the first hierarchy button.

- Mercado Libre by clicking on "Terms and Conditions" and "Privacy Policies", you will get to another site (see Fig. 6).
  The terms and conditions section works by listing in point form, which facilitates the search with a "search bar", which when used leads to the results located in the "Help" area. The use of bold is highlighted to facilitate scanning type reading (which is usually keywords). In the "privacy policies" section, it is handled visually attractive, with an index on the left, easy, simple and clear language. The use of enriched text is highlighted to promote relationships of trust, transparency and playfulness, optimal conditions to generate bonds of trust and understanding.
- Falabella presents a pop-up, on the same view of the account creation form. Language facilitation work is appreciated, but the text is long and fails to be concise (see Fig. 7).
- Ripley by selecting the terms and conditions sections and privacy policy, takes you to another site, also located in the "Help" area: (see Fig. 8).
- In the "terms and conditions" section an accordion-type index is used that when interacting generates an expectation that leads users to assume that the content appears immediately below but takes us to another page, where basically an endless flow is entered of related topics. In addition, formal language is used, with complex syntactic constructions, which makes it difficult to understand the contents. In the "privacy policies" section, the positive use of text blocks is highlighted. While there is no rich text, the structure allows for effortless and easy reading.

According to the analysis carried out, we could notice the following unethical practices facilitated by dark design patterns:

- Exploitation of human cognition by presenting long and difficult to read blocks of text. In the examples studied, Mercado Libre stands out positively by using rich text using bold type in the "Terms and Conditions", since it understands the natural way of reading people: scanning by keyword. Ripley, on the other hand, stands out negatively since it presents a solution that, although it helps to identify each section of the "Terms and Conditions", fails in the mode. Generally, interfaces with a higher cognitive load are difficult to navigate, and in this case, the user must remember not only how to return to the index but also avoid getting lost between related links. The text is not

Terms and conditions   Privacy policies

Fig. 6. Dark Patterns – Mercado Libre

Terms and conditions   Privacy policies

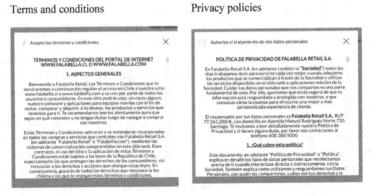

Fig. 7. Dark Patterns – Falabella

adapted or enriched, so reading and comprehension present barriers to access. It is worth highlighting the conscious effort to abbreviate the privacy policies.

- Absence of terms and policies. Paris presented the worst unethical practice by failing to indicate in the creation of an account the duties and responsibilities towards its consumers. People are trusted to access this information which is located at the far end of the site (see Fig. 9).

Not only are you unable to delete the account, but you also access a website/service marked by the absence of elements that Law No. 19,628/21,096 stipulates should be the minimum.

Terms and conditions   Privacy policies

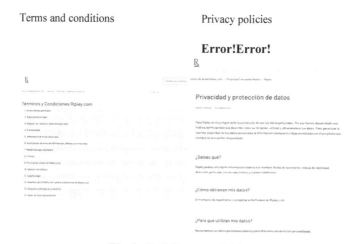

Fig. 8. Dark Patterns – Ripley

Fig. 9. Absence of terms and policies – Paris

Mercado Libre is concluded as the best example of good ethical practices due to its transparency and facilitation of rights and duties to its users. It also stands out as the only website in which users have power over the use of their cookies for personalized advertising (located in Account (login) > Settings > Privacy), although there is still work ahead, such as a total breakdown number of cookies, continues to far exceed the Chilean "state of the art".

5 Conclusions and Future Work

In order to understand the concept of ethics and its implication in digital products such as e-Commerce, we carried out a review on the etymology of the term, how it is applied to the business context and on the consumer, to then analyze a Chilean case. This first approach allowed us to understand the benefit between companies/consumers and their transactional relationship by reducing losses between both parties. To later understand the profound implications of the prevailing economic models of the world and national markets, the main causes of bad practices in the use and abuse of people's personal data.

While there is a lot of work ahead, especially in legal and auditing terms, we can approach a status quo of "correct" and "acceptable" in terms of ethical use of people's personal information by constantly reviewing the status of the art in countries that are ahead of us.

As professionals in the area of e-Commerce, it is not only necessary to ensure that a purchase can be carried safely, but also to avoid and point out unethical uses of obscure patterns of design/content of the interfaces. It is important to point out abusive, unclear interaction flows or that can lead to unpleasant situations that ultimately not only hurts a person's perceived experience with a service, but also the trust that a person can position on online transactions, as well as the losses that a company can suffer in the face of demands for unfulfilled service, terms not broken down/updated, etc.

For example, between the periods March-July 2020, the three most important retailers in the country concentrated 53% of the total complaints to the SERNAC. Within the investigation, unethical practices were detected such as: compensation in the form of a gift card that was later not fulfilled/delivered, abusive or ineffective "small bills", charges for each dispatch despite having only made one purchase and difficulties in accessing to the attention channels in case of problems, among other points indicated. And these problems do not even address the use and abuse of personal data of users, because at the country level we are not yet able to manage our privacy preferences in the vast majority of sites. How much data will we actually be delivering when we create an account for those we investigate? Have our decisions been influenced by content curated by advanced algorithms? How much net profit will these national companies be reporting profiting from our data?

Although all regulations protected by the legal frameworks of different countries have begun to integrate the digital paradigm in them, there are still no reliable and concrete ways to enforce them and that they are complied with. So far there have been few cases in which the GDPR has been invoked by fining a company, however, within the first eight months since the implementation of said regulation, about 60,000 self-reports of data leaks were reported throughout Europe.

Regarding Chilean legislation, irregularities are not yet systematically audited; furthermore, most of the terms and policies declared in the consulted sites cited Law No. 19,496, and not its updated version, Law No. 21,096, which became effective on 5 June 2018.

As future work we intend to evaluate the case studies with the CES scale to study the ethical behavior of users in e-Commerce.

Acknowledgements. The authors would like to thank the School of Informatics Engineering of the Pontificia Universidad Católica de Valparaíso (PUCV), Chile, and the Agencia Nacional de Investigación y Desarrollo (ANID).

References

1. Castelló S. F: Ética a Nicómaco. Universitat de Valencia (1993).
2. Cooper, L.: The rhetoric of Aristotle. Quart. J. Speech **21**(1), 10–19 (2009)
3. ¿Qué es la ética? https://www.ancmyp.org.ar/user/files/07Blaquier.pdf. Accessed 10 Jan 2021
4. Ética. http://www.juntadeandalucia.es/averroes/centros-tic/18008841a/helvia/aula/archivos/repositorio/0/23/html/cibernous/autores/taquino/teoria/etica/etica.html#:~:text=La%20%C3%A9tica%20de%20Tom%C3%A1s%20de,basa%20el%20pensamiento%20del%20aquinate.&text=Tom%C3%A1s%20de%20Aquino%20acepta%20las,teleol%C3%B3gico%20pero%20a%C3%B1adiendo%20elementos%20nuevos. Accessed 10 Jan 2021

5. Cortina, A., Orts, A.C., Navarro, E.M.: Ética. Ediciones Akal (1996)
6. Fraedrich, J., Ferrell, O.C., Ferrell, L.: Ethical Decision Making for Business. South-Western Cengage Learning, Mason (2011)
7. Ethical Design: The Practical Getting-Started Guide. https://www.smashingmagazine.com/2018/03/ethical-design-practical-getting-started-guide/. Accessed 10 Jan 2021
8. The Importance of Business Ethics. https://www.investopedia.com/ask/answers/040815/why-are-business-ethics-important.asp. Accessed 10 Jan 2021
9. What Are Business Ethics? Definition, Importance and Tips. https://www.indeed.com/career-advice/career-development/what-are-business-ethics. Accessed 10 Jan 2021
10. La Polar s.a. ¿era previsible la irregularidad, desde el análisis financiero?. http://www.asfae.cl/images/stories/papers/papers2011/603_LA_POLAR_SA_ERA_PREVISIBLE_LA_IRRE GULARIDAD_DESDE_EL_ANALISIS_FINANCIERO_2011.pdf. Accessed 10 Jan 2021
11. The Social Dilemma: A Horror Film in Documentary Clothing. https://www.psychologyto day.com/us/blog/positively-media/202010/the-social-dilemma-horror-film-in-documentary-clothing. Accessed 10 Jan 2021
12. Sorell, T.: Business ethics (1994)
13. Wright, L.T., Shaw, D., Newholm, T., Dickinson, R.: Consumption as voting: an exploration of consumer empowerment. European J. Market. (2006)
14. Vitell, S.J., Muncy, J.: Consumer ethics - an empirical investigation of factors influencing ethical judgments of the final consumer. J. Bus. Ethics **11**(8), 585–597 (1992)
15. Vitell, S.J., Muncy, J.: The muncy–vitell consumer ethics scale: a modification and application. J. Bus Ethics **62**(3), 267–275 (2005)
16. The Introduction To Consumer Ethics Business Essay. https://www.uniassignment.com/essay-samples/business/the-introduction-to-consumer-ethics-business-essay.php. Accessed 10 Jan 2021
17. Laudon, K.C., Traver, C.G: e-Commerce, negocios, tecnología y sociedad, Naucalpan de Juaréz, Estado de México, Pearson (2009)
18. Kracher, B., Corritore, C.L.: Is there a special e-commerce ethics? Bus. Ethics Quart. **14**(1), 71–94 (2004)
19. Ética empresarial ¿Es necesaria la Ética Empresarial? https://www.eade.es/blog/134-etica-empresarial-es-necesaria-la-etica-empresarial. Accessed 10 Jan 2021
20. Social Dilema. https://www.netflix.com/title/81254224. Accessed 10 Jan 2021
21. The History of the General Data Protection Regulation. https://edps.europa.eu/data-protec tion/data-protection/legislation/history-general-data-protection-regulation_en. Accessed 10 Jan 2021
22. How Is the GDPR Doing?. https://slate.com/technology/2019/03/gdpr-one-year-annive rsary-breach-notification-fines.html#:~:text=The%20EU%27s%20General%20Data%20P rotection,already%20scrutinizing%20the%20policy%27s%20effects.&text=Across%20E urope%2C%20nearly%2060%2C000%20breaches,by%20law%20firm%20DLA%20Piper. Accessed 10 Jan 2021
23. El nuevo entorno regulatorio de la protección de datos personales en Chile. https://iapp. org/news/a/el-nuevo-entorno-regulatorio-de-la-proteccion-de-datos-personales-en-chile/#: ~:text=La%20Ley%2021.096%20estableci%C3%B3%20que,condiciones%20que%20dete rmine%20la%20ley.&text=Esa%20ley%20es%20la%2019.628,que%20data%20del%20a% C3%B1o%201999. Accessed 10 Jan 2021
24. Ley 21096: consagra el derecho a protección de los datos personales. https://www.bcn.cl/ley chile/navegar?idNorma=1119730. Accessed 10 Jan 2021
25. Krafft, P.M., Donovan, J.: Disinformation by design: The use of evidence collages and platform filtering in a media manipulation campaign. Polit. Commun. **37**(2), 194–214 (2020)
26. Types of dark pattern. https://www.darkpatterns.org/types-of-dark-pattern. Accessed 10 Jan 2021

27. Falabella. https://www.falabella.com/falabella-cl/. Accessed 10 Jan 2021
28. Paris. https://www.paris.cl/. Accessed 10 Jan 2021
29. Ripley. https://simple.ripley.cl/. Accessed 10 Jan 2021
30. Mercado Libre. https://www.mercadolibre.cl/. Accessed 10 Jan 2021

Heuristics for Programming Codes

Jenny Morales[1]([⊠]) [iD] and Cristian Rusu[2] [iD]

[1] Facultad de Ingeniería, Universidad Autónoma de Chile, Av. 5 Poniente 1670,
3460000 Talca, Chile
jmoralesb@uautonoma.cl
[2] Pontificia Universidad Católica de Valparaíso, Av. Brasil 2241, 2340000 Valparaíso, Chile
cristian.rusu@pucv.cl

Abstract. A programming code includes statements written in a programming language and specifies a series of instructions that are processed in a computer to perform a specific task. The programming codes created over time are often reused and/or require maintenance. In both cases, the programmer's work is a difficult task to carry out if the programming codes are poorly written and documented, without following principles such as simplicity and order. User eXperience (UX) considers the perceptions of the users related to the use of products, systems, or services. In a broader approach, Customer eXperience (CX) refers to a person's interactions with various artifacts (products, systems, and services). A specific case of UX is the concept of the Programmer eXperience (PX). We can consider that the programmer is, to a certain degree, a "user" of programming codes, and the programmer could also be considered as a "customer" that is using several artifacts. We present the development of a set of heuristics that incorporate elements of usability and UX to evaluate the programming codes. The heuristics were developed under the methodology established by Quiñones et al. This methodology establishes 8 steps that allow obtaining a set of heuristics in a specific domain. Based on the methodology, we obtained a set of 8 heuristics aimed to evaluate the usability/UX for programming codes. We performed an initial validation, and the results are encouraging. However, we think that the set of heuristics requires further validation and can still be refined.

Keywords: Programming codes · Programmer eXperience · Usability · User eXperience · Customer eXperience · Heuristic evaluation

1 Introduction

The programming codes over time need to be maintained. This maintenance activity involves code reading and understanding its logical structure. Following principles such as readability, simplicity, and order help code understandability and facilitate its maintenance [1].

Various programming codes are available to programmers, such as Application Programming Interface (API), which are widely used. We found studies related to usability in APIs [2]. Also, we found sets of heuristics to evaluate the usability of the APIs [3, 4].

© Springer Nature Switzerland AG 2021
G. Meiselwitz (Ed.): HCII 2021, LNCS 12774, pp. 437–449, 2021.
https://doi.org/10.1007/978-3-030-77626-8_29

User eXperience (UX) considers perceptions of the users related to the use of products, systems, or services [5]. One of the key factors of UX is usability.

We developed a set of heuristics to evaluate the usability and UX of programming codes. The methodology followed to develop the heuristics was proposed by Quiñones et al. [6]. This methodology establishes 8 steps that allow obtaining a set of heuristics in a specific domain. We followed this methodology, and we obtained a set of 8 heuristics. This set was submitted to an initial validation through a survey; the results obtained were positive. However, we consider that the set of heuristics can be further validated and refined.

The paper is organized as follows: Sect. 2 introduces the background; Sect. 3 describes the methodology that we used, and the development of the set of heuristics; finally, in Sect. 4 we present conclusions and future work.

2 Background

2.1 User eXperience

The User eXperience (UX) considers various aspects of daily life. Garrett exposes it as "the experience the product creates for the people who use it in the real world" [7]. The ISO 9241–210 defines it as follows: "user's perceptions and responses that result from the use and/or anticipated use of a system, product, or service" [5]. Several models of UX have been proposed; one of them was proposed by Morville [8]. The model identifies 7 UX factors: (i) useful, it satisfies a need; (ii) usable, that is easy to use; (iii) desirable, that is attractive to the user; (iv) findable, that facilitates finding information; (v) accessible, the system can be used by different users with different capacities; (vi) credible, it must be trustworthy for the user; and (vii) valuable, it must provide value for the user.

We use this model in the development of heuristics considering six of the seven aspects. In this case we did not consider accessibility, as it is outside the scope of this work.

2.2 Usability

Usability is not a one-dimensional concept, according to Nielsen [9]; it is associated with 5 attributes, that are learning, efficiency, memorability, errors, and subjective satisfaction. The definition of usability has changed over time, initially it was defined only based on software, considering the following sub-attributes: understandable, learnable, and operable [10]. The ISO 9241–11 standard defines usability as "the extent to which a system, product or service can be used by specified users to achieve specified goals with effectiveness, efficiency and satisfaction in a specified context of use" [11]. This definition refers to a broad range of artifacts, including systems, products and services.

2.3 Heuristic Evaluation

Heuristics express usability principles, which are grouped into sets. There are general sets such as the one proposed by Nielsen [12], that can be used when evaluating any kind of interactive software system. Specific heuristics were proposed for specific domains, such as programming environments [13], mobile devices [14], among others.

Heuristic sets are used when performing a heuristic evaluation (HE). HE is an inspection method in which experts review an interface and judge its compliance with usability principles [15]. The heuristic evaluation process contemplates a group of experts who carry out individual activities that are later articulated in group work. HE based on specific set of heuristics usually generates better results than generic heuristics [16].

2.4 Programming Codes

Programming codes are instructions written by the programmer, expressed in a specific programming language. These instructions have a logical order, the number of instructions is finite, and also have the purpose of solving a problem. To run the programming code the computer compile or translate, depending on the language used by the programmer.

The programmer performs various tasks, including writing the programming codes and performing code maintenance [1]. Code maintenance is a difficult task because programmers must read the code and truly understand it. If the code is difficult to read, the task becomes more complex; for this reason, studies to improve the ability of programmers to write readable code have been carried out [17].

2.5 Programmer eXperience

The Programmer eXperience (PX) takes as reference a model and broader definition that is the User eXperience. The PX considers technical and social skills, as well as motivational components. Motivation can be influenced by the tools used and tasks that the programmer performs [1]. Considering the above, programmers are specific users and consumer of certain products such as website design templates, APIs, programming environments, among others. Usability is an important element within the UX. We found usability studies of APIs [2, 18], in addition to heuristic evaluation studies of APIs [3, 4]. The above shows concern for the PX, and the usability of programming codes.

3 Heuristics Development

3.1 Methodology

The methodology proposed by Quiñones et al. [6] allows developing set of usability and/or UX heuristics. This methodology proposes eight stages to be implemented flexibly, which can be done iteratively, overlapping, or skipping steps. The steps of the methodology are explained in Table 1.

3.2 Development Process

We started the process of developing the heuristics under the methodology described above (Sect. 3.1). In stage 1, we performed a search for information related to programming codes. We found several important features such as those related to the order and

Table 1. Steps of the methodology proposed by Quiñones et al. [6].

N°	Stage	Definition
1	Exploratory	Literature review must be carried out in relation to the specific domain, in which the set of heuristics is to be developed
2	Experimental	Collect additional information to that found in the literature review by conducting experiments
3	Descriptive	The information previously collected should be selected and prioritized
4	Correlational	Make the correlation among the characteristics found, attributes of usability and user experience, and the existing heuristics
5	Selection	In relation to the existing heuristics and the attributes considered, the decision must be made which heuristics must be maintained, modified, eliminated, or created, to form the new set
6	Specification	Detail each of the heuristics that make up the new set. The methodology suggests a template
7	Validation	The validation of the heuristics is carried out through experiments that consider various success criteria to validate the new set
8	Refinement	The refinement of the proposed set must be carried out considering the results of the validation stage

readability of the code. Concerning the set of heuristics, we found two sets aimed to evaluate APIs. The set proposed by Grill et al. (Table 2) includes 16 heuristics used to evaluate an API [4]. The set proposed by Mosqueira-Rey et al. (Table 3) contains 45 heuristics grouped into categories [3].

In stage 2, we conducted a brief interview about programming codes. Five experienced programmers with more than 10 years of experience in different languages and programming environments participated in the interview. The purpose was to collect relevant information from the professionals who are users of programming codes. The majority of the programmers considered important the following features: (i) indentation and order in the code; (ii) documentation within the code through comments; (iii) choice of representative names of the functions and/or variables, reflecting the context of the problem; (iv) modularity, related to functions or procedures created to solve specific problems separately; (v) simplify the code, avoiding multilevel inheritance, or code representations that can be described more simply and briefly; (vi) follow the logical structure of the program, that is, use the most logical places within the code where the definitions, classes, methods, functions, among others, must be located; and (vii) use adequate data types about the problem or specific information.

Following the methodology, in stage 3 and 4, the information collected in the previous stages was ordered and prioritized. A correlation was established among the features found in the descriptive stage, the selected attributes or aspects, and the sets of heuristics found in the exploratory stage. We obtained the detail of those characteristics that are covered by heuristics and those that are not.

Table 2. Set of heuristics proposed by Grill et al. [4].

N°	Heuristic	Definition
1	Complexity	An API should not be too complex. Complexity and flexibility should be balanced. Use abstraction
2	Naming	Names should be self-documenting and used consistently
3	Caller's perspective	Make the code readable, e.g. makeTV (Color) is better than makeTV (true)
4	Documentation	Provide documentation and examples
5	Consistency and conventions	Design consistent APIs (order of parameters, call semantics) and obey conventions (get/set methods)
6	Conceptual correctness	Help programmers to use an API properly by using correct elements
7	Method parameters and return type	Do not use many parameters. Return values should indicate result of the method. Use exceptions when exceptional processing is demanded
8	Parametrized constructor	Always provide default constructor and setters rather than constructor with multiple parameters
9	Factory pattern	Use factory pattern only when inevitable
10	Data types	Choose correct data types. Do not force users to use casting avoid using strings if better type exists
11	Concurrency	Anticipate concurrent access in mind
12	Error handling and exceptions	Define class members as public only when necessary. Exceptions should be handled near where it occurred. Error message should convey sufficient information
13	Leftovers for client code	Make the user type as few codes as possible
14	Multiple ways to do one	Do not provide multiple ways to achieve one thing
15	Long chain of references	Do not use long complex inheritance hierarchies
16	Implementation vs. interface	Interface dependencies should be preferred as they are more flexible

Table 3. Set of heuristics proposed by Mosqueira-Rey et al. [3].

N°	Id	Group	Heuristic
1	KCE-1	Knowability – clarity– clarity of elements	Names should be self-explanatory
2	KCE-2	Knowability – clarity– clarity of elements	Data types should be as specific as possible to make the code more readable
3	KCS-1	Knowability – clarity – clarity of structure	Inheritance hierarchies should not be too deep
4	KCS-2	Knowability – clarity – clarity of structure	When reading code that uses the API, it should be easy to understand what that code does
5	KCS-3	Knowability – clarity – clarity of structure	Do not expose core API functionality through secondary elements (attributes, annotations, etc.)
6	KCS-4	Knowability – clarity – clarity of structure	If the API is open source, the internal implementation should be also readable
7	KCS-5	Knowability – clarity – clarity of structure	The API should be loosely coupled
8	KCS-6	Knowability – clarity – clarity of structure	The different API elements (classes, methods, etc.) should be placed in the most logical place to be and where users expect to find them
9	KCF-1	Knowability – clarity – clarity in functioning	Functions should focus on doing one thing
10	KCF-2	Knowability – clarity – clarity in functioning	Functions should perform only the tasks described in their names
11	KCF-3	Knowability – clarity – clarity in functioning	When writing code, it should be easy to know what classes and methods of the API to use
12	KCF-4	Knowability – clarity – clarity in functioning	It should be possible to check where you are in a given scenario
13	KC-1	Knowability – consistency	The API should be consistent with itself
14	KC-2	Knowability – consistency	The API should be consistent with standard conventions
15	KC-3	Knowability – consistency	The API should be highly cohesive
16	KM-1	Knowability – memorability	The API should be easy to remember
17	KM-2	Knowability – memorability	The API should follow the terminology of the field

(*continued*)

Table 3. (*continued*)

N°	Id	Group	Heuristic
18	KHS-1	Knowability – helpfulness – suitability of documentation content	Every element of the API should be documented
19	KHS-2	Knowability – helpfulness – suitability of documentation content	Documentation and comments should only include relevant information
20	KHS-3	Knowability – helpfulness – suitability of documentation content	The API should properly identify deprecated classes and methods
21	KHS-4	Knowability – helpfulness – suitability of documentation content	The API should supply helpful error information and, if possible, suggest a solution
22	KHS-5	Knowability – helpfulness – suitability of documentation content	The API documentation should include code samples for the most common scenarios
23	OC-1	Operability – completeness	The API should provide the functionalities necessary to implement the tasks intended by the user
24	OC-2	Operability – completeness	The API should maintain backwards compatibility deprecating functions in a clear way
25	OP-1	Operability – precision	Numeric data types should be as precise as necessary
26	OP-2	Operability – precision	Data types should be as conceptually precise as necessary
27	OU-1	Operability – universality	The API should avoid the use of elements (units, formats, spellings, etc.) that are not universally recognized
28	OF-1	Operability – flexibility	The API should be easy to change
29	OFC-1	Operability – flexibility – controllability – workflow controllability – freedom in tasks	The API should not force users to make irreversible decisions without all the information available
30	OFC-2	Operability – flexibility – controllability – workflow controllability – reversibility	The API should allow reverting actions and returning to a previous state
31	EH-1	Efficiency – efficiency in human effort/task execution time	The level of abstraction of the API should be adequate for the users and the domain

(*continued*)

Table 3. (*continued*)

N°	Id	Group	Heuristic
32	EH-2	Efficiency – efficiency in human effort/task execution time	The API should require the user to type as little as possible
33	EH-3	Efficiency – efficiency in human effort/task execution time	If the API must be complex, establish layers of complexity for beginners and advanced users
34	ET-1	Efficiency – efficiency in task execution time	The API should not force the user to take actions that would affect performance
35	ER-1	Efficiency – efficiency in tied-up resources	The API should not excessively occupy limited resources
36	EC-1	Efficiency – efficiency in economic costs	The economic costs derived from using the API (if any) should be reasonable
37	RI-1	Robustness – robustness to internal error	The API should not have bugs in its functioning
38	RU-1	Robustness – robustness to improper use/third-party abuse	The API should allow detecting and managing errors without breaking the execution or leaving the error undetected
39	RU-2	Robustness – robustness to improper use/third-party abuse	The API should facilitate managing non common but correct situations without generating exceptions or forcing users to catch them
40	RU-3	Robustness – robustness to improper use/third-party abuse	The API should not expose vulnerabilities that would allow users to make errors
41	SUL-1	Safety – user safety/third-party safety – legal	The API should not put the user into legal trouble
42	SUL-2	Safety – user safety/third-party safety – legal	The API should clearly state its license of use
43	SUC-1	Safety – user safety/third-party safety – user confidentiality	The API should not compromise the confidentiality of the users' personal information
44	SUA-1	Safety – user safety/third-party safety – safety of user assets	The API should not compromise the security of the users' assets
45	SI-1	Subjective satisfaction – interest/aesthetics	Using the API should be satisfying

In stage 5 we decided actions like to create, adapt, maintain or eliminate the heuristics found in stage 1. In addition, we identified the applicability of each heuristic.

In relation to the set of heuristics showed in Table 2:

- We eliminated: heuristic 1, heuristic 5 and 6, heuristic 8 and 9, and heuristic 11 to 16.
- We adapted: heuristic 2 to 4, heuristic 7, and heuristic 10.

In relation to the set of heuristics showed in Table 3:

- We eliminated: heuristic 4 and 5, heuristic 7, heuristic 10 to 13, heuristic 15 and 16, heuristic 18, heuristic 20 to 25, and heuristic 27 to 45.
- We adapted: heuristic 1 to 3, heuristic 6, heuristic 8 and 9, heuristic 14, heuristic 17, heuristic 19, and heuristic 26.

Also, we created an additional heuristic to cover all the usability/UX features found in stages 1 and 2.

Table 4. Set of heuristics for programming codes.

ID	Heuristics	Description	Action
PC-1	Names self-explanatory	In the code the names of the variables, methods, among others, should be representative of the context of the problem	Adapted
PC-2	Data types specific	Data types should be as specific as possible, adjusting adequately to the type of data it represents and the operations that can be performed with them	Adapted
PC-3	Simplify the code	The code should be as simple as possible, avoiding inheritance of multiple levels, using an adequate number of parameters (no more than necessary), thus allowing an easier reading of the code	Adapted
PC-4	Follow the logical structure	The different elements in the codes (classes, methods, etc.) should be placed in the most logical location and where users expect to find them	Adapted
PC-5	Modularity	Functions and methods should focus on doing one thing	Adapted
PC-6	Consistent	The codes must be consistent and follow the conventions	Adapted
PC-7	Documentation and comments	Documentation within the code through comments must include relevant information	Adapted
PC-8	Aesthetic code	The code must be indented and in order	Created

In stage 6, we obtained the set of heuristics for the specific domain, programming codes. We used the abbreviation PC (Programming Codes) to identify the set of heuristics obtained. This set was formed with 8 heuristics, in Table 4 we can see detail of each one of them.

To describe the heuristics, we used the template proposed in the methodology proposed by Quiñones et al., which considers the following aspects: (i) id, which is the identifier associated with each heuristic; (ii) name, which is a representative and brief name of the heuristic; (iii) definition, a definition of the heuristic; (iv) explanation, a more extensive explanation of the heuristic and its compliance; (v) example figure, image showing the compliance of the heuristic as an example; (vi) benefits, the benefits are expressed has heuristic compliance; (vii) usability attributes and/or UX aspects, identifies the usability/UX aspects related to the heuristic; (viii) set of heuristics related, if the heuristics is based on an existing heuristic, it can be indicated in this section.

In Table 5, we can see an example of the definition of heuristic. The heuristic shown is Consistency, which was an adapted one, based on the set of heuristics proposed by Mosqueira-Rey et al. [3].

Table 5. Heuristic "Consistent".

Id	PC-6
Priority	3
Name	Consistent
Definition	The codes must be consistent and follow the conventions
Explanation	The denomination of variables, functions, classes, methods, among others, must follow writing conventions regarding the use of capitals, small letters, hyphens and / or numbers
Example figure	
Benefits	It facilitates the reading and understanding of the code. In addition to improve the visual aspect and facilitate the understanding of the meanings
Usability/UX attribute	Desirable (UX), Memorability (Usability)
Set of heuristics related	Mosqueira-Rey et al. [3]

Finally, in stage 7 we carried out an initial validation of the proposed set through a survey. The questionnaire was answered by five professionals with previous experience in at least one heuristic evaluation. The objective of the questionnaire was to evaluate the heuristics presented, in relation to useful, clarity, ease of use, and completeness. Also, we asked about the intention of use in a future heuristic evaluation of the set proposed on usability/UX problems in programming codes. We used a 5-point Likert scale, where the minimum score is 1 for strongly disagree and the maximum is 5 for strongly agree. In this case, 5 then fully meets the dimension. The results are detailed below (see Fig. 1).

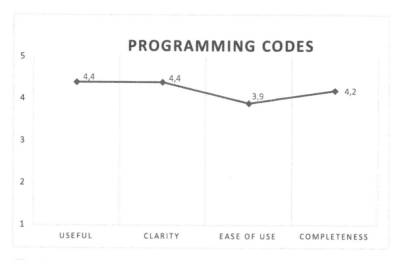

Fig. 1. Results of the validation of the set of heuristics for programming codes.

The set of programming codes obtained good results in general, obtaining in 3 out of 4 items averages equal to or greater than 4. The proposed set was considered useful and clear. Regarding the completeness, the question that evaluates whether the set covers the aspects to evaluate usability/UX in programming codes, the answers were between probably covers, and definitely covers the aspects, which allowed obtaining an average higher than 4. Concerning the ease of linking each heuristic with usability/UX problems in programming codes, the result was slightly lower, so it is an aspect to continue improving in later stages of new validations and refinement of the set.

Regarding intention of use, the participants unanimously responded that they would probably use the proposed set on future evaluations as an instrument to evaluate the usability/UX in programming codes, which is very positive.

4   Conclusion and Future Work

Considering that software maintenance is a complex and demanding activity for the programmer, we consider important to work on programming codes usability/UX. In this work we present a set of 8 heuristics developed under a formal methodology, to evaluate programming codes usability/UX aspects. During the development process of creating the heuristics, we found aspects such as readability, documentation and order are relevant. In addition, sets of heuristics were found to evaluate the usability of the APIs. However, we did not find sets to evaluate the usability of programming codes (in an overview not related to an API).

Following the methodology, we covered until the validation stage. We performed an initial validation by consulting professionals with experience in heuristic evaluation. In most dimensions we obtained good results, only in the ease of linking the heuristic with the problem we obtained a slightly better average result. However, we believe that the results achieved are positive and reinforce the idea that the development of the heuristics was carried out properly and considering the relevant aspects of the programming codes.

In future works, we intend to validate the heuristics with other type of experiment, such as a heuristic evaluation. This would help us to further refine the current set of heuristics.

Acknowledgment. We are grateful to all experts that participated in the survey. We also thank to Quimval SPA which provided example figures.

References

1. Morales, J., Rusu, C., Botella, F., Quiñones, D.: Programmer eXperience: a systematic literature review. IEEE Access **7**, 71079–71094 (2019)
2. Zibran, M.: What makes APIs difficult to use. Int. J. Comput. Sci. Netw. Secur. **8**(4), 255–261 (2008)
3. Mosqueira-Rey, E., Alonso-Ríos, D., Moret-Bonillo, V., Fernández-Varela, I., Álvarez-Estévez, D.: A systematic approach to API usability: taxonomy-derived criteria and a case study. Inf. Softw. Technol. **97**, 46–63 (2018)
4. Grill, T., Polacek, O., Tscheligi, M.: Methods towards API usability: a structural analysis of usability problem categories. In: Winckler, M., Forbrig, P., Bernhaupt, R. (eds.) Human-Centered Software Engineering. Lecture Notes in Computer Science, pp. 164–180. Springer, Heidelberg (2012). https://doi.org/10.1007/978-3-642-34347-6_10
5. ISO 9241–210. Ergonomics of human-system interaction- Part 11: usability: definitions and concepts. International Organization for Standardization, Geneva (2018)
6. Quiñones, D., Rusu, C., Rusu, V.: A methodology to develop usability/user experience heuristics. Comput. Stand. Interfaces **59**, 109–129 (2018)
7. Garrett, J.J.: The Elements of User Experience: User-Centered Design for the Web and Beyond, 2nd ed. Pearson Education (2010)
8. Morville, P.: User experience honeycomb. http://semanticstudios.com/user_experience_design/. Accessed 7 Jan 2021
9. Nielsen, J.: Usability Engineering. AP Professional (1993)
10. Pressman, R.: Ingeniería de Software. Un enfoque práctico, 7ma ed. McGraw-Hill (2010)
11. ISO 9241–11. Ergonomics of human-system interaction- Part 11: Usability: Definitions and concepts. International Organization for Standardization, Geneva (2018)
12. Nielsen Norman Group. 10 usability heuristics for user interface design. https://www.nngroup.com/articles/ten-usability-heuristics/. Accessed 7 Jan 2021
13. Morales, J., Rusu, C., Botella, F., Quiñones, D.: Programmer experience: a set of heuristics for programming environments. In: Meiselwitz, G. (ed.) Social Computing and Social Media. Participation, User Experience, Consumer Experience, and Applications of Social Computing. Lecture Notes in Computer Science, pp. 205–216. Springer, Cham (2020). https://doi.org/10.1007/978-3-030-49576-3_15

14. Inostroza, R., Rusu, C., Roncagliolo, S., Rusu, V., Collazos, C.A.: Developing SMASH: a set of SMArtphone's uSability Heuristics. Comput. Stand. Interfaces **43**, 40–52 (2016)
15. Nielsen, J.: Usability inspection methods. In: Conference Companion on Human factors in Computing Systems, pp. 413–414. (1994)
16. Quiñones, D., Rusu, C., Roncagliolo, S., Rusu, V., Collazos, C.A.: Developing usability heuristics: a formal or informal process? IEEE Lat. Am. Trans. **14**(7), 3400–3409 (2016)
17. Sedano, T.: Code readability testing, an empirical study. In: 2016 IEEE 29th International Conference on Software Engineering Education and Training (CSEET), pp. 111–117. IEEE (2016)
18. Zibran, M.F., Eishita, F.Z., Roy, C.K.: Useful, but usable? Factors affecting the usability of APIs. In: 2011 18th Working Conference on Reverse Engineering, pp. 151–155. IEEE (2011)

Why Do We Love Coffee Even Though It Is Bitter?

Takanobu Nakahara[✉]

School of Commerce, Senshu University, 3-8 Kanda Jinbocho,
Chiyoda-ku, Tokyo, Japan
nakapara@isc.senshu-u.ac.jp
http://www.nakapara.jp

Abstract. Sensory evaluation by taste sensitivity measurement differs depending on the evaluator, which means that there is a gap between the coffee that the average consumer finds tasty and the coffee that experts evaluate positively.

In this study, I used data from taste sensor measurements of coffee and a questionnaire survey of ordinary coffee drinkers to identify the characteristics of coffees with a high satisfaction level. The taste sensor uses a sebum film to identify and measure tastes, such as sourness, initial bitterness, initial astringency, umami, and after astringency. In the questionnaire survey, I asked the participants to select words to evaluate their coffee in order to show that even ordinary consumers can clearly evaluate the taste of coffee.

These data were used to develop a LASSO regression model to clarify the differences between high and low satisfaction coffees. The model obtained was sufficiently interpretable, and its discriminant accuracy was also high.

Results indicated that general consumers, prefer the fruity characteristics of coffee, such as aroma and mildness, rather than bitterness.

Keywords: Taste of coffee · Taste sensor · Verbal evaluation · LASSO regression

1 Introduction

In the past, research on taste has been conducted mainly by human sensory evaluation to measure taste. However, there is a difference in preferences between experts who perform sensory evaluation and ordinary consumers. While experts have sufficient knowledge and experience, and their evaluation ability is superior to that of ordinary consumers, general consumers have large individual differences in sensitivity, preference, and sense of value. These differences influence their overall preferences.

For example, in laboratory experiments with ordinary consumers, there is a context problem, where the laboratory context is very different from their usual drinking context. Their preferences are affected by that context. The same problem arose in the design of experiments I previously conducted to evaluate the taste of coffee [1].

© Springer Nature Switzerland AG 2021
G. Meiselwitz (Ed.): HCII 2021, LNCS 12774, pp. 450–460, 2021.
https://doi.org/10.1007/978-3-030-77626-8_30

The present study aims to identify the factors that affect the taste of coffee through a questionnaire survey on coffee with ordinary consumers. People perceive "deliciousness" when evaluating taste and a combination of the five senses: touch, sight, hearing, smell, and taste. They can smell the aroma of food, see the colors of foods, and hear the sound of chewing. Moreover, the context and their physical condition at the time of eating or drinking also affect the perceived taste of food.

Therefore, in the present study, I conducted a continuous questionnaire survey to consider consumers' usual coffee drinking conditions. In addition to the survey, the taste of coffees was quantitatively analyzed using a measurement device called a taste sensor in order to model the consumers' evaluations of deliciousness.

2   Analysis Framework

To clarify the factors that affect the deliciousness of coffee, this section describes the evaluation of coffee by a questionnaire survey and the measurement of coffee components by a taste sensor.

2.1   Taste Sensor

To quantitatively evaluate the taste of coffee, we used the TS-5000Z taste sensor (Fig. 1) from Intelligent Sensor Technology, Inc. Taste sensors use artificial lipid membranes that are used to detect and quantify food taste, similar to how the human tongue detects food components. The artificial lipid membrane utilizes four sensors to identify umami, acidity, bitterness, and astringency. The evaluation items were acidity, initial bitterness, initial astringency, umami, after bitterness, after astringency, and richness of the aftertaste The last three items represent the lingering taste in the mouth.

Table 1 shows the ten of 98 data by samples measured by the taste sensor. There were nine coffee samples, labeled from 1 to 9, in addition to a control sample labeled C1. During measurement, the value of the control sample was used as the standard. In the table, each measured value is expressed as a relative value; that is, the difference between the value of the control sample and that of the sample. For example, sample 7 has high acidity and high initial astringency.

Measurements of each sample were taken four times, and the average of the last three measurements was taken as the sensor measurement value of the sample. The control sample was UCC Gold Special (UCC Ueshima Coffee Co., Ltd.), which is the best-selling regular coffee in Japan. A total of 98 different coffee samples were measured.

Fig. 1. Taste sensor TS-5000z

Table 1. Measurements taken by the taste sensor

Sample	Acidity	Umami	Richness	Bitterness (initial)	Astringency (initial)	Bitterness (after)	Astringency (after)
C1	0	0	0	0	0	0	0
1	0.54	−0.35	−0.1	1.44	−0.59	1.48	−0.94
2	3.48	−1.06	0.5	1.68	0.44	0.7	0.51
3	2.96	−0.74	2.55	2.82	1.23	0.8	0.31
4	2.15	−0.66	0.94	2.99	0.81	1.74	0.82
5	−3.42	1.16	1.49	3.23	−0.18	5.21	0.3
6	3.9	−1.2	0.75	0.95	0.85	−0.18	0.31
7	6.65	−2.54	1.29	0.8	2.25	−2.64	1.45
8	2.53	−0.47	1.66	2.35	1.15	1.25	0.36
9	−0.24	0.78	1.53	3.46	1.04	3.86	0.9

Figure 2 shows the measurement values of a French roast coffee, which is a dark roast coffee. Both initial and after bitterness have higher values than the other evaluated items. Note that the values for all items were zero in the control sample. This method demonstrates that taste sensors can be used for measurements that quantitatively evaluate the taste of coffee.

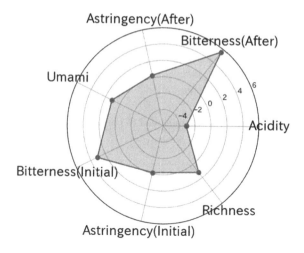

Fig. 2. The measured values of French roast coffee

2.2 Questionnaire Survey

The survey consisted of two parts: food preferences and individual coffee drinking habits and opinions. The food preferences questionnaire survey was conducted only once with each participant. The coffee drinking questionnaire survey was conducted multiple surveys with the participants who drank multiple coffees that were also measured by the taste sensor.

Table 2 shows an overview of the questionnaire on food preferences. Coffee preference was rated using a 5-point scale, and food preferences were rated using a 9-point scale. The questionnaire also asked about demographic data: occupation (14 types), sex, and age.

Table 2. Overview of the questionnaire survey on food preferences

Questions	Choices	Remarks
Preference for coffee	Bitterness, acidity, sweetness, richness	5-point scale
Food preference	Cake, lemon, Tabasco, etc. (30 items)	9-point scale
Occupation	Sales, engineering, etc.	14 types
Sex	Male, female	
Age (years)	10–90s	

In the coffee drinking questionnaire survey, a total of 161 responses were received from 38 participants. One participant provided 15 responses, which was the highest number of responses received from an individual participant. The coffee drunk by the highest number of participants (n = 8) was Tokugawa Shogun Coffee (Saza Coffee, Co. Ltd.).

Table 3. Overview of the questionnaire survey on coffee drinking

Questions	Choices	Remarks
Timing of drinking	Immediately after waking up, at breakfast, etc. (7 options)	
Emotion	Nervous, happy, etc. (20 options)	5-point scale
Coffee temperature	Hot, iced	
Drinking method	Black, sugar, milk, etc. (5 options)	
Coffee strength	Very strong - weak	4-point scale
Hunger	Hungry - full	5-point scale
Tiredness	Tired - energized	5-point scale
Storage	Frozen, refrigerated, room temperature	
Eaten together with	Bread, sweets, none, other	
Words to describe	Fruity, sharp, rich, etc. (35 options)	
Satisfaction	Satisfied - dissatisfied	5-point scale

Table 3 shows the contents of the questionnaire on coffee drinking. This survey was taken after the participants drank coffee. In the survey, the participants were asked to indicate the timing of drinking, their mood at the time of drinking, coffee temperature (hot or iced), their level of hunger, their level of tiredness, storage (frozen, refrigerated, or room temperature), foods eaten together with coffee, words to describe the taste of the coffee, and their satisfaction level.

The participants were provided with 35 different words to describe the taste of coffee, and they selected two or more words that corresponded to their evaluation of the coffee that they had just drunk. The most frequently used word to describe the coffee was "refreshing", which was selected 46 times. The next most frequently used words to describe the coffee were "full-bodied" (40 times) and "fragrant" (38 times). Using these expressions, I constructed a model to clarify the differences in the words used to describe coffee that was rated with high satisfaction versus low satisfaction.

3   Modeling

LASSO regression, a method of variable selection and regularization to enhance prediction accuracy, is used to construct a model for identifying coffee characteristics [2]. With the dependent variable in the classification model represented as $y \in \{0, 1\}$ (0: negative, 1: positive) and with the p explanatory variable vectors represented as $\mathbf{x} = (x_1, x_2, \cdots, x_p)$, the LASSO regression model is given by Eq. (1):

$$\Pr(y = 1|\mathbf{x}) = f\left(\boldsymbol{\beta}^\top \mathbf{x} + \beta_0\right), \tag{1}$$

where $f(\cdot)$ is a logistic function defined as $f(a) = 1/(1 + \exp(-a))$; $\boldsymbol{\beta} \in \mathbb{R}^p$ is a regression coefficient vector and $\beta_0 \in \mathbb{R}$ is a constant term, and both are estimated from training samples. The penalized estimation method gives the least-squares method a penalty for β and solves the minimization problem argmin $\{||y - \beta^T x||_2^2 + \lambda||\beta||_1$.

4   Calculation Experiment

4.1   Coffee Analysis Using the Taste Sensor Measurements

We obtained measurement values of 98 different kinds of coffee, as shown in Table 1. To capture the trends of these coffees, k-means clustering was applied to classify the coffees into four clusters using the measured values, and the results are shown in Fig. 3.

The values in the radar charts are the average values of each cluster. Figure 3(a) shows the average of 20 coffees classified into a cluster having high acidity, astringency, and low bitterness. Figure 3(b) shows the average of 13 coffees in a cluster with both high initial and high after bitterness and low acidity. Figure 3(c) shows the cluster with the highest number of coffees (n = 54), classified as having low values and no outstanding characteristics. Figure 3(d) shows a cluster of 11 coffees with high average values overall, which indicates that these coffees are well-balanced. Ultimately, this study develops a model of the relationship between the characteristics of coffee and the taste of coffee.

4.2   Analysis of Responses to the Coffee Drinking Questionnaire

Here we present the results of a fundamental analysis of coffee drinking using a total of 161 questionnaire surveys involving 38 participants. Among all the participants, the frequency of drinking black coffee was 93%, that of adding milk and sugar was 7%, that of drinking hot coffee was 87%, and that of drinking iced coffee was 13%. The most common timing of drinking coffee was between lunch and dinner (n = 81), between breakfast and lunch (n = 45), and at breakfast (n = 21). The values of hunger status while drinking coffee are shown in Table 4. The frequency of each hunger state was similar and fullness was related to the timing of drinking, possibly reflecting that the coffee might have been consumed after a meal. The values of tiredness status while drinking coffee are shown in Table 5. Most of the respondents were somewhat tired or neither tired nor energized, and somewhat energized.

The frequency of words used to describe coffee in the evaluation is shown in Table 6. The participants were asked to select two or more words for one type of coffee they drank. Satisfaction level was rated using a 5-point scale, where high satisfaction was indicated by 5 and 4, and low satisfaction was indicated by 3, 2, and 1. The relationship between the selected words and the evaluation of the coffee was examined. For example, the first word "refreshing" was used 46 times, and in 80 By this method, it was clear that most of the words were used when the level of satisfaction was high. On the other hand, words such as "watery" and "monotonous" were used when the level of satisfaction was low.

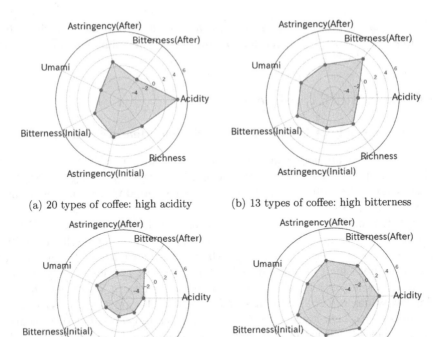

(a) 20 types of coffee: high acidity   (b) 13 types of coffee: high bitterness

(c) 54 types of coffee: low individuality   (d) 11 types of coffee: emphasis on balance

Fig. 3. Results of clustering coffees according to similar measured values

Table 4. Hunger state

Q12_How hungry	Freq.
Full	21
Somewhat full	53
Neither	36
Somewhat hungry	40
Hungry	11

Table 5. Tiredness state

Q13_How tired	Freq.
Tired	7
Somewhat tired	53
Neither	53
Somewhat energized	41
Energized	7

Table 6. Selected words in the coffee evaluation

Words	Frequency	Low satisfaction	High satisfaction
Refreshing	46	0.2	**0.8**
Full-bodied	40	0.12	**0.88**
Fragrant	39	0.051	**0.95**
Freshing	36	0.22	**0.78**
Well-balanced	36	0.056	**0.94**
Acidity	34	0.21	**0.79**
Light	34	0.38	**0.62**
Flavorful	33	0.03	**0.97**
Lingers on the tongue	33	0.33	**0.67**
Bitter	31	0.45	**0.55**
Mild	29	0.17	**0.83**
Savory	28	0.14	**0.86**
Strong taste	28	0.32	**0.68**
Smooth	27	0.26	**0.74**
Fruity	25	0.08	**0.92**
Good texture	24	0.17	**0.83**
Roasted aroma	24	0.21	**0.79**
Mellow	23	0.17	**0.83**
Rich	20	0.1	**0.9**
Deep taste	20	0.05	**0.95**
Soft	19	0.26	**0.74**
Sweet	14	0	**1**
Watery	14	**0.71**	0.29
Sharp	13	0.077	**0.92**
Monotonous	11	**0.64**	0.36
Sharp taste	**11**	0	**1**
Heavy	11	0.27	**0.73**
Relax	11	0.091	**0.91**
Strong	11	0.36	**0.64**
Miscellaneous taste	10	**0.8**	0.2
Flat	9	0.44	**0.56**
Sturdy	9	0.22	**0.78**
Harsh aftertaste	9	**0.89**	0.11
Astringent	5	**0.6**	0.4

4.3 Classification Model

A classification model is constructed using the LASSO regression model described in Sect. 3 using 116 coffees with a high satisfaction level (positive) and 45 with a low satisfaction level (negative). Explanatory variables for constructing the model utilize the values of the questionnaire and the values of the taste sensor explained in Subsect. 2.1. In the model construction, the training and test data were randomly sampled from the overall data set by cross validation. The prediction accuracy was 93.8%, indicating a relatively high accuracy rate.

Table 7. Selected explanatory variables in the model

Explanatory variable	Coefficient
(Intercept)	2.809
Q17_30_sharp taste	1.607
Q17_33_flavorful	1.470
Q17_8_fragrant	1.085
Q17_27_sweet	0.992
Q17_17_well-balanced	0.758
Q17_22_full-bodied	0.502
Initially astringent	0.428
Q17_28_mild	0.407
Q17_13_sharp	0.326
Q7S1_prefer cake	0.173
Q17_25_rich	0.162
Q7S18_prefer vinegared food	0.144
Q17_9_refreshing	0.108
Q7S3_prefer sweet buns	0.096
Q7S21_prefer parsley	0.017
Q7S29_prefer Tabasco	−0.032
Q7S19_prefer black coffee	−0.082
Q17_35_astringent	−0.098
Q17_7_bitter	−0.223
Q2S3_sweetness of coffee	−0.243
Q7S7_prefer potato chips	−0.308
Q13_tiredness	−0.351
Q17_26_miscellaneous taste	−0.769
Q17_19_watery	−1.084
Q17_29_harsh aftertaste	−2.111

Table 7 shows the results for the explanatory variables with coefficient values greater than zero selected by the LASSO penalty. Positive coefficients are the choice factors of coffees with a high satisfaction level, and negative coefficients are the choice factors of coffees with a low satisfaction level. Evaluation words are an important factor as a remarkable explanatory variable for coffee with a high satisfaction level. For example, words such as sharp taste, flavorful, fragrant, sweet, and well-balanced are factors that are associated with coffee with a high satisfaction level, while miscellaneous taste, watery, and harsh aftertaste are factors that are associated with coffee with a low satisfaction level.

In the taste sensor measurements, the initial astringency was found to be a factor that was associated with a high satisfaction level. The astringent taste of coffee is mainly derived from chlorogenic acid. Chlorogenic acid is abundant in green coffee beans, but is decreased in strongly roasted coffee. Many specialty coffees were drunk in this experiment, and the beans of these specialty coffees were relatively lightly roasted, which is a factor in the astringent component that was rated as tasty.

In terms of the other food preferences, those who preferred sweet foods, such as cakes and sweet buns, tended to be more satisfied with coffee than those who did not prefer sweet foods. On the other hand, those who preferred spicy and salty foods, such as Tabasco and potato chips, tended to be less satisfied with coffee than those who did not prefer spicy and salty foods.

These results suggest that coffees with a high satisfaction level are not characterized by bitterness, but are instead characterized by flavor, aroma, sweetness, mildness, and refreshing fruitiness.

5   Conclusion

In this study, we clarified the characteristics of coffee that general consumers find tasty by using quantitative measurement data obtained from a taste sensor and questionnaire surveys carried out after coffee drinking, rather than by a sensory evaluation of coffee.

In our method of asking people to evaluate coffee that they drank by selecting words that described the coffee's taste and aroma, we showed that even ordinary consumers could easily evaluate the taste of coffee. Sharp taste, flavorful, fragrant, sweet, and well-balanced were selected as the words to describe coffees with a high satisfaction level. On the other hand, miscellaneous taste, watery, and harsh aftertaste were selected to describe coffees with a low satisfaction level. These results clearly show that consumers differ in their level of satisfaction depending on the coffee's fruity characteristics, rather than on the bitterness of the coffee.

Acknowledgements. This work was supported by JSPS KAKENHI Grant Number 19H01542.

References

1. Nakahara, T., Kawahara, H., Hamuro, Y.: Design of experiments to evaluate the taste of coffee. In: The Fall National Conference of Operations Research Society of Japan, Abstracts, pp. 74–75 (2015). (In Japanese)
2. Tibshirani, R.: Regression shrinkage and selection via the lasso. J. Roy. Stat. Soc. B **58**, 267–288 (1996)

Effective Social Media Marketing Through Customer Journey Mapping

Marc Oliver Opresnik[✉]

Technische Hochschule Lübeck, Public Corporation, Mönkhofer Weg 239, 23562 Lübeck, Germany
Marc.Oliver.Opresnik@TH-Luebeck.de

Abstract. An essential pre-requisite of effective Social Media Marketing is a profound understanding of customers and their behaviour as this has been subject to dramatic changes.

Social Media marketing is about using social networks and tools to guide prospect (potential) customers through a series of steps – a funnel – to get them to take the desired action, e.g. becoming a new customer and buying the company's product and services, with the end-goal of turning new customers into loyal customers with a high lifetime value.

There are a lot of media tools. With all these Social Media marketing tools at the disposal, how should the company decide which ones fit to optimally to the social media funnel, and in which order they should be used? To answer this question, the company has to know who the potential customers are and how they can be reached most effectively. The social media marketer also has to know about the company's objectives, how it should measure these objectives (i.e. the metrics that should be analyzed) and what numbers should be set for those metrics. The social media funnel provides a comprehensive overview connected to the three stages of a typical customer buying process: Awareness, Engagement and Action.

Keywords: Social media marketing · Marketing planning · Marketing management · Web 2.0 · Marketing 4.0 · Integrated marketing communication · Social computing · Social media · Customer journey mapping · Customer touchpoint management

1 Online Segmentation of B2C and B2B Markets

Connected buyers toggle between online and offline channels to research, evaluate and buy products and to get customer service assistance, share experiences with others, and engage with brands and other shoppers. Global e-commerce sales account for only about 10% of all retail sales worldwide, but still digital marketing plays an important role in buyer behavior.

Once target segments are selected, analysis of buyer personas and customer journeys can be used to help understand the preferences, characteristics and online behaviours of different target customers, in order to make relevant segmentation procedures on the B2C market.

G. Meiselwitz (Ed.): HCII 2021, LNCS 12774, pp. 461–469, 2021.
https://doi.org/10.1007/978-3-030-77626-8_31

A buyer persona is a snapshot of a prototypical customer in the target segment. It tells the buyer's story using the information you used for segmentation (i.e. demographic, geographic, psychographic, benefit sought, occasion and behavior). With personas, marketers are better able to identify, understand, acquire, engage, and retain the target audience.

Today's online reality can be captured by describing customer decision processes in the context of a digital ecosystem, which recognizes a variety of influence sources, channels, behaviours, decision points, and experiences. We call this expanded view a customer journey. The details of customer decision-making are captured by the customer journey map-ping, which reflect how people travel through online and offline decision stages, which represent the series of interactions and touchpoints a customer has with a specific brand to accomplish typical tasks such as ordering, returning a product, or requesting an after-sales-service, such as a repair. The touchpoints are the individual online and offline interactions potential customers have before, during and after purchase of the product or service. Marketers care about touchpoints because they represent opportunities for customers and prospects to learn, have a positive experience, and form attitudes and associations about a brand that could lead to future purchases, brand loyalty and positive (digital) Word-of-Mouth (WOM) communication [1].

Like B2C industries, B2B buyer behavior (and segmentation) can be viewed as a buyer journey. Also, the principles of 'Buyer Personas' can be used on the B2B market.

Suppliers must ensure that relevant information about their solutions are findable, during the online information search stage. B2B buyers are often using a lot of time to search for the relevant supplier regarding a specific solution. The suppliers can help their potential customers in this process. For example, Monsanto (agrochemical & biotechnology company, acquired by Bayer in 2018) created an online brand community for its potential customers to provide complementary advice on product selection and business optimization strategies. A comparison engine (comparing key competitors' solutions) could provide information on energy requirements, installation costs, expected maintenance, lifetime ownership costs and other evaluation criteria for major competitors. In doing so, Monsanto positioned itself as a valuable partner and expert resource rather than one of many commodity suppliers.

Relevant B2B segmentation might be done according to the composition of the DMU (Decision Making Unit) and the needs among the different members in the DMU. Different members of the DMU may have different need for supplier information. Some DMU members may prefer a buyer journey without too much personal interaction with the suppliers' sales reps and may prefer digital 'self-services' with digitally enabled human interactions. Other DMU members may prefer a more personal face-to-face interaction with the supplier's sales reps [2].

Few companies have either the resources or the inclination to operate in all, or even most, of the countries in the world. Although some large organizations, such as Coca-Cola or Sony, sell products in more than 200 countries, most international firms focus on a smaller set. Operating in many countries presents new challenges as different countries may vary greatly in their economic, cultural, and political form. Thus, just as they do within their domestic markets, international companies need to group their world markets into segments with distinct buying need and behaviors and select appropriate target countries.

The assessment of international marketing opportunities usually begins with a screening process that involves gathering relevant information on each country and filtering out the less desirable countries. A 'top-down' model for selecting foreign markets is shown in Hollensen [3].

This model includes a series of four filters to screen out countries. The overwhelming number of market opportunities makes it necessary to break the process down into a series of steps. Although a firm does not want to miss a potential opportunity, it cannot conduct extensive market research studies in every country of the world.

The screening process is used to identify good prospects. Two common errors of country screening are (1) ignoring countries that offer good potential for the company's products and (2) spending too much time investigating countries that are poor prospects. Thus, the screening process allows an international company to focus efforts quickly on a few of the most promising market opportunities, by using published secondary sources available.

The first stage of the selection process uses macro variables to discriminate between regions and countries that represent basic opportunities and countries with little or no opportunity or with excessive risk. Macro variables describe the total market in terms of economic, social, geographic and political information. Often macroeconomic statistics indicate that the country is too small, as demonstrated by its gross national (or domestic) product. It may be that the gross national product seems large enough, but the personal disposable income per household may be too low. Political instability can also be used to remove a country from the set of possible opportunities.

In the second stage of the selection process, variables are used that indicate the potential market size and acceptance of the product or similar products. Often, proxy variables are used in this screening process. A proxy variable is a similar or related product that indicates a demand for your product.

The third stage of the screening process focuses on micro-level consider-actions such as competitors, ease of entry, cost of entry and profit potential. Micro-level factors influence the success or failure of a specific product in a specific market. At this stage of the process, marketers may be considering only a small number of countries, so it is feasible to get more detailed, up-to-date information via primary data-collection methods like specific potential customers. During the screening process the focus switches from potential market to actual market and, finally, to company profitability.

The market screening process requires a significant amount of effort. Once the target country has been selected, there is a tendency to focus on the selected markets and ignore the rejected countries. However, the world market is continually changing, and countries that were rejected last year may provide significant opportunities next year.

Increasing numbers of industries are global. To succeed in this environment, firms have to shift from a domestic perspective to considering the world as the arena of operations both with respect to the consumer markets for products and services and resources markets for raw materials, R&D, manufacturing, and human and capital resources.

The globalization of industries is also accompanied by trends towards regional economic integration: the European Union, NAFTA and the various other efforts for regional integration in Asia and Latin America. The implication for segmentation of these developments is that management has to consider portfolios of segments that include [3]:

1. global segments,
2. regional segments and
3. segments within specific countries.

Added to this complexity is the need to consider as the unit of analysis not just countries but countries by mode of entry, since both the risk and attractiveness of a country depend on the mode of entry. The selection and implementation of a portfolio of segments, which includes global segments, regional segments and segments within countries (by mode of entry), requires a significant amount of information on all relevant markets around the world. The creation and maintenance of such a data/knowledge base is not a trivial undertaking and is one of the major obstacles to the development of global segmentation strategies. The creation of processes for the development and maintenance of country, regional and world databases is a high-priority undertaking for all global firms. Yet the development of effective segmentation can take place even without such databases if the firm will proceed in an iterative bottom-up and top-down segmentation.

This process involves three bottom-up steps (contrary to the previous top-down model of country selection):

1. Segmentation of the market in each country (by mode of entry)
2. Examination of the resulting segments in all the selected countries to identify common segments across countries – clustering of country segments
3. Creation of a global portfolio based on various clusters of segments

The resulting portfolio of segments should be compared to a desired (top-down) conceptual portfolio of segments. The comparison and contrast of the two portfolios should be driven by the concept of global operation, which balances the need to develop strategies that best meet the needs of the local markets (given the idiosyncratic market, competitive and environmental conditions), while at the same time trying to achieve economies of scale and scope by focusing on cross-country segments in a number of markets [1].

2 The Internet-of-Things (IoT) and Its Use for Marketers

The Internet-of-Things (IoT) is a network of interconnected devices, systems and services within the existing Internet infrastructure. The core of the IoT is that it allows for 'all things connected' in the communication between devices and objects, creating a more direct integration between the physical world and computer-based systems.

By capturing and analyzing the data that come from the sensors at the endpoints of the connected objects, the IoT's value lies in its ability to track, measure and create 'smart' devices that bring considerable benefits to individuals and businesses.

Basically, an IoT system consists of three elements: [1].

Sensors.Sensors create data about the status of manufacturing equipment and its context, and work as an information interface between physical devices and the Internet. Sensors add connectivity to manufacturing equipment and material components, and are the building blocks of proactive and autonomous repair and maintenance concepts.

Actuators. Actuators are all sorts of components of automated systems that – based on signals from the sensors - drive movement of physical effects, such as moving robots, opening of windows in a house, etc. The IoT builds on Internet-connected actuators, which enable often centralized operators to remote control of a process, and to conduct remote repair and maintenance activities.

Cloud-driven services. IT-Internet ('Cloud') driven services, represented a smart phone app.

For example, a smartphone app, connects the physical objects in a house in order to create a good indoor climate. In this way, IoT may enhance customers' lives and make them 'smarter' (intelligent), while at the same time feed data to develop the firms' competitive advantages, making it possible to more directly, for example, target, monitor and deliver more specific and customized experiences. In order for IoT-oriented organizations to create and capture customer value, they must work together in order to solve customer problems, e.g. in order to create a good in-door climate. The challenge is to get different manufacturers' complementary IoT platforms to work together with the final goal of establishing a smartphone app, that can get the heating system to work together with the air condition system and opening of the windows at the right time.

Marketing has historically been about communicating messages and ensuring that it goes to the target persons – framing a product and then deciding what to tell the target market. The next phase takes marketing a step further – not only targeting the target audience but taking the next step for them and integrate a true Service-Dominant logic (SD-logic) by "doing the job for them".

IoT data is real usage data. Compare this to surveys or focus groups marketers have counted on for so long. We used these techniques because they provided us with some helpful insights but there is nothing more powerful than the insights, we can gain from IoT. Teams can see exactly how a customer is using a product, what specific features they are using and which they are not. Just pure facts without any bias or the risk of perception misguiding the feedback. And it is not only how they are using a product. Marketers can also identify design and performance issues, address them immediately and refine over time. Just imagine having a product that is constantly getting better rather than outdated by the next new gadget. When marketers correlate this with other information about their products and customers, they can get a much more sophisticated understanding of the people using their products.

Development and sustainability of IoT marketing is highly dependent on the acquisition of the new skills for the marketer. As the IoT solution becomes a reality, the interactions between consumers and things under-go emergence and contribute something greater than the sum of the parts resulting in new consumer experiences embodying design and complexity. For example, the connected devices in a home can create safe and secure home, with a good indoor climate.

The increasing challenge for marketers is shifting away from the traditional perspectives of marketing, sales and advertising towards design with a focus on architecting the interactions and orchestrating the consumer experiences underpinning IoT.

The role of the marketer greatly changes with IoT and responsibilities include developing IoT driven experiences through consideration of the product flows and integration with key consumer touch points, establishing the overall product interaction with customers and setting up pre-defined actions built on automating customer journeys.

This role is unique from previous marketing roles in the IoT has an ability to actually change customer behaviour for benefit of both the customer and marketer through monitoring the sensors. The data acquisition from sensors has not been available previously to marketers and represents an opportunity to add customer value through servicing and engaging the customer proactively in brand conversations.

The marketer can play a leadership role in making IoT data the means by which marketers can truly understand customers and products. Further-more, marketers can join forces with the heads of engineering, research and development, and sales. The use of IoT data to create more customer-centric products, offer new services, and find and sustain new competitive differentiation for the company.

Following steps are involved in the marketer's process of using IoT for gaining more customer insights and using appropriate marketing tools towards target customers [1].

1. Analyze customer buying habits across platforms
2. Gather previously unobtainable data about how consumers inter-act with devices and products
3. Gain deeper insights into where the customer is in the customer journey
4. Provide real-time point-of-sale notifications and targeted ads
5. Quickly resolve issues of 'getting the job done' and keep customers happy

3 From Single Channel to Omnichannel Strategy

Nowadays, there is an increasing integration of distribution channels, starting with the single-channel distribution, where the customers are being reached by only one type of distribution channel. This strategy will minimize the company's marketing expenses, but on the other hand the profound focus of a single channel strategy comes at the expense of missed opportunities in the huge variety of other channels.

A multichannel strategy is employed when a firm makes a product available to the market through two or more channels of distribution. Multiple channels include the Internet, salesforce, call centers, retail stores and direct mail. All the channels are in principle available to the customer but the channels are not themselves integrated.

This strategy has been a very popular channel design during the last decade. The increasing popularity of this strategy results from the potential advantages provided: extended market coverage and increased sales volume; lower absolute or relative costs; better accommodation of customers' evolving needs; and more and better information. This strategy, how-ever, can also produce potentially disruptive problems: consumer confusion; conflicts with intermediaries and/or internal distribution units; in-creased costs; loss of distinctiveness; and, eventually, an increased organizational complexity [1].

However, today more customers now navigate between many digital touchpoints for a single purchase. From the customer perspective, a typical journey might be searching the internet on the smartphone, investigate findings on the laptop, visit stores to review items, compare prices on the mobile while in the store, before the customer makes the final buying decision. This approach with different touchpoints requires more an omnichannel strategy, where all the channels are available to the customer, and the channels are also integrated and connected. The purpose is to deliver experiences and value through the whole customer journey. From a semantic standpoint, 'omni' means 'all'. In contradiction to Multichannel strategy, omnichannel strategy is not about maximizing channel efficiency. Instead it puts the customer, not corporate silos, at the core of the strategy. The omnichannel goal is to deliver seamless experiences for the customer to better engage and convert him or her. The delivered digital experience expectations are high through the customer journey. For in-stance, a store employee in a physical store should have key information on all past interactions at his fingertips when interacting with the customer. This also means that it is necessary to create a robust CRM system not only to track and contain data, but to provide a unique customer service experience [1].

4   Customer Journey Mapping

In order to design and produce online products and services that result in a good customer experience, the entire 'customer journey' must be viewed from the perspective of the customer. With the help of 'customer journey mapping', the customer journey and resulting customer experience can be understood, evaluated and improved.

Customer journey mapping is a technique for optimizing customer processes and developing innovative management concepts. It identifies exactly where improvements to the customer contact processes are possible in order to achieve an optimal customer experience across all channels. It also clarifies how and what can be organized more efficiently and with greater synchronicity to give a more joined-up (seamless) customer experience. The customer journey mapping is, when used properly, an easy and effective tool for improving customer experiences across channels as well as ensuring more efficiency in customer processes.

The customer journey map is an indispensable tool in the designing processes of effective websites and apps. Customer journey mapping (CJM) is also a method for visualizing the purchase process or service from the customer's decision perspective (see Fig. 1). It describes the customer's experience during the 'journey' a customer makes during the process of orientation, purchasing and eventual use of a product or service - at all points of contact and every 'touchpoint'. The customer's processing through the 'outer circle' represents the first-time buying process regarding the brand. Importantly, the conceptual model depicts a 'loyalty loop' by which customers who show post-purchase satisfaction develop brand loyalty. This would lead to future brand purchases in the 'inner circle' which would bypass some of the stages in the 'outer circle'. This provides opportunities for improvement across all channels and processes [1–5].

Advances in marketing technologies including marketing automation would make it possible (in Fig. 1) for subsequent purchase journeys to accelerate, speeding up the

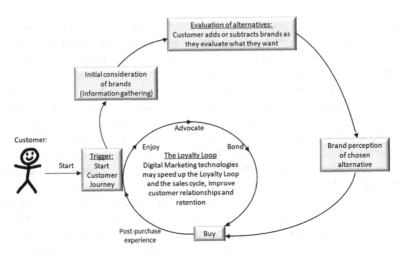

Fig. 1. The Customer Journey Mapping Model. Source: Hollensen and Opresnik (2020) based on Edelmam and Singer (2015) and Sciarrino et al. (2019)

sales cycle, improving customer retention and strengthening the customer relationship [5].

Effective customer journey mapping starts from the same place as the customer starts until the point what that decision-maker considers a successful outcome.

It is important to realize that different customer segments are likely to have different customer journeys. Thus, the holiday maker's journey will look very different from the business traveller's customer journey. Some-one who is actively shopping (with a deadline) may have a different journey from someone who is 'just browsing'.

5   Customer Touchpoint Management

Touchpoints are the individual interactions people have with brands before, during and after purchase. Marketers care about touchpoints because they represent opportunities for customers and prospects to learn, have a positive brand experience, and form attitudes and associations about the brand that could lead to future purchases, brand loyalty, and positive word-of-mouth communication.

Based on the visualization of the Customer Journey Mapping (CJM), offline touchpoints and online touchpoints can be recorded, the places where the target group and the organization meet each other. Based on this overview, the marketer can assess whether the most cost-effective solution has been and what adjustments are needed to realize or improve the product or service.

The stages and the touchpoints in the customer journey can be realized or supported via online communication media, such as websites and apps. A major advantage of online customer contact is that it allows the marketer to monitor customer behavior and with the use of advanced algorithms, elicit the most desirable response from the customer. It is possible to deliver bespoke and personalized customer experiences based on customer profiles. This allows an organization to design and provide products that enhance customer satisfaction, bind the customer to the organization and increase customer loyalty and of course Customer Lifetime Value (CLV).

Customer journey mapping including touchpoints can be applied at several different stages and for a variety of purposes [6]:

1. Identification of market and growth opportunities from the customer's perspective
2. For the organization and its employees to be able to view Digital Marketing from the perspective of the customer
3. Evaluation and improvement of the realized products
4. Providing direction for and keeping a handle on the process of measuring customer experiences
5. Development of ideas for products and services that provide the desired customer experience
6. Helping to identify that organizational changes are needed to facilitate product realization
7. Development of innovative operating concepts and new services
8. Gaining insight into synergy between channels

6 Conclusion

As digital communication becomes an increasingly dominant way for people exchange and share information, a sophisticated customer journey mapping along with a differentiated touchpoint management becomes an essential tool for any company and organization. The customer journey mapping model will help organizations and companies better understand customers and their behavior and outline the key activities they need to take to increase the effectiveness of their social media marketing actions.

References

1. Hollensen, S., Opresnik, M.: Marketing: Principles and Practice. A Management-Oriented Approach, 4th edition. Lübeck (2020)
2. Kotler, P., Hollensen, S., Opresnik, M.: Social Media Marketing – A Practitioner Guide, 4th ed. Lübeck (2020)
3. Hollensen, S.: Global Marketing, 8th ed. Harlow (2020)
4. Edelman, D.C., Singer, M.: Competing on customer journey. Harvard Bus. Rev. 93(11), 88–100 (2015)
5. Sciarrino, J., Friedman, J., Kirk, T., Kitchings, K.S., Prudente, J.: Quantifying the importance, contribution and efficiency of Cotton Inc.'s paid, owned and earned media through customer journey modelling. J. Digit. Soc. Media Mark. 6(4), 294–311 (2019)
6. Thomke, S.: The Magic that Makes Customer Experiences Stick, vol. 61, no. 1, pp. 56–63. MIT Sloan Management Review, Fall Issue (2019)

Mixed Reality Interface for Load Application in Finite Element Analysis

Emran Poh[1], Kyrin Liong[2], and Jeannie S. A. Lee[1(✉)]

[1] Infocomm Technology, Singapore Institute of Technology, Singapore, Singapore
[2] Engineering, Singapore Institute of Technology, Singapore, Singapore
{emran.poh,kyrin.liong,jeannie.lee}@singaporetech.edu.sg

Abstract. Finite Element Analysis (FEA) is an integral process in manufacturing design, providing assurance of quality and structural integrity of a manufactured item. FEA involves conducting rigorous stress simulations on a designed model to study its structural behaviour when under specific loading scenarios. Current FEA tools involve viewing and manipulating the 3D model displayed on a monitor screen. A Mixed Reality (MR) user interface allowing for direct manipulation and specification of loading scenarios on a designed model was developed, thus enabling design engineers to find new ways of interacting and visualising FEA results for analysis and thus reducing unnecessary prototyping costs. Three gesture interfaces were developed to allow application of load parameters on a surface of a model, namely: Point-Apply, Point-Hold, and Point-Drag. A pilot evaluation was conducted to study the suitability of each as an interface designed for engineers. Results suggest that Point-Hold is empirically the most usable interface compared to the other interfaces.

Keywords: Finite Element Analysis · Mixed reality · Gesture · 3D user interface · Digital twin

1 Introduction

Designing parts for manufacturing involves an iterative process studying the structural makeup of the 3D model also known as Finite Element Analysis (FEA) [35]. In this step, parts are placed under simulated stress and load to reveal any structural behaviour and irregularities which may delay production if not identified before during prototyping. Despite being highly functional and well-developed, current FEA tools are lacking in intuitiveness and implicate a steep learning curve onto anyone with little to no experience in the software. These tools allow for the manipulation of 3D models and their results, albeit on a 2D monitor with traditional user input devices such as a keyboard and a mouse.

MR offers significant application potential when it comes to engineering analysis. Mixed reality is a group of immersive experiential systems involving the varying levels of immersion, virtuality, and degree of interaction [33]. MR is represented as a form of continuum involving Augmented Reality (AR) as a subset

© Springer Nature Switzerland AG 2021
G. Meiselwitz (Ed.): HCII 2021, LNCS 12774, pp. 470–483, 2021.
https://doi.org/10.1007/978-3-030-77626-8_32

of this group which is most real environment augmented with some virtual over-lay [28]. The interaction between virtual 3D models and physical objects within an augmented environment [29] has the potential to reduce unnecessary proto-typing costs while maintaining the physical context. Working in such a manner assists designers in understanding and verifying structural assumptions within a real tangible context.

Existing approaches to develop FEA within the MR space often do not incor-porate interaction as an avenue for optimisation. Manipulation of FEA models are sometimes developed with bespoke tools specially designed for greater manip-ulation of FEA data that can be hard to replicate or acquire [6,16–18,36]. FEA may involve the modification of loading scenarios utilising physical input meth-ods such as force sensors or physical tools. These systems are able to provide a tangible method of modifying loading parameters, however such a methods would make room for hardware incompatibility and the time taken to setup and calibrate these sensors would not encourage rapid analysis which is necessary to improve workflow [5,15–17,31,34].

Knowing the requirements and use cases of FEA application applied within the context of an MR based system, the aim is to develop intuitive 3D user interactions built in MR for FEA. To study the feasibility of the proposed inter-face and draw meaningful conclusions on the compatibility and its effectiveness, a mixed-methods user study was conducted to qualitatively and quantitatively validate its usability.

2 Related Work

2.1 Computation of FEA in MR

FEA application tools are used by design engineers to optimise components in their design phase to reduce the number of physical prototypes and experiments, with the end goal of developing better products faster. FEA relies on scientific accuracy to produce meaningful insights when simulating structural behaviour.

Being able to visualise scientific information within a physical context is desirable, however, the visualisation complexity and its load onto the attached hardware will have to be considered. Computational limits to the visualisation of FEA results have to be balanced between the accuracy of the stress results and also usability. [16] underlined the real-time update speed limitation of dis-playing the FEA results in MR systems. A visualisation budget has to be put in place and adhered to when designing a visualisation strategy. Rendering an FEA model will require a considerable amount of calculation and rendering and any latency may significantly impact user experience and its accuracy in visual-ising scientific information. [12] explores the use of simplifying stress calculations and resulting in lighter processing loads on the device. Voxel-based visualisation of Finite Element Model (FEM) results [32] such as stress, temperature, and the resulting deformation provides an illustrative insight of physical parameters in an immersive workspace. The nodes are represented as tetrahedron and the physical attributes are manipulated to display numerous kinds of results without the extra visual complexity. It is worth noting that most suggestions provided above still involves the device connected to a PC or a laptop which does allow for some offloading of computational needs. Other offloading strategies such as cloud processing can be considered to offload much of its computational needs [24] but providing such a complex implementation may force it to only be only accessible to those with access to such resources. [26] suggest that dynamic results would be ideal, pre-calculated results could be considered as it does require intensive computing of results during run-time. Although a live computation is desirable in matters of convenience, an untethered head-mounted device has its computational limits. Calculating the FEA results of a simple object would require extensive processing, of which when done within the HoloLens, other features such as frame rate gets affected which will impact the usability of FEA interaction in MR greatly.

2.2   Interaction of FEA in MR

Interaction on a 2D monitor is still limited to traditional input devices. Being able to manipulate boundary conditions and view the results provides an opportunity to seek alternative natural direct manipulation interaction methods in MR. For most of the augmented reality (AR) systems built for engineering analysis simulation, there is a lack of an effective and intuitive interaction method [26].

[27] implements a dynamic object tracking of a magnet using a web camera and translates its position to derive its resultant magnetic field displayed on a background monitor. Through the literal movement of the magnet, the result could be calculated from its position. Using real force sensors [16,17] to enable live input of load boundaries by the user, greater control and realism can be introduced for load application. [12] allows the user to change the FEM boundary conditions. Through optical tracking and concurrent model update, an AR overlay is displayed upon the actual object allowing a high degree of cause-effect interaction visualisation. However, when dealing with flexible objects, the physical object's shape can change (possibly to the point where it is indistinguishable from the original object). This poses a mesh translation problem with using a single initial model and converting this mesh into a possibly same object.

Combining AR and the visualisation of FEA through seamlessly integrating FEA simulation techniques within AR space provides a much needed unified visualisation, would enable better understanding and interpretation of the displayed results. There is a need for seamlessly integrating FEA simulation techniques with AR as a necessary way to reduce system response time. In the likely case that the model is virtual, the user could be provided with a method to manipulate data or the user is provided a way to specify a location to apply stress or load.

2.3   Gesture Taxonomy

Human hands are dexterous and expressive [13] and are used to convey meaningful bodily motions to interact with the environment. [20] described a 'gesture continuum' defining five different kinds of gestures (Gesticulation, Language-like, Pantomimes, Emblems, Sign Language). Each of the gesture classification defined represents a certain method of conveying an action or thought. As the continuum progress from left to right, the association with speech and spontaneity declines and language properties and social regulation increases [21]. [22] went on to restructure gestures into four distinct groups (Iconic, Metaphoric, Beat, Deictic). Each of the gestures defined in Kendon's Continuum represents a gesture that is well used and would is vital to tap into this pool of gestures to come up with a natural interaction method. When comparing the conventional interaction devices such as keyboard and mouse, hand gestures may be more familiar and natural for human users and it is beneficial that computers should be made to understand and adapt to the gestures. Amongst the most well-known available MR systems, only a handful uses gesture tracking as part of the interaction system.

Point, Tap, and Hold. MR frameworks such as in HoloLens 1 provides a set of gestures such as *Point*, *Tap*, *Hold*. The pointing gesture is a straightforward method to direct attention onto a discrete subject [22] or even suggest a relationship between multiple objects by pointing at multiple subjects. Most gestures would involve the *Point* by mostly using the index finger to 'point', to bring attention to a discrete subject. In Hololens 2, the framework supports a hand ray that shoots out from the centre of the palm that would allow even greater precision and allow for the *Point* gesture to be used even from a distance.

The *Tap* gesture extends *Point* allows the freedom of selection (pointing) and the confirmation of said selection (tapping). Most MR platforms already have the *Tap* gesture set as the primary form of navigation.

The *Hold* gesture may not classify as a specific gesture but rather constitutes a form of gesture extension. Any gesture is maintained for an extended period could classify as 'holding'. The gesture could be represented as a physical application of force as if pressing onto a surface or translated to the uniform application of power to push the object. *Hold* has the potential be used to trigger a discrete event multiple times until the user releases the hold similar to that of pressing any character on a keyboard repeats the character when typing.

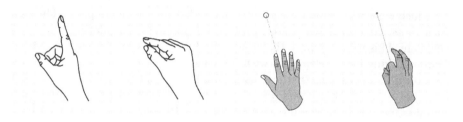

Fig. 1. Hand-Ray gestures supported and used in Microsoft Hololens 1 & 2

Extension of Simple Gestures. Composite gestures can be defined as uniquely designed gestures that combine multiple gestures. With the advent of bi-manual compatible systems, most mixed or AR systems often support the use of both hands in the interaction of the environment. Single-handed composite interactions such as *Drag* involve tapping as an initial trigger, maintaining and translating the gesture onto a different location in space and releasing the hold as a terminating gesture. A bimanual gesture like *Resize* in Hololens involves two hands in its gesture to physically pinch two corners of an object and manipulate its position, size and rotation. For bimanual compatible systems, the manipulation of the size of the object often involves the use of both hands to manipulate the position and size of the object. Such manipulation is best done with both hands as it allows for a higher degree of freedom in the three-dimensional shaping of the object.

The user can only effectively be familiar to a select intuitive few without training and for a couple more with training. Composite gestures could then be defined as a class of gestures that are built upon the strategic combination of simple gestures and their respective extensions.

Metaphoric and Iconic Gestures. Metaphoric and Iconic gestures likely contain cultural or social references that may not necessarily universal but rather unique enough to serve a specific purpose. Microsoft Hololens' Bloom allows the user to open and close the menu whenever using the system by carrying out a distinctive but easy to remember the gesture. The Magic Leap One's OK and Thumbs Up are then other interactions that simply translate the real-life interaction that is almost intuitive to users even without prior training. Such novel and exotic interactions have been proven to be useful in establishing a characteristically intuitive way of working with MR systems.

3   Gestures for FEA

FEA involves the modification and application of load parameters to be able to perceive and understand structural behaviour. Focus would be placed upon studying specific loading scenarios or conditions that may cause structural failures. Engineers would have to identify which faces of the model will be under load which faces will remain static for surfaces that are welded in place. Through which these same load parameters will be the input for calculating structural behaviour. This would require the design of a form of gesture for users to utilise when modifying load parameters with FEA models.

Natural hand gestures that are instinctive provide intuitive interactions that bridge both the real world and also the virtual environment. [1] Despite significant progress made in gesture interaction for MR [30] there has yet to be a consensus on the optimal combination of hand gestures mapped to the appropriate interactions in MR.

Point-Apply (PA). The *PA* gesture attempts to mimic the regular usage of the mouse and keyboard combination. Instead of the cursor of a mouse, the gaze cursor of the Hololens is used to *Tap* and select surfaces and loads for this interaction. This gesture has the potential to establish a baseline in determining the usability of the application. The user will be selecting the load from the menu using the tap gesture and proceeding to tap on the desired surface for load application. This interaction method is simplistic and could be the most familiar to the user. This gesture correlates to the *Deictic* gesture type as part of the Four Gesture Types described in [21]. The *PA* gesture uses only pointing gestures to accomplish the same task. Given the example of a metal beam, the application of load under *PA* would be similar to that of pointing to which surface the load is going to be and then pressing the next button.

Point-Hold (PH). The *PH* gesture aims to give the user a more natural feel to the application of load. The act of pressing is a pantomime of the natural 'pushing' or 'pressing' of an object. This continuous hold of the gesture *Tap* can be used to allow for manipulation of a numeric value based on the duration of the hold. This gesture correlates to the *Beat* gesture type as part of the Four Gesture Types described in [21]. The act of holding a gesture is minute and utilise the emphasis portion of the gesture to describe a certain action, in this case, a numeric manipulation. Given the example of a metal beam, the application of load under *PH* would be similar to that of pressing the load onto the surface of which the load is to be applied to.

Point-Drag (PD). The *PD* gesture allows for the application of load to happen as a seamless manoeuvre. As a form of gesticulation, the *PD* gesture is an exploitation of the dramatic change in the spatial position of the gesture. The further the gesture is dragged away from, the targeted value increments at a higher step. This gesture correlates to the *Metaphoric* gesture type as part of the Four Gesture Types described in [21]. The *PD* gesture could be seen as an attempt to metaphorically increase the numeric value through an imaginary line that extends from the start point of the gesture. Given the example of a metal beam, the application of load under *PD* would be similar to that of pressing the load onto the surface of which the load is to be applied to and adjusting the pressing force according to how much load is to be applied.

4   Implementation

For the development of the prototype gesture user interface, Microsoft HoloLens 1 was used as the testing headset for all gestures and interactions that were built using MRTK for the Microsoft Hololens 1 Mixed Reality headset. The prototype software application was built using:

- Microsoft HoloLens 1 with Mixed Reality Toolkit
- Unity Engine for development and testing
- Solidworks and Abaqus for simulation and export of stress results

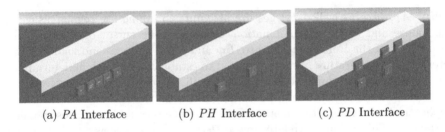

(a) *PA* Interface   (b) *PH* Interface   (c) *PD* Interface

Fig. 2. Load selection interface

PA as an interaction copies the usual activity of point and clicks and as such the selection of the surface and the application of load. Through the detection of the Raycast onto the specific side of the BoxCollider of the model, the load value can be applied onto any surface through a tapping gesture.

The *PH* gesture extends *PA* to produce a singular gesture. While *PA* is carried out through several trigger events, *PH* leverages on consistent manipulation handled by a modified ManipulationHandler where the increment function was implemented. The gesture is triggered through the start and the release of the pose.

PD adds on another layer of control allowing users to manage on the spot the rate of increase of the load. Intended to mimic the act of increasing strength while pressing on a surface to 'apply more force'. Depth tracking as a feature however is not supported till the release of HoloLens 2 and as such a workaround was made. This was carried out by placing incremental triggers in the form of buttons displaying a different rate of change linearly away from the point or surface of interaction. Fundamentally this gesture is still a 'Tap and Hold' but now involving translating the gesture onto a specific distance to mimic load application.

5   Evaluation

A pilot within-subjects usability experiment was conducted on a set of ten healthy participants to obtain data on the interface preferences and to evaluate the effectiveness and efficiency of the designed MR system. A post-experiment analysis was conducted to discern any possible effects that would allow us to understand further the learnability and usability of the interfaces. In this evaluation, we would attempt to observe the difference in relative usability, incurred workload, the flow of the application, and any possibility of simulator sickness. Different methods of interacting with the FEA results will be compared using a mixed-methods

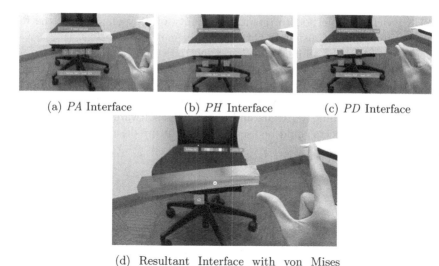

(a) *PA* Interface   (b) *PH* Interface   (c) *PD* Interface

(d) Resultant Interface with von Mises
Overlay

Fig. 3. Load selection interface

approach to find out more about the usability of the interactions. All 10 volunteer
participants were final year undergraduates with little to no experience in MR
or FEA, between the ages of 20–30. The interfaces are as follows:

1. Load Application through Point-Apply Interaction
2. Load Application through Point-Hold Interaction
3. Load Application through Point-Drag Interaction

While undergoing each interface, participants were asked to think-aloud. A
semi-structured interview was conducted with participants after completing all
three conditions.

A baseline SSQ score was recorded before the experiment and at the end of
each interface. The participant will also be required to complete the following
survey instruments:

– NASA Task Load Index Questionnaire (NASA TLX)
– Flow State Scale (FSS)
– System Usability Scale Questionnaire (SUS)
– Simulation Sickness Questionnaire (SSQ)

When considering the amount of mental load imposed onto the user, the
NASA-TLX is a tested method to quantitatively identify mental or physical
workload caused by the implementation of each interface [2]. The flow state scale
could be used to evaluate the correlation of skill, difficulty and the importance
of each task in providing a sense of "flow" [8,9,19]. A usability scale such as

the SUS provides a method to quantify usability of a system and as the final defining criteria when considered with the other metrics [3,4,25].

Using the SSQ, the simulator sickness metric would be able to inform any potential signs of motion sickness that may affect the user experience. Cases of simulator sickness for MR headsets are generally negligible or rare [37] compared to virtual reality headsets [11]. Simulation sickness may derive from other causes such as under performing hardware and ill-informed software design [10]. Understanding sickness aspects could be used to advise future design improvements to each of the interfaces.

6   Results

6.1   Simulator Effects, Workload, and Usability

Results for the simulator questionnaire [23] suggest that there was not any significant degradation of total simulator sickness for each interface (PA M = 26, SD = 8.5) (PH M = 26, SD = 9.6) (PD M = 29, SD = 14.5).

From the pilot test, findings show that PA (M = 38.8, SD = 19.1) and PH (M = 39.3, SD = 21.3) has similar workload [14] which is to be expected as the interactions were designed to mimic similar interactions that are relatively natural to a human user. However, PD (M = 47.6, SD = 28.3) reports as the most cumbersome interface due to its composite nature and will require a longer period for the user to get accustomed to such a complex interaction.

Results suggest that PH is empirically the most usable [4] interface (M = 67.8, SD = 16.1) as compared to PA (M = 67.5, SD = 19.4) and PD (M = 50.3, SD = 19.7). PH having involving one smooth movement and not requiring much work is expected to achieve a higher rating for usability.

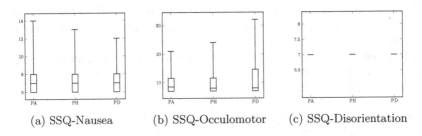

(a) SSQ-Nausea   (b) SSQ-Occulomotor   (c) SSQ-Disorientation

Fig. 4. SSQ results (n = 10)

6.2   Flow

Results reveal that while there is a consistent level of absorption throughout the interfaces (PA M = 18.7, SD = 5.4)(PH M = 19.5, SD = 5.3)(PD M = 20.3, SD = 5.6) and perceived importance (PA M = 8.3, SD = 3)(PH M = 8.1, SD = 2.8)(PD M = 9.6, SD = 2.8), the participants tend to feel that they are less fluent on the *PD* (M = 28.6, SD = 7.1) interface as compared to the *PA* (M = 30.9, SD = 8.9) and *PH* (M = 31, SD = 8.4). This is to be expected when considering that *PA* and *PH* are Deictic and Beat gestures they are much easier to learn and utilise as compared to a rather more Metaphoric gesture such as *PD* which could impose a steeper learning curve. The lower results for *PD* in Competency (M = 9, SD = 1.89) strengthens the claim that participants may not feel competent with the *PH* gesture. [7–9]

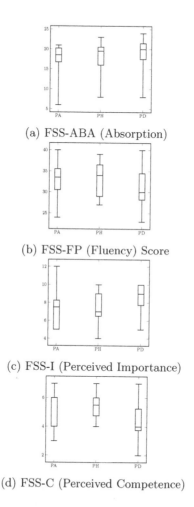

(a) FSS-ABA (Absorption)

(b) FSS-FP (Fluency) Score

(c) FSS-I (Perceived Importance)

(d) FSS-C (Perceived Competence)

Fig. 5. FSS scores for absorption and fluency

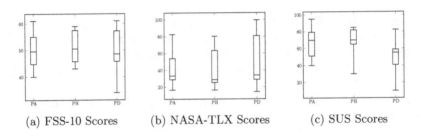

(a) FSS-10 Scores   (b) NASA-TLX Scores   (c) SUS Scores

Fig. 6. Overall flow, workload, and usability scores

6.3 Result Summary

Overall scores suggest that the *PH* interaction is the most usable interface. Although workload plays an important role in user experience, many participants were willing to choose an interface which slightly more complex in concept however brings forth a smoother user experience. Workload scores also suggest that as the interface complexity increases, the user experience may not necessarily be better even though more functionality is introduced. It is intended to recruit a larger and more varied population sample in a future study to further investigate the effectiveness of the interfaces. The MR headset such as the Hololens 1 may contain certain hardware limitations (such as refresh rates and ergonomic concerns) that may also affect the results.

7 Conclusion

The MR interface for FEA is a simple and intuitive interface designed to improve the efficiency of mechanical design engineers. The application leverages the advantages of MR to implement a 3D user interface to augment a FEA workflow. Results show that the *PH* interface is regarded as the most usable interface empirically. Nonetheless, the developed 3D interface could prove highly useful in supporting engineering designers in their processes to enhance their workflow productivity. The application has proved to be highly usable and learnable, which could potentially reduce training cost and resources for learning a new interface altogether.

Further enhancements could involve non-gaze based gesture design, and bimanual gestures using two hands for load application that is supported in future MR headsets. For FEA modelling, live von Mises calculation or other forms of structural or fluid simulation results could be overlaid onto real space and further interface interactions could be designed. Given its application for improving workflows for engineers, subsequent versions of the proposed interfaces could include extending them into a general-purpose library of useful singular gestures that could be matched into any future gesture-based engineering application in MR.

It is intended to conduct a future larger-scale evaluation with a larger population size and involving varied participant backgrounds to further understand the effectiveness of the user interface.

References

1. Azuma, R.T.: A survey of augmented reality. Presence Teleoperators Virt. Environ. **6**(4), 355–385 (1997)
2. Balk, S.A., Bertola, M.A., Inman, V.W.: Simulator sickness questionnaire: twenty years later (2013)
3. Bangor, A., Kortum, P.T., Miller, J.T.: An empirical evaluation of the system usability scale. Int. J. Hum. Comput. Interact. **24**(6), 574–594 (2008)
4. Brooke, J.: System Usability Scale (SUS): A Quick-and-Dirty Method of System Evaluation User Information, pp. 1–7. Digital Equipment Co. Ltd., Reading, UK (1986)
5. Carmo, M.B., et al.: Augmented reality for support decision on solar radiation harnessing. In: 2016 23rd Portuguese Meeting on Computer Graphics and Interaction (EPCGI), pp. 1–8. IEEE (2016)
6. Clothier, M., Bailey, M.: Augmented reality visualization tool for kings stormwater bridge. In: IASTED International Conference on Visualization, Imaging and Image Processing (VIIP) (2004)
7. Csikszentmihalyi, M., Abuhamdeh, S., Nakamura, J.: Flow. Flow and the Foundations of Positive Psychology, pp. 227–238. Springer, Dordrecht (2014). https://doi.org/10.1007/978-94-017-9088-8_15
8. Csikszentmihalyi, M., Abuhamdeh, S., Nakamura, J., et al.: Flow (1990)
9. Csikszentmihalyi, M., Csikszentmihalyi, I.S.: Optimal Experience: Psychological Studies of Flow in Consciousness. Cambridge University Press, Cambridge (1992)
10. Davis, S., Nesbitt, K., Nalivaiko, E.: A systematic review of cybersickness. In: Proceedings of the 2014 Conference on Interactive Entertainment, pp. 1–9 (2014)
11. Fernandes, A.S., Feiner, S.K.: Combating VR sickness through subtle dynamic field-of-view modification. In: 2016 IEEE Symposium on 3D User Interfaces (3DUI), pp. 201–210. IEEE (2016)
12. Fiorentino, M., Monno, G., Uva, A.: Interactive "touch and see" fem simulation using augmented reality. Int. J. Eng. Educ. **25**(6), 1124–1128 (2009)
13. Hale, K.S., Stanney, K.M.: Handbook of Virtual Environments: Design, Implementation, and Applications. CRC Press, Boca Raton (2014)
14. Hart, S.G.: Nasa-task load index (NASA-TLX); 20 years later. In: Proceedings of the Human Factors and Ergonomics Society Annual Meeting, vol. 50, pp. 904–908. Sage Publications, Sage, Los Angeles (2006)
15. Heuveline, V., Ritterbusch, S., Ronnas, S.: Augmented reality for urban simulation visualization. Prepr. Ser. Eng. Math. Comput. Lab **16** (2011)
16. Huang, J., Ong, S., Nee, A.: Real-time finite element structural analysis in augmented reality. Adv. Eng. Softw. **87**, 43–56 (2015). https://doi.org/10.1016/j.advengsoft.2015.04.014. http://www.sciencedirect.com/science/article/pii/S0965997815000733
17. Huang, J., Ong, S., Nee, A.: Visualization and interaction of finite element analysis in augmented reality. Comput. Aided Des. **84**, 1–14 (2017). https://doi.org/10.1016/j.cad.2016.10.004. http://www.sciencedirect.com/science/article/pii/S0010448516301300

18. Issartel, P., Guéniat, F., Ammi, M.: Slicing techniques for handheld augmented reality. In: 2014 IEEE Symposium on 3D User Interfaces (3DUI), pp. 39–42. IEEE (2014)

19. Jackson, S.A., Marsh, H.W.: Development and validation of a scale to measure optimal experience: the flow state scale. J. Sport Exerc. Psychol. **18**(1), 17–35 (1996)

20. Kendon, A.: Some relationships between body motion and speech. Stud. Dyadic Commun. **7**(177), 90 (1972)

21. Kendon, A.: Language and gesture: unity or duality. In: Language and Gesture, vol. 2 (2000)

22. Kendon, A.: Gesture: Visible Action as Utterance. Cambridge University Press, Cambridge (2004)

23. Kennedy, R.S., Lane, N.E., Berbaum, K.S., Lilienthal, M.G.: Simulator sickness questionnaire: an enhanced method for quantifying simulator sickness. Int. J. Aviat. Psychol. **3**(3), 203–220 (1993)

24. Kim, M., Yi, S., Jung, D., Park, S., Seo, D.: Augmented-reality visualization of aerodynamics simulation in sustainable cloud computing. Sustainability **10**(5), 1362 (2018)

25. Lewis, J.R., Sauro, J.: The factor structure of the system usability scale. In: Kurosu, M. (ed.) HCD 2009. LNCS, vol. 5619, pp. 94–103. Springer, Heidelberg (2009). https://doi.org/10.1007/978-3-642-02806-9_12

26. Li, W., Nee, A., Ong, S.: A state-of-the-art review of augmented reality in engineering analysis and simulation. Multimodal Technol. Interact. **1**(3), 17 (2017)

27. Matsutomo, S., Mitsufuji, K., Hiasa, Y., Noguchi, S.: Real time simulation method of magnetic field for visualization system with augmented reality technology. IEEE Trans. Magn. **49**(5), 1665–1668 (2013)

28. Milgram, P., Takemura, H., Utsumi, A., Kishino, F.: Augmented reality: a class of displays on the reality-virtuality continuum. In: Telemanipulator and Telepresence Technologies, vol. 2351 (January 1994). https://doi.org/10.1117/12.197321

29. Milgram, P., Takemura, H., Utsumi, A., Kishino, F.: Augmented reality: a class of displays on the reality-virtuality continuum. In: Telemanipulator and Telepresence Technologies, vol. 2351, pp. 282–292. International Society for Optics and Photonics (1995)

30. Piumsomboon, T., Clark, A., Billinghurst, M., Cockburn, A.: User-defined gestures for augmented reality. In: Kotzé, P., Marsden, G., Lindgaard, G., Wesson, J., Winckler, M. (eds.) INTERACT 2013. LNCS, vol. 8118, pp. 282–299. Springer, Heidelberg (2013). https://doi.org/10.1007/978-3-642-40480-1_18

31. Regenbrecht, H., Baratoff, G., Wilke, W.: Augmented reality projects in the automotive and aerospace industries. IEEE Comput. Graph. Appl. **25**(6), 48–56 (2005)

32. Scherer, S., Wabner, M.: Advanced visualization for finite elements analysis in virtual reality environments. Int. J. Interact. Des. Manuf. (IJIDeM) **2**(3), 169–173 (2008). https://doi.org/10.1007/s12008-008-0044-6

33. Speicher, M., Hall, B.D., Nebeling, M.: What is mixed reality? In: Proceedings of the 2019 CHI Conference on Human Factors in Computing Systems, p. 537. ACM (2019)

34. Sutherland, C., Hashtrudi-Zaad, K., Sellens, R., Abolmaesumi, P., Mousavi, P.: An augmented reality haptic training simulator for spinal needle procedures. IEEE Trans. Biomed. Eng. **60**(11), 3009–3018 (2012)

35. Szabó, B., Babuška, I.: Finite Element Analysis. Wiley, Hoboken (1991)

36. Valentini, P., Pezzuti, E.: Dynamic splines for interactive simulation of elastic beams in augmented reality. In: International Conference on Innovative Methods in Product Design, IMProVe 2011 (2011)
37. Vovk, A., Wild, F., Guest, W., Kuula, T.: Simulator sickness in augmented reality training using the Microsoft Hololens. In: Proceedings of the 2018 CHI Conference on Human Factors in Computing Systems, CHI 2018, New York, NY, USA, pp. 1–9. Association for Computing Machinery (2018). https://doi.org/10.1145/3173574.3173783

Identifying Customer eXperience Touchpoints in Tourism on the Hotel Industry

Luis Rojas[✉], Daniela Quiñones, and Cristian Rusu

Pontificia Universidad Católica de Valparaíso, Valparaíso, Chile
luis.rojas.c01@mail.pucv.cl, {daniela.quinones,
cristian.rusu}@pucv.cl

Abstract. Understanding the customer experience is important for practitioners and researchers to recognize customer perceptions and responses when interacting with different products, systems, and/or services. To achieve this, it is necessary to identify each direct or indirect interaction between customers and organizations, which are called touchpoints. Recognizing touchpoints throughout the customer's journey enables organizations to evaluate the customer experience and identify where to make improvements to satisfy customer needs.

This research identifies several touchpoints through the different stages of interaction with the hotel industry (before, during, and after the stay). Based on the experience of the authors and comments obtained in an experiment, 13 touchpoints were discussed and analyzed with the aim of grouping them. Thus, 8 touchpoints were recognized: (1) search for information, (2) book a room, (3) check-in, (4) room stay, (5) visit common areas, (6) order & receive food, (7) check-out, and (8) report experience. Finally, a customer journey map was created to represent the customer experience in the hotel industry identifying stages, touchpoints, channels, and emotions.

Keywords: Customer eXperience · Touchpoints · Channels · Customer journey map · Tourism · Hotel industry

1 Introduction

Customer eXperience (CX) has become one of the most decisive factors when we talk about achieving competitive advantage between companies or organizations from different industries. That is why it is important for organizations to correctly understand the CX concept, its definition, dimensions, touchpoints, channels, and methods or instruments to evaluate it correctly. However, over the years this concept and its dimensions have been presented in different ways by different authors so there are multiple variations according to the context being studied.

In simple terms, CX arises when customers interact with a company/organization through products, systems, or services. These interactions are called touchpoints and can occurs through multiple channels, which are the medium or place through which touchpoints take place [1–3]. Thus, it is important for companies to recognize their

© Springer Nature Switzerland AG 2021
G. Meiselwitz (Ed.): HCII 2021, LNCS 12774, pp. 484–499, 2021.
https://doi.org/10.1007/978-3-030-77626-8_33

touchpoints and channels because the experiences originate in each of these will directly influence on how the customer feels and will behave in the following interactions with them.

The hotel industry provides distinct products or services according to their classification (star rating); nonetheless, all of these should focus on knowing and meeting the needs of their customers independent of the type of hotel. To achieve this, it is necessary for hotels to clearly identify all the touchpoints and channels in which the different interactions with their customers originate, and subsequently to use different methods and/or instruments to evaluate the CX at those touchpoints. Nevertheless, the identification of the multiple touchpoints in which customers interact with hotels throughout the customer's journey is still limited in the literature.

To fill this gap, this article identifies several touchpoints, channels, and emotions related to the CX in tourism on the hotel industry and represents this information in a Customer Journey Map (CJM). We also discuss and analyze the different touchpoints and emotions of customers present at each stage of interaction with hotels. The document is organized as follows: Sect. 2 presents the concept of CX, touchpoints, CJM, and tourism and hotel industry; Sect. 3 presents the experiment design; Sect. 4 presents the results and analysis of the experiment conducted; and Sect. 5 presents the conclusion and future work.

2   Theoretical Background

To perform this research, it is necessary to understand certain key concepts relevant to this work. Thus, the concepts of CX, touchpoints, CJM, and tourism and hotel industry are briefly presented below.

2.1   Customer eXperience

Customer eXperience (CX) is a concept that currently has aroused the interest of companies from different sectors. However, there is still not generally accepted CX definition. Therefore, several authors have proposed different definitions over time, some of which are presented in Table 1.

Regarding Table 1, we can observe that each author highlights different aspects in their definitions. Meyer and Schwager [1] stress its subjective character and declare that it occurs with both direct and indirect contact with a company. Gentile et al. [2] approach their definition from the point of view of creation of CX emphasizing the customer's involvement at different levels. Finally, Lemon and Verhoef [3] focus on that CX occurs through interaction with brand offers –products or services– throughout the entire journey.

Concerning to CX dimensions, as shown in Table 2, there is no consensus among the authors when conceptualizing them. This variety of definitions and dimensions is due to the different domains/approaches in which CX is assessed. Therefore, the evaluation of the CX will be different when a customer interacts with a retail company and with a tourism company that is why different dimensions are proposed by the authors.

Table 1. CX definitions.

Author (year)	Definition
Meyer and Schwager (2007) [1]	"Customer experience is the internal and subjective response customers have to any direct or indirect contact with a company. Direct contact generally occurs in the course of purchase, use, and service and is usually initiated by the customer. Indirect contact most often involves unplanned encounters with representations of a company's products, services, or brands and takes the form of word-of-mouth recommendations or criticisms, advertising, news reports, reviews, and so forth"
Gentile et al. (2007) [2]	"The customer experience originates from a set of interactions between a customer and a product, a company, or part of its organization, which provoke a reaction. This experience is strictly personal and implies the customer's involvement at different levels (rational, emotional, sensorial physical and spiritual)"
Lemon and Verhoef (2016) [3]	"Customer experience is a multidimensional construct focusing on a customer's cognitive, emotional, behavioral, sensorial, and social responses to a firm's offerings during the customer's entire purchase journey"

Table 2. CX dimensions, attributes, and/or aspects.

Authors (Year)	Domain/Approach	Dimensions
Schmitt (1999) [4]	Marketing	Sense Feel Think Act Relate
Gentile et al. (2007) [2]	General	Sensorial Emotional Cognitive Pragmatic Lifestyle Relational
Alia et al. (2014) [5]	Resort hotels	Entertainment Esthetics Education Escapism

2.2 Touchpoints

The CX arises when customers interact with an organization/company through products, systems, or services. These interactions are called touchpoints and can occurs through multiple channels. Stein and Ramaseshan [6] states that "customers have experiences every time they 'touch' any part of the product, service, brand or organization, across multiple channels and at various points in time. Such moments of truth between the customer and any part of the company are known as touchpoints".

Lemon and Verhoef [3] in their research propose four categories of touchpoints that customers will experience on their journey:

- **Brand-owned touchpoints:** These touchpoints are interactions with customers during the experience which are designed and managed by a company and under its own control.
- **Partner-owned touchpoints:** These touchpoints are interaction with customers during the experience which are jointly designed, managed, or controlled by a company and any of its partners.
- **Customer-owned touchpoints:** These touchpoints are customer actions that are part of the CX, which are not influenced or controlled by a company or its partners.
- **Social/external touchpoints:** These are external touchpoints to a company that can influence customer perceptions and affect the customer's journey.

Furthermore, Stein and Ramaseshan [6] identifies seven distinct elements of CX touchpoints:

- **Atmospheric elements:** Covers the physical characteristics and surrounding that customers observe when interacting with a company.
- **Technological elements:** Customer's direct interaction with any type of technology through the customer journey.
- **Communicative elements:** One-way promotional and informative communication from a company to customers.
- **Process elements:** Necessary steps or actions that a customer must take to achieve a particular outcome with a company.
- **Employee–customer interaction elements:** Customer's direct or indirect interaction with an employee when interacting with any part of a company.
- **Customer–customer interaction elements:** Customer's direct or indirect interaction with other customer when interacting with any part of a company.
- **Product interaction elements:** Customer's direct or indirect interaction with products and/or services offered by a company.

As observed, categories allow to understand the origin of the touchpoints and the influence of companies on that interaction (e.g., brand-owned or social/external touchpoints). While elements allow to understand the nature of the touchpoints and the factors that affect that interaction. (e.g., physical characteristics, employees, or other customers). When considering both the categories and elements, a wide variety of touchpoints can be identified in order to correctly evaluate the CX throughout the customer's journey.

2.3 Customer Journey Map

A Customer Journey Map (CJM) [7] is a strategic management tool that provides a company with knowledge about CX. It consists of a visual representation of a sequence of events in which customers interact with a company identifying touchpoints, channels, expectations, and emotions throughout the customer's journey.

This representation can include different sections/contents to achieve its purpose effectively. However, CJM can be designed based on different approaches so there is no strict rule to define their structure or the elements it must have. Nevertheless, it is recommended that it be composed of at least four key elements [8, 9].

- **Persona:** It is important to identify what kind of customer interacts with the company. Therefore, it is necessary to include archetypal representations of customers that serve as patterns of behavior, motivations, habits, interests and needs.
- **Touchpoints:** It is essential to include the touchpoints as they provide relevant information to understand what the customer is doing. These should be represented as a logical sequence of interactions and if possible, grouped by stages.
- **Channels:** They are the medium or place through which touchpoints occur. Furthermore, they allow to know how and where the customers interact with the company.
- **Emotions:** It is crucial to understand how the customer feels at each of the multiple touchpoints. Knowing the emotions allows to the company to identify the critical points to take actions so as not to risk its relationship with the customer.

It is possible to incorporate other elements to the CJM such as: expectations, to know what customers expect; pain points, to identify what problems exist; recommendations, to suggest ideas for improvements; among others. It should be noted that including additional elements into a CJM involves greater effort and work as it will be necessary to collect, analyze, and discuss more data. Nevertheless, considering at least these 4 key elements allows to understand the CX through the customer's journey and then evaluate it correctly.

2.4 Tourism and Hotel Industry

The tourism area is currently one of the most important economic activities for several countries. Because this economic sector creates jobs, drives exports, and generates prosperity across the world [10]. According to Kaspar [11] tourism is "the entirety of interrelations and phenomena which result from people travelling to, and stopping at, places which are neither their main, continuous domiciles nor place of work".

The tourism area is composed of various sectors such as: accommodation, food & beverage, recreation & entertainment, transportation, and travel services [12]. The accommodation or lodging industry is made up of different establishments such as: hotels, motels, inns, bed & breakfast, guest houses, hostels, among others. However, this research was focused to identify several CX touchpoints specifically on the hotel industry during their journey.

Thus, a hotel is defined as "a managed building or establishment, which provides guests with a place to stay overnight - on a short-term basis - in exchange for money" [13]. There are different types of hotels that can provide additional products or services according to their classification (star rating). Nonetheless, regardless of the type of hotel, all these share certain interactions with their customers, i.e., check-in, check-out, among others.

3 Experiment Design

In order to obtain the necessary information to identify several touchpoints and create a CJM, a survey was carried out. The survey was composed of four main sections (see Table 3) which were focused on obtaining information about CX at the different interactions before, during, and after the stay in a hotel, i.e., touchpoints, channels, and emotions. Prior to the survey, a pilot study was conducted with four participants from different profiles to validate the correct understanding of the questions in the survey.

The experiment was conducted in May 2019, where multiple people who have stayed in a hotel in the last 12 months were contacted. We asked them via email for their participation. However, the survey was only answered by 18 participants, where 8 responses were discarded because they had incomplete sections, or because it did not correspond to what was asked. Thus, 10 responses were considered valid, 6 related to their experience in hotels and 4 related to why they are not staying in hotels (mainly related to a price factor).

Table 3. Survey design

Sections	Questions
Demographic	• Age • Gender • Civil status • Education level • No. of hotels visited last 12 months • Purpose of travel • Travel companion • Hotel location
Stage 1: CX before the stay Stage 2: CX during the stay Stage 3: CX after the stay	• Mention direct or indirect interactions with a hotel and the channels where they took place • How did you feel about these interactions? • If they existed, mention positive and negative experiences in each interaction • In a general way, how did you feel at this stage?

4 Results

After designing the experiment and obtaining the data, we discussed and analyzed the information obtained. This section briefly presents the profile of the participants, the touchpoints and emotions detected, and the CJM proposed.

4.1 Responders' Profile

As mentioned above, 18 participants participated in the experiment, nevertheless only 6 responses were considered valid. Thus, Table 4 below presents the demographic dimensions and experience related to the interaction with a hotel of the respondents.

Table 4. Demographic and travel profile of the respondents.

Dimension	Items	Percentage (participants)
Age	Under 20	17% (1)
	21–30	83% (5)
Gender	Female	67% (4)
	Male	33% (2)
Civil status	Single	100% (6)
Education level	Undergraduate	83% (5)
	Postgraduate	17% (1)
No. of hotels visited last 12 months	1 time	68% (4)
	2 times	16% (1)
	3 or more times	16% (1)
Purpose of travel	Leisure/vacations	100% (6)
Travel companion	Friends	17% (1)
	Family	50% (3)
	Couple	33% (2)
Hotel location	Chile	33% (2)
	Foreign country	67% (4)

As shown in Table 4, the demographic profile highlighted in the sample is a woman between 21–30 years old, whose civil status is single, and currently studying at undergraduate level. Regarding the travel profile she has preferences for traveling for leisure/vacation to a foreign country and with her family. This information will be used as a reference to create a customer profile and represent the CX through different interactions in a CJM. However, it is important to understand that this information corresponds only to one type of customer, therefore the results should not be generalized.

4.2 Touchpoints, Channels, and Emotions Identified

By analyzing the multiple responses obtained in the survey, it was possible to define various touchpoints present in the CX with hotels. Thus, Table 5 presents the touchpoints mentioned by the respondents in the different stages of interaction, and the related channels.

Table 5. Touchpoints and channels identified in the survey.

Stages	Touchpoints	Channels
Stage 1: CX before the stay	Search a hotel	Websites – Travel Agency
	Get features about the hotel	Websites – Email
	Compare hotels	Websites
	Choose a hotel	Websites – Email
	Book a room	Websites – Phone
Stage 2: CX during the stay	Check-In	Hotel Front Desk
	Receive room	Hotel Front Desk – Hotel Room
	Stay the night	Hotel Room
	Visit common areas	Hotel Front Desk – Hotel Restaurant – Hotel Lobby – Hotel Gym
	Order food	Hotel Restaurant – Room Service
	Check-out	Hotel Front Desk
Stage 3: CX after the stay	Receive a perception survey	Email
	Leave a review	Websites – Social Networks

As shown in Table 5, several touchpoints in the different stages of interaction with a hotel were identified. Each touchpoint is briefly explained below, and a general analysis of emotions is subsequently presented for each stage.

- **Search a hotel:** The customer enters different websites, either the hotel's own or an external one to search for a hotel in which he can stay on his trip.
- **Get features about the hotel:** The customer investigates about the characteristics of the hotel, e.g., services provided, location, prices, room types, among others.
- **Compare hotels:** The customer looks for similar hotels to have different options, usually checks other websites or reads reviews from other customers.
- **Choose a hotel:** The customer chooses the best option that satisfy their needs as his know the products and services offered.
- **Book a room:** The customer proceeds to make the reservation of the hotel room in which he wishes to stay by entering the reservation information, defining a method of payment and checking the terms and conditions.

- **Check-in:** The customer interacts with the reception staff by providing or confirming their personal information to validate a reservation made.
- **Receive room:** The customer receives the room key/card after the reception staff validates the booking information and gives him information of the hotel.
- **Stay the night:** The customer takes a shower and sleeps in the bed of his room.
- **Visit common areas of the hotel:** The customer interacts with different common areas of the hotel such as hotel front desk, hotel lobby, hotel restaurant, gym, bar, hall, among others.
- **Order food:** The customer orders food either for breakfast, lunch, and/or dinner by interacting directly with the restaurant or by calling the room service.
- **Check-out:** The customer interacts with the reception staff to end their stay; the staff checks for problems with their room and additional charges are made if the customer used a payment service.
- **Receive a perception survey:** The customer receives a survey thanking the visit and asking if he can evaluate his stay at the hotel and comment if there was any problem/inconvenience to improve it.
- **Leave a review:** The customer leaves a review on internet, whether it is on the hotel's website, an external one or a social network, telling their experience with the hotel.

The first stage consists of the various touchpoints before a customer stays in a hotel. At this stage, the most mentioned touchpoints were "search a hotel" and "choose a hotel", where half of the participants indicates their experiences in these interactions. In general, respondents indicated satisfaction with the different touchpoints, this can be observed in comments such as: "precise identification of the free and paid services offered by the hotel", "variety of options and prices for different needs", or "existence of several images of the hotel and its rooms".

The second stage involves several touchpoints that can happen from the moment the customer arrives at the hotel until he leaves. At this stage, the touchpoint "check-out" was mentioned by all participants. Nevertheless, no consensus was reached on the emotions of this interaction, as different comments were obtained such as: "check-out took a long time" or "the staff remembered my name and the process was fast". Furthermore, other of the most commented touchpoints were "check-in" and "order food", where very satisfactory experiences were obtained from respondents such as: "friendly and helpful staff" or "wide variety of food". Thus, although the experience at check-out was mostly negative, in general customer indicated a lot of satisfaction at this stage.

Finally, the third stage present touchpoints that can occur after the customer's stay in a hotel. In this experiment only two interactions were mentioned by the respondents, i.e., "receive a perception survey" and "leave a review". However, unlike other stages, no negative comments were obtained for these touchpoints by the participants. Therefore, the perception of customers at this stage varies from satisfactory to very satisfactory, this was observed in comments such as: "the hotel is concerned to know how the stay of its customers was and how can improve" and "the hotel responded the comments politely".

4.3   Customer Journey Map Proposed

Based on the experience of the authors and the comments obtained, it was possible to group and rename the touchpoints presented above into 8 interactions. This is because some of these touchpoints correspond to the same interaction with a hotel. Thus, Table 6 presents the grouped touchpoints used to create a CJM.

Table 6. Relationship between identified and refined touchpoints

Stages	Identified touchpoints	Grouped touchpoints
Stage 1: CX before the stay	Search a hotel	Search for information
	Get features about the hotel	
	Compare hotels	
	Choose a hotel	Book a room
	Book a room	
Stage 2: CX during the stay	Check-in	Check-in
	Receive room	Room stay
	Stay the night	
	Visit common areas	Visit common areas
	Order food	Order & receive food
	Check-out	Check-out
Stage 3: CX after the stay	Receive a perception survey	Report experience
	Leave a review	

As shown in Table 6 different touchpoints were grouped in order represent the CX in the hotel industry, a brief explanation of these touchpoints is presented below.

- **Search for information:** Includes touchpoints related to searching, find out and comparing hotels. Thus, at this touchpoint customers have the need to search for a hotel room on some website where they are informed about the characteristics of the hotel, offered services and amenities. Finally, customers compare between different hotels found by entering other websites or reading reviews.
- **Book a room:** Includes touchpoints related to choosing a hotel and booking a room. Thus, at this touchpoint the customers have knowledge about which hotel to choose because it best suits their needs. Therefore, the customers proceed to book a room checking the terms and conditions and entering the necessary data to make the reservation.
- **Check-in:** At this touchpoint, customers arrive at the hotel and interact with the front desk to validate a reservation, then the check-in staff registers them and gives them the key/card of their room.
- **Room stay:** Includes touchpoints related to receive room and stay the night. This touchpoint is related to the interaction of customers with booked room from the

moment they receive the keys and enters the room until the last day of their stay, including activities such as resting, showering or sleeping.

- **Visit common areas:** At this touchpoint, customers interact with different common areas of the hotel such as hotel front desk, hotel lobby, hotel restaurant, gym, bar, hall, among others.
- **Order & Receive food:** At this touchpoint, customers order and receive food/menu items either for breakfast, lunch, and/or dinner by interacting with the restaurant or the room service.
- **Check-out:** At this touchpoint, customers interact with check-out staff at the front desk to end their stay; the staff checks for problems with their room and make additional charges if customers used any paid product/service.
- **Report experience:** Includes touchpoints related to receive a perception survey and leave a review. At this touchpoint, customers indicate either in a survey or on some website/social network how his experience was interacting with that hotel. While the hotel is responsible for reviewing and responding to the comments of its customers.

As stated above, these touchpoints were used to propose a CJM. However, the CX is completely personal and/or subjective. Therefore, the Persona technique was used to create a representative customer profile using the information obtained in the survey (see Fig. 1). Thus, the CJM presented below (Fig. 2, 3 and 4) represents the journey of this type of customer and its emotions in different stages, touchpoints, and channels when interacting with the hotel industry.

Persona	 Jane
Profile	**Age:** 22-25 y/o **Gender:** Female **Civil Status:** Single **Education level:** Undergraduate **Purpose of travel:** Leisure **Travel Companion:** Family
Bio	"Jane is a young woman who likes to travel on vacation to foreign countries. Whenever she plans a trip, she look for the hotel that is closest to the city center and has the best ratings for other travelers. When she arrives at the hotel she expects the check-in to be efficient because long trips make her tired. She loves that her room and especially the bathroom has amenities as she never travels with products like shampoo or brushes. She likes to visit tourist places and taste their dishes, so she never visits the restaurants of hotels, however she eats at night using room service.Finally, she always plans her schedule so she hates the check-out being delayed."

Fig. 1. Persona used to represent the CJM

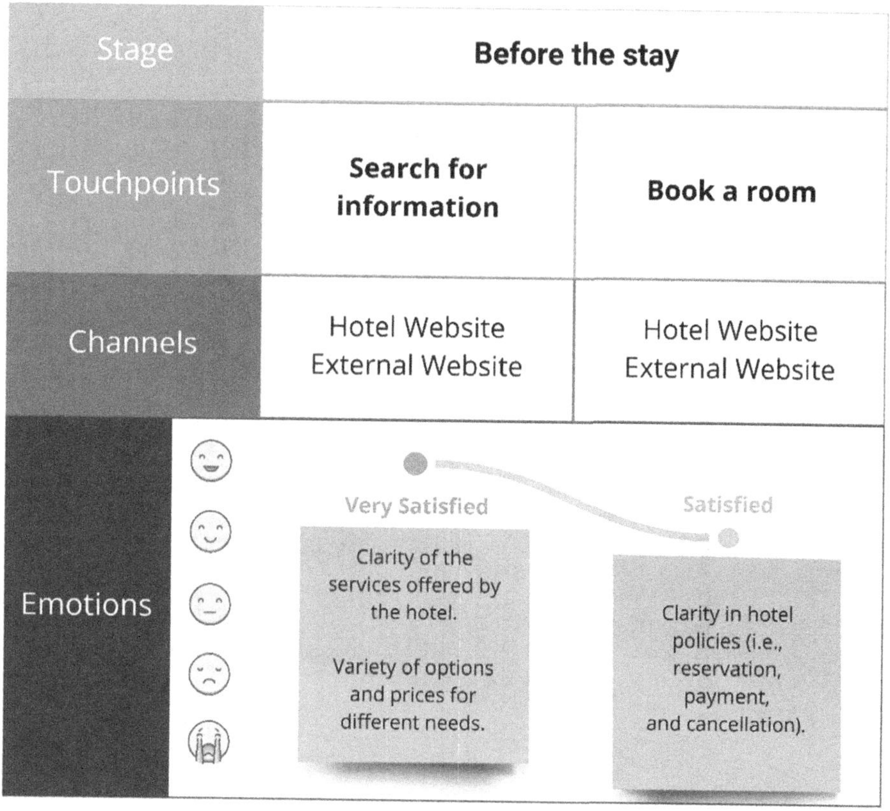

Stage	Before the stay	
Touchpoints	**Search for information**	**Book a room**
Channels	Hotel Website External Website	Hotel Website External Website
Emotions	Very Satisfied Clarity of the services offered by the hotel. Variety of options and prices for different needs.	Satisfied Clarity in hotel policies (i.e., reservation, payment, and cancellation).

Fig. 2. CJM – CX before the stay

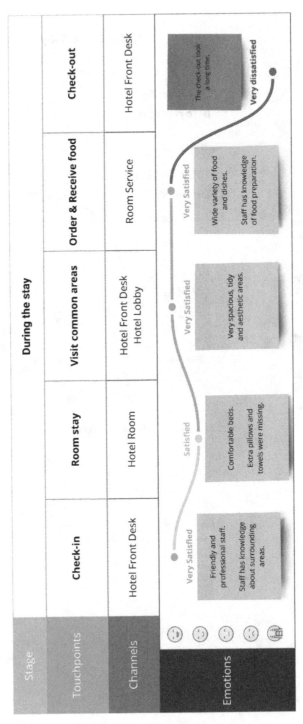

Fig. 3. CJM – CX during the stay

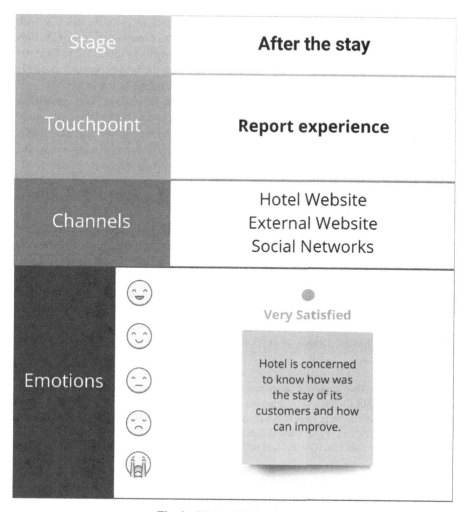

Fig. 4. CJM – CX after the stay

5   Conclusions and Future Work

This study was conducted with the purpose of identifying multiple touchpoints, channels and emotions of customers in different stages of interaction with hotels and represent them in a CJM. To achieve this, it was necessary to carry out an experiment to obtain feedback from different types of customers. Thus, after observing the results of the survey, 13 interactions with hotels could be identified preliminarily. However, when discussing and analyzing these results, they were grouped into 8 touchpoints: (1) search for information, (2) book a room, (3) check-in, (4) room stay, (5) visit common areas, (6) order & receive food, (7) check-out, and (8) report experience.

The results of this work provide important implications for researchers and practitioners. Regarding researchers, this work could help them to develop different methods and/or instruments such as scales, checklists, or heuristics to evaluate the CX with different types of hotels and correlating these touchpoints to dimensions of the CX. Furthermore, it can help practitioners to know the several interactions they need to focus on to satisfy the needs of their customers to provide them with the best experience possible in order to improve the CX and achieve a competitive advantage in the industry.

As this research progressed and developed, different limitations were identified. Firstly, the number of participants in the experiment was very limited; this is mainly because it was not possible to find customers with experience in the last 12 months with hotels due to "the social outbreak" in Chile and the coronavirus disease pandemic. Secondly, within the grouped touchpoints it was detected that "order & receive food" is a very specific interaction that does not usually occur in any type of hotel, and "visit common areas" is very general, as there are multiple areas inside hotels where customers interact and generate experiences.

As future work, we will intent to extend the study and fill the gaps found in the limitations. Regarding the first limitation, additional experiments will be carried out to validate the data obtained in the survey conducted and subsequently different CJM will be designed with new customer profiles. Concerning the second limitation, different groupings of touchpoints will be specified for different types of hotel, therefore there will be no limitations of very specific or general touchpoints. Finally, it is planned to use the information obtained in this research to propose checklists, scales, heuristics, and/or formal recommendations to improve the CX in hotel industry through products, systems or services.

Acknowledgment. This work was supported by the School of Informatics Engineering of the Pontificia Universidad Católica de Valparaíso – Chile. Luis Rojas has been granted the "INF-PUCV" Graduate Scholarship. Luis Rojas is supported by Grant ANID BECAS/DOCTORADO NACIONAL, Chile, N° 21211272. Daniela Quiñones is supported by Grant ANID (ex CONICYT), Chile, FONDECYT INICIACIÓN, Project N° 11190759.

References

1. Meyer, C., Schwager, A.: Understanding customer experience. Harv. Bus. Rev. **85**(2), 116 (2007)
2. Gentile, C., Spiller, N., Noci, G.: How to sustain the customer experience: an overview of experience components that co-create value with the customer. Eur. Manag. J. **25**(5), 395–410 (2007)
3. Lemon, K., Verhoef, P.: Understanding customer experience throughout the customer journey. J. Mark. **80**(6), 69–96 (2016)
4. Schmitt, B.: Experiential marketing. J. Mark. Manag. **15**(3), 53–67 (1999)
5. Ali, F., Hussain, K., Ragavan, N.A.: Memorable customer experience: examining the effects of customers experience on memories and loyalty in Malaysian resort hotels. Procedia Soc. Behav. Sci. **144**(1), 273–279 (2014)
6. Stein, A., Ramaseshan, B.: Towards the identification of customer experience touch point elements. J. Retail. Consum. Serv. **30**, 8–19 (2016)
7. Marquez, J., Downey, A., Clement, R.: Walking a mile in the user's shoes: customer journey mapping as a method to understanding the user experience. Internet Ref. Serv. Q. **20**(3–4), 135–150 (2015)

8. Van Hover, K.: How to create a Customer Journey Map (2018). https://www.ngdata.com/how-to-create-a-customer-journey-map/. Access 19 Jan 2021
9. Komninos, A.: Customer Journey Maps - Walking a Mile in Your Customer's Shoes (2019). https://www.interaction-design.org/literature/article/customer-journey-maps-walking-a-mile-in-your-customer-s-shoes. Accessed 19 Jan 2021
10. World Travel and Tourism Council. Travel & Tourism Economic Impact 2019 (2019)
11. Kaspar, C.: Leisure-Recreation-Tourism. An Introduction to the General Topic of the 31st AIEST Congress, AIEST Editions, Berne (1981)
12. North American Industry Classification System. https://www.census.gov/eos/www/naics/. Accessed 19 Jan 2021
13. Revfine: Hotel Industry: Everything You Need to Know About Hotels! (2020). https://www.revfine.com/hotel-industry/. Accessed 19 Jan 2021

Fairness in Design: A Tool for Guidance in Ethical Artificial Intelligence Design

Ying Shu[1]([✉]), Jiehuang Zhang[1,2], and Han Yu[1]

[1] School of Computer Science and Engineering, Nanyang Technological University,
Singapore, Singapore
{ying005,jiehuang001,han.yu}@ntu.edu.sg
[2] Alibaba-NTU Singapore Joint Research Institute, Singapore, Singapore

Abstract. As the artificial intelligence (AI) industry booms and the systems they created are impacting our lives immensely, we begin to realize that these systems are not as impartial as we thought them to be. Even though they are machines that make logical decisions, biases and discrimination are able to creep into the data and model to affect outcomes causing harm. This pushes us to re-evaluate the design metrics for creating such systems and put more focus on integrating human values in the system. However, even when the awareness of the need for ethical AI systems is high, there are currently limited methodologies available for designers and engineers to incorporate human values into their designs. Our methodology tool aims to address this gap by assisting product teams to surface fairness concerns, navigate complex ethical choices around fairness, and overcome blind spots and team biases. It can also help them to stimulate perspective thinking from multiple parties and stakeholders. With our tool, we aim to lower the bar to add fairness into the design discussion so that more design teams can make better and more informed decisions for fairness in their application scenarios.

Keywords: Design method · Design tool · Value sensitive design · Fairness in Artificial Intelligence · Ethical Artificial Intelligence · Responsible Artificial Intelligence

1 Introduction

With the speed of current breakthroughs, Artificial Intelligence (AI) has evolved to become a crucial backbone of society and a disruptor to almost every industry [26]. The influence is so huge that it is included as part of a technological revolution that will fundamentally change the way we live, work, and connect [23]. More algorithm tools are being used to supplement or replace human decision-making in all aspects of life [6], even in important and life-changing areas such as medicine and law. It is undeniable that with this level of power, there should be greater responsibility placed upon these AI systems.

For so long, key design metrics of AI systems were reliability, efficiency, and accuracy. We were mesmerized by the speed and capacity of these machines and

© Springer Nature Switzerland AG 2021
G. Meiselwitz (Ed.): HCII 2021, LNCS 12774, pp. 500–510, 2021.
https://doi.org/10.1007/978-3-030-77626-8_34

we aim to train them to be faster and better. However, the focus on these metrics above all else overlooked that these AI systems are not as impartial and reliable as we thought them to be. Even though they are machines that follow logic, biases and discrimination can creep into the data and models to affect outcomes to the point of causing harm [8,28]. The most notable example would be the Correctional Offender Management Profiling for Alternative Sanctions (COMPAS) software used in state courts systems in the U.S. whereby the model predicted twice as many false positives for recidivism for African-Americans offenders than white Americans [1]. In 2019, a healthcare risk-prediction algorithm that was used on more than 200 million people in the U.S. was found to show racial bias as it was less likely to identify eligible black people for high-risk care management due to a faulty metric [25].

Due to such serious negative consequences of algorithm bias, it is of utmost priority to develop responsible and ethical AI. This pushes us to re-evaluate the design process for creating such systems. One way is to start integrating human values early in the design process, especially when AI systems are capable of embodying political, social, and ethical values. Since product teams train AI with the data they choose, they have the power to ensure that machines hold up end-user values with a human-centric focus [18]. Therefore, methodologies for product teams to incorporate such values, as well as to avoid and minimize the negative impact of overlooking these values become crucial [14]. Mere awareness from product teams about the importance of human values in AI design is not enough. There needs to be tried and tested tools to help them identify the human values critical to the system, engage such values in their consideration, and discover any potential fatal problems, especially at the earliest stages of the design process when the specifications and prototypes are still fluid [11].

Even though they are of much importance, there are currently limited methodologies and tools available for product teams to incorporate ethical human values into their design process. Most of the methodologies come from the theoretical approach of Value Sensitive Design [14]. However, these methodologies tend to be generic without a focus on any human values. There are close to none that helps product teams to zoom in and dissect a human value deeper.

In this paper, we propose a methodology tool - Fairness in Design - to address this gap. We chose the ethical value of fairness to be the focal point of the tool as the lack of consideration for it showed us the danger of algorithm bias. Furthermore, it is a complex human value that has different meanings for different people. In the machine learning literature, there are already more than ten definitions and metrics for fairness [24]. Besides, there are also fundamental statistical incompatibilities between the fairness metrics such that there is no solution that can satisfy all metrics [5,21]. Thus, product teams are forced to consider the trade-offs between these metrics when considering fairness for their AI systems. It is therefore understandable that product teams will find it daunting to grasp all these in a short frame of time during their design process. A survey of industry practitioners in machine learning also indicated that they face problems in foreseeing trade-offs between fairness definitions, anticipating and overcoming blind spots, and auditing when designing fairer AI systems [19].

Our methodological tool aims to enable product teams to not only be more aware of fairness criteria for systems but also allow them to surface potential fairness concerns for their application scenario by stimulating perspective-taking from different stakeholders. In this paper, we will first elaborate on fairness in machine learning and value sensitive design as the foundation for the methodology tool. The instructions on using the tool as well as components of the tool will be described in detail subsequently. We conclude by discussing the potential benefits as well as outlining our future works. We also hope to inspire researchers to construct more methodological tools that enable the integration of human values into the design process.

2   Related Work

2.1   Fairness in Artificial Intelligence

There have been considerable efforts in the field of AI to determine how to operationalize fairness in a way algorithms can understand [4,20,27]. As the philosophical theories of fairness are discussed in words, the attempt is to construct similar concepts at a mathematical level. So far, two different categories have been distinguished for fairness definitions: individual and group fairness [9,22]. Individual fairness requires similarly situated individuals to be treated similarly [9]. It is fulfilled when the algorithm gives similar outputs to individuals who have similar attributes that determine the results. There are three statistical definitions under individual fairness which are fairness through awareness [9], fairness through unawareness [16], and counterfactual fairness [22]. Group fairness on the other hand requires different groups to be treated equally [9]. It is fulfilled when the distribution of outcomes is the same for each group. There are seven statistical definitions under group fairness which include demographic/statistical parity [27], conditional statistical parity [7], equalized odds [17], equal opportunity [17], test fairness [5], treatment equality [3], and fairness in relational domain [10]. We will be using these ten main fairness definitions as the focus of the tool.

2.2   Value Sensitive Design

Value Sensitive Design (VSD) is the most famous theoretical approach in value design of technology that focuses on integrating human values in a principled and methodical way throughout the design process [12]. It encompasses a large literature of targeted methods to engage with values differently. Qualities of VSD methods include being committed to the theoretical constructs of VSD, being in descriptive form to help designers gain more insights, and staying open to integration with other methods, adaptation and changes [15].

One method is direct and indirect stakeholder analysis. This analysis allows the identification and legitimation of stakeholders, as well as explores how they might be impacted [14]. This is useful as designers tend to focus on direct stakeholders, who are those that interact directly with the technology and often miss out on indirect stakeholders, those that do not interact directly with the technology but are still affected.

There are also two prominent methodology tools from VSD: Envisioning Cards and Judgment Call. Envisioning cards consist of 32 physical cards and are built on four criteria: stakeholders, time, values, and pervasiveness. The cards allow designers to think about the long-term and systemic issues in technology design [13]. Similarly, Judgement Call is a game that allows the design team to identify ethical concerns in a specific system via self-generated feedback [2]. It also consists of physical cards with four categories: the ethical value, the stakeholder, the number of stars, and wild cards. Our tool draws inspiration from both of them as they provide an open, engaging, and creative process to think about the impact of values in technology.

3   Fairness in Design: Introduction and Usage

Fairness in Design is in the form of physical cards and consists of five to six steps. It can be played in groups of minimum two and only requires pens or pencils. The cards can be used by a diverse range of users with varying expertise in AI from industry product teams to university students. It can also be used for different application areas involving AI systems. Users do not need any prior knowledge of fairness before using this tool. We have outlined the steps in Fig. 1 and we will elaborate more about the cards used in each step below.

3.1   Step 1: Write the Application Scenario

The first step involves the whole team identifying the application scenario they will use the tool for. It can be the actual product that they are working on or a fictional product. To have the most optimal effect, members should also be specific and elaborate on the component of the product that they want to assess fairness on. This will help to aid the discussion later by making the fairness criteria more relatable to the application scenario. As the tool can be used in any stage of the design process, product teams may choose to focus on an area that they have found or suspected to have fairness issues. This allows them to think about fairness concerns in a more open environment away from the technical details. Product teams developing complex AI systems can also consider breaking down the system into individual modules before starting so that the discussion will be focused and effective.

3.2   Step 2: Choose an Application Card

After indicating their application scenario, the team has to choose an application card that is the most relevant to their application scenario. There are five categories to choose from: 1) life-critical systems 2) industrial and commercial uses 3) office, home, and entertainment 4) exploratory, creative, collaborative applications 5) sociotechnical applications. They are adapted from Shneiderman's

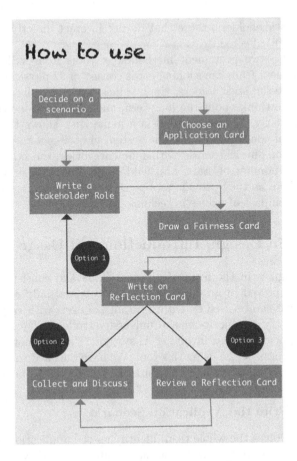

Fig. 1. A visual guide of Fairness in Design.

classification for usability motivation in the literature of Human-Computer Interaction (HCI). Similarly in ethical AI design, different AI applications will have different motivations and requirements for their design that will affect how they view fairness. Hence on each card, it will include thought-provoking statements and questions to provide a guide to the team in their evaluation of fairness criteria later on. It also includes application examples so that the team can more easily identify which application category their application scenario belongs to. Figure 2 shows an example of an application card.

3.3   Step 3: Identify the Stakeholders

Using the application scenario and application card as the background, the team will be given the definitions of direct and indirect stakeholders to read and understand. Each member will take a reflection card and write a stakeholder role on the space provided for it. The members have the flexibility to decide if

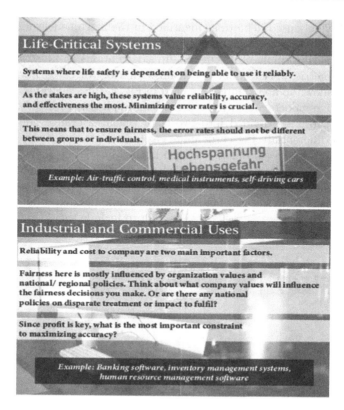

Fig. 2. Application card for life-critical systems and industrial and commercial uses.

they want to write a direct or indirect stakeholder role. This will be their identity for the remaining steps.

We adopt direct and indirect stakeholder analysis [14] to enable the teams to identify the stakeholders for their application scenario. Stakeholders are not only individuals and groups but can also be institutions and societies. We use the definitions described in Judgment Call as our definitions. Direct stakeholders refer to those who interact directly with the technology and can include end-users, designers, engineers, hackers, and administrators whereas indirect stakeholders do not interact with the technology but are affected by its use and can include advocacy groups, families of end-users, regulators, and society at large [2]. Identifying both categories is crucial as designers tend to focus on direct stakeholders and often miss out on indirect stakeholders in examining the impact on them.

3.4   Step 4: Draw a Fairness Card

Once every member has written their stakeholder role, they will draw one fairness card each and write it down on the reflection card as well. This will be their fairness metric to reflect on later. There are a total of ten fairness cards according to the most widely used definitions identified in the machine learning literature [24]. One side of the card contains the fairness metric name, definition, and the mathematical formula of it. On the flip side contains an illustration of how the fairness metric works under a certain scenario. All cards have the same scenario. As shown in an example of a card in Fig. 2, the scenario is a bank that has a predictive model to determine if the loan application will be approved or denied. The cards are divided into two color schemes: orange and blue. This is so to help differentiate the cards more easily into group fairness (in orange) and individual fairness (in blue). It is also labeled at the top right-hand corner to highlight to the members. We included the mathematical formulae as some engineers might understand the metrics easier by referring to them. As the cards are from the existing literature of fairness in AI, if new and better fairness metrics are operationalized, the tool is flexible enough to include them (Fig. 3).

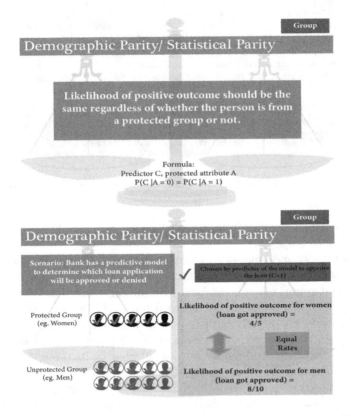

Fig. 3. An example fairness card (front and back). (Color figure online)

3.5   Step 5: Write a Reflection

After every member gets a fairness card, they will need to write their thoughts on the reflection card. With the application card as a guide, they are required to think about how the fairness metric will impact them from the perspective of their stakeholder role. Two questions are on the card to prompt the team in their thought process, namely asking them what could go right and what could go wrong with the fairness metric they have gotten. The team has to remember to think from the shoes of their stakeholder role and not as themselves.

3.6   Step 6: Go to Step 3 or Collect and Discuss or Write Review

When everyone has written their reviews, the team now has three different options to proceed. The first option is to go back to step 3 to write another round of stakeholder roles and start the process again. This is recommended for teams who want to cover more stakeholder roles as one round might not be enough to cover both direct and indirect stakeholders.

The second option is to collect the reflection cards, randomize them, and take turns reading them out loud. The cards will not contain any names for anonymity and will include the stakeholder role, the fairness metric that is chosen, and the reflection. Discussing the cards can surface potential benefits, harms, and tensions of fairness definitions. It can also help to discover potential blind spots. As everyone takes on a role, it differs from a normal brainstorming meeting whereby the only perspectives are usually of engineers and designers. This gives a more comprehensive overview without having to conduct extensive stakeholder studies and mitigates the potential team biases.

The third option is for each member to review another member's reflection card. Reflection cards will be collected, randomized, and given out. On the review card, members can give a rating of importance over a Likert scale of 1 to 5, 1 representing not important at all and 5 representing extremely important. The importance scale is to measure how important the reviewer thinks the fairness metric is to the product that they are creating. They can also add a comment to elaborate on why they give this rating. After everybody is done with the reviews, the cards will be collected, randomized, and shared out loud. This means that in addition to reflection cards in the previous option, the team can discuss the reviews as well. This is recommended for teams who want to work with a ranking of the fairness metrics that will likely be most important to their stakeholders and products.

4   Conclusions and Future Work

In this paper, we highlighted the gaps in ethical AI design methodologies and expressed the need for a tool that deciphers an ethical value deeper. We engaged the existing fairness literature in machine learning and the theory of VSD to create a tool that aims to help users to surface fairness concerns, navigate complex ethical choices around fairness, and overcome blind spots and team biases. The instruction for using the tool has also been described in detail.

With this methodological tool, product teams that view fairness as an important value in their AI system can now be focused on it. We understand that product teams often face barriers to improve fairness in their products even when they are motivated to do so. Since our tool takes a short amount of time and is easy to follow, we hope that the bar to include fairness into the design discussion will be lowered and more product teams can make better and more informed decisions for fairness in their application scenarios. We also hope to inspire researchers to construct more methodological tools that enable the integration of human values into the design process.

Our future work will be focused on conducting user studies to evaluate if the tool is effective in achieving the aims. We will be testing the tool with actual product teams that are working on different areas of AI systems. At the same time, due to Covid 19 and the increased uptake in working from home arrangements, we realize that most product teams will be working together online instead. This makes physical cards impractical since most employees will not be in the office together. As a result of this new norm, we are also extending efforts to digitalize our physical tool into a web application. Team members can collaborate and go through the methodology online. There will also be functions for facilitators to manage their teams and control the process. Having an online tool will help to reduce the need to arrange meetings and provide the flexibility to work on fairness at their convenience.

Acknowledgements. This research is supported, in part, by Nanyang Technological University, Nanyang Assistant Professorship (NAP); Alibaba Group through Alibaba Innovative Research (AIR) Program and Alibaba-NTU Singapore Joint Research Institute (JRI) (Alibaba-NTU-AIR2019B1), Nanyang Technological University, Singapore; the RIE 2020 Advanced Manufacturing and Engineering (AME) Programmatic Fund (No. A20G8b0102), Singapore; and the Joint SDU-NTU Centre for Artificial Intelligence Research (C-FAIR).

References

1. Angwin, J., Larson, J., Mattu, S., Kirchner, L.: Machine bias: there's software used across the country to predict future criminals and it's biased against blacks. ProPublica (2016)
2. Ballard, S., Chappell, K.M., Kennedy, K.: Judgment call the game: using value sensitive design and design fiction to surface ethical concerns related to technology. In: Proceedings of the 2019 on Designing Interactive Systems Conference, pp. 421–433 (2019)
3. Berk, R., Heidari, H., Jabbari, S., Kearns, M., Roth, A.: Fairness in criminal justice risk assessments: the state of the art. Soc. Meth. Res. **50**, 3–44 (2018)
4. Binns, R.: Fairness in machine learning: lessons from political philosophy. In: Conference on Fairness, Accountability and Transparency, pp. 149–159. PMLR (2018)

5. Chouldechova, A.: Fair prediction with disparate impact: a study of bias in recidivism prediction instruments. Big Data **5**(2), 153–163 (2017)
6. Coglianese, C.: Algorithmic Regulation. The Algorithmic Society, Technology, Power, and Knowledge (2020)
7. Corbett-Davies, S., Pierson, E., Feller, A., Goel, S., Huq, A.: Algorithmic decision making and the cost of fairness. In: Proceedings of the 23rd ACM SIGKDD International Conference on Knowledge Discovery and Data Mining, pp. 797–806 (2017)
8. Crawford, K.: Artificial intelligence's white guy problem. The New York Times, 25 June 2016
9. Dwork, C., Hardt, M., Pitassi, T., Reingold, O., Zemel, R.: Fairness through awareness. In: Proceedings of the 3rd Innovations in Theoretical Computer Science Conference, pp. 214–226 (2012)
10. Farnadi, G., Babaki, B., Getoor, L.: Fairness in relational domains. In: Proceedings of the 2018 AAAI/ACM Conference on AI, Ethics, and Society, pp. 108–114 (2018)
11. Flanagan, M., Howe, D.C., Nissenbaum, H.: Values at play: design tradeoffs in socially-oriented game design. In: Proceedings of the SIGCHI Conference on Human Factors in Computing Systems, pp. 751–760 (2005)
12. Friedman, B.: Value-sensitive design. Interactions **3**(6), 16–23 (1996)
13. Friedman, B., Hendry, D.: The envisioning cards: a toolkit for catalyzing humanistic and technical imaginations. In: Proceedings of the SIGCHI Conference on Human Factors in Computing Systems, pp. 1145–1148 (2012)
14. Friedman, B., Hendry, D.G., Borning, A.: A survey of value sensitive design methods. Found. Trends Hum. Comput. Interact. **11**(2), 63–125 (2017)
15. Friedman, B., Kahn, P., Borning, A.: Value sensitive design: theory and methods. University of Washington, Technical report 02-12-01 (2002)
16. Grgic-Hlaca, N., Zafar, M.B., Gummadi, K.P., Weller, A.: The case for process fairness in learning: feature selection for fair decision making. In: NIPS Symposium on Machine Learning and the Law, vol. 1, p. 2 (2016)
17. Hardt, M., Price, E., Srebro, N.: Equality of opportunity in supervised learning. arXiv preprint arXiv:1610.02413 (2016)
18. Havens, J.: Heartificial Intelligence: Embracing Our Humanity to Maximize achines. Jeremy P. Tarcher/Penguin (2016)
19. Holstein, K., Wortman Vaughan, J., Daumé III, H., Dudik, M., Wallach, H.: Improving fairness in machine learning systems: what do industry practitioners need? In: Proceedings of the 2019 CHI Conference on Human Factors in Computing Systems, pp. 1–16 (2019)
20. Hutchinson, B., Mitchell, M.: 50 years of test (un)fairness: lessons for machine learning. In: Proceedings of the Conference on Fairness, Accountability, and Transparency, pp. 49–58 (2019)
21. Kleinberg, J., Mullainathan, S., Raghavan, M.: Inherent trade-offs in the fair determination of risk scores. arXiv preprint arXiv:1609.05807 (2016)
22. Kusner, M.J., Loftus, J.R., Russell, C., Silva, R.: Counterfactual fairness. arXiv preprint arXiv:1703.06856 (2017)
23. Makridakis, S.: The forthcoming artificial intelligence (AI) revolution: its impact on society and firms. Futures **90**, 46–60 (2017)
24. Mehrabi, N., Morstatter, F., Saxena, N., Lerman, K., Galstyan, A.: A survey on bias and fairness in machine learning. arXiv preprint arXiv:1908.09635 (2019)
25. Obermeyer, Z., Powers, B., Vogeli, C., Mullainathan, S.: Dissecting racial bias in an algorithm used to manage the health of populations. Science **366**(6464), 447–453 (2019)

26. Schwab, K.: The Fourth Industrial Revolution. Currency (2017)
27. Verma, S., Rubin, J.: Fairness definitions explained. In: 2018 IEEE/ACM International Workshop on Software Fairness (Fairware), pp. 1–7. IEEE (2018)
28. Yapo, A., Weiss, J.: Ethical implications of bias in machine learning. In: Proceedings of the 51st Hawaii International Conference on System Sciences (2018)

Drone-Based AI and 3D Reconstruction for Digital Twin Augmentation

Alex To[1], Maican Liu[2], Muhammad Hazeeq Bin Muhammad Hairul[2],
Joseph G. Davis[1], Jeannie S.A. Lee[3], Henrik Hesse[4], and Hoang D. Nguyen[5(✉)]

[1] School of Computer Science, University of Sydney, Sydney, Australia
`duto3894@uni.sydney.edu.au, joseph.davis@sydney.edu.au`
[2] Aviation Virtual Pte Ltd., Singapore, Singapore
[3] Infocomm Technology, Singapore Institute of Technology, Singapore, Singapore
`Jeannie.Lee@singaporetech.edu.sg`
[4] James Watt School of Engineering, University of Glasgow, Singapore, Singapore
`Henrik.Hesse@glasgow.ac.uk`
[5] School of Computing Science, University of Glasgow, Singapore, Singapore
`Harry.Nguyen@glasgow.ac.uk`

Abstract. Digital Twin is an emerging technology at the forefront of Industry 4.0, with the ultimate goal of combining the physical space and the virtual space. To date, the Digital Twin concept has been applied in many engineering fields, providing useful insights in the areas of engineering design, manufacturing, automation, and construction industry. While the nexus of various technologies opens up new opportunities with Digital Twin, the technology requires a framework to integrate the different technologies, such as the Building Information Model used in the Building and Construction industry. In this work, an Information Fusion framework is proposed to seamlessly fuse heterogeneous components in a Digital Twin framework from the variety of technologies involved. This study aims to augment Digital Twin in buildings with the use of AI and 3D reconstruction empowered by unmanned aviation vehicles. We proposed a drone-based Digital Twin augmentation framework with reusable and customisable components. A proof of concept is also developed, and extensive evaluation is conducted for 3D reconstruction and applications of AI for defect detection.

Keywords: Digital Twin · 3D reconstruction · Artificial Intelligence (AI) · Information augmentation · Unmanned aerial vehicle (UAV)

1 Introduction

A Digital Twin is the virtual replication of a physical object. Through modelling and real-time data communication, the Digital Twin simulates the actual properties and behaviours of its physical counterpart in the physical space, thus, enable learning, reasoning, and dynamically re-calibrating for improved decision-making [19,21]. The tight and seamless integration between the physical and

© Springer Nature Switzerland AG 2021
G. Meiselwitz (Ed.): HCII 2021, LNCS 12774, pp. 511–529, 2021.
https://doi.org/10.1007/978-3-030-77626-8_35

virtual space in the Digital Twin paradigm makes it one of the most promising enabling technologies for the realization of smart manufacturing and Industry 4.0 [49].

To date, Digital Twin applications have seen success in various industries and domains, including product design, production, prognostic and health management, building and construction, and many others. Recent advances in sensor technologies, big data, cloud computing, social networks, Internet of Things (IoT), Computer-Aided-Design (CAD), 3D modelling, and Artificial Intelligence (AI) allow a massive amount of data to be collected while enabling real-time communication for the realization of the Digital Twin paradigm throughout the complete product's life-cycle [18,40,47,49].

In the Building and Construction industry context, physical objects are buildings and structural components. To generate and capture their virtual counterparts in the virtual space, Building Information Model (BIM) is a common standard that encompasses a large amount of detail on building dimensions and critical components. These components include façade features, dimensions of staircases, slopes of walls, height of railings, etc. The use of BIM provides high-quality preconstruction project visualisation, improved scheduling, and better coordination and issue management. The Digital Twin paradigm in this industry utilises BIM as one of the core technologies to facilitate information management, information sharing, and collaboration among stakeholders in different domains over the building life cycle [1,10].

In many cases, it is often desirable to obtain 3D models of the physical buildings and landscapes that can be used for enrichment, visualization, and advanced analytics of Digital Twin models [13,23,36,46]. Additionally, other sources of information can be useful for the Digital Twin models, such as contextual information and geographical information systems (GIS). However, there are some limitations with the current BIM technologies that hinder the capability to integrate multiple sources of data. For instance, BIM files are restricted in size, making it difficult to add large artefacts. The BIM format is neither initially designed for the integration of heterogeneous data sources nor capable of capturing real-time updates.

The process to obtain 3D models of the physical buildings and landscapes is also labour-intensive. When 3D reconstruction is done manually using a handheld device, the ability to capture an extensive model of the building is often limited due to physical constraints such as the size of tunnels or large constructions. These issues call for a new and more scalable approach in 3D reconstruction using unmanned aerial vehicles (UAV), optimal scanning methods, and advanced onboard processing algorithms [8,35,45,46].

On the other hand, real-time applications of AI and image analysis of BIM is also underdeveloped. One application of imaging in building maintenance for Digital Twin is defect detection, in which AI algorithms are employed to recognize defect regions such as cracks automatically. To develop such AI models, appropriate training data is required which, however, is often found in 2D format, prompting suitable methods on real-time transformation for AI applicability.

Motivated by the current limitations of building and construction technologies, we aim to innovate BIM for Digital Twin in two broad areas: 1) Develop an Information Fusion framework that extends BIM with a metadata layer to support heterogeneous data integration; 2) Enhance real-time synchronization between the physical space and virtual space in BIM through improved 3D reconstruction methods and real-time scanning.

To this aim, our approach is four-fold: First, we developed a proof of concept Information Fusion framework to facilitate the integration of multiple sources of information to produce useful data representations for BIM applications. It utilises a distributed and fault-tolerant database to store geometry objects (e.g., buildings and structural components) and meta-information (e.g., defects and tagged items) to provide maximal compatibility and highest/raw details; Second, we built a drone-based 3D reconstruction solution for scalable data collection and evaluate major scanning technologies including Light Detection and Ranging (LiDAR) sensor, stereovision, and single-lens camera; Third, we tested our real-time scanning capabilities by performing real-time 2D to 3D mapping from our camera feed at five frames per second. The mapping computation is done on the drone using an onboard miniature computer; Finally, we presented a defect detection use-case as an application of AI in real-time image scanning.

The contributions of our work are as follows. We provided a comprehensive review of Digital Twin technologies in conjunction with AI. We demonstrated an end-to-end proof of concept of the use of BIM for Digital Twin and information fusion. We conducted extensive experiments for the evaluation of 3D reconstruction techniques. Finally, we illustrated the feasibility of AI application in Digital Twin through defect detection with deep learning use-case. Our work provides some insights and theoretical and empirical implications for researchers as well as practitioners in this emerging field.

2   Background

2.1   Digital Twin Technologies And Applications

The concept and model of the Digital Twin were publicly introduced in 2002 by Grieves in his presentation as the conceptual model underlying Product Lifecycle Management [20]. Although the term was not coined at that time, all the Digital Twin's basic elements were described: physical space, virtual space, and the information flow between them. The key enablers of Digital Twin: sensor technologies, cloud computing, Big Data, IoT, and AI have since then experienced growth at an unprecedented rate. Recently, the concept of Digital Twin was formally defined by NASA as a multiphysics, multiscale, probabilistic, ultra-fidelity simulation that enables real-time replication of the state of the physical object in cyberspace based on historical and real-time sensor data.

Tao et al. extended the model and proposed that Digital Twin modelling should involve: physical modelling, virtual modelling, connection modelling, data modelling, and service modelling [49]. From a more structural and technological viewpoint, Digital Twin consists of sensor and measurement technologies, IoT, Big Data and AI [25,29].

The applications of Digital Twins span various domains from manufacturing, aerospace to cyber-physical systems, architecture, construction, and engineering.

Digital Twin in Manufacturing. Applications of Digital Twin are prominent in smart manufacturing. Due to ever-increasing product requirements and rapidly changing markets, there has been a growing interest in shifting problem identification and solving to early stages of product development lifecycle (also known as "front-loading") [51]. The Digital Twin paradigm fits perfectly because virtual replications of physical products allow early feedback, design changes, quality, and functional testing without entering the production phase.

Tao et al. suggested that a Digital Twin-driven product design process can be divided into conceptual design, detailed design, and virtual verification [48]. Throughout the process, various kinds of data such as customer satisfaction, product sales, 3D model, product functions, and configuration, sensor updates can be integrated to mirror the life of the physical product to its corresponding digital twin. With real-time closed-loop feedback between the physical and the virtual spaces, designers are able to make quick decisions on product design adjustment, quality control and improve the design efficiency by avoiding tedious verification and testing.

During production, simulation of production systems, the convergence of the physical and virtual manufacturing world leads to smart operations in the manufacturing process, including smart interconnection, smart interaction, smart control, and management. For example, Tao et al. proposed a shop-floor paradigm consists of four components physical shop-floor, virtual shop-floor, shop-floor service system driven by shop-floor digital twin data, enabled by IoT, big data, and artificial intelligence [50]. Modeling of machinery, manufacturing steps, and equipment also help in precise process simulation, control, and analysis, eventually leading to improvement of the production process [6]. A similar effort is observed in [36] to evaluate different methods in automated 3D reconstruction in SME factories. The authors explored the use of low-cost stereo vision techniques with Simultaneous Localization and Mapping (SLAM) to generate Digital Twin models of a physical factory floor and machinery.

Digital Twin in Building and Construction. Modelling physical buildings and landscapes with Digital Twin brought valuable opportunities to the architecture, construction, and engineering industry, such as improvements in urban planning, city analytics, environmental analysis, building maintenance, defect detection, and collaboration between stakeholders. An important concept in this domain is BIM [26], i.e. a process involving the generation and management of digital representations of physical and functional characteristics of places.

Yan et al. proposed a method for the integration of 3D objects and terrain in BIMs supporting the Digital Twin, which takes the accurate representation of terrain and buildings into consideration [53]. The authors discussed topological issues that can occur when integrating 3D objects with terrain. The key to solving this issue lies in obtaining the correct Terrain Intersection Curve (TIC) and amending 3D objects and the terrain properly based on it. Models developed by such methods are used for urban planning, city analytics, or environmental analysis.

For preventive maintenance of prestressed concrete bridges, Shim et al. proposed a new generation of the bridge maintenance system by using the Digital Twin concept for reliable decision-making [45]. 3D models of bridges were built to utilise information from the entire lifecycle of a project by continuously exchanging and updating data from stakeholders

Digital Twin also finds application in recording and managing cultural heritage sites. The work by [12] integrated a 3D model into a 3D GIS and bridge the gap between parametric CAD modeling and 3D GIS. The final model benefits from both systems to help document and analyze cultural heritage sites.

From most construction projects, the presence of BIM is prominent due to its wide range of benefits. BIM has received considerable attention from researchers with works aiming to improve or extend its various aspects for e.g. social aspect [1], elasticity and scalability [10], sustainability [28], safety [55] and many others.

Digital Twin in Smart Nations. Gartner's Top 10 Strategic Technology Report for 2017 predicted that Digital Twin is one of the top ten trending strategic technologies [39]. Digital Twin since 2012 has entered rapid growth stage considering the current momentum with applications in several industries and across variety of domains.

NASA and U.S Air Force adopted Digital Twin to improve production of future generations of vehicles to become lighter while being subjected to high loads and more extreme service conditions. The paradigm shift allowed the organisation to incorporate vehicle health management system, historical data and fleet data to mirror the life of its flying twin, thus, enabled unprecedented levels of safety and reliability [19].

The world's 11th busiest airport, the second largest in the Netherlands, Amsterdam Airport Schiphol built a digital asset twin of the airport based on BIM. Known as the Common Data Environment (CDE), Schiphol's Digital Twin solution integrates data from many sources: BIM data; GIS data; and data collected in real-time on project changes and incidents as well as financial information, documents, and project portfolios. The information fusion capability of Digital Twin presents opportunities to run simulations on potential operational failures throughout the entire complex [3].

Port of Rotterdam built a Digital Twin of the port and used IoT and artificial intelligence to collect and analyse data to improve operations. Digital Twin helps to better predict accurately what the best time is to moor, depart and how much cargo needs to be unloaded. Furthermore, real-time access to information enables better prediction of visibility and water conditions [7].

2.2   Artificial Intelligence in Digital Twin

The rapid adoption of enabling technologies such as IoT, cloud computing, and big data opens up endless opportunities for AI applications in Digital Twin. As a multidisciplinary field, AI encompasses Machine Learning, Data Mining, Computer Vision, Natural Language Processing, Robotics, among many others. AI emerges as a promising core service in Digital Twin to assist humans in decision making by finding patterns, insights in big data, generation of realistic virtual models through advanced computer vision, natural language processing, robotics, etc.

Li et al. proposed a method that uses a concept of dynamic Bayesian networks for Digital Twin to build a health monitoring model for the diagnosis and prognosis of each individual aircraft [31]. For example, in diagnosis by tracking time-dependent variables, the method could calibrate the time-independent variables; in prognosis, the method helps predict crack growth in the physical subject using particle filtering as the Bayesian inference algorithm.

In production, [2] introduced a Digital Twin-driven approach for developing Machine Learning models. The models are trained for vision-based recognition of parts' orientation using the simulation of Digital Twin models, which can help adaptively control the production process. Additionally, the authors also proposed a method to synthesize training datasets and automatic labelling via the simulation tools chain, thus reducing users' involvement during model training.

Chao et al. [14] described an insightful vision of Digital Twin to enable the convergence of AI and Smart City for disaster response and emergency management. In this vision, the authors listed four components in Disaster City Digital Twin, i.e. 1) multi-data sensing for data collection, 2) data integration and analytics, 3) multi-actor game-theoretic decision making, 4) dynamic network analysis, and elaborated the functions that AI can improve within each component.

Another interesting vision of Digital Twin in Model-Based Systems Engineering is described in [33] in which the realization of Digital Twin is progressively divided into four levels 1) Pre-Digital Twin, 2) Digital Twin, 3) Adaptive Digital Twin and 4) Intelligent Digital Twin. In the last two levels: Adaptive Digital Twin and Intelligent Digital Twin, the authors emphasized the tight integration of AI in engineering processes; for example, in level 3, an adaptive user interface can be offered by using supervised machine learning to learn the preferences and priorities of human operators in different contexts, therefore, support real-time planning and decision making during operators, maintenance and support; in level 4, additionally unsupervised machine learning can help discern objects, and patterns in the operational environment and reinforcement learning can learn from continuous data stream from the environment.

Power networks are the backbone of power distribution, playing a central economical and societal role by supplying reliable power to industry, services, and consumers. To improve the efficiency of power networks, researchers in the Energy industry have also been putting initial effort into integrating Digital Twin, and AI for informed decision-making in operation, support, and maintenance [34]. In particular, a virtual replication of the power network is developed. Various time-series measurements from the physical power networks, such as production values, loads, line thermal limits, power flows, etc., are streamed back to the virtual models. Based on the digital models, researchers exploit machine learning algorithms such as reinforcement learning to predict future states of the networks, as well as suggest possible optimal control actions.

2.3   3D Reconstruction

Various 3D scanning technologies are emerging for a range of applications, from outdoor surveying, 3D mapping of cities for digital twins, inspection to autonomous driving. Most of these applications and technologies rely on LiDAR sensors [32,38,41,52]. However, most LiDAR sensors tend to be expensive and heavy, making them less suitable for developing a drone-based surveying solution. Other 3D scanning solutions use a single lens [42,46] or stereo vision cameras [9,13,23,36] to compute a 3D model of the environment.

Photogrammetry. The most common method for 3D reconstruction of outdoor structures is photogrammetry. The 3D representation of complex structures such as buildings, bridges, and even 3D maps of a whole neighbourhood can be generated using a single-lens camera based on the concept of Structure from Motion (SfM) [43].

The steps to create a point cloud or textured mesh is to capture multiple photographs in sequence or randomising order with at least 70% overlapping and at angle part of around 5–10° [42]. This will ensure that the amount of overlap is sufficient for matching photos to have common feature points. Matching the features in different photos allows the SfM algorithm to generate a 3D point cloud [46]. The generated point cloud can be meshed to create a smooth or textured result of the 3D model.

Stereovision. Stereovision is a 3D scanning method suitable for smaller or indoor infrastructure projects where higher accuracy is required. The concept uses stereovision cameras (infrared or RGB) to estimate the depth in the field of view of the camera. Stereo Vision uses the disparity between images from multiple cameras to extract depth information [37]. Similar to the binocular vision in humans, when both eyes focus on an object, their optical axes will converge to that point at an angle. The displacement parallel to the eye base (the distance between both eyes) creates a disparity between both images. From the extent of disparity, it is possible to extract the distance of an object and pixel in an image through triangulation [17].

To generate the 3D model from the stereo or depth images, RGB-D cameras require an additional processor to run a process called Simultaneous Localisation and Mapping (SLAM) [5]. As the name suggests, the SLAM concept is able to build a 3D map of the environment in real-time and at the same time estimate the location and orientation of the camera. SLAM works by scanning the images for key features which can be extracted with Speeded Up Robust Features (SURF) [4] and matched with RAndom SAmple Consensus (RASAC) algorithm between multiple images [16]. These two algorithms work simultaneously, SURF compares two images and extracts matching key points. These key points are then combined with the depth data to allow RANSAC algorithm to determine the 3D transformations between the frames. The transformed key points are optimised into a graph representation resulting in a 3D representation of the environment.

LiDAR Scanning. Laser measurements provide another means to obtain depth information of the environment using the concept of time of flight of a light signal reflected at the surrounding. Hence, LiDAR also uses an active approach to obtain depth information similar to RGB-D technology. Still, LiDAR sensors have a much larger range of 100 m with accuracy in the millimetre range. In recent years, LiDAR sensors have received a lot of attention, mostly due to their extensive use in autonomous driving technologies. This resulted in many available LiDAR sensors, which are affordable and light enough to be installed on drones for aerial scanning of infrastructure projects.

Similar to RGB-D sensors, most LiDAR-based 3D scanning techniques also use a SLAM approach to convert the instantaneous laser-point measurements to 2D or 3D point-cloud representations. GMapping is a common SLAM technique introduced for LiDAR-based mapping, reducing the computation time for the SLAM algorithms [22]. HectorSLAM is the SLAM algorithm used here for the in-house development of a 2D mapping evaluation [27]. It was first developed for Urban Search and Rescue (USAR) scenarios and is suitable for fast learning of occupancy grid maps with low computational requirements. HectorSLAM presents a high update rate simultaneously on a 2D map for lower power platforms and the results yielded were a sufficiently accurate mapping. A more recent SLAM algorithm by Google is called Cartographer [24]. In a comparison study [15], GMapping produced an inaccurate mapping while both the HectorSLAM and Cartographer produced accurate and similar maps.

Many LiDAR-based 3D SLAM frameworks have been proposed specifically for 3D reconstruction and form the foundation for most commercial scanning technologies available. Among the many LiDAR-based 3D SLAM methods, LOAM is a widely used real-time LiDAR odometry estimation and mapping framework that uses a LiDAR sensor and optionally an inertial measurement unit (IMU) [54]. This method achieves real-time performance by separating the SLAM problem into odometry estimation algorithm and mapping optimisation algorithm. The odometry estimation algorithm runs at high frequency with low fidelity, while the mapping optimization algorithm runs at an order of magnitude lower frequency with high accuracy for scan-matching. Since its publication, LOAM has remained at the top rank in the odometry category of various benchmarks. LOAM has since then been commercialized, and its framework is no longer available in the public domain.

The current state-of-the-art 3D SLAM method for LiDAR odometry and mapping is LIO-SAM [44]. It utilizes factor graphs to incorporate multiple measurement factors for odometry estimation and global map optimization. The framework incorporates an IMU to improve the pose estimation and incorporate GPS as an option for additional key factors.

3 Solution Design

The backbone of our solution is an Information Fusion module to extend beyond the current limitations of BIM. The Information Fusion module has an extensive set of APIs, scalable storage, advanced search, and indexing capabilities to fuse multiple data streams, capture different types of BIM artefacts, AI models, and defects while supporting online communication from our drones and management site.

For 3D reconstruction, we present our drone-based setup. The drone has a stereovision camera attached as a cost-effective solution. The main computing unit is a miniature onboard computer responsible for processing the output from the camera feed via USB, and streaming it back to the Information Fusion module in a real-time manner.

To test our defect detection use-case as an application of AI in real-time image scanning, we deployed a deep learning model on the on-board computer. The defects detected from the camera feeds are sent back to the Information Fusion module to fuse with the 3D models and other BIM-related information.

The overall architecture is illustrated in Fig. 1. We also described each component in detail in the following sections.

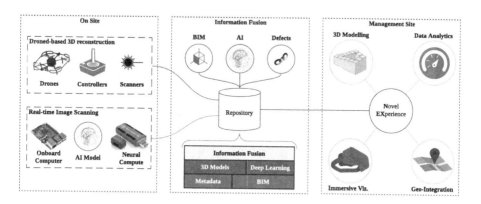

Fig. 1. Overall architecture

3.1 Information Fusion

To be able to capture heterogeneous data sources including structured, unstructured, images, 3D models, meta-information beyond BIM's capabilities, The Information Fusion module leverages one of the most efficient and well-established NoSQL database systems, Apache Cassandra, originally developed by Facebook, hence, is able to handle a huge amount of data across multiple locations, including on-site and off-site. With an extended database schema, the module offers the ability to store and replicate large BIM files with high data protection and fault-tolerance while also supporting imaging data, defects, and tagged items. We also added an extensive set of API to enable real-time communication from our drone for live streaming of RGB-D images and defect information.

3.2 Drone-Based 3D Reconstruction

The stereovision camera used in our drone is an Intel RealSense D435i camera which is more cost-effective compared to a LiDAR sensor. It is an RGB-D camera that produces point-clouds in color instead of black and white. The depth data provides the distance between the camera and the obstacle in its FOV. It has an integrated Inertial Measurement Unit to predict the orientation of the drone and provides a horizontal and vertical FOV of 87° by 58° that allows a 3D map to be generated. Our drone setup is shown in Fig. 2.

Fig. 2. Our drone configuration with integration of RPLidar A2 (bottom left) and Intel RealSense D435i (bottom right).

Flight Controller. Each drone requires a flight controller to allow the pilot to have precise control over the vehicle and its motors. Even in manual flight, the flight controller translates the throttle command on the radio control to individual motor commands to stabilize the drone. Flight controllers use several inbuilt sensors to control the vehicle response. In this work, we used a Pixhawk flight controller which allows us to operate the custom drone. The Pixhawk flight controller also supports many additional sensors and companion computers to be integrated.

Onboard Computing. We used a companion computer attached to our drone as the main processing unit. In our prototype, a Raspberry Pi4 single-board computer is added to allow additional sensors and features to be integrated. For e.g. it enables features such as obstacle avoidance, automated flight path tracking, or in this work, 3D scanning of the environment. Raspberry Pi4 is utilized in this prototype due to its low cost, high specifications, and large supporting community. The other significant factor for choosing the Raspberry Pi4 is its compatibility with the additional sensors and the Robotic Operating Software (ROS) used. The Intel RealSense D435i camera as mentioned in the previous sections is connected and executed by the Raspberry Pi4 via USB port.

Fig. 3. 3D reconstruction scanning.

Implementation of SLAM. Real-Time Appearance Based Mapping (RTABMap) is an open-source SLAM environment [30] with numerous tools to generate maps from RGB-D data. RTABMap has evolved to do online processing, minimal drift odometry, robust localization map exploitation, and multi-session mapping. The approach is based on the SLAM algorithm introduced before and is illustrated in Fig. 3, including the different algorithms used to extract the features into the point cloud. Using SLAM as the base to generate point clouds gives the user the flexibility to change parameters or adjust flight paths during the scanning process.

3.3   Real-Time Image Scanning

One limitation of Raspberry Pi 4 as compared to conventional computers is the limited processing power. This leads to low frame rates of only 5 frames per second. To provide more processing power to the Raspberry Pi 4 and allow more efficient Real-time Image Scanning, we explored the use of USB accelerators to increase the frame rate. A USB accelerator is a USB stick that contains a Vision Processing Unit aimed at boosting CPU performance. The USB accelerator used in this work is an Intel Neural Compute Stick 2 that is compatible with the Intel Real Sense D435. It also has a toolkit called the OpenVINO toolkit, which allows the companion computer to recognise the NCS2 and make full use of the additional CPU boost. After the implementation of the USB accelerator, the frames rate provided a boost to the CPU of the Raspberry Pi 4 resulting in an average of 12 fps.

3.4   AI for Defect Detection

To further evaluate our Real-time Image Scanning capability, we trained a deep learning model for defect detection using convolutional neural networks. We employed the SDNET 2018, a publicly available dataset, that contains 56,000 images of cracks and non-cracks [11]. The dataset provides various types of cracks, ranging from 0.06 mm to 25 mm, on different types of surfaces. We trained our classifier engine with multiple backbones, including ResNet18, ResNet50, and VGG; and then the classifiers' performance was evaluated against current baselines. We utilized the best model to classify 2D images, coming from streaming data sources. Our drone (in a simulated environment) captures the Red-Green-Blue (RGB) channels and the depth layer from RGBA images for processing. The drone position and intrinsic camera can be configured to provide the best 3D locationing of the defects for visualizing them in the simulation. The AI defect detection workflow is illustrated in Fig. 4.

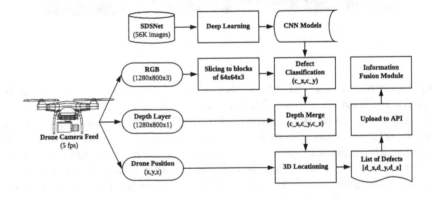

Fig. 4. AI defect detection

4   Experiments and Results

We conducted experiments to validate our solution and answer the following questions.

1. How do different scanning technologies perform compared to each other, and how do they perform compared to manual measurements?
2. How does a scanning technology perform when being used as a handheld device vs being used in a drone-based solution? And how are both approaches compared to manual measurements?
3. How do different CNN architectures perform in defect detection?

The detail of the experiments and results are given in the following sections.

4.1   Scanning Performance

Table 1. 3D scanning technologies

Area of Interest	Actual Dist (mm)	Stereovision M (mm)	Rel. %Err	3D LiDAR M (mm)	Rel. %Err	Photogrammetry M (mm)	Rel. %Err
1) Ceiling height							
Ceiling height (L1)	3185	3201	0.5%	3189	0.1%		
2) Height of safety barriers							
Balustrade (L2)	1120	1111	−0.8%	1007	−10.1%		
Staircase Railing (L2)	1110	1082	−2.6%	1018	−8.3%		
3) Profile of stairs							
Thread width	1817	1817	0.0%	1845	1.5%		
Riser height	148	149	0.7%	157	6.1%		
4) Dimensions of windows and doors							
Lift door width	1195	1199	0.3%	1204	0.8%		
Toilet door width	1135	1139	0.4%	1116	011.1%		
Corridor width (L2)	2100	2102	0.1%	1964	−6.5%		
5) Gradients of ramp							
Ramp length	3800	3845	1.2%	3851	1.3%	3890	2.4%
Ramp height	295	294	−0.3%	297	0.7%	330	11.9%
Ramp height/length	59/760	64/837	−1.5%	30/389	−0.7%	33/389	9.3%

We evaluated the performance of three different 3D scanning technologies with the following specific products.

1. Photogrammetry with Pix4D
2. Stereovision with Dot3D/Navisworks
3. 3D LiDAR with geoSLAM/Navisworks.

We manually measured selected areas of interest as well as scan them with the listed products. For photogrammetry, we only included the results for the ramp as the technology is deemed unsuitable for indoor scanning. The results are summarised in Table 1.

The evaluation of the methods showed that stereovision and 3D LiDAR achieve accuracies sufficient for indoor surveying, with stereovision achieving more consistent accuracies. Photogrammetry was found to not be suitable for indoor surveying due to the high inaccuracy of the results.

4.2 Measurement Errors

Drone-Based Inspection with Stereovision. We used the drone-based setup described in Sect. 3 to compare with manual measurements as well as when being used as a handheld device. The results are given in Table 2.

Table 2. Comparison between handheld and drone-based scanning using the stereovision approach against manual measurements

Area of interest	Measured distance	Handheld distance	Error	% Error	Drone-based distance	Error	% Error
Room width	9140 mm	9263 mm	123 mm	1.34%	9260 mm	120 mm	1.31%
Shelf width	690 mm	688 mm	2 mm	0.29%	691 mm	1 mm	0.14%
Shelf height	2130 mm	2127 mm	3 mm	0.14%	2127 mm	3 mm	0.14%

Both approaches produce very accurate results with the highest error of 1.3%. In addition, the flight scan results are slightly improved even since the drone only can move around in straight directions (up down, left right, front back) for the scan to be completed. This means that with lesser pitching of the drone the accuracy of results will be improved. This demonstrates that the drone-based concept using stereovision is a feasible approach for automated indoor scanning.

Drone-Based Inspection with 2D LiDAR. Next, we compared handheld and drone-based scanning using the 2D LiDAR approach against manual measurements. The result is given in Table 3.

Table 3. Comparison between handheld and drone-based scanning using the 2D LiDAR approach against manual measurements

Area of interest	Measured distance	Handheld distance	Error	% Error	Drone-based distance	Error	% Error
Room width	9140 mm	9103 mm	37 mm	0.40%	9104 mm	36 mm	0.39%
Shelf width	690 mm	695 mm	5 mm	0.72%	697 mm	7 mm	1.01%
Door height	950 mm	945 mm	5 mm	0.53%	949 mm	1 mm	0.11%

Similar to the stereovision approach, the drone-based scan for the 2D LiDAR also shows better accuracy compared to the handheld scanning. Although the difference between the handheld and drone-based readings is small, with the largest being at around 1%, it can be seen that the drone-based scan produces more consistent results, as the drone is more stable than the handheld method.

Comparison of the generated point-clouds from both scanning technologies, stereovision, and LiDAR, shows that using a drone to automate the scanning process has no detrimental effects. In fact, the results demonstrate that drone-based scanning provides a more accurate method compared to the handheld approach due to drone stability during flight. Hence, our work demonstrated that it is possible to use 3D scanning technologies integrated on a drone to enable automated indoor surveying.

4.3   Defect Detection Performance

Our drone-based setup scans the surrounding environment and uses the AI model deployed on the on-board computer for inference on the image stream as illustrated in Fig. 5.

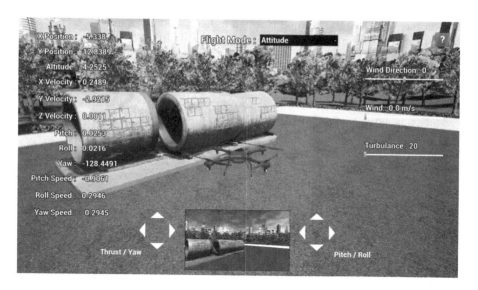

Fig. 5. Drone-based defect detection

The detection performance from our three trained models is given in the Table 4.

The ResNet-50 outperformed ResNet-18 by 2% in accuracy as well as a clear improvement of 9% in the recall of crack detection. The results showed that the deeper architecture allowed a better way to recognise cracks in different forms. VGG-16 has achieved comparable performance with ResNet-50. However, it has

Table 4. Performance evaluation of CNNs on crack detection

	Crack			No crack			Overall accuracy
	Precision	Recall	F1-score	Precision	Recall	F1-score	
Resnet18	0.86	0.52	0.65	0.92	0.98	0.95	0.91
Resnet50	0.86	0.61	0.72	0.93	0.98	0.96	0.93
VGG16	0.88	0.59	0.71	0.93	0.99	0.96	0.93

a slightly lower performance in terms of F1-score in the Crack category, hence, Resnet-50 is selected as our AI model of choice for defect detection

5   Conclusion

In this paper, we presented a drone-based AI and 3D Reconstruction for Digital Twin augmentation. We illustrated an Information Fusion framework that extends beyond BIM's capabilities to enable the integration of heterogeneous data sources. We developed a proof of concept drone-based 3D reconstruction and real-time image scanning and provided evaluation and comparison results from extensive experiments. Finally, we studied the feasibility of AI applications in real-time image scanning through a defect detection use-case. Our work shows that with Information Fusion, the applicability of BIM can be greatly enhanced because the additional data allows additional applications such as 3D reconstruction to be built on top of BIM. Our empirical experiments also give suggestions to researchers and practitioners that the use of drones, onboard computing, RGB-D cameras, and neural computing unit are viable options for the realisation of large-scale, real-time image scanning and AI in Digital Twin.

Acknowledgement. This research is conducted in collaboration with Aviation Virtual and Nippon Koei.

References

1. Adamu, Z.A., Emmitt, S., Soetanto, R.: Social BIM: co-creation with shared situational awareness. J. Inf. Technol. Constr. **20**, 230–252 (2015)
2. Alexopoulos, K., Nikolakis, N., Chryssolouris, G.: Digital twin-driven supervised machine learning for the development of artificial intelligence applications in manufacturing. Int. J. Comput. Integr. Manuf. **33**(5), 429–439 (2020)
3. Baumann, J.: Digital Twin Helps Airport Optimize Operations (2019). https://www.esri.com/about/newsroom/arcuser/digital-twin-helps-airport-optimize-operations/
4. Bay, H., Ess, A., Tuytelaars, T., Van Gool, L.: Speeded-up robust features (SURF). Comput. Vis. Image Underst. **110**(3), 346–359 (2008)
5. Beňo, P., Duchoň, F., Tölgyessy, M., Hubinskỳ, P., Kajan, M.: 3D map reconstruction with sensor kinect (2014)
6. Botkina, D., Hedlind, M., Olsson, B., Henser, J., Lundholm, T.: Digital twin of a cutting tool. Procedia CIRP **72**, 215–218 (2018)

7. Boyles, R.: How the Port of Rotterdam is using IBM digital twin technology to transform itself from the biggest to the smartest, pp. 1–4 (2019)
8. Chan, T., Hesse, H., Ho, S.: LiDAR-based 3D slam for indoor mapping. In: IEEE International Conference on Control, Automation & Robotics (ICCAR) (2021)
9. Choi, S., Zhou, Q.Y., Koltun, V.: Robust reconstruction of indoor scenes. In: Proceedings of the IEEE Conference on Computer Vision and Pattern Recognition, pp. 5556–5565 (2015)
10. Das, M., Cheng, J.C., Shiv Kumar, S.: BIMCloud: a distributed cloud-based social BIM framework for project collaboration. Comput. Civil Build. Eng. **2014**, 41–48 (2014)
11. Dorafshan, S., Thomas, R.J., Maguire, M.: SDNET 2018: an annotated image dataset for non-contact concrete crack detection using deep convolutional neural networks. Data in Brief **21**, 1664–1668 (2018)
12. Dore, C., Murphy, M.: Integration of historic building information modeling (HBIM) and 3D GIS for recording and managing cultural heritage sites. In: 2012 18th International conference on virtual systems and multimedia, pp. 369–376. IEEE (2012)
13. Dryanovski, I., Klingensmith, M., Srinivasa, S.S., Xiao, J.: Large-scale, real-time 3D scene reconstruction on a mobile device. Autonomous Robots **41**(6), 1423–1445 (2017). https://doi.org/10.1007/s10514-017-9624-2
14. Fan, C., Zhang, C., Yahja, A., Mostafavi, A.: Disaster city digital twin: a vision for integrating artificial and human intelligence for disaster management. Int. J. Inf. Manage. **56**, 102049 (2021)
15. Filipenko, M., Afanasyev, I.: Comparison of various slam systems for mobile robot in an indoor environment. In: 2018 International Conference on Intelligent Systems (IS), pp. 400–407. IEEE (2018)
16. Fischler, M.A., Bolles, R.C.: Random sample consensus: a paradigm for model fitting with applications to image analysis and automated cartography. Commun. ACM **24**(6), 381–395 (1981)
17. Fryer, J.G.: Photogrammetry (2010)
18. Fuller, A., Fan, Z., Day, C., Barlow, C.: Digital twin: enabling technologies, challenges and open research. IEEE Access **8**, 108952–108971 (2020)
19. Glaessgen, E., Stargel, D.: The digital twin paradigm for future NASA and US air force vehicles. In: 53rd AIAA/ASME/ASCE/AHS/ASC Structures, Structural Dynamics and Materials Conference 20th AIAA/ASME/AHS Adaptive Structures Conference 14th AIAA, p. 1818 (2012)
20. Grieves, M.: Conceptual ideal for PLM. University of Michigan, Presentation for the Product Lifecycle Management (PLM) center (2002)
21. Grieves, M.: Digital twin: manufacturing excellence through virtual factory replication. White Paper **1**, 1–7 (2014)
22. Grisetti, G., Stachniss, C., Burgard, W.: Improved techniques for grid mapping with Rao-Blackwellized particle filters. IEEE Trans. Rob. **23**(1), 34–46 (2007)
23. Henry, P., Krainin, M., Herbst, E., Ren, X., Fox, D.: RGB-D mapping: using depth cameras for dense 3D modeling of indoor environments. In: Khatib, O., Kumar, V., Sukhatme, G. (eds.) Experimental Robotics, pp. 477–491. Springer, Heidelberg (2014). https://doi.org/10.1007/978-3-642-28572-1_33
24. Hess, W., Kohler, D., Rapp, H., Andor, D.: Real-time loop closure in 2D LIDAR SLAM. In: 2016 IEEE International Conference on Robotics and Automation (ICRA), pp. 1271–1278. IEEE (2016)

25. Kaur, M.J., Mishra, V.P., Maheshwari, P.: The convergence of digital twin, IoT, and machine learning: transforming data into action. In: Farsi, M., Daneshkhah, A., Hosseinian-Far, A., Jahankhani, H. (eds.) Digital Twin Technologies and Smart Cities. IT, pp. 3–17. Springer, Cham (2020). https://doi.org/10.1007/978-3-030-18732-3_1

26. Kensek, K.M.: Building Information Modeling. Internet of Things. Springer, Cham (2018). https://doi.org/10.1007/978-3-319-92862-3_35

27. Kohlbrecher, S., Von Stryk, O., Meyer, J., Klingauf, U.: A flexible and scalable slam system with full 3D motion estimation. In: 2011 IEEE International Symposium on Safety, Security, and Rescue Robotics, pp. 155–160. IEEE (2011)

28. Krygiel, E., Nies, B.: Green BIM: Successful Sustainable Design with Building Information Modeling. Wiley (2008)

29. Kusiak, A.: Smart manufacturing must embrace big data. Nature News **544**(7648), 23 (2017)

30. Labbé, M., Michaud, F.: RTAB-map as an open-source LIDAR and visual simultaneous localization and mapping library for large-scale and long-term online operation. J. Field Robot. **36**(2), 416–446 (2019)

31. Li, C., Mahadevan, S., Ling, Y., Wang, L., Choze, S.: A dynamic Bayesian network approach for digital twin. In: 19th AIAA Non-Deterministic Approaches Conference, p. 1566 (2017)

32. Liu, X.: Airborne LIDAR for DEM generation: some critical issues. Prog. Phys. Geogr. **32**(1), 31–49 (2008)

33. Madni, A.M., Madni, C.C., Lucero, S.D.: Leveraging digital twin technology in model-based systems engineering. Systems **7**(1), 7 (2019)

34. Marot, A., et al.: L2RPN: learning to run a power network in a sustainable world NEURIPS2020 challenge design (2020)

35. Mauriello, M.L., Froehlich, J.E.: Towards automated thermal profiling of buildings at scale using unmanned aerial vehicles and 3D-reconstruction. In: Proceedings of the 2014 ACM International Joint Conference on Pervasive and Ubiquitous Computing: Adjunct Publication, pp. 119–122 (2014)

36. Minos-Stensrud, M., Haakstad, O.H., Sakseid, O., Westby, B., Alcocer, A.: Towards automated 3D reconstruction in SME factories and digital twin model generation. In: 2018 18th International Conference on Control, Automation and Systems (ICCAS), pp. 1777–1781. IEEE (2018)

37. Nair, D.: A guide to stereovision and 3D imaging - tech briefs: Tech briefs (2012). http://www.techbriefs.com/component/content/article/14925?start=1

38. Nys, G.A., Billen, R., Poux, F.: Automatic 3D buildings compact reconstruction from LIDAR point clouds. In: International Archives of the Photogrammetry, Remote Sensing and Spatial Information Sciences (XLIII-B2-2020), pp. 473–478 (2020)

39. Panetta, K.: Gartner's Top 10 Strategic Technology Trends for 2017 (2016). http://www.gartner.com/smarterwithgartner/gartners-top-10-technology-trends-2017/

40. Qi, Q., et al.: Enabling technologies and tools for digital twin. J. Manuf. Syst. **58**, 3–21 (2019)

41. Sampath, A., Shan, J.: Segmentation and reconstruction of polyhedral building roofs from aerial LIDAR point clouds. IEEE Trans. Geosci. Remote Sens. **48**(3), 1554–1567 (2009)

42. Santagati, C., Inzerillo, L., Di Paola, F.: Image-based modeling techniques for architectural heritage 3d digitalization: limits and potentialities. International Archives of the Photogrammetry, Remote Sensing and Spatial Information Sciences **5**(w2), 555–560 (2013)

43. Schonberger, J.L., Frahm, J.M.: Structure-from-motion revisited. In: Proceedings of the IEEE Conference on Computer Vision and Pattern Recognition, pp. 4104–4113 (2016)

44. Shan, T., Englot, B., Meyers, D., Wang, W., Ratti, C., Rus, D.: LIO-SAM: tightly-coupled LIDAR inertial odometry via smoothing and mapping. arXiv preprint arXiv:2007.00258 (2020)

45. Shim, C.S., Dang, N.S., Lon, S., Jeon, C.H.: Development of a bridge maintenance system for prestressed concrete bridges using 3d digital twin model. Struct. Infrastruct. Eng. 15(10), 1319–1332 (2019)

46. Spreitzer, G., Tunnicliffe, J., Friedrich, H.: Large wood (LW) 3D accumulation mapping and assessment using structure from motion photogrammetry in the laboratory. J. Hydrol. 581, 124430 (2020)

47. Tao, F., Cheng, J., Qi, Q., Zhang, M., Zhang, H., Sui, F.: Digital twin-driven product design, manufacturing and service with big data. Int. J. Adv. Manuf. Technol. 6, 3563–3576 (2017). https://doi.org/10.1007/s00170-017-0233-1

48. Tao, F., et al.: Digital twin-driven product design framework. Int. J. Prod. Res. 57(12), 3935–3953 (2019)

49. Tao, F., Zhang, H., Liu, A., Nee, A.Y.: Digital twin in industry: state-of-the-art. IEEE Trans. Ind. Informatics 15(4), 2405–2415 (2018)

50. Tao, F., Zhang, M.: Digital twin shop-floor: a new shop-floor paradigm towards smart manufacturing. IEEE Access 5, 20418–20427 (2017)

51. Thomke, S., Fujimoto, T.: The effect of "front-loading" problem-solving on product development performance. J. Prod. Innov. Manag. Int. Publ. Prod. Develop. Manage. Assoc. 17(2), 128–142 (2000)

52. Wu, B., et al.: A graph-based approach for 3D building model reconstruction from airborne LIDAR point clouds. Remote Sens. 9(1), 92 (2017)

53. Yan, J., Zlatanova, S., Aleksandrov, M., Diakite, A., Pettit, C.: Integration of 3D objects and terrain for 3D modelling supporting the digital twin. In: ISPRS Annals of Photogrammetry, Remote Sensing & Spatial Information Sciences, vol. 4 (2019)

54. Zhang, J., Singh, S.: LOAM: lidar odometry and mapping in real-time. In: Robotics: Science and Systems, vol. 2 (2014)

55. Zhang, S., Teizer, J., Lee, J.K., Eastman, C.M., Venugopal, M.: Building information modeling (bim) and safety: Automatic safety checking of construction models and schedules. Automation in construction 29, 183–195 (2013)

Estimating Interaction State from Nonverbal Cues and Utterance Events: A Preliminary Study to Support Ideation Facilitation in Living Lab

Ichiro Umata[1](✉), Sumaru Niida[1], Koki Ijuin[2], Tsuneo Kato[3], and Seiichi Yamamoto[3]

[1] KDDI Research, Inc, Garden Air Tower, 3-10-10, Iidabashi,
Chiyoda-ku, Tokyo 102-8460, Japan
ic-umata@kddi-research.jp
[2] The National Institute of Advanced Industrial Science and Technology,
2-3-26, Aomi, Koto-ku, Tokyo 135-0064, Japan
koki-ijuuin@aist.go.jp
[3] Department of Information Systems Design, Doshisha University, Kyotanabe-shi, Kyoto
610-0321, Japan
{tsukato,seyamamo}@mail.doshisha.ac.jp

Abstract. Living lab, where various stakeholders such as local residents, local governments and companies collaborate (cf. (European Networks of Living Labs. https://www.openlivinglabs.eu)), has been attracting attention as a design method for local community services. Running a living lab, however, requires the lab staff to have highly specialized skills, and ideation facilitation is one of the important skills required for successful Living Lab management. Supporting novice staff with information technologies is expected to contribute to the further spread and implementation of living labs. In this study, we conducted a preliminary study of interaction state estimation based on nonverbal and speech-event cues to support novice facilitators. The proposed method can serve as a basis for designing a supporting system for novice facilitators by detecting important interaction events.

Keywords: Interaction state estimation · Ideation · Collaboration · Body motion · Body synchrony · Living Lab

1 Introduction

Living lab, where various stakeholders such as local residents, local governments and companies collaborate (cf. [1], has been attracting attention as a design method for local community services. In such a citizen participatory design approach, stakeholders with various backgrounds are directly involved in the design process to tackle challenges in modern society [1, 2]. Bergvall-Kareborn and Stahlbrost argue that a Living Lab can be viewed as both an innovation milieu and an innovation approach [3], and five key principles of the Living Lab methodology have been suggested as follows [4]:

© Springer Nature Switzerland AG 2021
G. Meiselwitz (Ed.): HCII 2021, LNCS 12774, pp. 530–537, 2021.
https://doi.org/10.1007/978-3-030-77626-8_36

Continuity: This principle is important since good cross-border collaboration, which strengthens creativity and innovation, builds on trust, which takes time to develop.

Openness: The innovation process should be as open as possible since gathering of many perspectives and bringing enough power to achieve rapid progress is important. The open process also makes its possible to support the process of user-driven innovation, including users wherever and whoever they are.

Realism: To generate results that are valid for real markets, it is necessary to facilitate as realistic use situations and behavior as possible. This principle also is relevant since focusing on real users, in real-life situations, is what distinguishes Living Labs from other kinds of open co-creation environments, such as Second Life.

Empowerment of Users: The engagement of users is fundamental in order to bring innovation processes in a desired direction, based on humans' needs and desires. Living Labs efficiency is based on the creative power of user communities; hence, it becomes important to motivate and empower the users to engage in these processes.

Spontaneity: In order to succeed with new innovations, it is important to inspire usage, meet personal desires, and fit and contribute to societal and social needs. Here, it becomes important to have the ability to detect, aggregate, and analyze spontaneous users' reactions and ideas over time.

Group collaboration is one of the key elements to actualize the principles listed above, and face-to-face ideation sessions that involve a range of different stakeholders with various backgrounds need to be organized to give citizens or end users a direct role in the design of new services and technologies [2]. Thus, because running a living lab requires the lab staff to have highly specialized skills for managing, supporting and activating their collaborative ideation processes, this has made it difficult to popularize Living Lab projects where experienced facilitators need to guide the ideation processes that involves members of the public who lack expert knowledge. Supporting novice facilitators with information technologies is expected to contribute to the further spread and implementation of living labs. In this study, we conducted a preliminary study of interaction state estimation based on nonverbal and speech-event cues to support novice facilitators. We focus on body synchronization phenomena after extracting observed innovative idea presentation utterances contained in our pilot data, and propose an interaction estimation method with simple image processing technologies. We expect that the proposed method will serve as a basis for supporting inexperienced facilitators by detecting important interaction events that may not be noticed by novices, thereby helping to promote the further popularization of Living Labs.

2 Data Recording

To explore the possibilities of interaction state estimation based on objectively observable indices, we ran a pilot experiment that simulated a living lab ideation setting and analyzed the recorded interaction data. We asked 27 university students (aged from 19 to 24) to participate in the experiment and to select some problems encountered in campus life and to propose an ICT solution to one of the problems. Nine familiar triads engaged in three ideation sessions (27 sessions total). All the participants were students of the university where one of the authors is a member of the faculty. The length of each session was 15 min, and the total duration of our ideation session data was 405 min.

In the first session, they pointed out as many problems as they could think of in their campus life, and wrote each one down on a sticky label without considering if a solution to these problems was actually feasible (problem search). In the second session, they classified the problems they had selected and examined the relations among them using a whiteboard, then assessed the feasibility of an ICT solution to the problems (problem classification and feasibility assessment). In the third session, they designed an ICT solution to one of the problems (solution design). Only the first sessions were included in the current study (9 sessions, total 135 min).

They used pens and several sheets of B4 sized sticky notes during the interactions. Three participants were seated 1.5 m apart from each other in a triangular formation around a circular table (Fig. 1). The sessions were recorded via two Ricoh Theta omni-directional cameras: one was placed in the center of the circular table, and the other was fixed to the ceiling (Fig. 2). Their frontal images were recorded by the one set on the center of the circular table, and their utterances were recorded by wireless pin microphones.

Fig. 1. Experimental setup

Their utterances were transcribed, and utterances presenting an idea mentioned for the first time in the session were annotated as "New Idea" by two annotators. Utterances that were reactions to the previous utterance were annotated as "Reaction." We used the

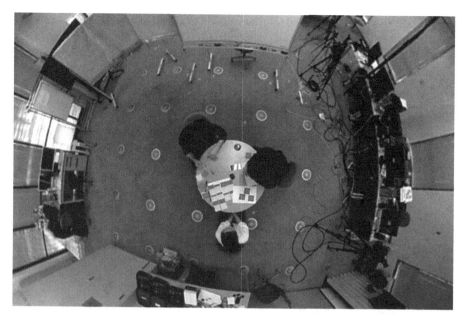

Fig. 2. Ceiling camera image.

EUDICO Linguistic Annotator (ELAN [5]) developed by the Max Planck Institute as a tool for annotation.

3 Analysis

Considering the feasibility of interaction estimation in actual ideation sessions, we adopted a simple approach combining image processing and utterance events, avoiding cumbersome devices and sensors that requires much effort and high skills and may even block the flow of discussion.

The relations between body-motion synchrony and the empathy among conversation participants have been pointed out by previous studies (ex. [6]), and Bernier et al. examined the possibility of empathy estimation based on body synchrony [7]. There have been studies that proposed an empathy estimation method based on body-motion synchrony calculated by image processing technology, without relying on human annotators [8, 9]. With those previous studies in mind, we observed our pilot sessions and found that the listeners tended to exhibit their body-motion synchrony through reactive utterances immediately following an utterance that presents an important new idea. Although there were wide variations in the form their body motions took, the timings of their body motions were closely synchronized.

Based on our observation, we examined the correlations between body-synchrony events with reactive utterances made by the listeners and important utterances that present a novel idea and drive the discussion. The omnidirectional camera images were trimmed for each participant, and optical flows were calculated for each participant. Then we calculated the correlations of those optical flows between participants. We modified a sample code "lk_track.py" included in OpenCV3 to calculate optical flows. The key points were detected using the "goodFeaturesToTrack" function of OpenCV (see Fig. 3 for a sample trimmed image and detected key points), and the shifts of key points were calculated using the Lucas-Kanade method [10].

Fig. 3. A sample trimmed image and detected key points

The formulae that calculate the amounts of key point shifts are as follows (t: number of frames; n: total number of key points):

$$\widehat{OF_{(t,x)}} = \frac{1}{n} \sum_{i=1}^{n} \left(P_{i(t,x)} - P_{i(t-1,x)} \right)$$

$$\widehat{OF_{(t,y)}} = \frac{1}{n} \sum_{i=1}^{n} \left(P_{i(t,y)} - P_{i(t-1,y)} \right)$$

$$\widehat{BodyMovement(t)} = \sqrt{\widehat{OF_{(t,x)}}^2 + \widehat{OF_{(t,y)}}^2}$$

Pearson product-moment correlation coefficients were used for the correlation analysis of the listeners. We slid a 1 s time frame in 0.5 s increments, and estimated that "body-motion synchrony" was happening when $r \geq .4$.

4 Results

We examined the relations between the estimated "body-motion synchrony" of the listeners with reactive utterances and the "New Idea" utterances. The results are shown in Table 1.

Table 1. The relations between "body-motion synchrony" events with reactive utterances and the "New Idea" utterances

Group no.	New idea utterance occurrences	Estimated body-motion synchrony occurrences	
		With "New Idea" utterances before body-motion synchrony	Without "New Idea" utterances before body-motion synchrony
1	16	2	0
2	9	0	0
3	25	2	0
4	18	1	0
5	17	0	0
6	16	0	0
7	29	4	0
8	18	2	2
9	30	1	1

As shown in the table above, "New Idea" utterances were often observed before "body-motion synchrony" events with reactive utterances. Six among the nine groups showed "body-motion synchrony" events with reactive utterances. For four of the six groups, there was always a "New Idea" utterance before a "body-motion synchrony" event with a reactive utterance. For the other two groups, a "New Idea" utterance was observed before 50% of the "body-motion synchrony" events with reactive utterances. A Wilcoxon signed-rank test showed that there was a marginally significant difference between the numbers of body synchrony preceded by new idea utterance and those not preceded by a new idea utterance ($p = .0975$).

5 Discussion

We have examined simulated triad ideation sessions and analyzed the relations between estimated "body-motion synchrony" of the listeners with reactive utterances and the "New Idea" utterances on the assumption that utterances with an innovative idea would be followed by listeners' body synchrony events coupled with the listeners' reactive utterances. The results showed that it was likely that there is a new idea event immediately before the listeners exhibit "body-motion synchrony" of the listeners with reactive utterances. This result suggests that body-motion synchrony and utterance serves as important cues that contribute to interaction state estimation. The proposed method is expected to serve as a basis for designing support systems for novice facilitators that will promote further popularization of Living Labs. In Living Lab ideation sessions, facilitators often have to manage several parallel ideation sessions by small subgroups, and grasping the state of each session requires highly specialized skills (see Fig. 4 for a sample image from an actual Living Lab ideation session). With the help of the supporting system based on the interaction state estimation method proposed here, even novice facilitators who do not have enough ability will be able to grasp the flow of parallel ideation sessions. The proposed method can also be applied for designing interaction data summary systems that select important interactional events or evaluate ideation activities based on recorded video data.

Fig. 4. A sample image from an actual Living Lab ideation session

However, there were also many occurrences of "New Idea" utterances not followed by a "body-motion synchrony" event with a reactive utterance. This may be because the "New Idea" utterances were often just new in the interaction, and not necessarily a "novel and useful" ones that drive the discussion: even commonplace and boring ideas were also labelled as a "New Idea" if they occurred for the first time in a particular session. Further studies with a more detailed standard for evaluating ideas will be required.

Moreover, the number of participants included in the sessions was small and they were all Japanese. Thus, the outcomes observed here may have been influenced by cultural and/or linguistic factors. Studies including a large number of participants with different cultural and linguistic backgrounds are also be needed.

The participants were limited to a narrow age range that included only young individuals, raising the possibility that the result may be specific to younger persons. There are also several other social factors that should be examined; for example, differences in the social status of participants may also affect the body-motion synchrony phenomena during collaborations. The current study is still in a preliminary stage, and further studies that includes more factors as suggested above are required to obtain more generalizable results.

6 Summary

We examined the relations between body-motion synchrony of the listeners with reactive utterances and the utterances presenting new ideas that were not observed in previous interactions in the session as a preliminary interaction estimation method for supporting novice facilitators in Living Lab projects. The results showed that it is likely that there is an utterance presenting a new idea occurs prior to body synchrony events between the listeners with their reactive utterances, suggesting the effectiveness of the proposed method in detecting important interaction events. However, the current work is still in a preliminary stage, and further studies that include cultural, linguistic, and social factors are needed.

References

1. European Networks of Living Labs. https://www.openlivinglabs.eu
2. Hagy, S., Morrison, G.M., Elfstrand, P.: Co-creation in living labs. In: Keyson, D.V., Guerra-Santin, O., Lockton, D. (eds.) Living Labs, pp. 169–178. Springer, Cham (2017). https://doi.org/10.1007/978-3-319-33527-8_13
3. Bergvall-Kareborn, B., Stahlbrost, A.: Living lab: an open and citizen-centric approach for innovation. Int. J. Innov. Reg. Dev. 1(4), 356–370 (2009)
4. CoreLabs. Living labs roadmap 2007–2010: recommendations on networked systems for open user-driven research, development and innovation. In: Open Document, Luleå: Luleå University of Technology, Centrum for Distance Spanning Technology (2007)
5. ELAN. http://www.lat-mpi.eu/tools/elan
6. Cappella, J.N.: Mutual influence in expressive behavior: adult-adult and infant-adult dyadic interaction. Psychol. Bull. 89, 101–132 (1981)
7. Bernier, F., Davis, J.M., Rosental, R., Knee, C.R.: Interactional synchrony and rapport: measuring synchrony in displays devoid of sound and facial affect. Pers. Soc. Psychol. Bull. 20, 303–311 (1994)
8. Nagaoka, C., Yoshikawa, S., Komori, M.: Embodied synchrony of nonverbal behavior in counselling: a case study of role playing school counselling. In: Proceedings of 28th Annual Conference of the Cognitive Science Society, pp. 1862–1867 (2006)
9. Nagaoka, C., Komori, M.: Body movement synchrony in psychotherapeutic counseling: a study using the video- based quantification method. IEICE Trans. Inf. Syst. 91(6), 1634–1640 (2008)
10. Lucas, B.D. and Kanade, T.: An iterative image registration technique with an application to stereo vision. In: Proceedings of 7th International Joint Conference on Artificial Intelligence, pp. 674–679 (1981)

A Preliminary Methodology to Evaluate the User Experience for People with Autism Spectrum Disorder

Katherine Valencia[1]([✉]) [iD], Cristian Rusu[1] [iD], and Federico Botella[2] [iD]

[1] Pontificia Universidad Católica de Valparaíso, Av. Brasil 2241, 2340000 Valparaíso, Chile
{katherine.valencia,cristian.rusu}@pucv.cl
[2] Universidad Miguel Hernández de Elche, Avienida de la Universidad s/n, 03202 Elche, España
federico@umh.es

Abstract. People with Autism Spectrum Disorder (ASD) have significant challenges in the development of their communication and social skills. They tend to enjoy interactions with computers, as these interactions offer a safe and structured environment.

Several studies have been dedicated to develop software systems and/or applications for people with ASD, trying to be as accessible and usable as possible. However, these studies do not present enough details on usability and User eXperience (UX) evaluation, nor empirical evidence in their research; therefore, we think it is necessary to formalize the process of UX evaluation, when working with people with ASD.

We stablish a preliminary methodology to evaluate UX for people with ASD. This methodology proposes 3 sequential stages, a planning stage, an execution stage and a results analysis stage. The methodology facilitates the correct selection of participants, evaluators and methods, as well as the execution of these methods, and the processing of the results. It aims to obtain valuable UX insights that can help the to improve users' skill learning, and thus their quality of life, through the use of technology.

Keywords: User experience · Autism spectrum disorder · User experience evaluation · Evaluation methodology

1 Introduction

Autism Spectrum Disorder (ASD) is a developmental disorder that affects people's communication and behavior. The fifth edition of the Diagnostic and Statistical Manual of Mental Disorders [1] (DSM-5) (American Psychiatric Association, 2013) states that autism spectrum disorder is a condition characterized by deficits in two core domains: (1) social communication and social interaction and (2) restricted repetitive patterns of behavior, interests, and activities.

The use of technology and software applications facilitates teaching language and social skills to people with ASD [2]. Studies such as the proposed by Kapp [3] mention

© Springer Nature Switzerland AG 2021
G. Meiselwitz (Ed.): HCII 2021, LNCS 12774, pp. 538–547, 2021.
https://doi.org/10.1007/978-3-030-77626-8_37

that people with ASD tend to have fun and participate more when technology is used, as it provides a safe and reliable environment.

Several studies have considered and evaluated the User eXperience (UX) in systems, products and/or technological applications used by people with ASD. Most of these studies do not present sufficient details of the evaluations and lack of empirical evidence in the research carried out [4].

Despite this, there are investigations that have proposed various evaluations of the usability and/or user experience of systems, products and/or technological applications developed for people with ASD, through the use of questionnaires, focus groups [5], under established scales [6] and/or use of Nielsen heuristics adaptations [7]. These studies demonstrate different possibilities to evaluate UX and/or usability in systems and/or products used with people with ASD, but empirical details and evidence are lacking.

Given the need formalize this evaluation process, we propose a preliminary methodology to evaluate UX for people with ASD. To accomplish this, we searched and selected UX and/or usability evaluation methods that could be applied in systems or products focused on people with ASD. In future works, we plan to adapt and specify those methods to be used in UX evaluations for people with ASD, considering the specific characteristics of these users.

This document is organized as follows: Sect. 2 presents the theoretical background; Sect. 3 describes relevant related work; Sect. 4 shows the UX methods selected; Sect. 5 presents a preliminary proposal of the UX evaluation methodology for people with ASD; and Sect. 6 presents conclusions and future works.

2   Theoretical Background

2.1 Autism Spectrum Disorder

In 1943 Leo Kanner [8] defined the term autism as a developmental disorder characterized by delays in language, stereotyped movements, self-stimulating behaviors, and alterations in relationship, communication, and flexibility. The concept of autism was considered conceptually different from the Asperger Syndrome described by Hans Asperger in 1944 [9], given its qualitative differences. In 1979 Lorna Wing and Judith Gould [10], stated that despite the qualitative differences between Autism and Asperger's Syndrome, people with these conditions share difficulties in: communication, social interaction and cognitive rigidity. Since 2013, in the fifth edition of the Diagnostic and Statistical Manual of Mental Disorders (DSM-5) [1], both concepts are considered within the broader definition of Autism Spectrum Disorder (ASD), as a condition characterized by deficits in two core domains: (1) social communication and social interaction and (2) restricted repetitive patterns of behavior, interests, and activities.

2.2 Usability

The international standard on ergonomics of human system interaction, ISO 9241–11 [11] defines usability as the "extent to which a system, product or service can be used by specified users to achieve specified goals with effectiveness, efficiency and satisfaction in a specified context of use".

In addition, Nielsen [12] defines usability as "a quality attribute that assesses how easy user interfaces are to use. The word "usability" also refers to methods for improving ease-of-use during the design process". Nielsen highlights that usability is defined by five quality components: learnability, efficiency, memorability, errors and satisfaction.

2.3 User Experience

The international standard on ergonomics of human system interaction, ISO 9241–11 [11] defines user experience as "user's perceptions and responses that result from the use and/or anticipated use of a system, product or service". It considers that UX "users' perceptions and responses include the users' emotions, beliefs, preferences, perceptions, comfort, behaviours, and accomplishments that occur before, during and after use". In other words, the user experience is the degree of "satisfaction" that the end user has with the system or service after using it, that is based on each of the interactions that he or she has.

In addition, the ISO 9241–11 standard [11] mentions that UX is a "consequence of brand image, presentation, functionality, system performance, interactive behavior, and assistive capabilities of a system, product or service. It also results from the user's internal and physical state resulting from prior experiences, attitudes, skills, abilities and personality; and from the context of use".

3 Related Work

Providing positive experiences, ensuring comfort in the use of products, systems or services, considering the needs of people with ASD is a priority when interacting with these artifacts.

Few studies have developed and evaluated UX in this context, and many of these studies did not provide enough detail about the use of these concepts, as evidenced in our previous work [4]. This shows us that many studies have deficiencies in evaluating the UX, as well as lack of empirical evidence when working with people with ASD.

Studies such as those proposed by De Los Rios [13], Backman et al. [5], Khowaja and Salim [14], Vallefuoco et al. [15] and Caria et al. [6] propose various evaluations of the usability and/or UX of systems and/or technological applications used by people with ASD.

De Los Rios [13], suggests evaluating the usability of the application used based on users' eye tracking. In Backman et al. [5], a questionnaire after the use of the system and focus groups has been applied to the users, parents and teachers of the users who participated in the case study. Khowaja and Salim [14], evaluated their proposed solution using an adaptation of the heuristics proposed by Nielsen [7] to the context of the study. Vallefuoco et al. [15], performed a usability test with children under the methodology proposed by Moreno Ger [16]. And finally, Caria et al. they used the "System Usability Scale" (SUS) [17] to evaluate the usability of their applications.

We have reviewed proposals for instruments to evaluate the usability and/or UX of systems and/or applications for people with ASD through heuristic evaluations, as proposed in the "Heuristics to Evaluate Interactive Systems for Children with Autism Spectrum Disorder (ASD)" [14]. In this research, Khowaja. K and Salim. SS propose a set of 15 heuristics, as adaptation of Nielsen's heuristics [7], to inspect features such as visibility, match, consistency, recognition, minimalist, control, error, flexibility, recover, documentation, personalization, screens, responsiveness, track and multi-modalities.

These studies demonstrate different approaches to assess UX and/or usability of the systems and/or applications used in their research. But these studies do not provide enough details of the evaluations performed, and many of these studies do not present empirical evidence of positive results when working with people with ASD [4].

4   UX Evaluation Methods for People with ASD

Given the lack of specific methods to evaluate UX in people with ASD [4], we investigated general UX methods that can be used in systems or products to be used by people with ASD. We selected six methods based on the information found in previous work [4] and methods presented on the website www.allaboutux.org [18].

The selection criteria have been based on our previous work where we studied the affinities and characteristics of people with ASD [4, 19]. In [4] a systematic literature review was carried out on the use of technology to teach people with ASD, and how these studies consider and evaluate usability, accessibility and UX. In [19] a total of eleven studies were analyzed, which were selected from the category of "social skills" of the previous systematic review of the literature [4], in order to understand how they characterize the difficulties of people with ASD, how these characteristics are used to design their proposals, the results obtained, and possible recommendations, in order to define design guidelines and best practices for future technology interventions that meet specific needs in people with ASD.

One of the most recurrent criteria we used to exclude methods was reviewing if they use individual and group questionnaires, are focused on emotions, and if they use images with facial expressions. The six selected methods are presented below:

1. **Controlled Observation** [20]: This method is focused on evaluating the effect of particular design decisions over the user satisfaction when using of a product or system, isolating these decisions to obtain noise-free data. This is achieved by individually controlling each of the design decisions through hard and balance controls over the order and execution of specific tasks by the participants within a controlled environment (often carried out in specific laboratories). Some of the controls used are task-ordering, which eliminates noise caused by prior knowledge when performing similar activities, and applying extremely controlled conditions by eliminating any environmental distraction that could affect the user's response to the product, including noise from conversations or other elements in the participant's field of vision. This method allows obtaining "pure" information and detecting less visible or specific effects on design decisions.

2. **Property Checklists** [20]: This method consists of a checklist related to a series of design properties that would affect the utility of the product, in order to verify that design objectives are met. This list refers to high-level properties, such as consistency, compatibility and good feedback, and low-level properties, such as the color, position and size of characters on the screen. The purpose of these checklists is that an expert usability evaluator can verify that the design of the product is adjusted to what is described in the list.

3. **Field Observations** [20]: This method is based on observing the users/participants in the environment in which they would naturally interact with the system or product. The purpose of this evaluation is to understand how participants experience the interaction of the system in natural conditions without limiting restrictions that could arise from a pre-established investigation. The role of the evaluator during the observation process should be as minimal as possible, since the participants can modify their behavior consciously or unconsciously during the observation.

4. **Group-based Expert Walkthrough** [21]: This method considers usability inspections based on task scenarios, in order to identify usability problems, design improvements and successful/good design solutions of a product or system. In order to carry out this evaluation, it is suggested to be carried out between 5–6 expert evaluators in the domain, which may not have knowledge in usability inspections, guided by a leader who must be a usability expert. The Walkthrough consists of task scenarios, structured enough for any non-usability evaluator to be able to participate, where the leader guides evaluators step-by-step through the product or system and evaluators take notes individually, and then in a second walkthrough, each of the evaluators' opinions is compiled through a group discussion for each of the tasks performed.

5. **Perspective-Based Inspection** [22]: This method applies a usability inspection of several sessions, which focus on detecting a subset of usability problems by inspectors/evaluators who perform a set of tasks considering different perspectives. These perspectives should be mutually exclusive, since it is stated that the set of perspectives would help to detect more problems than the use of traditional inspection techniques. The authors detail that the model helps to identify two categories of usability problems, such as "gulf of execution", which refers to the differences that arise between the intentions that users have and the actions that the product allows or system, and "gulf of evaluation", which refers to the discrepancy between the system's representation and the expectations of the user of this system.

6. **Heuristic Evaluation** [7]: This evaluation consists of examining and judging the compliance of selected usability principles ("heuristics") of an interface/system, by the inspection of a group of evaluators (ideally between 3 to 5). This evaluation presents four sequential stages, (1) each of the evaluators evaluates the system and generates a list with the potential usability problems that were detected. (2) All evaluators together make a unique list of potential problems detected based on the findings in the previous stage, associating each of these with a heuristic from the selected set of heuristics. (3) Each evaluator rates each of the potential problems based on its frequency, occurrence of the problem during the use of the system/interface, and its severity, the negative impact that the problem generates on the use of the system. Then, frequency and severity are added, resulting in the criticality of that

problem. And (4) all evaluators together gather the information in the previous stage and calculate the averages of the frequency, severity and criticality for each problem.

5   A Methodology Proposal

We propose a 3-stage methodology to formalize the process of evaluating the UX when working with people with ASD. This methodology has been created based on the information collected in systematic literature review [4], and considering previous works and sources detailed in this document, such as the evaluation methods presented in the previous section.

We propose 3 sequential stages: A Planning Stage, followed by the Execution Stage, and ending with the Results Analysis Stage. Processes and/or evaluations have been planned for each of the stages, as can be seen in Fig. 1.

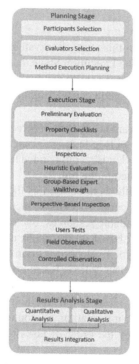

Fig. 1. Detailed UX evaluation methodology proposal for people with ASD.

5.1   Planning Stage

The purpose of this initial stage is to choose and select the necessary information for the Execution stage. As can be seen in Fig. 1, three activities have been considered:

Participants Selection. This aims to define and select the users who will be participants in the experiments to be carried out the next stage of the methodology. It is recommended to have a diversity and a significant number of participants, considering at least 10 participants with and without ASD, in order to have a better representation of the end users. If possible, it is recommended to include the participation of their learning companions, and/or their tutors, to create a safe environment for the participants.

Evaluators Selection. We propose to select and have the support of multiple evaluators during the execution of the UX evaluation methods proposed in the Execution Stage. Those professionals can be: experts in usability, UX, and experts in the specific domain, such as professionals who work with people with ASD like psychologists, speech therapists and differential teachers.

It is recommended to have between 3 to 5 professionals from the UX area, and between 3 to 5 professionals from the domain, that work with people with ASD, for each of the inspection methods. Having the support of different professionals will help to include different views to the analysis, and eventually, find a greater diversity of potential UX problems.

Method Execution Planning. In this stage, the evaluators must determine and select the methods to be performed in the Execution Stage, based on the objective, scope and available time of the UX evaluation. To select the methods to use and based on the time and resources available, we recommend considering the following criteria:

- If time and available resources are not critical, it is recommended to carry out each of the methods presented (shown in Fig. 1).
- If time and resources are limited, it is recommended to use fewer evaluation methods, following the sequence presented in the Fig. 2.
- It is possible to decide the methods to be used as the execution stage progresses. It is recommended that the "Property Checklists" method is always carried out, and depending on the time and available resources, one or more inspection methods can be carried out, selecting them based on the needs of the case study and considering the following order: Heuristic Evaluation, Group-Based Expert Walkthrough and Perspective-Based Inspection. The order is based on time and resources required. If time and resources are limited, it is recommended to perform the "Field Observations". Otherwise, "Controlled Observation" method would be recommended, since it allows obtaining clean noise information, by controlling the effect of distractions and prior knowledge caused by the order of tasks to be performed by the user, as detailed in Sect. 3.

5.2 Execution Stage

In this stage we propose the implementation and execution of methods to evaluate the user experience of the system or products for people with ASD. As shown in Fig. 1, the use of 6 methods is proposed, described in Sect. 3, which were classified into 3 sequential sub-stages: "Preliminary Evaluation", "Inspections" and "Users Tests".

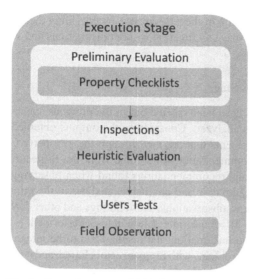

Fig. 2. Execution stage with limited time sequence.

Preliminary Evaluation. In this first stage we apply methods that focus on evaluating the usability and UX of the system or product in a preliminary manner, in order to discriminate and/or filter if it meets certain predefined primary criteria. The use of the "Property Checklists" method is proposed, which uses of a checklist made by the evaluator in order to evaluate the usability of the system or product (as detailed in Sect. 3). At the time of creating the "Property Checklists" method, it is recommended to elaborate a checklist that considers the characteristics, affinities and difficulties of people with ASD. We also recommend that each one of the aspects described by the 7 guidelines, that we defined in [19] (Structured and Predictable Learning Environment, Generalization to Daily Life, Learning Dynamics: Individual and Collaborative, Engagement Through Activity Cycles and Game Elements, Error Managing, Mixed Activities, No-touch and Hybrid Interfaces), should be considered and incorporated, since they provide a set of good practices and recommendations validated by the literature for this context.

Inspections. Once the preliminary evaluation has been carried, the implementation of inspection methods is proposed. The "Group-Based Expert Walkthrough", "Perspective-Based Inspection" and "Heuristic Evaluation" methods described in Sect. 3 are proposed to be carried out with the support of the evaluators selected in the previous stage, "Evaluators Selection". It is recommended that these inspections should be designed considering the characteristics of the users with ASD.

User Tests. It is proposed to carry out methods to evaluate UX with the participation of users, in order to assess the perception of the users in the interaction with the system or product. In this sub-stage, we recommend the use of the "Controlled Observation" and "Field Observations" methods with the participants selected in the previous stage, "Participants Selection". It is recommended to design these tests based on the characteristics, affinities and difficulties of people with autism spectrum disorder, in order to encourage the participation of the participants, by providing them a safe and structured environment in which they can function without distractions and stress.

5.3 Results Analysis Stage

Once UX evaluations have been carried out in the previous stage, the results obtained must be collected and analyzed. Considering the outputs obtained from each method, such as the design elements that are met through the "Property Checklist", problems identified, design recommendations that come from the inspections, as well as other relevant information and recommendations found when observing the users, it is recommended to do a quantitative and qualitative analysis of the information obtained, in order to gather problems, observations, shortcomings and other design elements that are frequent and critically affect user interaction in tests performed.

After analyzing the information, the results need to be integrated, which includes matching the potential problems with frequent errors found, and creating descriptive stats and observations so we can evaluate the user's perceptions, the efficiency and effectiveness of the system or product, and also provide solutions and design recommendations to improve said experience in future iterations of the system or product.

6 Conclusions

People with ASD often communicate, interact, behave and learn in very different ways from other people. Providing a positive experience is essential when people with ASD interact with technology. Studies have evaluated and developed systems and/or applications in order to develop various skills in people with ASD, trying to provide a comfortable and satisfactory experience, but these studies lack details in the evaluations and empirical evidence in the investigations carried out.

Literature mentions and declares the importance of aspects such as UX and usability when working with people with ASD. However, these aspects are generally not considered or validated in detail. Using a formal UX evaluation process would provide reliable results. That is why we are proposing a methodology to evaluate the UX for people with ASD, in which we have described the methodology, its stages, suggested evaluation methods and several considerations, regarding mainly the available time and resources.

We expect to validate and refine this preliminary methodology in future works, adding depth, elaborating about the details of its use, and including particular method adaptations for users with ASD.

Acknowledgments. Katherine Valencia is a beneficiary of the ANID-PFCHA/ Doctorado Nacional/2019–21191170.

References

1. American Psychiatric Association: Diagnostic and Statistical Manual of Mental Disorders, 5th edn. American Psychiatric Publishing, Arlington (2013)

2. Grynszpan, O., Weiss, P.L., Perez-Diaz, F., Gal, E.: Innovative technology-based interventions for autism spectrum disorders: a meta-analysis. Autism **18**(4), 346–361 (2014)
3. Kapp, K.: The Gamification of Learning and Instruction: Game-Based Methods and Strategies for Training and Education, 1st edn. Pfeifer, San Francisco (2012)
4. Valencia, K., Rusu, C., Quiñones, D., Jamet, E.: The impact of technology on people with autism spectrum disorder: a systematic literature review. Sens. **19**(20), 4485 (2019)
5. Backman, A., et al.: Internet-delivered psychoeducation for older adolescents and young adults with autism spectrum disorder (SCOPE): an open feasibility study. Res. Autism Spectrum Disord. **54**, 51–64 (2018)
6. Caria, S., Paternò, F., Santoro, C., Semucci, V.: The design of web games for helping young high-functioning autistics in learning how to manage money. Mobile Netw. Appl. **23**(6), 1735–1748 (2018). https://doi.org/10.1007/s11036-018-1069-0
7. Nielsen, J., Molich, R.: Heuristic evaluation of user interfaces. In: Proceedings of the SIGCHI Conference on Human Factors in Computing System, Association for Computing Machinery, Seattle, USA, pp. 249–256 (1990)
8. Kanner, L.: Autistic disturbances of affective contact. Nerv. Child **2**(3), 217–250 (1943)
9. Asperger, H.: Die "Autistischen Psychopathen" im Kindesalter. Arch. Psychiatr. Nervenkr. **117**(1), 76–136 (1944)
10. Wing, L., Gould, J.: Severe impairments of social interaction and associated abnormalities in children: epidemiology and classification. Autism Dev. Disord. **9**(1), 11–29 (1979)
11. Ergonomics of human-system interaction — Part 11: Usability: definitions and concepts, https://www.iso.org/obp/ui/#iso:std:iso:9241:-11:ed-2:v1:en. Accessed 23 Jan 2021
12. Usability 101. Introduction to Usability. https://www.nngroup.com/articles/usability-101-int roduction-to-usability/. Accessed 23 Jan 2021
13. De Los Rios, C.: Adaptable user interfaces for people with autism: a transportation example. In: 15th International Web for All Conference: Internet of Accessible Things. Association for Computing Machinery, Lyon, France (2018)
14. Khowaja, K., Salim, S.: serious game for children with autism to learn vocabulary: an experimental evaluation. Int. J. Hum.-Comput. Inter. **35**(1), 1–26 (2019)
15. Vallefuoco, E., Bravaccio, C., Pepino, A.: Serious games in autism spectrum disorder: An example of personalised design. In: 9th International Conference on Computer Supported Education, SciTePress, Porto, Portugal, pp. 567–572. (2017)
16. Moreno-Ger, P., Torrente, J., Hsieh, Y.G., Lester, W.: Usability testing for serious games: Making informed design decisions with user data. Adv. Hum.-Comput. Inter. **2012**(2), (2012)
17. Brooke, J.: SUS: a 'quick dirty' usability scale. Usability evaluation in industry. Taylor and Francis (1996)
18. All About UX. http://www.allaboutux.org/all-methods. Accessed 02 June 2020
19. Valencia, K., et al.: Technology-based social skills learning for people with autism spectrum disorder. In: Meiselwitz, G. (ed.) Social Computing and Social Media. Participation, User Experience, Consumer Experience, and Applications of Social Computing. Lecture Notes in Computer Science, vol. 12195, pp. 598–615. Springer, Cham (2020). https://doi.org/10.1007/978-3-030-49576-3_44
20. Jordan, P.W.: Designing Pleasurable Products. An Introduction to the New Human Factors, 1st edn. Taylor & Francis, London (2000)
21. Følstad, A.: Group-based Expert Walkthrough. In: R^3 UEMs: Review, Report and Refine Usability Evaluation Methods, pp. 58–60 (2007)
22. Zhang, Z., Basili, V., Shneiderman, B.: Perspective-based usability inspection: an empirical validation of efficacy. Empir. Softw. Eng. **4**(1), 43–69 (1999)

One Profile, Many Memories: Projecting Memorials for Instagram via Participatory Design

Aline E. C. Verhalen[1]([⊠]), Cristiano Maciel[1,3]([⊠]), Hélia Vannucchi[2]([⊠]),
and Daniele Trevisan[3]([⊠])

[1] Institute of Computer Sciences - Federal University of Mato Grosso,
Cuiabá – Mato Grosso, Brazil
`alineverhalen@usp.br`, `cmaciel@ufmt.com`
[2] School of Communication and Arts - Federal University of Mato Grosso,
Cuiabá – Mato Grosso, Brazil
`helia@ufmt.br`
[3] Graduate Program in Education - Federal University of Mato Grosso,
Cuiabá – Mato Grosso, Brazil
`daniele109926@estudante.ufmt.br`

Abstract. As the popularity of social networks continue to increase, numerous profiles created daily tend to evolve as software. As they represent people in the online environment, these profiles are digital assets that, after their user's death, represent a digital legacy, even if it only represents emotional value. In some social networks, these legacies become digital memorials. Currently, on the social network Instagram, there is no difference between an active account and an account that has become a memorial, thus is a source of confusion to anyone who visits these profiles. Instagram moreover does not provide options for users to configure their future memorials, which can affect aspects of a person's identity after his or her death. A problem therefore emerges: how to maintain the aspects of identity, volition and privacy from the moment of the configuration of a memorial until its creation/transformation. In view of the above, this research has the means to raise questions and propose solutions for an Instagram digital memorial, while maintaining the three aspects. From a methodological point of view, this qualitative exploratory research was based on bibliographic reviews, observation on the web, and a survey and participatory design involving the participation of a focus group. The result includes a set of requirements and interface prototypes that are focused on digital memorials and useful for system developers.

Keywords: Digital legacy · Instagram · Digital memorial · Participatory design · Terms of use · Privacy policies

1 Introduction

Smartphones are thus defined because they combine the functions of personal computers with those of mobile phones. Torres [28] points out that, since the

G. Meiselwitz (Ed.): HCII 2021, LNCS 12774, pp. 548–566, 2021.
https://doi.org/10.1007/978-3-030-77626-8_38

arrival of the BlackBerry and the expansion of the market by using the Internet on mobile phones, smartphones have become a bigger phenomenon. Companies fueled their strength with a rush in production, as they endeavored to offer more features on their devices to render them unique and more attractive in the eyes of consumers.

Thus, several platforms, which had previously been designed for viewing in desktop devices, have been adapted in order to be easily accessed by mobile devices. E-mails, online shopping, and especially social networks have developed applications to facilitate the access of its target customer. According to a survey called "Global Digital Report 2018" [15], 62% of the Brazilian population use social networks.

Used by more than half of the population, social networks are easily accessible tools and act as facilitators for their users, who are able to share a photo and post a text with a click of a button and post their own photo with another click. Consequently, there is an increase in the production of digital assets, which are the assets produced by a person in the digital medium, such as photos, videos and messages [7,22]. These digital assets are almost always linked to a single account and compose a part of their legacy in the digital medium, so when the account owner dies, his or her assets cannot simply be deleted. Therefore, companies should provide mechanisms to deal with these assets.

We are experiencing a pandemic due to the new coronavirus, COVID-19, so there is constant encounter with death on social media, which reinforces the need to think about the composition of memorials. The creation of digital memorials provides a destination for users' digital data, comparable to what happens with dead bodies in a physical cemetery. They are lives that leave us in the real world and become immortal in our hearts by means of technology and this reinforces the need to think about solutions to configure digital memorials.

Facebook already allows users to designate an heir to manage their digital memorial or delete their account, as described in [9], after their death. While Google has the option of sharing its data with people previously designated by the user. In the case of Instagram, it is possible to request the "memorialization" of an account, by filling out a form sent by relatives or friends. Currently, an update is under work in order to render this process simpler, in addition to changes in the design, which signals that the account has become a memorial. These changes are still undergoing the testing phase and there are still no updates on the designation of an heir.

However, regardless of this solution, how is it possible to maintain the aspects of identity, volition and privacy when setting up a memorial until its creation on Instagram?

This work aims to raise questions and propose solutions regarding Instagram digital memorials, while preserving identity, volition and privacy. The methodology to search for these results is an exploratory research of a qualitative nature, which seeks to achieve the proposed objective using bibliographic reviews, web observations, surveys and participatory design sessions involving a focus group.

In this text, we initially present the theoretical framework in which we address guiding concepts that was underlying in the research. Then we present the chosen methodology describing how the research was developed. Next, the results and their analysis are presented. Finally, we present the final considerations of the research and the bibliographical references.

2 Guiding Concepts

In the case of human values, the identity that people develop about themselves is of supreme importance. The Merriam-Webster [1] defines identity as: "the distinguishing character or personality of an individual". Brubaker and Vertesi [6] explain that identity is built through interactions. Leaver and Highfield [17] reaffirm this concept and state that online identity is a co-creative process, in which other individuals participate. The identity that a user leaves in the digital environment is important for the construction of their online memory, including the digital memorial.

In a digital memorial, it is important that the heir has knowledge about the identity that the individual has developed in that social network, as stated by Gach and Brubaker [11], who mention how even small changes to the memorial settings performed by the heir can change the entire identity of the person who has passed away. The settings of a memorial are of the utmost importance so that, when an account becomes a memorial, it is able to represent who its late owner was. The power of choice given to the user, inserted in these settings, is called volition.

Maciel and Pereira [22] understand volition as the user's decision-making power regarding what will happen with their accounts, profiles, data, among others. Maciel [19] demonstrates in his work some volitional solutions that can be applied in Social Web, some of which can be:

1. The system checks from time to time whether the user is active;
2. The system asks the user about procedures in case death is notified.

Regarding volition, de Toledo *et al.* [9] studied issues such as identity and volition on the social network Facebook, looking for solutions in these two aspects, in order to make Facebook's digital memorial more user-friendly and grant more freedom to its heir.

Viana, Maciel and Souza [29] discuss how terms of use and privacy policies are essential for social networks, since they will define the destination of both the account and the assets of that account. In view of a more legal approach, Edwards and Harbina [10] bring the prospect of death and privacy online. They bring up the idea of social privacy, which is defined through interactions between profiles, such as comments, shared photos, among others. This opens the debate about whether comments are good for those who commented, or for those who received the comments? The authors point out that there is still no answer to this question, as there is still a debate about the legal point of view, and image interests are not necessarily protected by law. It is important to note that the authors base their view on the Anglo-American legal system when developing this analysis.

2.1 Instagram

Instagram was launched in 2010 and purchased by the social network Facebook in 2012. It is a social network focused on sharing photographs, videos and, more recently and popularly, stories, which are videos or photos that are temporarily accessible to followers. When it was launched, Instagram's goal was to be used for snapshots, alluding to popular instant-film Polaroids. However, over time, a considerable niche was found for advertising and publicity. This is because its feed is used solely for photos, so a message can be easily transmitted and, furthermore, can be directly linked to the advertiser's store.

Instagram has a web version, whose access is similar to the app, containing messages, likes and comments, but with some restrictions. In this version, the Terms of Use and Privacy Policies were read in order to investigate the network's position in relation to digital memorials. Currently, it does not permit the user to define an heir to his or her accounts. Nor does it allow any modifications in the profile photo, comments or other characteristics when the account is transformed into a memorial. However, one of the most noticeable factors found during the study of Instagram was the lack of identification of a memorial.

Besides the studies by Leaver and Highfield [17] on the development of identity on Instagram until death and by Gibbs et al. [14] on Instagram practices that involve mourning rites, no other studies were found concerning Instagram's digital memorials.

3 Methodology

The objective of this qualitatively based work was sought by formulating a survey that was submitted to a focus group. Two focus group meetings were held about participatory design. The first meeting discussed the topic and conceptions of design. The second meeting was dedicated to the applying these requirements in low fidelity designs.

As for the composition of the focus group, according to Barbosa and Silva [3], it is appropriate for focus groups to have 3 to 10 people to ensure the discussion progresses well. The focus group allows an idea or impression to be analyzed from different perspectives and produce different or equivalent impressions on certain points [2,13].

According to Bjögvinsson [5], participatory design (PD) arose out of a concern for how design could support diverse groups with few resources, especially at a time when information technology was being introduced. They emphasize that PD must start from a simple viewpoint and the people affected by the design must have a voice in the process. For people to participate, Rocha and Baranauskas [26] argue, the workplace is a common choice, as the subject becomes incorporated as a member of the design team. The authors additionally highlight three important characteristics: context-oriented discussions, involvement of collaboration at many levels, and interactive approach.

A survey inquiring about interest in participation was sent through messages, emails and Facebook groups, in order to reach the largest possible number of interested parties. It was not anonymous because the people who responded showing interest in participating in the focus group would then be contacted. It should be noted that the survey was used solely for inviting participants. To compose the participant profile, there were questions about their education level and area of expertise. The selected participants belonged to fields of knowledge that were different from the researcher's in attempt to assure variety in the discussion. The questionnaire was available for 3 d, and had a reach of 62 people, of whom 13 were interested, 9 confirmed their participation, and only 6 attended. This number was within the expectations of the research and in accordance with the numbers of academic literature [3].

For the participation of the focus group, it was clarified that the participants would be videotaped for the purpose of analyzing the discussion, but that none of them would be identified. All participants agreed by signing a Free and Informed Consent Form. The first stage of the focus group consisted of introducing the participants, through a group dynamic called an "icebreaker", so that they could get to know each other a little and feel more comfortable in starting the discussion.

The group dynamic was shortly followed by introducing and putting into context the main terms that would be used to provide a basis for the discussion, namely: Instagram, Digital Legacy, Digital Memorial, Digital Asset, Digital Heir, Volition and Privacy. This contextualization included examples of profiles belonging to celebrities who passed away. In some cases, it was detectable that, due to the person's fame both in life and in death, the social media profiles witnessed an increase in the number of followers and expressions of mourning. The examples included Brazilian television presenter Gugu Liberato, singer Gabriel Diniz and actor Cameron Boyce.

Subsequently, for the group discussion, questions were asked to investigate what the participants' views were on Instagram digital memorials, and how, in their perspective, these digital memorials could be improved. The following questions were asked during the focus group: 1) Do you think it is important that digital memorials exist?; 2) It has been noticed that, in some cases, when a person dies, the number of followers increases. What makes Instagram profiles of people who have passed away more attractive?; 3) When the owner of the profile dies, what should happen to the account? How can the person determine what will happen to his or her account? 4) And what should happen if the profile is private?; 5) What should be the responsibilities of a digital heir? 6) Regarding business accounts: who should have access?; 7) In the case of digital influencers, what is the impact on the profile when the owner dies?

In addition to the scripted questions, the moderator was completely free to add questions that arose during the discussion, as there could be experiences underwent by the users that could be discussed. Moreover, adding questions could help prolong a subject, thus stimulating the group to think about more questions and answers.

For analyzing the focus group, the entire footage was transcribed, using strategies recommended in academic literature [12,23], for a document in the

Libre Office Writer tool. The transcript of the video, which was 1 h long, resulted in 20 pages of content. The members were anonymized with the nomenclature H (1–4) for male participants and F (1–2) for female participants.

After transcription, the text was analyzed in order to find excerpts that addressed aspects of: volition/settings, privacy, digital heir and digital memorial, which were the terms contextualized at the beginning of the focus group. However, as the reading and analysis took place, other aspects were identified as relevant to the development of the requirements: identity, system, interaction, and homage. The participants' sentences could have more than one important aspect. This analysis resulted in 17 requirements that will be presented in the results section.

At the next meeting, where the same people from the first meeting participated, the generated requirements were presented, in addition to new concepts, such as prototypes. Participants were divided into two groups (hereby named G1 and G2), each composed of 3 people, and were given stationery material, sheets of paper with printed requirements, in addition to templates that simulated mobile phones, and were instructed to redraw the settings and Instagram memorial screen based on the requirements. There was no designer to assist them, only two moderators to answer questions. Participants were asked to label what requirement each aspect of the design represented.

They could also modify the requirements if they felt that they did not cover the ideas presented by the group in the previous discussion. And they were told it was not necessary to include all requirements. Additionally, they were also asked to create terms of use and privacy policies that would be compatible with the new requirements.

At the end of the participatory design, the participants delivered the prototypes created to the researcher, who analyzed them and separated the ideas presented by the two groups based on the requirements that were used by both.

This analysis was performed so that the researcher could then generate prototypes of medium fidelity, aligning both ideas, based on design and usability studies, generating a total of 6 screens created in the Balsamiq Mockup tool.

4   Results

This section will present the results found through the analysis of the questionnaire and focus groups. It was divided into four parts: Survey Analysis, Generation of Requirements, Design Solutions and Elaboration of Terms of Use.

4.1   Survey Analysis

The survey made it possible to list the profiles of people interested in participating in the focus group. Thirteen people were interested, but one did not use any social network, so he was discarded, leaving 12 people to be contacted, 9 confirmed that they could attend the section, which would be held on January 21, 2020. Out of 9 people, 6 attended – 4 men and 2 women, between the ages of 18 and 25. The 6 participants were enrolled in university or already had an undergraduate degree, and belonged to different fields, such as Medicine, Law, Chemistry, Physics, Pedagogy and Computer Science.

Of the 12 interested people, 3 responded that they had never heard of the term "digital memorials" before the survey. When asked about "What did they understand by digital memorials", some of the responses from interested people were: "A space reserved for everything you left online, everything you 'planted' on networks during your life"; "A memory created on the Web"; "It is the data stored in a lifetime"; and "It is a place where friends and family can pay tribute to and remember the deceased through the internet".

Indeed, memorials can encompass all these responses, and the question was posed to determine how much more should be explained about the topic. Hence, thanks to that question, the group that was reached by the survey already had a certain knowledge about the theme, even though it is a theme that is still not very widespread.

4.2   Generation of Requirements

For the identification of requirements we use the caption FRn, where n corresponds to the number of requirements, for functional requirements. And NFRn, for non-functional requirements.

The next table (Table 1) presents the functional requirements generated from the analysis of the transcript of the first meeting and which excerpts of the focus group were used to generate these requirements.

FR01 was conceived after questioning participants about the importance of memorials. H3 said: "(...) It is important for you to differentiate between people who are alive and people who are dead (...)". Which reinforces the issue that Instagram does not explicitly inform when a profile becomes a memorial. Regarding digital memorials [18, 20] addresses some aspects of memorials that may be essential to make a visual distinction between the profile of a living person and that of a person who has died, such as showing the name of the heirs.

In the second question, "Sometimes, after a person dies, the number of his/her followers increases. What do you think makes Instagram more attractive in profiles of people who have already died?". Using examples of profiles shown at the beginning of the focus groups meeting, H2 stated that: "(...) after death, the act of following the person becomes even more meaningful (...)" and, when asked about the fact that respect can be shown by comments, he states: "It is so much easier just to follow someone, all you have to do is click on a button". F1, on the other hand, showed a different perspective: "(...) The way I see it, you follow someone to see an update on their life (...)". Thus, for some of them, the act of following would be a kind of tribute. With this discussion among the participants, the second requirement (FR02) emerged. As the act of following would be merely symbolic, in the view of the participants, it is possible to relate this with Ribeiro [25], who states that: "what man wants when creating places of memory, is, in a way, to develop places that can remain: eternal places, even

Table 1. Functional requirements

ID	Requirements	ID	Requirements
[FR01]	The application should change the layout of a digital memorial for it to become different from a user's profile	[FR09]	The application should, when not configured in memorial, disable the account when there is no access within a period of 5 (five) years
[FR02]	The application should modify the status of the option "follow" for a memorial	[FR10]	The application should send a verification message to the owners of deactivated accounts
[FR03]	The application should make it clear in the settings where to configure a memorial	[FR11]	The application should delete accounts that do not reply to the verification messages by a given period
[FR04]	The application should let the user choose what is going to happen to his or her account after passing away	[FR12]	The application should delimit all the heir's activity based on the choices previously made by the deceased user
[FR05]	The application should allow business owners designate heirs to their accounts	[FR13]	The application should clearly identify who is the heir of that account
[FR06]	The application should give the option of: deleting the account, designating it to an heir and transforming it into a memorial in case death of the user is detected or just turning it into a memorial	[FR14]	The application should allow complaints to be filed against the account heir
[FR07]	The application should periodically remind the user to configure their future memorial	[FR15]	The application should notify the heir in case of a complaint and warn that the account can be banned
[FR08]	The application should contact the heir and question him/her about the confirmation of death, before turning it into a memorial	[FR16]	The application will issue up to n warnings about misuse of account before the heir is banned

though, paradoxically, these places are in increasingly fluid devices, which bring back our memories."

The group was asked: "When the owner of the profile dies, what should happen to the account?", Which raised questions about the profile settings. F2 talked about how each person should be able to determine what happens in their account. F1 pointed to the place where this should happen: "In the settings, I think, it is easier." To what H4 retorts: "But Instagram's settings are super confusing." H4 was echoed by F1, who granted that they really are confusing. Thus, FR03 was created. Still on this question, a discussion was initiated on how users will know that they must make these changes in the settings. H1 says: "(...) I think you have to have the option, the person can choose if it stays online, as a memorial, or if it is disabled". H2 asked what would happen if the person had not made this choice in life and thus started a discussion about a standard procedure for unconfigured accounts. Participants raised that if there is no user choice, the account must be closed, leaving only the current followers, as suggested by F2. When asked about business accounts, H2 made the following note: "if it is a business account, the person would generate a certain type of income with that account, if that account goes to another partner, the family who should have inherited the dead person's property becomes totally forsaken". This discussion resulted in the creation of FR04 and FR05, and is a clear demonstration of volition, discussed by Maciel and Pereira [22], since it is something that can be determined only by the user.

An issue was raised by H4: whether or not there is an heir. F2 stated that: "(...) What I think should happen to the account is, I think it should close, leaving only those who are already there (...)". H2 added: "(...) If the person hasn't defined what happens to her account after she dies, I think it would be interesting to do as Facebook does, which is at least to identify that it has become a digital memorial". Thus, FR06 was proposed in light of the options that the network should make available to its user.

F2 suggested that the settings should be available "when she creates her profile, (...) it should appear every time she logs in, right? To remind her to answer". But it was refuted by H3 who thinks "it would drive people away". H3 then suggested the use of pop-up screens, a suggestion that was well received by others, and H2, exemplified: "(...) After a period of time using the social network, a little pop-up screen appears that says: What would you like to happen to your account after you pass away?". Finally, the whole group agreed that periodic or discreet notices would be the best option to remind the user. This resulted in FR07.

The system in relation to the heir was sometimes mentioned, as well as how to identify the user's death. In a scenario where there is an heir, participants find that notifying the latter is the most practical action. This is the foundation for FR08. In this case, one of the biggest challenges for detecting death is: What should be considered? Since words of comfort and reminiscing can be used in other cases, such as the death of a pet, or parting of ways.

But what if there is no heir? F1 pointed out: "If you have no heir, there's no one to contact". There was then a discussion about how long the system should take to disable a profile. H1 argued five years would be an ideal period ("no one stays away for five years without logging in"). And F2 pointed out that it should be a process "without deleting anything". And F1 added that the user could reactivate the account if "(...) after a while, after you send this photo, they activate your account back. Which proves you're alive (...)". With this photo,

F1 referred to an Instagram security method, in which a message with a security code is sent, and the user must return with a photo of his or her face, and a paper written with the code on the same photo, thus proving their identity. H2 then added that, in order not to accumulate inactive accounts, the system should "(...) Wait for a period of time, disable it, then wait another period of time, then if there really is no sign of life, then you [deactivate the account]". Based on this discussion, requirements FR09, FR10 and FR11 were generated.

Regarding the settings, the role of the heir was debated based on the question: "Can the heir change the person's settings?" H4 partook the opinion that: "(...) in the settings that the heir made, in the settings of the deceased, they are different, and think that it should have a different priority (...)", meaning that the person who died should pre-configure the settings of the heir, while he or she is still alive. This issue was discussed by de Toledo *et al.* [9], who questioned why Facebook only allows one heir and there is no freedom for the heir's powers to be modified.

H3 added that the heir would not have the opportunity to be more open: "It is because it is a restriction, like, he can't open more, but he can restrict more." Still on the freedoms of the heir, issues regarding tributes were addressed again, which had been mentioned earlier when participants mentioned that the act of following a person was a type of tribute. Instagram's current rule is not to allow changes to a memorial, but there was a general consensus in the focus group that the social media platform should allow the existence of an heir, and this heir should be able to post from the account, such as photos and videos. H4 mentions questions of homage to justify his point of view: "(...) A famous person who has an event to celebrate her death later, or announcing Requiem Mass, or posting something about the person's funeral (...)". This discussion was what determined FR12.

FR13 was prepared based on the moderator's following provocation: do participants think it is ethical for other people to have the account of the person who died? This caused the discussion to merge identity and heir, as when H1 states that: "If they kind of make it explicit that this person died, and this is a memorial, I think it is". H3 adds that: "You put a marker there that this is not the [dead] person's original post."

The question "What would the responsibilities of an heir be?" goes back to the user definitions when changing the profile settings, but it also becomes a discussion about the limits the software imposes to an heir. There must be freedom of action in the system, but certain control is also needed regarding what is possible to accomplish in another person's memorial. H2 reports that, in order to control an heir who could be abusive with the account, "everybody could check", which suggested that everyone would have the right to report a post. F2 proposed that, in order to protect against false reports, "the agent (the system) checks later". F1 complemented with the evaluating the number of complaints, and H1 brought up the idea of issuing warnings: "(...) Should give one or two warnings, like: look, this was ... you performed an action that violates such and such. . ." This generated the following three requirements (FR14, FR15 and FR16).

Maciel and Pereira [21] comment on the existence of a misalignment between processes of identification, registration and documentation of individuals in real life and in digital life. This results in a great challenge for software developers in terms of addressing these issues. Leal [16] states that the Judiciary Power will be increasingly called upon to solve problems resulting from the mismatch between physical death and the permanence of contents available online, which reveals the pressing need to discuss the topic. Furthermore, there is growing concern about privacy and data protection, especially if we consider the General Data Protection Law, as discussed by Beppu and Maciel [4].

H3 spoke about the comfort of other people and the privacy of the deceased person, emphasizing that the systems must: "(...) be informed about who has died, in order to deal with it differently and to present this profile to them in a different way or not to present them at all." Thus, the last requirement, FR17, was established.

For the non-functional requirements, ideas were used from earlier discussions, such as the difficulty in finding the configurations, which generated the first non-functional requirement (NFR01) (Table 2).

Table 2. Non-functional requirements

ID	Requirements	ID	Requirements
[NFR01]	The application should have easily accessible settings for the user	[NFR03]	The application should use an algorithm to search for patterns in comments for detecting death
[NFR02]	The application should respect the user's privacy, based on the settings of the account and the Terms of Use	[NFR4]	TThe application should respect the terms signed externally by the account owners

During the discussion, participants emphasized the importance of privacy, recalling the terms of use and raising the question of whether these terms explicitly allude to this type of information. Schaub *et al.* [27] mention how companies that offer services and process data should inform what information is collected and how long it is retained, as well as with whom it is shared. In its Terms of Use, Instagram only specifies that, after deleting the account, the user's data will still be stored for some time; furthermore, if not deleted, data from the account will become public domain. Thus, the second non-functional requirement (FRN02) was considered.

Another point that was discussed concerned how the social network will know how to contact the heir to confirm death. H2 and H4 talked about using an algorithm, and despite the cons of a mistaken detection of death, participants agree that this would be the most practical option. Thus, NFR03 was defined. As for the public domain issue, a discussion was also initiated regarding the user profiles of famous people, which brought H3's observation about image rights associated with inheritance and privacy: "(...) In the case of famous people, the heir's responsibility ends where the rights of the person who owns the image rights, the copyrights of the person who passed away, begin". Hence was defined the last non-functional requirement (NFR04).

In general, throughout the focus group, the mediator did not need to interfere much, and the participants, most of the time, waited for each other to finish speaking before explaining their counterargument. Moreover, the participants were quick to understand the questions and were engaged in the discussion, and even raised issues themselves. The interrupted moments were also transcribed in the analysis document, making it clear that the mediator had interfered, and clarified to the participants the reason for the interruption.

4.3   Design Solutions

The results of the second meeting were the low-fidelity prototypes generated by the participants, in addition to an eighteenth requirement generated by G2, which was: FR18 - The application should allow the user to search for and choose an heir among people that follow him/her.

G1 was the only one using FR15, FR16 and NFR02, while G2 used FR02 and created a new requirement, which he named FR19, but which would become FR18 to suit the order of requirements. G1 and G2 referred to FR01 in a similar way, as shown below, using the profile screen.

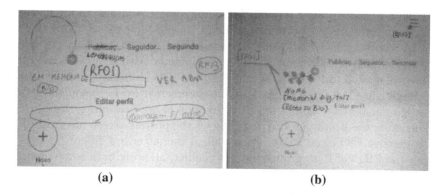

Fig. 1. a. and b.: Low-fidelity prototype developed by the focus group (In Portuguese)

G1 chose to replace the word 'publication' with the word 'memories'(Fig. 1 a.), and G2 chose to place flowers around the photo (Fig. 1 b.). Since both ideas did not conflict, both were used in the first screen of the prototype (Fig. 2 a.). For this screen, it was decided to leave the words "In memory of ...", by G2, so that it would be less polluted. He also used the FR13 designed by G1 Which specifies who is the heir to the account and FR07 that G2 developed, to warn users about the settings of the future digital memorial.

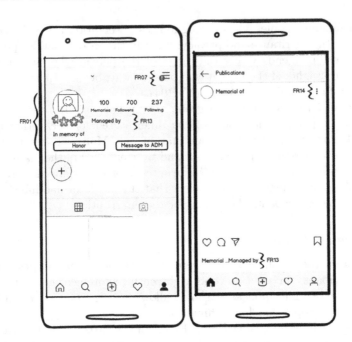

Fig. 2. a. and b.: Prototype of screen of the profile transformed into a memorial and Prototype of a memorial post screen

While G1 chose to use FR13 on the profile screen, G2 chose to use it on the screen that represents the posting of a photo. On this same screen, G2 added the FR14 to report against heirs, and G1 represented it the same way, but added FR15 and FR16 in the same space used for complaints. Although FR15 and FR16 are directly related to FR14, after analyzing the idea, only the use of FR14 was considered, since the three points that the groups marked for complaints, from the design perspective, cannot have the function of notification.

Therefore, the prototype (Fig. 2 b.) shows the posting screen after this decision to remove FR15 and FR16. Even though the latter are different representations, the FR13 of both groups did not conflict, allowing both to be used.

When analyzing the way in which the groups thought about the settings of future digital memorials, it is clear that the ideas of the path that the user should take were similar. Both used the FR03 and FR06 requirements. First, the user should find settings and then digital memorials. G2 kept the settings notice (FR07) on the memorial access tab.

The user's path begins in the main settings page and covers FR03 (Fig. 3 a.). In the "Digital Memorial", FR04 is addressed, including FR06 and FR02. The FR02 idea was used only by G2, so it is not necessary to choose the best representation. It was decided to mix the ideas of G1 with those of G2, which puts all the configuration options on the screen. This combination of ideas means that, when the user interacts with the system, he does not have to click on many buttons in order to find what he is looking for.

During the generation of prototypes, it was decided that an exclusive tab would be developed for the heir, which delimits his or her activity. Thus, the idea of G2 was limited to only exposing the destinations of the account (Fig. 3 b.) and, using G1's idea, the heir's permissions were for the settings involving the heir.

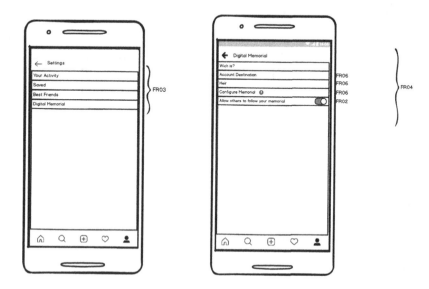

Fig. 3. a. and b.: Prototype of the settings screen

In the heir permissions prototype (Fig. 4 a.), both the FR12 ideas developed by G1 and those of G2 were used, but with the change of artifacts used to represent them. The On /Off switch was chosen because it is more used in the Instagram interface when the person has only two options.

Regarding the FR05 requirement, used by both groups, the idea of G2 was adopted, which was to select the heir of your account from the profiles with which you already have contact on Instagram. G1's proposal was to collect data from the future heir, such as: name, phone number, and e-mail. However, this is an issue that may border privacy issues since the user would be handing out someone else's information to the social network. This personal information would be part of Instagram's database from the moment the social network had access to it, with no specifications on how to deal with the data, since the image implies that even a person who does not use Instagram could be the heir. One solution would be to link the phone number to an Instagram account, as this data has already been provided by the user.

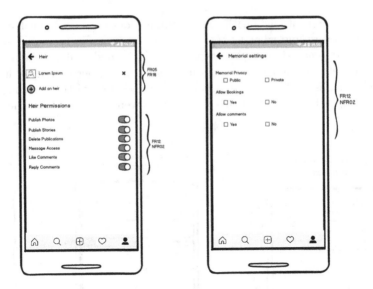

Fig. 4. a. and b. Prototype of the heir permissions screen

Finally, there are the memorial settings (Fig. 4 b.). They are directly linked to NFR02, and only G1 made a representation of it: their idea was used to prototype the settings of this memorial.

On this screen, it is possible for the user to choose the settings of the future memorial, so that, when death is confirmed, these decisions will remain, and cannot be modified by the heir, such as the privacy of the memorial, and if people will be able to comment on photos. Unlike the settings for the heir, these settings are designed to define the interactions with the memorial, while the heir settings better define the interactions of the heir through the memorial.

Both the settings of the heir and the settings of memorials address the terms mentioned by Maciel [19] about volition since, on both screens, the user is not only informed about what will happen to his account after his death, but also is presented with options to decide where the account will go.

4.4   Elaboration of Terms of Use

Much was mentioned about not wanting others to see the users' data, and how the rules between system and user could be established in the Terms of Use. Thus, during Focus Group 2, the groups also developed how certain clauses of the Terms of Use and Privacy Policies would be if the requirements were applied, with G1 using the FR06, FR09, FR10 and FR11 requirements, while G2 used FR9, FR10 and FR11. Custers *et al.* [8] talks about how Facebook has a very transparent privacy policy with many examples of how the data will be used. But they can still be very confusing for a regular user to understand, especially due to their size.

The terms of use clauses developed by G1 are: 1) The user will be able to choose whether he wishes to transform his account into a digital memorial or exclude it in the event of death. 2) If the user does not select one of the available options, the account will be deactivated after 3 years of inactivity and proof will be required for reactivation. 3) For proof of death, the heir will be called upon to provide documentation for proof. If there is no heir, proof can be provided by any family member.

The terms of use clauses created by G2 are:1) If the destination of the "post-mortem account" is not defined by the user, the profile will be disabled when no access is detected within a period of 5 (five) years.2) After deactivation, the application will send a verification email to the user to verify activity.3) If there is no response to this email within a period of 5 (five) years, the account will be deleted.

When observing the terms of use above, it is possible to notice a few similarities between them, such as the fact that both defined a time frame for the account to be deactivated; however, following the elaborated requirements, G2 established the way in which the user would be notified. The question of proof of death established by G1 already occurs in parts on Instagram, since it requests that only a family member can ask for the deletion of an account. G1 also does not establish the account to be deleted, only deactivated, while G2 determines a period for this exclusion, thus elucidating the term when determining the data storage.

5   Final Considerations

Through the user's view, it can be seen that it is possible to maintain the aspects of identity, volition and privacy from the moment a memorial is set up until its creation/transformation, in which case adjustments to Instagram digital memorials are needed. In this sense, the Participatory Design method was fundamental for exploring user perception. By adopting this approach, the construction of requirements became easy and dynamic, since in the group discussion and in the transcription and analysis of the material it was possible to see agreement among participants in many points, despite the difference in the backgrounds and experiences of each participant.

Maciel and Pereira [21] emphasize how it is up to the designers to give users the options, through the system, so that they can decide the best way for their account regarding issues of "digital mourning", transfer of assets to heirs, among others. In this sense, the function of the requirements created here is to serve as a bridge between the designer and the end user through effective communication.

Based on the presentations made on the concepts of identity, volition and privacy, as well as discussions with the participants, it was possible to note that, even though they are not fully aware of these aspects, the participants expect them to exist on their social networks, and they expect to choose what will happen with their image even after death.

When evaluating low-fidelity prototypes, produced during focus group sessions, the user's decision-making is noticeably a predominant factor that should be prioritized, as is demonstrated by the use of buttons, checkboxes and others, as well as in the attempt to be sufficiently elucidatory for the people who will use the system. The medium-fidelity prototypes were produced to be as true as possible to the ideas presented in the focus group; however, in order to adapt to the standards already used by Instagram, some ideas were merged and modified.

Discussions about digital memorials are crucial because social networks profiles partly compose the construction of a person's identity; hence this includes the moment this person dies. It is also essential that social networks begin to clarify how their users can set up their memorials, so that users may continue to protect their image while maintaining their legacy in the digital environment.

As for suggestions of future studies, it would be interesting to analyze designs created with people who did not participate in the first meetings, in order to validate them from the perspective of someone who was not present during their development. Additionally, there could be usability and communicability tests applied in the prototypes of this research. Also, there are plans to study the impact on the mourning of family members and followers of deleting the profile of a person immediately after death is confirmed, not only in the immediate issue after death, but also over a longer period. Also, if Instagram launches any solution, it could be compared with the proposal in this research, evaluating them and considering the Interaction Anticipation Challenges [24].

Finally, it is worth emphasizing that it is important that digital memorials are explored in greater depth, so that they can be improved and adapted and result in a place of comfort for those who stayed and good memories of those who left.

Acknowledgments. The authors would like to thank the volunteer participants of the participatory design activities; the Conselho Nacional de Desenvolvimento Científico e Tecnológico (CNPq); the Pró-reitoria de Pesquisa (PROPeq) of the Federal University of Mato Grosso, and the Uniselva Foundation; for their partial support of this publication in Brazil.

References

1. The Merriam-Webster Dictionary. https://www.merriam-webster.com/dictionary/identity. Accessed 1 Oct 2020
2. Aarts, B., Bauer, M.: A construçao do corpus: um princípio para a coleta de dados qualitativos. In: Editora Vozes, pp. 39–63 (2002)
3. Barbosa, S., Silva, B.: Interação Humano-Computador. Elsevier, Brasil (2010)
4. Beppu, F., Maciel, C.: Perspectivas Normativas para o Legado Digital Pós-Morte Face à Lei Geral de Proteção de Dados Pessoais. Anais do I Workshop sobre as Implicações da Computação na Sociedade, pp. 73–84. SBC (2020). https://doi.org/10.5753/wics.2020.11038
5. Bjögvinsson, E., Ehn, P., Hillgren, P.: Design things and design thinking: Contemporary participatory design challenges. Des. Issues **28**(3), 101–116 (2012). https://doi.org/10.1162/DESI_a_00165
6. Brubaker, J.R., Vertesi, J.: Death and the social network. In: Proceedings of CHI Workshop on Death and the Digital (2010)

7. Carroll, E., Romano, J.: Your Digital Afterlife: When Facebook, Flickr and Twitter are your Estate, What's your Legacy?. New Riders, Berkeley (2010)
8. Custers, B., van der Hof, S., Schermer, B.: Privacy expectations of social media users: the role of informed consent in privacy policies. Policy Internet 6(3), 268–295 (2014). https://doi.org/10.1002/1944-2866.POI366
9. de Toledo T.J., Maciel, C., Muriana, L.M., de Souza, P.C., Pereira, V.C.: Identity and volition in Facebook digital memorials and the challenges of anticipating interaction. In: Proceedings of the 18th Brazilian Symposium on Human Factors in Computing Systems, pp. 1–11. (2019). https://doi.org/10.1145/3357155.3358454
10. Edwards, L., Harbina, E.: Protecting post-mortem privacy: reconsidering the privacy interests of the deceased in a digital world. Cardozo Arts Ent. LJ. 32, 83 (2013)
11. Gach, K.Z., Brubaker, J.R.: Experiences of trust in postmortem profile management. ACM Trans. Soc. Comput. 3(1), 1–26 (2020). https://doi.org/10.1145/3365525
12. Garcez, P.M.: Transcrição como teoria: a identificação dos falantes como atividade analítica plena. Identidades: recortes multi e interdisciplinares. Campinas, SP: Mercado de Letras, pp. 83–95 (2002)
13. Gatti, B.A.: Formação de grupos e redes de intercâmbio em pesquisa educacional: dialogia e qualidade. Revista Brasileira de Educação 30, 124–132 (2005). https://doi.org/10.1590/S1413-24782005000300010
14. Gibbs, M., Meese, J., Arnold, M., Nansen, B., Carter, M.: # Funeral and Instagram: death, social media, and platform vernacular. Inf. Commun. Soc. 18(3), 255–268 (2015). https://doi.org/10.1080/1369118X.2014.987152
15. Kemp, S.: Digital in 2018: World's internet users pass the 4 billion mark. https://wearesocial.com/blog/2018/01/global-digital-report-2018. Accessed 16 May 2021
16. Leal, L.T.: Internet e morte do usuário: a necessária superação do paradigma da herança digital. Revista Brasileira Direito Civil 16, 181 (2018)
17. Leaver, T., Highfield, T.: Visualising the ends of identity: pre-birth and post-death on Instagram. Inf. Commun. Soc. 21(1), 30–45 (2018). https://doi.org/10.1080/1369118X.2016.1259343
18. Lopes, A.D., Pereira, V.C., Maciel, C.: Recomendações para o design de memórias digitais na web social. In: Proceedings of the 13th Brazilian Symposium on Human Factors in Computing Systems, pp. 275–284 (2014). https://doi.org/10.5555/2738055.2738099
19. Maciel, C.: Issues of the social web interaction project faced with afterlife digital legacy. In: Proceedings of the 10th Brazilian Symposium on Human Factors in Computing Systems and the 5th Latin American Conference on Human-Computer Interaction, pp. 3–12 (2011). https://doi.org/10.5555/2254436.2254441
20. Maciel, C., Lopes, A., Carvalho Pereira, V., Leitão, C., Boscarioli, C.: Recommendations for the design of digital memorials in social web. In: Meiselwitz, G. (ed.) HCII 2019. LNCS, vol. 11578, pp. 64–79. Springer, Cham (2019). https://doi.org/10.1007/978-3-030-21902-4_6
21. Maciel, C., Pereira, V.C.: The fate of digital legacy in software engineers' view: technical and cultural aspects. In: Maciel, C., Pereira, V. (eds.) Digital Legacy and Interaction, pp. 1–30. Springer, Cham (2013) https://doi.org/10.1007/978-3-319-01631-3_1
22. Maciel, C., Pereira, V.C.: The internet generation and its representations of death: considerations for posthumous interaction projects. In: IHC, pp. 85–94. Citeseer (2012). https://doi.org/10.5555/2393536.2393548

23. Marcuschi, L.A.: Análise da enunciação. Editora Ática, São Paulo (1986)
24. Prates, R.O., Rosson, M.B., de Souza, C.S.: Interaction anticipation: communicating impacts of groupware configuration settings to users. In: Díaz, P., Pipek, V., Ardito, C., Jensen, C., Aedo, I., Boden, A. (eds.) IS-EUD 2015. LNCS, vol. 9083, pp. 192–197. Springer, Cham (2015). https://doi.org/10.1007/978-3-319-18425-8_15
25. Ribeiro, R.R.: A morte midiatizada: como as redes sociais atualizam a experiência do fim da vida. Eduff (2015)
26. Rocha, H.V., Baranauskas, M.C.C.: Design e Avaliação de Interfaces Humano-Computador. Edição disponível em (2003) http://www.nied.unicamp.br/publicacoes
27. Schaub, F., Breaux, T.D., Sadeh, N.: Crowdsourcing privacy policy analysis: potential, challenges and best practices. It Inf. Technol. **58**(5), 229–236 (2016). https://doi.org/10.1515/itit-2016-0009
28. Torres, C.: A bíblia do marketing digital: tudo o que você queria saber sobre marketing e publicidade na internet e não tinha a quem perguntar. Novatec Editora (2018)
29. Viana, G.T., Maciel, C., de Arruda, N.A., de Souza, P.C.: Análise dos termos de uso e políticas de privacidade de redes sociais quanto ao tratamento da morte dos usuários. In: Anais do VIII Workshop sobre Aspectos da Interação Humano-Computador para a Web Social, pp. 82–93. SBC (2017)

Author Index

.

Printed in the United States
by Baker & Taylor Publisher Services